Ethical Dimensions of the Foreign Policy of the European Union

This book analyses the theory and practice of the European Union's 'ethical foreign policy', arguing that current practices dilute the impact and efficacy of EU policies but that an effort which is at times effective is being made to protect certain values in the Union's international relations. Beginning with an investigation of the international rules authorising or obliging the Union/Community or the Member States to promote certain values in third states or take action to protect them, Khaliq goes on to examine the limits under international law which constrain such policies. The issues are then assessed from an EU/Community law perspective, and the importance attached to ethical values and their relationship with other priorities and objectives is analysed in the context of relations with Myanmar, Nigeria, Pakistan, Israel and the Palestinian Authority. The European Community's humanitarian aid policy is also discussed.

Cambridge Studies in European Law and Policy

This series aims to produce original works which contain a critical analysis of the state of the law in particular areas of European Law and set out different perspectives and suggestions for its future development. It also aims to encourage a range of work on law, legal institutions and legal phenomena in Europe, including 'law in context' approaches. The titles in the series will be of interest to academics; policymakers; policy formers who are interested in European legal, commercial, and political affairs; practising lawyers including the judiciary; and advanced law students and researchers.

Joint Editors

Professor Dr. Laurence Gormley, *Rijksuniversiteit Groningen, The Netherlands*
Professor Jo Shaw, *University of Edinburgh*

Editorial advisory board

Ethical Dimensions of the Foreign Policy of the European Union

A Legal Appraisal

Urfan Khaliq

CAMBRIDGE
UNIVERSITY PRESS

CAMBRIDGE UNIVERSITY PRESS
Cambridge, New York, Melbourne, Madrid, Cape Town, Singapore, São Paulo,
Delhi

Cambridge University Press
The Edinburgh Building, Cambridge CB2 8RU, UK

Published in the United States of America by
Cambridge University Press, New York

www.cambridge.org
Information on this title: www.cambridge.org/9780521870757

First published 2008

Printed in the United Kingdom at the University Press, Cambridge

A catalogue record for this publication is available from the British Library

Library of Congress Cataloguing in Publication data
Khaliq, Urfan, 1970–
Ethical dimensions of the foreign policy of the European Union : a legal
appraisal / Urfan Khaliq.
    p.   cm. – (Cambridge studies in European law and policy)
Includes bibliographical references.
ISBN 978-0-521-87075-7
1. European Union countries – Foreign relations – Moral and ethical aspects.
2. European Union countries – Foreign relations – Moral and ethical aspects –
Case studies.   I. Title.   II. Series.
JZ1570.K53   2008
172′.4094–dc22

                                                        2008018935

ISBN 978-0-521-87075-7 hardback

Table of Contents

Series Editors' Preface

The foreign policy of the European Union as such has so far received relatively little attention from lawyers, although there are excellent works on the Union's external relations in general. *Ethical Dimensions of the Foreign Policy of the European Union* seeks at once to fill that gap and to present, both in the wider perspective and, through the use of well-thought-out case studies, by reference to the major ethical themes of denial of democratic rights, participation in the Middle East peace process, and humanitarian aid, a considered, scholarly and critical assessment of the Union's foreign policy objectives and achievements. The promotion of ethical values in foreign policy forms an essential part of good neighbourhood policy and the promotion of respect for fundamental rights and the rule of law; and, as Dr Khaliq rightly observes, the litmus test for an ethical foreign policy lies in its application. He assesses ethical foreign policies from the perspective first of public international law, and then turns to the policy and practice of the European Union. Although the Union is firmly anchored on such concepts as liberty, democracy, respect for human rights and fundamental freedoms, and social rights, he notes that the link between these principles and external relations is weak; this is certainly institutionally so, although in practice the link is more frequently paraded, even if perhaps not always as much observed as might be desired. All foreign policies must, to varying degrees, take account of *Realpolitik*, as well as of accepted or disputed principles, whether those principles be self-adopted or encouraged, stimulated or imposed by (elements of) the world order. The chicken and egg relationship between principles and policies is never far from the surface, demonstrating that politics remains the art of the possible.

The European Union has had to tread a careful path, ensuring that the right measures are adopted on the basis of the right powers, not least because the European Court of Justice will be keen to ensure that (at the very least) the prerogatives of the Community are not infringed, and that the Institutions have acted within the limits of their powers. The use of Community or Union *vires* as appropriate is dramatically illustrated and brought to life in Dr Khaliq's book. Of particular interest is his illustration of the use of the Community's development cooperation powers to pursue a global humanitarian policy, while leaving the Member States free to pursue their own development cooperation agendas. His case studies illustrate powerfully how the Union uses the means at its disposal, but they also demonstrate the shortcomings in its relationships with third countries, some of which result from inherent contradictions in granting aid, and some from the need to rely on other organisations to carry out the activities. Yet more generally, the structure of the Union's approach to foreign policy (even if the Treaty of Lisbon comes into force, there will still be more than one person seeking to speak for Europe) and the plethora of actors within the Union offer plenty of room for turf wars at the expense of a coherent foreign policy. While the overall picture of the promotion of ethical values and principles in third countries which Dr Khaliq paints is positive, he does not gloss over the need for reform and reassessment if the Union's contribution is to be more meaningful still.

This book will be of enormous value to lawyers, policy-makers and all concerned with foreign policy analysis and the external aspects of the Union's activities in the broadest sense. It is, therefore, with great pleasure that we welcome this important and invigorating book in the series *Cambridge Studies in European Law and Policy*.

Laurence Gormley
Jo Shaw

Acknowledgements and Preface

This monograph is based upon a very substantially revised and expanded version of a PhD thesis successfully defended at University College, London in 2004. In the course of writing the thesis and subsequently the book, I have become indebted to many people who have helped in different ways. I would like to thank each of you individually but it is impossible to do so here so I will thank you all collectively. There are, however, a few people who I must mention.

I would like to thank Margot Horspool, Prof. David O'Keeffe and especially Prof. Eileen Denza for supervising my doctoral work. Without their encouragement, patience and advice it would not have been possible for me to finish the thesis. My examiners, Prof. Marise Cremona and Prof. Dominic McGoldrick, provided very detailed and insightful feedback on the thesis with a view to it being revised for publication. I have tried to address each and every one of their suggestions. I am extremely grateful to them all.

I would particularly like to thank Dr Heli Askola and Dr Stewart Field for their many detailed and insightful comments and suggestions. I would also like to thank Mauro Barelli, Dr Jo Hunt and James Young for commenting upon earlier versions of particular chapters. I further wish to express my immense gratitude to Prof. Robin Churchill and Prof. David Campbell for their suggestions, support and advice, not only with regard to this work but on all matters since I first had the pleasure to work with them.

The anonymous readers for Cambridge University Press provided detailed comments and insights which I have tried to address; the editorial staff of Cambridge University Press were efficient at all times; and I was awarded a year's sabbatical by Cardiff Law School to allow me to finish the book. I am very grateful to them all. I would also like to thank the Law School of the University of Michigan, Ann Arbor, where I spent a summer carrying out some of the research for this book. Furthermore, I would also like to thank a substantial number of EU officials and members of the ministries of various governments who took the time to respond to my numerous queries by email, over the telephone and also for meeting with me in person to discuss aspects of my work. The usual disclaimer of course applies to all of the above.

In my undertaking such a lengthy and time-consuming project, my loved ones have invariably suffered (or benefited, depending on the point of view) from my either not being around very much, being too busy to do certain things with them or not turning up for the odd event. This book or my finishing it will not make up for any of these short-comings in my behaviour over the years but it would have been impossible without you. Thank you.

I have sought to state the law and facts as I understood them on 30 June 2007 although it was possible to take account of events in the Middle East and Pakistan up until the end of July 2007. It has not been possible to take account of the subsequent uprising in Myanmar, the Annapolis Conference on the Middle East or the state of emergency in Pakistan, all of which occurred before the end of 2007 but after the manuscript was submitted. It has also not been possible to take account of and discuss the Treaty Amending the Treaty on European Union and the Treaty Establishing the European Community (EU Reform Treaty) as approved during the informal European Council in Lisbon on 18–19 October 2007. Those provisions of the Constitutional Treaty which are discussed in the text are substantively not very (if at all) different from those which are in the EU Reform Treaty. It is, of course, still uncertain if the EU Reform Treaty will enter into force and, if it does, when it will do so. So as to allow the interested reader to more easily compare the position under the Constitutional Treaty with the EU Reform Treaty, I have created a Table of Equivalences of the main provisions of the former discussed in the text. Where the provisions of the EU Reform Treaty amend existing provisions in the current treaties they must be read in conjunction with them. It is hoped that by creating such a table this will prove a satisfactory way of trying to take account of the Reform Treaty at this stage in the production process.

Urfan Khaliq
Cardiff

The Constitutional Treaty and the Reform Treaty: Table of Equivalences

Constitutional Treaty Provisions	Reform Treaty Provisions	Existing EU/EC Treaty Provisions Amended
Article I-2	Article 1(3)	
Article I-3	Article 1(4)	Articles 2 TEU, TEC
Article I-7	Article 1(55)	
Article I-9	Article 1(8)	
Article I-58	Article 1(57)	Article 49 TEU
Article III-292	Article 1(24)	
Article III-308	Article 1(45)	Article 47 TEU
Article III-309	Article 1(49)	Article 17(2) TEU
Article III-316	Article 2(161)	Articles 177 and 178 TEC
Article III-318	Article 2(163)	Article 180 TEC
Article III-321	Article 2(168)	
Article III-328	Article 2(175)	Article 20 TEU
Article III-376	Article 2(223)	
Article III-426	Article 2(281)	Article 282 TEC

Table of Cases

European Court of Justice

Cases:

Opinions

Permanent Court of International Justice
and International Court of Justice

Advisory Opinions:

Awards and Decisions of Other International Tribunals

Decisions of Domestic Courts

Table of Treaties

EC and EU Treaties

Treaty Establishing the European Community,1957 298 UNTS 11.
Adopted 25 March 1957, Rome, entered into force 1 January 1958 as amended by the Treaty of Nice [2002] OJ C325/33, 24 December 2002, adopted 26 February 2001, entered into force 1 February 2003.

Treaty on European Union [1992] OJ C 191/1, 29 July 1992. Adopted 7 February 1992, Maastricht, entered into force 1 November 1993 as amended by the Treaty of Nice [2002] OJ C325/33, 24 December 2002, adopted 26 February 2001, entered into force 1 February 2003.

Treaties to Which the EC Is Party

Other Treaties

Abbreviations

ACHR	American Convention on Human Rights, 1969
ACP	African, Caribbean and Pacific Group of States
AJIL	*American Journal of International Law*
ALA	Asian and Latin American states
APMC	ASEAN Post-Ministerial Conference
ARF	ASEAN Regional Forum
ASEAN	Association of South East Asian Nations
ASEM	Asia Europe Meetings
AYBIL	*Australian Yearbook of International Law*
Boston College ICLR	*Boston College International and Comparative Law Review*
Brooklyn JIL	*Brooklyn Journal of International Law*
BYBIL	*British Yearbook of International Law*
California Western ILJ	*California Western International Law Journal*
CAP	Common Agricultural Policy
Case W Res. JIL	*Case Western Reserve Journal of International Law*
CAT	Committee Against Torture
CCP	Common Commercial Policy
CCPM	Community Civil Protection Mechanism
CDE	*Cahiers de Droit Européen*
CEDAW	Committee on the Elimination of Discrimination Against Women
CEECs	Central and Eastern European Countries
CERD	Committee on the Elimination of Racial Discrimination
CESCR	Committee on Economic, Social and Cultural Rights

CFI	Court of First Instance
CFSP	Common Foreign and Security Policy
CJEL	*Columbia Journal of European Law*
CMLRev.	*Common Market Law Review*
COHOM	Council Working Party on Human Rights
Columbia HRLR	*Columbia Human Rights Law Review*
Columbia JEL	*Columbia Journal of European Law*
Columbia JTL	*Columbia Journal of Transnational Law*
Columbia LR	*Columbia Law Review*
Conn. JIL	*Connecticut Journal of International Law*
Cornell Int'l LJ	*Cornell International Law Journal*
CRC	Convention on the Rights of the Child, 1989
CSP	Country Strategy Paper
CTBT	Comprehensive Test Ban Treaty, 1996
DAC	Development Assistance Committee (OECD)
DDA	Doha Development Agenda
Denver JILP	*Denver Journal of International Law and Policy*
DFID	Department for International Development (United Kingdom)
DG	Directorate-General (European Commission)
DG ECHO	European Community Humanitarian Office
DG RELEX	Directorate-General for External Relations
DRR	disaster risk reduction
EAC	East African Community
EBA	Everything But Arms
ECHR	European Convention for the Protection of Human Rights and Fundamental Freedoms, 1950
ECJ	European Court of Justice
ECPT	European Convention for the Prevention of Torture and Inhuman or Degrading Treatment or Punishment, 1987
ECtHR	European Court of Human Rights
EDF	European Development Fund
EFARev.	*European Foreign Affairs Review*
EfD	Energy for Democracy
EHRLR	*European Human Rights Law Review*
EIB	European Investment Bank
EIDHR	European Initiative (now Instrument) for Democracy and Human Rights

EJIL	*European Journal of International Law*
ELJ	*European Law Journal*
ELRev.	*European Law Review*
ENP	European Neighbourhood Policy
ENPI	European Neighbourhood Policy Instrument
EPA	Economic Partnership Agreement
EPC	European Political Cooperation
EPL	*European Public Law*
ESC	Economic and Social Committee
ESDP	European Security and Defence Policy
EU	European Union
EU BAM	European Union Border Assistance Mission
EU COPPS	European Union Coordinating Office for Palestinian Police Support
EU EOM	European Union Election Observation Mission
EUEU	European Union Electoral Unit
EUPOL COPPS	EU Police Mission for the Palestinian Territories
FAC	Food Aid Convention
FAO	Food and Agriculture Organisation (United Nations)
FCO	Foreign and Commonwealth Office (United Kingdom)
Fordham ILJ	*Fordham International Law Journal*
FPA	Framework Partnership Agreement
GATT	General Agreement on Tariffs and Trade, 1994
Geo. JICL	*Georgia Journal of International and Comparative Law*
Geo. Wash. JILE	*George Washington Journal of International Law and Economics*
GNI	gross national income
GSP	Generalised System of Preferences
GYBIL	*German Yearbook of International Law*
Harvard ILJ	*Harvard International Law Journal*
Harvard LR	*Harvard Law Review*
Hastings ICLR	*Hastings International and Comparative Law Review*
HHRJ	*Harvard Human Rights Journal*
HPG	Humanitarian Policy Group (Overseas Development Institute)
HRC	Human Rights Committee
HRQ	*Human Rights Quarterly*
IAEA	International Atomic Energy Agency

ICCPR	International Covenant on Civil and Political Rights, 1966
ICERD	International Convention on the Elimination of All Forms of Racial Discrimination, 1966
ICESCR	International Covenant on Economic, Social and Cultural Rights, 1966
ICFTU	International Confederation of Free Trade Unions
ICJ	International Court of Justice
ICLQ	*International and Comparative Law Quarterly*
ICRC	International Committee of the Red Cross
IDF	Israeli Defence Force
IDI	Institut de Droit International
IHT	*International Herald Tribune*
ILA	International Law Association
ILC	International Law Commission
ILCASR	International Law Commission's Articles on State Responsibility, 2001
ILO	International Labour Organisation
Iowa LR	*Iowa Law Review*
IPA	Instrument for Pre-Accession Assistance
IRRC	*International Review of the Red Cross*
IYBIL	*Italian Yearbook of International Law*
JCMS	*Journal of Common Market Studies*
JEPP	*Journal of European Public Policy*
JHA	Justice and Home Affairs
JIA	*Journal of International Affairs*
JIEL	*Journal of International Economic Law*
JJSO	Juvenile Justice System Ordinance, 2000 (Pakistan)
JPA	Joint Parliamentary Assembly
JWT / JWTL	*Journal of World Trade / Journal of World Trade Law*
LDCs	Least Developed Countries
LICs	Low Income Countries
LIEI	*Legal Issues of European / Economic Integration*
LMICs	Lower Middle Income Countries
LRRD	linking relief, rehabilitation and development
MDGs	Millennium Development Goals
MEPP	Middle East Peace Process
MJIL / MYBILS	*Michigan Journal of International Law / Michigan Yearbook of International Legal Studies*

MSF	Médecin Sans Frontières
NEC	National Electoral Commission (Nigeria)
NGO	non-governmental organisation
NILR	*Netherlands International Law Review*
NLD	National League for Democracy (Burma/Myanmar)
Nordic JIL	*Nordic Journal of International Law*
NPT	Treaty on the Non-Proliferation of Nuclear Weapons, 1968
NQHR	*Netherlands Quarterly of Human Rights*
NYBIL	*Netherlands Yearbook of International Law*
NYL Sch. LR	*New York Law School Law Review*
NYRB	*New York Review of Books*
NYUJILP	*New York University Journal of International Law and Politics*
OAS	Organization of American States
ODI	Overseas Development Institute
ODI Review	*Overseas Development Institute Review*
OECD	Organisation for Economic Cooperation and Development
PCIJ	Permanent Court of International Justice
PCPDP	Palestinian Civil Police Department Programme
PLC	Palestinian Legislative Council
PLO	Palestinian Liberation Organisation
RRM	Rapid Reaction Mechanism
SAARC	South Asian Association for Regional Cooperation
SALW	small arms and light weapons
SEA	Single European Act, 1986
SPDC	State Peace and Development Council (Burma/Myanmar)
Stanford JIL	*Stanford Journal of International Law*
Syracuse JILC	*Syracuse Journal of International Law and Commerce*
TEC	Treaty Establishing the European Community
TEU	Treaty on European Union
Texas ILJ	*Texas International Law Journal*
TIM	Temporary International Mechanism
UMICs	Upper Middle Income Countries

UNCAT	Convention Against Torture and Other Cruel, Inhuman or Degrading Treatment or Punishment, 1984
UNDP	United Nations Development Programme
UNHCR	United Nations High Commissioner for Refugees
UNRWA	United Nations Relief and Works Agency
Vanderbilt JTL	*Vanderbilt Journal of Transnational Law*
VCLT	Vienna Convention on the Law of Treaties, 1969
VCLTSIO	Vienna Convention on the Law of Treaties between States and International Organisations or between International Organisations, 1986
Virginia JIL	*Virginia Journal of International Law*
WHO	World Health Organisation
WTO	World Trade Organisation
YEL	*Yearbook of European Law*

1   Introduction

In their foreign policies states have historically, in the main, sought directly to protect only their own interests. During the last thirty years or so, various administrations have formally declared that in their foreign policy formulation, acting either individually or collectively, they will take account of human rights, good governance and democracy, among other values. The European Union's current constitutive treaties expressly refer, for example, to the objectives of promoting and protecting human rights and democracy in third states. The Council, Presidency, the European Parliament, various Commissioners and the Commission have all on numerous occasions declared their desire to achieve those objectives and the methodology to be used in their pursuance.

Foreign policies which promote certain 'ethical' values and principles have often been theoretically analysed by International Relations scholars. This work is of interest and value but 'ethical foreign policies' also involve many questions of domestic and international law. Law is, therefore, as important a tool as International Relations in the analysis of such policies. This book analyses the European Union's efforts to this end in legal terms, to understand how and on what basis action (if any) is taken and how effective it has been or is likely to be. This study will focus on the European Union's relations with a number of primarily developing states. As a legal analysis of the European Union's 'ethical foreign policies' and practice, this study does not attempt to engage itself in the International Relations debates, although it does refer to them where necessary. It is concerned with a number of different legal questions.

Chapter 2 assesses 'ethical foreign policies' from a public international law perspective. It first discusses what such policies are and what the Union considers them to be. It then investigates which international legal rules, if any, oblige or allow the Union, Community and/or the Member States to promote certain values in third states or in certain circumstances to take action if they are being violated. It further examines the legal constraints on taking such action and whether it may be seen as intervention in the internal affairs of a non-Member State.

Chapter 3 examines legal policy and practice from the perspective of the European Union. Foreign policy powers are likely, in a nation state, to be among the powers exclusively reserved for the central or federal government or an inherent part of the royal or executive prerogative. With a system based on the principle of conferred powers, however, it must be positively established to what extent the Union has competence to act externally to promote and protect certain values and interests and the methods by which it can do so. The aim of Chapter 3 is to determine the scope of this competence, the legitimacy of acting under available powers and the extent to which they have been exercised in practice. Initially, it examines the instruments available to the Union and Community in the pursuance of foreign policy objectives. The main part of the chapter is concerned with the various relevant Community policies in this field as this is most relevant to the case studies which follow. In particular, this part of the chapter analyses how the Community has attempted to use all of its external competences to pursue its objectives, among others, in its development cooperation, trade and humanitarian aid policies.

The next three substantive chapters analyse practice. The litmus test for an 'ethical foreign policy' lies in its application. Policy statements and legal obligations are one thing, implementation quite another. Although a number of general surveys now exist on conditionality and its use in practice, the aim in chapters 4 and 5 is to look at the multitude of instruments and policies that the European Union has used in its relations with particular countries.[1] This allows analysis of the circumstances which are taken into account when acting and also how priorities are identified and furthered in the relationship that exists with

---

[1] In particular, K. Tomaševski, *Responding to Human Rights Violations 1946–1999* (The Hague: Kluwer Law International, 2000); E. Fierro, *The EU's Approach to Human Rights Conditionality in Practice* (The Hague: Kluwer Law International, 2002); M. Bulterman, *Human Rights in the Treaty Relations of the European Community: Real Virtues or Virtual Reality?* (Antwerp: Intersentia, 2001) and L. Bartels, *Human Rights Conditionality in the EU's International Agreements* (Oxford: Oxford University Press, 2005).

those states. It also allows the opportunity to analyse the importance attached to ethical values and their relationship with other priorities and objectives. Chapter 4 examines relations with Myanmar, Nigeria and Pakistan.[2] Chapter 5 looks at relations with the Palestinian Authority and Israel in the overall context of the Middle East Peace Process (MEPP).

Nigeria, Pakistan and Myanmar have been chosen in Chapter 4 as the Union has a different legal relationship with each of them. There are, however, similarities between some of the domestic problems in each of these countries, in particular, in relation to democracy. Nigeria is a member of the African, Caribbean and Pacific (ACP) group of states and has been chosen as it allows for an evaluation of the role of the Lomé/Cotonou institutions.[3] In the context of relations with ACP states there are a number of examples of those Agreements being suspended and a number of other states could have been discussed: Rwanda, Haiti, Sierra Leone, Fiji, Sudan, Niger and Cote d'Ivoire to name just a few. Nigeria does, however, offer the opportunity to look at relatively recent practice and also consider the circumstances in which all punitive measures have been withdrawn and full relations resumed, something some of the other potential ACP case studies did not offer. Furthermore, Nigeria is politically and economically one of the most important ACP states.

Pakistan has been selected as a developing country which is outside of the Lomé/Cotonou scheme but is covered by the scope of some of the Community's other development cooperation programmes. It has a close trading relationship with the Union and its Member States and has concluded bilateral treaties with the Community. Two military coups and the subsequent suspension and limited reintroduction of the democratic process have occurred while formal relations have been in existence. Pakistan is also in many ways unique. It is in many respects a failing state: it has major constitutional and legal problems as well as widespread problems with human rights, democracy, corruption, good governance and extreme poverty. Military coups, its hugely important role in the 'war on terror' and the resumption of full cooperation with a military regime are distinguishing features. Chile, Brazil,

---

[2] Although a number of states, such as the United Kingdom, still prefer to use Burma, Myanmar will be used throughout this book.

[3] The Lomé Conventions (as is the case now with the Cotonou Convention) were between, on the one hand, the Community and its Member States and, on the other, the ACP group of states. These conventions are discussed in detail in Chapter 3.

Columbia, Bangladesh, Sri Lanka, China and India, among others, would have been equally valid case studies.

Myanmar has been selected as another developing state, this time within the ASEAN[4] group of states, but one which has had all assistance, with the exception of humanitarian aid, suspended by the Community and with which the Union and its Member States have very limited contact. It is, however, a part of ASEAN, the other Member States of which enjoy bilateral treaty relations with the Community. It thus poses unique policy and strategic problems for the Union as to the approach to be adopted. The current military government has annulled previous democratic elections and is one of the more repressive regimes currently in power anywhere. Myanmar has also been selected as it is one of the few examples where it is possible to assess the full scope of the Community and Union's spectrum of measures against a state, taken in the absence of a sanctions regime imposed by the United Nations. Where the United Nations takes such action, the implementation of measures through the Common Foreign and Security Policy (CFSP) and/ or Community legal orders is primarily intended to enable the Member States to comply with their obligations under the Charter of the United Nations. Myanmar, however, is an example of action taken by the European Union in the absence of measures having been adopted by the Security Council of the United Nations or in other international fora which are binding upon the Member States.

Chapter 5, as noted above, describes the role of the Union in the overall context of the MEPP and more specifically its relations with the Palestinian Authority and Israel. Although the 1995 Agreement between the Community and Israel is not a classic development cooperation-based one (the Community historically has had no definition of 'developing state' to determine which type of instrument it utilises),[5] it does contain an 'essential elements' clause. Israel's problems with its Arab populations both within its internationally recognised boundaries and in the Occupied Territories are well documented. Union relations with Israel and the Palestinian Authority also provide an ideal case study to examine the relationship between the CFSP and the Community legal orders, and other Union initiatives such as the Barcelona Process and the European Neighbourhood Policy (ENP), to assess the promotion of Union objectives.

---

[4] Association of South East Asian Nations.   [5] See further the discussion in Chapter 3.

In Chapter 5, many of the Maghreb and Mashreq countries could have made suitable case studies, as they are also part of the ENP and the Barcelona Process. Similarly, relations with, for example, Iran, Saudi Arabia and a number of other Middle Eastern states would have offered valid studies for analysis. A central focus of the Union's relationship with many Middle Eastern states, however, is the 'Palestinian issue'. The European Security Strategy 2003 considers resolution of the Arab/Israeli conflict to be a strategic priority for the European Union for this very reason.[6] Thus it was the logical choice to examine the relationship between the Union, on the one hand, and, on the other, Israel and the Palestinian Authority. Furthermore, as noted above, the case study with Israel allows the opportunity to investigate the pursuance of ethical values where the Community does not have a development-based competence and other geopolitical considerations play a role in that dialogue, in particular, the MEPP.

Having justified the selection of the case studies in chapters 4 and 5, it is equally important to explain why some other states, also worthy of discussion, have been excluded. The most obvious category of states not to be specifically discussed are the central, eastern and south-eastern European states. As the majority of these countries have already become or are to be future members of the Union or have a very close or 'special' relationship with the Union, they have by and large been subjected to different legal and political criteria by the Union and its Member States compared to other third states. For the purposes of the Organisation for Economic Cooperation and Development (OECD), World Bank and the United Nations Development Programme (UNDP) many of these countries are considered to be 'economies in transition', as opposed to developing countries, although they have in financial terms been the largest recipients of overseas aid from the Union and its Member States since the early 1990s. The Union and the Member States included human rights guarantees as a condition for the recognition of the statehood of many of the new states which emerged from the Soviet Union and Yugoslavia, following the end of the Cold War. These conditions went beyond the traditional criteria for statehood. Since then the Copenhagen criteria have established the basic requirements for all prospective members.[7] There is also already a very

---

[6] J. Solana, *A Secure Europe in a Better World: the European Security Strategy*, p. 8. The strategy was approved by the European Council, 12–13 December 2003, Doc. 5381/04, para. 84.

[7] See further the discussion in chapters 2 and 3.

substantial literature on relations with these states[8] and furthermore the monograph as a whole primarily addresses the relationship between the Union and developing countries and thus it was not felt necessary to discuss relations with these states separately. This also explains the absence of specific discussion of relations with a number of other important third states, such as the United States, Japan and the rest of the Western developed world, including Canada, New Zealand and Australia.

The final substantive chapter on practice, Chapter 6, looks at the issue of humanitarian aid. A study of humanitarian aid is important for a number of reasons. In the first instance, the European Union considers that the humanitarian aid it distributes is clear evidence of its commitment to human rights, protecting human dignity and the upholding of certain other values and principles in relations with third countries. Furthermore, the theory of humanitarianism to which the Union subscribes should allow no influences, other than need, to dictate its actions and funding programmes. Humanitarian aid is, in this context, the ultimate test of the equal application of the principles and policies which are the subject of this monograph.

Chapter 7 draws some conclusions as to the legality and efficacy of the various policies and instruments used by the Union and the approaches adopted in practice.

---

[8] See, in particular, M. Cremona (ed.), *The Enlargement of the European Union* (Oxford: Oxford University Press, 2003) and C. Hillion (ed.), *EU Enlargement: a Legal Approach* (Oxford: Hart Publishing, 2004).

2 Promoting Values in Foreign Relations: Policy and Legal Issues

2.1 Introduction

Foreign polices which have an ethical or principled dimension to them, or more conveniently but less accurately 'ethical foreign policies', are closely tied up with ideology and the desire to project a particular identity to the wider world.[1] The decision to promote such values also stems from the desire, or at the least acquiescence, of the domestic constituency to engage in such practices. Prior to the 2004 enlargement of the European Union it was estimated, for example, that 81 per cent of the Union's population felt that the Union should promote human

---

[1] For example, Jose Pereira, during the Portuguese Presidency of the Council at a conference entitled, 'The EU and the Central Role of Human Rights and Democratic Principles in Relations with Third Countries', Venice, 25 May 2000, stated '[E]ncouraging respect for human rights and fundamental freedoms is at the centre of the relations between the EU and third countries . . . it is what we are about', available at http://ec.europa.eu/comm/external_relations/human_rights/conf/third/open_per.htm. Also see Robin Cook, who as Foreign Secretary of the United Kingdom, in a speech entitled, 'Human Rights into a New Century', London, 17 July 1997, stated 'human rights are at the heart of our foreign policy'. Although the Labour government which came into power in 1997 is widely credited with adopting the United Kingdom's 'ethical foreign policy', a number of Foreign and Commonwealth Office (FCO) policy papers illustrate that previous Labour and Conservative governments had also adopted documents advocating such an approach: see FCO, *British Policy Towards the United Nations*, Foreign Policy Doc. No. 26 (London: HMSO, 1978); FCO, *Human Rights in Foreign Policy*, Foreign Policy Doc. No. 215 (London: HMSO, 1991); FCO, *Human Rights in Foreign Policy*, Foreign Policy Doc. No. 268 (London: HMSO, 1996); and further R. Little and M. Wickham-Jones (eds.), *New Labour's Foreign Policy: a New Moral Crusade?* (Manchester: Manchester University Press, 2000). Also see J. Carter, 'Address on Foreign Affairs', University of Notre Dame, 22 May 1977; ICJ, *Human Rights in United States and United Kingdom Foreign Policy: a Colloquium* (London: International Commission of Jurists, 1978); and Dutch Ministry of Foreign Affairs, 'Human Rights and Foreign Policy' (1980) 11 *NYBIL* 193. Although such policies are generally considered to be a relatively recent development in international relations, the United States, for example, has (very)

rights abroad.[2] The pursuit of ideological goals that are perceived as being moral and legitimate in domestic policy, such as, for example, protecting human rights, provides an accessible and easily understood rationale in the formulation of a polity's foreign policy.[3] Although foreign policy has many objectives, the pursuit of emotive ideological goals such as the protection of human rights in third states is newsworthy, leading to a pressure to act, whereas many other foreign policy objectives are far less visible and more abstract. Spokespersons for the European Union have made clear on numerous occasions its position on the promotion and protection of certain values in the Union's external relations. For example, Javier Solana, the EU High Representative for the Common Foreign and Security Policy at the Fifty-eighth Session of the UN Commission on Human Rights stated:

the European Union is determined fully to assume ... international responsibilities ... on account of our size, our wealth, our history and our geography. Our Union is set to play a prominent international role in the century to come. Human rights will remain at the heart of that role because human rights are at the core of European integration ... Ours is a Union of values.[4]

In a similar vein, the Council's first *Annual Report on Human Rights* stated:

Human rights ... are the foundations of freedom, justice and peace in the world ... [T]he Union's headway towards integration is paralleled in the field of human rights. In a world where human rights ... continue to be violated daily, the Union's commitment to human rights is continuously being translated into action.[5]

Such sentiments have been, *inter alia*, repeated consistently in the *Annual Report on Human Rights* since 1999. The Laeken Declaration of 2001 has

selectively promoted democracy in third states since the nineteenth century. See M. Light, 'Exporting Democracy' in K. Smith and M. Light (eds.), *Ethics and Foreign Policy* (Cambridge: Cambridge University Press, 2001) p. 75. For a comparative overview of the history of such policies see K. Sikkink, 'The Power of Principled Ideas: Human Rights Policies in the United States and Western Europe' in J. Goldstein and R. Keohane (eds.), *Ideas and Foreign Policy: Beliefs, Institutions and Political Change* (Ithaca: Cornell University Press, 1993) p. 139.

[2] J. Gras, *The European Union and Human Rights Monitoring* (Helsinki: University of Helsinki, 2000) p. 1.

[3] See F. Berman, 'The Role of the International Lawyer in the Making of Foreign Policy' in C. Wickremasinghe (ed.), *The International Lawyer as Practitioner* (London: BIICL, 2000) pp. 3, 9.

[4] Geneva, 19 March 2002, available at www.europa-eu-un.org/articles/es/article_1232_es.htm

[5] Council of the European Union, *European Union Annual Report on Human Rights, 1998-1999* (Luxembourg: OOPEC, 2000) p. 7.

been significant in both asking questions and providing answers regarding the perception that European leaders have about the Union's values and its role and responsibilities in a globalised world. It states:

What is Europe's role in this changed world? Does Europe not, now that it is finally unified, have a leading role to play in a new world order, that of a power able both to play a stabilising role worldwide and to point the way ahead for many countries and peoples? Europe as the continent of humane values, the Magna Carta, the Bill of Rights, the French Revolution and the fall of the Berlin Wall; the continent of liberty, solidarity and above all diversity, meaning respect for others' languages, cultures and traditions . . .

Now that the Cold War is over and we are living in a globalised, yet also highly fragmented world, Europe needs to shoulder its responsibilities in the governance of globalisation. The role it has to play is that of a power resolutely doing battle against all violence, all terror and all fanaticism, but which also does not turn a blind eye to the world's heartrending injustices. In short, a power wanting to change the course of world affairs in such a way as to benefit not just the rich countries but also the poorest. A power seeking to set globalisation within a moral framework.

The Declaration fails to mention, of course, that Europe is also the continent of the Holocaust and the home of states who through colonial empires brutally oppressed and plundered large parts of the world for a number of centuries, but the process started by the Laeken Declaration led to the clearest and most important articulation of the Union's perceived values: Article I-2 of the proposed Treaty Establishing a Constitution for Europe.[6] The fact that at the time of writing the Constitutional Treaty is not in force does not change that.[7] Article I-2 of the proposed Constitutional Treaty identifies the Union's different values (some of which are stated more than once) by declaring:

The Union is founded on the values of respect for human dignity, freedom, democracy, equality, the rule of law and respect for human rights, including the rights of persons belonging to minorities. These values are common to the Member States in a society in which pluralism, non-discrimination, tolerance, justice, solidarity and equality between women and men prevail.

---

[6] [2004] OJ C310/1, 16 December 2004.
[7] At the informal European Council held in Lisbon on 18–19 October 2007, the Treaty Amending the Treaty on European Union and the Treaty Establishing the European Community, which is to replace The Constitutional Treaty, was agreed. See the Table of Equivalences between the Constitutional Treaty and the Reform Treaty.

In its relations with the wider world Article I-3(4) of the Constitutional Treaty states:

the Union shall uphold and promote its values and interests. It shall contribute to peace, security, the sustainable development of the Earth, solidarity and mutual respect among peoples, free and fair trade, eradication of poverty and the protection of human rights, in particular the rights of the child, as well as to the strict observance and the development of international law, including respect for the principles of the United Nations Charter.

These statements, declarations and treaty texts are a part of the European Union's international identity, whereby it represents itself as an entity constructed on a normative basis. As a consequence, the Union is predisposed 'to act in a normative way in world politics'.[8] It is certainly true that much of the Union's rhetoric in this regard is about external relations inspired by an 'ethics of responsibility' towards others due to its possession of political and economic power.[9] Lucarelli has argued, for example, that the Union is increasingly seen as an actor with principled behaviour in foreign policy, that behaves according to a set of dynamic yet identifiable values, principles and images of the world.[10]

These texts also illustrate, in part, the rationale upon which the Union wishes to legitimise its practices and identify some of the ethical values it considers itself founded upon and those which it wishes to promote. 'Ethical values' in this sense refers to the Union's perception of its disposition concerning a purpose and way of conducting itself in international affairs. Ethics can be encapsulated in a monolithic set of principles, in which case such an approach could amount to a 'morality' but that would narrow its scope.[11] Ethics in this sense concern the

---

[8] I. Manners, 'Normative Power Europe: a Contradiction in Terms?' (2002) 40 *JCMS* 235, 252.

[9] For an example of where the Union attempts to seduce the Chinese to adopt the same approach see B. Ferrero-Waldner, 'The EU and China: Moving Forward', Beijing, China, 18 January 2007, available at http://ec.europa.eu/comm/external_relations/china/docs/07_speech_renmin_university.pdf. It should also be noted that in the Millennium Declaration, General Assembly Resolution 55/2, 8 September 2000, para. 2, all states declared, 'we have a collective responsibility to uphold the principles of human dignity, equality and equity at the global level'.

[10] S. Lucarelli, 'Values, Principles, Identity and European Union Foreign Policy' in S. Lucarelli and I. Manners (eds.), *Values and Principles in European Union Foreign Policy* (London: Routledge, 2006) pp. 1, 2.

[11] J. Wallach, 'Human Rights as an Ethics of Power' in R. Wilson (ed.), *Human Rights in the 'War on Terror'* (Cambridge: Cambridge University Press, 2006) pp. 108, 111.

practical realisation of a purpose and shape the Union's exercising of power and politics.[12] Kagan has argued that as the United States believed it had discovered the secret to human happiness, so the Union (although he refers to 'Europeans') considers that it wishes to transport its miracle of reconciliation, compromise after generations of bitter conflict, prosperity and basis for the 'good life' to third states.[13] The realisation of such a purpose or at least the decision to share it with third states has both policy and legal implications. This chapter will deal first with some of the policy issues and then with the legal considerations which arise under international law from adopting and implementing such an approach to foreign policy.

2.2 Ethical Values and Foreign Policy: Choices and Implications

Schenbaum has, in the context of inter-state relations, helpfully classified state interests into three categories: individual state interests; state interests rooted in cooperation with closely associated and allied states; and interests held in common with all of international society, such as poverty reduction and the fight against instability and disease.[14] The pursuance and promotion of the values as presented and identified by the Union in its foreign policy formulation is primarily concerned with the third of these categories, although it can encompass the first and second of these categories also. Pursuing values will require the Union to take into account and be sensitive to the interests of individuals in third states. It may sometimes require acting in a manner which is detrimental to the interests of some of the Union's own citizens. There is no overriding moral consensus in international relations that such an approach be adopted. Consequently, as Light and Smith note, there is nothing wrong in states (or in our case the Union) not doing so.[15] The decision by a state or a group of states to promote and protect certain values in relations with third states is replete with policy

---

[12] See further Lucarelli and Manners, *Values and Principles*.

[13] R. Kagan, *Of Paradise and Power: America and Europe in the New World Order* (New York: Vintage Books, 2004) p. 61.

[14] T. Schenbaum, *International Relations: the Path Not Taken – Using International Law to Promote World Peace and Security* (Cambridge: Cambridge University Press, 2006) p. viii.

[15] K. Smith and M. Light, 'Introduction' in Smith and Light, *Ethics and Foreign Policy*, p. 3.

implications. The aim of this section is not to discuss all of them comprehensively but to highlight and identify certain issues which will be referred to in the later parts of the book, which examine practice, to provide a yardstick against which to measure EU actions.

It is apparent that the Union's decision to promote values such as democracy, human rights and equality in its relations with third states is an attempt to give further effect to values, which can be considered Liberal ones, in a global political order in which Realism is currently the prevailing ideology.[16] A common theme throughout the various strains of the Realist tradition of International Relations is an emphasis upon the power and interest equilibrium and the protection of state security and interests.[17] Realism in its classic form is the view that international society is essentially anarchical and emphasises the necessity of power arrangements to advance state interests. Thus for Morgenthau, for example, principles are subordinate to politics and the ultimate skill for any leader is to adapt to changing political configurations to protect the survival of the state.[18]

It is not contentious, however, to say that some of the values which the Union has identified and seeks to promote, in particular human rights, are now an entrenched feature of international relations. Michael Ignatieff, for example, has described human rights and their promotion as the *lingua franca* of global moral thought.[19] The issue is how to reconcile the fundamental and essential interests of an entity, be it a state or an international organisation, and the promotion of such values where the two appear to be incompatible? Jimmy Carter, whose US administration adopted a human rights dimension to its foreign policy which was narrower than the values identified by the Union, has stated

---

[16] See D. Forsythe, *Human Rights in International Relations* (Cambridge: Cambridge University Press, 2000) and J. Donnelly, *Realism and International Relations* (Cambridge: Cambridge University Press, 2000). For extensive discussion of the different variants of Realist thought see M. Smith, *Realist Thought from Weber to Kissinger* (Baton Rouge, La.: Louisiana State University Press, 1998); J. Haslam, *No Virtue like Necessity: Realist Thought in International Relations since Machiavelli* (New Haven: Yale University Press, 2002); and M. Doyle, *Ways of War and Peace: Realism, Liberalism and Socialism* (New York: W. W. Norton & Co Ltd, 1997) p. 41 *et seq.*

[17] See further Donnelly, *Realism*. Realists are sometimes referred to as Statists due to their emphasis on the preeminence of the state.

[18] H. Morgenthau, *Politics Among Nations: the Struggle for Power and Peace* (London: McGraw Hill, 1992) *passim.*

[19] M. Ignatieff, *Human Rights as Politics and Idolatry* (Princeton: Princeton University Press, 2003) p. 53.

that they had no idea how complicated such an orientation would be and what the ramifications of it would be.[20]

Some states acting unilaterally or collectively may wish to stand for something other than simply interest and power in their international relations. Choosing to do so, however, is not straightforward. There are difficult choices to be made concerning priorities and objectives in international relations and the relative weight to be attached to them, as well as the methods used to further those identified aims. To take an obvious example in the context of the European Union, the Union has since the Lisbon European Council in 2000 sought to work towards 'sustainable economic growth with more and better jobs and greater social cohesion'.[21] At the same time manufacturing industries have suffered significantly in Europe during the transition from manufacturing-based economies to knowledge and services-based ones. A question which must be posed, therefore, is: does the promotion of the values identified by the Union prohibit sales of armaments to a repressive regime, where this may be crucial for the economic survival of that part of manufacturing industry? Even if the policy is formulated so as to prohibit arms sales to repressive recipients, will the answer be the same if the regime is a crucial ally for security purposes, such as Pakistan or Egypt, in the proclaimed 'war on terror' to which all Member States (even if some of them are more enthusiastic about it than others) and the Union as a whole have subscribed?

Most Realists who have analysed foreign policies with such an orientation consider that even attempting to formulate such a policy is naïve, as it is ultimately futile. Vincent, for example, has argued that '[t]here is an inescapable tension between human rights and foreign policy'.[22] Trimble in a similar vein has noted that foreign policy is inherently an 'unprincipled enterprise, reflecting compromises of values

---

[20] J. Carter, *Keeping Faith: Memoirs of a President* (New York: Bantam Books, 1982) p. 144. Harold Koh, who was Assistant Secretary of State for Democracy, Human Rights and Labour in the United States under the Clinton administration, has said that for the United States the most difficult issue in this context was dealing with crisis management, as there were public expectations of a response even if state interests were not at stake. H. Koh, 'A United States Human Rights Policy for the 21st Century' (2002) 46 *Saint Louis University Law Journal* 293, 299.

[21] Lisbon Extraordinary European Council, 23–24 March 2000, (2000) 3 *Bull. EU* I.5.5. See further COM(2005)24 which attempts to identify a strategy for the Union to give effect to the Lisbon agenda.

[22] R. Vincent, *Human Rights and International Relations* (Cambridge: Cambridge University Press, 1986) p. 129.

and objectives on an *ad hoc* basis'.[23] Human rights, he argues, 'embody principle, universally and consistently applied. Foreign policy is about politics; human rights is about law. It is neither realistic nor desirable for the values of human rights ... to be perpetually paramount to all other values sought to be protected by ... foreign policy.'[24] Henry Kissinger, in the context of US policy, has gone further by stating:

> I believe it is dangerous for us to make the domestic policy of countries around the world a direct objective of ... foreign policy ... The protection of basic human rights is a very sensitive aspect of the domestic jurisdiction of ... governments.[25]

From this perspective, national interest and security are considered the ultimate objectives of foreign policy and all others will be compromised if they are endangered. The Realist approach in the context of inter-state relations also insists that the morality one expects in relations between the state and its citizens need not play a role in relations between states, as there is no single shared universal morality.[26] States, according to this approach, formulate their policies in moral language when it suits them and to cloak their other interests.[27] To take a recent example, the foreign policy formulated by President George W. Bush in the aftermath of September 2001 is cast in terms of values and moral language such as the 'fight against evil' but there is significant force in the argument that in reality this is all about *Realpolitik* and protecting the most fundamental and essential US economic and political interests.[28]

Most Realist studies on ethical or principled approaches to foreign policies, however, tend to be dismissive of them without a detailed examination of practice.[29] Despite the cynicism about such foreign

---

[23] P. Trimble, 'Human Rights and Foreign Policy' (2002) 46 *Saint Louis University Law Journal* 465, 467.

[24] *Ibid.*

[25] Cited by P. Baehr, *The Role of Human Rights in Foreign Policy*, 2nd edn (London: Macmillan Press, 1996) p. 85.

[26] Haslam, *No Virtue*, p. 250.

[27] M. Hollis and S. Smith, *Explaining and Understanding International Relations* (Oxford: Clarendon Press, 1990) p. 27.

[28] Schenbaum, *International Relations*, p. xi. See the State of the Union Address, Washington, 29 January 2002, available at www.whitehouse.gov/news/releases/2002/01/ 20020129–11.html and further the various National Security Strategies of the United States since 2002.

[29] See e.g., H. Kissinger, *Diplomacy* (New York: Touchstone, 1994) and H. Kissinger, *Toward a Diplomacy for the Twenty-First Century: Does America Need a Foreign Policy?* (London: Simon and Schuster, 2001) and further the work in n. 16 above.

policies among Realists, some adherents to this school do not entirely reject a role for ethical objectives, values and morality in foreign policy formulation. Such values are simply subordinate to other essentials. Kissinger, for example, as a leading proponent of that school of thought, notes:

America should give preference to democratic governments over repressive ones and be prepared to pay some price for its moral convictions ... there is an area of discretion which should be exercised in favour of governments ... promoting democratic values and human rights ... The difficulty arises in determining the precise price to be paid and its relationship to other essential American priorities.[30]

The role played by the values and principles identified in foreign policy formulation in the creation of a new legal and political order will, however, still be marginal. Those theorists who subscribe to the Liberal school of thought feel that such values can play a greater role (although it is not a central one) in the formulation of foreign policy than many Realists consider they should.[31] A 'weak liberal' such as Keohane,[32] while discussing values in foreign policy, has noted in the context of international cooperation that it does not 'necessarily depend upon altruism, idealism ... or a shared belief in a set of values embedded in a culture. At various times and places any of these ... may indeed play an important role ... but cooperation can be understood without reference to any of them.'[33]

Other schools of thought, however, consider that the role such values play in foreign policy formulation should be much more central. Those who advocate this approach do so for different reasons. Some adopt a philosophical approach, based on natural law, utilitarianism or religious

---

[30] Kissinger, *Diplomacy*, p. 811.
[31] The description 'liberal school' or 'liberal internationalism' encompasses an extremely broad tapestry of views. For a useful analysis in this context see K. Jørgensen, 'Theoretical Perspectives on the Role of Values, Images and Principles in Foreign Policy' in Lucarelli and Manners, *Values and Principles*, pp. 42, 44 *et seq.* and more generally Doyle, *Ways of War and Peace*, p. 205 *et seq.*; S. Burchill, R. Devetak, A. Linklater, M. Paterson, C. Reus-Smit and J. True, *Theories of International Relations*, 3rd rev. edn (Basingstoke: Palgrave Macmillan, 2005) p. 29 *et seq.*; and R. Jackson and G. Sørenson, *Introduction to International Relations: Theories and Approaches*, 2nd edn (Oxford: Oxford University Press, 2003) p. 105 *et seq.*
[32] I am using Jørgensen's description, Jørgensen, 'Theoretical Perspectives' p. 45.
[33] R. Keohane, *International Institutions and State Power: Essays in International Relations Theory* (Boulder: Westview Press, 1989) p. 159.

convictions.[34] Those who subscribe to the English School of International
Relations, for example, tend to argue that a foreign policy which places
the defence of human rights at the centre of its ethical code will make
an important contribution to both protecting national interests and
also strengthening the pillars of an international order.[35] The former
British Prime Minister, Tony Blair (in a major foreign policy speech
approximately ten years after Robin Cook announced that the United
Kingdom would have an 'ethical foreign policy') while in power seems
to have adopted this approach. Blair stated that British foreign policy
between 1997 and 2007 has 'been governed as much by values as
interests; indeed ... it is by furthering our values that we further our
interests in the modern era'.[36]

   This approach is unsurprisingly commensurate with policy documentation stemming from the British Foreign and Commonwealth Office.
The Foreign and Commonwealth Office, in identifying nine strategic
international priorities for the United Kingdom, has noted how these
priorities intersect and cannot be pursued in isolation. The priorities
identified include: making the world safer from global terror and weapons of mass destruction; supporting the economy and business through
an open and expanding global economy; and promoting sustainable
development and poverty reduction underpinned by human rights,
democracy, good governance and environmental protection.[37]

   The Union's approach is almost identical to this. The European Security
Strategy is a clear example, as it notes '[i]n a world of global threats, global
markets and global media, our security and prosperity increasingly
depend on an effective multilateral system. The development of a stronger international society, well functioning international institutions

---

[34] For a sample of views, see D. Forsythe, *Human Rights and World Politics*, 2nd edn (Lincoln:
    University of Nebraska Press, 1989); Forsythe, *Human Rights in International Relations*;
    Baehr, *Human Rights in Foreign Policy*; Smith and Light, *Ethics and Foreign Policy*; Donnelly,
    Realism; T. Dunne and N. Wheeler (eds.), *Human Rights in Global Politics* (Cambridge:
    Cambridge University Press, 1996); D. Hill and R. Beddard (eds.), *Human Rights and
    Foreign Policy: Principles and Practice* (Basingstoke: Macmillan Press, 1989) and Jørgensen,
    'Theoretical Perspectives'.
[35] See e.g., N. Wheeler, *Saving Strangers* (Oxford: Oxford University Press, 2000).
[36] T. Blair, 'Our Nation's Future: Defence', London, 12 January 2007, available at
    www.numberten.gov.uk/output/Page10688.asp
[37] FCO, *Active Diplomacy for a Changing World: the UK's International Priorities* (London: HMSO,
    2006) p. 28. Cf. a senior advisor involved in drafting the priorities, who stated in person
    that the exercise essentially involved identifying what the Foreign Office already did
    and then coming up with the priorities and not by identifying priorities first and
    adjusting the work of the Foreign Office in response to them.

and a rule-based international order is our objective.'[38] This is an attempt to reconcile essential interests with the creation of a stable international order in which its values are reflected. It can be argued, for example, that the European Union's adherence and commitment to the rule of law in international affairs is in part due to its absence of military power to rival that of the United States (and thus about constraining the latter's influence and trying to maintain a balance of power through 'soft power') and not solely about a commitment to the inherent value in the international rule of law.[39] The Union's 'soft power' in this context is being exercised in an attempt to get the outcomes it seeks through attracting others to its way of thinking as opposed to coercing them.[40]

From a long-term perspective, the interests of a polity's citizens can be best protected and promoted through a change in international thinking and in the behaviour of other states. The promotion of ethical values in third states, therefore, benefits the citizens of all states. As the former Commissioner for External Relations, Chris Patten noted in a speech 'human rights make moral, political and economic sense ... But it is also sensible for strategic reasons. Free societies tend not to fight one another or to be bad neighbours. Countries that treat their citizens decently are the best countries in which to do business.'[41] Foreign policies with an ethical dimension to them must, if they are to be sustainable, serve the long-term interests of the promoter. A long-term perspective requires implementation in the short term, however, and a careful balance must be struck between them.

Moving from the reasons for having such a policy (or not as the case may be) to giving effect to it, there are a number of general issues which should be borne in mind. For an ethical foreign policy to be meaningful, it must be clearly formulated and some order of priorities of the values and interests that are being pursued needs to be established. Furthermore, there must be some identification of how those objectives are to be achieved.

By and large positive measures, for example preferential trade agreements as a reward for approved and encouraged reforms, are not where

---

[38] J. Solana, *A Secure Europe in a Better World: the European Security Strategy*, p. 9. The strategy was approved by the European Council, 12–13 December 2003, Doc. 5381/04, para. 84.
[39] See Kagan, *Of Paradise and Power*, pp. 66 and 130.
[40] J. Nye, *Soft Power: the Means to Success in World Politics* (New York: Public Affairs, 2004) p. 5.
[41] Speech by Commissioner Patten, Human Rights Discussion Forum, Brussels, 30 November 1999, Speech 99/193.

the conceptual problems tend to lie. The formulation of such mechanisms and standards are not, on the whole, problematic. It is with regard to punitive, condemnatory or negative action that policy considerations and dilemmas become most apparent. The failure to systemise the evaluation process where punitive measures may be taken can lead to *ad hoc* decision-making. This runs a greater risk of inconsistency and incoherence with other policies and activities. In such circumstances, criticism of human rights and a lack of democratic instruments, for example, can be used strategically (and this is often the case): the absence of certain institutions and procedures or a failure to respect certain principles by third states becomes another ideological weapon by which to demonise a regime without any cost.

Some International Relations scholars argue that foreign policy decisions are usually made by utilising 'the rational model'.[42] According to this model, decision-makers look for the 'cost-benefit analysis' of any action and this is done by clarifying the goals in a situation; identifying their relative importance; identifying the alternative methods to achieving the goals; investigating the consequences and probable and possible implications of those alternatives; and then choosing the action that produces the best outcome in the situation.[43] Publicly identifying in advance and stating the priorities and weight to be attached to state objectives, in the above model, runs the risk of an administration being held a hostage to fortune. It limits flexibility and the ability to respond to changing international events and circumstances. Harold Koh, however, who was the Assistant Secretary of State for Democracy, Human Rights and Labour in the United States, has stated that one of the best ways to get such a policy enacted and implemented consistently is to announce your principles and policies in advance. He considers that there is then always a pressure to comply with the identified priorities and to take them into account when any decisions are being made.[44] Even where priorities are identified in political speeches and in policy documents, it is often difficult to determine the extent to which they are rhetoric and the extent to which they contain concrete legal undertakings, if any, and the relationship between the priorities, as some will be more important than others.

The pursuit of an ethical foreign policy also requires the utilisation of appropriate instruments. In the implementation of such a policy, there

---

[42] See e.g., J. Goldstein, *International Relations*, 3rd edn (Harlow: Longman, 1999) p. 150.
[43] *Ibid.*   [44] Koh, 'A United States Human Rights Policy', 300.

is discretion in deciding which instruments to use. The effectiveness and impact of differing instruments require careful consideration. The Union and Community have various instruments at their disposal by which to promote and protect ethical values in third states, which are discussed in Chapter 3. The discussion now turns to the general legal considerations in the promotion and protection of certain values in third states.

2.3 Legal Considerations and the Policy of Promoting and Protecting Ethical Values in Third States

The decision to promote certain ethical values and principles in relations with third states raises numerous legal questions. It is clear that there are legal limits to the permissibility of such a policy and the manner in which it can be pursued. The Union and Member States cannot unilaterally act in any manner they wish, without due regard to their international legal obligations. The principles of the sovereign equality of states and non-interference in the internal affairs of another state are central to determining the prima facie legality or otherwise, under international law, of a decision to promote and protect ethical values in third states. It may also be the case that the Member States, and possibly the Community and/or Union, are with regard to some values, legally obliged to promote and protect them in third states. This section deals with these issues. The discussion initially analyses the relationship between the Union and Community and international law. It then discusses more generally the legal limits, imposed by international law, upon a foreign policy which seeks to promote certain values and principles. The final section of the chapter examines the content of those values under international law which, according to their constitutive treaties, the Community and Union are obliged to promote in third states.

2.3.1 International Legal Obligations and the Member States, Community and Union

Before defining the content of any relevant international legal obligations, it must first of all briefly be determined in what way the Member States, Community and Union are recognised as being bound by international law. With regard to the Member States the issue is not subject to any difficulties. With regard to the Community and Union the issue is more complex. Two issues need to be examined: first, the extent to which they possess international legal personality; secondly, the approach of Community/Union law to public international law. The discussion on the latter point deals primarily with customary international law, as it is this body of law which is most relevant to the analysis which follows in later parts of the chapter.[45]

2.3.1.1 International Legal Personality and the Community and Union

In international law, personality is the basic proposition that an entity, whether it is a state, intergovernmental organisation or person, has in a specific context some legal capacity. Personality is relative. All legally recognised persons do not have identical powers and rights. Only states possess the totality of rights and duties.[46] Article 281 TEC states that the Community 'shall have legal personality'. The conferral of international legal personality in Article 281 TEC may be contrasted with the conferral of capacity in domestic law by Article 282 TEC. Article 281 TEC does not impose an obligation upon those states which are not a party to the Treaty, and for many years the Soviet Union and its allies declined to accept the personality of the EC. Article 310 TEC confers express power to the EC to conclude treaties with third states and organisations. Numerous provisions, such as Articles 133 and 181 TEC, in the fields of the common commercial policy and development cooperation respectively, confer competence to conclude Agreements with third states in a specific area. By looking at these provisions and practice,[47] it is clear that the EC has international legal personality.

---

[45] This is because the Community/Union cannot, as a non-state entity, currently be a party to, for example, international human rights treaties. The United Nations Convention on the Rights of Persons with Disabilities, 2007, opened for signature 30 March 2007, is an exception as Article 44 allows 'regional international organisations' to become party to it. The EC is among the signatories. The situation is also different in theory (as many practical obstacles will still have to be overcome in the Council of Europe) with regard to the Convention for the Protection of Human Rights and Fundamental Freedoms, 1950, ETS No. 5, once Protocol No. 14, ETS No. 194, is in force. Article I-9(2) of the proposed Constitutional Treaty imposes an obligation upon the Union to accede to the Convention. This, however, is supplemented by Protocol 32 to the Constitutional Treaty which allows each EU Member State to maintain the right to veto the EU's accession to the Convention in the Council of Europe's political bodies.

[46] See Advisory Opinion, *Reparations for Injuries Suffered in the Service of the United Nations* [1949] ICJ Reports 174, 179.

[47] The Community is now a party to literally hundreds of treaties.

With regard to the Union the issue is less clear-cut.[48] As is well known, it was expressly decided not to include references to the Union's legal personality in the TEU, primarily due to the intransigence of the United Kingdom on this matter.[49] A lack of express conferment of personality does not, however, preclude it. This is especially the case if reference is made to the aims and objectives of the entity and personality is deemed necessary to fulfil those objectives.[50] Academic commentary on the legal personality of the Union has, by and large, argued that full international legal personality may be implied from the treaty-making capacity of the European Union, but without addressing the implication of this conclusion.[51] Articles 24 and 38 TEU confer the ability to conclude Agreements with third states. Many authors who consider the Union to have personality do so because they consider it a pre-requisite for it to enter into an Agreement.[52] Yet this is not the case.[53]

---

[48] See, among others, J. Klabbers, 'Presumptive Personality: the European Union in International Law' in M. Koskenniemi (ed.), *International Law Aspects of the European Union* (The Hague: Martinus Nijhoff, 1997) p. 231; E. Paasivirta, 'The European Union: From an Aggregate of States to a Legal Person?' (1997) 2 *Hofstra Law and Policy Symposium* 37; N. Neuwahl, 'Legal Personality of the European Union: International and Institutional Aspects' in V. Kronenberger (ed.), *The European Union and the International Legal Order* (The Hague: Kluwer, 2001) p. 3; N. Neuwahl, 'A Partner with a Troubled Personality: EU Treaty Making in Matters of CFSP and JHA after Amsterdam' (1998) 3 *EFARev.* 177; R. Wessel, 'The International Legal Status of the European Union' (1997) 2 *EFARev.* 109; P. Eeckhout, *External Relations of the European Union: Legal and Constitutional Foundations* (Oxford: Oxford University Press, 2004) p. 154 *et seq.*; P. Koutrakos, *EU International Relations Law* (Oxford: Hart Publishing, 2006) p. 406 *et seq.*; J. Piris 'Comment on the Draft Amendments to Article 24 TEU', submission to Working Group III on Legal Personality of the European Convention, 24 November 2000, SN 5332/1/00 Rev.1; and R. Gosalbo Bono, 'Some Reflections on the CFSP Legal Order' (2006) 43 *CMLRev.* 337.

[49] See M. Eaton, 'Common Foreign and Security Policy' in D. O'Keeffe and P. Twomey (eds.), *Legal Issues of the Maastricht Treaty* (Chichester: Wiley & Sons, 1994) p. 215.

[50] See the *Reparations* opinion, n. 46 above, 179.

[51] The works cited in n. 48 above. For a contrary view see, among others, M. Bulterman, *Human Rights in the Treaty Relations of the European Community: Real Virtues or Virtual Reality?* (Antwerp: Intersentia, 2001) p. 53 and E. Denza, *The Intergovernmental Pillars of the European Union* (Oxford: Oxford University Press, 2002) p. 173.

[52] For a very express statement to this effect see J. Piris, *The Constitution for Europe: a Legal Analysis* (Cambridge: Cambridge University Press, 2006) p. 60.

[53] See further R. Higgins, 'The Legal Consequences for Member States of the Non-Fulfilment by International Organisations of their Obligations Toward Third Parties' (1995) 66 *AIDI* 249, 254; I. Brownlie, 'The Responsibility of States for the Acts of International Organisations' in M. Ragazzi (ed.), *International Responsibility Today: Essays in Memory of Oscar Schachter* (Leiden: Martinus Nijhoff, 2005) p. 355; and the Reports of the International Law Association Committee on the Accountability of International Organisations: *Report of the 68th ILA Conference* (London: International

Even after the Nice amendments to Article 24 TEU and in the light of a substantial amount of subsequent practice,[54] it is still not entirely clear if in these Agreements it is the Member States acting together but using the Council as a negotiating instrument, or if it is the Council acting for the Union.[55] Article 24 TEU can be seen to refer only to the internal decision-making process without any external implications. Declaration No. 4 to the Amsterdam Treaty on Article 24 TEU notes that such Agreements 'shall not imply any transfer of competence from the Member States to the European Union'. Gosalbo Bono has noted, however, that Nice reworded Article 24 TEU to make sure that international Agreements concluded by the Council under the CFSP are binding on the institutions of the Union – thus this underlines, it is argued, that the Agreements are concluded on behalf of the Union as a distinct entity rather than the Member States acting collectively.[56] Taking into account that Agreements are negotiated by the Presidency, which pursuant to Article 18(1) TEU represents the Union and not the Member States, subsequent practice and the number of Agreements concluded with a wide variety of third parties, the Union does seem to be adopting unilateral acts autonomously and distinctly from its Member States through the Council and thus personality can be seen on this basis as argued by Gosalbo-Bono to exist objectively as well as on an implied basis.[57]

The issue is still not, however, fully settled. The Final Report of Working Group III on Legal Personality of the European Convention[58] came out strongly in favour of the Union having its own explicit single legal personality with the proposal being that the Union absorb the separate legal personalities of the various Communities. In the reasoning of the Working Group, the Union had, in part, to have personality as the existing Communities already have express personality and if

---

Law Association, 1998) p. 584; *Report of the 69th ILA Conference* (London: International Law Association, 2000) p. 875; *Report of the 70th ILA Conference* (London: International Law Association, 2002) p. 772; and *Report of the 71st ILA Conference* (London: International Law Association, 2004) pp. 164, 190 *et seq.*

[54] See e.g., Council Decision 2001/352 Concerning the Conclusion of the Agreement between the European Union and the Federal Republic of Yugoslavia on the Activities of the European Union Monitoring Mission, [2001] OJ L125/1, 5 May 2001. For a list of most of the Agreements which have been concluded so far see Gosalbo Bono, 'Some Reflections', 356.

[55] See Declaration No. 4 to the Amsterdam Treaty on Article 24 TEU. For a contrary view, see Eeckhout, *External Relations*, p. 158 and the work cited therein.

[56] Gosalbo Bono, 'Some Reflections', 352.   [57] *Ibid.*

[58] CONV 306/02 WG III 16.

they were to be merged then it followed that the Union needed to have express personality as well. This view is reflected in Article I-7 of the proposed Constitutional Treaty and is accompanied by Article III-426 which is the conferral of capacity in domestic law, equivalent to Article 282 TEC. The Convention Working Group on Legal Personality considered that all too often the ambivalence of the current system leads to confusion both in relations with states which are not members of the Union and among Member States. This confusion was seen to undermine the affirmation of the Union's identity at the international level and legal certainty.[59] A substantial number of the fifty or so Agreements concluded using Article 24 TEU had already been finalised at the time of the Convention Working Group reaching its conclusions but it was still felt that the position was uncertain; it is on the basis of these Agreements that most commentators conclude categorically that personality already exists. In addition, if the basis for the Union having international legal personality is its powers under the CFSP then it should be noted that Common Strategies under Article 13 TEU are to be implemented by the Union in areas in which the *Member States* (not Union) have important interests in common.[60] As the Community has its own distinct legal personality, any legal personality enjoyed by the Union can only be based upon the CFSP. Furthermore, the Commission has clearly distinguished between the Community and Union in terms of legal personality when making representations to the ILC Special Rapporteur on the Responsibility of International Organisations.[61] All representations in terms of international responsibility refer to the European Community, not the European Union. It is the Community which is clearly and expressly seen as the legal person in these submissions.

It does seem clear that the issue of the Union's personality will not finally be laid to rest until there is an express conferral of personality in a treaty text which is in force. If the Union has personality, it has responsibility for its international actions. If it does not, the Community

---

[59] *Ibid.* para. 8.
[60] Although the Common Strategy is a failed legal instrument. See further the discussion in Chapter 3.
[61] See 'Responsibility of International Organisations', Comments and Observations from International Organisations, ILC 56th Session, A/CN.4/545. For an excellent discussion see S. Talmon, 'Responsibility of International Organizations: Does the European Union Require Special Treatment?' in Ragazzi, *International Responsibility*, p. 405.

and /or its Member States, and not the Union, are responsible for any unfulfilled obligations entered into or any acts which violate international law, which are carried out in its name. The important point is that personality only determines where responsibility lies, not whether it exists or not.[62]

2.3.1.2 Relationship between International Law and the Community and EU Legal Orders

From an international law perspective, it is clear that the Community and Union are bound in their activities to respect custom and the peremptory norms of international law in relations with third states and other international organisations. The International Court of Justice (ICJ), in assessing the Agreement of 25 March 1951 between the World Health Organisation (WHO) and Egypt, held that international organisations are subjects of international law and are bound by general rules of international law, under their constitutions and other international agreements to which they are parties.[63] The principle that international organisations may be held internationally responsible for their acts is now a part of customary international law.[64] The Community and Union are a party to neither the 1969 Vienna Convention on the Law of Treaties (VCLT) (as it is only open to states), nor the 1986 Vienna Convention on the Law of Treaties Between States and International Organisations, to which they can become a party.[65] Nevertheless, any treaty relationships they enter into with third states or organisations are regulated by the provisions of the Conventions to the extent that

---

[62] See G. Conway, 'Breaches of EC Law and the International Responsibility of Member States' (2002) 13 *EJIL* 679 and ILA, *Report on Accountability of International Organisations* (2004) p. 196 *et seq.* and more generally, M. Hirsch, *The Responsibility of International Organisations Towards Third Parties: Some Basic Principles* (Dordrecht: Martinus Nijhoff, 1995); K. Wellens, *Remedies Against International Organisations* (Cambridge: Cambridge University Press, 2002); and D. Sarooshi, *International Organizations and their Exercise of Sovereign Powers* (Oxford: Oxford University Press, 2005). The real problem is with mixed Agreements, entered into by the Community and Member States, which are outside the scope of this discussion.

[63] Advisory Opinion, *Interpretation of the Agreement of 25 March 1951 between the WHO and Egypt* [1980] ICJ Reports 73, 89. Also see Advisory Opinion, *Difference relating to Immunity from Legal Process of a Special Rapporteur of the Commission on Human Rights* [1999] ICJ Reports 62, para. 66.

[64] ILA, *Report on Accountability of International Organisations* (2004) p. 196.

[65] Vienna Convention on the Law of Treaties, 1969, 1155 UNTS 331 and the Vienna Convention on the Law of Treaties between States and International Organisations or between International Organisations, 1986, UN Doc.A/Conf.129/15, (1986) 25 *ILM* 543.

they reflect custom. Furthermore, Article 103 of the United Nations Charter, an organisation of which all Member States of the Union are also party, obliges all states to give priority to their obligations under the Charter, as opposed to those entered into under other treaties.

The now defunct European Commission of Human Rights and the European Court of Human Rights (ECtHR) on a number of occasions have adopted the same approach and made clear that a State Party does not evade responsibility under the European Convention on Human Rights (ECHR) if it acts in a manner contrary to its other international legal obligations.[66] In the context of the obligations stemming from the treaties establishing the Community, the European Commission in its submission to the ECtHR in the *Bosphorus* case argued that 'while a State retained some Convention responsibility after it had ceded powers to an international organisation, that responsibility was fulfilled once there was proper provision in that organisation's structure for effective protection of fundamental rights at a level at least "equivalent" to that of the Convention'.[67] The ECtHR, while accepting this submission in part, stated that:

In the Court's view, State action taken in compliance with such legal obligations is justified as long as the relevant organisation is considered to protect fundamental rights, as regards both the substantive guarantees offered and the mechanisms controlling their observance, in a manner which can be considered at least equivalent to that for which the Convention provides (... an approach with which the parties and the European Commission agreed). By 'equivalent' the Court means 'comparable': any requirement that the organisation's protection be 'identical' could run counter to the interest of international co-operation pursued. However, any such finding of equivalence could not be final and would be susceptible to review in the light of any relevant change in fundamental rights' protection.

If such equivalent protection is considered to be provided by the organisation, the presumption will be that a State has not departed from the requirements of the Convention when it does no more than implement legal obligations flowing from its membership of the organisation. However, any such presumption can be rebutted if, in the circumstances of a particular case, it is considered that the protection of Convention rights was manifestly deficient. In such

---

[66] For example, in 1958, the European Commission made it clear that any State Party to the ECHR remained liable if it concluded any other international agreement which required the State Party to act in a manner contrary to its obligations under the Convention: *X v. Federal Republic of Germany* (1958) 2 *YB* 256.

[67] *Bosphorus Hava Yollari Turzm ve Ticaret Anonim Şirketi v. Ireland* (2006) 42 EHRR 1, para. 122. Also see *Matthews v. United Kingdom* (1999) 28 EHRR 361.

cases, the interest of international co-operation would be outweighed by the Convention's role as a 'constitutional instrument of European public order' in the field of human rights.[68]

The ECtHR has in the *Bosphorus* case left itself with ample discretion to enquire into the level of protection provided under Community law and to reach different assessments as to whether State Parties are complying with their Convention obligations on a case by case basis. Even though the standard is a high one, manifest deficiency, the Member States are responsible for any violations of the ECHR they may commit in the course of carrying out their legal obligations under the Community Treaty.

What is clear is that states cannot evade their obligations under the UN Charter or international human rights treaties to which they are party, such as the ECHR, by delegating powers to other organisations which they establish. While this may be obvious, the pertinent question is: what is the legal approach of the Community to these issues?

The European Court of Justice (ECJ) considers the Community to be a legal order *sui generis*.[69] As de Witte notes, the ECJ has never stated 'in so many words that EC law is entirely outside the scope of public international law but some of its dicta seem to point in that direction'.[70] Notwithstanding the unique qualities the ECJ considers the Community to possess, the ECJ does show a large measure of deference to international law and the decisions or the judgments of other international tribunals, in particular the ECtHR.[71] The fact that the Community legal order owes a great deal to international law and forms part of the international legal order is indisputable. Community law is nothing more than treaty law at its most integrated. Article 307 TEC does recognise that the legal obligations of the Member States, entered into prior to becoming members of the Community, should be respected vis-à-vis third parties. This is opposed to relations between states which are members of the EC, where Community law supersedes it in the areas it regulates.

---

[68] *Bosphorus*, n. 67 above, paras. 155–6.
[69] Case 26/62 *NV Algemené Transport–en Expeditie Onderneming Van Gend en Loos* v. *Nederlandse Adminstratie der Belastingen* [1963] ECR 1, 12.
[70] B. De Witte, 'Rules of Change in International Law: How Special is the EC?' (1994) 25 *NYBIL* 299, 300.
[71] See M. Bronckers, 'The Relationship of the EC Courts with Other International Tribunals: Non-Committal, Respectful or Submissive?' (2007) 44 *CMLRev.* 601.

The position of international law within the EC legal order can be seen to be analogous to the relationship between international law and the national law of a state. States can be monist or dualist; both are permissible – international law is concerned not with the method but the end result.[72] On the occasions the ECJ has looked at the role of custom and its impact in the Community legal order, it has tended to be in the context of the ability of individuals to challenge Community acts on the basis that they conflict with customary international law.[73] In *Racke*, Advocate General Jacobs explored the relationship between custom and the legal systems of the Member States but came to an ambivalent conclusion.[74] This was of importance in the context of custom binding the Community's actions as general principles of Community law resulting from the constitutional traditions common to the Member States. The ECJ has also displayed uncertainty as to the rights custom provides individuals and the circumstances in which it can be invoked by them under Community law. It did, however, state in *Racke* that:

> It should be noted in that respect that, as is demonstrated by the Court's judgment in *Poulsen and Diva Navigation* ... the *European Community must respect international law in the exercise of its powers*. It is therefore required to comply with the rules of customary international law when adopting a regulation suspending the trade concessions granted by, or by virtue of, an agreement which it has concluded with a non-member country.[75]

The Court of First Instance (CFI) has also discussed the relationship between the 'domestic or Community legal order' vis-à-vis that of the United Nations in a number of cases.[76] The CFI has been bolder in its

---

[72] See E. Denza, 'The Relationship between International and National Law' in M. Evans (ed.), *International Law*, 2nd edn (Oxford: Oxford University Press, 2006) pp. 423, 427.

[73] Case C-286/90 *Poulsen and Diva Navigation* [1992] ECR I-6019; Case T-115/94 *Opel Austria* [1997] ECR II-39 and Case C-162/96 *A. Racke GmbH & Co.* v. *Hauptzollant Mainz* [1998] ECR I-3655.

[74] See para. 89 of his Opinion.

[75] *Racke*, n. 73 above, para. 45. Emphasis added. See also para. 46 *et seq.*

[76] See Case T-315/01 *Yassin Aduallah Kadi* v. *Council and Commission* [2005] ECR II-3649 (at the time of writing on appeal as C-402/05 P) para. 228 and Case T-306/01 *Ahmed Ali Yusef and Al Barakat International Foundation* v. *Council and Commission* [2005] ECR II-3533 (at the time of writing on appeal as C-415/05 P). These cases have been upheld in Case T-253/02 *Chafiq Ayadi* v. *Council* [2006] ECR II-2139; Case T-228/02 *Organisation des Modjahedines du Peuple d'Iran* v. *Council* [2007] 1 CMLR 34; Case T-49/04 *Faraj Hassan* v. *Council and Commission* [2006] ECR II-52 (at the time of writing on appeal as C-399/06 P); Case T-362/04 *Leonid Minin* v. *Commission*, judgment of 31 January 2007, nyr; and Case T-47/03 *Jose Maria Sison* v. *Council* [2007] 3 CMLR 39.

approach than the ECJ and in a series of cases it has expressly asserted the primacy of international law and the obligations stemming from the Member States' membership of the United Nations over that of Community law. In *Ahmed Ali Yusuf*, for example, the CFI noted in the context of the relationship between Community law and obligations stemming from the Security Council that 'the Community must be considered to be bound by the obligations under the Charter of the United Nations in the same way as its Member States, by virtue of the Treaty establishing it'.[77] The CFI made it clear that it is in terms of Community not international law that the Community is bound by Charter obligations.

The exact impact of custom, and the significance of international law more generally, in the Community legal order depends on the circumstances in which it is being invoked. Lenearts and De Smijter have argued that the views of the ECJ and generally understood inter-pretations of international law do not always coincide.[78] Taking a restrictive view, the ECJ's dicta in *Racke* above can be read to mean that an individual would not be able to challenge a treaty which con-flicted with customary international law through the judicial review procedures of the Community, solely on that basis.[79] In practical terms, however, notwithstanding the criticism of Lenearts and De Smijter, the ECJ does in its jurisprudence take account of the international legal obligations which regulate its activities. The dicta from *Racke*, cited above, should be read more broadly as a general recognition of the binding nature of customary international law upon the Community in all its activities. This has been the approach of the CFI in cases such as *Yusuf*, *Kadi* and *Ayadi*. The CFI can in fact, if anything, be accused of being excessively eager in its recognition of which norms (and their content) it considers to be peremptory ones.[80]

---

[77] Case T-306/01 *Ahmed Ali Yusef*, n. 76 above, para. 243.

[78] K. Lenearts and E. De Smijter, 'The European Union as an Actor under International Law' (1999/2000) 19 *YEL* 95, 122.

[79] The point here is that no matter what the status of the norm violated, unless the individual can rely on another rule of Community law, it cannot be challenged. The ICJ adopted this exact approach in *Bosnia and Herzegovina* v. *Serbia and Montenegro – Case concerning the Application of the Convention on the Prevention and Punishment of the Crime of Genocide*, judgment of 26 February 2007, para. 147, nyr.

[80] The CFI in, for example, Case T-306/01 *Ahmed Ali Yusef*, n. 76 above, at para. 284 *et seq.* considered the right to property, the right to a fair hearing and the right to an effective judicial remedy to be peremptory norms, which they clearly are not. See further the discussion below.

The reference by the ECJ in *Racke* to the adoption of a regulation, as an exercise of its powers, is simply one example of when regard must be had to custom. Where treaty relations are under consideration before the ECJ, for example, reference to the terms of the two Vienna Conventions is commonplace and the ECJ always perceives them to bind the Community on the basis that they represent customary international law.[81] The Community was created by states, which do not have the power to establish any entity outside the rules of the international legal order. Even if the Community is said to be a legal order *sui generis*, there is little doubt that it and the Union are bound in their activities to comply with the general rules of international law and the ECJ, and especially the CFI, as far as the Community is concerned, recognise this.[82]

2.3.2 Legal Limits to Ethical Foreign Policies under International Law

The principles of the sovereign equality of states and non-interference in the internal affairs of another state are central in determining the prima facie legality or otherwise, under international law, of the Union's ethical foreign policies. This section is primarily concerned with the legality of the nature of such policies *per se*, rather than the manner in which the Union's policies are implemented in practice. The latter issue will be developed in Chapter 3, although some general comments are made in the following sections. The following two sections of the chapter discuss first, as noted above, the legality of an ethical foreign policy in general, and secondly, the legal limits on implementing such a policy.

2.3.2.1 State Sovereignty and the Principle of Non-Interference

When the Union promotes the values it considers important in third states, it must be careful to ensure that it simply exerts its influence in requesting them to adhere to certain standards and does not intervene in their internal affairs. In many senses, this is the crux of the issue which this section deals with. It is concerned with what Falk has referred to, in a narrower context, as the reconciliation between

---

[81] For example, the ECJ referred to the 1986 VCLTSIO in Case C-158/91 *Ministère Public et Direction du Travail et de l'Emploi* v. *Jean-Claude Levy* [1993] ECR I-4287, para. 19 and to the 1969 VCLT in Opinion 2/00 *Cartagena Protocol on Biosafety* [2001] ECR I-9713, para. 24.

[82] For a narrower discussion in the context of human rights, see further T. Ahmed and I. Butler, 'The European Union and Human Rights: an International Law Perspective' (2006) 17 *EJIL* 771.

sovereignty and human rights.[83] There are two different but related issues of concern: first, the extent to which international law limits the sovereignty of a state vis-à-vis the nature and actual relationship in existence between it and those within its jurisdiction;[84] secondly, the extent to which international law allows, or at least does not forbid, third states acting in an attempt to influence that relationship.

The principles of state sovereignty and the equality of all states prima facie preclude external coercion upon a state to adhere to certain values. The internal regulation of relations between a state and its citizens is, generally speaking, within the *domaine réservé* of that state. The complexity of the interrelationship which exists between sovereignty, non-intervention in internal affairs and values, such as human rights, is reflected in Articles 1, 2, 55 and 56 of the UN Charter (UNC), in particular, Article 2, on the one hand, and, on the other, Articles 55 and 56.[85] The relevance and importance of Article 2(7) of the Charter and the principle it encapsulates cannot be overestimated.[86] It is difficult to find any resolution adopted in any of the UN organs or bodies

---

[83] See R. Falk, *Human Rights Horizons: the Pursuit of Justice in a Globalising World* (London: Routledge, 2000) Ch. 4.

[84] With regard to sovereignty Henkin wryly noted, '[s]overeignty is a bad word … [i]t means many things, some essential, some insignificant, some agreed, some controversial'. See L. Henkin, 'International Law: Politics, Values and Functions' (1989) 216 *RDC* 9, 24.

[85] Article 2(7) UNC is concerned with the United Nations intervening in the internal affairs of its members and not with relations between them. In the light of Article 2(1) UNC it does not legitimise intervention by others. For detailed discussion, see B. Simma (ed.), *The Charter of the United Nations* (Oxford: Oxford University Press, 1994) p. 139 *et seq.*; L. Preuss, 'Article 2, Paragraph 7 of the Charter of the United Nations and Matters of Domestic Jurisdiction' (1949) 74 *RDC* 553; A. Trindade, 'The Domestic Jurisdiction of States in the Practice of the United Nations and Regional Organisations' (1976) 25 *ICLQ* 715; F. Ermacora, 'Human Rights and Domestic Jurisdiction' (1968) 124 *RDC* 371; L. Henkin, *The Age of Rights* (New York: Columbia, 1990) Ch. 4; H. Waldock, 'General Course on Public International Law'(1962) 106 *RDC* 5, 173 *et seq.*; R. Higgins, *The Development of International Law through the Political Organs of the United Nations* (London: RIIA and Oxford University Press, 1963) p. 58 *et seq.*; J. Alvarez, *International Organizations as Law-Makers* (Oxford: Oxford University Press, 2005) p. 156 *et seq.*; K. Zemanek, 'Human Rights Protection vs. Non Intervention: a Perennial Conflict?' in L. Vohrah, F. Pocar, Y. Featherstone, O. Fourmy, C. Graham, J. Hocking and N. Robson (eds.), *Man's Inhumanity to Man: Essays on International Law in Honour of Antonio Cassese* (The Hague: Kluwer Law International, 2003) p. 383; and R. Jennings and A. Watts (eds.), *Oppenheim's International Law*, 9th edn (Harlow: Longman, 1992) p. 427 *et seq.*

[86] The principle is one of customary international law, notwithstanding Article 2(7) UNC. See *Nicaragua* v. *United States of America – Case concerning Military and Paramilitary Activities in and Against Nicaragua* [1986] ICJ Reports 14, paras. 174 and 202 (hereinafter 'the *Nicaragua* case'). Higgins, *Development of International Law*, p. 61, writing in 1963 argued

which, when dealing with, for example, international cooperation and assistance between states in the fields of human rights and democracy, does not refer to Article 2(7) UNC either expressly or implicitly. The now defunct Commission on Human Rights[87] and the General Assembly,[88] for example, have adopted dozens of resolutions concerned with the promotion and protection of human rights and democracy, which require cooperation between states. These resolutions consistently reiterate that when states cooperate with or assist one another, they should respect the provisions of the Charter. Either the principle of non-interference or Article 2(7) UNC is almost always referred to.

It is possible to argue that international society is now undergoing a paradigmatic shift from the era of geopolitics to one of geogovernance, where the broader interests of social justice, such as the protection of human rights, take priority over the doctrine of non-intervention.[89] According to this approach, the human rights treaties which have been negotiated under the auspices of the United Nations and subsequent state practice have changed the nature and scope of that which is defined as within the 'domestic affairs' of a state. As Reisman has argued, 'no serious scholar still supports the contention that internal human rights are "essentially within the domestic jurisdiction of any State" and hence insulated from international law'.[90] Similarly, McGoldrick has argued that the once central issue of domestic jurisdiction is now largely peripheral.[91] Conversely it can be argued, however, that such

that the assumption that the manner in which a state treated its own citizens was a matter of domestic jurisdiction was open to serious doubt.

[87] For example, see the following resolutions: Promotion of a Democratic and Equitable International Order, CHR Resolutions 2003/63, 2002/72, 2001/72 and 1999/68; Enhancement of International Cooperation in the Field of Human Rights, CHR Resolutions 2002/86, 2001/67 and 2000/70; The Role of Good Governance in the Promotion of Human Rights, CHR Resolution 2003/65; and Further Measures to Promote and Consolidate Democracy, CHR Resolution 2002/46.

[88] For example, see the following resolutions: Enhancement of International Cooperation in the Field of Human Rights, A/RES/57/224 and A/RES/55/109; Promotion of a Democratic and Equitable International Order, A/RES/57/213, A/RES/56151 and A/RES/55/107; Strengthening the Rule of Law, A/RES/57/221; and Promoting and Consolidating Democracy, A/RES/55/96.

[89] See C. Chinkin, 'Human Rights and the Politics of Representation: Is there a Role for International Law?' in M. Byers (ed.), *The Role of Law in International Politics: Essays in International Relations and International Law* (Oxford: Oxford University Press, 2000) p. 131.

[90] M. Reisman, 'Sovereignty and Human Rights in Contemporary International Law' (1990) 84 *AJIL* 866, 869.

[91] See D. McGoldrick, 'Approaches to the Assertion of International Jurisdiction: the Human Rights Committee' in P. Capps, M. Evans and S. Konstadinidis (eds.), *Asserting Jurisdiction: International and European Legal Perspectives* (Oxford: Hart Publishing, 2003)

treaties are only elaborating upon, and not transforming, the nature of the relationship between human rights and that which is within the 'domestic affairs' of a state.[92] There is no need, however, to perceive the relationship between human rights and other values such as democracy, on the one hand, and, on the other, sovereignty, as a zero-sum game as is often contended.[93] Neither is it necessary to define sovereignty to encapsulate responsibility for a population.[94] The soundest way to examine the relationship between sovereignty and values such as human rights is to question what amounts to interference and the extent to which such matters are actually within the internal affairs of a state. If 'ethical values' are not within the internal affairs of a state or if the 'interventions' of a third state or organisation do not amount to interference then state sovereignty is not an impediment to an ethical foreign policy.[95]

The views of the Union and its Member States on where the boundaries lie between what is and is not within the internal affairs of a state and what amounts to interference in such situations have undergone a fundamental shift. During the negotiation of the First Lomé Convention ('Lomé 1'), for example, the ACP states and Commission resisted the inclusion of references to human rights precisely because it was felt that it would interfere in the internal affairs of the states in question.[96] The 1986 Declaration on Human Rights of the twelve EU Member States, however, states quite clearly that, 'the protection of human rights is the legitimate and continuous duty of the world community and of nations

---

pp. 199, 200 and D. McGoldrick, 'Human Rights and Non-Intervention' in V. Lowe and C. Warbrick (eds.), *The United Nations and the Principles of International Law: Essays in Memory of Michael Akehurst* (London: Routledge, 1994) p. 85.

[92] M. Byers, *Custom, Power and the Power of Rules* (Cambridge: Cambridge University Press, 1999) p. 43.

[93] See M. Kamminga, *Inter-State Accountability for Violations of Human Rights* (Philadelphia: University of Pennsylvania Press, 1992) p. 1; Henkin, 'International Law: Politics, Values and Functions'; I. Brownlie, *Principles of International Law*, 6th edn (Oxford: Oxford University Press, 2003) p. 294; and McGoldrick, 'Human Rights and Non-Intervention', p. 85.

[94] See Reisman, 'Sovereignty and Human Rights'; R. Falk, 'Sovereignty and Human Dignity: the Search for Reconciliation' in F. Deng and T. Lyons (eds.), *African Reckoning: a Quest for Good Governance* (Washington, DC: Brookings Institute, 1998) p. 14; and International Commission on Intervention and State Sovereignty, *The Responsibility to Protect* (Ottawa, On.: International Development Research Centre, 2001).

[95] This is recognised in most of the works cited in the previous two notes, it is just that other approaches are also adopted.

[96] See T. King, 'Human Rights in the Development Policy of the EC: Towards a European World Order?' (1997) 27 *NYIL* 51, 54.

individually. *Expressions* of concern at violations of such rights cannot be considered interference in the domestic affairs of a State.'[97] More recently in a statement at the Fifty-sixth Session of the Commission on Human Rights, a spokesperson on behalf of the Presidency noted:

> human rights ... are ... about universality. No country should be free to invoke sovereignty or interference in internal affairs to prevent people under its jurisdiction from fully enjoying their human rights. It is the duty of the international community to call upon those States ... to cease those practices and bring the perpetrators to justice.[98]

The approach the Union has adopted is that it is perfectly legitimate for it to comment upon the protection or violation of any rights in any state.[99] An examination of Union practice, especially the issuing of declarations and démarches, illustrates that this is indeed its practice and view.[100] It is worth questioning, however, to what extent the approach of the Union is in accordance with international law. In the *Nationality Decrees* cases the Permanent Court of International Justice (PCIJ) stated:

> within the domestic jurisdiction seems ... to contemplate certain matters which ... are not in principle matters regulated by international law ... The question whether a certain matter is or is not solely within the jurisdiction of a State is an essentially relative question; it depends upon the development of international relations.[101]

In the later *Lotus* case[102] the approach adopted by the PCIJ was essentially that states are free to engage in any act they wish, as it emanates from their own will, so long as another rule of international law does

---

[97] Declaration on Human Rights, 21 July 1986, (1986) 7/8 *Bull. EC* 2.4.4. Emphasis added.

[98] Statement by Mr J. Gama, on behalf of the Portuguese Presidency, Geneva, 21 March 2000.

[99] The view of the United States, although similar to that of the European Union with regard to third states, is somewhat different (as is that of most states) when it is the subject of criticism. After the decision of the ICJ in the *Nicaragua* case, US State Department Legal Advisor Abraham Sofaer stated, 'we reserve to ourselves the power to determine which matters fall essentially within the domestic jurisdiction of the United States'. Cited by N. Chomsky, *Hegemony or Survival: America's Quest for Global Dominance* (London: Penguin, 2004) p. 14. This is, of course, reiterating the terms of the so called 'Connally reservation' as devised by the United States in accepting the ICJ's jurisdiction under Article 36(2) of the ICJ Statute.

[100] See Chapter 3.

[101] Advisory Opinion, *Nationality Decrees Issued in Tunis and Morocco*, PCIJ (1923) Series B, No. 4, 1, 24.

[102] *France v. Turkey*, PCIJ (1927) Series A, No. 10, 1.

not prohibit it. This position has been repeated on numerous occasions.[103] Furthermore, in the *Reparations* opinion, it was stated that a state is an entity which 'possesses the totality of international rights and duties *recognised by international law*'.[104] In each case the fundamental limit of 'domestic jurisdiction' is the extent to which international law, at that time, prohibits the activity in question or requires states to act in a particular manner.

In the *Nicaragua* case, the ICJ had to determine the legality of US acts which included assisting the *contras* in Nicaragua and laying mines in Nicaraguan territorial waters. The ICJ drew heavily upon the definitions of non-intervention which had been formulated in two General Assembly Declarations: On the Principles of International Law Concerning Friendly Relations and Cooperation Among States in Accordance with the Charter of the United Nations 1970[105] and On the Inadmissibility of Intervention in the Domestic Affairs of States and the Protection of their Independence and Sovereignty 1965.[106] With regard to non-intervention in general, it noted:

in view of the generally accepted formulations [i.e., the two declarations], the principle forbids all States or groups of States to intervene directly or indirectly in the internal or external affairs of other States. A prohibited intervention must accordingly be one bearing on matters in which each State is permitted, by the principle of State sovereignty, to decide freely.[107]

Citing examples, the ICJ noted that the 'choice of political, economic, social and cultural system and the formulation of foreign policy' were all matters within the domestic jurisdiction of a state.[108] Subsequent General Assembly declarations have also dealt with non-intervention in internal affairs but essentially none of them actually touch upon the fundamental issue of what is and is not generally within the 'domestic affairs' of a state.[109] The reason for this is clear; it is not fixed but dependent upon the development of international law. As Rosalyn Higgins noted in 1963 in what is still one of the most insightful and detailed discussions on this issue, 'the legal principle of domestic

---

[103] See e.g., Advisory Opinion, *Legality of the Threat or Use of Nuclear Weapons* [1996] ICJ Reports 226 and the *Nicaragua* case, n. 86 above.

[104] Advisory Opinion, *Reparations*, n. 46 above, para. 180. Emphasis added.

[105] GA Resolution 2625 (XXV) 24/10/1970. See the *Nicaragua* case, para. 191.

[106] GA Resolution 2131 (XX) 21/12/1965. See the *Nicaragua* case, para. 203.

[107] *Ibid.* para. 205.   [108] *Ibid.*

[109] Most importantly, the Declaration on the Inadmissibility of Intervention and Interference in the Internal Affairs of States, A/RES/36/103.

jurisdiction is ... singularly susceptible to development by the process of interpretation by political bodies'.[110]

This same fluid approach was also adopted by the Institut De Droit International (IDI) in its 1954 declaration 'la détermination du domaine réservé et ses effets'.[111] The Institut's 1989 declaration on 'The Protection of Human Rights and the Principles of Non-Intervention in Internal Affairs of States',[112] however, indicates where the boundaries lie between domestic jurisdiction and international regulation and the permissibility of measures which may be taken to persuade third states to uphold and protect human rights. Article 1 of the Declaration considers the protection of human rights to be an obligation *erga omnes*. Having attained such a status, such rights are no longer considered matters which are essentially within the domestic jurisdiction of a state. Articles 2 and 3 of the Declaration deal with the legality of action by third states in response to the violation of human rights by another state. Article 3 contends that diplomatic representations, as well as purely verbal expressions of concern or disapproval, regarding violations of any human rights are lawful in all circumstances. Article 2 considers that retorsion, reprisals and other countermeasures are legitimate responses to the violation of human rights in a third state, provided such measures are permitted under international law and do not involve the use of force. The Declaration considers that 'such measures cannot be considered an unlawful interference in the internal affairs of that State'. Article 2 also draws a distinction between non-derogable and derogable rights. In the case of the former, violations do not have to be gross or systematic to justify third state action, whereas in the case of the latter, the implication is that individual violations will not be enough.[113]

Although the Declaration is not legally binding, it does raise a number of issues which necessitate further discussion. The Declaration does not attempt to define the term 'human rights', all of which are considered to be obligations *erga omnes*, although it does draw a distinction in terms

---

[110] Higgins, *Development of International Law*, p. 61. The exact same point is also made by T. Farer, 'Promoting Democracy: International Law and Norms' in E. Newman and R. Rich (eds.), *The UN Role in Promoting Democracy: Between Ideals and Reality* (Tokyo: United Nations University Press, 2004) pp. 32, 34.

[111] Session d'Aix-en-Provence 1954. Article 1 states, 'le domaine réservé est celui des activités étatiques où la compétence de l'Etat n'est pas liée par le droit international. L'étendue de ce domaine dépend du droit international et varie suivant son développement.'

[112] Session of Santiago de Compostela.   [113] See Article 2(3).

of the appropriate action in response to violations of different rights. Nor is it concerned with 'ethical values' beyond human rights and thus only considers 'interference' by third states permissible when human rights are being violated. Unless issues such as the rule of law, democracy and good governance directly impact upon the protection of such rights, then they are within the domestic jurisdiction of a state. Furthermore the Declaration does not deal with the positive aspect of promoting ethical values (which is addressed below), but simply with action by third states in response to the violation of human rights. It considers that responses are legitimate, under international law, notwithstanding the existence of procedures under various international human rights treaties to deal with their violation. General self-help or horizontal mechanisms for the enforcement of international law, in this case human rights, have supposedly remained intact. As these above issues are vital in determining the legality of an ethical foreign policy under international law, they will be examined in turn.

2.3.2.1(a) Human Rights and Obligations Erga Omnes

There are certain international legal norms in whose violation all states have a legal interest. These are the obligations *erga omnes*, as identified by the ICJ in its dictum in the *Barcelona Traction* case.[114] The ICJ stated:

> an essential distinction should be drawn between the obligations of a State towards the international community as a whole, and those arising vis-à-vis another State ... By their very nature the former are the concern of all States. In view of the importance of the rights involved, all States can be held to have a legal interest in their protection; they are obligations *erga omnes* ... Such obligations derive, for example, in contemporary international law, from the outlawing of acts of aggression, and of genocide, and also from the principles and rules concerning the basic rights of the human person, including protection from slavery and racial discrimination.[115]

The ICJ only gave an illustrative list of such obligations. *Third Restatement of the Foreign Relations Law of the United States*, section 702, in this context considers that any state 'violates international law if, as a matter of state policy, it practices, encourages, or condones' violations of certain

---

[114] See *Belgium* v. *Spain – Barcelona Traction, Light and Power Company, Limited*, Second Phase, [1970] ICJ Reports 3.

[115] *Ibid.* paras. 33–34. The status of genocide as an obligation *erga omnes* has subsequently been confirmed, *inter alia*, in *Bosnia and Herzegovina* v. *Yugoslavia – Case concerning Application of the Convention on the Prevention and Punishment of the Crime of Genocide*, Preliminary Objections [1996] ICJ Reports 595, para. 31.

rights. In addition to those rights listed by the ICJ in the *Barcelona Traction* case, section 702 makes specific reference to murder or disappearances; torture or other cruel, inhuman or degrading treatment or punishment; prolonged arbitrary detention; and a 'consistent pattern of gross violations of internationally recognised human rights'.[116] The Human Rights Committee (HRC), established by the International Covenant on Civil and Political Rights, 1966 (ICCPR), has also contributed to this debate.[117] In General Comment 24 it stated that all states party to the Covenant are prohibited from entering reservations to key provisions, that is, those which are considered to be peremptory norms.[118] The list of rights includes: slavery; torture and other forms of inhuman treatment; executing pregnant women; presuming a person guilty until they prove their innocence; arbitrarily arresting and detaining persons; and permitting the advocacy of national, racial or religious hatred.[119] The General Comment is, strictly speaking, only of relevance to those states which are a party to the Covenant.

Both General Comment 24 and the *Third Restatement* take a very expansive approach to those rights which, when violated, all states have an interest in. Beyond those norms referred to by the ICJ in the *Barcelona Traction* case, there is disagreement over which others can be considered to be obligations *erga omnes*.[120] At the very least, however,

---

[116] *Restatement (Third) of Foreign Relations Law* (1987), s.702. Section 702(m) considers that 'any State is liable under customary law for a consistent pattern of violation of any such right as State policy'. With regard to the rights listed, so long as the violations are state policy, responsibility is invoked. The scale is not important. With regard to the other norms referred to in s.702 (privacy; arbitrary arrest and detention; denial of fair trial; grossly disproportionate punishment; freedom of conscience and religion; and invidious racial or religious discrimination) only gross violations invoke responsibility. Also see further Comment O on s.702, which states that '[v]iolations of the rules stated in this section are violations of obligations to all other States'.

[117] 999 UNTS 171. All of the Member States of the Union are a party to the Covenant.

[118] Peremptory norms of international law or principles *jus cogens* and obligations *erga omnes* are not synonymous, although in substantive terms there is a very significant overlap between them. See further, M. Ragazzi, *The Concept of Obligations Erga Omnes* (Oxford: Oxford University Press, 1997) p. 43 *et seq.*; J. Crawford, *The International Law Commission's Articles on State Responsibility* (Cambridge: Cambridge University Press, 2002) p. 244 *et seq.*; and G. Gaja, 'Obligations *Erga Omnes*, International Crimes and *Jus Cogens*: a Tentative Analysis of Three Related Concepts' in J. Weiler, M. Spinedi and A. Cassese (eds.), *International Crimes of States: a Critical Analysis of the ILC's Draft Article 19 on State Responsibility* (Berlin: Walter de Gruyter, 1989) p. 151.

[119] *Issues Relating to Reservations Made upon Ratification or Accession to the Covenant or the Optional Protocols*, UN Doc. CCPR/C/21/Rev.1/Add.6 (1994) para. 8.

[120] See further Ragazzi, *Obligations*, p. 132.

self-determination,[121] certain obligations under international human-itarian law[122] and torture[123] are now also universally accepted as having achieved that status. The list does not extend to all human rights as the IDI's 1989 declaration implies.

2.3.2.1(b) Human Rights Obligations, the Limits of Domestic Jurisdiction and the Legality of Horizontal Enforcement

There is little doubt that those treaties which primarily protect human rights are considered to be somewhat different in nature from other international agreements.[124] The ICJ in its Advisory Opinion on *Reservations to the Genocide Convention* stated that in such Conventions '[c]ontracting states do not have interests of their own; they merely have, one and all, a common interest, namely the accomplishment of those high purposes which are the *raison d'être* of the Convention'.[125] In the *Barcelona Traction* case, although dealing with a somewhat different issue, the ICJ's sentiment is much the same, as is the approach of the HRC in General Comment 24. In this sense it can be argued that all states which are party to a human rights treaty have an interest in compliance with it, even though they are not being directly affected by violations of its provisions in a third state. There are, however, two considerations which need to be addressed. First, is the state which is the target of disapproval violating a legal obligation? Secondly, if there is a legal obligation, where does it stem from?

A distinction must be drawn between legal obligations stemming from custom and those stemming from treaties. With regard to treaties which protect human rights, utilising the approach discussed above

---

[121] See *Portugal* v. *Australia* ('East Timor Case') [1995] ICJ Reports 90, para. 29 and Advisory Opinion, *Legal Consequences of the Construction of a Wall in the Occupied Palestinian Territory* [2004] ICJ Reports 136, para. 155.

[122] See Advisory Opinion, *Nuclear Weapons*, n. 103 above, para. 79 and Advisory Opinion, *Legal Consequences of the Wall*, n. 121 above, paras. 157–9.

[123] See e.g., *R* v. *Bow Street Metropolitan Magistrate, ex parte Pinochet Ugarte* (No. 3) [1999] 2 WLR 827, 841; *Filartiga* v. *Pena-Irala*, 630 F.2d 876 (1980) and *Al Adsani* v. *United Kingdom* (2002) 34 EHRR 11, para. 151.

[124] See e.g., M. Craven, 'Legal Differentiation and the Concept of the Human Rights Treaty in International Law' (2000) 11 *EJIL* 489 and R. Higgins, 'Introduction' in P. Gardner (ed.), *Human Rights as General Norms and a State's Right to Opt Out* (London: BIICL, 1997) p.vx. Although see the responses of the United Kingdom, United States and France to General Comment 24 of the Human Rights Committee.

[125] Advisory Opinion, *Reservations to the Convention on the Prevention and Punishment of the Crime of Genocide*, [1951] ICJ Reports 15, 23. Article 60(5) Vienna Convention on the Law of Treaties, 1969, 115 UNTS 331, also recognises this.

(that of the ICJ in the *Genocide* opinion among others) it can be argued that all states which are party to any such treaty have an interest in ensuring its provisions are being complied with by others and, beyond this, a right to act to protect that interest. Issues such as valid reservations will be a consideration in determining the extent of that right. Notwithstanding the existence of reservations, the ratification of a treaty entails the state's consent to international regulation in such matters. The jurisprudence of international tribunals, such as the ECtHR, has clearly held that once a state becomes a party to such a treaty, those matters regulated by it are no longer within the exclusive preserve of the state's discretion. In the *Belgian Linguistics* case,[126] for example, in response to Belgium's argument that its policy on education was within its domestic jurisdiction, notwithstanding its obligations under the Convention system, the ECtHR noted:

the Convention and the Protocol, which relate to matters normally falling within the domestic legal order of the Contracting States, are international instruments whose main purpose is to lay down certain international standards to be observed by the Contracting States in their relations with persons under their jurisdiction.[127]

It does not automatically follow, however, that because a state has ratified an international treaty protecting such rights that other states have a right to comment or take other action in response to its violations of that treaty. This is especially the case as almost all such conventions have their own specific enforcement mechanisms.[128] The issue, therefore, is to what extent are methods of enforcement, other than those provided for in the treaties themselves, legitimate? The answer depends on the treaty in question; they take different approaches. The ICCPR and the ECHR are exceptional in that they are the only major international human rights treaties that specifically refer to this issue. The Covenant, in Article 44, states that the 'provisions for the implementation of the present Covenant ... shall not prevent

---

[126] Application Nos. 1474/62, 1677/62, 1691/62, 1769/63, 1994/63 and 2126/64 *Case Relating to Certain Aspects of the Laws on the Use of Languages in Education in Belgium* v. *Belgium* ('Belgian Linguistics Case (No. 1)'), judgment on Preliminary Objections, Series A, No.5, (1979–80) 1 EHRR 241.

[127] *Ibid.* Conclusions of the Court, para. [e], 250.

[128] There are notable exceptions, such as Convention Relating to the Status of Refugees, 1951, 606 UNTS 267; Convention on the Prevention and Punishment of the Crime of Genocide, 1948, 78 UNTS 277; and Slavery Convention, 1926, 60 LNTS 253, as amended by the Protocol to the 1926 Slavery Convention, 1953, 212 UNTS 17.

the State Parties to the present Covenant from having recourse to other procedures for settling a dispute in accordance with general or special international agreements in force between them'. The ECHR, however, takes the opposite approach. Article 55 requires that parties to it shall 'except by special agreement ... not avail themselves of treaties, conventions or declarations in force between them for the purpose of submitting, by way of petition, a dispute arising out of the interpretation or application of this Convention to a means of settlement other than those provided for in this Convention'.[129] All other international human rights treaties, whether regional or universal, are either silent on this issue[130] or do not exclusively reserve the resolution of any disputes to the competent named bodies.[131] As both the ICCPR and ECHR refer only to dispute settlement procedures contained in treaties, it can be concluded that no human rights treaty actually prohibits the use of methods, other than those provided for, to encourage or persuade states party to them to comply with their obligations.[132] The adoption of resolutions on cooperation and assistance in human rights in the United Nations, as discussed above, is consistent with this understanding. A state bound by certain international obligations in the field of human rights is thus entitled to require another state, bound by those same obligations, to perform them.[133] The procedures

---

[129] See further M. Novak, *U.N. Covenant on Civil and Political Rights: CCPR Commentary*, 2nd edn (Kehl: Engel, 2005) p. 789 *et seq.*

[130] See International Covenant on Economic, Social and Cultural Rights, 1966, 993 UNTS 3; Convention on the Rights of the Child, 1989, 1577 UNTS 3; American Convention on Human Rights, 1969, Pact of San José, Costa Rica, (B-32) (1970) 9 *ILM* 674; and African Charter on Human and People's Rights, 1981, 1520 UNTS No. 26, 363.

[131] See Article 22 of the International Convention on the Elimination of All Forms of Racial Discrimination, 1966, 660 UNTS 195; Article 29 of the Convention on the Elimination of All Forms of Discrimination Against Women, 1979, 1249 UNTS 13; Article 30 of the Convention Against Torture and Other Cruel, Inhuman or Degrading Treatment or Punishment, 1984, 1464 UNTS 85; Article 92 of the International Convention on the Protection of the Rights of all Migrant Workers and Members of their Families, 1990, General Assembly Resolution Doc. A/45/158, 18/12/1990; Article 3 of the Protocol to the African Charter on the Establishment of an African Court on Human and Peoples' Rights, 1998, 9 June 1998, OAU Doc. OAU/LEG/EXP/AFCHPR/PROT (III).

[132] For a concurring view, see Henkin, *Age of Rights*, p. 59. A. Cassese, *International Law*, 2nd edn (Oxford: Oxford University Press, 2004) p. 302 and Kamminga, *Inter-State Accountability*, p. 189 consider that the ECHR does not allow this. The distinction is that the ECtHR has the exclusive right to settle disputes, but not over other methods of ensuring compliance with Convention rights.

[133] See L. Henkin, 'Human Rights and State "Sovereignty"' (1996) 25 *Geo. JICL* 31, 43 and L. Henkin, 'Inter-State Responsibility for Compliance with Human Rights Obligations' in Vohrah *et al.*, *Man's Inhumanity*, p. 383.

provided for by a treaty coexist alongside those traditional mechanisms for ensuring compliance, in international law, which exist between states.[134] Taking action against a state for failing to comply with its legal obligations requires no injury in the traditional sense.[135]

It is only the Member States which are parties to human rights conventions, rather than the Community or Union. Thus, where *all* of the Member States are party to a treaty, they have a collective interest, as do all other parties to it, to ensure compliance with those legal obligations they have all accepted. The issue of reservations by the Member States of the Union will be a consideration. If, in their capacity as States Parties to a treaty, they choose to speak or act through the Union's institutions, that is their choice.

With regard to human rights obligations which derive from custom, the issue of the legality of horizontal enforcement is more straightforward.[136] The practice of Charter-based bodies and procedures, such as ECOSOC Resolutions 1235[137] and 1503[138] and the work of the Special Rapporteurs, illustrates clearly that states can legitimately seek to ensure that others comply with their human rights obligations. Unilateral action is not necessarily problematic either, as each state has an interest in compliance with those obligations, whether they are directly affected or not. Thus measures which seek to ensure compliance with such norms are, subject to compliance with other international rules, perfectly legitimate. With regard to the content of such norms, it is difficult to contend that they extend beyond those which are recognised as obligations *erga omnes*. By definition, all states are bound by them and have a right to act when they are breached. The fact that states are selective as to when they choose to act, does not

---

[134] Section 703 of the *Third Restatement*, however, considers that the specific treaty-based machinery 'supplements' traditional remedies.

[135] See further O. Schachter, 'International Law Implications of US Human Rights Policies' (1978/9) 24 *NYLSch.LR* 63.

[136] See J. Frowein, 'Reactions by Not Directly Affected States to Breaches of Public International Law' (1994) 248 (IV) *RDC* 349 and B. Simma, 'From Bilateralism to Community Interest in International Law' (1994) 250 (VI) *RDC* 221. For more general discussion see L. Damrosch, 'Enforcing International Law Through Non-Forcible Measures' (1997) 269 *RDC* 19 and O. Elagab, *The Legality of Non-Forcible Countermeasures in International Law* (Oxford: Oxford University Press, 1989).

[137] ECOSOC Resolution 1235 (XLII), 42 UN ESCOR Supp. (No. 1) 17, UN Doc. E/4393 (1967).

[138] ECOSOC Resolution 1503 (XLVIII), 48 UN ESCOR (No. 1A) 8, UN Doc. E/4832/ Add.1 (1970).

invalidate their legal right to do so,[139] although it may detract from their credibility when they do act.

2.3.2.1(c) Violation of International Norms by Third States and Member State Obligations

The Member States and Community also have an obligation (as opposed to a right) to respond, in certain circumstances, when third states violate certain norms. Although the International Law Commission's Articles on State Responsibility (ILCASR) do not apply to international organisations, many of the provisions are a reflection of custom.[140] The principle in Article 16 ILCASR, which prohibits aid or assistance in the commission of an 'internationally wrongful act', therefore, also applies to any other entity which has legal personality and has the capacity to act in that regard.[141] Article 16 establishes a relatively high threshold before a state or other entity is considered to be aiding or assisting in the commission of an internationally wrongful act by another.[142] The definition of an 'internationally wrongful act' in Article 2 is, however, broad enough to encompass violations of any legal obligation.[143] If entities with legal personality are considered to be aiding or assisting a third state in the violation, for example, of its human rights obligations, then they are internationally responsible for their actions and obliged to stop doing so.[144] Due to the manner in which the relevant articles of the ILCASR are drafted, aiding or assisting, for example, an isolated incident of torture will be enough to invoke responsibility.[145]

---

[139] Schachter, 'International Law Implications', 79 argues that a legal right to act does not impose an obligation to do so in every case.

[140] See Articles 55 and 57. Professor Giorgio Gaja has been appointed by the International Law Commission (ILC) as a Special Rapporteur for the 'Responsibility of International Organisations' in its programme of work. His reports can be found at http://untreaty.un.org/ilc/summaries/9_11.htm

[141] The ICJ in Advisory Opinion, *Legal Consequences of the Wall*, n. 121 above, para. 159 referred to a number of principles which can be found in the ILCASR, including Article 16, but did not expressly mention them. In the later *Bosnia and Herzegovina* v. *Serbia and Montenegro* case, n. 79 above, at para. 402, however, it does expressly refer to Article 16 ILCASR and considers that it reflects customary international law.

[142] For discussion of the conditions see Crawford, *State Responsibility*, p. 148.

[143] Article 2 states that '[t]here is an internationally wrongful act of a State when conduct of an action or omission: (a) is attributable to the State under international law; and (b) constitutes a breach of an international obligation of the State'.

[144] See Article 30 ILCASR.

[145] See also, Article 40(2) ILCASR, which deals with aiding and assisting violations of peremptory norms.

Accordingly, the Member States and Community must cease any activities which aid or assist in the commission of such acts.

The question of whether the Community and its Member States are obliged to act, where they are not aiding or assisting in the commission of an internationally wrongful act, is somewhat different. Chapter III of Part Two of the ILCASR contains Articles 40 and 41, which deal with breaches of peremptory norms of international law[146] and the consequent responsibility of states. Article 40 applies to the 'international responsibility [of a state] entailed by a *serious breach* ... of an obligation arising under a peremptory norm of ... international law'.[147] Article 41 details the obligations of other states in response to serious violations of peremptory norms by another. States must cooperate to bring the violation to an end through lawful means and not recognise as lawful a situation created by a serious breach within the meaning of Article 40.[148] The general nature of a state's obligations in such circumstances is relatively clear, even if the actual content of the obligation may not be.[149]

Whether these obligations also extend to the Community and Union is more complex. The commentary on Article 40 of the ILC Articles refers back to Article 53 of the 1969 Vienna Convention on the Law of Treaties.[150] This provision considers a peremptory norm of general international law to be one recognised 'by the international community of States as a whole'. Palchetti implies that this excludes the Community acting in such circumstances.[151] It is questionable on

---

[146] Article 26 ILCASR also refers to peremptory norms. It is concerned, however, with the circumstances precluding the wrongfulness of an internationally wrongful act.

[147] Emphasis added.

[148] This principle was also used by the ICJ in Advisory Opinion, *Legal Consequences of the Wall*, n. 121 above, para. 159, but without referring to the ILCASR. The Separate Opinions of Judge Higgins at para. 37 *et seq.* and that of Judge Kooijmans at para. 40 *et seq.* are, however, worth noting as to the responsibility of third states.

[149] See further below and more generally P. Klein, 'Responsibility for Serious Breaches of Obligations Deriving from Peremptory Norms of International Law and United Nations Law' (2002) 13 *EJIL* 1241 and G. Gaja, 'Do States Have a Duty to Ensure Compliance with Obligations *Erga Omnes* by Other States?' in Ragazzi, *International Responsibility*, p. 31.

[150] Crawford, *State Responsibility*, p. 245.

[151] P. Palchetti, 'Reactions by the European Union to Breaches of *Erga Omnes* Obligations' in E. Cannizzaro (ed.), *The European Union as an Actor in International Relations* (The Hague: Kluwer, 2002) pp. 219, 221. J. Klabbers, 'Comment on Case C-162/96, *A. Racke GmbH & Co.* v *Hauptzollant Mainz*' (1999) 36 *CMLRev.* 179, considers that *Racke* presented the ECJ with the opportunity to make pronouncements on the Community's duties vis-à-vis obligations *erga omnes*, as opposed to peremptory norms, but it chose not to

policy grounds, however, whether the 'international community of States' should be read so restrictively as to exclude international organisations in the obligations they may owe to ensure that such norms are not violated. States may still have the monopoly in recognising such principles[152] but that is not to say that the entities they create cannot act in that regard.

Article 41 of the ILC Articles provides a possible solution. Article 41(1), as noted above, obliges states to cooperate together to bring to an end, through lawful means, serious breaches of peremptory norms.[153] Action taken by states individually, however, is not excluded by this formula. The provision does not prescribe the action to be taken and it is clear that where the Member States have transferred competence to the Community, then under Community law, action must be taken by it.[154] How that action is taken or through which forum is not relevant for the purposes of state responsibility. The obligation upon states is to act. Whether an obligation exists on the Community independently of the Member States is unclear. There is no reason, in principle, why it should not where the Member States have transferred their competence to it. Palchetti argues in this regard that the Community acts on behalf of the Member States and is not obliged to act independently of them.[155] Yet the bestowal and recognition of legal personality arguably means that, within its competence, the Community is obliged to act even if that obligation is ultimately owed by the Member States. If the action required is outside the scope of Community competence and the Member States choose to act through the CFSP or independently, that is their prerogative. In practical terms, in such circumstances, whether an obligation is owed by the Community, Member States or by both makes little difference. Action is being taken ultimately by a state in

take it. The CFI has, of course, done so with regard to peremptory norms in, *inter alia*, *Yusef*, *Kadi* and *Ayadi*.

[152] Simma, 'From Bilateralism', 243 has referred to this as 'the foxes guarding the chickens'.

[153] N. Jørgensen, *The Responsibility of States for International Crimes* (Oxford: Oxford University Press, 2000) p. 215 argues, however, that the role of third states in such circumstances is limited to assisting and enforcing any decisions made by a determining body (probably the Security Council) as to whether such obligations have been violated or not.

[154] The issue with the Union is slightly different. Under the CFSP, where such action would be taken, there is no permanent limitation of the sovereign rights of the Member States in the sense there is under the EC Treaty. Whether obligations would, therefore, exist on the Union independently of the Member States is far less certain.

[155] Palchetti, 'Reactions by the Union', p. 228.

response to the systematic breach of peremptory norms and that is what is legally required. There is nothing to stop the EU Member States acting through whichever forum their other legal obligations require. In this limited respect, therefore, there is an obligation, as opposed to right, upon the Community to respond to violations of such norms. Similarly, the Member States may wish to utilise Union instruments to act. That is within their discretion.

On the basis of the preceding discussions, the following conclusions can be drawn. Those norms which are recognised as obligations *erga omnes* are no longer within a state's domestic jurisdiction. This is also the case with regard to those obligations a state has accepted by becoming party to a human rights treaty. With regard to obligations *erga omnes* all states have an interest in their compliance and a right to act when they are violated by a third state. Where all of the Union's Member States are party to a human rights treaty, they have a legitimate interest in ensuring that other states comply with their obligations under it. They also have a right to act if the treaty is violated by a third state, so long as they all have also accepted the obligation in question. All other issues are within the domestic jurisdiction of a state. The Community and its Member States, as is the case with all other states, must not aid or assist in the commission of any internationally wrongful acts by another state. Furthermore, where there are serious breaches of peremptory norms of international law, the Community and its Member States must cooperate together with others to bring to an end, through lawful means, such violations. Regardless of whether there is a right to act or an obligation, the responses must be lawful. The next section deals, in part, with this issue.

2.3.2.2 Legal Limits on the Implementation of Policy

Ethical foreign policies are both positive and negative in nature and the values which they seek to promote and protect extend beyond the relatively narrow ambit of certain human rights. Thus, as regards positive measures, programmes are often funded by donors to help raise awareness of particular rights and issues, where an identified problem is seen to exist. The Community, for example, has consistently funded seminars in third states which attempt to ensure that journalists are aware of the international rules protecting freedom of expression.[156] Furthermore, the Community routinely provides food

---

[156] See the Council's *Annual Report on Human Rights* for examples of such activities.

aid for distribution.[157] Positive rewards for compliance with certain norms, such as through the Generalised System of Preferences (GSP) scheme as implemented by the Community, are in principle perfectly lawful under international law. In most cases, positive measures cannot function without the consent of the third state. Such policies are, however, legally limited to encouraging and persuading other states to comply with those standards without intervening, in the sense of acting without or beyond the consent granted, in the internal affairs of the recipient state. Thus the Community can provide assistance and any other help requested or agreed upon with the consent of all parties involved. Positive measures tend to pose few legal problems.

Legal problems do exist when states, in objecting to the policies and practices of a third state, take punitive action, such as withdrawing preferential trade arrangements. Such acts may be part of the objecting donor's prerogative but they are not completely unregulated by international law. In a 1994 Communication the Commission stated that in response to human rights violations in a third state the European Union may issue confidential or public démarches; change the content of cooperation programmes or the channels used; defer signature or the decisions needed to implement a cooperation Agreement; reduce cultural, scientific or technical cooperation; defer the holding of joint committee meetings; suspend all bilateral contact; postpone new projects; refuse to act on new initiatives; impose trade embargoes; or suspend all cooperation.[158] A number of such actions, which straddle retorsion and reprisals, have legal consequences. The legal issues involved will depend, among other things, on the exact factual circumstances, the legal provisions regulating relations between the parties and the nature of the violation. A more detailed analysis of the legal limits of the instruments used by the Union is undertaken in Chapter 3. This discussion is concerned more generally with the legal limits of implementing an ethical foreign policy.

In the first instance states, through some means or other, must be aware of a situation in a third state of which they disapprove. The former Commissioner for External Relations, Chris Patten noted that human rights promotion by the Union is a preemptive measure as there is no *droit de regard* on the part of foreign governments.[159] Simma and

---

[157] See the discussion below.   [158] COM(1994)42, p. 11.

[159] C. Patten, 'Current and Future Trends of the Human Rights Agenda', 14 July 2003, Speech 03/364.

Alston have argued, however, that such a right has evolved and is also broadly accepted.[160] This view is certainly the correct one. All states observe and gather information, through various means, on compliance by others with legal obligations in which they have an interest. In the case of human rights, that would entail violations of all human rights protected by a treaty to which both states are a party or of those protected by custom. Despite Patten's comment, this does not pose a legal problem. Supervising a third state's compliance with its legal obligations is not prohibited so long as it does not amount to intervention in its internal affairs.

Intervention, like many of the terms discussed in this chapter, has proved a controversial term. During the drafting of the Friendly Relations Declaration, 1970 the Mexican representative noted that 'intervention, like life itself, was so fluid and changeable that it would always escape the confines of any definition'.[161] Some commentators have argued that it should have a broad interpretation which would mean that much UN action and unilateral state action is prohibited.[162] Others, such as Lauterpacht, argued that it should be interpreted narrowly and amount to 'dictatorial interference' meaning that far more action through the United Nations is permissible.[163] It is the latter approach which has prevailed. Alvarez has noted that as far as human rights and the practice of the United Nations' political bodies are now concerned 'there is precious little of a State's residual right to be left entirely alone'.[164] Accordingly, any interference that is not dictatorial does not amount to intervention. The IDI's 1989 Resolution and the Union, as noted above, now consider that purely verbal expressions of concern are lawful in all situations. Such expressions of concern, whether or not the issue is considered to be a part of the state's domestic jurisdiction, are legitimate according to this approach, because they do not satisfy the threshold to amount to intervention. As the Reporter's

---

[160] B. Simma and P. Alston, 'The Sources of Human Rights Law: Custom, *Jus Cogens* and General Principles' (1992) 27 *AYBIL* 82, 98.

[161] Cited by Zemanek, 'Human Rights Protection', p. 961.

[162] See further the works cited in n. 85 above.

[163] See H. Lauterpacht, 'The International Protection of Human Rights' (1947) 62 *RDC* 1, 19. On its background and usage see Preuss, 'Article 2, Paragraph 7', 605. The term is still widely used in the literature, see Jennings and Watts, *Oppenheim*, p. 430; Henkin, *Age of Rights*, p. 55; and L. Damrosch, L. Henkin, R. Pugh, O. Schachter and H. Smit, *International Law: Cases and Materials*, 4th edn (St Paul, Minn.: West Publishing, 2001) p. 951.

[164] Alvarez, *International Organizations as Law-Makers*, p. 156.

Notes to the *Third Restatement* state, 'virtually every State has criticised some other for its human rights practices, both directly and by statement or vote in international bodies'.[165] The approach to intervention adopted by the ICJ in the *Nicaragua* case supports this. The ICJ relied heavily upon the 1965 and 1970 General Assembly Declarations, discussed above, both of which adopt a similar formula. The 1970 Declaration considers that:

No State or group of States has the right to intervene, directly or indirectly, *for any reason*, whatever, in the international or external affairs of another State. Consequently … all … *forms of interference* … are in violation of international law. No State may use or encourage the use of economic, political or any other type of measure to *coerce* another State in order to obtain from it subordination of the exercise of its sovereign rights and to secure from it advantages of any kind.[166]

The ICJ stated:

As regards the content of non-intervention … the principle forbids all States or groups of States to intervene directly or indirectly in internal or external affairs of other States. A prohibited intervention must accordingly be one bearing on matters in which each State is permitted … to decide freely … Intervention is wrongful when it *uses methods of coercion* in regard to such choices, which must remain free ones.[167]

On the basis of the *Nicaragua* case it is clear that the Union, whether it is dealing with a legally binding obligation or not, may publicly unilaterally criticise any situation in a third state of which it disapproves. The issues of domestic jurisdiction or sovereignty are not an impediment, as verbal expressions of concern are not coercive and thus do not amount to intervention. This is further supported by the ICJ in the *Nicaragua* case, which also considered that action on the economic plane against Nicaragua by the United States, namely the cessation of economic aid, the reduction of sugar quotas and trade embargoes, despite their economic consequences, did not amount to intervention.[168] In this case it does not amount to intervention in the affairs of a third state, if a donor changes its trade policies, as a response to behaviour it disapproves of, because it is within its discretion to afford those facilities to a third state. Foreign policy formulation is a part of the state's prerogative.[169] Section 703 of the *Third Restatement* goes further, however,

---

[165] *Third Restatement*, Reporter's Notes (9).   [166] Emphasis added.
[167] *Nicaragua* case, n. 86 above, para. 205.   [168] *Ibid*. para. 245.   [169] *Ibid*. para. 205.

in considering that 'a State does not violate international law when it shapes its trade, aid or other national policies to influence a State to abide by recognised human rights standards'. Such acts have traditionally been considered to be retorsion and thus legal.[170] It can be questioned, however, whether they are always legal. When donating aid, it is possible for states to undertake unilateral obligations which are legally binding and thus they may be estopped from rescinding from them.[171] In the alternative, suspension of a development cooperation treaty with a third state, in the absence of an 'essential elements' clause, will only be a lawful response if one of the situations identified in Articles 54 to 64 of the Vienna Convention on the Law of Treaties exists. This is the case even if the donor is, of its own volition, granting to a third state preferential access to its markets. Furthermore, Article 60(5) VCLT, which deals with treaties of a humanitarian character, is relevant if the treaty in question is poverty-orientated and individuals are perceived to be the identified beneficiaries. Suspension or termination not only of a treaty but also of other bilateral aid, can also potentially lead to the legal responsibility of the former donor for violations of certain economic, social and cultural rights in the target state.[172]

In the absence of treaty relations, states often resort to countermeasures, including sanctions, retorsion and non-forcible reprisals, in an attempt to convince or coerce another state to act in a manner which is deemed appropriate. While this area of law is not well regulated, it is not entirely without rules. Again, such measures should not amount to coercion.[173] The debate as to where the boundaries lie between economic coercion and lawful responses to the violation of human rights is routinely played out in the political organs of the United Nations.[174]

---

[170] See L. Damrosch, 'Politics Across Borders: Non-intervention and Non-forcible Influence over Domestic Affairs' (1989) 83 *AJIL* 1, 54 and Crawford, *State Responsibility*, p. 281.

[171] For the general principle see *Australia* v. *France – Nuclear Tests Case* [1974] ICJ Reports 253, para. 43 and *New Zealand* v. *France – Nuclear Tests Case* [1974] ICJ Reports 457, para. 46.

[172] See General Comment 8 of CESCR, E/C.12/1997/8, para. 11.

[173] If they are simply symbolic that poses no problem, although if they are punitive in nature the considerations are the same as for those which are coercive. See M. Craven, 'Humanitarianism and the Quest for Smarter Sanctions' (2002) 13 *EJIL* 43, 47. Also see G. Abi-Saab, 'The Concept of Sanction in International Law' in V. Gowlland-Debbas (ed.), *United Nations Sanctions and International Law* (The Hague: Kluwer, 2001) pp. 29, 32.

[174] See the various Resolutions adopted by the General Assembly and Commission on Human Rights entitled 'Human Rights and Unilateral Coercive Measures and Unilateral Economic Measures as a Means of Political and Economic Coercion Against Developing Countries': A/RES/57/222, A/RES/56/148, A/RES/55/110, A/RES/54/172, A/RES/53/141,

Such measures can be considered to be coercion if the target state is not violating a legally binding obligation or the issue is within the scope of its discretion. In the *Nicaragua* case, the ICJ considered that choices as to 'political, economic, social and cultural system, and the formulation of foreign policy' are entirely within the discretion of the state. Thus the implementation of broad-ranging sanctions to express disapproval of a non-democratic or corrupt regime, for example, may amount to coercion.

If the issue is not within the domestic jurisdiction of a state, for example it is engaging in violations of obligations *erga omnes*, then although an objecting state has a right to respond, any countermeasures taken must still be proportionate.[175] Article 48(1) ILCASR notes, in this context, that a state may invoke the responsibility of a wrongdoing state if the *obligation breached* is 'owed to a group of States, including that State, and is established for the protection of a collective interest of the group'. Commenting on Article 54 ILCASR, which permits 'lawful measures' by states other than those who are injured, Crawford considers that currently international law 'on countermeasures taken in the general or collective interest is uncertain ... At present there appears to be no clearly recognised entitlement of States ... to take counter-measures in the collective interest.'[176] The fact that there is no 'clearly recognised entitlement' to act does not mean that states cannot do so; they simply must ensure that in doing so they respect other principles of international law. Article 54 ILCASR very pointedly uses the language of 'lawful measures'.

The ICJ, on the occasions it has referred to the duty of states to react to infringements of obligations *erga omnes*, has not provided any guidance as to what they should do. In the *Namibia* opinion it stated:

A/RES/52/120, CHR Resolution 2002/22, CHR Resolution 2001/26 and A/RES/56/179, A/RES/54/200, A/RES/52/181 respectively.

[175] See Article 51 ILCASR and *Hungary* v. *Slovakia – Case concerning the Gabčíkovo-Nagymaros Project* [1997] ICJ Reports 7, para. 87: 'in the view of the Court, an important consideration is that the effects of a countermeasure must be commensurate with the injury suffered, taking account of the rights in question'. Reprisals must also be proportionate. The classic authority is *Portugal* v. *Germany – the Naulilaa Case* (1928) 2 RIAA 1012, 1026. See further E. Cannizzaro, 'The Role of Proportionality in the Law of International Countermeasures' (2001) 12 *EJIL* 889.

[176] Crawford, *State Responsibility*, p. 305. See further M. Craven, 'For the "Common Good": Rights and Interests in the Law of State Responsibility' in M. Fitzmaurice and D. Sarooshi (eds.), *Issues of States Responsibility Before International Judicial Institutions* (Oxford: Hart Publishing, 2005) pp. 105, 109.

A binding determination ... to the effect that a situation is illegal cannot remain without consequence ... the Court ... would be failing in the discharge of its judicial functions if it did not declare that there is an obligation especially upon members of the United Nations, to bring that situation to an end. [177]

In the *Wall* opinion it noted that all States Parties to Geneva Convention IV are under an obligation while respecting 'the United Nations Charter and international law' to ensure compliance by Israel with that Convention.[178] Simma and Alston have argued that where there are gross and persistent abuses of obligations *erga omnes*, countermeasures *are* lawful in the absence of treaty relations.[179] The use of 'lawful measures' in Article 54 ILCASR implies that, notwithstanding the seriousness of any such breach, countermeasures will not always be lawful; it depends on *their* nature. In the case of values which have not attained that normative status and may not even be legally binding upon the target state, there are significant constraints on the responses which are legitimately available to third states.[180]

2.3.3 Legal Obligations to Promote Ethical Values in the Treaty Framework

The objective in this section is to determine which values the Community and Union are legally obliged to promote and protect and the content of those values in international law. Reference is made only to the constitutive treaties. The secondary legislation that has been adopted, practice and the treaties entered into with third states and organisations, which aim, in part, to give effect to these obligations, are discussed in Chapter 3.

2.3.3.1 Introductory Comments

The starting point for this discussion is Title XX of the EC Treaty which contains Articles 177 to 181 dealing with development cooperation. Article 177(1) TEC refers to the fact that the Community '*shall* foster'

---

[177] Advisory Opinion, *Legal Consequences for States of the Continued Presence of South Africa in Namibia Notwithstanding Security Council Resolution 276(1970)* [1971] ICJ Reports 16, para. 117.

[178] Advisory Opinion, *Legal Consequences of the Wall*, n. 121 above, para. 159.

[179] Simma and Alston, 'Sources', 98.

[180] For more general discussion see N. White and A. Abass, 'Countermeasures and Sanctions' in Evans, *International Law*, p. 509 and Gowlland-Debbas, *United Nations Sanctions*.

the campaign 'against poverty in the developing countries'[181] and in Article 177(2) TEC that this policy '*shall* contribute to the general objective of developing and consolidating democracy and the rule of law, and to that of respecting human rights and fundamental freedoms'.[182] Furthermore, Article 177(3) TEC obliges the Community and its Member States to comply with 'the commitments and take account of the objectives they have approved in the context of the United Nations and other competent organisations'. Article 177(3) TEC does not, however, contain a general obligation vis-à-vis all commitments undertaken in the United Nations but concerns solely those relating to development cooperation.

Article 177 TEC is further supplemented by the TEU. There is reference in the Preamble to the TEU to the Union's attachment to the principles of liberty, democracy and respect for human rights and fundamental freedoms as well as the social rights contained in the European Social Charter 1961 and the Community Charter on Fundamental Social Rights of Workers 1989. However, it is not specified whether this attachment is limited to the 'internal sphere' of the Union or also applies to the Union's external relations. Beyond this, the relationship between human rights and democracy, among other principles, in external relations and the objectives of the Common Provisions is weak. Article 11 TEU, which established the CFSP, specifically states that the Union shall 'develop and consolidate democracy and the rule of law, and respect for human rights and fundamental freedoms', but this is not a free-standing obligation for the Union but one of the objectives of the CFSP. Richardson has argued that this provision is evidence of the European Union's commitment to safeguarding the values of the Union in conformity with the United Nations Charter. As he notes, it is evidence of a 'foreign policy clearly based on principles and not on *Realpolitik*'.[183]

Article 2 TEU, which establishes the Union's objectives as a whole, only implicitly refers to such questions with, for example, the creation of Union citizenship. The link between these objectives and the

---

[181] Article III-316 of the proposed Constitutional Treaty is more ambitious in that the primary objective of development cooperation shall be 'the reduction and, in the long term, the eradication of poverty'.

[182] Emphasis added.

[183] J. Richardson, 'The European Union in the World: a Community of Values' (2002) 26 *Fordham ILJ* 12. For a contrary view, see E. Duquette, 'Human Rights in the European Union: Internal Versus External Objectives' (2001) 34 *Cornell Int'l LJ* 363, 378, who argues that the Union acts on the basis of power, not morality.

promotion of human rights in external relations is not apparent. Article 6 TEU does, however, give a hint on issues of cultural relativity. Article 6, which reaffirms that the Union is founded on the principles of liberty, democracy, respect for human rights and the rule of law, states in its second paragraph that:

The Union shall respect fundamental rights, as guaranteed by the European Convention for the Protection of Human Rights and Fundamental Freedoms ... and as they result from the constitutional traditions common to the Member States, as general principles of Community law.

The listed sources of fundamental rights upon which the Union is said to be founded all advocate a 'European standard' of human rights protection. Implicitly this means that this is the standard which the Union as a whole should promote both in the CFSP and in the Community's development cooperation policies. This seems to be the case even though 'European standards' may not be applicable or relevant to third states, which are either committed to other international treaties or consider that they have a different set of cultural values.[184] In many senses, the idea of 'European standards' is as culturally relative and objectionable as the 'Asian values' argument which has at times bogged down international human rights debates.[185] There is thus a desire to impose or at least achieve 'our standards' elsewhere, due to an inherent belief in the superiority of those values, without necessarily realising or seriously considering that they may not be appropriate or applicable outside of a particular social and historical context. The principles advocated by the European Union are far from universal. While human rights are not a Western idea, there is significant force in the argument that the specific philosophy on which the current universal regime is based is Western in essence. As Mutua notes:

that Africa merely needs a liberal democratic, rule of law State to be freed from despotism is mistaken. The transplantation of the narrow formulation of Western liberalism cannot adequately respond to the historical reality and the political and social needs of Africa ... The supremacy of the jurisprudence of

---

[184] In practice, however, the approach is sometimes subtly different. See further Chapter 4.
[185] For a more general discussion of European attitudes see P. Leino, 'European Universalism? The EU and Human Rights Conditionality' (2005) 24 *YEL* 329.

individual rights ... is not a natural ... or universal phenomena, applicable to all societies, without regard to time and place.[186]

Yet in some of the most important Communications on external policy and values, the Commission has noted that its actions in the field of external relations will be guided by compliance with the rights and principles contained in the EU Charter of Fundamental Rights, as opposed to the ECHR to which the TEU refers, as this will promote coherence between internal and external approaches.[187]

Beyond these references, there is nothing else in the constitutive treaties, as they currently exist, which creates an obligation to eradicate poverty or promote human rights and the rule of law in third states. Nor is there any articulation of what is meant by these principles or why it is that they have been identified as global goals to be pursued.

In the proposed Constitutional Treaty, Article III-292 adopts a broader approach. In addition to the objectives mentioned above it also refers to, for example: preserving peace and preventing conflicts; preserving and improving the quality of the environment; assisting populations confronting man-made and natural disasters; and promoting an international system based upon multilateral cooperation and good global governance.[188] There is no discussion in the treaties as they currently stand, or in the proposed Constitutional Treaty, of the weight to be attached to these principles in relation to other policies or their content.

The legal obligations imposed by the treaties vis-à-vis the promotion of these values are, as one would expect, extremely flexible. They do not expressly articulate, for example, that there is a general obligation upon the Community to take account of poverty reduction policies vis-à-vis the Common Commercial Policy; this only exists with regard to development cooperation. Article 3 TEU, however, in imposing an obligation on the institutions to ensure consistency and continuity of all activities, should prevent the Community, for example, in the World

---

[186] M. Mutua, 'The Banjul Charter and the African Cultural Fingerprint: an Evaluation of the Language of Duties' (1995) 35 *Virginia JIL* 339, 341. Also see further M. Mutua, *Human Rights: a Political and Cultural Critique* (Philadelphia: University of Pennsylvania Press, 2002).

[187] See COM(2001)252, SEC(2001)380/3 and COM(2005)172. See further the discussion in Chapter 3.

[188] This is further supplemented by Article III-316 of the proposed Constitutional Treaty on development cooperation which, with the exception of referring to the eradication of poverty, is not substantively very different from the current provisions, and Article III-321 on humanitarian aid, which is recognition of the de facto situation.

Trade Organisation from adopting a position which would undermine its own development programmes in developing states.[189] The position under the proposed Constitutional Treaty is different as Article III-292 imposes an express obligation upon the Union to ensure 'consistency between the different areas of its external action and between these and its other policies'.

2.3.3.2 Obligation to Promote and Protect Human Rights in Third States

In the context of the CFSP, the Union is obliged to contribute to the global development and consolidation of respect for human rights and fundamental freedoms. Much of the Union's external activities in the context of the promotion of human rights and other ethical values takes place in the more specific context of the Community's development cooperation policy and the interrelationship between development, human rights, the rule of law and democracy. This is dealt with in the following sections. It is initially worth addressing, however, to what extent the Member States of the Union are generally obliged to protect and promote human rights in third states by their human rights treaty obligations. This is as opposed to the protection of norms in which they have an interest and the limits of responding to breaches of such norms, which were discussed above. This is so that it can be determined whether the Union's Member States are giving effect to existing legal obligations or acting of their own volition.

2.3.3.2(a) Member States and Treaty Obligations to Promote and Protect Human Rights in Third States
The issue we are concerned with here is the 'territorial applicability' of human rights treaties and whether those treaties generally oblige states to protect and promote such rights outside of their jurisdiction.[190] Notwithstanding the fact that a number of treaties contain similar language, there is no overall consistency in relation to this issue. The two 1966 Covenants, for example, take differing approaches. The Covenant on Economic, Social and Cultural Rights makes no specific reference to its jurisdictional application.[191] Article 2 ICCPR, on the

---

[189] Although this is not the case in practice, see the discussion in Chapter 3.
[190] More specific obligations are discussed below.
[191] This is also the case in the Women's Convention, although the Optional Protocol of 1999 (Optional Protocol to the Convention on the Elimination of All Forms of Discrimination Against Women,1999, 2131 UNTS 83) in Article 2 refers to the

other hand, obliges each state to 'undertake to respect and ensure to all individuals within its territory and subject to its jurisdiction the rights recognized in the present Covenant'. Most other treaties do not expressly limit their applicability to the territory of a state and require that effect be given by the Contracting State to the rights protected to 'all within their jurisdiction', although that term is understandably never defined.[192]

By looking at the practice of the tribunals established to interpret these treaties and the background to some of them, it is clear that there was (and is) no general intention to impose an obligation upon states to protect human rights in third states. For example, examination of the drafting history of Article 2 ICCPR makes it clear that the term 'jurisdiction' was added to ensure that states would be responsible for the acts of their agents outside of the state's geographical territory. As Novak notes, however, the discussions on these issues reveal that the intention of the final wording was to avoid obligating States Parties to protect persons who are under their jurisdictional authority but *outside* their sovereign territory.[193] Despite generally taking a very expansive approach to asserting its jurisdiction,[194] in the light of the *travaux préparatoires* the Human Rights Committee has not obliged any state party to protect Covenant rights outside its jurisdiction, where its agents are not involved.

The Strasbourg organs of the ECHR have on a number of occasions determined the applicability of the Convention outside of the physical territory of the Contracting States and their respective responsibilities. In the *Cyprus* v. *Turkey* cases of 1975, for example, it was held that a Contracting State may be responsible for the acts of its authorised agents outside of its territory.[195] The ECtHR has subsequently further

---

communications submitted by 'individuals, under the jurisdiction of a State Party'. Similarly, the African Charter does not have such a clause.

[192] The following relevant treaties take this approach: Article 6 ICERD; Article 2 CRC; and Article 1 ECHR. The approach of the European Social Charter, 1961, ETS No. 35, is different. Article 34 of the 1961 Charter applies to 'metropolitan territory' although a state can extend it to non-metropolitan territories under Article 34(2). Article 10(1) of the 1988 Additional Protocol, ETS No. 128 and Article L(1) of the Revised European Social Charter, ETS No. 163, are substantively identical.

[193] Novak, *U.N. Covenant*, p. 43. Also see Advisory Opinion, *Legal Consequences of the Wall*, n. 121 above, paras. 109–11.

[194] For more general discussion see McGoldrick, 'Approaches to the Assertion of International Jurisdiction'.

[195] Applications 6780/74 and 6950/75 (First and Second Applications) *Cyprus* v. *Turkey* (1976) 4 EHRR 482.

defined the 'extra-territorial' application of the Convention on numerous occasions,[196] most importantly in *Banković*.[197] It is clear from the ECtHR's jurisprudence that it does not oblige Contracting States to protect or promote Convention rights outside of their jurisdiction. As is the case with the ICCPR, a state may, however, be responsible for the acts of its agents outside of its territory.[198] As far as is known, on no occasion, under any of the major human rights treaties to which the EU Member States are a party, has a tribunal considered that states parties generally have an obligation to promote and protect human rights in third states. This does not mean, however, that obligations vis-à-vis third states do not exist with regard to specific issues, particularly in the context of development.

2.3.3.2(b) Development Cooperation, Human Rights and the Legal Obligations of Third States

The relationship between development and human rights is a complex and multifaceted one.[199] The right to development has been recognised on a number of occasions in declaratory documents, but always with a

---

[196] See e.g., *Soering* v. *United Kingdom*, Series A, 161 (1989) 11 EHRR 439; *Loizidou* v. *Turkey*, Preliminary Objections (1995) 20 EHRR 99; and *Loizidou* v. *Turkey* (1996) 23 EHRR 513.

[197] Application No. 52207/99, *Banković and others* v. *Belgium and 16 other States* (2007) 44 EHRR SE5.

[198] See, in particular, *Banković*, paras. 57–73. For a scathing critique see, L. Loucaides, 'Determining the Extra-territorial Effect of the European Convention: Facts, Jurisprudence and the Banković Case' (2006) *EHRLR* 391.

[199] See, among many others, the chapters in P. Alston and M. Robinson (eds.), *Human Rights and Development: Towards Mutual Recognition* (Oxford: Oxford University Press, 2005) and P. Gready and J. Ensor (eds.), *Reinventing Development: Translating Right-Based Approaches from Theory into Practice* (London: Zed Books, 2005); S. Marks, 'The Human Right to Development: Between Rhetoric and Reality' (2004) 17 *HHRJ* 137; K. Kumado, 'An Analysis of the Policy of Linking Development Aid to the Implementation of Human Rights Standards' (1993) 50 *The Review–The ICJ* 23; H. Madsen, 'Development Assistance and Human Rights Concerns' (1994) 61/62 *Nordic JIL* 129; J. O'Manique, 'Human Rights and Development' (1992) 14 *HRQ* 78; J. O'Manique, 'Development, Human Rights and Law' (1992) 14 *HRQ* 383; J. Donnelly, 'Human Rights, Democracy and Development' (1999) 21 *HRQ* 608; J. Paul, 'The Human Right to Development: Its Meaning and Importance' (1992) *Third World Legal Studies* 17; P. Alston, 'Ships Passing in the Night: the Current State of the Human Rights and Development Debate Seen Through the Lens of the Millennium Development Goals' (2005) 27 *HRQ* 755; Common Understanding on the Human Rights Based Approach to Development Cooperation, available at www.unescobkk.org/fileadmin/user_upload/appeal/human_rights/ UN_Common_understanding_RBA.pdf; and the Draft Guidelines on Human Rights and Poverty Reduction Strategies, available at www.unhchr.ch/development/ povertyfinal.html#

substantial dissenting or abstaining minority.[200] Arguments for the recognition of such a right are partly based on the principle, articulated in the UN Charter, that all states have an obligation to work together in an attempt to achieve global welfare.[201] Furthermore, Article 28 of the Universal Declaration of Human Rights recognises the right of everyone to a 'social and international order in which the rights and freedoms set forth in this Declaration can be fully realised'; this provision is, however, rarely referred to in international discourse.[202] In the same vein, the two 1966 Covenants refer to the idea that the human rights recognised in those documents can only be achieved 'if conditions are created where everyone may enjoy his civil and political rights, as well as his economic, social and cultural rights'.[203] These declarations and provisions do not in themselves impose legal obligations upon states to assist others. The 1986 Declaration on Development has, however, caused the relationship between human rights and development to become increasingly intertwined and complex.[204] The Rio Declaration of 1992,[205] as well as the reports of the Independent Expert on the Right to Development, initially appointed by the Commission on Human Rights, consider that the relationship between human rights and development has now gained universal acceptance.[206] What is in all probability legally recognised under customary international law, is 'the right to development ... as a universal and inalienable right and an integral part of fundamental human rights'.[207]

---

[200] The Commission on Human Rights expressly recognised the human right to development in 1977, see UN Doc. E/CN.4/SR.1389, p. 1392. More important is the 1986 Declaration on the Right to Development, GA Resolution 41/128, GAOR, 41st Session Supp.53, p. 186.

[201] In particular, Articles 1, 55 and 56 UNC. See further T. Franck, *Fairness in International Law and Institutions* (Oxford: Oxford University Press, 1995) chs. 13 and 14.

[202] The Charter of Economic Rights and Duties of States, GA Resolution. 3281(XXIX), UNGAOR, 29th Sess., Supp. No. 31 (1974) 50 is an exception.

[203] See the Preambles to the 1966 Covenants.

[204] Uppendra Baxi has been one of the most vocal critics of the vision of human rights which has been linked to development. His basic view is that a narrow market-oriented version of human rights is being used in development discourse to promote economic liberalisation and globalisation. See U. Baxi, *The Future of Human Rights*, 2nd edn (New Delhi: Oxford University Press, 2005).

[205] (1992) 31 *ILM* 874.

[206] *Report of the Independent Expert on Development*, 11/09/2000, E/CN.4/2000/WG.18/CRP.1, para. 5. See further A. Sengupta, 'On the Theory and Practice of the Right to Development' (2002) 24 *HRQ* 837.

[207] See the Vienna Declaration and Programme of Action 1993, A/CONF.157/23, reprinted (1993) 32 *ILM* 1667 para. 10. The eighth Millennium Development Goal is essentially

What the exact content of the right to development is and which obligations it imposes upon all states, however, are more difficult to determine. Development can be seen as a process, which aims to eliminate poverty and also allows other rights to be protected.[208] Development can also be seen as a value-based, culturally particular discourse.[209] Development, however, has a number of dimensions, implications and conceptual aspects which are of relevance to this discussion. First, why in the development discourse has poverty been so specifically highlighted, not only at the international level but also by the Union? Secondly, what is the actual role and place of human rights in the development process? Thirdly, do legal obligations to provide some form of assistance exist? Finally, are there possible obligations not to hinder the development of others? These questions are addressed in turn.

The trend towards identifying poverty as a primary objective of development cooperation policies began with the World Bank's 1990 *World Development Report*. This signalled recognition of the importance of a focus on the poor, to ensure that they were not excluded from the benefits of development. The OECD now considers that the commitment of *all* development agencies to poverty reduction is 'most tangibly reflected by their across the board support for the international development targets'.[210] This was established in the context of several UN Conferences and Summits.[211] Poverty is not perceived to be a high priority simply for the sake of relieving suffering. The *Human Development Report 2000*, for example, argues that human rights are not a reward of

---

defined as to 'develop a global partnership for development'. It is this goal which is the most unlikely to represent customary international law, see further Alston, 'Ships Passing in the Night', 774.

[208] Sengupta, 'Theory and Practice', 848.

[209] B. Rajagopal, *International Law from Below: Development, Social Movements and Third World Resistance* (Cambridge: Cambridge University Press, 2003) p. 138 argues that the effect of this approach has been to add another layer to the meaning of development. As he argues, it is now not merely poverty alleviating, environmentally sustainable or gender equalising, it is also, among other things, democracy dependent, democracy enhancing and peace building.

[210] DAC, *Shaping the 21st Century: Scoping Study, Donor Poverty Reduction and Practices* (Paris: OECD, 1996) p.vii.

[211] In particular, the World Summit for Social Development in Copenhagen in 1995. This has been developed (not always successfully) in a number of subsequent summits and meetings both under the auspices of the United Nations, such as the Monterrey Consensus of March 2002 and also of the G8, especially the Gleneagles Summit of 2005.

development but they are critical to achieving it.[212] It notes a 'decent standard of living, adequate nutrition, health care, education and decent work and protection against calamities are not just development goals – they are also human rights'.[213] As development and poverty are seen as being multidimensional it becomes far easier to absorb a human rights dimension into them.[214] One in five of the global population lives on less than US$ 1 per day.[215] For this reason it is argued that poverty eradication is not only a development goal but *the* central challenge for human rights in the twenty-first century.[216]

A recent example of an integrated approach to development and human rights comes from *In Larger Freedom: Towards Development, Security and Human Rights for All*, the report submitted to the World Summit by the then UN Secretary-General, Kofi Annan, in 2005.[217] In the report it is stated 'the world must advance the cause of security, development and human rights together otherwise none will succeed … In a world of interconnected threats and opportunities, it is in each country's self interest that all of these challenges are addressed effectively.'[218] Those living in extreme poverty are clearly, in practice, not benefiting from many of the rights which states have committed themselves to protecting and promoting. It is now considered that poverty can only be eradicated as part of the development process. The collateral respect for certain human rights this entails, as part of the more general relationship between development and human rights, is obvious.[219]

The role of human rights in the development process is relevant in two different respects. First, there is the relationship between human

---

[212] UNDP, *Human Development Report 2000, Human Rights and Development* (Oxford: Oxford University Press, 2000) p. 8. The report, which is one of the most comprehensive in its approach to poverty and development, built upon Amartya Sen's work and understanding of poverty and his capabilities argument. See A. Sen, *Inequality Reexamined* (Cambridge: Harvard University Press, 1992) and A. Sen, *Development as Freedom* (Oxford: Oxford University Press, 1999).

[213] *Human Development Report 2000*, p. 8.

[214] See OHCR, *Human Rights and Poverty Reduction: a Conceptual Framework* (New York and Geneva: United Nations, 2004).

[215] World Bank, *World Development Indicators 2006*. Poverty using a capabilities approach is, of course, much broader than income alone, but income is one of the more stark indicators of poverty. See further Chapter 3.

[216] *Human Development Report 2000*, p. 8.

[217] K. Annan, *Report of the Secretary General: In Larger Freedom: Towards Development, Security and Human Rights for All*, A/59/2005, 21 March 2005, available at http://daccessdds.un.org/doc/UNDOC/GEN/N05/270/78/PDF/N0527078.pdf?OpenElement

[218] *Ibid.* para. 18.   [219] See further the discussion in Chapter 3.

rights and the recognition of a right to development and what this entails. Secondly, there is the relationship between the protection of human rights and the economic development of the state in question. It has been argued that the right to development centres primarily upon the individual.[220] It has, in the alternative, also been argued that the right to development is actually nothing other than the recognition that, in the development process, the state should take account of and protect the already existing rights of those individuals who are affected by its development policies.[221] It is certainly without doubt that a large number of 'development' projects cause and create legally prohibited harms to some categories of project-affected persons.[222] But a 'rights-based' approach to development in this context is not easy to realise.[223] It assumes that rights can be defined and given effect in ways that facilitate planning and programming for their realisation. As Rajagopal has noted, how, for example, 'would one define freedom of speech and access to information in the context of a development project or program?'[224] Is it a right to participate in the decision-making process or would it simply recognise the right of project-affected people to express their opinions, or does it go further and grant a substantive right of veto over parts of or even the entire project?[225]

The argument that the development process is focused upon the individual is now the more widely accepted formulation and this is the approach which the Community has adopted in its policies.[226] There is no reason, though, why the right to development does not also encompass the differing approaches mentioned above. They are not necessarily incompatible; it is a question of where the emphasis lies. The individual, not the state, is seen as the main beneficiary of the development process

---

[220] Article 2 of the 1986 Declaration.

[221] See, F. Stewart, 'Basic Needs Strategies, Human Rights and the Right to Development' (1989) 11 *HRQ* 347; M. Nayar, 'Human Rights and Economic Development: the Legal Foundations' (1980) 2 *Universal Human Rights* 55 and I. Shihata, 'Democracy and Development' (1997) 46 *ICLQ* 635.

[222] Paul, 'The Human Right to Development', 20.

[223] As Gready and Ensor, *Reinventing Development*, p. 1 note, there is a huge diversity of opinions over what a 'rights-based' approach to development should be. See also, P. Alston and M. Robinson, 'The Challenges of Ensuring the Mutuality of Human Rights and Development Endeavours' in Alston and Robinson, *Human Rights and Development*, p. 1.

[224] Rajagopal, *International Law from Below*, p. 223.

[225] This is adapted from Rajagopal, *International Law from Below*, p. 223.

[226] See e.g., Article 9 of the Cotonou Convention and discussion in Chapter 3.

and is its focus. This requires that in the development process his or her legally protected or defined rights are not violated. It can also mean that as the state develops economically and politically, individual rights are increasingly realised, promoted and protected.

What these principles entail for the Community and its Member States is that when providing assistance and, in particular, funding for specific projects, these should not have an adverse impact upon the legally recognised rights of individuals in that state. It is difficult to think of a situation likely to arise in practice, however, in which the Community and or Member States could be held responsible for the role they have played in development projects they have funded, if any recognised rights have been violated as a part of that process. The recipient state, in conjunction with whom such projects are initiated and usually completed, is responsible and accountable before national and or international mechanisms, to which it is a party, for any possible breaches of its obligations.

The next question is to what extent does an obligation to assist, in this context, exist? In 1969 the Development Assistance Committee (DAC) of the OECD agreed a target for developed countries to donate 0.7 per cent of their gross national product for overseas development assistance. This commitment has been reaffirmed on a number of occasions since.[227] The provision of assistance to states, in this context, was described by Addo, writing in 1990, as nothing more than soft law.[228] Subsequently the Vienna Declaration of 1993 noted that 'states should cooperate with each other in ensuring development and eliminating obstacles to development', as have other documents which have been adopted at major international conferences.[229] Such commitments and statements cannot and do not, however, amount to unilateral statements in the sense required for the formation of a legally binding obligation to provide assistance.[230] Most, if not all, developed states provide some assistance. They do not, however, consider that

---

[227] Most importantly the Millennium Declaration. With regard to the European Union see COM(2005)311, p. 12 and further the discussion in Chapter 3.

[228] M. Addo, 'Some Issues in European Community Aid Policy and Human Rights' (1988) *LIEI* 55, 62.

[229] See para. 10 of the Vienna Declaration. See also, the Declarations of the Cairo World Population and Development Summit, 1994, the Copenhagen World Summit for Social Development, 1995, the Beijing Fourth World Conference on Women, 1995 and the Millennium Declaration.

[230] See the *Nuclear Tests Cases*, n. 171 above, para. 45.

they are obliged to do so, unless they have entered into a specific treaty agreement to do so. The recognition and acceptance by consensus at Vienna in 1993 of the right to development as 'a universal and inalienable right and an integral part of fundamental human rights' and subsequent reiterations to this effect in, for example, the Millennium Declaration, do not mean that states feel legally obliged to provide a certain amount of development assistance. 0.7 per cent of gross national product is accepted as being a target and the European Union, for example, has agreed dates by which all of the old Member States should reach it, but these are not legally binding obligations.[231] For the purposes of custom the requisite *opinio juris* and practice is absent.[232] The United States, for example, has stated on a number of occasions that it does not recognise a legal obligation to provide a certain amount of aid[233] and the European Union has stated that it considers a legally binding treaty obligation to do so would be unhelpful.[234]

A legal obligation, which has now arguably been accepted in the development process, is that a state or group of states should not hinder the development of others. This is because development is perceived to be the best manner in which human rights can be protected.[235] Articles 55 and 56 of the UN Charter read in conjunction with the Vienna Declaration, the 1986 Declaration on the Right to Development and Part III of the Millennium Declaration impose obligations upon states to cooperate and take action to work towards development for all states. What the potentially 'obstructive states' must not do, however, is unclear. It is difficult to define a core obligation that the principle entails. A developing state would not be able to hold a group of developed states responsible for not removing trade barriers, for example,[236] if it

---

[231] See COM(2005)311.

[232] The lack of a legal obligation is recognised most importantly by Sengupta in his capacity as the then Independent Expert on the Right to Development.

[233] At the UNCHR 59th session in a comment in the Working Group on the Right to Development on 10 February 2003, the US representative is reported as having stated 'states ... have no obligation to provide guarantees for implementation of any purported "right to development"': cited by Marks, 'Human Right to Development', 137.

[234] With regard to the Union's position see European Council, *EU Annual Report on Human Rights 2003* (Luxembourg: OOPEC, 2003) section 4.3.8 where it is noted 'the EU has serious doubts as to whether the option of a legally binding instrument [in the context of the United Nations] would provide an appropriate or practicable way forward'.

[235] See further below.

[236] The eighth Millennium Declaration goal refers to such undertakings; as noted above, it is the least likely to represent customary law.

considers its development is being hindered, unless there is a breach of a specific treaty obligation. There is a well-established practice for developing states to be treated in a different or preferential manner in certain international treaties. The obligation not to hinder or to provide assistance in practical terms, however, means little outside of such a treaty.

The content of the obligations discussed above and the responsibilities and duties of states are both unquantified. More precise legal obligations, however, do exist upon developed states. These are in the context of providing assistance in certain circumstances to developing states.

2.3.3.2(c) Development Cooperation, Humanitarian Assistance and the Obligation to Assist

In a more limited context, it is arguable that developed states are, in certain circumstances, under a legal obligation to provide humanitarian aid to third states. With regard to human rights, states are obliged, as noted above, to protect the rights only of those under their jurisdiction. Humanitarian assistance is concerned with providing assistance to those in another jurisdiction. Here the state, if it still exists, is unable or unwilling to provide its population with protection from a situation which threatens their very existence. There is thus an overwhelming necessity for other states, agencies or organisations to act to alleviate the suffering of those affected.

Humanitarian assistance is usually considered to be a component of development assistance. There is in practice a continuum between the two. The provision of emergency relief can be substantially reduced if development projects, as understood in the strict sense, establish an infrastructure which lessens the long-term dependency on emergency aid in the eventuality of a disaster. Conversely humanitarian assistance can be concerned with the rehabilitation of affected populations, as well as alleviating immediate danger, and thus merge into development cooperation. It is also usually only in the developing world that a natural or man-made disaster will put a population in a situation where the state does not have the resources to alleviate their suffering. It is the overwhelming necessity to assist in the alleviation of that suffering that compels others to take action to assist the affected state in its efforts, if there are any. The two can be conceptually and legally distinguished, although the boundaries between them are sometimes unclear. Humanitarian assistance is seen to be subject to a different set of principles.[237] Development cooperation is an inherently long-term and political activity while humanitarian assistance is an altruistic and short-term one, the defining principles of which are, or at least should be, urgency, neutrality and impartiality. Assistance is to be provided on the basis of need and nothing else. In the suspension of development cooperation, for whatever reason, an exception is always made for humanitarian assistance.

Although distinguishable from development cooperation, there is still a relationship between human rights and humanitarian assistance. They are related in the sense that a humanitarian emergency, whatever its cause, will interfere with the enjoyment of rights such as those to health, food and shelter. While a lack of development can also interfere with such rights, the threat posed in a humanitarian situation is more urgent than would normally be the case in the context of economic, social and cultural rights.[238]

Numerous declarations and resolutions currently exist which urge states to contribute and assist those in desperate and urgent need but they do not currently impose a legally binding obligation to do so.[239] The Millennium Declaration of the UN General Assembly, for example, recognises that each state has a separate as well as collective responsibility to uphold the principles of human dignity, equality and equity at the global level.[240] It does not, however, encompass a specific obligation to assist. Similar commitments have also been made, for example, at the Rome Declaration on World Food Security 1996[241] and the World Food Summit Plan of Action.[242] The earlier General Assembly Resolution 45/102[243] encouraged the international community to contribute substantially and regularly to international humanitarian activities and stressed the importance of further developing international cooperation in the humanitarian field to better facilitate

---

[237] See further Chapter 6.

[238] The CESCR has in General Comment 3, 12 December 1990, noted at para. 1 that the Covenant does impose immediate obligations but also allows for progressive realisation acknowledging the constraints due to limits of available resources.

[239] For a contrary view see P. Laurent, 'Humanitarian Assistance is a Right' in C. Pirotte, B. Husson, and F. Grunewald (eds.), *Responding to Emergencies and Fostering Development* (London: Zed Books, 1999) p. 122.

[240] Millennium Declaration, para. 2.

[241] Adopted under the auspices of the UN Food and Agricultural Organisation, see www.fao.org/docrep/003/w3613e/w3613e00.htm

[242] Objective 7.4 of the Plan of Action, available at www.fao.org/docrep/003/w3613e/w3613e00.htm

[243] Promotion of International Cooperation in the Humanitarian Field, A/RES/45/102.

understanding, mutual respect, confidence and tolerance among the planet's countries and peoples. Again, no legally binding obligation to assist exists. In two resolutions, however, the General Assembly does seem to recognise a very limited right to assistance. This is where there is a starving population involved, although the resolutions do not elaborate upon whom the duty is placed.[244]

This is not to state, however, that there is no rights discourse in the humanitarian assistance field.[245] General Assembly Resolution 43/131 on Humanitarian Assistance to Victims of Natural Disasters and Similar Emergency Situations, for example, considers that a right exists for those providing assistance to demand access to victims of natural disasters and other emergency situations, although the nature of the obligation on those hindering access is not elaborated upon.[246] If such a right were accepted, the question of whether the consent of the state in question would be required still needs to be resolved. The position reflected in treaties concerned with this area of law would certainly answer this in the affirmative.[247] Generally, however, consent can be implied. There are relatively few examples of states making clear that they do not wish for outside assistance.[248]

---

[244] Humanitarian Assistance to Victims of Natural Disasters and Similar Emergency Situations, A/RES/45/100 and Strengthening of the Co-ordination of Humanitarian Emergency Assistance of the United Nations, A/RES/46/182.

[245] In the more general context see Chapter 6.

[246] GA Resolution, A/RES/43/131. Also see A/RES/45/100 and further Chapter 6.

[247] The Four Geneva Conventions of 1949 as well as the 1977 Protocols all require the consent of the state to be granted: Geneva Convention for the Amelioration of the Condition of the Wounded and Sick in Armed Forces in the Field, 1949 ('Geneva Convention I') 75 UNTS 31; Geneva Convention for the Amelioration of the Condition of the Wounded, Sick and Shipwrecked Members of the Armed Forces at Sea, 1949 ('Geneva Convention II') 75 UNTS 85; Geneva Convention Relative to the Treatment of Prisoners of War, 1949 ('Geneva Convention III') 75 UNTS 135; Geneva Convention Relative to the Protection of Civilian Persons in Time of War, 1949 ('Geneva Convention IV') 75 UNTS 287; Protocol Additional to the Geneva Conventions of 12 August 1949, and Relating to the Protection of Victims of International Armed Conflicts (Protocol I), 1125 UNTS 3; and Protocol Additional to the Geneva Conventions of 12 August 1949, and Relating to the Protection of Victims of Non-International Armed Conflicts (Protocol II), 1125 UNTS 609. In the *Nicaragua* case, n. 86 above, paras. 242–3, the ICJ held that there was no doubt that the provision of strictly humanitarian aid cannot amount to unlawful intervention or be contrary to international law, so long as such aid was without discrimination of any sort. Whether this position is an evolution of the Protocols and Conventions is unclear.

[248] Zimbabwe, for example, has occasionally refused humanitarian assistance at which the Union Presidency has expressed dismay. See Presidency Statement, 7 November 2005, Doc. 13969/05.

Article 11 of the International Covenant on Economic, Social and Cultural Rights (ICESCR) can be said, however, to contain legal undertakings which may be relevant in imposing an obligation upon the Member States of the Union to provide assistance in the context of the right to adequate food and the right to be free from hunger.[249] Article 2 ICESCR which establishes the general nature of a state's obligations under the Covenant seems to imply, when read in conjunction with Article 11, that in times of crisis, for example famine, a state is obliged to seek international assistance.[250] The exact nature and extent of the legal obligation this imposes on Contracting States is not easy to ascertain. General Comment 3 of the Committee on Economic, Social and Cultural Rights (CESCR), in referring to Articles 55 and 56 of the UN Charter, recognises that the obligation to assist is 'particularly incumbent upon those States in a position to assist others in this regard'.[251] Shelton, in particular, has argued that general principles of law and human rights treaties impose a duty on states to provide famine assistance.[252] The Limburg Principles,[253] however, note that international cooperation and assistance must be based on the sovereign equality of states,[254] and Article 11 ICESCR refers to the fact that the realisation of rights and international cooperation should be based upon 'free consent'. The CESCR in its General Comment 12 on Article 11, on the other hand, notes that States Parties should take steps to protect the right to food in other countries, and to provide the *necessary* aid when

---

[249] This also extends to access to water under Article 11 ICESCR, see CESCR, General Comment 15, E/C.12/2002/11, especially paras. 30–6. See also, the reports of the Special Rapporteur on the Right to Food, especially E/CN.4/2002/58 and E/CN.4/2003/54 and W. Vandenhole, 'Third State Obligations under the ICESCR: a Case Study of EU Sugar Policy' (2007) *Nordic JIL* 73.

[250] See P. Alston, 'International Law and the Human Right to Food' in P. Alston and K. Tomaševski (eds.), *The Right to Food* (Dordrecht: Martinus Nijhoff, 1984) pp. 9, 43. This is very much in line with para. 26 of the Limburg Principles, UN Doc. E/CN.4/1987/17. See also, M. Craven, *The International Covenant on Economic, Social and Cultural Rights: a Perspective on its Development* (Oxford: Oxford University Press, 1998) p. 144 and A. Eide, 'The Right to an Adequate Standard of Living including the Right to Food' in A. Eide, C. Krause and A. Rosas, *Economic, Social and Cultural Rights: a Textbook* (Dordrecht: Martinus Nijhoff, 2001) p. 133 *et seq.*

[251] General Comment 3 of the CESCR, para.14.

[252] D. Shelton, 'The Duty to Assist Famine Victims' (1984–5) 70 *Iowa Law Review* 1279. This view is now substantiated by para. 38 of General Comment 12 on Article 11 ICESCR, E/C.12/1995/5 CESCR.

[253] The Limburg Principles are not legally binding, although they are highly persuasive.

[254] *Ibid.* para. 33.

required.[255] States must also ensure an equitable distribution of world food supplies in relation to need.[256] Alston has argued that these obligations can be interpreted to mean that states have a duty to avoid international policies which deprive other states of their means of subsistence or which promote an inequitable distribution of food supplies. It also implies a duty to mitigate national policies which promote inequality and to ensure that international trade works towards an equitable distribution of food.[257] It can further be argued that states have a joint and individual responsibility to cooperate in providing disaster and humanitarian assistance in times of emergency, including to refugees, although each state is only obliged to contribute to this task in accordance with its ability.[258] States in need are entitled to ask for assistance; developed states, however, are not individually obliged to make up the shortfall but must attempt to meet the assessed need, to the extent they can.

Many of these obligations have now been expressly recognised by the CESCR in a *sui generis* statement.[259] The Committee considers that those in a position to provide 'international assistance and cooperation, especially economic and technical' to enable developing countries to fulfil their core obligations (under the ICESCR) must do so. Such core obligations give rise to national responsibilities for all States Parties to the Covenant, and international responsibilities for developed states, as well as others that are 'in a position to assist'.[260] Core obligations are considered by the Committee to have a crucial role to play in international development policies. As it notes, 'it is particularly incumbent upon those who can assist, to help developing countries to respect this international minimum threshold ... [I]f an international anti-poverty strategy does not reflect this minimum threshold, it is inconsistent with the legally binding obligations of the State parties.'[261]

Although the exact legal significance of this statement is uncertain, it is in many senses an express consolidation and elaboration of the

---

[255] General Comment 12, para. 36. See also, General Comment 15, para. 31, with regard to water.
[256] Article 11(2)(b) ICESCR.   [257] See Alston, 'Human Right to Food' p. 9.
[258] Limburg Principles, para. 38.
[259] CESCR, *Substantive Issues arising in the Implementation of the ICESCR: Poverty and the ICESCR*, UN Doc E/C.12/2001/10, (2002) 9 IHRR 889. It is not a General Comment and there are, to date, no other statements similar to it.
[260] *Ibid.* para. 16.   [261] *Ibid.* para. 17.

ICESCR's provisions and the Committee's earlier General Comments. The Member States of the Union, therefore, as States Parties to the Covenant, individually have a legal obligation under it to provide assistance to developing states and are obliged to work together and with others to avoid policies which lead to an inequitable global distribution of food. The fact that they may coordinate their action in response to such obligations through DG ECHO or the other Directorates-General of the Commission is perfectly compatible with their obligations under the ICESCR. Despite the existence of these obligations, it is clear that while the Commission and DG ECHO consistently refer to the human rights nature of their work with regard to humanitarian aid, there is no reference to these legal obligations.[262] With regard to development, the right to food and humanitarian assistance, the ICESCR is the clearest relevant set of legal obligations requiring the Member States of the Union to provide assistance to third states. The content of these obligations is not particularly clear.

2.3.3.3 Obligation to Promote and Protect Democracy and the Rule of Law in Third States

2.3.3.3(a) Democracy
The development and consolidation of democracy and the rule of law are objectives shared by both the CFSP and the Community's development cooperation policy. They are also considered by the proposed Constitutional Treaty to be some of the values upon which the Union is based. As far as its own Member States are concerned, the Union has, since the Copenhagen Declaration on Democracy of 1978, insisted that 'respect for and maintenance of representative democracy and human rights in each Member State are essential elements of membership of the European Community'.[263] In more recent years, significant amounts of capital and energy have been invested by the Union in ensuring the existence of liberal democratic states on its eastern and southern borders. If one accepts Slaughter's argument that liberal (as opposed to non-liberal) democracies: do not tend to engage in armed conflicts with

---

[262] See further Chapter 6.
[263] (1978) 3 *Bull. EC* 5. The position for new prospective Member States is laid down in the Copenhagen Criteria of the Copenhagen European Council, 21–22 June 1993, (1993) 6 *Bull. EC* I.13. Article I-58 of the Constitutional Treaty permits any European state which respects the Union's values as articulated in Article I-2 to apply to become a member.

one another; obey their international obligations; enforce agreements; are respected; and take the unpredictability factor out of international development projects and investment by multinationals, then the logic of such an approach is apparent.[264]

A similar argument was put forward by King who, writing in 1996, argued that the Union is convinced that liberal democracies will prove to be the most peaceful neighbours.[265] This has been borne out by the Union's practice since the end of the Cold War, in particular the adoption of the European Neighbourhood Policy.[266] As the Union and its Member States contributed the most assistance to these states (with some of them subsequently becoming members of the Union) and accounted for the vast bulk of trade, they had little choice but to accept conditions on the recognition of their statehood, which clearly added criteria which were then not broadly or generally accepted as prerequisites for statehood in customary international law.[267]

As Tomaševski notes, whereas states have traditionally engaged in relations with one another on the basis of their ability to satisfy the criteria of statehood, some states are now increasingly passing judgment on whether they consider a particular regime to be legitimate or not.[268] Whether a right to democratic governance currently exists or not and what its contents are, is controversial.[269] Academic

---

[264] A. Slaughter, 'International Law in a World of Liberal States' (1995) 6 *EJIL* 503. J. Crawford, 'Democracy and the Body of International Law' (1993) 44 *BYBIL* 113, note 1, comments, that while this may be broadly true for war it is not the case for covert action. See S. Marks, 'International Law, Democracy and the End of History' in G. Fox and B. Roth (eds.), *Democratic Governance and International Law* (Cambridge: Cambridge University Press, 2000) p. 532 and J. Alvarez, 'Do Liberal States Behave Better? A Critique of Slaughter's Liberal Theory' (2001) 12 *EJIL* 183, for critiques of Slaughter's argument.

[265] T. King, 'The European Community and Human Rights in Eastern Europe' (1996) *LIEI* 93.

[266] See further the discussion in Chapter 5.

[267] The traditional criteria for statehood do not include democratic institutions or respect for human rights or minority groups. See C. Warbrick, 'Recognition of States: Part 2' (1993) 43 *ICLQ* 433 and Denza, *Intergovernmental Pillars*, p. 49 on how the Community and the Member States, in terms of competence, ensured 'an immaculate fudge' by not distinguishing who proposed the new criteria.

[268] K. Tomaševski, *Development Aid and Human Rights Revisited* (London: Pinter Publishers, 1993) p. 123. See also, S. Murphy, 'Democratic Legitimacy and the Recognition of States and Governments' (1999) 48 *ICLQ* 545 and J. Crawford, *The Creation of States in International Law*, 2nd edn (Oxford: Oxford University Press, 2006).

[269] The seminal article is T. Franck, 'The Emerging Right to Democratic Governance' (1992) 86 *AJIL* 46. Fox and Roth, *Democratic Governance*, contains an excellent collection of essays, many of which are critical of Franck's argument.

commentary can be found in support of rereading Article 2(4) of the UN Charter, in certain circumstances, to allow the unilateral use of force to restore democracy.[270] Yet as Crawford notes, the invasions in Panama and Nicaragua were routinely condemned in the United Nations and OAS[271] and as the ICJ noted in the *Nicaragua* case, there is no right for one state 'to intervene' in the affairs of another, simply because it has chosen a particular ideology or political system.[272] Intervention and the use of force to restore democracy are only permissible where they are authorised by the Security Council, as in the case of Haiti.[273]

Discussion of the role and status of democracy in international law can be approached from the point of view that such a right now exists and what its contents are or how international law should develop and respond to democracy as a norm? Claims for a right to democratic entitlement require that international rules judge the legitimacy of regimes and that democracy is essential in domestic law.[274]

Relations between those states which are most keen on the promulgation of a right to democratic governance and non-democratic regimes, however, are far from consistent.[275] The EU Member States, for example, have friendly relations with, among others, Saudi Arabia, Dubai, Kuwait, Bahrain, Singapore, China and Musharaff's regime in Pakistan; but not with Zimbabwe or Myanmar, illustrating that democracy, or the lack thereof, is sometimes, in part, an ideological weapon in inter-state relations. The so-called 'Bush Doctrine for Democracy in the Middle East' of 2003 illustrates just how the lack of democracy in a region can be used selectively and inconsistently. President George W. Bush, without any sense of contradiction, stressed how regimes in the region needed to become democratic yet in the previous months had been putting pressure on the Palestinians to elect

---

[270] See for differing views, A. D'Amato, 'The Invasion of Panama was a Lawful Response to Tyranny' (1990) 84 *AJIL* 37; Reisman, 'Sovereignty and Human Rights' and M. Byers and S. Chesterman, 'You the People: Pro Democratic Intervention in International Law' in Fox and Roth, *Democratic Governance*, p. 259.

[271] J. Crawford, 'Democracy and the Body of International Law' in Fox and Roth, *Democratic Governance*, p. 106.

[272] *Nicaragua* case, n. 86 above, paras. 102–10 and 265.

[273] Security Council Resolution 940 (1994), 31 July 1994.

[274] Marks, 'International Law', p. 546.

[275] For EU practice see Chapter 4 and more generally R. Youngs, *The European Union and the Promotion of Democracy* (Oxford: Oxford University Press, 2001).

new leaders democratically, who could not include Yasser Arafat.[276] For many states, democracy (or its absence) in other states plays no real role in determining relations between them, as it is perceived as being part and parcel of a state's internal affairs. The inconsistent practice of some states does not, however, necessarily undermine the evolution of a norm at the international level. For example, the now defunct UN Commission on Human Rights and the General Assembly have adopted a number of resolutions which reaffirm that democracy is important for the protection of other rights, although they rarely, if ever, make reference to a 'right to democratic governance' itself.[277]

The traditional view has clearly been that international law has no business with domestic constitutional issues and the formation of government. Fox and Roth note, however, that since the events of 1989–91, international law has begun to address the issue.[278] There clearly has been a major shift in practice; for example, self-determination now plays a more significant role in questions of recognition than was the case in the past.[279] Not only have international tribunals dealing with human rights issues begun to stress the importance of democracy for the protection of human rights[280] but international declarations have continually affirmed that 'democracy fosters the full realisation of all

---

[276] G. W Bush, Speech on the 20th Anniversary of the National Endowment for Democracy, 6 November 2003, available at www.whitehouse.gov/news/releases/2003/11/20031106-2.html. For discussion on the approach to Arafat and the differing attitudes of the European Union and United States towards him see further Chapter 5.

[277] See e.g., CHR 1999/57, The Promotion of the Right to Democracy; GA Resolution 55/96, 'Promoting and Consolidating Democracy'; GA Resolution 59/201, Enhancing the Role of Regional, Subregional and Other Organizations and Arrangements in Promoting and Consolidating Democracy; CHR 2000/47, Promoting and Consolidating Democracy; CHR 2001/41, Continuing Dialogue on Measures to Promote and Consolidate Democracy; CHR 2002/46, Further Measures to Promote and Consolidate Democracy; CHR 2003/36, Interdependence between Democracy and Human Rights; CHR 2005/32, Democracy and the Rule of Law; and Part V of the Millennium Declaration.

[278] Fox and Roth, *Democratic Governance*, p. 1.

[279] See further J. Crawford, 'Democracy in International Law: a Reprise' in Fox and Roth, *Democratic Governance*, p. 114.

[280] See e.g., the Human Rights Committee's General Comment 25, 12 July 1996 and a number of decisions of the ECtHR concerning Turkey, such as *United Communist Party of Turkey v. Turkey* (1998) 26 EHRR 121, para. 45. For a good survey of many of these cases, see P. Harvey, 'Militant Democracy and the European Convention on Human Rights' (2004) *ELRev.* 407.

human rights and vice versa'.[281] The Commission on Human Rights, for example, has urged the:

continuation and expansion of activities carried out by the United Nations system, other intergovernmental and non-governmental organisations and Member States to promote and consolidate democracy within the framework of international cooperation and build a democratic political culture through the observance of human rights, mobilisation of civil society and other appropriate measures in support of democratic governance.[282]

The UN General Assembly has also, as noted above, adopted a number of different resolutions concerning democracy and electoral assistance. One of the first of these resolutions is entitled 'Respect for the Principles of National Sovereignty and Non-Interference in the Internal Affairs of States in their Electoral Process' which declares very clearly that:

any ... attempt, directly or indirectly, to interfere in the free development of national electoral processes, in particular in the developing countries, violates the spirit and letter of the principles enshrined in the Charter and in the Declaration on the Principles of International Law Concerning Friendly Relations and Cooperation Amongst States in Accordance with the Charter of the United Nations.[283]

Another resolution entitled 'Strengthening the Role of the United Nations in Enhancing the Effectiveness of the Principle of Periodic and Genuine Elections and the Promotion of Democratisation' commends the assistance that has been provided to states and requests that further post-election assistance be provided to requesting states in order to sustain the electoral process.[284] The basic sentiment of the resolutions is that states or international organisations may provide assistance for the electoral process, if they are so requested, but must not interfere in the development of that process, in particular, in developing countries.

Democracy can be seen as being compatible with respecting all five types of rights: economic, social, cultural, civil and political. The implementation of democratic institutions is in itself also an exercise of various rights. The holding of fair elections, for example, is seen to contribute to the fulfilment of the right to political participation as

---

[281] CHR 1999/57.   [282] *Ibid.* para. 4.   [283] A/RES/52/119.   [284] A/RES/52/129.

found in Article 25 ICCPR.[285] While democracy may be conducive to the protection of human rights it is not essential or indeed sufficient. Questions concerning the arbitrary exercise of power or even majority rule, in particular where political parties are defined along ethnic or religious lines, would still need to be addressed. In majoritarian democracies, for example, discrimination may be rife.[286] In the development context, democratisation is often pursued alongside economic liberalisation and thus it can be challenged by powerful sets of economic interests which can actually distort the democratic process. The existence of democratic institutions and the protection of human rights are not necessarily synonymous.

The EC Treaty and the CFSP, as stated above, set as a policy objective the promotion and consolidation of democracy in dealings with all states. The perceived importance of the role of democracy in the development context is, however, more advanced than its evolution as a general normative value. Various international organisations, such as the United Nations and European Union, have emphasised the importance of democracy, not only as a condition for the respect for human rights, as discussed above, but also because it is conducive to the development of the state in question as opposed to a right per se.[287] The European Commission has noted on numerous occasions that 'developing states can only develop and reduce poverty where functioning democracies and accountable governments are in power'.[288] The OECD has also placed a great deal of stress on the fact that democracy and good governance are central to the achievement of the development goals of the twenty-first century.[289] A lack of democracy is thus seen to be fatal to the development process. Conflicts between ethnic groups, for example, arguably often break out due to a lack of democratic representation within domestic institutions. As Held has noted, 'democracy suggests a way of relating values to each other and of leaving the resolution of value conflicts open to participants in a public

---

[285] Article 3 of the First Protocol to the ECHR and Article 13 of the African Charter are narrower in scope.

[286] Israel is a classic example of this. See e.g., the Concluding Observations of CERD, CERD/C/52/Misc.29 and further Chapter 5.

[287] Although see the resolutions which were regularly adopted by the Commission on Human Rights which seemed to emphasise all aspects of democracy, e.g., CHR 2002/46, Further Measures to Promote and Consolidate Democracy.

[288] See e.g., COM(2001)252, p. 4.

[289] See OECD, *Final Report of the Ad Hoc Working Group on Participatory Development and Good Governance* (Paris: OECD, 1997).

process'.[290] Thus if states and organisations are to assist others in the development process, it is on the basis that democratic institutions exist and the mechanisms are in place to ensure that grievances of such a nature can be redressed. Clark, for example, has argued that what has taken place in Eastern Europe and in Latin America is the realisation that human rights and democracy are not luxuries, nor are they the result of being developed or wealthy, but conditions which make wealth develop.[291]

It can be appreciated that liberal democracies may prefer to deal with other democratic states, as opposed to totalitarian ones.[292] However, the basis for the connection between democracy and development (and this is limited only to the Community's development cooperation policy) is the argument that democracy assists the development process, increases trade and thus benefits the population. The perception seems to be that human rights will be respected and this will also lead, over a period of time, to wealth creation within the state itself. Democratic states are also seen, as discussed above, as being less prone to civil strife and unlikely to slide into civil conflict.[293]

While this approach may have an intrinsic appeal, it is questionable whether it is correct. A number of Asian states, such as Malaysia, Taiwan, Indonesia, South Korea and China, have developed rapidly without the presence of democratic institutions but due to the implementation of sound economic policies. Well-functioning firms and markets with significant government intervention and regulation have been heavily involved. The Union, among others, seeks the liberalisation of markets in its trading relationships, which does not allow for the careful management of that process and this can have many negative consequences. In terms of poverty reduction, for example, India and China have in real terms lifted more people out of poverty in recent years than at any time throughout human history.[294] One is democratic and in political terms relatively free, the other is neither.

---

[290] D. Held, *Models of Democracy* (Cambridge: Polity Press, 2006) p. 260.

[291] J. Clark, 'Human Rights and Democratic Development' in K. Mahoney and P. Mahoney (eds.), *Human Rights in the Twenty First Century* (Dordrecht: Martinus Nijhoff, 1993) p. 683.

[292] It is always worth noting the distinction which is drawn by some governments between states which are described as 'totalitarian' and those considered to be 'authoritarian'.

[293] See further the discussion in Chapter 3.

[294] See J. Wolfensohn, 'Some Reflections on Human Rights and Development' in Alston and Robinson, *Human Rights and Development*, pp. 19, 24 and J. Bhagwati, *In Defence of Globalization* (Oxford: Oxford University Press, 2005) p. 65. See further Chapter 3.

Freedom, be it democratic, economic or in terms of liberties does not seem to be directly related to economic growth.[295] Political credibility, as opposed to democratically held elections, is certainly a factor in how a state develops economically. Multinational corporations are far more likely to invest, as economic studies show, in countries which implement sound fiscal policies and where institutions have credibility as opposed to those which are democratic but lack such credibility or where corruption at all levels is rife. As investment from multinational corporations outweighs development assistance by a ratio of approximately five to one, it is these factors which are more important for the economic development of the state than democracy alone.[296]

As noted above, democratic states may ideologically prefer to cooperate with other democracies but in practice they have no hesitation in dealing with non-democratic regimes, or seeing election results set aside, when they perceive it to be in their interests. Events in Algeria are a classic example of this. In the context of this book, Denza has noted that the Union lacks any international legal basis for imposing democracy on non-Member States.[297] States may assist each other in the development and consolidation of democracy but it is essential that this must not amount to interference in their internal affairs. Democracy as a right per se is not yet established in international law; at most it is *lex ferenda*. Democracy as a right, as protected in multilateral treaties, is only a procedural one. For it to be substantively effective it must be accompanied by the rule of law. Without it, procedural democracy in real terms means little to the average person. It is probably for this reason that the EC and EU Treaties and the proposed Constitutional Treaty refer to the consolidation and development of both democracy and the rule of law.

2.3.3.3(b) *The Rule of Law*

As with democracy, the rule of law is seen as being of most importance, in its promotion, in developing states. The World Bank's annual *World Development Report*, for example, consistently recognises and affirms that establishing the rule of law is one of the five 'fundamental tasks'

---

[295] See J. Sachs, *The End of Poverty: How We Can Make it Happen in Our Lifetime* (London: Penguin Books, 2005) p. 319, who cites the Index of Economic Freedoms, 1995–2003.

[296] See e.g., S. Borner, A. Bunetti and B. Weder, *Political Credibility and Economic Development* (London: St Martin's Press, 1995) p. 62 and further the discussion in Chapter 3.

[297] Denza, *Intergovernmental Pillars*, p. 89.

which governments must perform in the pursuit of development.[298] The reports emphasise a number of functions which governments must fulfil in order to support the rule of law: providing a set of rules which are known in advance and which are actually implemented as opposed to simply existing on the statute book; the equal and consistent application of those legal rules; a judicial system which is reasonably effective and impartial in the resolving of disputes between parties; and a clear process by which rules and procedures are amended to avoid abuse.[299] Many of these criteria also overlap with the concept of 'good governance' which is a 'fundamental element' of the Cotonou Agreement.[300] Good governance is perceived to include support for the rule of law by providing assistance to improve and reinforce the legal, judicial and enforcement systems; strengthening public sector management; controlling corruption; reducing excessive military expenditure; and promoting and defending human rights by adherence to internationally agreed principles.[301]

The OECD, like the World Bank, now places a great deal of stress on the fact that democracy, good governance and the rule of law are central to the achievements of the development goals of the twenty-first century.[302] Invoking and ensuring respect for the rule of law, as well as implementing policies concerned with good governance, are undeniably among the most difficult aspects of reform which any state can

---

[298] See e.g., World Bank, *World Development Report: the State in a Changing World* (New York: Oxford University Press, 1997) p. 4. See also, D. Kennedy, 'Laws as Development' in J. Hatchard and A. Perry-Kessaris (eds.), *Law and Development: Facing Complexity in the 21st Century* (London: Cavendish, 2003) p. 17.

[299] For the link between poor laws and law enforcement see R. Sherwood, G. Shephard and C. Marcos de Sousa, 'Judicial Systems and Economic Performance' (1994) 34 *Quarterly Review of Economics and Finance* 101. A lack of effective institutions can also hamper economic development; see H. De Soto, *The Other Path* (New York: Harper and Rowe, 1989) and H. De Soto, *The Mystery of Capital: Why Capital Triumphs in the West and Fails Everywhere Else* (London: Black Swan Books, 2001).

[300] In the context of developing countries, see further, J. Faundez (ed.), *Good Government and Law: Legal and Institutional Reform in Developing Countries* (London: Macmillan, 1997) and H. Sano, G. Alfredsson and R. Clapp (eds.), *Human Rights and Good Governance: Building Bridges* (The Hague: Martinus Nijhoff, 2002).

[301] See K. Ginther, E. Denters and P. de Waart (eds.), *Sustainable Development and Good Governance* (The Hague: Kluwer, 1995) and Sano, Alfredsson and Clapp, *Human Rights and Good Governance*, for more on the notion of good governance in the context of development cooperation. The list here is based upon regularly cited features of good governance derived from the reports cited above.

[302] See OECD, *Report of the Working Group*, p. 223.

undertake.[303] As noted above, it is a widely held belief in development circles that the rule of law will help to eradicate corruption and this is of benefit to the development process, even though this view is not uncontested.[304] Tom Carothers, one of the leading experts on rule of law and democracy promotion, has noted that the rule of law is now seen as an 'elixir' which will remove all obstacles to development in the transition to democracy and capitalism.[305] Certainly it is less ideological and perceived as being less culturally loaded than human rights by some, but in the development context it is always part of a package deal.[306] It is undeniably the case that most rule of law projects which are implemented by the Union or other organisations are aimed at partially liberalised autocracies as opposed to totally repressive societies. In the latter they will have no chance of getting off the ground so it is perceived as being futile, but in the former they may make a difference. As Carothers notes, however, semi-authoritarian regimes are masters at absorbing liberalising reforms without really changing their core political structures.[307]

The practical problem is that many rule of law projects are designed by lawyers who look at legal institutions and the actual content of the law. Thus reform exists on various levels, such as reforming or reviewing the laws themselves; strengthening legal institutions through, for example, training lawyers and members of the judiciary; and trying to ensure that the authorities themselves comply with the law. As noted above, such reforms are undeniably among the most difficult aspects of change which any state can undertake and it is even harder for a third party to make a difference where there is some resistance to these objectives.

The essential question, however, is the extent to which international legal rights or obligations exist, requiring states not only to respect the

---

[303] See in this regard the argument that good enough governance as opposed to good governance is sufficient, M. Grindle, 'Good Enough Governance: Poverty Reduction and Reform in Developing Countries' (2004) 17 *Governance* 525.

[304] See Kennedy, 'Laws as Development', p. 23.

[305] T. Carothers, 'The Rule of Law Revival' in T. Carothers, *Critical Mission: Essays on Democracy Promotion* (Washington, DC: Carnegie Endowment for International Peace, 2004) pp. 121, 124.

[306] Although the rule of law is seen as being less loaded, it has been argued that good governance and administrative law in that sense are Western concepts and not universal, see C. Harlow, 'Global Administrative Law: the Quest for Principles and Values' (2006) 17 *EJIL* 187.

[307] T. Carothers, 'Is Gradualism Possible?' in Carothers, *Critical Mission*, pp. 237, 245.

rule of law but also to promote it.[308] The rule of law is essential to the protection of other rights. Furthermore, as noted above, democracy in the procedural sense is only meaningful if it is accompanied by the rule of law. In this context, the rule of law is also procedural, in the sense that Raz argued for, as opposed to substantive.[309] If the rule of law is seen as being separate but probably related to democracy, it is difficult to see states being obliged to comply with the rule of law outside of the treaty obligations they have undertaken. There is certainly no general legal obligation for it to be promoted in third states.

2.4 Conclusions

The promotion of certain values and principles in foreign policy requires serious consideration of numerous issues if it is to be pursued in a meaningful manner. It requires the balancing of different, at times competing, interests. The promoters of such values are in a stronger moral position if they themselves comply with the standards they espouse for others. In a major Commission Communication on human rights and democracy in external relations, for example, it was argued that the European Union's moral and political authority to engage in such practices stemmed from the fact that 'the EU and all its Member States are democracies espousing the same policies both internally and externally'.[310] Ethical policies are a part of 'enlightened self-interest' and worth pursuing – but without consistency and uniform application they have little credibility in third states.

In terms of legal obligations, it is clear that international law does give rights and imposes obligations upon states, and in some instances the organisations they have established, to act in certain limited circumstances. There are also legal limits as to how those values should be promoted in third states. Most of the law in this field, however, is uncertain or controversial. It is difficult to determine, in specific cases, what is required or prohibited. The law is, however, evolving so as to

---

[308] Article 8 ACHR; Article 7 Banjul Charter; Article 6 ECHR; and Article 14 ICCPR, to the extent that they cover the rule of law, do not impose obligations for the promotion of the concept in third states.

[309] J. Raz, *The Authority of Law* (Oxford: Oxford University Press, 1979) p. 214. For an eloquent overview of differing approaches to the rule of law see P. Craig, 'Formal and Substantive Conceptions of the Rule of Law: an Analytical Framework' (1997) *Public Law* 467.

[310] COM(2001)252.

limit the 'protection' provided by the principle of 'domestic jurisdiction' and strengthen the possibilities of international support for the enforcement of certain norms. International society is undergoing a paradigmatic shift, as a result of which interests such as human rights and democracy will further limit state sovereignty, but it has almost certainly not yet reached its destination.

3 Promoting Values and the International Relations of the Union and Community: Competence and Practice

3.1 Introduction

This chapter aims to assess the competence of the European Community and European Union to promote human rights, democracy and other ethical values in third states.[1] As systems based upon the conferral of powers, the Community and Union are only competent to act where powers have been transferred to them.[2] The first part of the chapter examines the relationship between the Union and Community and the instruments through which they pursue their foreign policy objectives. The remainder of the chapter adopts a thematic approach to competence and examines how it has been used in practice. The discussion is focused on those aspects of practice which are most relevant to relations between the Union and developing states.

---

[1] The discussion does not specifically deal with the general relationship between the Community/Union and international organisations concerned with such matters, for example, the Council of Europe or the United Nations.

[2] Article 5 TEC and Article 5 TEU. This principle is reiterated and clarified in Articles I-11, I-12, I-13 and I-14 of the proposed Constitutional Treaty, [2004] OJ C310/1, 16 December 2004. (At the informal European Council held in Lisbon on 18–19 October 2007, the Treaty Amending the Treaty on European Union and the Treaty Establishing the European Community, which is to replace the Constitutional Treaty, was agreed. See further the Table of Equivalences between the Constitutional Treaty and the Reform Treaty.) As I. Macleod, I. Hendry and S. Hyett, *The External Relations of the European Communities* (Oxford: Oxford University Press, 1996) p. 38 state in the context of the Community, the legally correct question is actually 'whether one of the objectives of the Treaties would be attained by the measures proposed, and whether adoption of such measures would be consistent with the procedures envisaged in the Treaty, in conformity with any conditions imposed by the Treaties ... and with other principles of Community law'.

3.2 Relationship between the Union and Community and the Instruments Available for Implementing an Ethical Foreign Policy

3.2.1 Relationship between the Component Parts of the Union[3]

Article 1 TEU states that the Union is founded on the European Communities. The Union is built upon the foundations laid by the Communities but it is not confined to them. Whether the structure of the Union is considered to be a Greek temple, a cathedral or a layered organisation,[4] it is clear that, as it exists at the time of writing, there is a significant overlap between the objectives of the Communities in relation to third states and those of the Common Foreign and Security Policy (CFSP), which are defined in broader and less precise terms.[5] In public international law, in such circumstances, the more specialised body should carry out its functions and not cede its powers to the more general institution of which it is a part.[6] The CFSP's objective of international cooperation, for example, can absorb or at least encroach upon the

---

[3] See more generally, among others, E. Denza, *The Intergovernmental Pillars of the European Union* (Oxford: Oxford University Press, 2002); G. Isaac, 'Le "pilier" communautaire de l'Union Europe, un "pilier" pas comme les autres' (2001) 37 *CDE* 45; P. Eeckhout, *External Relations of the European Union: Legal and Constitutional Foundations* (Oxford: Oxford University Press, 2004) p. 138 *et seq.*; and R. Baratta, 'Overlaps between European Community Competence and European Union Foreign Policy Activity' in E. Cannizzaro (ed.), *The European Union as an Actor in International Relations* (The Hague: Kluwer, 2002) p. 51.

[4] See, among others, B. de Witte, 'The Pillar Structure and the Nature of the European Union: Greek Temple or French Gothic Cathedral?' in T. Heukels, N. Blokker and M. Brus (eds.), *The European Union after Amsterdam* (The Hague: Kluwer, 1998) p. 51; A. von Bogdandy and M. Netteshein, 'Ex Pluribus Unum: Fusion of the European Communities into the European Union' (1996) 2 *ELJ* 267; R. Wessel, *The Constitutional Relationship between the European Union and the European Community: Consequences for the Relationship with the Member States*, Jean Monnet Working Paper 9/03; W. Schroeder, *European Union and European Communities*, Jean Monnet Working Paper 9/03; and D. Curtin and I. Dekker, 'The EU as a "Layered" International Organisation: Institutional Unity in Disguise' in P. Craig and G. de Bùrca (eds.), *The Evolution of EU Law* (Oxford: Oxford University Press, 1999) p. 84.

[5] If the proposed Constitutional Treaty had come into force, then the pillar structure would not exist, which is not to say, however, that the procedures would have been the same for all policy areas. Under the Constitutional Treaty, specific procedures remained for the CFSP. For discussion of the structure of the Union under the Constitutional Treaty, see J. Piris, *The Constitution for Europe: a Legal Analysis* (Cambridge: Cambridge University Press, 2006) p. 56 *et seq.*

[6] See e.g., Advisory Opinion, *Legality of the Threat or Use of Nuclear Weapons* [1996] ICJ Reports 226, para. 29.

development cooperation competence of the Community.[7] Neither the Union nor Community Treaties, however, provides much clear guidance on the nature of the relationship between the Union's constituent parts, although the TEU does require consistency between their activities.[8]

Article 2 TEU requires the Union to assert its identity on the international scene in particular through the CFSP. Article 11 TEU furthermore states that the CFSP 'will cover all aspects of foreign and security policy'. If Community external relations competence is to remain intact, as Article 47 TEU requires, then the differing character and nature of cooperation requires that the powers being exercised under the different legal orders should be defined as such. As Eeckhout notes in this regard, the paradox of the relationship between EC and CFSP external action (indeed he calls it the 'original sin of EU external action') is that the CFSP supplements the first pillar with a less intrusive policy, but yet is to cover all areas of foreign and security policy.[9] As a consequence of the Union's structure, where the Community is exercising its development cooperation competence, this needs to be distinguished from action taken under the CFSP more generally. All external competences are not exclusively within the scope of the latter, even though the Council, when acting under the second pillar and defining policies with regard to a particular country, has on occasion defined all areas of foreign policy.[10]

The distinctions between development and foreign policy are now certainly not hard and fast, if indeed they ever were. The EU Security Strategy makes clear that development policy will be absorbed into more general foreign policy objectives.[11] In 2006 the External Relations Commissioner, Benita Ferrero-Waldner noted on the distinctions between foreign and development policy, '[t]he truth is these distinctions are losing their meaning. Or perhaps I should say, they have already lost their meaning.'[12] It is not necessary to take the approach forwarded by Wessel, however, who considers that any indistinctiveness in cases of

---

[7] Article 11 TEU.

[8] Article 3 TEU. As does Article III-292 of the proposed Constitutional Treaty.

[9] Eeckhout, *External Relations*, p. 145.   [10] See further the discussion below.

[11] J. Solana, *A Secure Europe in a Better World: the European Security Strategy*, approved by the European Council, 12–13 December 2003, Doc. 5381/04, para. 84.

[12] B. Ferrero-Waldner, 'Human Security and Aid Effectiveness: the EU's Challenges', 26 October 2006, Speech 06/636.

overlap should be resolved to the benefit of the Community.[13] It is simply the case that a distinction should be maintained which is based upon the purpose and function of the legal base to determine its scope. Competence under the CFSP is different in nature from that under the Community. The different instruments, for example, reflect the different scope and objectives of the acts.

Some of the difficulty in defining the relationship between the CFSP and Community results from the failure of the Intergovernmental Conferences to provide the ECJ with jurisdiction over decisions taken by the European Council/Council where they do not utilise Community procedures.[14] The ECJ has, however, ensured that Community procedures and institutions are not circumvented. In the *Airport Transit Visas* case,[15] and the *Criminal Sanctions* case,[16] the ECJ has held that it does have jurisdiction to determine the scope of a measure adopted under what were the Justice and Home Affairs (JHA) provisions of the TEU. This was not because it had jurisdiction over such acts but so that it could determine whether a provision of the EC Treaty should have formed the legal basis instead.[17] Although Articles 230 and 234 TEC grant the ECJ jurisdiction only over acts adopted under the EC Treaty,[18] the Court may state that a Community legal base should have been used, which is a de facto declaration of illegality.

It is only in instances in which the Community has exclusive competence that the Council must not encroach upon its powers. If the Member States enjoy shared competence, the choice is theirs as to how they exercise it. In the context of development cooperation and

---

[13] R. Wessel, *The European Union's Foreign and Security Policy: a Legal Institutional Perspective* (The Hague: Kluwer, 1999) p. 14.

[14] This is not rectified by the proposed Constitutional Treaty. The first paragraph of Article III-376 states that the ECJ will have no jurisdiction with respect to the CFSP and defence except that under Article III-308 (as is the case now under Article 47 TEU), it will be able to review compliance with the 'non-affectation' clause and under the second paragraph of Article III-376 it will have the power to review the legality of Council decisions providing for restrictive measures against natural or legal persons adopted on the basis of Chapter II of Title V, i.e., the CFSP Chapter. See further M. Ketvel, 'The Jurisdiction of the European Court of Justice in respect of the Common Foreign and Security Policy' (2006) 55 *ICLQ* 77.

[15] Case C-170/96 *Commission* v. *Council* [1998] ECR I-2763.

[16] Case C-176/03 *Commission* v. *Council* [2005] ECR I-7879.

[17] See *Airport Transit Visas* case, paras. 16–17 and *Criminal Sanctions* case, paras. 38–40. See also e.g., Case T-228/02 *Organisation des Modjahedines du Peuple d'Iran* v. *Council* [2007] 1 CMLR 34, para. 40.

[18] For confirmation of this, see e.g., Case C-167/94 *Criminal Proceedings Against Juan Carlos Grau Gomis and others* [1995] ECR I-1023, para. 6.

humanitarian aid, for example, it is perfectly possible for both the Community and the Member States, unilaterally or through the CFSP, to exercise their competence.[19] The CFSP '*acquis*' can be amended at any time and does not carry a permanent limitation of the sovereign rights of the Member States in the sense that Community law does.[20] There is in principle no reason why some of the non-exclusive powers currently exercised by the Community cannot also be exercised by the Member States under the CFSP.

The *Airport Transit Visas* and *Criminal Sanctions* cases confirm that the ECJ may determine if acts adopted by the Council outside of the Community Treaty should have been based on EC powers and polices the boundaries of its jurisdiction. The ECJ has ensured that the Member States do not circumvent the Community by resorting to other aspects of the Union. The conclusion that can be drawn is that the relationship between the CFSP and Community cannot be precisely described even though the Union has been in existence for a decade and a half.

3.2.2 Union and Community Instruments Relevant to the Pursuit of Ethical Values in Third Countries

3.2.2.1 Union Instruments

3.2.2.1(a) Common Strategies

The aim of Common Strategies is to enhance the coherence of the Union's international action. Such measures should be adopted by the European Council where the Member States have important interests in common.[21] Common Strategies do not have to develop a new approach to a particular country or region but may build upon pre-existing arrangements and coherently present in one document the objectives,

---

[19] See Cases C-181/91 and 248/91 *European Parliament* v. *Council and Commission* [1993] ECR I-3685 (the *Bangladesh* case) and Case C-316/91 *European Parliament* v. *Council* [1994] ECR I-625 (the *EDF* case). See also the Joint Statement by the Council and the Representatives of the Governments of the Member States Meeting within the Council, the European Parliament and the Commission, 'The European Consensus on Development', 22 November 2005, [2006] OJ C46/1, 24 February 2006, which states throughout that Community policy is complementary to that of the Member States and shared. Eeckhout, *External Relations*, p. 151, writing in the more general context, argues, however, that the CFSP should only cover those aspects of foreign policy in which the Community does not have competence.

[20] See further R. Gosalbo Bono, 'Some Reflections on the CFSP Legal Order' (2006) 43 *CMLRev*. 337, 359.

[21] Article 13 TEU.

interests and priorities of the Union and Member States.[22] Common Strategies are decided upon unanimously by the European Council and though they are usually implemented by Joint Actions and Common Positions, they may require action to be taken under any of the pillars or by the Member States. Dehousse warned after the Amsterdam Treaty had been finalised that even if a Common Strategy was adopted, this did not guarantee a smooth process of implementation. He argued that Member States may contest whether proposed Joint Actions and Common Positions fall within the framework of the Common Strategy or that they relate to another topic.[23]

The Common Strategy has not been successful as a legal instrument.[24] The reason for this, as Gosalbo Bono has noted, is due to the fact that they 'have been too broadly defined and too thoroughly negotiated, with the result that they have become little more than inventories of existing policies and activities'.[25] The Common Strategies adopted by the Cologne European Council on Russia,[26] the Helsinki European Council on the Ukraine[27] and the Feira European Council on the Mediterranean, all reflect this. They also illustrate that the promotion of human rights, fundamental freedoms, the rule of law and democracy will form part of the Union's strategy towards those countries or regions.[28] The Common Strategies commit the Union to respect the

---

[22] See e.g., 2000/458/CFSP, Common Strategy of the European Council of 19 June 2000 on the Mediterranean Region, [2000] OJ L183/5, 22 June 2000, para. 4.

[23] F. Dehousse, 'After Amsterdam: a Report on the Common Foreign and Security Policy of the European Union' (1998) 9 *EJIL* 525.

[24] The Common Strategies are limited in time, e.g., para. 36 of the Mediterranean Common Strategy limits its duration to four years. The Russian and Ukraine Common Strategies have been renewed but for one-year periods at a time, see e.g., 2003/471/CFSP, Common Strategy of the European Council of 20 June 2003 amending Common Strategy 1999/414/CFSP on Russia in order to extend the period of its application, [2003] OJ L157/68, 26 June 2003. The Mediterranean Common Strategy was renewed until 23 January 2006, see 2004/763/CFSP, Decision of the European Council of 5 November 2004 amending Common Strategy 2000/458/CFSP on the Mediterranean Region in order to extend the period of its application, [2004] OJ L337/72, 13 November 2004. For detailed analysis of these strategies see P. Koutrakos, *EU International Relations Law* (Oxford: Hart Publishing, 2006) p. 394 *et seq.*

[25] Gosalbo Bono, 'Some Reflections', 364.

[26] 1999/414/CFSP, Common Strategy of the European Union of 4 June 1999 on Russia, [1999] OJ L157/1, 24 June 1999.

[27] 1999/887/CFSP, European Council Common Strategy of 11 December 1999 on Ukraine, [1999] OJ L331/1, 23 December 1999.

[28] Mediterranean Common Strategy, para. 14; Ukraine Common Strategy, para. 10; Russia Common Strategy, para. 1.

separation of powers between the CFSP and Community.[29] They do nothing, however, to help demarcate that separation of powers. One of the problems with these Strategies is that there is some doubt as to the exact nature of the legal obligations they impose.[30] In practice, however, Common Strategies contain few, if any, precise commitments; these are rather found in the Joint Actions and Common Positions adopted to implement such Strategies.

3.2.2.1(b) Common Positions, Joint Actions and Decisions

According to Article 13 TEU, Common Strategies are to be implemented, in particular by adopting Common Positions and Joint Actions. The Council also has the power to adopt 'decisions' as referred to in Article 13(3) TEU. Joint Actions, Common Positions and Decisions can also be used independently of a Common Strategy to introduce, implement or amend policy vis-à-vis a third country, a group of countries or a region. All such measures impose a legal obligation upon the Member States to comply with them, although the nature of this differs.[31]

Articles 14 and 15 TEU, which provide for the adoption of Joint Actions and Common Positions respectively, do not provide for any hierarchy between them. The Treaty adopted at Maastricht did not explain when one should be used in preference to the other. Article 14 TEU now states that, '[j]oint actions shall address specific situations where operational action by the Union is deemed to be required'.

Common Positions are the more general measure which define 'the approach of the Union to a particular matter of geographical or thematic nature'.[32] The choice as to whether a Joint Action or Common Position should be adopted is, generally speaking, within the discretion of the Council and it has not always followed the guidelines in Articles 14 and 15 TEU.[33] Common Positions, for example, have routinely been used to reduce economic and financial relations with third countries or,

---

[29] Mediterranean Common Strategy, para. 24, for example, states: '[t]his Common Strategy shall be implemented by the EU institutions and bodies, each acting within the powers attributed to them by the Treaties, and in accordance with the applicable procedures under those Treaties'.

[30] For discussion see F. Pagani, 'A New Gear in the CFSP Machinery: Integration of the Petersburg Tasks in the Treaty on European Union' (1998) 9 *EJIL* 737 and Denza, *Intergovernmental Pillars*, p. 140 et seq.

[31] See in particular, Articles 14(3) and 15 TEU.   [32] Article 15 TEU.

[33] See Denza, *Intergovernmental Pillars*, p. 151.

for example, to impose arms embargos.[34] They have also, on occasion, been partly used as an instrument by which to condemn a third state.[35] Joint Actions have, on the whole, been more specific in their content and concentrated on operational issues.[36]

On numerous occasions, as noted above, however, the Council has also used Decisions – usually to implement, amend or give further effect to the detail of a Common Position or a Joint Action already adopted.[37] The Council, after the Amsterdam amendments, also has a specific power under Article 18(5) TEU to appoint a Special Representative with a mandate in relation to particular policy issues. This provision reflects preexisting practice. Such representatives have usually been appointed by Joint Actions but have, on occasion, had their mandate terminated by Decisions.[38] The work of the Special Representatives is primarily of a diplomatic nature.[39]

A problem in preparing legally binding measures to implement the CFSP is finding common ground between the Member States. The need for negotiation and compromise between the Member States may also slow down the decision-making process. In terms of foreign policy, what is especially problematic is the fact that the Member States have differing approaches to the promotion and protection of ethical values in third states. The strategic, security, material and economic interests, historical allegiances, animosities, priorities and preferred techniques of action of the Member States differ. Finding an approach which is acceptable to all and as effective as possible in the circumstances will rarely be straightforward. The fundamentally differing positions of the Member States in

---

[34] See further the discussion in chapters 4 and 5 and more generally, Eeckhout, *External Relations*, p. 401 *et seq* and Koutrakos, *EU International Relations Law*, p. 399 *et seq.*

[35] See e.g., Common Position 95/515/CFSP, on Nigeria, [1995] OJ L298/1, 11 December 1995 which is discussed in Chapter 4.

[36] See Eeckhout, *External Relations*, p. 401 *et seq* and Koutrakos, *EU International Relations Law*, p. 399 *et seq.*

[37] See e.g., Council Decision 1999/75/CFSP, [1999] OJ L23/5, 30 January 1999 and more generally Denza, *Intergovernmental Pillars*, p. 151.

[38] The current nine Special Representatives (Middle East, Great Lakes, former Yugoslav Republic of Macedonia, Bosnia and Herzegovina, Afghanistan, South Caucasus, Moldova, Central Asia and Sudan) have all been appointed by Joint Actions, except Pierre Morel who replaced Jan Kubis, who resigned as Special Representative for Central Asia and was appointed by Council Decision 2006/670/CFSP, [2006] OJ L275/65, 6 October 2006. The sixteen former Special Representatives were also appointed by Joint Actions, except Panagoitis Roumeliotis, who was appointed by Council Decision 1999/361/CFSP, [1999] OJ L141/1, 4 June 1999.

[39] See the discussion in Chapter 5.

2003 over events in Iraq highlight how difficult it can be for there to be an effective CFSP. This is not to say that the Union is any better or worse than individual states in formulating foreign policy, if indeed they are comparable. The Union faces a unique set of considerations.

Joint Actions, Common Positions and Decisions, however, also have their advantages. An agreed position and policy by twenty-seven states is potentially far more effective than unilateral measures by a solitary one. Heavyweight foreign policy players, such as France, Germany and the United Kingdom (the 'EU 3') often have significant influence in their relations with third states and the value of collective action by them, for example in discussions with Iran over nuclear proliferation, along with others in persuading states to amend their behaviour can be substantial.[40] A joint approach is also useful if such action is unpopular in the third country or region targeted, as the burden of any retaliatory action will be shared, theoretically at least, by all of the Union's Member States.

3.2.2.1(c) Diplomatic and Other Legally Non-binding Measures and Instruments

In some cases legally binding measures are either not appropriate or cannot be adopted. For these reasons the Union also uses classic instruments of diplomacy, such as démarches, declarations and statements. The Union also uses political dialogue as an instrument to pursue its political objectives. These are discussed in turn.

Démarches are usually carried out by the Presidency or by the Troika. Although it is difficult to ascertain exactly how many démarches are delivered annually, their frequency indicates that they are considered to be an invaluable tool. Approximately 100 démarches were delivered in 1986, the figure for 1990 was 120.[41] The number of démarches delivered annually now is substantially higher;[42] in 2006, for example, démarches

---

[40] For detailed discussion on the role of the EU 3 in relations with Iran, see E. Denza, 'Non-Proliferation of Nuclear Weapons: the European Union and Iran' (2005) 10 *EFARev.* 289 and below.

[41] See [1986] OJ C86/137, 2 November 1986 and Statement of 15 December 1990 on the Activity of the Community and its Member States in the Field of Human Rights in 1990, (1990) 12 *Bull. EC* 1.5.3.

[42] European Council, *1998 Annual Report of the CFSP* (Luxembourg: OOPEC, 1999) npg, refers to 138 being made. In the 2002 Report, no number is given but each démarche and statement which is not completely confidential is listed and there are over 200: see European Council, *2002 Annual Report of the CFSP* (Luxembourg: OOPEC, 2003) p. 78. Under the British Presidency of the European Union for the six-month period between July and December 2005, the Union issued démarches with regard to the situation in

with regard to torture and ill-treatment only were carried out with regard to the situation in over fifty states.[43] Démarches take a number of forms. They can be: completely confidential; confidential in part; initially confidential in part or full and then later published; or published in full when the démarche is made.[44] The advantage of confidential démarches is that a particular case or situation can be discussed at the appropriate level with the state in question, with no public loss of face for either side. Confidential démarches are made if there is a danger that publicity will damage or harm the interests of a particular individual. Public démarches concerned with an individual are very sensitive and relatively rare, usually only being issued in instances involving high profile individuals.[45] Démarches which are concerned with a particular situation tend to be public, as there is usually no direct individual interest and often public interest in the Union taking action. States rarely, if ever, respond to démarches dealing with human rights issued by the Union. In terms of their content, démarches mostly deal with civil and political rights issues and there is only occasionally reference to the legal obligations a state may have breached.[46]

The former External Relations Commissioner, Chris Patten has rightly noted that few authoritarian governments go weak at the knees at the prospect of a European démarche.[47] Although a démarche may be dismissed as meaningless, some states who are addressed by them no longer consider them to be so. Harold Koh, who was Assistant Secretary of State

thirty countries and delivered over forty statements on human rights. See Foreign and Commonwealth Office, *Human Rights Annual Report 2005* (HMSO: London, 2006) p. 129.

[43] European Council, *Annual Report on Human Rights, 2006* (Luxembourg: OOPEC, 2006) p. 27.

[44] For an outline of the common elements in a torture démarche, see European Council, *Annual Report on Human Rights, 2006*, p. 28.

[45] For example, the initiation of proceedings by Malaysia against UN Special Rapporteur Cumaraswamy led to named démarches being delivered by the Union: démarche of 11 August 1999 cited in European Council, *1998 Annual Report of the CFSP*, npg. In the European Council's *Working Paper on the Implementation of the EU Guidelines on Efforts to Prevent and Eradicate Torture* (available at http://consilium.europa.eu/uedocs/cmsUpload/workingpaperTortures.pdf) adopted 10 December 2002, para. 3.3, it is clear that non-confidential individual démarches will be carried out where there are well-documented individual cases of torture.

[46] M. Kamminga, *Inter-State Accountability for Violations of Human Rights* (Philadelphia: University of Pennsylvania Press, 1992) p. 29 argues that as far as démarches on human rights are concerned, little reference is made to law, as the obligations in question are usually uncertain and thus it is more credible to refer to morality. The Union does sometimes refer to human rights treaty obligations but reference to the provisions of international humanitarian law treaties is much more common in statements and démarches. See in particular, the discussion in Chapter 5.

[47] C. Patten, *Not Quite the Diplomat* (London: Penguin Books, 2006) p. 194.

for Democracy, Human Rights and Labour under the Clinton administration, stated in 2002 that the European Union's routine démarches on the use of the death penalty in the United States were 'no longer minor diplomatic irritants'.[48]

The Presidency on behalf of the Union and the European Council also routinely issues declarations and statements, either unilaterally or in multilateral fora, on notable events in many third states.[49] Declarations and statements are usually used to condemn certain practices and situations or to commend developments. The wording of statements and declarations is a product of compromise and negotiation. As a consequence of the unanimity rule, declarations and statements require formulation of a form of wording acceptable to all of the Member States. In multilateral fora, whether declarations or statements can be issued is often determined by the agreed agenda of a meeting or session. In the annual sessions of the United Nations Commission on Human Rights, for example, where only relatively brief opportunities existed to make statements, the Union on occasion compiled an annual volume of its views on the human rights situation in third states to supplement its oral statements.[50] Whereas the Presidency or Council are tempered by diplomatic constraints, in particular when criticising third states, the European Parliament which adopts many resolutions on third states tends to be much more forthright in its criticism.

The implementation of a foreign policy which seeks to promote issues such as human rights, the rule of law and democracy requires discussion on them to be introduced into the political dialogue that exists with third states. Political dialogue takes place in a number of different fora. An Agreement between the Community and a third state usually establishes an institutional framework for such discussion.[51] This is especially the case if it contains an 'essential elements' clause,

---

[48] H. Koh, 'A United States Human Rights Policy for the 21st Century' (2002) 46 *Saint Louis University Law Journal* 293, 310.

[49] In 2002, a total of 204 declarations and statements were issued; see European Council, *2002 Annual Report of the CFSP*, p. 77.

[50] These can be found at http://ec.europa.eu/comm/external_relations/human_rights/unhrcom.htm for the period 1998–2002. For subsequent years, most statements and explanations in the Commission on Human Rights and subsequently Human Rights Council and the relevant Committees of the General Assembly and other bodies, such as ECOSOC, concerning human rights and the political situation in third states can be found at either www.europa-eu-un.org/articles/articleslist_s9_en.htm or www.consilium.europa.eu/cms3_fo/showPage.asp?id=403&lang=EN&mode=g

[51] See further the discussions in Chapters 4 and 5 on political dialogue in practice.

which gives legitimacy and focus to such discourse.[52] Dialogue also takes place between the Union and third states in the absence of formal treaty relations or outside any institutional framework.

Although they are not entitled to perform the full range of diplomatic functions, the Communities have established over 145 Commission delegations in third states.[53] It is also common practice for the majority of third states to send ambassadors to the Union and establish diplomatic missions in Brussels.[54] Diplomatic relations between the Union and third states are well established in practice and can be used to commence a political dialogue on, among other things, ethical values. The Council can also appoint Special Representatives to be a part of such dialogues.[55] The fora can be multilateral or bilateral in nature.[56] An example of the former is the Union's participation in the Middle East Peace Process as a member of the Quartet.[57]

The Union's political dialogue with China is bilateral in nature, and with Iran was bilateral in nature but it is now essentially a 'unilateral dialogue' and a clear example of how changing political circumstances and priorities can affect an ongoing 'human rights' dialogue.[58] It is to these political dialogues, and the human rights guidelines that may inform them, that the discussion now turns.

The European Union has no contractual relations with Iran. Further to a Commission Communication of 2001, an effort was made to improve

---

[52] See the discussion further below.

[53] Article 20 TEU does not confer any competence in this regard. See the External Services Directory at http://europa.eu.int/comm/external_relations/repdel/index_rep_en.cfm and further Denza, *Intergovernmental Pillars*, p. 164 and Macleod, Hendry and Hyett, *External Relations*, p. 208. Under Chapter VII of the proposed Constitutional Treaty (Articles III-327 and III-328) there will be 'Union delegations' and essentially a 'Union diplomatic service'. Under the terms of Articles 5 and 6 of the Vienna Convention on Diplomatic Relations, 1961, 500 UNTS 95, European Commission delegation heads should not be described as 'ambassadors' as they are in practice.

[54] Denza, *Intergovernmental Pillars*, p. 164 and Macleod, Hendry and Hyett, *External Relations*, p. 208.

[55] Article 18(5) TEU. The EU High Representative for the CFSP, Javier Solana on 29 January 2007 appointed Riina Kionka as his Personal Representative for Human Rights. She replaced Michael Matthiessen who was appointed on 17 January 2005. The Brussels European Council, 16–17 December 2004, Doc. 16238/1/04, para. 52 of its conclusions, created the post of the Personal Representative.

[56] With mixed Agreements, one side will be composed of the Community and its Member States.

[57] See further Chapter 5.

[58] Although they are referred to as 'human rights dialogues' in documentation and the term is now widely used, the dialogues also cover, *inter alia*, democracy and the rule of law.

relations between the parties and a trade and cooperation Agreement was subsequently discussed.[59] As part of the process, a political dialogue which concentrated on terrorism, nuclear proliferation, reform of the political process, including progress towards democracy and protection of human rights, was initiated in December 2002. In June 2003, however, relations between the parties began to strain over the ongoing Iranian nuclear programme. Led by the EU 3 of Germany, United Kingdom and France (with both the latter, of course, possessing nuclear weapons), a relatively attractive prospective Agreement was offered by the Union to Iran in October 2003. In return, the expectation was that Iran would cease its nuclear activities and allow inspection of its nuclear facilities by the International Atomic Energy Agency (IAEA).[60] Although negotiations on an Agreement between the Community and Iran did resume they ceased in August 2005 once it was considered that Iran had reneged on its obligations regarding uranium enrichment under the terms of an Agreement signed in Paris in November 2004 between the EU 3, on the one hand, and, on the other, Iran.[61] Relations took a

---

[59] COM(2001)071.

[60] This is required by Article III of the Treaty on the Non-Proliferation of Nuclear Weapons, 1968, 729 UNTS 10485 (NPT) to which Iran and the EU 3 are party. Under the terms of Article III NPT, Iran has also negotiated with the IAEA a Safeguards Agreement: Agreement between Iran and the Agency for the Application of Safeguards in Connection with the Treaty on the Non-Proliferation of Nuclear Weapons, 1974, IAEA, INFCIRC/214, 13 December 1974. This Agreement sets out the legal terms of the relationship between the IAEA and Iran as far as inspections of its nuclear facilities are concerned.

[61] Agreement between the Government of the Islamic Republic of Iran and the Governments of France, Germany and United Kingdom, Paris, 15 November 2004. The text of the Paris Agreement is reproduced in IAEA, INFCIRC/637, 26 November 2004. This Agreement built on the 'Tehran Agreed Statement' of 21 October 2003 between the same parties. For discussion of the negotiations between the EU 3 and Iran, see Denza, 'Non-Proliferation of Nuclear Weapons'. The Union is active in this field and has adopted numerous measures to that end; see e.g., Council Joint Action 2006/418/CFSP on Support for the IAEA Activities in the Areas of Nuclear Security and Verification and in the Framework of the Implementation of the EU Strategy Against Proliferation of Weapons of Mass Destruction, [2006] OJ L165/20, 17 June 2006. Article 11(b) of the Revised Cotonou Convention (Partnership Agreement between the Members of the African, Caribbean and Pacific Group of States, of the one Part and the European Community and its Member States, of the other Part, [2000] OJ L317/3, 15 December 2000 as revised [2005] OJ L209/27, 11 August 2005) also contains a clause on nuclear non-proliferation. Although most provisions of the revised Cotonou Convention have been provisionally applied since 25 June 2005, this is not one of them; any measures which at the time of writing have already been adopted to give effect to this provision are being funded by Regulation 1717/2006 Establishing an Instrument for Stability, [2006] OJ L327/1, 24 November 2006 (the 'Stability Instrument').

further turn for the worst after Mahmoud Ahmadinejad became President in 2005.

The 'human rights dialogue' effectively ceased in June 2004 since when the Union has dealt with the situation in Iran primarily by condemning the situation through issuing declarations and démarches; the General Affairs and External Relations Council adopting conclusions which refer to its concerns; or by sponsoring or supporting resolutions in multilateral fora.[62] The reason for the human rights dialogue effectively stopping is not a refusal on the part of the European Union to continue with it – the Union would welcome the opportunity to continue to do so – but intransigence on the part of the Iranian authorities. Under pressure from the Union, which has shown flexibility in agreeing revised modalities to continue with the dialogue, Iran has agreed to meetings but then cancelled them, which has led to condemnation from the Council.[63]

The Union's ability to engage with Iran on the issue of human rights, which since the 1979 revolution has adopted a very culturally/religiously relative perspective on the matter, was closely connected for the Iranians with envisaged treaty relations with the Community. In many senses, while Iran continues to adopt a very religiously relative perspective on human rights, such a dialogue can at best only contribute to limited change and even then only with regard to certain issues. A general deterioration in relations with the Union over Iran's continued uranium enrichment, however, further aggravated by the election of a President who took a very confrontational approach to relations with the Union and many of its Member States, led to the effective abandonment of the human rights dialogue alongside that on the trade and cooperation Agreement.

Although Iran is party to the Treaty on the Non-Proliferation of Nuclear Weapons (NPT), 1968, and has signed the Comprehensive Nuclear Test Ban Treaty (CTBT), 1996,[64] it is not under any legal obligations which prohibit it from enriching uranium, so long as it is for

---

[62] See http://ec.europa.eu/comm/external_relations/iran/intro/gac.htm for extracts of the Council's debates and conclusions.

[63] For discussion of the Union's view see European Council, *EU Annual Report on Human Rights 2005* (Luxembourg: OOPEC, 2005) p. 27, *Annual Progress Report of the Implementation of the European Union's Policy on Human Rights and Democratisation in Third Countries*, Doc. 5180/07, p. 6 and Council Conclusions, 11 December 2006, Doc. 16289/06, p. 20, 23.

[64] Comprehensive Nuclear Test Ban Treaty, 1996, GA Resolution A/RES/50/245. The CTBT is not yet in force.

peaceful purposes. Iran has always maintained that its uranium enrichment is not for a weapons programme and that it is in compliance with
its obligations under Article II of the NPT.[65] The legal problem stems
from Iran's refusal to cooperate fully with the IAEA who are entitled to
inspect Iran's nuclear facilities under the terms of the NPT and the 1974
Safeguards Agreement with Iran. The EU 3 as signatories to the NPT are
entitled to try and ensure that Iran complies with its obligations under
that treaty.

Spokesmen for Iran have repeatedly noted how it has been singled
out for its nuclear programme.[66] There is some merit in this argument;
Iran was, of course, identified by President Bush in 2002 as a part of an
'axis of evil' which had to be addressed as a part of the 'war on terror'.[67]
As far as the Union is concerned, it is certainly true that there has not
been any public comment on not only Israel's ability to enrich uranium
but also its possession of nuclear weapons.[68] In legal terms, however,
Israel is not in violation of its obligations as it is not party to the NPT.
Nor has the Union put pressure on, for example, India either, over its
possession of such weapons. India again is not party to the NPT.[69]

Notwithstanding its laudable objectives, the NPT is an inherently
inequitable treaty which attempts to preserve the right to nuclear
weapons technology to a very limited number of states. Even within
the confines of the regime it establishes, however, it is debatable
whether the United Kingdom, a member of the EU 3, by renewing its
Trident missile is complying with its own NPT obligations. The United
Kingdom contends, as does Iran, that it is not violating the terms of the
NPT.[70] In any case, two nuclear armed states trying to pressure Iran to

---

[65] See e.g., the statement made by Javid Zarif on behalf of Iran in the Security Council
in the debate after the adoption of Security Council Resolution 1696 (2006), 31 July
2006, available in Press Release, SC/8792, 31 July 2006.

[66] For example, see the statement by Mr Zarif, Press Release, SC/8792.

[67] President G.W. Bush, State of the Union Address, Washington DC, 29 January 2002.

[68] See the statement by Mr Zarif, Press Release, SC/8792.

[69] The Union does, as discussed in Chapter 5, discuss nuclear proliferation with Israel but
does not (publicly at least) question Israel's possession of such weapons. Israel has
traditionally adopted a 'no comment' approach to the issue of its nuclear capabilities.
Israeli governments use every opportunity to condemn Iran's nuclear programme and
to highlight the threat Israel feels Iran poses to it. Iran is widely seen as being involved
in a proxy war against Israel by helping to fund Hezbollah and also Hamas. The Union,
as will be discussed in Chapter 4, condemned the Indian nuclear tests in May 1998 but has
not subsequently taken action against India for its possession of such weapons.

[70] For the British government's arguments that it is not in violation of the NPT, see *The
Future of the United Kingdom's Nuclear Deterrent*, CM 6994 (London: HMSO, 2006).

abandon its nuclear programme appears hypocritical, even if the legal arguments concerning Iran's failure to comply with the NPT are correct.

In the light of the EU 3 sponsoring the two Security Council resolutions, adopted on the basis of Chapter VII, obliging Iran to suspend all enrichment-related activities and imposing punitive measures against it, the ability of the Union to engage with Iran on human rights issues, as things stand, is certainly at an end.[71] The Union's ability to engage with Iran on human rights related issues was directly related to the envisaged political and cooperation Agreement, but as other priorities have came to the fore, the human rights dialogue, which was effectively moribund, has been abandoned by the Union.

The human rights dialogue with China, on the other hand, was initiated in 1996 in the absence of existing or envisaged treaty relations establishing an institutional framework for discussion of human rights.[72] It formed part of a more general strategy towards closer relations.[73] As political relations and economic ties have evolved, the Union has become more ambitious in the nature of the relationship it envisages and its expectations as far as the outcomes of the human rights dialogues are concerned. In the ninth European Union–China Summit which was held in Helsinki in September 2006, the parties agreed to negotiate a Partnership and Cooperation Agreement.[74] In the subsequent Communication from the Commission to give effect to this, the bi-annual human rights dialogue between the parties has been described as being 'fit for purpose' but it then goes on to note that the Union's expectations, which have increased in line with the quality of the partnership, are 'increasingly not being met'. To that end the Commission considers that the dialogue should now be 'more focused and

---

[71] Security Council Resolution 1696 (2006), 31 July 2006 and subsequently Security Council Resolution 1737 (2006), 27 December 2006. In the latter the Security Council imposed punitive measures against Iran. In the EU context, Common Position 2007/140/ CFSP, [2007] OJ L61/49, 27 February 2007 was adopted and in turn, in the Community context, Council Regulation 423/2007 concerning Restrictive Measures Against Iran, [2007] OJ L103/1, 20 April 2007, was implemented to give effect to Security Council Resolution 1737 (2006).

[72] Agreement on Trade and Economic Cooperation between the European Economic Community and the People's Republic of China, [1985] OJ L250/1, 19 September 1985. This Agreement was complemented in 1994 and 2002 by an exchange of letters, establishing a broad European Union–China political dialogue. Although now quite dated on this point, see further E. Fierro, *The EU's Approach to Human Rights Conditionality in Practice* (The Hague: Kluwer, 2002) p. 191 *et seq.*

[73] See COM(1995)279, COM(1998)191, COM(2001)265 and COM(2003)533.

[74] See COM(2006)631.

results-oriented, with higher quality exchanges and concrete results', 'more flexible' and better coordinated with Member State dialogues.[75]

The Communication notes that the 'Chinese leadership has repeatedly stated its support for reform, including on basic rights and freedoms' and thus seeks to justify the Union's intervention by considering that it will contribute to an already ongoing process.[76] The Communication further seeks to justify its promotion of human rights in its relationship with China by stressing the economic benefits to China of the greater protection of such principles by noting that the 'better protection of human rights, a more open society, and more accountable government would be beneficial to China, and essential for continued economic growth'.[77] The Communication does not limit its activities in this field to bilateral fora. As it notes the 'EU will also encourage China to be an active and constructive partner in the Human Rights Council, holding China to the values which the UN embraces'.[78] By trying to put pressure on China in the Human Rights Council,[79] as well as using soft power to persuade China of the political and economic benefits of respecting rights in bilateral fora, the Union is reemphasising the holistic approach it has already in practice been taking to the issue of human rights, democracy and the rule of law in China.[80]

Whether the Union will get its way with China still remains to be seen. Less powerful states, such as Australia, New Zealand and Mexico, have resisted the inclusion of 'essential elements' clauses in Agreements with the Community and sometimes got their own way.[81] What is clear, however, is that the 'human rights dialogue' with China was initiated as part of a process of building closer relations and as the relationship has evolved the ambitions of that dialogue have increased commensurately. The Council has in the past issued benchmarks for the

---

[75] Ibid. p. 4.   [76] Ibid.   [77] Ibid.   [78] Ibid.

[79] In 1997 the human rights dialogue was interrupted by China for the best part of a year after ten Member States tabled a resolution in the Human Rights Commission, later withdrawn by all except Denmark, on the human rights situation in China. The Council position with respect to tabling a resolution on China in the Human Rights Commission has included: a decision not to table or cosponsor a resolution (1998, 1999); voting against a no-action motion (1998, 1999, 2001, 2002, 2003); and voting in favour of a resolution if tabled (2001, 2002, 2003). See further FIDH, Preliminary Assessment of the EU–China Human Rights Dialogue (2004) available at www.fidh.org/IMG/pdf/cn2502a.pdf

[80] See further below on the human rights guidelines and their implementation.

[81] This is particularly true in the case of New Zealand and Australia. Mexico also resisted strongly but ultimately attached a unilateral statement to its Agreement with the EC and its Member States. See Declaration by Mexico on Title I, [2000] OJ L276/68, 28 October 2000.

dialogue. China has certainly undertaken to and ratified a number of international human rights treaties, but it is impossible to determine if the dialogue with the European Union has played any role in this. The issue, however, is that at least the Union is in a position where it can make its concerns and position known at the higher echelons of the Chinese government.

The two human rights specific dialogues discussed above are noteworthy in that they have been established in the absence of treaty relations which provide for such discussion.[82] Bilateral dialogue usually takes place in the context of institutions which are established by Agreements between the Community and/or the Member States, on the one hand, and, on the other, the non-Member State(s). Until the end of 2001, however, there were no overall guidelines as to when such issues should be raised in political dialogue or in which fora.[83] The Council addressed this by adopting the EU Guidelines on Human Rights Dialogue in December 2001, seeking to integrate discussion on human rights and democracy into all aspects of relations with a third country.[84] Five other sets of guidelines have also been adopted, although they all differ as far as legal obligations are concerned. They deal with the death penalty,[85] torture,[86] human rights defenders,[87] children and armed conflict,[88] and international humanitarian law.[89]

The 2001 Guidelines on Human Rights Dialogue, which are the broadest ranging and most general, state that a specific human rights dialogue can be initiated for any issue of concern.[90] Torture, the death

---

[82] The Union also has an institutional human rights-specific dialogue with Russia and consults with 'like-minded' states so as to adopt common positions prior to, for example, sessions of the Human Rights Council. See European Council, *EU Annual Report on Human Rights 2005*, p. 30 for examples of the issues discussed in these dialogues.

[83] Although right-specific dialogues already existed on the death penalty. See further below.

[84] EU Guidelines on Human Rights Dialogue. These were approved, without debate, by the Economic and Financial Affairs Council on 13 December 2001, Doc. 15139/01. The Laeken European Council started the day after. The death penalty guidelines, which were drafted in 1998, predate this set of guidelines, as do the torture guidelines which were adopted in April 2001. The human rights dialogue with Iran, as discussed above, was the first to be established under the 2001 guidelines.

[85] Adopted by the General Affairs Council, 29 June 1998, Doc. 9730/98.

[86] Adopted by the General Affairs Council, 9 April 2001, Doc. 7833/01.

[87] Adopted by the General Affairs Council, 14 June 2004, Doc. 10189/04.

[88] Adopted by the General Affairs Council, 8 December 2003, Doc. 15535/03.

[89] [2005] OJ C327/4, 23 December 2005.

[90] EU Guidelines on Human Rights Dialogue, para. 3.

penalty, children's rights,[91] freedom of expression, equality, promotion of the processes of democratisation and good governance, among others, are a part of all dialogues and, as noted above, some of these topics (for example, torture) now have their own separate guidelines. The general obligation to initiate a human rights specific dialogue in the 2001 Guidelines is extremely vague and based upon political expediency rather than consistency. Any human rights dialogue must define the practical aims to be achieved as well as the added value to be gained. A 'degree of pragmatism and flexibility' is an inherent part of the process.[92] While the assessment and any decision to initiate such a dialogue requires the agreement of the Council Working Party on Human Rights (COHOM), the final decision to initiate it lies with the Council of Ministers.[93]

The objectives to be pursued and the issues to be covered in all dialogues will vary from one to the next and will be defined on a case-by-case basis.[94] This built-in flexibility is to be expected, to accommodate the different basis and nature of relationships with third countries. It is noticeable, though, that despite the numerous occasions on which the Union has committed itself to consistency and coherence of action between institutions and policies, it has never explained how to achieve it between all third states.[95] What the Council has done recently, however, as part of mainstreaming human rights across the CFSP and other EU policies, is to take preemptive action to address accusations of double standards in human rights dialogues. This is not with regard to the Union's various attitudes and approaches towards different third states but with regard to dialogue partners raising the issue of human rights protection in the Member States. The Council Secretariat has identified a number of issues which are systematically raised by third countries; these include the universal character of human rights;

---

[91] See also, COM(2006)367 which is entitled *Towards an EU Strategy on the Rights of the Child.*
[92] Guidelines on Human Rights, para. 3.
[93] *Ibid.* para. 6. The Working Party on Human Rights (COHOM) must work with geographical working parties, the Working Party on Development Cooperation (CODEV) and the Committee on Measures for the Development and Consolidation of Democracy and the Rule of Law. COHOM now draws up an annual progress report on the Union's policy on human rights and democratisation in third countries. The report for 2006, e.g., is Doc. 5180/07.
[94] Guidelines on Human Rights, paras. 4–5.
[95] See COM(2000)212 for one example, from many.

racism; the indivisibility of rights; the right to development; and counter-terrorism and human rights.[96]

The 'issue specific guidelines' on torture, the death penalty, human rights defenders, international humanitarian law and children in armed conflict, as mentioned above, are noteworthy because of their differing approach to legal obligations and competence. The torture and human rights defender guidelines expressly state that they only apply to the CFSP.[97] Yet, it is difficult to see why they cannot be part of the Community dimension as well. There is no obvious reason why, for example, the death penalty can be raised within Community competence but not torture. This is, in particular, the case as the prohibition on torture is an obligation *erga omnes*.[98] The torture, children in armed conflict and international humanitarian law guidelines refer to numerous treaty obligations which already bind all of the Member States and large parts of which represent customary international law and in some cases obligations *erga omnes*. The death penalty guidelines specially refer to the fact that they are aiming to work 'towards the progressive development of human rights'.[99]

With regard to the guidelines on human rights defenders, there is a clear lack of legal obligations which are binding on third states. The Union has identified the protection of human rights defenders, especially women human rights defenders, as one of the top priorities in this field. Human rights defenders are clearly important to the evolution and development of civil society. The Union relies upon civil society for many of its policies in this field and provides funding to encourage its flourishing in third states. The normative basis for these guidelines is the UN Declaration on the Right and Responsibility of Individuals, Groups and Organs of Society to Promote and Protect Universally

---

[96] Council Secretariat, *Mainstreaming Human Rights Across CFSP and Other EU Policies*, 7 June 2006, Doc. 10076/06, Part I.1(3).

[97] Guidelines on Torture, para. 1 and Guidelines on Human Rights Defenders, para. 7. The others do not differentiate between the Community or CFSP dimension.

[98] See the discussion in Chapter 2.

[99] The Commission in 2002 also proposed a regulation concerning trade in certain equipment and products which can be used for the purposes of capital punishment, torture, inhuman and degrading treatment. See COM(2002)770. It was subsequently adopted as Council Regulation 1236/2005 Concerning Trade in Certain Goods which could be Used for Capital Punishment, Torture or Other Cruel, Inhuman or Degrading Treatment or Punishment, [2005] OJ L200/1, 30 July 2005. See further the discussion below on this regulation.

Recognised Human Rights and Fundamental Freedoms.[100] In terms of obligations in general international law, this is the weakest normative basis for any of the issue specific guidelines. The guidelines on children in armed conflict refer to the Children's Convention, which all Member States have ratified, but is specifically concerned with children in armed conflict, which is addressed in the Optional Protocol to the Children's Convention, to which a number of Member States are not party.[101] It is, however, a widely ratified treaty and the parts of it which deal with 'child soldiers' can strongly be argued to represent custom.[102] The normative basis is even stronger with the regard to the guidelines on international humanitarian law. Here, the legal obligations both on all the Member States and on third states are perfectly clear and the basic principles of the Geneva Conventions are undeniably customary international law and in some cases obligations *erga omnes*.[103]

The lack of a firm normative basis for the human rights defenders guidelines is not a practical hindrance, however, to their implementation. In the case of international humanitarian law, torture and in more limited cases the death penalty, the Member States will have a legal obligation to act if those norms are being seriously breached. The guidelines on human rights defenders, as is the case with children and armed conflict, in the practical sense are more about recognising operational priorities for foreign policy and trying to address these issues, where relevant, either in bilateral dialogues or in multilateral fora and to ensure that these are targeted as far as funding is concerned.[104] A potential problem with all of these guidelines, however, is that unless they are well known among the relevant Commission delegations and the EU Missions in third states they will not be utilised. A study

---

[100] Declaration on the Right and Responsibility of Individuals, Groups and Organs of Society to Promote and Protect Universally Recognised Human Rights and Fundamental Freedoms, 1999. Adopted by the General Assembly, A/RES/53/144, 8 March 1999.

[101] Optional Protocol to the Convention on the Rights of the Child on the Involvement of Children in Armed Conflict, UNGA Res. 54/263, 25 May 2000. At the time of writing some Member States, such as Estonia, Hungary and the Netherlands, have signed but not ratified the Protocol. Some Member States, such as Germany and Luxembourg, ratified the Protocol after the Council had adopted the Guidelines in 2003.

[102] See further the discussion in Jean-Marie Henckaerts and L. Doswald-Beck, *Customary International Humanitarian Law* (Cambridge: Cambridge University Press, 2005) vol. I, *Rules*, p. 482 *et seq.*

[103] See the discussion in Chapter 2.

[104] To this end see the Action Plan for the children and armed conflict guidelines, available at www.consilium.europa.eu/cms3_fo/showPage.asp?id=944&lang=EN&mode=g

commissioned by the European Parliament's Subcommittee on Human Rights which reported in March 2007 found, for example, that a number of individuals in the relevant Commission delegations and EU Missions in third states were not aware of the torture guidelines.[105] Considering that the torture guidelines were the earliest set of issue specific guidelines, having been adopted in 2001, and in terms of legal obligations represent one of the (if not the) most important guidelines adopted by the Union, this does not bode well for the other guidelines adopted by the Union.

3.2.2.2 Community Instruments

The Community also has at its disposal a number of instruments to promote and protect certain values in third states. In terms of external relations, one of the most important powers at its disposal is the ability to negotiate new Agreements or become a party to existing ones with states or international organisations. Article 281 TEC expressly confers legal personality upon the Community.[106] The Community is now a party to a wide variety of Agreements with third states and organisations. Their scope and whether or not they are mixed in nature, is determined by the Community's competence. Any Community Agreement must be based upon both the relevant paragraphs of Article 300 TEC, which sets out the procedural steps to be followed, and those Treaty articles which confer substantive competence to act. Numerous Treaty provisions, such as Articles 133, 149, 151, 174, 181, 181a, 308 and 310 TEC, provide that competence. The Community is a party to treaties which can be broadly classified as Association, Cooperation and Sectoral Agreements. The Community can also adopt unilateral measures which assist in its pursuance of foreign policy objectives and have legal consequences for third states and/or their nationals. The 2006 Regulation, which establishes a financial instrument for development cooperation, is an example.[107] These powers enable the Community to pursue its political objectives in different ways. Agreements and regulations provide a legal basis for a broad scope of Community activities, ranging from assisting a third state with infrastructure projects to funding the

---

[105] European Parliament, *The Implementation of the EU Guidelines on Torture and Other Cruel, Inhuman or Degrading Treatment or Punishment* (Brussels: European Parliament, 2007).

[106] Article 184 of the EURATOM Treaty and Article 6 of the now expired ECSC Treaty are in identical terms.

[107] Regulation 1905/2006 Establishing a Financing Instrument for Development Cooperation, [2006] OJ L378/41, 27 December 2006.

promotion of certain values, such as democracy or freedom of expression. The Community can, in the context of a regulation, change the content of cooperation programmes or the channels used; reduce cultural, scientific or technical cooperation; refuse to act on new initiatives or postpone new projects. In the case of an Agreement which has been negotiated, it can defer signature or its implementation and, in the case of one already in force, defer holding joint committee meetings.[108] It is further open to the Community to suspend all or part of its assistance to a third state, suspend all contact and association with a regime in power in a third state, or ultimately to take punitive measures against a third state and or individuals associated with it.[109]

3.3 The Exercise of Competence and the Pursuit of Ethical Foreign Policy Objectives

The utility of the instruments at the disposal of the Community/Union will depend upon the scope of the measures which are actually adopted. This is ultimately limited by the competence actually enjoyed and the political will to adopt such measures. It is to this issue the discussion now turns.

3.3.1 Development Cooperation

The Community's main commitment in international development terms has always been to the group of countries now known as the ACP states.[110] The relationship between these countries, the Community and its Member States is currently regulated by the Cotonou Convention.[111]

---

[108] Agreements have been delayed over human rights concerns with, for example, Russia (1995), Croatia (1995), Algeria (1998) and Pakistan (1999). See [2003] OJ C280/63, E, 21 November 2003. At the time of writing, the 1998 Partnership and Cooperation Agreement with Turkmenistan still has not been approved by the Member States or Parliament, due to such concerns.

[109] See COM(1994)42, p. 11, where some of these options are mentioned and chapters 2, 4 and 5 where some such measures and their utilisation in practice are discussed.

[110] Originally known as the Associated African States and Madagascar.

[111] Partnership Agreement between the Members of the African, Caribbean and Pacific Group of States, of the One Part and the European Community and its Member States, of the Other Part, [2000] OJ L317/3, 15 December 2000 as revised [2005] OJ L209/27, 11 August 2005. Some of the revised provisions have, as noted above, been applied since 25 June 2005; see [2005] OJ L287/4, 28 October 2005; all the revisions to the Convention will take effect once it has been ratified by all EU Member States and two-thirds of ACP states.

This Convention (like the earlier ones)[112] is mixed in nature.[113] In the vast majority of the Community's other Agreements with developing countries the Member States are not also parties to the Agreement. The tension between the now global reach of Community development policy and a special commitment to the ACP states can still be seen in Article 179(3) TEC, which provides that the development cooperation provisions of the TEC are without prejudice to treaty relations with those states. The Community's development cooperation policy originally had a limited focus and was concentrated on the then colonies of the Member States, the first of them soon to be given independence. It now has a global reach and substantively is all encompassing, covering issues such as armed conflict, sustainable development, climate change, debt relief, tourism, poverty reduction and migration.[114] Such a broad approach to development is not unique to the Community; this has been one of the definitive patterns of all actors in this policy field in recent years.

The relationship between the violation of human rights and development assistance has been extensively discussed since the first Lomé Convention and the situation in Uganda under Idi Amin.[115] The provisions and mechanisms which have been inserted into the subsequent Lomé/Cotonou Conventions[116] to deal with such eventualities, however, are still unclear as to whether it is the Member States, the Community or both who are exercising their competence in such matters. The Agreement amending the Fourth Lomé Convention, for example, ensured that a commitment to human rights became an 'essential

---

[112] Yaoundé I and II, Convention d'association entre la Communauté économique européenne et les Etats africains et malgache associés à cette Communauté, [1964] OJ L93/1431, 11 June 1964 and [1970] OJ L282/2, 28 December 1970, respectively; and the four Lomé Conventions, ACP-EEC Convention of Lomé, [1976] OJ L25/2, 30 January 1976; Second ACP-EEC Convention, [1980] OJ L347/1, 22 December 1980; Third ACP-EEC Convention, [1986] OJ L86/3, 31 March 1986; Fourth ACP-EEC Convention, [1991] OJ L229/3, 17 August 1991; and the Agreement amending the Fourth ACP-EEC Convention, [1998] OJ L156/3, 29 May 1998.

[113] See Article 1 of the respective Conventions.

[114] See the discussion below on some of these issues.

[115] See the statement issued by the Council on 21 June 1977 with regard to Uganda, (1977) 6 *Bull. EC* 77.

[116] From the voluminous literature on this issue, see in particular, K. Arts, *Integrating Human Rights into Development Cooperation: the Case of the Lomé Conventions* (The Hague: Kluwer, 2000) p. 167 *et seq.* and M. Bulterman, *Human Rights in the Treaty Relations of the European Community* (Antwerp: Intersentia, 2001) p. 151 *et seq.*

element' of the Convention and that its provisions could be suspended if fundamental and systematic abuses of those values occurred.[117] The amended Article 366a of the Convention provided a clear legal base for the suspension or termination of the Agreement, if either party considered that the other had failed to fulfil an obligation to respect the 'essential elements' referred to in Article 5.[118] In Council Decision 1999/214/EC, which adopted a procedure in case of violations of Article 366a by an ACP state, the question of competence between the Member States and the Community vis-à-vis such violations was unresolved.[119] For the purposes of Articles 9 and 96 of the Cotonou Convention, the Member States have adopted an internal agreement for the procedures to be followed in areas that come within their competence, in which the issue is still not clear.[120] In the Community's development cooperation Agreements to which the Member States are not also a party, these complications do not exist.

Before discussing the competence granted by the development cooperation provisions of the EC Treaty, which provide one of the legal bases for such Agreements, it is necessary to discuss the November 1991 Resolution of the Council and the Member States Meeting within the Council on Human Rights, Democracy and Development.[121] This Resolution is a watershed in the Community's perception of the relationship between development cooperation and the promotion of ethical values and objectives.

---

[117] Article 5 Lomé IV (bis).

[118] Article 366a is further elaborated upon in Annex LXXXIII to the Fourth Lomé Convention.

[119] Council Decision 1999/214/EC on the Procedure for Implementing Article 366a of the Fourth ACP-EC Convention, [1999] OJ L75/32, 20 March 1999. The final paragraph of the Preamble to Council Decision 1999/214/EC states: 'Whereas in fields covered by the Convention and falling within the competence of Member States, the representatives of the governments of the Member States meeting within the Council may authorise in parallel the Council, if need be, also to cover these fields in adopting decisions pursuant to Articles 1 and 2 of this decision.'

[120] Internal Agreement between the Representatives of the Governments of the Member States, Meeting within the Council, on Measures to be Taken and Procedures to be Followed for the Implementation of the ACP-EC Partnership Agreement, [2000] OJ L317/376, 15 December 2000, as amended [2006] OJ L247/48, 9 September 2006. See in particular, Article 3 of the amended Annex on competence.

[121] Reprinted (1991) 11 Bull. EC 122. The Resolution developed an earlier Commission document, SEC(1991)61.

3.3.1.1 1991 Resolution of the Development Council and the Member States

In a declaration adopted by the Luxembourg European Council of 28–29 June 1991, it was stated that respect for human rights, the rule of law and the existence of political institutions which are effective, accountable and enjoy democratic legitimacy are the basis for equitable development.[122] The later Development Council Resolution of November 1991 had as one of its primary objectives the improvement of the cohesion and consistency of initiatives taken both by the Community and by its Member States in the promotion of human rights and democracy in relations with developing countries. It very clearly recognised the central place of the individual in the development process, which should be designed to promote economic and social rights as well as civil and political liberties through representative democracy.

A high priority was also given to a positive approach that stimulates respect for human rights and encourages democracy. Examples of such positive measures included assistance in the holding of elections, promoting the role of non-governmental organisations and ensuring equal opportunities for all.[123] While priority would be given to such measures, negative measures would also be used, in appropriate circumstances, taking account of the gravity of the breach and guided by objective and equitable criteria. The most important aspects of the relationship between the Community and other states, however, would be the Community's emphasis on sensible economic and social policies; democratic decision-making; adequate governmental transparency and financial accountability; the creation of a market-friendly environment for development; measures to combat corruption; and respect for the rule of law, human rights, freedom of the press and expression in third states.[124] The Council also attached a great deal of importance to the question of military spending in developing countries. It was considered that since donor countries were engaged in a process whereby *their* military spending was being reduced, it would be difficult to justify granting aid if its recipients did not adopt the same policy.[125] This final aspect of the Resolution has not been elaborated upon by the Commission in the various Communications it has since adopted. Otherwise, the Resolution has acted as a catalyst for the

---

[122] Declaration on Human Rights of the Luxembourg European Council (1991) 6 *Bull. EC* I.4.
[123] Resolution on Human Rights, Democracy and Development, para. 4.
[124] *Ibid.* para. 5.   [125] *Ibid.* para. 9.

integration of its various different aspects into the Community's relations with the ACP states and other developing countries, as well as the Central and Eastern European states.

The 1991 Resolution signified a major shift in approach for the Community's development cooperation policy and the promotion of ethical values. The Resolution firmly placed human rights and other ethical values on the Community's agenda in its relations with third states prior to the coming into force of the TEU, which expressly makes reference to these issues for the first time in the treaties. Although the Resolution is a joint one and thus does not clarify the issue of competence, it implies that the Community can take action in the fields addressed by the Resolution either solely or jointly with the Member States.

The Resolution's addition of new objectives and conditions to the Community's development cooperation policy is, as noted above, in line with the general policy being pursued by all donors, in the last twenty years or so. The number of development success stories is relatively few and far between, so donors seek to condition their schemes, in an attempt to make them more effective. Although recipient states have an interest in expanding the number of objectives, as it provides them with alternative sources of funding for projects, most conditions have been added at the insistence of donors, including the Community.[126] At the same time nothing seems to be removed from the list of objectives and criteria and there is no identification of the relationship between them.[127]

The majority of recipient states have little or no real choice in the imposition of conditionality. Conditionality has often been pursued by donors without assessing its effectiveness and the burdens it imposes upon recipient states. A number of programmes funded by different bodies all requiring the satisfaction of various conditions can create a huge administrative burden for a developing state. For example, in Cameroon in 2004, 14 donors had established 400 project missions which required 60 coordination management units to try and run them.[128] In the Union context, therefore, coordination between the Community and the Member States becomes exceptionally important

---

[126] See Arts, *Integrating Human Rights*, p. 167.

[127] C. Pollit and H. O'Neil, *An Evaluation of the Process of Evaluation of EC External Aid Programmes* (Brussels: COTA, 1999) p. 17.

[128] OECD, *OECD Workshop on the Paris Declaration: Implications and Implementation* (Paris: OECD, 2006) p. 5. Similarly, in 2000 there were 405 projects in Mozambique's health sector alone which had differing reporting requirements for various donors, see World

as a way to reduce that burden.[129] There is usually little systematic relationship between conditionality and policy changes, unless conditionality supports reforming groups and there is some domestic will to reform in general.[130] The adjustments required to satisfy conditionality criteria can be very difficult to implement. Yet, the relationship between the implementation of policies stipulated by the Community and the continued flow of funding to help with reform has traditionally been weak.[131] States therefore may lose the incentive to implement reform policies, as not only are the promised benefits not being realised but they cannot be afforded either.

Where the Community takes or threatens to take negative measures under the 1991 Resolution, it is worth questioning which standards are being applied in the determination of 'equitable and objective factors'. The Resolution says the Community will avoid penalising the population for governmental actions. Thus it may have to adjust activity with a view to ensuring that development aid benefits more directly the poorest sections of the population. As will be discussed below, the adjustment of such programmes will not always be possible with the new focus in mind, and the relationship with other foreign policy objectives will also be relevant.

3.3.1.2 Competence under Articles 177 to 181 TEC

Article 177 TEC establishes the general objectives to be pursued by the Community in its development cooperation policy: the sustainable economic and social development of the developing countries, and more particularly the most disadvantaged among them; the smooth and gradual integration of the developing countries into the world

Bank, *World Development Report 2000/2001: Attacking Poverty* (Washington DC: World Bank, 2000) p. 193.

[129] This is now repeatedly emphasised in the European Consensus on Development.

[130] See A. Alberto and D. Dollar, *Who Gives Foreign Aid to Whom and Why*, NBER Working Paper 6612, cited in *World Development Report 2000/2001*, p. 193. It is also the case, as obvious as it seems, that there is a very strong correlation between how well projects are designed and the impact they have. The point here is that 'low capacity governments' have no choice but to accept poorly designed projects which have little impact; whereas states with strong, effective central government can refuse certain aid projects if they feel the costs will outweigh the benefits. India and Thailand are examples of states now refusing some projects on these grounds. See further W. Warne, *The Quality of Foreign Aid: Country Selectivity or Donors Incentives?*, WBPRWP 3325 (Washington DC: World Bank, 2004).

[131] See further, Court of Auditors, *Special Report 12/2000: The Management by the Commission of the European Union on Support for the Development of Human Rights and Democracy in Third Countries*, [2000] OJ C230/1, 10 August 2000.

economy; and the campaign against poverty in the developing countries. Article 177 TEC does not clarify the relationship between these objectives. If the proposed Constitutional Treaty had become law the position would have been clearer. Paragraph 1 of Article III-316, which notes that EU policy in the field of development cooperation shall be conducted within the framework of the principles and objectives of the Union's external action, states that it shall have as its 'primary objective the reduction and, in the long term, the eradication of poverty'. It further notes that the Union shall take account of the objectives of development cooperation in the policies that it implements which are likely to affect developing countries. Both Article 177 TEC and Article III-316 of the proposed Constitutional Treaty note that policy in this area should be consistent with Member States' policies and expressly state that competence is complementary to that of the Member States.[132]

Some of the uncertainties inherent in Article 177 TEC were addressed by the ECJ in the well-known case of *Portugal* v. *Council*.[133] Portugal sought the annulment of Council Decision 94/587/EC concerning the conclusion of the Cooperation Agreement on Partnership and Development between the EC and India.[134] The decision was based upon Articles 133, 181 and 300 TEC.[135] The Agreement dealt with a variety of issues, such as energy, intellectual property, tourism and drug abuse.[136] Article 1(1) of the Agreement provided that, '[r]espect for human rights and democratic principles is the basis for the cooperation between the Contracting Parties and for the provisions of this Agreement, and it constitutes an essential element of the Agreement'. 'Essential elements' clauses, as is well known, have been standard Community practice since 1995.[137] Article 1(2) of the Agreement with India provided its

---

[132] Article III-318 of the proposed Constitutional Treaty and Article 180 TEC develop this further by imposing express obligations with regard to the complementarity and efficiency of Member State and Union action, although it should be borne in mind that such references are commonplace in policy documents. See e.g., the numerous references in the European Consensus on Development.

[133] Case C-268/94 *Portuguese Republic* v. *Council* [1996] ECR I-6177.

[134] 94/578/EC, [1994] OJ L223/23, 27 August 1994.

[135] At the time, Articles 113, 130y, 228(2) and 228(3) TEC. For the purposes of this discussion, the Amsterdam and Nice amendments have not changed the substantive scope of the provisions in question.

[136] Articles 7, 10, 13 and 19 of the Agreement.

[137] The policy was formally adopted in the November 1991 Development Council Resolution at para. 10 and further developed in COM(1995)216. For discussion of the policy in general, see E. Reidel and M. Will, 'Human Rights Clauses in External Agreements of the EC' in P. Alston, M. Bustelo and J. Heenan (eds.), *The EU and Human*

principal objective: to enhance and develop through dialogue and partnership cooperation between the parties in order to achieve a closer and upgraded relationship.

Portugal challenged the Agreement, arguing, in particular, that the legal bases used did not confer on the Community the necessary powers to include the 'essential elements' clause or the provisions on tourism and energy. With regard to the 'essential elements' clause, Portugal argued that Article 308 TEC should have been used. This article provided the Community with an appropriate legal basis for such commitments prior to the TEU. In addition, Portugal argued that while observance of human rights may be mandatory in the Community legal order, this did not provide a competence to act in that sphere in either internal or external matters.[138] Article 177(2) TEC was considered merely to define a general objective and not to confer a competence to include such provisions in an Agreement.

The ECJ held that while Article 308 TEC had been used prior to the coming into force of the TEU as the basis for such measures, it could only be used in the absence of more specific provisions granting that power. As Article 177 TEC declared that, 'Community policy … shall contribute to the general objective of developing and consolidating the rule of law … respecting human rights and fundamental freedoms', the decision should have referred to Article 308 TEC only if the terms of the Agreement extended beyond the competence granted by that provision.[139] The ECJ further stated:

The mere fact that Article 1(1) of the Agreement provides that respect for human rights and democratic principles 'constitutes an essential element' of the Agreement does not justify the conclusion that the provision goes beyond the objective stated in Article 130u(2) of the Treaty. The very wording of the latter provision demonstrates the importance to be attached to respect for human rights and democratic principles, so that, *amongst other things, development cooperation policy must be adapted to the requirement of respect for those rights and principles.*[140]

This paragraph of the ECJ's judgment can be read in two different ways. The first is that in its formulation, the Community's development policy must take account of other conditions and objectives, such as

---

Rights (Oxford: Oxford University Press, 1999) p. 723; Bulterman, *Human Rights in Treaty Relations*; Fierro, *The EU's Approach*; and L. Bartels, *Human Rights Conditionality in the EU's International Agreements* (Oxford: Oxford University Press, 2005).

[138] *Portugal* v. *Council*, n. 133 above, paras. 1–16.   [139] *Ibid.* paras. 17–23.
[140] *Ibid.* para. 24. Emphasis added.

human rights and democracy. There is no hierarchy between the different objectives and principles; development policy must simply take account of other relevant principles. The alternative reading, which is supported by paragraph 26 of the judgment, is that development policy is subordinate to the objective of protecting human rights and democratic principles and must be conditioned towards that aim.[141] It was open to the Court to take one of a number of approaches to the relationship between development and human rights. It could have decided that the Community must adopt a 'human rights perspective' to development which is a perspective but not a set of obligations; or that it must 'mainstream human rights' into its development efforts which requires all development efforts to be considered from a human rights angle; or, finally, that it must take a 'human rights based approach' which transforms the way in which development is conceptualised and is the most burdensome for donors. The ECJ seems to have taken the latter approach.

The ECJ did not, however, elaborate on whether Article 177 TEC could lawfully form the basis of an Agreement in which the protection of human rights was a specific field of cooperation. It would seem, however, that the legal base was valid precisely because, in the Agreement with India, the observance of human rights and democratic principles were not specific fields of cooperation. If human rights were included as a field of cooperation this would possibly go beyond the relationship between human rights and development cooperation established by the ECJ. This view is further supported by paragraph 39 of the Court's judgment where, referring to *Opinion 1/78*,[142] the ECJ declared that clauses dealing with specific matters should not impose such extensive obligations that they de facto constitute distinct objectives. While this approach is consistent with the ECJ's earlier case law on this issue and also, in this context, a literal reading of Article 177(2) TEC, the relationship developed between development policy and human rights in paragraphs 24–26 of the judgment goes beyond it.

---

[141] *Ibid.* para. 26 states, '[w]ith regard, more particularly, to the argument of the Portuguese Government that the characterisation of respect for human rights as an essential element in cooperation presupposes specific means of action, it must first be stated that to adapt cooperation policy to respect for human rights necessarily entails establishing a certain connection between those matters whereby one of them is made subordinate to the other'.

[142] *Opinion 1/78* [1979] ECR 741.

It was Advocate General La Pergola, not the ECJ, however, who addressed one of the most important matters raised by the case. The inclusion of an 'essential elements' clause is necessary if the Community wishes to invoke violation of its terms to legitimately suspend or terminate, under international law, an Agreement between itself and a third state.[143] Articles 60–62 of the Vienna Convention on the Law of Treaties, 1969, codified the customary law on the suspension or termination of a treaty, as a consequence of its provisions being breached.[144] The requirement in Article 60(3)(b) VCLT for the suspension of an Agreement is that a provision which is 'essential to the accomplishment of the object and purpose of the treaty' must have been breached. A narrow reading of Article 60 VCLT could mean that the 'essential elements' clause cannot form the basis for suspension or termination of the Agreement. This is precisely because cooperation in human rights is not provided for. The basic objective of the Agreement, set out in Article 1(2), is to enhance and develop the relationship between the parties. The ECJ's reading of the relationship between the 'essential elements' clause and Article 1(2) of the Agreement in the *Portugal* case is that human rights and democracy are the foremost objectives, with the broader notion of development subservient to them, although this is far from clear in the Agreement itself. Protecting or promoting human rights is not an objective in Article 16, which deals expressly only with development cooperation. The observance of human rights and democratic principles by both the Community and India, however, is the basic condition for its continuing application.

The *travaux préparatoires* of the 1969 Vienna Convention suggest, however, that Article 60 has a broader application. Paragraph 9 of the

---

[143] *Portugal* v. *Council*, n. 133 above, para. 28 of his Opinion. The 'essential elements' clause in the Agreement with India is different in nature from the clause in the Cotonou Agreement. There is no one 'essential elements' clause as the content tends to differ depending upon the third state(s) with whom the Community is concluding the Agreement. For analysis of the different clauses, see Bulterman, *Human Rights in Treaty Relations*, p. 167 *et seq.*; Fierro, *The EU's Approach*, p. 213 *et seq.*; and Bartels, *Human Rights Conditionality*, p. 32 *et seq.* While the content of the clauses may differ, in bilateral treaties at least, the suspension mechanisms usually do not. For recent and critical analysis of the clauses and their use see the report submitted to the European Parliament by R. Agnoletto, MEP, *Report on the Human Rights and Democracy Clause in European Union Agreements*, Final A6-0004/2006.

[144] Vienna Convention on the Law of Treaties, 1969, 1155 UNTS 331. For an early confirmation of the status of these principles as customary rules, see Advisory Opinion, *Legal Consequences for States of the Continued Presence of South Africa in Namibia Notwithstanding Security Council Resolution 276(1970)* [1971] ICJ Reports 16, para. 87.

International Law Commission's 1966 commentary on Article 60(3) VCLT states:

> The Commission ... was unanimous that the right to terminate or suspend must be limited to cases where the breach is of a serious character. It preferred the term 'material' to 'fundamental' to express the kind of breach ... 'fundamental' might be understood as meaning that only the violation of the provision directly touching the central purposes of the treaty can ever justify the other party in terminating the treaty. But other provisions considered by a party to be essential to the effective execution of the treaty may have been very material in inducing it to enter into the treaty at all, even although these provisions may be of an ancillary nature.[145]

The inclusion of provisions defining human rights and democratic principles as 'essential elements' should therefore allow suspension or termination in accordance with Article 60 VCLT.[146] Although the application of Article 60 must be determined by the facts of the case itself, the *travaux préparatoires* and terms of the provision make it clear that the breach must be a serious or 'material' one. The suspension or termination of such an Agreement would only be lawful, therefore, in response to new and systematic breaches of human rights or the dismantling of democratic institutions. Furthermore, an 'essential elements' clause cannot be invoked by the Community for human rights violations which were ongoing at the time an Agreement was concluded and where the Community was aware of them.[147] The clause is designed to ensure that human rights do not seriously deteriorate within those states, not to improve them. That must be achieved through other mechanisms.

There is also a further possible limitation to an 'essential elements' clause. Article 60(5) VCLT prohibits the suspension of 'provisions relating to the protection of the human person contained in treaties of a humanitarian character'. This is arguably drafted broadly enough to refer to any treaty which creates rights intended to protect the individual, whether or not the treaty is primarily humanitarian, so long as it

---

[145] (1966) *Yearbook of the International Law Commission*, Part II, p. 255, cited by S. Rosenne, *Breach of Treaty* (Cambridge: Grotius, 1985) p. 21.

[146] See COM(1995)216, p. 8, for a confident assertion that suspension or termination would be legally permissible under Article 60 VCLT.

[147] See Article 45 VCLT.

has a substantial humanitarian element to it.[148] Bulterman has argued that the principle in Article 60(5) is not applicable in the context of Community Agreements as the 'essential elements' clause serves no purpose, if the values it aims to protect are violated.[149] She further argues that such provisions are ancillary in nature and thus not central to the objective of the treaty.[150] The extent to which this is correct regarding all the Agreements to which the Community is a party and which have such a clause, must be questioned. In the *Portugal* case the ECJ held that development cooperation should work towards the protection of certain values, such as human rights and democracy.

The discussion below stresses that poverty reduction and its eventual eradication, which should focus on the individual, is now the primary aim of the Community's development cooperation policy.[151] Due to the conceptual approach the Community has adopted towards the relationship between human rights and democracy, on the one hand, and poverty reduction and development cooperation, on the other, the relevance of Article 60(5) VCLT cannot be dismissed. Whether it precludes relying on an 'essential elements' clause must be determined in the light of the actual content of an Agreement with a third state and the programmes the Community has initiated in that state.

The suspension or termination by the Community of an Agreement for violation of an 'essential elements' clause by a third state has moreover no bearing upon the legal obligations owed under international law by that state. The ILC's Articles on State Responsibility and the Vienna Convention on Treaties create two distinct legal regimes.[152] The Community is thus still free to use other methods, as discussed in Chapter 2, to pursue its objectives in its relations with the state in question.

Since the *Portugal* case it has been clear that the development cooperation provisions of the EC Treaty grant the Community competence

---

[148] See e.g., A. Aust, *Modern Treaty Law and Practice* (Cambridge: Cambridge University Press, 2000) p. 238 who argues that Article 60(5) VCLT applies to a treaty which creates 'rights intended to protect individuals'.

[149] Bulterman, *Human Rights in Treaty Relations*, p. 223.   [150] *Ibid.*

[151] See Declaration by the Council and European Commission on the European Community's Development Policy of 16 November 2000, Doc. 13458/00 (2000 Development Policy Statement), COM(2000)212, p. 5, and the European Consensus on Development.

[152] See Article 56 of the International Law Commission Articles on State Responsibility and Article 43 VCLT, and further the discussion in the *Third Report on State Responsibility*, A/CN.4/507/Add.3, para. 324.

to include 'essential elements' clauses in its development cooperation Agreements and to adopt other measures to further the objectives referred to in Article 177 TEC. This has also been the case on the basis of Article 181a TEC in relations with all third states.[153] The ECJ in the *Portugal* case did not, however, address the issue of subsidiarity. Article 177(1) TEC makes clear that the Community's competence in this area is complementary to the policies pursued by the Member States – it is neither superior to Member State competence nor inferior to it. Article I-14(4) of the proposed Constitutional Treaty affirms this relationship between Member State and EU competence by stating that in development cooperation (and humanitarian aid) the Union shall have competence to carry out activities and conduct a common policy, however, 'the exercise of that competence shall not result in Member States being prevented from exercising theirs'. This is also the case under the TEC. Advocate General Jacobs in the *EDF*[154] case and the ECJ in the *Bangladesh* case[155] highlighted that until rules in the *AETR*[156] sense develop (if they can develop) Member States retain their competence to engage in development cooperation activities both outside the Community system as well as in cooperation with it.[157] Even though it is a non-exclusive competence, subsidiarity is unlikely to be a major obstacle in its exercise. The underlying approach of the ECJ in the *Portugal, EDF* and *Bangladesh* cases meant that the Member States were not going to be deprived of their competence to act in this field and the proposed Constitutional Treaty has confirmed that this is most unlikely to happen in the future either.

---

[153] Article III-319 of the proposed Constitutional Treaty is the equivalent of Article 181a TEC but does not expressly state as the latter does that 'policy in this area shall contribute to the general objective of developing and consolidating democracy and the rule of law, and to the objective of respecting human rights and fundamental freedoms'. This objective is referred to instead in Article III-292 which establishes general foreign policy, as opposed to development cooperation, objectives.

[154] Case C-316/91 *European Parliament* v. *Council* [1994] ECR I-625, paras. 42–47 of his Opinion.

[155] Cases C-181/91 and 248/91 *European Parliament* v. *Council and Commission* [1993] ECR I-3685, para. 16.

[156] Case 22/70 *Commission* v. *Council* [1971] ECR 263. The ECJ has recently reaffirmed the importance of the *AETR* test in *Opinion 1/03 of 7 February 2006 on the Competence of the Community to Conclude the New Lugano Convention on Jurisdiction and the Recognition and Enforcement of Judgements in Civil and Commercial Matters* [2006] ECR I-1145.

[157] See further, Declaration 10 attached to the TEU, COM(1995)160 and COM(1999)218.

3.3.1.2(a) Poverty Reduction and Development Cooperation

One express objective of Article 177(1) TEC is the 'campaign against poverty in developing countries'. Poverty reduction has been affirmed on a number of occasions as the overriding focus of Community development cooperation policy[158] as well as that of the Member States[159] and all major development agencies.[160] The Community continuously reaffirms its commitment to the Millennium Development Goals (MDGs) and states how it is working towards achieving those objectives.[161]

The Community has affirmed its commitment to help reduce the number of persons living in absolute poverty by one-half by 2015 and for developed states to donate 0.7 per cent of their gross national product for overseas development assistance, although the record of its Member States in living up to their agreed commitments is patchy.[162] The Commission has also issued a substantial number of Communications dealing with these issues and the Council has adopted a number of

---

[158] See e.g., 2000 Development Policy Statement, para. 7; COM(2000)212, p. 5; and the European Consensus on Development, para. 42.

[159] See Part I of the European Consensus on Development.

[160] See e.g., World Bank, *Building Poverty Reduction Strategies in Developing Countries* (Washington, DC: World Bank, 1999) and the discussion in Chapter 2.

[161] See the European Consensus on Development; European Commission, *European Commission Report on the Millennium Development Goals, 2000–2004* (Brussels: Directorate-General for Development, 2005); and the many Commission communications attempting to give effect to these commitments, e.g., COM(2004)150, COM(2005)132 final/2, COM(2005)134, COM(2007)164 and SEC(2007)415. The eight MDGs are to: eradicate extreme poverty and hunger; achieve universal primary education; promote gender equality and empower women; reduce the mortality rate of children; improve maternal health; combat HIV/AIDS, malaria and other diseases; ensure environmental sustainability; and develop a global partnership for development. European Consensus on Development, para. 6 makes the Union's commitment to the eight MDGs clear.

[162] See e.g., COM(2000)212, p. 5; the Preamble to the Cotonou Agreement; Monterrey Consensus of the International Conference on Financing for Development, 18–22 March 2220, A/CONF.198/11; Conclusions of the Barcelona European Council, 15–16 March 2002, para. 13, where (the old) Member States agreed to aim for 0.39 per cent of GNP by 2006 with a long-term commitment to 0.7 per cent; the conclusions of the Council, 23–24 May 2005, Doc. 8817/05, p. 20 *et seq.* where the subsequent detailed targets are set out for 'old' and 'new' Member States; and the European Consensus on Development. The *2006 EU Donor Atlas* illustrates that while Denmark, Sweden, The Netherlands and Luxembourg have already hit the long-term target of 0.7 per cent of their gross national product for overseas development assistance (with Sweden having a commitment to 1 per cent), Italy only donates 0.15 per cent of its gross national product for this purpose and Greece 0.22 per cent. European Commission/OECD, *EU Donor Atlas 2006: Mapping Official Development Assistance*, vol. 1, p. 6, available at http://ec.europa.eu/development/body/publications/docs/eu_donor_atlas_2006.pdf

important conclusions which address poverty reduction. An effectively implemented poverty reduction policy is, without doubt, the most important contribution the Community can make to promoting human rights and the other ethical values the Union states it is committed to in its relations with third states.[163]

Defining poverty or how to tackle it is not straightforward. There is no one universal formula as to how to tackle poverty. The causes of and solutions to eradicating poverty differ between states and each one needs to be looked at individually. A substantial percentage of a state's population may live in poverty, however defined, due to a number of variables. Conflict, natural disasters, adverse weather conditions, a lack of resources, corruption and failing social structures, for example, all play a role. The causes of poverty in each state are multidimensional. In this regard the Paris Declaration on Aid Effectiveness is very important as ministers from both developing and developed countries expressly recognised that for aid to be effective it must be adapted to differing country situations – a broad brush approach was not seen as the way to tackle it.[164] There is also widespread agreement that for aid projects, both generally and specifically for those that emphasise poverty, to be successful each project needs to emphasise participation and partnership.[165] Poverty reduction is deemed to require ownership of the development process by those most in need and an increased focus on the social dimension of growth and development.[166]

The Community's approach to the relationship between poverty reduction and principles such as democracy, good governance, human rights and the rule of law has not been entirely consistent. The April 2000 Commission Communication entitled 'The European Community's Development Policy' states that to achieve their objectives poverty

---

[163] For a more general discussion see OHCHR, *Human Rights and Poverty Reduction: a Conceptual Framework* (New York and Geneva: United Nations, 2004).

[164] The Paris Declaration, which was adopted on 2 March 2005 under the auspices of the OECD by over one hundred ministers, heads of agencies and other senior officials, committed countries and organisations to continue to increase efforts in the harmonisation, alignment and managing of aid. It is particularly important as it lays down a 'road-map' to improve the quality of aid and its impact. See further www.oecd.org/document/18/0,2340,en_2649_3236398_35401554_1_1_1_1,00.html. See also on this point DAC, *Guidelines on Poverty Reduction* (Paris: OECD, 2001) p. 10.

[165] See Pollit and O'Neil, *Evaluation*, p. 21; Paris Declaration, Part II; European Development Statement 2000, para. 11; and the European Consensus on Development, para. 14.

[166] See DAC, *Guidelines*, p. 10 and European Consensus on Development, paras. 11 and 14.

reduction policies must exist in a context in which democracy, good governance, human rights and the rule of law are respected. These are all to be cross-cutting principles – to be integrated into the implementation of development policies which support economic growth and focus on poverty reduction.[167] This approach can be found in a number of subsequent policy papers emanating from the Commission and is in tune with the Millennium Declaration as far as good governance is concerned, although this is not the case with regard to human rights and democracy.[168] Paragraph 24 of the Millennium Declaration notes that '[w]e will spare no effort to promote democracy and strengthen the rule of law, as well as respect for all internationally recognized human rights and fundamental freedoms, including the right to development'. Human rights, the rule of law and democracy are to be pursued as ends in their own right and not expressly as part of the development and poverty eradication process.

In the 2005 European Consensus on Development, which takes priority over the MDGs as far as the Community and Member States are concerned, the interrelationship between poverty reduction, human rights, democracy and governance is more ambiguous. The Council and Commission in this document note that 'development is a central goal by itself; and that sustainable development includes good governance, human rights and political, economic, social and environmental aspects'.[169] The European Consensus later elaborates upon the relationship between development, poverty and these principles. In this regard it notes that 'Community development policy will have as its primary objective the eradication of poverty in the context of sustainable development, including pursuit of the MDGs, as well as the promotion of democracy, good governance and respect for human rights … At the Community level, these objectives will be pursued in all developing

---

[167] COM(2000)212, p. 27. The UK's Department for International Development has since 2000 adopted a somewhat different approach as set out in DFID, *Realising Human Rights for Poor People* (HMSO: London, 2000). Instead of placing human rights within the democratisation and rule of law agenda, its policy focuses on how the impoverished can be empowered to claim their rights. See further on this, L. Piron, *Learning from the UK Department for International Development's Rights-based Approach to Development Assistance* (London: ODI, 2003).

[168] See e.g., COM(2003)615 and COM(2006)421, both of which concern good governance in development policy. See also para. 13 of the Millennium Declaration.

[169] European Consensus on Development, para. 7.

countries and applied to the development assistance component of all Community cooperation strategies with third countries.'[170]

For the purposes of poverty eradication it is debatable which approach (if they are mutually exclusive which they may not be) is more effective. There is a substantial disagreement, for example, whether the presence of good governance is necessary for development projects to be effective or whether other factors such as the design of the project, the capacity of the recipient state (or population) to utilise the aid and continuity of funding are more important.[171] The danger from a poverty reduction perspective with the approach espoused in the 2005 European Consensus on Development is that, for example, human rights and the rule of law projects will be funded and those objectives pursued as ends in themselves as opposed to where they will help to contribute directly to poverty reduction. Where principles such as the rule of law and human rights are only cross-cutting principles, however, there is the possibility that poverty reduction projects will have less impact than would otherwise be the case. A careful balance, therefore, must be struck in identifying and funding projects to ensure that the ultimate objective of poverty reduction is maintained but that other projects are also funded which create or support an environment in which the poverty reduction projects are as effective as they can be. The simple funding of human rights or rule of law projects (narrowly

---

[170] *Ibid.* para. 42.

[171] The debate as to the need for good governance for development projects which pursue economic growth to work as a means to poverty reduction has led to very divergent views. The arguments essentially come down to the following views: that aid increases economic growth in all countries, but with limited effects (see e.g., H. Hansen and F. Tarp, 'Aid and Growth Regressions' (2001) 64 *Journal of Development Economics* 547; R. Rajan and A. Subramanian, *What Undermines Aid's Impact on Growth*, NBER Working Paper 11657; and R. Lensink and H. White, 'Are there Negative Returns to Aid?' (2001) 37 *Journal of Development Studies* 42); that aid increases economic growth, but only in countries where good governance and economic policies are present, but even then up to a certain point (see e.g., P. Collier and D. Dollar, 'Aid Allocation and Poverty Reduction' (2002) 46 *European Economic Review* 1475; C. Burnside and D. Dollar, 'Aid, Policies and Growth' (2000) 90 *American Economic Review* 847; P. Collier and D. Dollar, 'Can the World Cut Poverty in Half? How Policy Reform and Effective Aid Can Meet International Development Goals' (2001) 29 *World Development* 1787); and finally that aid has no effect on economic growth at all (see e.g., W. Easterly, 'Can Foreign Aid Buy Growth?' (2003) 17 *Journal of Economic Perspectives* 23). For further discussion of some of these studies see E. Anderson and H. Waddington, *Aid and the MDG Poverty Target: How Much is Required and How Should it be Allocated?*, ODI Working Paper 275.

defined) will have less impact if they are not designed with a view to their contribution to poverty reduction. This approach, where a careful balance is struck between potentially competing aims, is also commensurate with a multifaceted definition of poverty so that it is not only economic poverty that is being addressed but poverty as a lack of capabilities in the sense argued by Amartya Sen.[172]

The Community's approach to poverty reduction, however, suffers from a number of problems. One of the most notable is the definition of poverty. An early Communication on this issue, from 1993, only really noted that poverty and its causes were multidimensional.[173] A later Communication (from 2000) suggests that the deprivation of basic capabilities and a lack of access to education, health, natural resources and political participation, as well as a lack of income, are all relevant.[174] Poverty can be defined in a number of other ways, as the Community repeatedly notes in policy documents, including taking into account: consumption, level of assets, lack of dignity or autonomy, social exclusion, equality in terms of gender and race, political freedom and security, avoiding preventable morbidity and premature mortality, being adequately sheltered, having basic education, taking part in the life of a community and deprivation of a long and healthy life.[175] The 2000 Communication, however, in no way elaborated upon the relevance of factors other than income in its definition; it did stress though that an integrated approach to institutional support and capacity building is required.[176] In the past this narrow focus has been one of the criticisms of the Community's policies. Audits of such policies had highlighted that if the Community focused greater attention upon institutions and policies within recipient states, then its impact on

---

[172] See A. Sen, *Inequality Re-examined* (Cambridge: Harvard University Press, 1992) and A. Sen, *Development as Freedom* (Oxford: Oxford University Press, 1999).

[173] COM(1993)518. See also, European Consensus on Development, para. 11, which notes that the manifestation of poverty is multidimensional.

[174] COM(2000)212, p. 16.

[175] These approaches to poverty are an amalgamation of differing factors utilised in UNDP, *Human Development Report 2000* (New York: Oxford University Press, 2000) p. 17; DAC, *Shaping the 21st Century, Scoping Study, Donor Poverty Reduction and Practices* (Paris: OECD, 1996) p. 12; and UNHCHR, *Draft Guidelines: A Human Rights Approach to Poverty Reduction Strategies*, para. 47. The Draft Guidelines are available at www.unhchr.ch/development/povertyfinal.html#guid1. The Community refers to some of these factors in its recent policy papers (e.g., European Consensus on Development, para. 11) but the issue is how much attention it pays to criteria other than income in practice.

[176] COM(2000)212, p. 16.

poverty reduction would be significantly greater.[177] The political responsibility of governments for macro-economic reforms, gender issues, social policies such as health, food security education and training, and the sustainable management of natural resources are also of the utmost importance.

The Community has identified three ways in which a poverty focus can be implemented.[178] First, by concentrating on the least developed countries, with a special emphasis on sub-Saharan Africa, who will get half of the extra EU overseas development assistance.[179] Secondly, by implementing a more poverty-focused cooperation programme with middle-income countries. In the 2000 Communication those middle-income countries where more than 20 per cent of the population live on or under US\$1 per day are particularly identified as those to be assisted but in subsequent policy documents this criteria has been dropped. In the 2005 European Consensus on Development, for example, it is simply noted that 'support to the middle-income countries also remains important to attaining the MDGs'.[180] The third way is by improving the focus on poverty reduction in cooperation programmes with all other developing countries.[181]

There are a number of theoretical and practical problems with this approach. One of the methods by which the Community has attempted to implement its poverty reduction strategies has been through the identification of 'poor groups'. Yet the identification and targeting of the poor by donors often adopts a 'broad brush approach' and treats

---

[177] See European Commission, *Synthesis of EC (ACP, MED, ALA, Humanitarian) Aid Evaluation* (Brussels: European Commission, 1999) p. 13. See also, Court of Auditors, *Special Report 8/2003: Concerning the Execution of Infrastructure Work Financed by the EDF, Together with Commission Replies*, [2003] OJ C181/1, 31 July 2003, para. 35, which notes that the EDF can make a significant and relevant contribution to national infrastructure development strategies but all too often the end results, costs and time were very different from the initial terms of the contract; ECDPM, *Assessment of the EC Development Policy* (Maastricht: ECDPM, 2005) which while generally positive notes a number of shortcomings in this regard; and Court of Auditors, *Special Report 4/2005: Concerning the Commission's Management of Economic Cooperation in Asia, Together with the Commission's Replies*, [2005] OJ C260/1, 19 October 2005.

[178] COM(2000)212, p. 20. In subsequent policy documents neither the Commission nor Council have elaborated upon poverty reduction priorities as clearly as in this Communication. Later documents are, however, more or less consistent with the approach articulated in COM(2000)212.

[179] The European Union is, with regard to Africa, implementing the agreement made by the G8 at Gleneagles in 2005. See e.g., European Consensus on Development, para. 23.

[180] European Consensus on Development, para. 61.   [181] COM(2000)212, p. 20.

target groups as homogeneous socio-economic groups.[182] Studies have shown that the Community has often adopted this 'one approach fits all' perspective.[183] As noted above, this ignores the fact that the causes of poverty in each state vary considerably. It is also the case that, in the past, not all Directorates-General in the Commission received training in poverty reduction and that some personnel in the other Directorates-General felt that major development statements such as the 2000 Development Policy Statement belonged to the Development Directorate-General and had little or no relevance to them.[184] In the past, for example, there was no emphasis on poverty reduction in the Directorate-General of the Commission (DG IB) which dealt with the Asian and Latin American countries as well as the Mediterranean countries and is now part of the External Relations Directorate-General.[185] In the Development Directorate-General, which deals with the ACP states, poverty reduction is the overriding priority but in the External Relations Directorate-General, when other developing countries are being dealt with, statements such as the 2000 Development Policy Statement or now the 2005 European Consensus on Development are simply one amongst a number of texts, which are of equal importance, to which they must refer.[186] An emphasis on poverty reduction has also had the consequence of all aspects of development cooperation being

[182] See DAC, *Guidelines*, p.xiii.
[183] See C. Loquai, K Hove and J. Bossuyt, *The European Community's Approach towards Poverty Reduction in Developing Countries*, ODI Working Paper 111, p. 78. See also, J. Carlsson, P. Chibbamullilo, C. Orjueal and O. Saasa, *Poverty and European Aid in Zambia*, ODI Working Paper 138. The Court of Auditors, *Special Report 10/2003: Effectiveness of the Commission's Management of Development Assistance to India in Targeting the Poor and Ensuring Sustainable Benefits*, [2003] OJ C211/21, 5 September 2003, paras. 11–37, notes that the Community had been reasonably successful in targeting and identifying poor groups although systematic attention to these issues throughout the project would have improved its results.
[184] See e.g., ECDPM, *Assessment of the EC Development Policy* (2005).
[185] DAC, *Shaping the 21st Century*, p.xviii.
[186] The structures delivering EU development assistance are less than ideal. The Commissioner for Development and Humanitarian Aid (at the time of writing Louis Michel) is in charge of EU development policy for the ACP states. The Commissioner for External Relations, Benita Ferrero-Waldner deals with Asia, Latin America and all other states but she is still in charge of EuropeAid, the agency responsible for the delivery of all development aid. Notwithstanding these structures the general consensus is that the delivery and effectiveness of EC aid has continued to improve. For assessments to this effect see e.g., DAC, *Development Cooperation Review: European Community* (OECD: Paris, 2002) and DAC, *Development Assistance Committee Peer Review: European Community* (OECD: Paris, 2007).

portrayed as being poverty oriented, even when a programme has little direct connection with it. Admittedly part of the reason for this more recently is that seven of the eight MDGs are poverty oriented,[187] and due to a multifaceted approach to it, the Community has greater latitude in being able to justify its projects as being poverty oriented even where their impact in that regard is likely to be tangential at best.

Although the emphasis in the proposed Constitutional Treaty is different, under the development cooperation provisions of the TEC the Community's development cooperation policy is not focused on the dignity of the individual and their autonomy but is seen as a means to ensure the general integration of developing countries into the world economy.[188] It is for this reason that economic growth and trade are seen as being important to eradicating poverty.[189] It is argued that a focus on such an approach will not only help to reduce poverty levels but will also ensure developed countries integrate into the global economy. The Community sees supporting trade as a contribution to the first and eighth Millennium Development Goals, which are to reduce the proportion of people living on less than US$1 per day and the establishment of a global partnership for development, respectively.[190]

For the Community this means that the objective is to create a sustainable economic development process, which can then benefit the poor through a trickle-down process. This perspective, however, may conflict with its approach to the more general relationship between development and human rights, which is based on a grass-roots approach.[191] Of crucial importance, therefore, is that the overall balance of policy towards a state takes account of the aims and objectives identified in development policy. Yet, this is not the case, especially when the Community's poverty reduction and development cooperation policies compete with its more general foreign policy objectives. For example, in a number of policy papers since 2001 there is a notable tension between poverty reduction and development cooperation more

---

[187] See European Commission, *European Commission Report on Millennium Development Goals*, p. 12 *et seq.*

[188] The development cooperation provisions of the proposed Constitutional Treaty do not refer, as Article 177 TEC does, to the general integration of developing countries into the world economy. The integration of developing countries into the world economy is in Article III-292.

[189] See e.g., COM(2000)212, p. 20; COM(2005)134, p. 6; Council Conclusions, 16 October 2006, Doc. 14018/06; European Consensus on Development, para. 36; and COM(2007) 163, p. 2.

[190] COM(2007)163, p. 2.   [191] See Chapter 2 and the discussion below.

generally, on the one hand, and, on the other, political objectives, especially the fight against international terrorism and illegal migration.[192] As the *World Development Report* for 2003 notes, effective policies aimed at eradicating poverty should, in any case, contribute to a safer world.[193]

The tensions between security and development concerns that sometimes arise have become further apparent in the light of Community measures to implement a Council Joint Action which attempts to contribute to stopping the spread of small arms and light weapons (SALW) which has a Community dimension.[194] This also raises inter-pillar issues. The European Parliament has lodged an action against the Commission for funding a border security project in the Philippines using a budget line associated with the (now repealed) ALA Regulation in which it seeks to give effect to the Joint Action.[195] The European Parliament argues that the Joint Action aims to give effect to measures concerned with combating terrorism, whereas the ALA Regulation aims to aid development by means of financial, technical and economic cooperation. A measure which aims to assist the Philippines government to make its borders more secure, with the aim of combating terrorism, is considered by the Parliament to go beyond the competence the Community has under the terms of the ALA Regulation. Although the ALA Regulation has now been repealed, the case when it is heard by

---

[192] See e.g., COM(2003)299/4; COM(2002)340; the European Security Strategy; and the Agreement Establishing an Association between the European Community and its Member States, of the One Part, and the Republic of Chile, of the Other Part, [2002] OJ L352/3, 30 December 2002.

[193] World Bank, *World Development Report 2003: Sustainable Development in a Dynamic World* (Washington, DC: World Bank, 2003) p. 1.

[194] Council Joint Action, 2002/589/CFSP, On the European Union's Contribution to Combating the Destabilising Accumulation and Spread of Small Arms and Light Weapons and Repealing Joint Action 1999/34/CFSP, [2002] OJ L191/1, 19 July 2002. The Council has also adopted Common Position 2003/468/CFSP, On the Control of Arms Brokering, [2003] OJ L156/79, 25 June 2003 and the European Council, 16 December 2005, Doc. 13066/05, approved the EU Strategy to Combat Illicit Accumulation and Trafficking of SALW and their Ammunition, Doc. 539/06. The Council also on 12 December 2003 adopted an EU Strategy Against the Proliferation of Weapons of Mass Destruction, but although related this is beyond the scope of this discussion. For comprehensive discussion of EU policy in this field, see House of Lords European Union Committee, *Preventing Proliferation of Weapons of Mass Destruction: the EU Contribution*, Thirteenth Report of the Session 2004–2005 (London: HMSO, 2005) and Denza, 'Non-Proliferation of Nuclear Weapons'.

[195] Case C-403/05 *European Parliament v. European Commission*, [2006] OJ C10/14, 14 January 2006.

the ECJ will raise very interesting issues concerning the demarcation between pillars and the relationship between development and security.

There is a second related case which, at the time of writing, is also pending before the ECJ, which will lead to an examination of the relationship between development and more general foreign policy objectives.[196] The European Commission has lodged a case against the Council seeking the annulment of a Council Decision implementing the SALW Joint Action.[197] The Commission's argument centres on the fact that the Council by enacting measures under the CFSP is allegedly affecting Community powers in the field of development cooperation. This is, in particular, as Article 11(3) of the (revised) Cotonou Agreement covers actions, *inter alia*, against the spread of SALW and a number of projects have now been funded under the European Development Fund (EDF) to that effect. The Commission's argument thus centres on an alleged infringement of Article 47 TEU. Both 'security' and 'development' as utilised by the Community, especially after the adoption of the European Security Strategy, are fairly flexible terms and the potential for overlap between them is obvious. This is especially the case with security measures seen as dealing with terrorist-related threats. The court thus has two opportunities to delineate the boundaries between these areas as well as dealing with the inter-pillar issues they raise.

The tension between development cooperation and general foreign policy objectives has been long-standing. The situation in Liberia in 2000 is a good example. The (then) Development Council was trying to adjust programmes to ensure that those in power would not benefit from Community aid. It found, however, that the General Affairs Council took action to suspend all aid to that country in pursuit of its more general foreign policy objectives, although the aid suspended was directly earmarked for poverty reduction programmes.[198] The danger of short-term priorities consistently prevailing over long-term objectives is particularly acute following the absorption of the Development Council into the General Affairs and External Relations Council.

---

[196] Case-C91/05 *European Commission v. European Parliament*, [2005] OJ C115/10, 14 May 2005.

[197] Council Decision 2004/833/CFSP, Implementing Joint Action 2002/589/CFSP with a view to a European Union Contribution to ECOWAS in the Framework of the Moratorium on Small Arms and Light Weapons, [2004] OJ L359/65, 4 December 2004.

[198] See House of Commons Select Committee on International Development, *The Effectiveness of EC Development Aid*, Ninth Report of the Session 1999–2000 (London: HMSO, 2001) Evidence, Question 43.

Although a single Council can balance competing objectives, the General Affairs Council has repeatedly stated that development priorities should be integrated into more general foreign policy ones.[199] It has further approved the European Security Strategy.[200] The preeminence of general foreign policy objectives may relegate poverty reduction to an ancillary status. For the General Affairs and External Relations Council, development cooperation and poverty reduction are one consideration in the 'foreign relations mix'; security, migration and trade policy, for example, are no less important.

As noted above, poverty is now usually defined by reference to more than just income. The focus on income levels is, however, tangible, relatively easily identifiable, transparent and progress is measurable even if it is less than satisfactory as a definition of poverty. The MDGs also clearly adopt an approach primarily based upon income in identifying the global population living in extreme poverty, one-half of which it is intended will be lifted out of poverty by 2015. The Community has repeatedly stated that its aid should prioritise the Least Developed Countries (LDCs) and other Low Income Countries (LICs).[201] Yet the allocation of EC aid to developing countries is not focused on the most deprived in terms of income. The allocation was described in 2001 by the International Development Select Committee of the House of Commons in the United Kingdom as giving 'more to the better off and less to the poor'.[202]

Although things have improved they are not much better now. The World Bank's *World Development Indicators 2006*, show that just over 2 per cent of the population of Eastern Europe and Central Asia live on US$1 per day.[203] The corresponding figures for south Asia and sub-Saharan Africa are 31.2 per cent and 44 per cent respectively. If the level of abject

---

[199] See e.g., General Affairs Council, 18 September 2002, Doc. 6266/02.
[200] Solana, *European Security Strategy*. See further, House of Lords European Union Committee, *EU Development Aid in Transition*, Twelfth Report of the Session 2003–2004 (London: HMSO, 2004) p. 28 *et seq.*
[201] The OECD/UN/World Bank classification of states on the basis of gross national income (GNI) per capita is currently as follows: least developed or low-income country (LDC/LIC), US$735 or less; middle-income country (MIC), US$726–9,075; high-income country (HIC), above US$9,076. The World Bank distinguishes between lower and upper middle-income countries. Lower middle-income countries (LMICs), US$726–2,935, and upper middle-income countries (UMICs), US$2,936–9,075.
[202] Select Committee, *Effectiveness of EC Development Aid*, para. 4.
[203] World Bank, *World Development Indicators 2006*, Table 2.7 (Washington, DC: World Bank, 2006). 2002 is the last year included in these statistics.

poverty is drawn at US$2 per day the figures for Asia and Africa rise to 77.8 per cent and 74.9 per cent respectively.[204] The corresponding rise for Eastern Europe and Central Asia is to 16 per cent. In real terms this translates to 1.5 billion people in south Asia and sub-Saharan Africa living on US$2 per day or less and 76 million in Central Asia and Eastern Europe. Although there has clearly been a reduction in poverty levels in Central Asia and Eastern Europe the real problem lies in south Asia (which of course does not include China) and sub-Saharan Africa.[205]

The Community's allocation of aid commitments would have to undergo a fundamental shift if poverty reduction were indeed to become a central objective. Between 1990 and 2000 the top ten recipients of EC development assistance included: Morocco, Bosnia and Herzegovina, the former Yugoslavia, Egypt, Tunisia, South Africa, Turkey, Albania and Macedonia.[206] None of these are classified as low-income countries by the OECD. Between 1980 and 1998, of the (then) ACP states, only Ethiopia ranked among the top beneficiaries of EC aid. That list was again dominated by the former Yugoslavia, Poland, the Russian Federation and other central and eastern European states.[207] According to the *EU Donor Atlas 2006*, the top twenty recipients of EC aid for 2004 are again dominated by a number of countries some of whom cannot be classified as those in the most need. The top five recipients are: Serbia and Montenegro, Turkey, Democratic Republic of Congo, Morocco and Afghanistan. Egypt, South Africa, Bosnia and Herzegovina and Tunisia all make the list of top twenty recipients.[208] If EC figures for 2004 are considered in terms of percentages they are as

---

[204] World Bank, *World Development Indicators 2006*, Table 2.7.

[205] The reduction of people in real and percentage terms living in poverty in China between 1981 and 2002 is staggering. In 1981, 64 per cent of the Chinese population (at that time estimated at 634 million) lived on less than US$1 per day. The figures for 2002 are 14 per cent of the population, which equates to 180 million people. If poverty is defined at US$2 per day, the figures have still dropped by 50 per cent.

[206] Select Committee, *Effectiveness of EC Development Aid*, para. 19. The distinction should be drawn between aid which is donated by the EU Member States and that which is donated by the Commission; the figures differ as the Member States continue to donate aid according to their own unique preferences although, as noted above, under the terms of the European Consensus on Development the priority of all EU aid is poverty reduction.

[207] For a long-term breakdown, see A. Cox and J. Chapman, *The European Community External Cooperation Programmes: Policies, Management and Distribution* (London: ODI, 1999) p. 129. Poland, for example, between 1990 and 2001 received more aid than all of Asia together. See Select Committee, *Effectiveness of EC Development Aid*, para. 24.

[208] *EU Donor Atlas 2006*, p. 27.

follows: 42 per cent for the LDCs which includes almost all of sub-Saharan Africa; 13 per cent for other LICs; 41 per cent for Lower Middle Income Countries (LMICs); and 4 per cent for Upper Middle Income Countries (UMICs).[209]

The justification for the allocation of very substantial amounts of aid to middle-income countries is that substantial pockets of abject poverty are also present in these states and that some of these countries are very effective at reducing poverty.[210] This is somewhat disingenuous as it underplays the strategic and political importance of most of the countries benefiting. It cannot be denied that aid targeted towards middle-income countries which promote growth and have sound economic policies and institutions, can be extremely effective.[211] It is, however, still difficult to defend the Community's actions in the light of its proclaimed priorities and objectives. The allocation of EC aid to middle-income countries is not correlated with measured levels of poverty. These states are, of course, a diverse group; however, they differ from lower-income countries in having less poverty, greater access to international capital markets, more domestic resources for tackling poverty, lower dependence on aid, better macro-economic policies and higher quality social and political institutions.[212] EC aid can, of course, be justified by other considerations, including geopolitical factors, special transitional circumstances and alternative non-income measures of poverty. What seems clear, however, is that the Community budget continues to be spent in particular regions, usually for reasons related to geography and history, and not for the primary purpose of poverty reduction.

There are other aspects, however, of poverty reduction policies and development cooperation generally where the Community is trying to and has improved its record. Of particular importance is the attempt to

---

[209] *Ibid.* p. 30.
[210] Select Committee, *Effectiveness of EC Development Aid*, para. 19. See also, European Consensus on Development, para. 61.
[211] E. Anderson and H. Waddington, *Aid and the MDG Poverty Target: How Much is Required and How Should it be Allocated?*, ODI Working Paper 275, have argued that a much larger number of people could be lifted out of poverty if aid was allocated on a poverty-efficient basis (and many middle-income states are more efficient in this regard) rather than so as to halve the US$1 a day poverty headcount in individual countries. These gains would be achieved in practice by allocating a greater share of total aid to south Asia and a smaller share to sub-Saharan Africa.
[212] See E. Anderson, S. Grimm and C. Montes, *Poverty Focus in EU Support to Middle Income Countries* (London: ODI, 2004).

eradicate the practice of tied-aid. It has been estimated that over 66 per cent of all grants awarded to African countries have been recycled back to EU states.[213] The OECD and a number of aid agencies have long been campaigning to bring the practice of tied-aid to an end.[214] Aid donations are sometimes only agreeable to donor states on the basis that they also assist the home economy. The untying of aid makes it far more effective in achieving its objectives. It allows for more competitive tendering, ensuring funds go further. It helps facilitate expertise in recipient countries and breaks the cycle of dependency on companies and experts in donor states, and finally it assists with local ownership of projects, which are deemed essential for their success.[215] The Commission and Council identified the untying of aid to least developed countries as one of eight priorities in the context of the Monterrey Consensus.[216] An important Commission Communication[217] has addressed the issue as did the OECD's Paris Declaration on Aid Effectiveness to which the EC has committed itself.[218] Furthermore, the Community and Member States have committed themselves to the untying of aid in the European Consensus on Development.[219] Two 2005 financial regulations which regulated access to Community external assistance referred in strong terms to the untying of aid, although this was not an aim of the regulations nor were the provisions on untying aid legally binding.[220] The two regulations did make apparent, however, that aid should not be tied. They have now been repealed by the new regulations concerned with external aid.[221] None of these six regulations refer to the untying of aid in terms as strong as the 2005 regulations. Figures from the OECD

---

[213] See the Annex to Select Committee, *Effectiveness of EC Development Aid*.

[214] See DAC, *Recommendation on Untying Official Development Assistance to the Least Developed Countries* (Paris: OECD, 2001). The 2001 recommendation was amended in 2006; for all documents see www.oecd.org/department/0,2688,en_2649_18108886_1_1_1_1_1,00. htm. See also, ActionAid's campaign at www.actionaid.org

[215] See DAC, *Recommendation on Untying Official Development Assistance*.

[216] 'The Monterrey Consensus and the European Union', MEMO/04/05, 11 March 2004. Nine of the 'old' fifteen Member States had already legislated to untie their aid by 2004.

[217] COM(2002)639.   [218] Paris Declaration, para. 31.

[219] European Consensus on Development, paras. 29 and 50.

[220] See the Preambles to Regulation 2110/2005 on Access to Community External Assistance, [2005] OJ L344/1, 27 December 2005 and Regulation 2112/2005 on Access to Community External Assistance with EEA Relevance, [2005] OJ L344/23, 27 December 2005.

[221] This is part of the new external relations framework proposed in COM(2004)101final/ 2. There are six new regulations which replace a mass (approximately 100) of earlier regulations concerned with external aid, such as the ALA Regulation. The new regulations came into force on 1 January 2007. The new regulations are as follows: Regulation 1905/2006 Establishing a Financial Instrument for Development

continue to highlight, however, how since 2001 the amount of tied-aid from both EU and non-EU OECD members has been falling steadily, and collaterally the effectiveness of aid has been improving.[222]

3.3.1.2(b) Poverty Reduction, Development Cooperation and Trade

As an instrument to alleviate poverty, trade has far greater potential than aid.[223] World Bank figures show that developing countries earn US $322 per capita through exports as opposed to US$10 from aid.[224] Even a modest increase in exports can far outweigh the impact of all aid initiatives in developing countries. Trade is widely regarded as the most powerful instrument available to alleviate poverty.[225] Economic development driven by trade as in Japan, India, Singapore, South Korea, Thailand, Taiwan, Hong Kong, Indonesia, Malaysia and China all prove this to be the case.

Trade-driven poverty alleviation, however, is not without negative repercussions for either the Union or those developing states who are supposed to benefit from it. The Union, which adheres to the Washington Consensus in its trade negotiations, subscribes to the liberalisation of markets which does not allow them to be carefully managed and this can have many negative consequences in developing states.[226] Furthermore, as opposed to other initiatives and instruments, trade-based development can also directly affect the commercial and economic

Cooperation, [2006] OJ L378/41, 27 December 2006; Regulation 1717/2006 Establishing an Instrument for Stability, [2006] OJ L327/1, 24 November 2006; Regulation 1638/2006 Laying Down General Provisions Establishing a European Neighbourhood and Partnership Instrument, [2006] OJ L310/1, 9 November 2006; Regulation 1889/2006 Establishing an Financing Instrument for the Promotion of Democracy and Human Rights Worldwide, [2006] OJ L386/1, 29 December 2006; Regulation 1085/2006 Establishing an Instrument for Pre-Accession Assistance, [2006] OJ L210/82, 31 July 2006; and Regulation 1934/2006 Establishing a Financing Instrument for Cooperation with Industrialised and Other High-Income Countries and Territories, [2006] OJ L405/41, 30 December 2006. These regulations are discussed below.

[222] See DAC, *Implementing the 2001 DAC Recommendation on Untying Official Development Assistance to the Least Developed Countries, 2006 Progress Report to the High Level Meeting* (Paris: OECD, 2006).

[223] See OECD, *The Development Dimension of Trade* (Paris: OECD, 2002) and OECD, *Strengthening Trade Capacity for Development* (Paris: OECD, 2002).

[224] World Bank, *World Development Indicators 2006*.

[225] Although see J. Bhagwati, *In Defence of Globalization* (Oxford: Oxford University Press, 2005) p. 55 *et seq.*, who has argued that trade growth can 'immiserize' a country and its poor as well. On balance, however, he does argue that growth does reduce poverty as the reduction in the numbers of the world's poor in Africa and Asia show.

[226] See J. Stiglitz and A. Charlton, *Fair Trade for All: How Trade Can Promote Development* (Oxford: Oxford University Press, 2005) p. 15.

interests of donor states. In any case as Jonathan Sachs has noted, markets are only powerful engines of development when the preconditions of basic infrastructure and human capital are in place.[227] Trade-based initiatives will not lead to the alleviation of poverty, therefore, without basic infrastructure and human capital being in place. The focus on trade as an instrument to alleviate poverty must be part of a holistic approach towards developing countries if it is to be effective.

The Community, as noted above, considers trade to be crucial in assisting the integration of developing countries into the world economy and helping to alleviate poverty and has on numerous occasions adopted policy papers to try and help developing countries to benefit from trade.[228] The Doha Development Agenda (DDA) as part of the WTO Ministerial Conference, alongside the commitments undertaken in Johannesburg at the World Summit for Sustainable Development and Monterrey at the International Conference on Financing for Development, now form the basis for initiatives and action to be taken by the Community in this regard.[229] The approach adopted by the Community towards developing countries in trade negotiations is, however, often protectionist and detrimental to their interests.[230] The Community may wish to alleviate poverty in developing states through trade but is not necessarily willing to pay the price for doing so. An economic analysis of the Community's position in the WTO in 2002 stated:

---

[227] J. Sachs, *The End of Poverty: How We Can Make it Happen in Our Lifetime* (London: Penguin Books, 2005) p. 3.

[228] See COM(2002)82; COM(2002)513; COM(2005)134; Council Conclusions, 16 October 2006, Doc. 14018/06; European Consensus on Development, para. 36; and COM(2007)163.

[229] Seville European Council, 21–22 June 2002, para. 40 of its conclusions confirmed the commitment to Doha and Monterrey, as a means to sustainable development. See also, COM(2002)513, COM(2004)150 and COM(2007)158, which deal with how to 'translate the Monterrey Consensus into practice'. Article 2 of the Doha Ministerial Declaration (available at www.wto.org/English/thewto_e/minist_e/min01_e/mindecl_e.pdf) states that 'international trade can play a major role in the promotion of economic development and the alleviation of poverty. We recognise the need for all our peoples to benefit from the increased opportunities and welfare gains that the multilateral trading system generates. The majority of WTO members are developing countries. We seek to place their needs and interests at the heart of the Work Programme adopted in this Declaration.'

[230] See e.g., C. Bjørnskov and K. Lind, 'Where Do Developing Countries Go After Doha? An Analysis of WTO Positions and Potential Alliances' (2002) 36 *JWT* 543; Oxfam, *Rigged Rules and Double Standards* (London: Oxfam, 2002); and the rebuttal, European Commission, *Rigged Rules and Double Standards: Trade, Globalisation and the Fight Against Poverty – Comments from the Commission*, issued 17 April 2002.

contrary to official declarations, analysis demonstrates that the EU is not a staunch defender of developing countries in the WTO ... [m]ost of the African Group actually has a large negative correlation with EU positions ... [t]he relatively protectionist policies ... are in opposition to the declared interest of most developing countries ... although ... the EU believe themselves to be more friendly to the developing countries than the rest of the world ... They ... are isolated in strong opposition to the developing countries in the WTO.[231]

Pascal Lamy, when he was the EU Commissioner for Trade, in the negotiations for the Doha Round made a bold gesture in 2004 when he talked about developing countries having the 'round for free'.[232] He was subsequently forced to abandon this in the face of opposition from EU Member States (especially France) and conceded that developing countries would have to make concessions and commitments on tariffs in some areas and in particular on trade facilitation. He thus subsequently used the less catchy phrase that developing countries could have the 'round at a modest price'.[233] Similarly, Peter Mandelson, upon becoming Trade Commissioner, stated '[m]y mission, as Europe's new Trade Commissioner, is to make trade fair for the many, not just free for the few. By fairness, I mean enabling all countries, including the poorest, to share in rising global prosperity.'[234] Yet his subsequent approach to trade negotiations in the WTO and for the Economic Partnership Agreements (EPAs) with the ACP states has not lived up to his rhetoric.[235] On 28 October 2005, for example, Commissioner Mandelson tabled a second offer on agriculture as part of the DDA;[236]

---

[231] Bjørnskov and Lind, 'Developing Countries', 547 and 560–2.

[232] P. Lamy, 'Where Next for EU Trade Policy?' Berlin, 11 June 2004.   [233] *Ibid.*

[234] P. Mandelson, 'This is our 21st Century Challenge', *Guardian*, 1 December 2004.

[235] See the discussion below.

[236] The EU offer proposed: an average cut in agriculture tariffs of 46 per cent; a maximum agricultural tariff of 100 per cent, as demanded by developing countries; a reduction in the number of sensitive products designated by the Union; reductions in tariffs for sensitive products; a 70 per cent reduction in trade distorting agricultural subsidies, as agreed in the Union's 2003 CAP reform, and tighter disciplines on 'Blue Box spending'; the total elimination of all agricultural export support by an agreed date, if others discipline their export support; and differential treatment for developing countries: higher tariff bands, lower tariff cuts and a maximum tariff of 150 per cent. See 'EU Tables New Offer in Doha World Trade Talks', 28 October 2005, available at www.europa.eu.int/comm/trade/issues/newround/doha_da/pr281005_en.htm. The second EU offer was in response to an earlier offer which had been rejected by developing countries. According to Oxfam, under the first proposal the Union would not have had to reduce the amount of money paid to farmers by a single euro. Oxfam Press Release, 'No Real Gains for Poor in EU Trade Offer', 12 October 2005, cited by House of Commons International Development Select Committee, *The WTO Hong Kong*

disagreements over agriculture have been a central cause of the failure to conclude the talks.[237] Commissioner Mandelson argued that this was a credible and substantial offer but it was expressly conditional upon satisfactory concessions from developing countries on non-agricultural market access and services.[238] It has been estimated that under the deals being discussed in 2006, 83 per cent of the DDA benefits would have gone to developed countries and that in sub-Saharan Africa poverty would have increased.[239] It is, therefore, not surprising that the director of Oxfam at the 2006 World Economic Forum in Davos noted on the Union's approach to the WTO negotiations in the Doha Development Round that:

They [the Union and United States] have turned this trade round on its head; from one that was meant to reform trade rules for the benefit of poor countries, to one which is about aggressive corporate gain in industrial products and services and indefensible northern protectionism in agriculture.[240]

The Community considers the GSP and Everything But Arms (EBA) initiative[241] to be its major contribution to alleviating poverty through trade.[242] The Commission has argued that it has fully opened its

---

Ministerial and the Doha Development Agenda, Third Report of the Session 2005–2006 (London: HMSO, 2006) para. 18.

[237] Agriculture may be small in value terms for Africa, but in the poorest developing countries agriculture represents 40 per cent of GDP, 35 per cent of exports and between 50 and 70 per cent of total employment. See UN Millennium Project Task Force on Trade, *Trade for Development* (New York: United Nations, 2005) p. 46. It is for this reason that agricultural earnings are so important to a large number of developing countries and that the subsidies and protective agricultural policies of the Union and other developed nations have been at the centre of the debate. See further, Select Committee, *The WTO, Hong Kong and Doha*, para. 12.

[238] See 'EU Tables New Offer in Doha World Trade Talks', 28 October 2005.

[239] See C. Kirkpatrick, C. George and S. Scrieciu, *Sustainability Impact Assessment of Proposed WTO Negotiations: Final Global Overview – Final Report* (Manchester: IDPM, 2006) and ActionAid, *Mission Unaccomplished: One Year On from Gleneagles, Is the G8 Hitting its Targets on Debt, Trade and Aid?* (London: ActionAid, 2006).

[240] Oxfam Press Release, 'Rich Countries Must Not Pursue "Business as Usual" in Trade Talks', 26 January 2006. For general discussion of the European Union's approach to the DDA, see Select Committee, *The WTO, Hong Kong and Doha*.

[241] See COM(2004)461. The original EBA was in Council Regulation 416/2001, [2001] OJ L60/43, 1 March 2001 and is now Article 12 of Council Regulation 980/2005, [2005] OJ L169/1, 30 June 2005, which is the current GSP scheme.

[242] Although the GSP does not incur costs charged to the EC budget, it does entail a loss of customs revenue. The Commission has estimated that the 2005 GSP Regulation entails an annual loss of customs revenue of around €2.2 billion, see COM(2004)699, p. 2. In 2002, imports under the GSP amounted to €53.2 billion out of €360 billion worth of imports from all developing countries, see European Council, *EU Annual*

internal market to all products, except weapons, from the forty-nine least developed countries[243] although tariffs on sensitive goods such as bananas, sugar and rice are only gradually being removed for some states.[244] The Commission has argued that these measures are part of its attempt to 'ensure that the concerns of developing countries are at the heart of the discussions under the DDA'.[245]

Most of the extreme poor in the developing world, however, work in agriculture and labour intensive industries where the European Community's tariffs are still possibly the highest in the developed world. Oxfam, in its 2002 analysis of trade rules, showed that the tariffs applied to agricultural goods by the Community are double that of the United States and can be significantly higher than that of almost all other states.[246] Other audits paint a slightly different picture[247] but what is inescapable is that the agricultural subsidies awarded by developed states to their farmers are still about six times greater than the development assistance they grant to developing states.[248]

The EBA is only of benefit to the LDCs if they have the capacity to respond to the further opening up of European markets and if there is a demand for products for which they can meet the supply. In many cases,

---

Report on Human Rights 2005, p. 57. C. Michalopoulos, Developing Countries in the WTO (London: Palgrave, 2001) p. 30 has noted that 'the GSP turned out to be less than it has been touted to be at its inception. It was important for some products, for some countries, for some of the time. But it [has] not served to strengthen the integration of developing countries into the world trading system.'

[243] For the purposes of the EBA, the defining of a state as a 'least developed country' is based on a composite indicator; it is not a direct measure of either poverty or trade disadvantage. With the exception of Bangladesh, all countries with a population over 75 million are excluded from it. Thus, countries like Kenya which are only marginally richer than the LDCs and the very big but poor developing countries such as India, Pakistan and Indonesia all miss out on the benefits under it. See House of Commons International Development Committee, Sixth Report, Fair Trade? The European Union's Trade Agreements with African, Caribbean and Pacific Countries (London: HMSO, 2005) para. 35.

[244] See Regulation 1401/2002 Laying Down Detailed Rules of the Opening and Administration of the Tariff Quotas for Rice, Originating in the Least Developed Countries, [2002] OJ L203/42, 1 August 2002 and Regulation 1381/2002 Laying Down Detailed Rules of the Opening and Administration of the Tariff Quotas for Raw Sugar Cane, Originating in the Least Developed Countries, [2002] OJ L200/14, 30 July 2002.

[245] European Commission, Rigged Rules, p. 1.

[246] Oxfam, Rigged Rules and Double Standards, p. 99.

[247] See European Commission, Rigged Rules, and J. Gallezot, Real Access to the EU's Agricultural Market (2003), available at http://trade-info.cec.eu.int/doclib/docs/2003/july/ tradoc_113490 and the literature cited therein.

[248] World Bank, World Bank Development Report 2003 (Washington DC: World Bank, 2003) p. 12. This was, of course, before the 2003 reform of the CAP.

non-sensitive goods are already subject to duty-free access. The danger, though, is not to producers based in the European Union but to producers in states not classified as LDCs. The EBA benefits producers in the LDCs at the expense of those elsewhere, who are only entitled to take advantage of the general GSP or GSP+ scheme. Where the goods they export to the European Union are in competition with those exported by the LDCs, those producers and their economies will suffer. This is particularly the case with sugar.[249]

What should be borne in mind, however, is that even if the level of subsidies which are paid under the Common Agricultural Policy falls further, and tariffs are reduced on sensitive goods, the consequences of this for developing states are not clear-cut or easily predictable.[250] If less subsidies are paid, for example, the prices of commodities may go up as a consequence; many developing countries are net importers of food and thus while some local farmers will do well, other locals may not and this may actually increase poverty in some developing states.[251]

Another trade and poverty-related area in which the Union's rhetoric and deeds are not entirely commensurate is, as noted above, in the ongoing EPA negotiations with the ACP states.[252] Under the terms of Articles 36 and 37 of the Cotonou Agreement, the ACP states, on the one

---

[249] See the studies available at www.acpsugar.org/ and C. Stevens and J. Kennan, *The Impact of the EU's Everything But Arms Proposal: a Report to Oxfam* (London: Oxfam, 2001) and House of Lords European Union Committee, *Too Much or Too Little? Changes to the EU Sugar Regime*, Eighteenth Report of Session 2005–06, vol. I (London: HMSO, 2005). Brazil and Thailand (neither of whom is a LDC) along with Australia successfully challenged the EC's tariff regime on sugar in October 2004 under the WTO dispute resolution mechanism. The WTO ruled that the EC was subsidising sugar exports excessively, in violation of its WTO commitments. This finding was subsequently essentially upheld on appeal, see WTO Report of the Appellate Body, *European Communities – Export Subsidies on Sugar*, 28 April 2005, WT/DS265/AB/R, WT/D266/AB/R and WT/DS283/AB/R 05-1728.

[250] After reforms to the Common Agricultural Policy in 2003, most domestic support measures have been placed in the 'Green Box' and thus deemed minimally or non-trade distorting.

[251] Sachs, *The End of Poverty*, p. 282.

[252] A very large coalition (171) of non-governmental organisations such as Oxfam, ActionAid, Christian Aid, Traidcraft and War on Want have formed a movement known as the 'Stop the EPA Campaign'. See further www.stopepa.org and www. epawatch.net. On the EPAs and the negotiating process more generally see further, Open Europe Working Paper, *Five Ways to Make Trade Work for Development*, available at www.openeurope.org.uk/research/; Oxfam, *Unequal Partners: How EU-ACP Economic Partnerships Could Harm the Development Prospects of Many of the World's Poorest Countries* (London: Oxfam, 2006); and International Development Committee, *EU Development and Trade Polices: an Update*, Fifth Report of Session 2006–2007 (London: HMSO, 2007).

hand, and, on the other, the EC and its Member States are required to negotiate EPAs which are WTO compatible and which must come into force by 1 January 2008.[253] Negotiations on the EPAs have been ongoing since 2002. The ACP states have been split into four groups for these purposes and different EPAs are being negotiated with each group.[254] Analysis of the proposed EPAs and the possible alternatives to them have shown that switching from the Cotonou preferences to the GSP and the EBA initiative will be more beneficial for most ACP states than agreeing to an Economic Partnership Agreement. The GSP+ scheme (which is extended to encompass more sensitive products than the standard GSP) is the optimum choice for those ACP states which are classified as being the least developed.[255] This, along with the splitting of the ACP states into groupings, has a number of consequences.

The East African Community (EAC), which includes Kenya, Uganda and Tanzania, provides a stark example. These countries have already engaged in a process of economic collaboration and are establishing a customs union. As LDCs, both Uganda and Tanzania already enjoy the benefits of the EBA. Consequently they have little, if anything, to gain in joining an EPA. Kenya, on the other hand, as the only low-income (as opposed to least developed) country in the EAC, is now particularly isolated. The least developed ACP states, such as Uganda and Tanzania, thus have to decide whether to continue with their unlimited, non-reciprocal, duty-free access for non-sensitive goods to the market of the EC Member States and leave their regional grouping, or should they negotiate alongside their regional partners and face reciprocal market opening? The least developed countries such as Uganda and Tanzania have nothing to gain from the EPAs, while Kenya, their non-LDC neighbour, has a great deal to lose.[256]

The Community and its Member States, by splitting up the ACP states, have of course weakened the latter's collective bargaining position in any trade negotiations. It should, of course, be remembered that many

---

[253] Under the terms of Article XXIV GATT 1994, 1867 UNTS 187.

[254] See the Appendix to International Development Committee, *Fair Trade? The European Union's Trade Agreements with African, Caribbean and Pacific Countries*, for the detailed configurations.

[255] See R. Perez, 'Are the Economic Partnership Agreements a First-Best Optimum for the African Caribbean Pacific Countries' (2006) 40 *JWT* 999.

[256] This example is adapted from Joint Memorandum Submitted by Several Non-Governmental Organisations to the International Development Committee. See *Fair Trade? The European Union's Trade Agreements with African, Caribbean and Pacific Countries*, Evidence 39.

of the ACP states have little in common, in terms of size, population, natural resources or geography and are only linked as the vast majority have a European colonial past. Each of the new groups has different strengths and weaknesses and while it will be possible for there to be differentiated treatment to take account of the particular circumstances of each grouping, there is also the danger that a weaker grouping will have far more concessions wrung out of it than a stronger one. It is also the case that as the groupings are made up of countries with quite different interests, it is harder for them to agree a common position. In addition, the regional integration which the EC wishes to promote amongst these states and which has already taken place in some regions is somewhat ironically now being undermined by the Community. The vulnerability of the divided ACP states is clear from the fact that the EC is strongly pushing with them the so-called Singapore issues (trade facilitation, investment, competition and government procurement) even though after the collapse of WTO talks in Cancún, WTO members agreed to drop all the Singapore issues, except trade facilitation, from the Doha Round.

For the Community, the EPAs will assist in the development process by liberalising trade between the ACP states by creating free trade areas which it is hoped will lead to investment, increased productivity and consequentially economic development, prosperity and a reduction in poverty.[257] Negotiations with the ACP states, however, are being led by the Directorate-General for Trade. According to the House of Commons Select Committee for International Development, the role of the Development Directorate-General appears to be minimal and confined to supporting the EPA process through funding initiatives via the EDF.[258] As they note, 'this is of concern because it may mean that the poverty implications of trade policies proposed and negotiated by DG Trade are not properly taken into account'.[259]

---

[257] See S. Bilal, 'Redefining ACP-EU Trade Relations: Economic Partnership Agreements', available at www.ecdpm.org

[258] It is worth noting that the Council has agreed to provide €2 billion in total for 'Aid for Trade' initiatives in addition to funding under the EDF. These conclusions establish an explicit link between the Aid for Trade initiative and development support for the EPAs. See General Affairs and External Relations Council, 16 October 2006, Doc. 14018/06.

[259] International Development Committee, *Fair Trade? The European Union's Trade Agreements with African, Caribbean and Pacific Countries*, para. 54.

For many ACP states, however, trade liberalisation and regional integration are not sufficient. Many of the regional groupings the Community is negotiating with are, as noted above, already composed of a number of free trade areas or economic communities.[260] Without the ability to produce manufacturing or agricultural goods, for which there is demand, a free trade area by itself does little for development. The 'Stop EPA Campaign' has argued that the current approach of the Community will disrupt local production and government revenues, create unemployment and ultimately increase poverty rather than reduce it.[261] It has further been argued that market liberalisation by cutting fiscal revenues will consequently limit the capacity of ACP governments.[262] It has been estimated, for example, that Kenyan revenues will decrease by 17 per cent as a result of the market liberalisation process.[263] Considering the Union's emphasis on governance in its external relations, the fact that its own policies may undermine the capacity of third state governments seems somewhat paradoxical.

The essential problem with EPAs, however, is the EC's insistence on reciprocity, which is a fundamental about-turn from the position under the Cotonou Agreement, the GSP scheme and the EBA initiative. The impact of reciprocity may be devastating on certain sectors, in particular agriculture and manufacturing in ACP states.[264] The EC's position can, however, be defended as it is attempting to ensure that the EPAs are compliant with Article XXIV of the General Agreement on Tariffs and Trade (GATT) and cannot be challenged by non-ACP states. This requires ACP states to remove customs duties on over 90 per cent of EU goods and services within a ten-year period. The Trade Commissioner, Peter Mandelson has undertaken to try and ensure that it is possible within the WTO to allow for special and differential treatment for the EPAs with the LDCs although this may well not be possible.[265] He has also stated that the LDCs will not be any worse off from joining an EPA than they would be if they used the EBA initiative.[266] Even if this is correct

---

[260] For example, the ESA-EU EPA is composed of ACP states who are also members of the following regional free trade areas or economic communities: Common Market for Eastern and Southern Africa (COMESA), Eastern African Community (EAC) and Indian Ocean Commission (IOC).

[261] See the campaign statement at www.stopepa.org

[262] Joint Memorandum Submitted by Several Non-Governmental Organisations to the International Development Committee, *Fair Trade? The European Union's Trade Agreements with African, Caribbean and Pacific Countries*, Evidence 39.

[263] *Ibid.*   [264] *Ibid.*   [265] *Ibid.* para. 39.   [266] *Ibid.* para. 40.

(and it will not know be known until the negotiations are complete) it is certain that the big losers from the EPA process will be those developing ACP states who are not classified as the 'least developing' by the Community.

Effective poverty reduction in third states requires a refocusing of approach and the Member States must be willing to sacrifice some of their own interests. Despite its rhetoric with regard to poverty reduction, the Community has been much more active in protecting and promoting ethical values through other mechanisms, such as funding projects. This has been easier for the Community as it does not require it fundamentally to reassess its relationships with all third states. It is to such mechanisms that the discussion now turns.

3.3.1.2(c) Funding the Pursuance of Ethical Values and Practice
3.3.1.2(c)(i) General Legal Basis for Funding Development Projects Pursuing Ethical Values   EC development aid is primarily funded through a number of different sources: the EDF in the case of the Lomé/Cotonou Conventions[267] and Heading 4 of the Budget for external action in general.[268] Notwithstanding the rhetorical emphasis the Community accords to issues such as human rights and democracy as opposed to aid in the strict sense, it should be noted that in actual terms, such allocations amount to no more than between 1 and 2 per cent of the external relations budget lines.[269] This expenditure is dwarfed by other categories of assistance, such as Programme or Humanitarian Aid.

---

[267] There has been long-standing debate on whether or not the EDF should be integrated into the Community budget, see e.g., COM(2004)101final2, p. 27 where the Commission argues for the 'budgetisation' of the EDF. In December 2005, the European Council adopted a financial envelope for the Tenth EDF which comes to €22.7 billion for the period 2008–2013. The Ninth EDF which covered the period 2003–2007 had been allocated the sum of €13.5 billion.

[268] Although the general budget is also used in ACP states. For general (if now dated) analysis of external aid budgets, see Cox and Chapman, *External Cooperation Programmes*; Select Committee, *Effectiveness of EC Development Aid*; and House of Lords, *EU Development Aid in Transition*. This discussion does not extend to the work of the European Investment Bank.

[269] Approximately €100–120 million has been allocated per year since 2001, see the *EU Annual Report on Human Rights* for the period between 2001–2006 for detailed breakdowns. For the period 2007–2013, the new financial framework allocates approximately 10 per cent of the annual budget for the classification 'The EU as a Global Actor', see COM(2004)101, p. 29 which will include not only the EIDHR but is also assumed to include the EDF. Cox and Chapman, *External Cooperation Programmes*, p. xviii of the 1997 version of their report gave a figure of 2 per cent of the external relations budget.

The European Parliament originally instigated the initiative to move all budget lines relating to the promotion of human rights and democratic principles together into a single chapter of the budget to be called the 'European Initiative in Support of Democracy and the Protection of Human Rights'.[270] Despite the consolidation, the expansion of budget lines concerned with aspects of human rights and democracy has continued. A reason for this is the introduction of *ad hoc* budget lines by the Parliament, where it has considered the general allocation to be deficient. The Commission has also stressed the need for the various financial instruments used to promote ethical values to be flexible, so as to ensure compatibility with their specific objectives and to guarantee the availability of financial resources at a minimum of notice.[271]

Community expenditure, however, is only legitimate if it has both a budgetary appropriation and is also authorised by the adoption of a basic act which provides the appropriate legal base. The ECJ's decision in *United Kingdom* v. *European Commission* (the *Social Funds* case),[272] which reaffirmed this, led to 100 budget headings (equating to 1 per cent of the Union's budget for 1998) being suspended for non-compliance.[273] As the Financial Report for 1998 notes, a number of different budget heads concerned with the promotion of democracy, the rule of law and human rights had to be suspended. The earmarked funds were eventually released under the terms of an *ad hoc* agreement between the institutions.[274]

In the light of the *Social Funds* case, it was clear that many projects promoting ethical values in third states were not lawful where there was significant expenditure without an appropriate legal base. Some projects, however, were based on an appropriate unilateral instrument.

---

[270] Resolution on a European Democracy Initiative [1992] OJ C150/281, 15 June 1992. Subsequently referred to as the European Initiative for Democracy and Human Rights and now as the European Instrument for Democracy and Human Rights (EIDHR).

[271] See COM(1995)567, section 2(b). Court of Auditors, *Special Report 12/2000*, para. 75 urged the Commission to simplify the number of budget heads to allow evaluation of them, which in its response the Commission refused to do. The new financial regulations have provisions which allow a significant degree of flexibility; see e.g., the Preamble to Regulation 1889/2006 on Establishing a Financing Instrument for the Promotion of Democracy and Human Rights Worldwide. The Commission has also confirmed the need for flexibility; see e.g., COM(2006)23 which sets out the programme for the promotion of human rights and democracy until 2013.

[272] Case C-106/96 *United Kingdom* v. *European Commission (Payments to Combat Social Exclusion)* [1998] ECR I-2729.

[273] *European Communities Financial Report 1998* (Luxembourg: OOPEC, 1999) p. 53.

[274] *Ibid.* p. 54.

Article 6 of the Asia and Latin America Regulation (the ALA Regulation) for example, specifically referred to the fact that financial and technical assistance was to be extended, in particular, with regard to the spread of democracy and human rights.[275] The fact that the Commission and the other institutions understood beforehand the weakness of the legal basis for some of the human rights and democracy-based projects can be ascertained from a 1997 Communication. This proposed a 'human rights regulation' to provide the various different headings for such projects with a clear legal basis,[276] but the Council rejected the proposal.[277] The decision of the ECJ in the *Social Funds* case, however, made it necessary to ensure the legality of such funding.

Although the two 'human rights regulations' which were eventually adopted in 1999[278] have now been repealed, it is worth examining their legal base and scope to determine how they differ from the current regulations which now provide the legal basis for such activities.

The original proposal from the Commission for a 'human rights regulation' in the aftermath of the *Social Funds* case was based exclusively on Article 179 TEC. This was clearly inadequate for countries with which the Community has relations outside of the development cooperation context. It was for this reason that the proposed regulation was then split into two, with one regulation relying upon Article 179 TEC

---

[275] See e.g., the report issued by the Commission on the implementation of the Regulation which was published as COM(1998)40. The ALA Regulation as of 1 January 2007 has been repealed by Regulation 1905/2006 Establishing a Financial Instrument for Development Cooperation.

[276] COM(1997)357.

[277] Although the Opinion of the Legal Service of the Council was confidential, J. Weiler and S. Fries, 'A Human Rights Policy for the European Community and Union: the Question of Competences' in Alston, Bustelo and Heenan, *The EU and Human Rights*, p. 147 claim it was widely leaked in the press and led to an agreement where the Council would turn a blind eye to the Commission's practices, if the Commission expunged any official reference to a Community human rights policy relating to any activity in and by the Member States.

[278] Council Regulation 975/1999 Laying Down the Requirements for the Implementation of Development Cooperation Operations which Contribute to the General Objective of Developing and Consolidating Democracy, and the Rule of Law and to that of Respecting Human Rights and Fundamental Freedoms, [1999] OJ L120/1, 8 May 1999 (as amended by Regulations 1882/2003, 2240/2004 and 2110/2005) and Council Regulation 976/1999, Laying Down the Requirements for the Implementation of Community Operations, Other than those of Development Cooperation, which within the Framework of Community Cooperation Policy, Contribute to the General Objective of Developing and Consolidating Democracy, and the Rule of Law and to that of Respecting Human Rights and Fundamental Freedoms in Third Countries, [1999] OJ L120/8, 8 May 1999 (as amended by Regulations 907/2003, 2242/2004 and 2112/2005).

and the other Article 308 TEC. In substantive terms the proposals were identical.[279]

Article 308 TEC, however, unlike Articles 177–179 TEC makes no reference to human rights or other principles such as democracy. The practice of the Community prior to the Maastricht amendments was to use Article 308 TEC to fund all such projects, and the specific competence was derived from Article 2 TEC. Once Article 179 TEC provided a more specific legal base for developing states, Article 308 TEC can only continue to be used in this context in relation to other states. Although the ECJ did not address this issue directly in the *Portugal* case, this approach was upheld in rejecting Portugal's arguments on Article 308 TEC in the Agreement with India. A similar conclusion can be drawn from *Opinion 2/94*.[280] There the ECJ did not, as such, reject the use of Article 308 TEC as a provision granting competence to the Community to undertake or pursue human rights objectives in its external relations. It only rejected the use of Article 308 TEC when it amounted to a de facto circumvention of the procedure for treaty amendment.[281] The use of Article 308 TEC for measures pursuing such objectives in third states, in the absence of constitutional implications, was not questioned. As the ECJ noted in *Opinion 2/94*, Article 308 TEC:

is designed to fill the gap where no specific provisions of the Treaty confer on the Community institutions express or implied powers to act, if such powers appear none the less to be necessary to enable the Community to carry out its functions with a view *to attaining one of the objectives laid down by the Treaty*.[282]

Article 308 TEC must respect limits in its text and scope as defined by the ECJ. The use of Article 308 TEC to pursue ethical values in non-developing third states is not without problems, however, even though it has been extensively used for that purpose. Article 181a TEC, after the Nice amendments, grants competence to the EC to adopt measures (not just Agreements) so there is no need, after it came into force, to rely upon

---

[279] The Commission also presented an earlier amended proposal for the regulation in COM(1999)13. The following discussion, however, is based upon the re-examined proposals for the regulations in COM(1999)206 and COM(1999)207.

[280] *Opinion 2/94* [1996] ECR I-1759.

[281] See further, G. Gaga, 'Opinion 2/94' (1996) 33 *CMLRev.* 973; S. Mathieu, 'L'adhésion de la communauté à la CEDH' (1998) 414 *RMUE* 31 and M. Cremona, 'The EU and the External Dimension of Human Rights Policy' in S. Konstadinidis (ed.), *A People's Europe: Tuning a Concept into Content* (Aldershot: Dartmouth, 1999) p. 155.

[282] *Opinion 2/94*, para. 29. Emphasis added. See also, *Opinion 2/92* [1995] ECR I-521, para. 36.

Article 308 TEC to promote human rights in non-developing states. It had to be relied upon, however, for what became Regulation 976/1999 as there was no other legal base for a regulation concerning the promotion of human rights and democracy in non-developing states at the time.

This raises the long-standing question of whether the protection of human rights is one of the objectives of the Community.[283] The ECJ had the opportunity in *Opinion 2/94* to declare whether the protection of human rights was one of the Community's general objectives, a question of disagreement among the Member States.[284] It avoided addressing it. Before the ECJ five Member States argued that the protection of human rights was not a Community objective and that neither the Community nor Union had specific powers in the field. They relied upon the fact that it was not mentioned in either Articles 2 or 3 TEC. It is clear, however, that the 'activities' listed in Article 3 of the Treaty are not exhaustive. Article 2 TEC sets out the Community's tasks with Article 3 stipulating the activities of the Community which 'shall include' but are not limited to the list in that provision. The task of 'raising . . . the standard of living and quality of life' as found in Article 2 can be seen as having a human rights objective. Furthermore, the Preamble to the Universal Declaration of Human Rights says that the protection of human rights leads to the promotion of social progress and 'better standards of life'. The means may be different but the objectives are ultimately much the same. A number of commentators attach importance to the fact that the ECJ did not declare that the Community does not have a human rights objective.[285]Others have argued that the protection of human rights is a transverse objective.[286]

---

[283] For a detailed analysis see Bartels, *Human Rights Conditionality*, p. 169 *et seq.*

[284] Austria, Belgium, Denmark, Finland, Germany, Greece, Italy, Sweden, the Commission and the European Parliament all considered the protection of human rights to be a Community objective. France, Portugal, Spain, Ireland and the United Kingdom all opposed the idea.

[285] P. Alston and J. Weiler, 'An Ever Closer Union in Need of a Human Rights Policy: the EU and Human Rights' in Alston, Bustelo and Heenan, *The EU and Human Rights*, pp. 3, 24 and A. Arnull, '*Opinion 2/94* and its Implications for the Future Constitution of the Union' in *The Human Rights Opinion of the European Court of Justice and its Constitutional Implications*, CELS Occasional Paper No. 1 (Cambridge: Centre for European Legal Studies, 1996) p. 7.

[286] B. Brandtner and A. Rosas, 'Human Rights and the External Relations of the European Community: an Analysis of Doctrine and Practice' (1998) 9 *EJIL* 468, 472 and the Commission in *Opinion 2/94*, 1773. A number of Member States in their submissions considered the protection of human rights to be a horizontal principle as opposed to an objective.

The objectives in the EC Treaty are expressly supplemented by the Common Provisions of the TEU which apply to all aspects of the Union. Article 6(1) TEU which affirms that the Union is founded on the principles of liberty, democracy and respect for human rights and fundamental freedoms and the rule of law, is relevant here.[287] Article 6(4) TEU further provides that the 'Union shall provide itself with the means necessary to attain its objectives and carry through its policies'. Article 6(4) TEU also makes an appearance in the Protocol on the Application of the Principles of Subsidiarity and Proportionality which was attached to the EC Treaty at Amsterdam. Paragraph 2 of the Protocol specifically notes that reference should be had to Article 6(4) TEU in the application of the principles of subsidiarity and proportionality. This reinforces the argument, if there are still any doubts, that those objectives of the Union which are found in the Common Provisions can be pursued through the Community pillar.[288] If the provisions in both the Community and Union Treaties are considered in conjunction, then Article 308 TEC within the confines of the scope of the EC Treaty can provide a basis to achieve those objectives. Any measures taken on the basis of Article 308 TEC, however, still have to satisfy the link with the functioning of the common market and be necessary.

These criteria have routinely been ignored in the presence of political will for measures to be adopted.[289] Although *Opinion 2/94* was in a different context, no Member State challenged Community competence to accede to the Convention before the ECJ on the basis that it was not connected to the functioning of the common market. Dashwood considers that the ECJ did not address the issue as there obviously is no such link.[290] An alternative view is that there seems to have been a general acceptance that there *was* such a link and the ECJ did not address it for

---

[287] A use of language which draws heavily not only on the ECJ's own jurisprudence but also the Preamble to the Universal Declaration on Human Rights, 1948.

[288] This is made expressly clear in some of the new external relations financial regulations; see e.g., the Preamble to Regulation 1889/2006 Establishing a Financing Instrument for the Promotion of Democracy and Human Rights Worldwide.

[289] For detailed historical analysis on the use of Article 308 TEC, see J. Weiler, 'The Transformation of Europe' (1991) 100 *Yale Law Journal* 2403 and for a more recent perspective, R. Schütze, 'Organized Change Towards an "Ever Closer Union": Article 308 TEC and the Limits to the Community's Legislative Competence' (2003) 22 *YEL* 79. For a detailed recent judicial assessment of the scope of Article 308 TEC, see *Ahmed Ali Yusef and Al Barakat International Foundation* v. *Council and Commission* [2005] ECR II-3533 (at the time of writing on appeal as C-415/05 P), paras. 80–170.

[290] A. Dashwood, 'Commentary' in *The Human Rights Opinion of the European Court of Justice and its Constitutional Implications*, p. 24.

that reason. In the case of the proposed regulation on funding for human rights projects in non-developing third states, Article 308 TEC was used because there was eventual political agreement between the Member States to use it and the criteria for a link with the functioning of the common market and being necessary, in the sense the provision refers to, were set to one side.

In terms of substantive competence, the use of Article 308 TEC as the legal base for what became Regulation 976/1999 on funding for human rights projects in non-developing third states was problematic. In the Preamble to both Regulation 976/1999 and Regulation 975/1999, which provided the basis for funding human rights and democracy-related projects in developing countries, the principle of the indivisibility of rights, as proclaimed in the Vienna Declaration, was seen as a principle that 'underpins the international system for the protection of human rights' and therefore 'constitutes the very foundation of European integration'. Regulation 976/1999 also provided a basis to fund projects aimed at giving effect to many other related principles and concepts. This is questionable as far as non-developing states were concerned. Article 6 TEU refers to the respect of 'fundamental rights, as guaranteed by the European Convention ... on Human Rights ... and as they result from the constitutional traditions common to the Member States, as general principles of Community law'. This is significantly narrower than the ambit that was encompassed by Regulation 976/1999. Article 11 TEU does refer more generally to the development and consolidation of 'democracy and the rule of law, and respect for human rights and fundamental freedoms' but is limited to the CFSP and is not one of the Common Provisions. Regulation 975/1999, which used Article 179 TEC as a legal base, was less susceptible to criticism on this basis.

After the Nice amendments Article 181a TEC is a more appropriate legal basis than Article 308 TEC and the latter is no longer one of the provisions that is relied upon in the relevant new external relations regulations concerned with promoting human rights. The six new regulations that have come into force have replaced over a hundred different instruments[291] such as the ALA Regulation[292] but not others such as the GSP or Humanitarian Aid Regulations. The new regulations have

---

[291] COM(2004)101final/2, p. 33.

[292] Regulation 443/1997 on Operations to Aid Uprooted People in Asian and Latin American Developing Countries, [1997] OJ L68/1, 8 March 1997.

attempted to consolidate the legal instruments which can be used and to make the planning and delivery of assistance more coherent and effective. Each regulation also has a financial envelope attached to it so as to provide adequate funding. The regulations do, however, differ in a number of respects.

Regulation 1905/2006 which establishes a financing instrument for development cooperation (the Development Cooperation Instrument) relies solely upon Article 179(1) TEC. As a measure designed to replace most of the Community's existing extra-EU regional development cooperation instruments the sole legal base is to be expected. It is complemented by Regulation 1934/2006 which establishes a financing instrument for cooperation with industrialised and other high-income countries and territories. The legal basis for Regulation 1934/2006 is, as to be expected, Article 181a TEC.

The initial Commission proposal was for one instrument which would have not only replaced the two 1999 human rights regulations but also the various development cooperation instruments, as well as covering economic cooperation with developed states.[293] The proposal was strongly opposed in the European Parliament and the legislative process for the instruments which eventually transpired has been described as 'tortuous, convoluted and at time fraught with difficulties'.[294] The insistence (and ultimate success) of the European Parliament's Development Committee in having a specific instrument for development cooperation has ensured that there are clearly defined objectives for relations with developing states, whereas in the original proposal there was very little clarity in the identification of priorities. The Commission was essentially trying to ride too many horses at the same time. The consequence of the instruments being separated out, however, has been that trade and economic issues are the primary focus of what has become Regulation 1934/2006 (which deals with cooperation with industrialised and other high-income countries) and the role of ethical values in relationships with these states based upon the

---

[293] See COM(2004)629. Pre-accession states (it was proposed that a new instrument would replace, *inter alia*, the PHARE and TACIS programmes) and states covered by the then proposed European Neighbourhood Policy Instrument (ENPI) would not have been covered by the original Commission proposal.

[294] European Parliament Committee on Development, *Recommendation for Second Reading on the Council Common Position for Adopting a Regulation of the European Parliament and of the Council Establishing a Financing Instrument for Development Cooperation*, FINAL A6-0448/ 2006, p. 6.

regulation will be almost non-existent. While this is a recognition of the reality of the respective bargaining parity of the EC and the other high-income states, it is unfortunate as it again (and justifiably so) exposes the Community to accusations of double standards in its differing treatment of developing and developed states.

This inconsistency is not rectified by the new European Instrument for Democracy and Human Rights (EIDHR), which is now Regulation 1889/2006. Although it extends to all states, the regulation is clear that it is developing states that will receive most of the assistance. The Preamble makes it clear, for example, that the regulation aims to contribute to the aims of the MDGs and the European Consensus on Development. The EIDHR is, however, complementary to the other new external relations regulations. The EIDHR has a financial envelope which amounts to just over €1 billion for the period between 2007 and 2013. This envelope is to be used to supplement the financial envelopes to the other regulations, some of which also provide competence to the Community to fund projects which seek to promote and protect, *inter alia*, democracy, the rule of law and human rights.

Whereas Regulation 1905/2006 (the 'Development Cooperation Instrument') has a very strong emphasis on the promotion of democracy, human rights, good governance and the rule of law in developing countries, there is a very notable absence of such issues in Regulation 1934/2006, which establishes a financing instrument for cooperation with industrialised and other high-income countries and territories. Although Regulation 1934/2006 refers to the fact that the European Union is founded upon the principles of liberty, democracy, human rights and the rule of law and will seek to promote commitment to these principles in partner countries,[295] the promotion of these principles is not expressly considered to be an area of cooperation under Article 4 of the regulation. As the regulation is designed to cover cooperation with, among others, Bahrain, Brunei, Chinese Taipei, Kuwait, Oman, Qatar, Saudi Arabia, Singapore, the UAE and the United States,[296] not all of which are paragons of democracy, good governance or the rule of law, the absence of cooperation on such issues on the basis of the regulation is noteworthy. The fact that no suspension mechanism exists either under Regulation 1934/2006, as it does under a number of the others, notably Article 37 of Regulation 1905/2006 which deals with developing countries, further affirms that principles and values such as

---

[295] Article 3(1) Regulation 1934/2006.   [296] See the Annex to Regulation 1934/2006.

human rights and good governance are not high on the Community's list of priorities in relations with these states and territories.

Regulation 1889/2006 (the EIDHR) which establishes a financing instrument for the promotion of democracy and human rights worldwide, however, as noted above, gives the Community scope to promote ethical values in all states, including developed ones. Regulation 1889/2006 replaces the two previous human rights regulations, Regulations 975/1999 and 976/1999, and utilises a dual legal basis of Articles 179(1) and 181a(2) TEC, as is to be expected.

The EIDHR, the Development Cooperation Instrument and the regulation establishing a financing instrument for high-income countries are accompanied by three further regulations. The Instrument for Pre-Accession Assistance (IPA), the Instrument for Stability (the 'Stability Instrument') and the European Neighbourhood Policy Instrument (ENPI) are all also in part concerned with the promotion of ethical values. The IPA solely utilises Article 181(a) TEC as a legal base, whereas the Stability Instrument and ENPI also use Article 179 TEC.[297] The Stability Instrument is more tangentially related to the promotion of values and principles than the IPA and ENPI as its aim is in part to stop states sliding into conflict or to assist with the transition from conflict back to normality.[298]

Neither of these six new regulations, nor those that they have replaced, however, defines what is meant by terms such as human rights, the rule of law, good governance or democracy.[299] But this is not unexpected, as it enables flexibility in funding. It is also notable that in the new regulations it is made clear that there is, for example, no one model of democracy which the Community wishes to support.[300] This is in part a further recognition of democracy as a process which will differ according to the constitutional and historical environment of a state. Additionally, the regulations do not provide an exhaustive list of

---

[297] The original Commission proposal was based upon Article 308 TEC and Article 203 EURATOM. See COM(2004)630.

[298] It is discussed further below and in Chapter 6.

[299] This lack of clarity is a common feature of all Community documents which address issues such as human rights and democracy, although there are separate Communications which further discuss issues such as good governance in the development context. See, e.g., COM(2003)615 and COM(2006)421.

[300] See e.g., the Preamble to Regulation 1889/2006 Establishing a Financing Instrument for the Promotion of Democracy and Human Rights Worldwide.

those operations for which the Community shall provide technical and financial aid.

All of the regulations provide a very long and expansive list of the types of 'human rights projects' which can be funded. Article 2 of the EIDHR, which establishes the scope of the instrument, casts its net even wider than Article 2 of Regulation 975/1999 which it in part replaced. For example, projects which aim to strengthen the rule of law; promote the independence of the judiciary; promote pluralism; promote equal participation of men and women; facilitate the peaceful conciliation of group interests; support human rights defenders; help in the fight against racism; support indigenous people; support civil society; and promote and strengthen ad hoc international criminal tribunals and truth and reconciliation mechanisms, can all be funded. Essentially, Article 2 of the EIDHR is so widely defined that it is difficult to think of projects which would not in some way or other be related to human rights, democracy, good governance or the rule of law and thus be outside the scope of initiatives that can be funded under it. Numerous Commission reports and the Council's *EU Annual Report on Human Rights* illustrate the sheer breadth of projects funded and their geographic scope under the original EIDHR and the subsequent 1999 regulations.[301] The scope of funded projects is unlikely to be any narrower under the current scheme.[302] This is not to say, however, as discussed above, that the funding of projects has gone unchallenged where they are deemed to be pursuing non-development-based objectives and come within the scope of the CFSP.

3.3.1.2(c)(ii) Funding and Promoting Democracy   In its activities in promoting and protecting certain values in its relations with third states, the Union has placed very considerable emphasis on the promotion of democracy. A link is seen to exist between development, human rights and democracy. Human rights are necessary for the full development of the individual, whereas democracy is a necessary condition for the exercise of

---

[301]   See e.g., COM(1994)42, COM(1995)191, COM(1996)672, COM(2000)726, SEC (2004) 1041, the *EIDHR Compendiums* available at http://ec.europa.eu/europeaid/projects/eidhr/documents_en.htm and the *EU Annual Report on Human Rights* for the period between 1998 and 2006.

[302]   This is confirmed by COM(2006)23 which sets out the thematic programme for the promotion of democracy and human rights worldwide under the future financial perspective.

those rights.[303] This approach is expressed in the Resolution on Human Rights, Democracy and Development, 1991.[304] It is similar to that in the Declaration on the Right to Development, 1986, which recognises man as the main beneficiary of the right to development, as opposed to the text of the EC Treaty which is more concerned with the integration of developing economies into the world economy.[305] The earlier Luxembourg European Council Resolution on Human Rights had stated that respect for human rights and democracy was part of the economic development process and without it economic growth would not occur.[306] The concept of development has thus metamorphosised from one concerned with the economic development of states, as stated in Article 177 TEC, to one that primarily promotes human rights and democracy.

The Court of Auditors has argued, however, that the Community's purpose in combining democracy, development and human rights, was to promote them as a political good which would improve the lives of citizens by bringing more freedom, political representation and account-ability.[307] In this respect, combining the concepts is an essential part of the process of furthering sustainable social and economic development. It should create economic wealth which will eventually benefit all.[308]

Supporting democracy in third states can take a number of different forms. One of the Union's primary practical contributions to democ-racy, following the 1991 Resolution, is through the sponsoring and observation of elections in developing or transitional countries. Election observation as an activity is relatively cheap,[309] it is only for a limited period of time[310] and requires only a limited number of

---

[303] See e.g., COM(1995)567, the Preamble to Regulation 1889/2006, the multitude of references in the European Consensus on Development and the discussion in Chapter 2.
[304] See at para. 3.
[305] Declaration on the Right to Development, GA Resolution 41/128, GAOR, 41st Session Supp. 53, p. 186.
[306] See the discussion above.   [307] Court of Auditors, *Special Report 12/2000*, p. 3.
[308] See further T. King, 'Human Rights in the Development Policy of the European Community: Towards a European World Order?' (1997) *NYBIL* 51, 61 *et seq.* and B. Simma, J. Aschenbrenner and C. Schultze, 'Human Rights Considerations in the Development Cooperation Activities of the EC' in Alston, Bustelo and Heenan, *The EU and Human Rights*, p. 571.
[309] The election observation budget was approximately €13 million per year between 2000 and 2004 when on average there were nine observation missions per year. In 2005 and 2006 there were thirteen missions and the budget was increased to €27 million, MEMO/06/107.
[310] On average each mission is in the host state for a six-week period. See COM(2001)191.

observers.[311] The holding of elections and their monitoring is also likely to obtain some media coverage. Election observation, therefore, provides an opportunity to display to the international community a commitment to democracy and reform.[312]

The Union has extensively developed its involvement in the observation of multiparty parliamentary elections from the early 1990s. Since then it has observed and assisted in numerous elections, including those held in South Africa, the West Bank and Gaza, Sierra Leone, Ecuador, Kenya, Madagascar, Mozambique, Malawi, Indonesia, Nigeria, Pakistan, Zambia, Fiji, Haiti, Zimbabwe and Togo, to name but a few.[313] The basis for the expenditure incurred has at times been unsystematic and dependent on whether it is the Community that has engaged in election assistance or the Union that engaged in election observation under the second pillar.[314] Competence for the Community has been derived from Articles 179, 308 or 310 TEC, depending upon the region in question. In the context of the ACP states, the Lomé/Cotonou Conventions have also been used as a legal basis. With regard to other countries the specific basis for election assistance has sometimes been the partnership or cooperation Agreement with the country in question or the regulation in force at the time, for example the ALA Regulation,[315] governing relations between the Community and country in which elections were

---

[311] The number of observers differs substantially between each mission. For the Presidential elections in Zimbabwe in 2002 there were a total of 198 observers, yet for the Presidential elections in Afghanistan in 2004 there were only 25. For further details on the election observer missions see http://ec.europa.eu/comm/external_relations/human_rights/eu_election_ass_observ/archive.htm

[312] Although paradoxically the Member States and European Parliament have in the past criticised the Union's lack of visibility in monitoring elections, see COM(2000) 191, p. 9.

[313] In the period between 1992 and 1994, for example, the Community provided such assistance to forty-one countries. See COM(1995)567. See further COM(2000)191 on election observation and SEC(2003)1472 which is the report on the implementation of COM(2000)191. See also, the section in the Council's *Annual Report on Human Rights* for a summary of the previous year's EU election observation activities. The Union has tended in recent years not to send separate election observers where the Organisation for Security and Cooperation in Europe (OSCE) is fully involved.

[314] Article 6(1) TEU and Article 11 TEU, although it has all been referred to as Union activity. See e.g., with regard to South Africa, where Decision 93/678/CFSP, [1993] OJ L316/45, 17 December 1993 established the principle for the Union's support in the election process but where the funding came from Community Budget Line B7-5070. COM(2000)191 was in part an attempt to systematise the Community's election observation and to move away from *ad hoc* interventions and since 2000 all EU Election Observer Missions have been funded by the EIDHR Budget Line. See SEC(2003)1472, p. 9.

[315] Article 5 ALA Regulation.

taking place. The Community's support for the election process has also been funded from the electoral processes budget heads.[316]

Electoral assistance as a form of aid has been considered to be within the Community pillar, whereas election observation has been funded either through the first or second pillar, or both.[317] The primary reason for this approach was to ensure the adequacy of funding. The 2000 Communication on election observation noted that whereas second pillar Joint Actions have been used to observe elections, funds had never been sufficient to cover all of the expenses of EU involvement and have, therefore, been combined with complementary Community action.[318] The strategy between 2000 and 2006 has been for all observations and assistance to be based upon the competence granted by paragraph (f) of Article 2.2 of Regulation 975/99 and Article 3.2 of Regulation 976/99, respectively.[319] Article 2(1)(a) of Regulation 1889/ 2006 (the current EIDHR) has provided the requisite competence since January 2007.

Election assistance, which is complementary to election observation, is an effort to improve the electoral process prior to the election itself. It can involve a variety of different interventions, such as capacity building for election management bodies, assisting with voter registration or voter education.[320] For any assistance rendered to be meaningful there must be enough time for it to have an impact prior to the election itself. Community election assistance is usually preceded by a request from the host state and the Community will still only assist if the state is willing to invest in the process itself.[321]

Generally speaking, the Community has committed its energies to election observation as opposed to election assistance. By and large the Community has deployed election observation missions (known as an EU EOM) for national elections, but has at times (for example, Pakistan in 2002) sent observers for local elections as well. This is only the case where it is considered that such events are of significant political importance in the democratisation process.[322]

Each EU EOM publishes a detailed report at the end of its mission outlining its findings. Almost all national elections anywhere in the world are commented upon by the Presidency, usually in a statement. The Presidency also almost always issues a statement on an election

---

[316] COM(2000)191, p. 11.   [317] Ibid.   [318] Ibid. p. 14.   [319] Ibid. p. 11.
[320] For examples of EU election assistance see SEC(2003)1472, p. 13 et seq.
[321] Ibid.   [322] Ibid. p. 4.

once an EU EOM issues its preliminary statement and upon publication of the final report. On more than one occasion, there has been a very noticeable difference of emphasis between the approaches of the Presidency and the EU EOM. For example, in the aftermath of the 2002 elections in Pakistan, the EU EOM was very critical of the blatant vote-rigging. The Council, however, welcomed the elections as a welcome step towards democratisation in Pakistan. This was at a time when Pakistan (and in particular Pervez Musharraf) had, after being an international pariah, been rehabilitated and was seen by, among others, the EU Member States as a key ally in the 'war on terror'.[323] It should be borne in mind, however, that the EU EOMs are independent of the Council, the Member States, Commission and the European Parliament. The commitment of all EU EOMs to independence and impartiality has been reinforced since the adoption of the Declaration of Principles for International Election Observation and the Code of Conduct for International Election Observers, 2005, of which the European Commission is an endorsing organisation.[324]

While supporting the electoral process displays the Community's commitment to reform and democratic rule, it is not the end of its involvement. In transitional countries, in particular, democratic institutions need to be consolidated and supported. A democratically elected government may, for example, dismantle institutions or remove obstacles which limit its exercise of power.[325] In fact, studies have shown that although aid can contribute to democratisation in several ways, such as through the type of technical assistance to the electoral processes that the Community routinely provides, there is no evidence that aid actually promotes democracy. While there has been a process of democratisation in the past thirty years or so across the globe, studies argue that little if any of that change is attributable to foreign aid.[326] The 2000 Communication on election observation accepts the limitations of electoral assistance, for example, when it notes that the ultimate aim of such assistance is that such activities should 'become superfluous by

---

[323] See further the detailed discussion in Chapter 4.

[324] The declaration and code were 'commemorated' on 27 October 2005, at the United Nations in New York.

[325] For discussion in the context of Pakistan, see Z. Maluka, *The Myth of Constitutionalism* (Karachi: Oxford University Press, 1996) and the discussion in Chapter 4.

[326] See S. Knack, 'Does Foreign Aid Promote Democracy?' (2004) 48 *International Studies Quarterly* 251, 262.

entrenching democracy deep within each nation through the deployment of national capacities'.[327]

The Community also recognises that democracy is a dynamic process by which citizens are able to get involved in the decision-making processes that affect their lives. The 2005 *EU Annual Report on Human Rights* gives a clear indication of the characteristics the Union considers democratic societies should possess. It notes that:

[t]here is no single model of democracy, but genuine democracies have common features in line with international standards that include: control over government decisions about policy constitutionally vested in elected representatives, who are chosen in regular and fair elections; all adult citizens have the right to vote and to run for public office; people have the right to express themselves on political issues without the risk of punishment, and have the right to seek information from a diversity of sources; people have the right to form independent associations and organisations, including political parties, and to disseminate their opinions; government is autonomous and does not face overriding opposition from groups like un-elected officials or the military or international blocs.[328]

Simply assisting with elections or observing them is thus not enough to support or consolidate democracy. It is for this reason that the Community has also undertaken measures to support pluralism, civil society, good governance and the rule of law, all of which it is assumed will assist in entrenching democratic values in a state.

3.3.1.2(c)(iii) Good Governance, the Rule of Law and Civil Society   In its 1991 Resolution on Human Rights and Democracy the Council stressed the importance of good governance and the rule of law. While recognising that sovereign states have the right to institute their own administrative structures and establish their own constitutional arrangements, the Council stressed that equitable development could only be achieved effectively and sustainably if a number of general principles were followed. Those are: sensible economic and social policies; adequate government transparency and financial accountability; creation of a market-friendly environment; democratic decision-making; measures to combat corruption; as well as respect for the rule of law, human rights and freedom of the press and expression. The Community and the Member States

---

[327] COM(2000)191, p. 5.
[328] European Council, *EU Annual Report on Human Rights 2005*, p. 61.

considered that these principles would be central in both existing and new relationships with other states.

The rule of law and good governance are now considered to be areas of common interest, fundamental to the dialogue between the parties and central to the achievement of development goals.[329] The OECD and the World Bank adopt a similar approach.[330] The Community has recently provided some guidance as to what it means by the rule of law and good governance.[331] While there is substantial overlap with the approaches adopted by the World Bank and the OECD, they are not identical.[332] For the Community, the rule of law entails the effective implementation of legal rules; the separation of powers; institutional arrangements for participation in decision-making at all levels; political and institutional pluralism and transparency; and the integrity of institutions. Furthermore, the legislature and an independent judiciary must respect and give effect to human rights and fundamental freedoms and there must be equality before the law.[333]

With regard to good governance the following are perceived as being vital: equity and the primacy of the law in the management and allocation of resources; the institutional capacity to manage resources effectively in the interests of economic and social development; accountability and measures aimed at preventing and combating corruption; and public participation in the decision-making process.[334] In its 2003 Communication on governance, the Commission stated,

---

[329] COM(1998)146, p. 2 and COM(2003)615, p. 3.

[330] See e.g., OECD, *Final Report of the Ad Hoc Working Group on Participatory Development and Good Governance* (Paris: OECD, 1997) *passim* and World Bank, *World Development Report* (Washington DC: World Bank, 1997) p. 4 *et seq*. See further, J. Faundez (ed.), *Good Government and Law: Legal and Institutional Reform in Developing Countries* (London: Macmillan, 1997) and K. Ginther, E. Denters and P. de Waart (eds.), *Sustainable Development and Good Governance* (The Hague: Kluwer, 1995) p. 20 for more on good governance in this context.

[331] See COM(2003)615 and COM(2006)421.

[332] In part, because there are no internationally agreed definitions. See further, J. Court, G. Hyden and K. Mease, *Making Sense of Governance: Empirical Evidence from Sixteen Transitional Societies* (London: Lynne Reinner, 2004) who identify six key arenas for governance: civil society, political society, government, bureaucracy, economic society and the judiciary. The UN Commission on Human Rights in Resolution 2000/64 (E/CN.4/RES/2000/64, 2 April 2000) entitled 'The Role of Good Governance in the Promotion of Human Rights', identified five governance principles: transparency, responsibility, accountability, participation and responsiveness.

[333] See COM(1998)146, p. 6.

[334] *Ibid*.; COM(2003)615, p. 3; Article 9(3) of the Cotonou Convention and also the 'good governance incentive scheme' under the GSP Regulation, as discussed below.

'governance refers to the rules, processes, and behaviour by which interests are articulated, resources are managed, and power is exercised'.[335] The Commission has thus increasingly become more holistic in its theoretical approach, as opposed to simply concentrating on technocratic issues.[336]

The overlap between the rule of law and good governance can be seen from the 2005 European Consensus on Development. It notes that 'good governance requires a pragmatic approach based on the specific context of each country. The Community will actively promote a participatory in-country dialogue on governance, in areas such as anti-corruption, public sector reform, access to justice and reform of the judicial system.'[337] Both principles, in particular good governance, to the extent that they are defined are referred to in a fluid manner and it is questionable to what extent the definitions provided are meaningful.

It is certainly noteworthy that both good governance and the rule of law have been increasingly prioritised and mainstreamed at the policy level. The advantage in stressing good governance and the rule of law in relations with third states is that these principles are more pragmatic than, and not as culturally loaded as, human rights.[338] Both principles must be introduced or improved by states which are recipients of Community aid. What is apparent, however, is that the Community is demanding relatively high standards from third states, especially developing countries. For example, for the rule of law (as defined) to be implemented in a society where in the past it has not been respected requires a fundamental redistribution of power – which is exceptionally difficult to achieve or impose.

The Union's 'rule of law' missions in Georgia, Iraq and Kosovo highlight perfectly that such undertakings require consistent and concerted efforts and substantial funds to make a notable contribution.[339] The Iraq mission, for example, was allocated €10 million for a fifteen-month

---

[335] COM(2003)615, p. 3.
[336] This refers to good governance in the sense of the Community wishing to fund projects. Under the GSP scheme, the Community does take a very narrow approach but in this instance it is limited by the absence of relevant international conventions. See the discussion below.
[337] European Consensus on Development, para. 86.   [338] COM(2003)615, p. 3.
[339] Council Joint Action 2004/523/CFSP on the European Rule of Law Mission in Georgia, EUJUST THEMIS, [2004] OJ L228/21, 29 June 2004; Council Joint Action 2005/190/CFSP on the European Union Integrated Rule of Law Mission for Iraq, EUJUST LEX, [2005] OJ L62/37, 9 March 2005; and Council Joint Action 2006/304/CFSP on the Establishment of an EU Planning Team (EUPT Kosovo) regarding a Possible EU Crisis Management

period.[340] The figure for Kosovo is just under €14 million for a fourteen-month period.[341] If one considers that the entire EIDHR budget line on average amounts to just over €100 million per year, then this gives an indication of the financial commitments required. In each of these cross-pillar initiatives there is a Community dimension and the Commission has agreed to work toward the objectives of the Joint Actions by adapting or using relevant Community instruments.[342]

Although the Community, along with the World Bank and the OECD, argues that good governance and the rule of law are indispensable to development, it is not clear to what extent it has considered the appropriateness of their application in practice. In April 2000 the now defunct Commission on Human Rights of the United Nations adopted a resolution entitled The Role of Good Governance in the Promotion of Human Rights,[343] where it noted that good governance necessarily varies according to the particular circumstances and needs of different states. The Resolution further noted that the responsibility for determining and implementing such practices, based on transparency and accountability and which aim to create and maintain an environment conducive to the protection and promotion of human rights, rests with the state concerned. As has been noted on a number of occasions throughout this chapter, the Community refers to the principles of ownership, partnership and pragmatism in its development projects and also recognises in policy documents that good governance is country specific. The Community's rhetoric and its practice, however, do not always coincide. Togo, Kenya, and Cote d'Ivoire, for example, have had aid suspended or delayed over accusations of corruption but this seems to have been more to do with the misappropriation of donor funds than shortcomings in good governance in general.[344] The real concern, however, lies not in the unwillingness or inability of third states to

---

Operation in the Field of Rule of Law and Possible Other Areas in Kosovo, [2006] OJ L112/19, 26 April 2006.

[340] Article 11 of Joint Action 2005/190/CFSP.

[341] See Article 4 of Joint Action 2006/918/CFSP amending and extending Joint Action 2006/304/CFSP on the Establishment of an EU Planning Team (EUPT Kosovo) regarding a Possible EU Crisis Management Operation in the Field of Rule of Law and Possible Other Areas in Kosovo, [2006] OJ L349/57, 12 December 2006.

[342] E.g., Article 11 of Joint Action 2004/523/CFSP and Article 12 of Joint Action 2005/190/CFSP.

[343] RES/2000/64, 2 April 2000.

[344] See House of Lords, EU Development Aid in Transition, p. 74.

adopt and implement appropriate policies, but in the scope of the Community's ambition.

Good governance is difficult to achieve and, in practice, projects dealing with public procurement and tackling corruption have historically attracted the most funding from the Community.[345] Recent evaluations of Community practice, however, indicate that a large share of governance funding is increasingly dedicated to capacity building.[346] This is part of the more holistic approach mentioned above. The problem with such a broad approach, however, is that the sheer scope of the governance agenda becomes so wide that, much like poverty, almost all projects can be seen as governance related. It also means that there will be a differing emphasis on the various aspects of the governance agenda depending upon the Directorate-General of the Commission and the country delegations involved. As a consequence, it becomes very difficult to determine how effective or not, as the case may be, the Community's interventions are and if indeed any improvements in a state in this respect can be attributed to Community support. As a 2006 evaluation on governance notes, 'governance as a key political priority has not yet been properly "digested" and internalized by the EC ... There is still substantial confusion on what governance really means and how best to support it.'[347]

The Community's initiative to promote its objectives through funding is not only ambitious but also stretches the Community's budget lines over a vast geographic region and a vast area of reforms, so that it is not able to give effective support to a reform process that it may have instigated. Reports on the funding of external relations projects illustrate the great diversity of Community assisted projects concerned with good governance, civil society and the rule of law.[348] The striking breadth of projects which the Community has funded has obviously contributed to the fact that the Community's project portfolio has been spread far too thinly over different areas, resulting in the dilution of their impact. The Court of Auditors, for example, has noted that the Commission in funding projects has rarely addressed their continuity. Valuable and worthy projects which have not been able to attract

---

[345] Ibid. p. 67.
[346] Particip, *Thematic Evaluation of the EC Support to Good Governance, Final Report* (Synthesis Report, June 2006) vol. I, p. 3.
[347] Ibid.
[348] See COM(1994)42, COM(1995)191, COM(1996)672, COM(2000)726, the *EIDHR Compendiums* and the *EU Annual Report on Human Rights* for the period 2000–2006.

funding other than from the Commission have stopped functioning when Community funding has dried up.[349] Even though Country Strategy Papers exist, the lack of long-term strategic planning by the Community, which includes continuity of funding, has consequently ensured that the Community has had a limited impact when it could have achieved significantly more.

The funds committed by the Community would have had a far greater impact if they were part of a coherent overall strategy which assessed needs and aimed to address particular issues identified as needing support within the context of policy towards a third state. Such an approach would not only focus the Community's effort but would also lead to more tangible benefits for the citizens and the state in question. While this may be laborious and difficult to undertake, it would provide real benefits. It is true, however, that such efforts can usually only tinker with the edges. This is especially true in Asian and Latin American states, where the ratio is most stark between the size of the populations and the amount of funding from the Community.

3.3.2 Humanitarian Aid and Food Aid

3.3.2.1 Community Competence in Humanitarian Aid

The Community has, like most other donors, considered humanitarian aid within the development cooperation context. The Union and Community Treaties still do not establish a humanitarian aid policy. Historically, practice was conducted on an *ad hoc* basis using a variety of legal bases. The Yaoundé/Lomé Conventions, for example, contained provisions which allowed the Community and the Member States to provide emergency assistance to ACP states, funded out of the EDF, the general budget, or both. In non-ACP states the Community either relied upon a provision in a framework regulation or, where there was none, funds were allocated on the basis afforded by the general budget procedure.[350] Prior to the TEU, Article 308 TEC was used for such action with the addition of Article 37 TEC where food aid was involved.

The European Community Humanitarian Office (now DG ECHO) was eventually set up in 1992, partly in response to the humanitarian crises resulting from the conflict in the Balkans and Persian Gulf in the early

---

[349] Court of Auditors, *Special Report 12/2000*, paras. 33 and 47.
[350] See, for examples, DG ECHO, *Annual Report on Humanitarian Aid 1993*, p. 10.

1990s.[351] The aspiration for the Union to become an international actor arose when the end of the Cold War left a power vacuum.[352] Humanitarian aid was perceived to be one means towards that end. The creation of what is now DG ECHO streamlined the procedural aspects of the Community's activities in this field. It brought within its scope activities carried out by several services within the Commission structure, such as humanitarian aid, emergency food aid, and prevention and disaster preparation activities. It did nothing, though, to clarify the scope of the Community's competence in this field.[353]

Eventually a 1995 Communication,[354] which became the 1996 Council Regulation on Humanitarian Aid,[355] attempted to establish objectives and to set out the general criteria for the humanitarian aid provided by the Community. It also addressed the issue of competence and the scope of activity. The legal base for the regulation is Article 179 TEC, but it has been used for a global humanitarian aid policy. The logic behind splitting the proposal for what became the 1999 regulations on human rights and democracy into two, as explained above, was because development cooperation provisions can only lawfully extend to developing countries. Article 308 TEC had to be used for non-developing countries in what became Regulation 976/1999, even though, as noted above, this was not unproblematic. The Humanitarian Aid Regulation, however, is careful not to limit its application to developing countries. Article 1 states:

[t]he Community's humanitarian aid shall comprise assistance ... to help people in third countries, particularly the most vulnerable among them, and as a priority those in developing countries, victims of natural disasters, man-made crises ... or exceptional situations or circumstances.

Assistance can thus be provided to any third country. It is not clear that assistance to those in developing countries must be due to a humanitarian incident – it must simply aim to alleviate suffering of the most

[351] The European Community Humanitarian Office (ECHO) is now officially a Directorate-General in the Commission and known as DG ECHO.

[352] M. Holland, *The European Union and the Third World* (Basingstoke: Palgrave, 2002) p. 100.

[353] Mandate from the Commission to ECHO, 6 November 1999. See also, *Annual Report on Humanitarian Aid 1993*, p. 2 where ECHO's *raison d'être* is explained and Court of Auditors, *Special Report 2/1997: Concerning Humanitarian Aid from the European Union between 1992 and 1995*, [1997] OJ C143/1, 12 May 1997 which deals with the background to the administrative shake-up.

[354] COM(1995)201.

[355] Council Regulation 1257/96 concerning Humanitarian Aid, [1996] OJ L163/1, 2 July 1996.

vulnerable in such countries. A distinction between developing and non-developing countries can be seen to lie within the regulation. Assistance can be provided to a developing country, regardless of an emergency, to alleviate suffering, but to non-developing countries only if an emergency situation of some sort exists. In practice, however, it does not seem that this distinction is in any way observed. The Commission has considered that Article 179 TEC is a perfectly adequate legal base for the Community's activities in this field.[356] The Humanitarian Aid Regulation has not been repealed or amended as part of the wholesale consolidation of the Community's external relations regulations which took effect at the start of 2007.[357]

The objectives and general principles of humanitarian aid in the regulation are broad in nature and provide the Community with competence beyond what can be strictly considered to be of a humanitarian nature. The principal objectives in the regulation are: to save and preserve life during emergencies and their immediate aftermath; to provide the necessary assistance and relief to people affected by longer lasting crises; and to take steps to carry out short-term rehabilitation and reconstruction work with a view to facilitating the arrival of aid.[358] The regulation also grants powers for operations to prepare for or prevent disasters or comparable emergencies.[359] With regard to its preparatory work, the Community's humanitarian activities merge into development cooperation.

The demarcation between development, rehabilitation and humanitarian aid has historically been further muddied by two more regulations – the Regulation on Operations to Aid Uprooted People in Asian and Latin American Developing Countries and the Regulation on Rehabilitation and Reconstruction of Operations in Developing Countries.[360] Although these regulations are no longer in force, having

---

[356] See COM(1999)468.
[357] Regulation 1257/96 has been amended by Regulation 1992/2003, [2003] OJ L284/1, 31 October 2003 (this not a substantive amendment).
[358] Article 2 Regulation 1257/96.   [359] *Ibid.* Article 1.
[360] The original measure was Regulation 443/1997 on Operations to Aid Uprooted People in Asian and Latin American Developing Countries, [1997] OJ L68/1, 8 March 1997. It was replaced in 2001 by Regulation 2130/2001 on Operations to Aid Uprooted People in Asian and Latin American Developing Countries, [2001] OJ L287/3, 31 October 2001 which was extended by Regulation 107/2005, [2005] OJ L23/1, 26 January 2005 to apply until 31 December 2006. Council Regulation 2258/96 on Rehabilitation and Reconstruction Operations in Developing Countries, [1996] OJ L306/1, 28 November 1996.

been replaced by the Stability Instrument which came into force on 1 January 2007,[361] they are worth discussing briefly so as to assess Community practice and competence until the end of 2006. The discussion will then move on to competence in this field under the Stability Instrument.

The Regulation on Rehabilitation and Reconstruction of Operations in Developing Countries stemmed directly from the 1996 Communication entitled 'Linking Relief Rehabilitation and Development' (LRRD).[362] The practice of linking such aid was widespread prior to the 1996 LRRD Regulation coming into force.[363] This regulation, which was based upon Article 179 TEC, provided the Community with an express competence to fund projects which overlap with both emergency humanitarian assistance as well as infrastructure projects, which would normally come within the ambit of development cooperation. Projects designed to help re-establish a working economy, and the institutional capacity needed to restore social and political stability, could all be funded.[364] The distinction between the scope of the 1996 LRRD Regulation and that concerned with humanitarian aid was that the former was clearly limited to developing countries.

Operations under the LRRD Regulation were seen as forming part of a continuum between humanitarian action and development aid. These operations permitted refugees and other internally displaced persons to return home and assisted the population to resume normal civilian life.[365] Such operations were not to be implemented by DG ECHO, however, but by the Commission.[366] The adoption of these different measures led to a situation where some forms of rehabilitation assistance to non-developing countries were based upon the Humanitarian Aid Regulation and implemented by DG ECHO, but the Commission (through EuropeAid)[367] was responsible for the implementation of rehabilitation aid in developing countries. DG ECHO, however, usually had a

---

[361] Regulation 1717/2006, the Stability Instrument.   [362] COM(1996)153.

[363] See e.g., Articles 255 and 257 Lomé IV. See also, COM(1993)204 and Court of Auditors, *Special Report 4/2000: On Rehabilitation Action for ACP Countries as an Instrument to Prepare for Normal Development Aid*, [2000] OJ C113/1, 19 April 2000, p. 3.

[364] See Article 1 Council Regulation 2258/96.   [365] *Ibid*. See further below.

[366] See Article 7 Council Regulation 2258/96.

[367] EuropeAid was established in 2001 with the aim of creating a single department to coordinate non-humanitarian aid destined for all third countries. Some aid agencies initially had reservations about its effectiveness but the general consensus now is that it has substantially helped to improve the quality and delivery of aid. As noted above, EuropeAid is part of the portfolio of the Commissioner for External Relations not the

far clearer idea of where such funding was most needed and the necessary coordination was often lacking.

The distinction between humanitarian and rehabilitation aid was
further muddied by the aforementioned Regulation on Operations to
Aid Uprooted People in Asian and Latin American Developing
Countries. This assistance was distinct from that under Article 1 of the
LRRD Regulation which also covered such persons. The purpose of a
separate regulation was to provide support and assistance for uprooted
persons who were not covered by the Humanitarian or LRRD
Regulations and was thus distinguishable from them both. Whereas
rehabilitation under the LRRD Regulation would provide for assistance
to such persons it did not lawfully permit the extent of funding provided by the Uprooted Persons Regulation.

The Stability Instrument, which from January 2007 has replaced these
regulations along with a raft of others, provides exceptionally broad
powers to the Community to assist both developing and developed
states outside the scope of what is strictly speaking emergency aid.[368]
The Stability Instrument, which utilises both Articles 179 and 181a TEC,
identifies two main objectives which are 'in a situation of crisis or
emerging crisis to contribute to stability by providing an effective
response to help preserve, establish or re-establish the conditions essential to the proper implementation of the Community's development
and cooperation policies' and 'to help build capacity both to address
specific global and transregional threats having a destabilising effect
and to ensure preparedness to address pre- and post-crisis situations'.[369]
Articles 3 and 4 of the Stability Instrument, which list the areas in which
the Community will provide technical and financial assistance, is far
broader than the scope of competence in the LRRD Regulation. The
Stability Instrument essentially allows the Community to fund any
projects which are needed and these do not have to be limited to
those that are humanitarian in nature. There will be many instances,
however, in which the decision as to whether to use the Stability
Instrument, the Development and Cooperation Instrument and in
some cases the Humanitarian Aid Regulation will be determined by
budgetary or political considerations, as opposed to the nature and
objectives of the project to be funded. While this pragmatism is

Commissioner for Development and Humanitarian Aid. EuropeAid is also known as
AIDCO.
[368] Article 11(3) Regulation 1717/2006.   [369] *Ibid*. Article 1(2).

welcome in that it still allows the Commission and DG ECHO flexibility to implement and fund projects in accordance with their assessment of priorities and needs on the ground, it does have the effect of ensuring that the Community's competence and activities are becoming less demarcated between its different component parts. The problems this may cause are discussed in Chapter 6.

3.3.2.2 Community Competence in Food Aid and Security

The Community's humanitarian and development aid activities often involve it in the distribution of food aid. The competence for this, however, has not been solely derived from the 1996 Humanitarian Aid Regulation. Until the end of 2006 it was also, depending upon the context, based upon the 1996 Regulation on Food Aid Policy and Management.[370] If such assistance is now of a humanitarian nature it is based upon the Humanitarian Aid Regulation[371] and, if not, it is based upon Article 15 of the Development Cooperation Instrument.

The Common Agricultural Policy (CAP) has meant that a policy on food aid has been in existence since July 1968 when the Community joined the Food Aid Convention (FAC) of the International Wheat Agreement and the European Food Aid programme was established.[372] European Food Aid programmes started as a means of using surplus agricultural commodities for the purposes of economic development and emergency relief in developing countries.[373] Such programmes have evolved over time to accommodate changing international circumstances, as well as the Community's evolving competence and approach. It is, for example, only twenty-five years since a Communication on such assistance stated that one of the reasons

---

[370] Regulation 1292/96 on Food Aid Policy and Food Aid Management and Special Operations in Support of Food Security, [1996] OJ L166/1, 5 July 1996 as amended by Regulation 1726/2001, [2001] OJ L234/10, 1 September 2001.

[371] See COM(2006)21, p. 3.

[372] Food Aid Convention of 1967, [1968] OJ L305/1, 19 December 1968. See also, Council Decision 2000/421/EC on the Conclusion on behalf of the European Community of the Food Aid Convention 1999, [2000] OJ L163/37, 4 July 2000 with regard to the Food Aid Convention 1999.

[373] See [1975] OJ C170/28, 28 July 1975 where the Commission provides a summary of all Community food programmes between 1969 and 1975. More recent surveys of Community food aid programmes can be found in the *Annual Report on Humanitarian Aid*, e.g. see DG ECHO, *Annual Report 2003*, COM(2004)583 and DG ECHO, *Annual Report 2005*, COM(2006)441.

for the Community providing food aid was to help pull *it* out of recession.[374]

The inherently differing objectives of agricultural and development policy ensured that while dual legal bases were being used, the Community's actions with regard to food shortages were driven less by concern for the alleviation of hunger than by the objectives of Article 33 TEC.[375] It is for this reason, among others, that Snyder described food aid as 'one of the most visible, most frequently praised, yet also most vociferously criticised facets' of the relationship between the developed and developing world.[376] Cathie maintains, however, that the Community has never argued the case for food as a form of aid on the grounds of the interests of its own producers.[377] This is highly questionable. The legal basis for the Community to become party to the Food Aid Conventions and for the early regulations concerned with food aid matters was Articles 42 and 43 TEC.[378] Where the Community's agricultural competence was relied on, it is difficult to argue that development cooperation was the primary aim. Article 235 (now 308) TEC would have allowed for a development-based approach, if the political will had existed. It did not.[379]

With Regulation 3331/82, a discernible shift from previous practice can be detected. This regulation followed shortly after the November 1981 Resolution of the Council on Aid to Agricultural Products and Food Aid, which stated that the Community had a responsibility to ensure that the aid it supplied was used effectively to relieve hunger and improve the self-reliance of the targeted countries.[380] The regulation used the same double legal base and did not take the full step towards

---

[374] See COM(1982)640.

[375] See further P. Macalister-Smith, 'The EEC and International Humanitarian Assistance' (1981) *LIEI* 89, 98.

[376] F. Snyder, 'The European Community's New Food Aid Legislation: Towards a New Development Policy?' in F. Snyder and P. Slinn (eds.), *International Law of Development: Comparative Perspectives* (Abingdon: Professional Books, 1987) p. 271.

[377] J. Cathie, *European Food Aid Policy* (Aldershot: Ashgate, 1997) p. 6.

[378] See e.g., Regulation 2721/72, [1972] OJ L29/28, 28 December 1972 and Regulation 2727/1975, [1975] OJ L281/1, 1 November 1975. Regulations strictly concerned with food aid used the then Articles 42 and 43 TEC. Other measures concerned with cereals and food which may have been used as aid also relied upon the now Articles 133 and 300 TEC.

[379] See further, COM(1974)300 as an early example of the Commission's approach to questions of food policy and aid.

[380] Reproduced in *Compilation of Texts Adopted by the Council January 1981–December 1988* (Luxembourg: OOPEC, 1989) p. 13.

humanitarian objectives. As Snyder notes, the use of the two bases meant it was a mixture of 'ideology, strategy, technology and surpluses'.[381]

The Community's policy vis-à-vis food aid since 1996 has been based on the development cooperation provisions of the EC Treaty. The now repealed 1996 Regulation on Food Aid Policy and Management shows how the Community's approach had evolved from that adopted in the earlier legal instruments.[382] It highlighted the objectives of Community food aid policy, which were no longer solely or even largely to be driven by the welfare of the Community's own agricultural producers. The basic aim was to provide food aid in situations in which food insecurity existed, whatever its basic cause, and to increase food security in developing countries.[383] The Community's broadly defined competence to act was not limited to emergency situations, although such emergencies were also covered. The Community could also respond in different ways to promote food security; in particular, it could act to raise the nutritional level of the recipient population or promote the availability of foodstuffs to the public, although this is no longer an express objective in the Development Cooperation Instrument.[384] This is because Community food aid interventions, despite their good intentions, had long been recognised as sometimes having adverse effects on local production and markets.[385]

The Community does, however, have powers to act with long-term solutions in mind, for example, to support the efforts of recipient countries to improve their own food production and thus reduce their dependence on food aid.[386] This can involve financial support for domestic structural reform as opposed to the more short-term measures, noted above, which would primarily involve sending food aid. This again involves more than humanitarian or emergency aid. Agricultural development, however, has to fit within the overall context of the Community's development policy and this raises the importance

---

[381]   Snyder, 'The European Community's Food Aid Legislation', p. 281 quoting R. Talbot, 'The European Community's Food Aid Programme: an Integration of Ideology, Strategy, Technology and Surpluses', Food Aid, November 1979, 269. Also see F. Snyder, 'European Community Law and Third World Food Entitlements' (1989) 32 GYBIL 87.

[382]   COM(1995)283 provides further background to the Food Aid Regulation.

[383]   Article 1(1) Regulation 1292/96.   [384] Ibid. Article 1(3).

[385]   This is expressly recognised in the Preamble to the Development Cooperation Instrument and is given as part of the reason for the repeal of the 1996 Regulation. See further, COM(2006)21 which is the Commission's food security agenda.

[386]   Article 15(2)(b)(iii) Regulation 1905/2006.

of the coherence between the Community's differing sectoral competences described above. For example, under its development competence the Community routinely helps fund irrigation projects in Africa so that local farmers can supply produce to regional markets. Yet by subsidising its own farmers, the Community can help to depress the global prices for goods which compete with those grown as a consequence of those very same irrigation projects.[387]

The Community's extensive general competence in development cooperation and humanitarian aid covers almost all conceivable situations concerning food security and aid. But it can only achieve its objectives if adequate resources are committed. In financial terms the amount of European food aid distributed is impressive. In 1998 and 2001, for example, it accounted for approximately 8 per cent of the Community's total aid budget, which in the latter year equated to €484 million.[388]

The Community's food security policy in general has displayed an acute awareness of the priorities and needs of low-income countries, many of which desperately need assistance to feed their populations. As noted above, the 1996 Regulation on Food Aid Policy and Food Aid was very much aimed at pursuing a food security policy and not a food aid one. A key aspect of the regulation was that it changed the approach of the Community by aiming to increase the purchasing power of vulnerable groups. The 1996 Regulation also recognised that priority must be given to targeting the food security programme of the most vulnerable populations in the LDCs. Community intervention under the food security programme has been directed at 34 low-income countries, which are not self-sufficient.[389] These interventions are classifiable as structural and the states as crisis or post-crisis countries. Close to half (48 per cent) of the food security programme has gone to direct aid. This has allowed the Commission to intervene directly, either by funding government programmes via budget support or by giving direct support to private or

---

[387] See House of Commons International Development Committee, *The Commission for Africa and Policy Coherence for Development: First Do No Harm*, 1st Report of Session 2004–2005 (London: HMSO, 2004) Evidence, Question 8 *et seq.*

[388] The figure in real terms is more or less consistent between 1989 and 2001. See EuropeAid, *External Aid Programmes: Financial Trends, 1989–2001*, p. 8. Under the terms of the new Financial Perspectives, covering the years 2007–2013, all activities of a humanitarian nature have been integrated. The current budgetary allocations are thus not directly comparable to the earlier allocations. See further Chapter 6.

[389] See e.g., Working Document (2001) 32947.

public bodies.[390] Such assistance is only provided, however, if there is a funding agreement between the beneficiary government and the Commission, specifying the implementation arrangements as well as the conditions to which this aid is subject.[391] Between 1996 and 2001, for example, most aid in this context was given to the ACP states (57 per cent), followed by Asia (15 per cent), Latin America (8 per cent) and the Near and Middle East (6 per cent). Of the ACP's share, the vast majority (61 per cent) was given to East Africa where need has, over a prolonged period of time, been the greatest. A further 20 per cent was given to Southern Africa, where there has been, more recently, a substantial famine.[392]

As of 1 January 2007, the legal basis for the Community's food aid programme has been overhauled. Council Regulation 1292/96 has been repealed but the Community will still pursue food security as part of its development cooperation policy.[393] It is to be hoped that the Community's practice in this regard will continue in the current vein where it has been targeted at where need is greatest.

The Community's competence in terms of food aid, as with development cooperation, does not encroach upon the competence of the Member States to act in parallel. The policy now reflects the reorientation of food aid from the purpose of disposal of the Community's surplus agricultural produce to that of the Community's development cooperation policy.

3.3.3 Competence in Trade and the Pursuit of Ethical Values

The final area of substantive competence to be discussed is that of trade. International trade is considered in the context of the development cooperation provisions to be a tool by which developing states can be brought into the global economy. Trade is also crucial, as discussed above, to the Community's efforts to help eradicate and reduce poverty in third states. The demarcation between competence in trade and

---

[390] Ibid.   [391] Ibid.   [392] Ibid.

[393] See Article 15 Regulation 1905/2006 Establishing a Financing Instrument for Development Cooperation, [2006] OJ L378/41, 27 December 2006. See further, COM(2006)21 which outlines Community policy for advancing the food security agenda so as to achieve the Millennium Development Goals; Court of Auditors, *Special Report 2/2003: On the Implementation of the Food Security Policy in Developing Countries Financed by the General Budget of the European Union*, [2003] OJ C93/1, 17 April 2003; and Particip, *Thematic Evaluation of Food-Aid Policy and Food-Aid Management and Special Operations in Support of Food Security: Synthesis Report–Evaluative Report* (Brussels: European Commission, 2004) vol. I.

development cooperation is, however, at times very unclear. The Community's role in trade is also relevant in other ways to the pursuit of ethical values in third states. Some of these are tangentially related, others more directly so. The globalisation of trade, in which the Community has played a substantial role, has arguably resulted in an increase in the rule of law in international economic relations.[394] As a commitment to the rule of law is considered imperative for economic development, as well as the establishment of democracy and protection of human rights, trade policy has in this tangential way also contributed to the Community's development cooperation objectives.

For third states, trade with and possibly assistance from the Union will be among the most important considerations when they seek to establish, enhance or break-off, as the case may be, relations with the Union. The pursuit of ethical values in third states and a trade-based relationship are, however, not always compatible. Trade relies on economic efficiency, which can interfere with the enjoyment of certain human rights, for example, minimum labour standards.[395] The enforcement of minimum labour standards is, however, sometimes perceived to be driven by protectionism. There is a difficult balance to be struck. Linking trade to a respect for ethical values does provide an enforcement mechanism to those states who are in a position to offer concessions or other trade-related benefits. Within the Community context, the relationship between ethical values in third states, primarily human rights, and trade arises directly in a number of different contexts. First, there is a relationship between the protection of certain rights in third states and the granting or withdrawing of benefits under the Generalised System of Preferences (GSP). Secondly, there is the imposition of restrictive measures against a third state for its violation of certain principles and usually in addition restrictive measures which target certain individuals. Thirdly, restrictive measures can be imposed on the export to certain or all third states of goods which may be used either for purposes of which the Union does not approve or in the

---

[394] See F. Garcia, 'The Global Market and Human Rights: Trading Away the Human Rights Principle' (1999) 25 *Brooklyn JIL* 51, 53 and P. De Waart, 'Quality of Life at the Mercy of WTO Panels: GATT's Article XX: an Empty Shell?' in P. De Waart and F. Weiss (eds.), *International Economic Law with a Human Face* (Dordrecht: Nijhoff, 1988) p. 109.

[395] See more generally, L. Compa and S. Diamond (eds.), *Human Rights, Labour Rights and International Trade*, 2nd edn. (Philadelphia: University of Pennsylvania Press, 1996) and T. Cottier, J. Pauwelyn and E. Bürgi (eds.), *Human Rights and International Trade* (Oxford: Oxford University Press, 2005).

pursuance of the other legal obligations of the Member States. Each of these will be discussed in turn below.

3.3.3.1 GSP Scheme

In the Community context, the GSP and the removal of all tariffs for the LDCs under the EBA Initiative increasingly blur the distinction between trade and development cooperation. An expansive approach to both development and trade makes the demarcation between the two increasingly difficult but the demarcation is important as the Community's competence in trade in external relations is exclusive in nature, while in development cooperation it is not.

The Community first established a GSP in 1971 with the regulations which formed the scheme either based on Articles 235 (now 308) or 113 (now 133) TEC.[396] The scheme was updated in the 1980s by Regulations 3599/85[397] and 3600/85,[398] in which there was no reference to a legal base. These measures were subsequently challenged by the Commission to determine whether Article 113 (now 133) TEC could extend to incorporating development cooperation aims or whether reference to Article 235 (now 308) TEC was required. Both Advocate General Lenz and the ECJ held that Article 113 TEC could be used for development-based measures. The rationale was that the link between development and trade was progressively stronger and it was therefore legitimate for development aims to play a role in international trade relations.[399] As the ECJ, relying upon *Opinion 1/78*,[400] stated:

> the existence of a link with development ... does not cause a measure to be excluded from the sphere of the common commercial policy ... it would no longer be possible to carry on any worthwhile common commercial policy if the Community were not in a position to avail itself also of means of action going beyond instruments intended to have an effect only on the traditional aspects of external trade.[401]

---

[396] Règlement 1314/1971 du Conseil, du 21 Juin 1971, établissant, pour certains produits des chapitres 1 à 24 du tarif douanier commun, un système de préférences généralisées en faveur des pays en voie de développement, [1971] OJ L142/85, 28 June 1971; Règlement 1313/1971 du Conseil, du 21 Juin 1971, portant ouverture de préférences tarifaires pour certains produits textiles et des chaussures, originaires de pays en voie de développement, [1971] OJ L142/76, 28 June 1971.

[397] [1985] OJ L352/1, 30 December 1985.   [398] [1985] OJ L352/107, 30 December 1985.

[399] Case 45/86 *Commission* v. *Council* [1987] ECR 1493, paras. 17–18.

[400] *Opinion 1/78* [1979] ECR 2871.

[401] Case 45/86 *Commission* v. *Council*, n. 399 above, para. 20.

The link is now well established in Community law. The Community has competence to include development objectives in trade measures and these should be based upon Article 133 TEC. In the context of the current GSP scheme,[402] there are two principal dimensions to the relationship with ethical values. These are the withdrawal of preferences for the violation of certain principles or the awarding of greater preferences for compliance with specified international instruments.

3.3.3.1(a) GSP Scheme and the Withdrawal of Benefits

In the 2005 GSP Regulation, the Community has provided that it may temporarily withdraw the preferential arrangements in respect of all of or certain products originating in a beneficiary country for one or more of a number of reasons.[403] This is not new and such a provision was also present in the previous GSP regimes.[404] The Community, in providing such benefits to third states, has sought to protect its own interests under the various GSP schemes by giving itself latitude to withdraw those preferences. These include: the export of goods made by prison labour; shortcomings in customs controls on export or transit of drugs (illicit substances or precursors), or the failure to comply with international conventions on money laundering; unfair trading practices which have an adverse effect on a Community industry; and the violation of certain human rights related norms. What is particularly noteworthy about these justifications for the temporary withdrawal of the GSP is not only the expanding list of reasons which protect the Community's direct financial interests but also the expansion of the human rights related norms in the latest GSP scheme as compared to the earlier ones.

---

[402] Council Regulation 980/2005 Applying a Scheme of Generalised Tariff Preferences, [2005] OJ L169/1, 30 June 2005.

[403] Article 16 Regulation 980/2005. As a unilateral measure the Community, as discussed in Chapter 2, has latitude under international law to withdraw such preferences. The importance of the provision lies in the fact that it puts beneficiary states on notice of the circumstances under which the Community is likely to withdraw benefits to a third state.

[404] See Article 9 of Council Regulation 3281/1994 Applying a Four-Year Scheme of Generalised Tariff Preferences (1995 to 1998) in respect of Certain Industrial Products Originating in Developing Countries, [1994] OJ L348/1, 31 December 1994; Article 9 of Council Regulation 1256/1996 applying Multi-annual Schemes of Generalised Tariff Preferences (1996 to 1999) in Respect of Certain Agricultural Products Originating in Developing Countries, [1996] OJ L160/1, 29 June 1996; and Article 26 of Council Regulation 2501/2001 Applying a Scheme of Generalised Tariff Preferences for the Period 1 January 2002 to 31 December 2004, [2001] OJ L346/1, 31 December 2001.

Under the 1994 GSP Regulation, benefits could be withdrawn for violation of either the 1926 Slavery Convention or International Labour Organisation (ILO) Conventions Nos. 29 and 105 on forced labour.[405] As the prohibition on slavery and slave-like practices is an obligation *erga omnes* there is support in international law for the Community taking such an attitude toward the violation of such a fundamental norm. Under Article 26 of the 2001 GSP Regulation the list was expanded to encompass all eight of the ILO's 'core' conventions.[406] The approach of the 2001 GSP Regulation towards the norms in question was preferable to that adopted under the 1994 scheme, in the sense that under the latter scheme the rights in some core ILO conventions were considered to be worthy of protection and others were not.[407] Although there was widespread agreement within the ILO as to which conventions should be considered to be 'core' ones, not all of the rights they protect can be considered to be custom, let alone obligations *erga omnes*. This is especially the case regarding the 1951 Equal Remuneration Convention.

Under the 2005 GSP Regulation the list of conventions has been further expanded. Preferences can be withdrawn for violations of not only the eight 'core' ILO conventions but also eight UN human rights conventions. These are the two 1966 International Covenants; the Race Convention; the Women's Convention; the Convention on the Rights of the Child; the Torture Convention; the Genocide Convention; and the

---

[405] Convention No. 29, Forced Labour Convention, 1930, 39 UNTS 55; Convention No. 105, Abolition of Forced Labour Convention, 1957, 320 UNTS 291; and Slavery Convention, 1926, 60 LNTS 253 as amended by the Protocol to Slavery Convention, 1953, 212 UNTS 17. ILO Convention No. 29 provides a definition of forced labour and is supplemented by Convention No. 105. Article 1 of Slavery Convention, 1926, as amended by the Protocol to Slavery Convention, 1953, still provides the basic definition of slavery in international law.

[406] The other six conventions are: Convention No. 87, Freedom of Association and Protection of the Right to Organise Convention, 1948, 68 UNTS 17; Convention No. 98, Right to Organise and Collective Bargaining Convention, 1949, 96 UNTS 257; Convention No. 100, Equal Remuneration Convention, 1951, 165 UNTS 304; Convention No. 111, Discrimination (Employment and Occupation) Convention, 1958, 363 UNTS 31; Convention No. 138, Minimum Age Convention, 1973, 1015 UNTS 14862; and Convention No. 182, Worst Forms of Child Labour Convention, 1999, 2133 UNTS 37245.

[407] See Article 9 Council Regulation 3281/1994 and Article 9 Council Regulation 1256/1996. This anomaly was not the fault of the Community; it was not until the 86th Session of the ILO in Geneva in June 1998 that the ILO Declaration on Fundamental Principles and Rights at Work was adopted.

Convention on the Suppression and Punishment of the Crime of Apartheid.[408]

While the link between labour standards and trade is not new, the linking of UN human rights conventions and trade by the Community in this context certainly is.[409] Article XX(e) GATT 1947, for example, has allowed the banning of goods made by prison labour, although the provision has not as far as is known been invoked by the Community.[410] In the Community context, the Commission first made the link between trade and labour standards in a 1978 Communication, but this highlighted some of the pitfalls inherent in doing so.[411] The standards used by the Commission were derived from an amalgamation of a number of ILO Conventions, to which most of the Community's then Member States were not party.[412] Accusations of protectionism in such circumstances are perfectly understandable. Furthermore, in the past the language used by the Commission did nothing to clarify which standards were to be used, as 'international labour standards' and 'fair labour standards' were used interchangeably to mean the same thing.[413]

The Community now uses the term 'core labour standards'[414] in line with the approach adopted by the OECD[415] as well as the ILO itself. In Article 50 of the Cotonou Convention, for example, the parties 'reaffirm their commitment to the internationally recognised core labour standards, as defined by the relevant International Labour Organisation (ILO)

---

[408] Convention on the Prevention and Punishment of the Crime of Genocide, 1948, 78 UNTS 277; International Covenant on Civil and Political Rights, 1966, 999 UNTS 171; International Covenant on Economic, Social and Cultural Rights, 1966, 993 UNTS 3; International Convention on the Elimination of All Forms of Racial Discrimination, 1966, 660 UNTS 195; International Convention on the Suppression and Punishment of the Crime of Apartheid, 1973, 1015 UNTS 243; Convention on the Elimination of All Forms of Discrimination Against Women, 1979, 1249 UNTS 13; Convention Against Torture and Other Cruel, Inhuman or Degrading Treatment or Punishment, 1984, 1464 UNTS 85; and Convention on the Rights of the Child, 1989, 1577 UNTS 3.

[409] See Compa and Diamond, *Human Rights, Labour Rights*, p. 273, E. Wet, 'Labour Standards in the Globalised Economy: the Inclusion of a Social Clause in the General Agreement on Tariffs and Trade/World Trade Organisation' (1995) 17 *HRQ* 443 and P. Waer, 'Social Clauses in International Trade' (1996) 30 *JWT* 25.

[410] This is because it is almost impossible for customs authorities to determine the conditions under which particular goods are produced in third countries.

[411] COM(1978)492.

[412] See further, P. Alston, 'International Trade as an Instrument of Positive Human Rights Policy' (1982) 4 *HRQ* 155.

[413] See e.g., COM(1996)402.   [414] See COM(2001)416.

[415] OECD, *International Trade and Core Labour Standards* (Paris: OECD, 2000).

Conventions'.[416] A similar approach has been adopted in the dialogue between the EC and China regarding China's failure to sign up to the core ILO conventions.[417] With regard to the link between trade and specified UN human rights treaties in the Community context there are a number of noteworthy issues.

First, a large number of states who benefit from the GSP scheme are certainly not party to the UN treaties specified, and even where they are, compliance is often patchy at best. The GSP scheme is thus holding them accountable under treaty regimes which they may not have accepted. While a number of the rights protected or prohibited by these treaties are undeniably customary and some, such as the prohibition on genocide, apartheid and slavery, obligations *erga omnes*, there is legitimate disagreement over the scope of the definitions of some of the rights in question. States do not ratify treaties for various reasons and have the right not to do so. At the very least, therefore, the negative aspect of the Community GSP scheme should relate to only those rights which are widely accepted as being binding upon states under customary international law. As will be discussed below, the issue is different where benefits are being awarded to states under the GSP scheme.

Secondly, even where a state is party to a treaty, not all the treaties in question have established treaty bodies to supervise compliance with them. This is the case for both the Convention Against Genocide and the Convention Against Apartheid. In such cases the Commission will have to make an assessment of the situation in a third state. While the basic prohibitions in both of these conventions are undeniably accepted as being obligations *erga omnes*, such an assessment by the Commission will be fraught with political considerations. An accusation of genocide is extremely contentious and controversial with regard to any state (even if it is historic as is the case, for example, with Turkey and the Armenian minority) and while the Community is on sound legal ground under public international law in wishing to take action for violations of such fundamental norms, the Commission will need strong political backing from the Member States if any such action is to be meaningful.

Thirdly, what is the relationship between the position of the Community and the findings of the treaty bodies for those conventions where they exist? As discussed in Chapter 2, no human rights treaty actually prohibits the use of methods other than those provided for, to encourage or persuade states party to them to comply with their

---

[416] [2000] OJ L317/3, 15 December 2000.   [417] See COM(1998)181, section B1.

obligations. The treaty bodies, however, are the most authoritative and credible organs to determine a state's compliance with its obligations. Article 19 of the GSP Regulation notes that the Commission shall seek all the information it considers necessary 'including the available assessments, comments ... of the UN, the ILO and other competent international organisations. These shall serve as the point of departure for the investigation as to whether the temporary withdrawal is justified.'[418] This certainly gives the Commission scope to go beyond the findings of the relevant treaty bodies and while such findings are to 'serve as the point of departure', if this aspect of the GSP scheme is to be credible, it should not be the case that the Community comes to a different assessment from the relevant treaty body, as doing so may in part undermine it. In practice, where the GSP benefits have been withdrawn the Commission's conclusions have relied heavily, in these instances, on the findings of the requisite ILO bodies and did not come to a divergent finding.[419] It is hoped that this approach continues.

Fourthly, many states, including those who are members of the Union, have only become party to the UN treaties in question upon entering very substantial reservations. France and the United Kingdom, for example, have entered broad-ranging reservations to the ICCPR. A number of states which benefit from the GSP, such as Bangladesh (which is widely regarded as having a number of development success stories), have entered reservations to a number of the UN human rights treaties which are legally questionable. This is in particular the case, as is well known, with regard to the Women's and Children's Conventions. The Nordic states, in particular, have been very active in objecting to such reservations and trying to influence the future development of the law of reservations as far as human rights treaties are concerned.[420] If an allegation were brought under the GSP against Bangladesh, for example, that it was systematically violating its obligations under the Women's Convention, this would raise very difficult but interesting questions regarding the validity of reservations and the approach of the EU Member States towards such practice. Political and diplomatic considerations, and not only legal ones, will play a major role in any such determination as it is the Council under Article 19 of the GSP

---

[418] Emphasis added.
[419] See further the discussion below and in Chapter 4 on Myanmar.
[420] See further J. Klabbers, 'Accepting the Unacceptable: a New Nordic Approach to Reservations to Multilateral Treaties' (2000) 69 *Nordic JIL* 179.

Regulation which has the power ultimately to decide whether the benefits in question should be withdrawn or not.

Finally, while all EU Member States are at least party to the conventions specified in the GSP scheme, it is worth pointing out that the conclusions of the treaty bodies, as far as Member State compliance is concerned, routinely highlight substantial shortcomings. For example, the Committee Against Torture between 2004 and 2006 in its conclusions highlighted substantial problems as far as the 1984 Torture Convention was concerned in France, Austria, Greece and the United Kingdom.[421] Unless the compliance of all EU Member States with such human rights treaties is exemplary (which it is not although it is much better than that of many other states), the Union is exposing itself to further accusations of double standards.

As was the case under the 2001 GSP Regulation, is it not necessary under the current GSP scheme that goods produced under conditions which are in violation of the relevant norms, are actually exported to the Community. It is simply the fact that such practices occur in the state in question. Any Member State, natural or legal person can bring to the attention of the Commission violations of the requisite conventions in the territory of a state benefiting under the GSP.[422] The investigative procedure initiated as a result of such a complaint allows the Commission to obtain information from a broad array of individuals and organisations.[423] Once the Commission has concluded its investigations, the preferences can be suspended by the Council, if appropriate.[424]

The withdrawal of preferences under the GSP is not formally linked with other aspects of Community development cooperation.[425] If a state is considered to be in serious and systematic breach of core ILO conventions or various UN human rights treaties, then it is also likely to be in breach of any 'essential elements' clause of any Agreement in force between it and the Community. While there is no formal link between suspension of the GSP scheme and other measures, for reasons of

---

[421] Conclusions and Recommendations of the Committee Against Torture: France, 3 April 2006, CAT/C/FRA/CO/3; Austria, 15 December 2005, CAT/C/AUT/CO/3; Greece, 10 December 2004, CAT/C/CR/33/2; and United Kingdom, 10 December 2004, CAT/C/CR/33/3.

[422] Article 18 Regulation 980/2005.   [423] Article 19 Regulation 980/2005.   [424] Ibid.

[425] For confirmation of the view that the removing of the GSP had no link with other measures, see [1998] OJ C21/75, 22 January 1998. Such a provision has not been introduced in subsequent revisions to the GSP scheme.

consistency it should follow that withdrawal of benefits under the GSP should lead to commensurate action with regard to other assistance.

Where the Commission has some latitude under the GSP Regulation is with regard to the fact that any breach of the UN or ILO conventions must be considered to be a 'serious and systematic' one.[426] This certainly gives the Commission the opportunity to keep the situation under review, in particular where the beneficiary state agrees to take some remedial steps. This was the case when a complaint was submitted against Pakistan in 1996. Benefits were not withdrawn due to the commitment of the Pakistani authorities to try and tackle the problems highlighted by the complaint.[427] Where the benefits have been withdrawn, in 1997 with regard to Myanmar[428] and Belarus in June 2007,[429] the failure of the national authorities to take any action in response to the Commission request (or to make undertakings to that effect) played a major role in suspending the benefits. In the case of Myanmar, the fact that the national authorities did not assist or cooperate with the fact-finding mission sent by the Commission seems to have been almost as crucial to the determining of a breach as the practices themselves.[430]

3.3.3.1(b) GSP Incentive Scheme

An incentive scheme under the Community GSP scheme was one of the innovative features of the GSP as formulated in the 1994 and 1996 regulations. Each subsequent version of the GSP Regulation has contained an incentive scheme but they have been recognised by the Commission as having failed to act as an attraction to developing states to make the changes to their domestic legislation and practices that the

---

[426] Article 16(1)(a) Regulation 980/2005.   [427] See the discussion in Chapter 4.

[428] Council Regulation 552/1997, [1997] OJ L85/8, 27 March 1997, as subsequently amended and extended. The current GSP Regulation specifically does not apply to Myanmar as a consequence of this measure.

[429] Regulation 1933/2006 Temporarily Withdrawing Access to the Generalised Tariff Preferences from the Republic of Belarus, [2006] OJ L405/35, 30 December 2006. Under Article 3 the regulation only entered into force on 21 June 2007 if Belarus did not take adequate remedial action in the intermediate; it was deemed not to have done so. For the background to the complaint against Belarus see Commission Decision, 29 December 2003, Providing for the Initiation of an Investigation Pursuant to Article 27(2) of Council Regulation 2501/2001 with respect to the Violation of Freedom of Association in Belarus, [2004] OJ L5/90, 9 January 2004 and Commission Decision, 17 August 2005, on the Monitoring and Evaluation of the Labour Rights Situation in Belarus for Temporary Withdrawal of Trade Preferences, [2005] OJ L213/16, 18 February 2005.

[430] See the Preamble to the regulation and further the detailed discussion in Chapter 4.

Community would like to encourage.[431] The current scheme is the most expansive in terms of the norms which states must accept to benefit from it[432] and has also been adopted subsequent to India's successful challenge before the WTO dispute settlement bodies against part of the previous scheme.[433]

The current incentive scheme seeks to replace and simplify the various schemes which existed under the 2001 GSP Regulation. That scheme also covered the eight 'core' ILO conventions, treaties concerned with the environment and measures which combat drug production and trafficking.[434] It was with regard to the incentive scheme under the 2001 Regulation concerned with the combating of drug production and trafficking that India complained to the WTO. India claimed that states were being granted benefits under the incentive scheme when this was not objectively justifiable. The underlying rationale of the complaint was India objecting to Pakistan being granted extra concessions under the scheme as part of the European Union's reward package to Pakistan for siding against the Taliban regime in Afghanistan in the aftermath of the attacks in the United States in September 2001.[435] The WTO Appeals Panel upheld the Indian complaint and also accepted

---

[431] See COM(2003)634, p. 3 and COM(2004)461, p. 9.

[432] Although it should be pointed out that Article 14(2)(b) was part of the amendments made to the 2001 Regulation by Article 4 of Regulation 2211/2003 amending Regulation 2501/2001 applying a Scheme of Generalised Tariff Preferences for the Period 1 January 2002 to 31 December 2004 and extending it to 31 December 2005, [2003] OJ L332/10, 19 December 2003. This was so as to allow states to benefit from the incentive scheme if they were engaged in applying legislation to give effect to the conventions then in question in a 'clear and significant way'. This effectively lowered the threshold from the standard required in the earlier schemes and has been carried over to the current scheme.

[433] WTO Panel Report, EC – Tariff Preferences, WT/DS246/R, 1 December 2003 as upheld in WTO Appellate Body Report, EC – Tariff Preferences, WT/DS246/AB/R, 7 December 2004. For discussion of these complaints see J. Harrison, 'Incentives for Development: the EC's Generalized System of Preferences, India's WTO Challenge and Reform' (2005) 42 CMLRev. 1663 and L. Bartels, 'Conditionality in GSP Programmes: the Appellate Body Report in European Communities – Conditions for the Granting of Tariff Preferences to Developing Countries and its Implications for Conditionality in GSP Programmes' in Cottier, Pauwelyn and Bürgi, Human Rights and International Trade, p. 463. For a more general, if now slightly dated, discussion of the compatibility of the EC GSP incentive scheme with the WTO Enabling Clause, which is beyond the scope of this work, see L. Bartels, 'The WTO Enabling Clause and Positive Conditionality in the European Community's GSP Program' (2003) 6 JIEL 507.

[434] Measures concerning the environment were dealt with by Articles 21–24 and to combat drug trafficking under Article 25 of Regulation 2501/2001.

[435] See further the discussion in Chapter 4.

the compatibility of the incentive scheme with the Enabling Clause so long as the scheme is applied in an objective manner which is non-discriminatory.[436]

The current incentive scheme encourages states to ratify and effectively implement the same eight UN human rights treaties and eight core ILO conventions in respect of which, as discussed above, beneficiary states may find their preferential treatment withdrawn if they systematically and seriously violate them. For the incentive scheme, however, states must not only ratify and effectively implement those sixteen conventions but in addition must also ratify and effectively implement at least seven of the eleven conventions which relate to the environment and good governance and are listed in the Annex to the regulation;[437] undertake to ratify and effectively implement by the end of 2008 those remaining treaties which they are not already party to; undertake not to denounce those conventions and accept all monitoring and review mechanisms that those treaties may entail; and be considered a 'vulnerable country'.[438] To be considered a 'vulnerable country', a state must not be classified as a high-income country by the World Bank; the five largest sections of its GSP-covered imports to the Community must represent more than 75 per cent in value of its total GSP-covered imports; and those imports to the Community must represent less than 1 per cent in value of all GSP imports to the Community.[439]

In essence, therefore, any state which (if it is not already a party to the eight UN human rights treaties, the eight 'core' ILO conventions and at least seven of the eleven good governance and sustainable development conventions) is willing to become party to a number of treaties, is

---

[436] WTO Appellate Body Report, *EC – Tariff Preferences*, para. 165.

[437] The eleven conventions are the: Montreal Protocol on Substances that Deplete the Ozone Layer, 1987, (1987) 26 *ILM* 1550; Basel Convention on the Control of Transboundary Movements of Hazardous Wastes and their Disposal, 1989, (1989) 28 *ILM* 649; Stockholm Convention on Persistent Organic Pollutants, 2001, (2001) 40 *ILM* 532; Convention on International Trade in Endangered Species of Wild Fauna and Flora, 1973, (1973) 12 *ILM* 1085; Convention on Biological Diversity, 1992, (1992) 31 *ILM* 818; Cartagena Protocol on Biosafety to the Convention on Biological Diversity, 2000, (2000) 37 *ILM* 1027; Kyoto Protocol to the United Nations Framework Convention on Climate Change, 1997, (1998) 37 *ILM* 22; United Nations Single Convention on Narcotic Drugs, 1961, 520 UNTS 204; United Nations Convention on Psychotropic Substances, 1971, 1019 UNTS 175; United Nations Convention Against Illicit Traffic in Narcotic Drugs and Psychotropic Substances, 1988, (1989) 28 *ILM* 493; and the United Nations Convention Against Corruption, 2003, (2004) 43 *ILM* 37.

[438] Article 9(1) Regulation 980/2005.   [439] *Ibid.* Article 9(3).

hugely dependent upon the Community as an importer of its products but whose value is minimal in relative terms to the Community can, depending on the product,[440] gain a greater reduction than that enjoyed under the GSP scheme under the Common Customs Tariff.[441] This is the so called GSP+. Any state which wished to benefit from the scheme had to do so by 31 December 2005. Fifteen states were awarded the extra benefits. Sri Lanka had applied and been successful under the incentive scheme established under the 2001 Regulation. Subsequently, eleven Latin American countries,[442] Moldova, Georgia and Mongolia were granted the extra benefits available under the GSP+ scheme for the two-year period from 1 January 2006 to 31 December 2008.[443] According to the well-regarded non-governmental organisation Transparency International, in 2006 twelve of the twenty countries in the world which are perceived to be the least corrupt are EU Member States.[444] It is not amiss, however, to point out that a number of the developing states which have been awarded benefits under the GSP+ scheme are, according to the same organisation, less corrupt and thus more success-ful in giving effect to that aspect of their good governance obligations than some EU Member States. Costa Rica and El Salvador, for example, are considered to be less corrupt than Romania and Poland and only marginally less corrupt than Cyprus, Italy and Greece.[445]

Where a state benefits from the EBA initiative, the GSP+ provides no incentive at all. The scheme is of utility, therefore, only for countries not classified as being amongst the least developed. The incentive scheme was only an inducement to states where the products in ques-tion were significant foreign currency earners, were not classified as

---

[440] The current general GSP scheme covers about 7,200 products, this is up from around 6,900 products under the 2001 scheme.

[441] Article 8 Regulation 980/2005.

[442] Bolivia, Columbia, Ecuador, Peru, Venezuela, Costa Rica, El Salvador, Guatemala, Honduras, Nicaragua and Panama.

[443] Commission Decision, 21 December 2005, on the List of Beneficiary Countries which Qualify for the Special Incentive Arrangement for Sustainable Development and Good Governance, provided for by Article 26(e) of Council Regulation 980/2005 applying a Scheme of Generalised Tariff Preferences, [2005] OJ L337/50, 22 December 2005.

[444] For Transparency International's Corruption Perception Index Table see www. transparency.org/news_room/in_focus/2006/cpi_2006_1/cpi_table

[445] Costa Rica is also considered to be less corrupt than Bulgaria and is ranked as the fifty-fifth least corrupt state. Greece was considered by Transparency International to be the fifty-fourth least corrupt country in 2006.

being sensitive and the reduction in tariffs made enough of a difference for it to be worthwhile to go through the onerous procedure entailed.[446]

Few states are likely to have amended their legislation solely due to the inducements described. Those states which have taken advantage of the scheme were all already party to the UN human rights treaties and the ILO conventions in question and are likely to have already adopted or were in the process of adopting domestic legislation giving effect to those treaties. The amendments made in the 2005 Regulation, however, are enough of a positive development from the 2001 Regulation to have made a difference. As noted above, only Sri Lanka was granted benefits under the previous scheme.

The utility of the current scheme is, however, a limited one. If the Community wishes states to take full advantage of the GSP+ scheme it must provide the opportunity to others to apply to take advantage of it. The Commission considers the GSP scheme as now formulated as being fully WTO compliant and thus, so long as the scheme is applied in a non-discriminatory objective manner there is nothing under the WTO Agreement to prevent it being extended to states who did not meet the 31 December 2005 deadline for applications, as established under the current scheme.[447] The GSP+ may possibly act as an incentive to other states to ratify the specified conventions and to give effect to them in domestic law, if the option is open to them. In practice, however, such states are likely already to be engaged in such a process. The Community, in specifying that to benefit under the GSP+ a state must be classifiable as 'vulnerable', is clearly seeking to provide incentives to those most likely to be (adversely) affected by large movements in price to one or two key commodities, as well as ensuring that it is protecting its own financial interests. Even allowing for the protection of its financial interests the Community should consider allowing other states to apply for the GSP+ if it wishes to influence positively the behaviour of a wider number of states.

3.3.3.2 Restrictive Trade Measures

A decision to interrupt or reduce economic relations between the Member States and a third state or to take punitive action against certain individuals, for matters within the scope of its competence,

---

[446] The Commission decision granting the benefits acknowledged the procedure was fairly onerous, see the Preamble to Commission Decision, 21 December 2005.

[447] See COM(2004)461, p. 6.

must be given effect by the Community, notwithstanding the forum in which such action is agreed. Action outside of the Community would encroach on its exclusive competence, and the danger exists that, if such measures are enacted by individual Member States, distortions of competition may arise. It has long been the practice to implement the commercial aspects of any such decision through the Community.[448] The standard modern practice is for the Council to adopt a Common Position, which outlines the measures to be taken, and for it to be implemented by the requisite actors depending on the allocation of competence.[449] Some aspects need to be implemented by the Member States and the others by the constituent parts of the Union. The Community has express competence under Articles 60 and 301 TEC to give effect to Common Positions or Joint Actions where they relate to third states. If measures not only in respect of third countries but also in respect of individuals and non-state bodies which are not necessarily linked to the governments or regimes of those countries are to be adopted, then Article 308 TEC must also be included as a legal basis for any measures to be adopted.[450]

The decision on restrictive measures in the CFSP, which are then in part implemented by the Community, may be unilaterally adopted by the Council[451] or may give effect to a resolution adopted by the Security Council acting under Chapter VII of the UN Charter.[452] This is binding on the Member States as UN members[453] and, according to the CFI, on

---

[448] For discussion of early practice, see P. Kuyper, 'Sanctions against Rhodesia and the European Economic Community and the Implementation of General International Legal Rules' (1975) 12 *CMLRev.* 231 and P. Kuyper, 'Community Sanctions Against Argentina: Lawfulness under Community and International Law' in D. O'Keeffe and H. Schermers (eds.), *Essays in European Law and Integration* (The Hague: Kluwer, 1982) p. 141.

[449] Although not all are very clear on this, for discussion of such measures see Denza, *Intergovernmental Pillars*, p. 296 *et seq.*

[450] See *Ahmed Ali Yusef and Al Barakat International Foundation* v. *Council and Commission*, n. 289 above, paras. 108–170.

[451] See e.g., Council Common Position 2006/51/CFSP Renewing Restrictive Measures Against Zimbabwe, [2006] OJ L26/28, 31 January 2006.

[452] E.g., Council Regulation 423/2007 concerning Restrictive Measures Against Iran, giving effect to Common Position 2007/140/CFSP, which in turn was adopted to give effect to Security Council Resolution 1737 (2006).

[453] Article 103 UNC and Article 307 TEC. Economic sanctions agreed by the Security Council and which are then implemented by the Member States through the Community legal order are perfectly compatible with the Member States' obligations under the UN Charter, see Article 48(2) UNC.

the Community as a result of Community law.[454] Such measures can be punitive in order to bring pressure to bear on a third state for its policies or acts.[455] They may also aim to ensure that the Member States, possibly again with others, do not provide a state or insurgents with some of the materials and instruments needed to engage in practices and policies they do not approve of; for example, the measures noted above adopted with regard to Iran and its uranium enrichment programme.[456]

The Community has also adopted more general measures which do not apply to a specified state or individuals but to particular types of exports. In this vein the Community has adopted a regulation concerning trade in equipment and products which can be used for capital punishment, torture or other cruel, inhuman and degrading treatment[457] and a regulation on dual-use goods. These will be discussed in turn.

The regulation concerning trade in equipment and products which can be used for capital punishment, torture or other cruel, inhuman or degrading treatment is based upon Article 133 TEC. The first part of the regime established by Regulation 1236/2005 imposes a ban on exports to any third state of products which have no practical use, other than for the purposes of torture, inhuman and degrading treatment or capital punishment.[458] The purpose of this is to prevent violation of human rights and it is aimed at giving further effect to the aforementioned specific guidelines on torture and the death penalty.[459] In a series of cases, the ECJ has held that the Common Commercial Policy can encompass regimes which have a foreign policy aspect.[460]

---

[454] See *Ahmed Ali Yusef and Al Barakat International Foundation* v. *Council and Commission*, n. 289 above, para. 243.

[455] E.g., Common Position 2006/51/CFSP concerning Zimbabwe.

[456] Council Regulation 423/2007 concerning Restrictive Measures Against Iran, [2007] OJ L103/1, 20 April 2007.

[457] Council Regulation 1236/2005 Concerning Trade in Certain Goods which Could be Used for Capital Punishment, Torture or Other Cruel, Inhuman or Degrading Treatment or Punishment, [2005] OJ L200/1, 30 July 2005.

[458] Articles 3 and 4 Council Regulation 1236/2005.

[459] See COM(2002)770, Explanatory Memorandum, para. 5 and the Preamble to Regulation 1236/2005.

[460] Case C-83/94 *Criminal Proceedings Against Peter Leifer, Reinhold Otto Krauskopf and Otto Holzer* [1995] ECR I-3231, paras. 10–13. See also, among others, Case C-70/94 *Fritz Werner Industrie-Ausrüstungen GmbH* v. *Germany* [1995] ECR I- 3189; Case C-367/89 *Aimé Richardt* [1991] ECR I-4621; and Case C-124/95 *R, ex parte Centro-Com Srl* v. *HM Treasury and the Bank of England* [1997] ECR I-81, especially Advocate General Jacobs's opinion at para. 27. The first three cases were in the context of dual-use goods.

This regulation, however, is the first attempt specifically to prohibit the export to all states of goods irrespective of their origin, which have no other use but, according to the Community, to contribute to human rights violations. The prohibition is notwithstanding the fact that the imposition of capital punishment, at least in a third state, may be legitimate under both domestic and international law. The regulation also prohibits the importing of any such goods into a Member State.

The second part of the regime established under this regulation deals with 'dual-use goods', in the sense that they can also be used for the purpose of inflicting torture, cruel, inhuman or degrading treatment or punishment upon another person. This part of the regime does not expressly extend to goods which could also be used for the purposes of capital punishment. Although such goods may also be covered by Regulation 1334/2000,[461] which establishes the current Community regime on dual-use goods, the regime under Regulation 1236/2005 is phrased in more mandatory terms, although it is too early to tell if it makes any difference in practice. Under Article 5 of Regulation 1334/2000, Member States may prohibit or impose an authorisation requirement on the export of certain goods. Under Regulation 1236/2005, if any goods (listed in Annex III to the regulation) that can be used for the purpose of torture or other cruel, inhuman or degrading treatment or punishment are to be exported, then an authorisation must be applied for.[462]

The relevant Member State authorities do have discretion as to whether such authorisations will be granted and the regulation speci- fies the criteria which must be taken into account. The competent authorities must not grant any authorisation if there are reasonable grounds to believe that they will be used for prohibited purposes, taking into account 'available international court judgments' and the findings of competent bodies of the United Nations, Council of Europe, the European Committee for the Prevention of Torture and the UN Special Rapporteur on Torture, as well as the findings of non-governmental organisations.[463] If such information is considered seriously it is

---

[461] Council Regulation 1334/2000 Setting up a Community Regime for the Control of Exports of Dual-Use Items and Technology, [2000] OJ L159/1, 30 June 2000. It has been subsequently amended on a number of occasions, most recently by Council Regulation 394/2006 amending and updating Regulation 1334/2000 Setting up a Community Regime for the Control of Exports of Dual-Use Items and Technology, [2006] OJ L74/1, 13 March 2006.

[462] Article 5 Regulation 1236/2005. There are some very limited exceptions.

[463] Article 6(2) Regulation 1236/2005.

difficult to envisage that goods which may be used for prohibited purposes under this regulation will be exported to many third states. The reality, however, is likely to be that the national authorities will take a variable approach (as has been the case under the Dual-Use Goods Regulation)[464] and that while the scheme will work effectively in some Member States it will leave something to be desired in a number of others. It is to the Dual-Use Goods Regulation that the discussion now turns.

The original Community dual-use goods regime was implemented by Regulation 3381/94.[465] It was with respect to this regulation that the ECJ in the *Werner* and *Leifer* cases, confirmed that restrictions on the export of dual-use goods fell within the exclusive competence of the Community. Article 8 of Regulation 3381/94 referred to Annex III of Council Decision 94/942/CFSP. This set out the considerations the competent authorities should take into account when deciding whether or not to grant an export authorisation.[466] These included obligations under Security Council Resolutions, the non-proliferation of sensitive goods and an obscure reference to human rights in terms of the June 1991 Luxembourg European Council Resolution. This said that the export of conventional arms to states should take its human rights record and internal situation into account. Cross-pillar action was thus taken to regulate trade in dual-use goods.

In Regulation 1334/2000, which replaced that regime with a purely Community system, Article 5 allows, as noted above, a Member State to prohibit or impose an authorisation requirement on the export of goods, for public security reasons or due to human rights considerations.[467] The Member State in so doing must inform the Commission of its reasoning. The state has discretion on the matter and if it decides that it does not wish to permit the export of such goods it may legitimately do so, so long as the restriction is proportionate to the risk to the protection of human rights in the state of destination.

---

[464] See SEC(2004)1158, point 3. This Commission paper assesses the implementation of the regulation between 2000 and 2004 and only deals with the 'old' fifteen Member States.

[465] Council Regulation 3381/94 Setting up a Community Regime for the Control of Exports of Dual-Use Goods, [1994] OJ L367/1, 31 December 1994. For detailed discussion of this regime and how it differs from the current one, see Koutrakos, *EU International Relations Law*, p. 419 *et seq*.

[466] OJ L 278/1, 30 October 1996.

[467] Although this is not to say that it still does not have inter-pillar dimensions to it, for further discussion see Koutrakos, *EU International Relations Law*, p. 442 *et seq*.

Decision 94/942/CFSP has now been repealed,[468] but Annex III is still applicable.[469] The general regime has also occasionally been supplemented by regulations which specifically prohibit the exportation of dual-use goods to a named third state because they may be used for the purposes of internal repression.[470] This is so as to remove any discretion as far as these third states and the particular goods in question are concerned. All of these measures rely on human rights violations in the states in question, among the reasons behind their adoption.[471]

Such considerations are also relevant in the EU Code of Conduct on Arms Exports.[472] Arms exports are outside the Community's competence but not outside the scope of the CFSP.[473] In the Code of Conduct on Arms Exports, 'Criterion Two' is based upon the respect for human rights in the country of final destination and declares that Member States will not issue export licences if there is a clear risk that the proposed export will be used for repressive measures. Respect for human rights is, however, only one of seven detailed criteria in addition to which the measure is not legally binding.[474]

3.4 Conclusions

This chapter has shown that the Community and Union have a wide range of instruments and strategies at their disposal to pursue their ethical objectives in third states. Although the Community and Member States were slow to introduce such values into their relations with third

---

[468] 2000/402/CFSP, Council Decision Repealing Decision 94/942/CFSP on the Joint Action Concerning the Control of Exports of Dual-Use Goods, [2000] OJ L159/218, 30 June 2000.

[469] Preamble to Regulation 1334/2000.

[470] See e.g., Council Regulation 2158/1999 Concerning a Ban on the Supply to Indonesia of Equipment which might be Used in Internal Repression, [1999] OJ L265/1, 13 October 1999 (this measure is no longer in force) and Council Regulation 817/2006 Renewing the Restrictive Measures in respect of Burma/Myanmar and repealing Regulation 798/2004, [2006] OJ L148/1, 2 June 2006.

[471] See in particular, the Preambles to the regulations cited above.

[472] Adopted 8 June 1998. See Denza, *Intergovernmental Pillars*, p. 104.

[473] Article 11(1) TEU.

[474] An annual report is published on the national measures taken to give effect to the Code; see e.g., Eighth Annual Report according to Operative Provision Eight of the European Union Code of Conduct on Arms Exports, [2006] OJ C250/1, 16 October 2006. The reports indicate that some Member States regularly refuse to grant export licences. Amnesty International, however, has been very critical of the Code, see Amnesty International, *Undermining Global Security: the European Union's Arms Exports* (London: Amnesty International, 2004). A number of third states, such as Canada, Iceland and Norway, have officially aligned themselves to the criteria in the Code.

states, the end of the Cold War and the lack of a rival political ideology and provider of ideologically tied funds strengthened their bargaining position.[475] The changing global political climate, coinciding with the adoption of the Maastricht Treaty, enabled a more proactive approach to be adopted. Not only have policies which place an emphasis upon certain values been introduced in relations with most third states, but there has also been a refocusing of approach. The transformation in the Community's competence and attitude has been significant. Food aid, for example, has gone from being a policy concerned with equally promoting the interests of Community producers to one primarily cast in terms of alleviating hunger.

The Union has used the CFSP, Community and cross-pillar action to implement the policies it wishes to pursue. Where the Community does not have competence, for example with regard to arms controls, the CFSP has been used instead. Where Community competence does exist, its breadth is more than apparent. The projects which have been and can be funded under the various human rights regulations, for example, illustrate the scope of the Community's activities and ambition. The competence under Articles 177–181 TEC is, however, expressly limited to relations with developing states. The Community has also used its development cooperation powers to pursue a global humanitarian aid policy. Articles 308, 133 and 310 TEC have also been used to pursue ethical values in relations with third states. The use of Article 133 TEC, where the Community has exclusive competence, still does not substantially affect the competence of the Member States in their development cooperation policies.

The ECJ and Member States have allowed a very broad approach to development cooperation because it is about coordinated action and providing funds. Community policies do not prohibit the Member States from pursuing any policies they so wish, so long as they are broadly complementary to and coordinated with Community action. Development aid is most effective when it both supports economic growth and is focused on poverty reduction. The Community, in line with all other major donors, now considers poverty reduction to be the major objective of development policy. The obstacles all donors face are substantial, especially considering the institutional structures in

---

[475] This, of course, is now changing with the rise of China as an aid donor (without political conditionality but not without strings) in particular, to resource rich but impoverished developing countries.

recipient states with which they often have to contend. There is no one formula to purge poverty from third states or make them democratic and accountable to their citizens. As the House of Lords Committee on the European Union noted in 2004, despite these problems, '[t]here is little doubt that EU aid is achieving better results than it has in the past, but is capable of achieving even better results'.[476] The Union certainly has the powers, instruments and economic influence to pursue an effective ethical foreign policy. The major consideration facing the Union in the pursuit of such a policy, however, is the balance to be struck, in practice, between its sometimes competing foreign policy objectives. The next two chapters of the book deal with this issue in the context of relations with specific third states.

---

[476] House of Lords, *EU Development Aid in Transition*, p. 8. See also, Department for International Development, *Eliminating World Poverty: Making Governance Work for the Poor* (HMSO: London, 2006) p. 115, where the DFID considers that the European Union is now better at distributing aid than it was. This is not faint praise: the DFID in the United Kingdom has been very critical over the years about EU aid, and considers itself to be a far more effective aid donor than the Commission.

4 Ethical Values and Foreign Policy in Practice: Responses to the Denial of Democracy in Myanmar, Nigeria and Pakistan

The next two chapters of the book deal with examples of the practice of the Union in its relations with specific third countries. In this chapter, relations with Myanmar, Pakistan and Nigeria are discussed. In all three countries democracy has been interrupted at one stage or another and all have well-documented problems relevant to those values and principles the European Union seeks to promote and protect in third states. The aim in this chapter is to assess how the scope and type of legal and diplomatic instruments selected by the Union to achieve its objectives have been influenced by differing approaches and tactics, as well as geopolitical considerations.

4.1 Myanmar

In 1980 the (then) European Economic Community entered into a Cooperation Agreement[1] with the (then) Member States of the Association of South East Asian Nations (ASEAN).[2] With the exception of Myanmar, the Community has subsequently extended relations with those states who have joined ASEAN after the 1980 Cooperation Agreement came into force.[3] In April 2007 the Council issued a mandate to the

---

[1] Cooperation Agreement between the European Economic Community and Indonesia, Malaysia, The Philippines, Singapore and Thailand – Member Countries of the Association of South-East Asian Nations, [1980] OJ L144/2, 10 June 1980.
[2] Singapore, Malaysia, The Philippines, Indonesia and Thailand. Brunei joined in 1984, Vietnam in 1995, Laos and Myanmar in 1997 and Cambodia in 1999. ASEAN is not an international organisation nor does it have international legal personality.
[3] This has been through either the adoption of a Protocol to the Agreement with the ASEAN states (e.g., Brunei) or the adoption of both a separate bilateral Agreement and a Protocol (e.g., Cambodia and Laos).

Commission to negotiate a Free Trade Agreement between the European Community and the ASEAN states.[4] Any such future Agreement, however, as is the case with the 1980 Cooperation Agreement, will not extend to Myanmar. This is due to the existing situation in that country and the Community's long-standing refusal to enter into treaty relations with that country. In the absence of a development-based treaty relationship with Myanmar, if the Union wishes to promote and protect certain values and principles in that country, the primary techniques and instruments will be those of the Common Foreign and Security Policy (CFSP) as supplemented by the Community exercising its development-based competence and funding various projects in Myanmar.

Until the end of 2006, Myanmar came under the scope of the Asian and Latin American Regulation (ALA Regulation).[5] Since January 2007, it has come within the scope of Regulation 1905/2006 Establishing a Financing Instrument for Development Cooperation.[6] It has thus been eligible, depending upon the time in question, for projects to be funded under these two regulations, as well as under the various incarnations of the EIDHR.[7] The ALA Regulation stated that in relations with Asian and Latin America countries, emphasis should be placed on strengthening the cooperation framework and on making an effective contribution, through institutional dialogue and economic and financial cooperation, to sustainable development, security, stability and democracy.[8] The ALA Regulation further stipulated that indicative multi-annual guidelines should apply to the main partner countries and accordingly in the Country Strategy Papers (CSP) for these countries, the promotion of effective democracy and protection of human rights and fundamental freedoms had been identified as major objectives.[9] Under the terms of Regulation 1905/2006, the commitment to the

---

[4] General Affairs and External Relations Council, 23–24 April 2007, Doc. 8425/07.
[5] Council Regulation 443/92 on Financial and Technical Assistance to, and Economic Cooperation with, the Developing Countries in Asia and Latin America, [1992] OJ L52/1, 27 February 1992.
[6] Regulation 1905/2006 Establishing a Financing Instrument for Development Cooperation, [2006] OJ L378/41, 27 December 2006.
[7] Council Regulation 975/1999, [1999] OJ L1201/, 8 May 1999 as repealed and replaced by Regulation 1889/2006 Establishing a Financing Instrument for the Promotion of Democracy and Human Rights Worldwide, [2006] OJ L386/1, 29 December 2006.
[8] Articles 4–6 Regulation 443/92.
[9] A CSP does not exist for Myanmar. Although see COM(2003)399/4, p. 19 with regard specifically to ASEAN states.

Millennium Development Goals (MDGs) and human rights, the rule of law and democracy is as clear, if not even clearer.[10]

Before discussing relations between the Union and Myanmar in detail, it is worth briefly discussing the situation there.[11] A highly authoritarian regime has been in power in Myanmar since 1962, when an elected civilian government was overthrown. Since 1988, when the armed forces suppressed a massive pro-democracy movement, a junta composed of senior military officers have ruled by decree, without a Constitution or legislature. On 27 May 1990, by most accounts the military permitted relatively free elections for a parliament to which they announced they would transfer powers. Voters overwhelmingly supported anti-government parties, with the National League for Democracy (NLD) winning 80 per cent of the parliamentary seats. Since the election, the military has systematically and brutally suppressed the democracy movement. The reports of the Special Rapporteur appointed by the Commission on Human Rights and the Special Envoy of the Secretary-General of the United Nations,[12] submissions made to US courts,[13] and reports from the International Labour Organisation (ILO)[14] and respected non-governmental organisations (NGOs)[15] highlight and document gross and systematic human rights violations. In brief (and the list is not exhaustive), the following violations of international norms are all well documented and widely verified: torture; extra-judicial killings; disappearances; arbitrary arrest and detention; denial of fair trials; excessive use of force and violations of humanitarian law; widespread rape by military officials; severe restrictions on the freedoms of expression, assembly and movement;

---

[10] Article 2 Regulation 1905/2006.
[11] This information is derived from the Reports of the UN Special Envoy and Special Rapporteur to Burma/Myanmar, especially E/CN.4/2006/34, E/CN.4/2005/36, E/CN.4/2003/41, E/CN.4/2000/38, E/CN.4/1999/35, E/CN.4/1999/129, E/CN.4/1997/64, E/CN.4/1996/65, E/CN.4/1994/57, E/CN.4/1993/37, A/61/369, A/58/219, A/57/290 and A/56/312.
[12] *Ibid.*
[13] See *Doe* v. *Unocal*, 963 F. Supp. 880 (2002) and *National Foreign Trade Council* v. *Andrew S. Natsios and Philmore Anderson, III*, 118 F.3d.38 (1999).
[14] See e.g., *Report of the Commission of Inquiry appointed under Article 26 of the Constitution of the ILO to Examine the Observance by Myanmar of the Forced Labour Convention 1930 (No. 29)* Geneva, 2 July 1998.
[15] See, for specific examples, Amnesty International, *Myanmar: Travesties of Justice – Continued Misuse of the Legal System* (December 2005) and Human Rights Watch, '*They Came and Destroyed Our Village Again': the Plight of Internally Displaced Persons in Karen State* (2005) 17(4)(c), 1.

persecution of ethnic groups; and the systematic and widespread use of slavery and slave-like practices.

The military government, known as the State Peace and Development Council (SPDC),[16] has routinely refused to meet with representatives of the United Nations and has on numerous occasions denied the Special Rapporteur entry into the country, although some visits have been permitted since 1998.[17] In 1998 the ILO in a report on Myanmar referred to the regime engaging in 'clear flagrant violations of a peremptory norm of international law' (referring to slavery and slave-like practices) and 'crimes against humanity'.[18] Myanmar was suspended from the ILO in 2000, due to its failure to ensure compliance with the ILO Forced Labour Convention, 1930.[19] The NGOs Freedom House, Amnesty International and Human Rights Watch all consider the military regime to be one of the most repressive in power anywhere in the world.[20] According to Transparency International, in 2006 it was the second most corrupt country in the world[21] and the Fund for Peace and

---

[16] Previously the State Law and Order Restoration Council.

[17] Ibrahim Gambari, the UN Undersecretary-General for Political Affairs, was sent as the Secretary-General's Special Envoy and was granted permission in May 2006 to visit Myanmar. It is worth noting that this was after Myanmar had become an issue of discussion in the Security Council and Gambari had briefed the Council on the situation in Myanmar in December 2005. The former Special Envoy to Myanmar, Razali Ismail, resigned in January 2006. The authorities in Myanmar had refused him entry for the previous two years. In the past the Special Rapporteurs on the Human Rights Situation in Myanmar (Professor Yozo Yokota (1992–6), Judge Rajsoomer Lallah (1996–2000) and Professor Paulo Sergio Pinheiro (2000– present)) have also routinely been denied entry to Myanmar. Pinheiro, for example, has been denied entry since November 2003. His November 2003 visit had to be cancelled after secret listening devices were found in a room he was using to conduct interviews.

[18] *Report of the Commission of Inquiry appointed under Article 26 of the Constitution of the ILO*, Part V, para. 538.

[19] Convention No. 29, Forced Labour Convention, 1930, 39 UNTS 55. Report of the Governing Body of the ILO, 276th Session, November 1999. Of the ILO's 'core' conventions, Myanmar is also a party to Convention No. 87, Freedom of Association and Protection of the Right to Organise Convention, 1948, 68 UNTS 17.

[20] See Freedom House, *Country Report 2006 – Burma*, available at www.freedomhouse.org/template.cfm?page=22&year=2006&country=6932: the situation with regard to political rights and civil rights in Myanmar are both rated 7, the lowest possible rating (for Freedom House's methodology and raking system see www.freedomhouse.org/template.cfm?page=351&ana_page=298&year=2006); Amnesty International, *Report 2006*, available at http://web.amnesty.org/report2006/mmr-summary-eng; and Human Rights Watch, *World Report 2007* (New York: Human Rights Watch, 2006) p. 248.

[21] The Transparency International Corruption Perception Index Table can be found at www.transparency.org/policy_research/surveys_indices/cpi/2006

Foreign Policy 'Failed States Index' considered it the eighteenth most unstable state in 2006.[22]

The SPDC, for its part, considers that it is the victim of propaganda and misinformation. According to it, those human rights obligations which are culturally applicable to the people of Myanmar are respected.[23] Myanmar is a party to the 1926 Slavery Convention,[24] the Genocide Convention,[25] the UN Conventions on the rights of women[26] and children[27] and a total of nineteen ILO Conventions, although it is only party to two of the eight ILO 'core' conventions.[28] It is also party to the Four Geneva Conventions of 1949.[29]

Economic data on Myanmar is either very sketchy or considered unreliable. For this reason the World Bank Development Indicators do not have a per capita GDP figure for Myanmar. The United Nations Development Programme estimated the per capita GDP in 2004 to be US$1,027.[30] According to the Human Development Index, Myanmar

---

[22] The Fund for Peace and Foreign Policy 'Failed States Index' can be found at www.fundforpeace.org/programs/fsi/fsindex.php

[23] See the SPDC's webpage www.myanmar-information.net/truth/truth.html

[24] Slavery Convention, 1926, 60 LNTS 253.

[25] Convention on the Prevention and Punishment of the Crime of Genocide, 1948, 78 UNTS 277.

[26] Convention on the Elimination of All Forms of Discrimination Against Women, 1979, 1249 UNTS 13.

[27] Convention on the Rights of the Child, 1989, 1577 UNTS 3.

[28] Myanmar is party to Convention No. 29, Forced Labour Convention, 1930 and Convention No. 87, Freedom of Association and Protection of the Right to Organise Convention, 1948. The 'core' conventions to which it is not party are Convention No. 98, Right to Organise and Collective Bargaining Convention, 1949, 96 UNTS 257; Convention No. 100, Equal Remuneration Convention, 1951, 165 UNTS 304; Convention No. 105, Abolition of Forced Labour Convention, 1957, 320 UNTS 291; Convention No. 111, Discrimination (Employment and Occupation) Convention, 1958, 363 UNTS 31; Convention No. 138, Minimum Age Convention, 1973, 1015 UNTS 14862; and Convention No. 182, Worst Forms of Child Labour Convention, 1999, 2133 UNTS 37245.

[29] Geneva Convention for the Amelioration of the Condition of the Wounded and Sick in Armed Forces in the Field, 1949 (Geneva Convention I), 75 UNTS 31; Geneva Convention for the Amelioration of the Condition of the Wounded, Sick and Shipwrecked Members of the Armed Forces at Sea, 1949 (Geneva Convention II), 75 UNTS 85; Geneva Convention Relative to the Treatment of Prisoners of War, 1949 (Geneva Convention III), 75 UNTS 135; and Geneva Convention Relative to the Protection of Civilian Persons in Time of War, 1949 (Geneva Convention IV), 75 UNTS 287.

[30] See UNDP, *Human Development Report 2006: Beyond Scarcity – Power, Poverty and the Global Water Crisis* (New York: Palgrave Macmillan, 2006) p. 285. The European Commission considers the figure to be €1,590, see http://ec.europa.eu/comm/external_relations/myanmar/intro/index.htm

is ranked 130th out of 177 countries in terms of development.[31] It is classified as a low-income country. In 1993, trade between the European Union and Myanmar amounted to ECU 28 million.[32] In 2005 this trade was worth €370 million.[33] Myanmar is very rich in natural resources such as gas, oil, timber and gems but does not control sufficient quantities on a global scale of any vital resources to be particularly important, in the sense that, for example, Iran is with regard to oil. It is of negligible importance, relatively speaking, in trade terms to the Union and it does not pose a security threat to it. Nor is it likely that a large influx of refugees from Myanmar will arrive at the Union's borders; those who have fled persecution have largely sought refuge in India, Thailand and Bangladesh. Thus, with little else at stake, there are few interests which can impede any decision of the Union and its Member States to take punitive action against Myanmar or, indeed, little tangible benefit to them in promoting certain values and principles in it either.

The Union's relationship and dealings with Myanmar have been conducted on both a regional and a bilateral basis. The latter is dealt with in detail below. Although it is not possible within the scope of this chapter to discuss the regional dialogue between the Union and the ASEAN states in detail, the following section provides some context and background to that dialogue and discusses the approach to ethical values in it.

4.1.1 Role of Ethical Values and Principles in Regional Dialogue Involving Myanmar and the Union

The Union was slow to realise the growing importance of South-East Asia in global terms. It was not until the Essen European Council of 1994 that a New Asia Strategy (NAS) recognised that the existing relationship with the ASEAN states had undergone a fundamental shift and was increasingly one of equals. The relationship thus required a review of the presumptions upon which it had been based. One of the consequences of the NAS was the establishment of the Asia Europe Meetings (ASEM) in 1996 which are intended to function outside formal regional structures.[34] The political dialogue undertaken in ASEM is in addition to

---

[31] UNDP, *Human Development Report 2006*, p. 285.

[32] See [1995] OJ C91/53, 6 December 1995.

[33] See the webpage of the Commission Delegation to Thailand, Cambodia, Laos and Myanmar at www.deltha.ec.europa.eu/Myanmar/MM_trade.htm

[34] ASEM is composed of the ASEAN states, China, Japan, South Korea and the EU Member States. In September 2006, the Sixth ASEM summit decided to admit Pakistan, India, Mongolia, the ASEAN Secretariat and the new EU Member States, Romania and

those arrangements which have been established with a more formal structure. These include the ASEAN Regional Forum (ARF),[35] ASEAN Post-Ministerial Conferences (APMC) and the ASEAN-EU Joint Cooperation Committee (JCC), which is based upon the 1980 Cooperation Agreement with the ASEAN Member States.[36] With the exception of the ASEAN-EU Joint Cooperation Committee, all fora come within the scope of the CFSP.

The Union and its Member States have, in accordance with the objectives of the CFSP and Community development cooperation provisions, introduced discussion on human rights, democracy and other values and principles into their regional dialogue with these Asian states. The Union has encountered differing levels of resistance from them. Furthermore, the Union has at times vetoed the admission into the dialogue of certain states, namely Myanmar, Laos and Cambodia, due to their lack of democratic institutions and the human rights situation within them. The situation in Laos and Cambodia has been deemed to have improved sufficiently with regard, for example, to human rights and democracy for the Union to have agreed to admit them to the various fora and the Community has consequently also entered into treaty relations with them.[37] The Community still does not, as noted above, have any treaty relations with Myanmar.[38]

Bulgaria. See also, the declaration on behalf of the Commission, (1996) 1/2 *Bull. EU* 1.4.139; further the Commission's perspective on the ASEM meeting, COM(1996)4; and the Opinion of the Economic and Social Committee on Relations between the European Union and Asia, [1996] OJ C97/31, 1 April 1996.

[35] The ARF primarily provides a setting in which members can discuss regional security and political concerns in the Asia Pacific region. All ARF documents are available at www.dfat.gov.au/arf/

[36] Although now dated see further, D. Mahncke, 'Relations between Europe and South East Asia: the Security Dimension' (1997) 2 *EFARev.* 291; P. van Dijk, 'Meeting Asia and Latin America in a New Setting' in P. van Dijk and G. Faber (eds.), *The External Economic Dimensions of the European Union* (The Hague: Kluwer, 2000) p. 292; M. Kagami, 'Europe and Asia: Too Faraway' in Dijk and Faber, *External Economic Dimensions*, p. 341; and J. McMahon, 'ASEAN and the Asia-Europe Meeting: Strengthening the European Union's Relationship with South East Asia?' (1998) 3 *EFARev.* 233.

[37] See Cooperation Agreement between the European Community and the Lao People's Democratic Republic, [1997] OJ L334/15, 5 December 1997 and Cooperation Agreement between the European Community and the Kingdom of Cambodia, [1999] OJ L269/18, 19 October 1999. Both Agreements have an 'essential elements' clause.

[38] The Council on 26 June 1997, e.g., stated that the situation in Myanmar precluded starting negotiations on that country's accession to the EC-ASEAN Cooperation Agreement and that Myanmar's membership of ASEAN did not imply its involvement in the Asia-Europe dialogue. See (1997) 6 *Bull. EU* 1.2.112.

This approach, where the Union insists upon third states respecting certain norms, can in some respects disadvantage it, as the Asian states may respond by taking their business where such commitments are not necessary. China and India are rivals for political and economic dominance in South-East Asia and Russia has increasingly sought to strengthen its economic position in the region as well.[39] None of these countries insists that third states respect the norms the Union refers to. In the First ASEM meeting held in Bangkok in 1996, for example, the different priorities and perspectives of the Union and Asian states was more than apparent. In paragraph five of the statement adopted at the conclusion of the meeting, the Asian states managed to ensure that the commitment to the dialogue, among the participating countries, was being conducted 'on the basis of mutual respect, equality, promotion of fundamental rights and, in accordance with the rules of international law and obligations and non-intervention, whether direct or indirect, in each other's internal affairs'.[40] This form of wording was clearly a compromise between the parties. The Union wished to ensure that some commitment to human rights was agreed upon whereas the Asian states wanted to ensure that the impact of that commitment was, as far as possible, diminished. Unlike the approach of the Union, the position of many Asian states is that matters such as human rights and democracy are within a state's domestic jurisdiction and any criticism of them is an interference in its internal affairs.[41] The wording was thus one both parties could live with, as they took it to mean different things.

The description by a leading Commission official of some of the documents adopted in the Third ASEM summit in Seoul in 2000 as a 'breakthrough vis-à-vis human rights', simply highlights the limited ambitions and prospects that have been held out for such objectives being effectively addressed in this forum.[42] In the light of the attacks in Bali and Jakarta in 2002 and 2003 respectively, the Union has very clearly shifted its focus to cooperating on and dealing with terror in the region. This has now been recognised as one the key objectives of

---

[39] See 'ASEAN Hails the Benefits of Friendship with China', *IHT*, 2 November 2006 and 'Sanctions Won't Work on Myanmar – ASEAN Official', *Taipei Times*, 12 June 2007.

[40] See (1996) 3 *Bull. EU*, Doc. 2.3.1.   [41] See further the discussion below.

[42] M. Rieterer, 'ASEM – The Third Summit in Seoul 2000: a Roadmap to Consolidate the Partnership between Asia and Europe' (2001) 6 *EFARev.* 1, 13.

ASEM.[43] With regard to the question of participation in ASEM, the Union has stood its ground on the human rights records of some of the Asian states. Laos, Cambodia and Myanmar all became parties to ASEAN, albeit after the ASEM process had begun. The European Union has accordingly stated very clearly that it did not wish to negotiate or engage in dialogue with these states due to their human rights records. As was noted above, it is only with regard to Myanmar that the Union continues to adopt this approach.

In the Fifth ASEM meeting in Hanoi in 2004 the Union, under pressure from the other participants, accepted the participation of Myanmar but only on the understanding that the representatives from Myanmar would be from a level lower than that of the Head of State or Government. The European Parliament, however, adopted a resolution 'deploring' the EU decision to allow Myanmar to participate in the Fifth ASEM Summit. The Parliament insisted that Myanmar's participation should be conditional on the regime recognising that the National League for Democracy (led by Aung San Suu Kyi) won the 1990 election, transferring power to civilian authorities, releasing all political prisoners and respecting human rights.[44] Finland's decision to grant a visa to the Foreign Minister of Myanmar to allow him to attend the Sixth ASEM summit, which was held in Helsinki in September 2006, also caused controversy in some circles. The European Union, as will be discussed below, has placed travel restrictions on some members of the regime in Myanmar. The Finnish authorities, acting within their discretion, decided to grant a visa to the Foreign Minister of Myanmar so that he could attend the meeting, a move which caused brouhaha among certain human rights activists.[45] In 2005, the Dutch Presidency had refused to issue visas to officials from Myanmar to participate in an ASEM Finance Ministers meeting. There is a clear difference in approach between some of the Member States of the Union as how best to deal with Myanmar, a difference which is more apparent in meetings solely with the ASEAN states, as will be discussed below. What the Union has attempted to do, however, is use the opportunity the ASEM summits provide to discuss with the other participants the democratisation process (or lack thereof) in Myanmar.

---

[43] See the Chair's Statements at the Fifth ASEM Foreign Ministers Meeting, 24 July 2003 and at the Sixth ASEM Foreign Ministers Meeting, 10–11 September 2006.

[44] (2004) 3 *Bull. EU* 1.2.7.

[45] 'Finland Causes Controversy with Burma Invitation', *euobserver.com*, 26 July 2006 and 'Finland Takes Flak for Inviting Burma to Asia-EU Meet', *Newsroom Finland*, 27 July 2006.

The Community, as noted above, also has a Cooperation Agreement with the Member States of ASEAN. The Union has continually (although quite selectively at times) plugged away at discussions on ethical values with the ASEAN states, even though the 2003 Commission Communication on relations with them highlights a distinct focus on tackling terrorism.[46] The Union, on the one hand, considers that they have problems with human rights and democracy and, on the other, maintains a dialogue with them encouraging cooperation in trade matters, countering terrorist activities and the greater protection of intellectual property, among a host of other issues. There are, however, major shortcomings in the approach of the Union toward the ASEAN states on matters such as human rights and democracy.

The Union has, by and large, treated the ASEAN states in a homogeneous manner. Yet, there is no shared Asian culture or a uniform view on the role of human rights and democracy.[47] Some of the ASEAN states are Islamic in nature, although this is expressed in very different ways; others are Buddhist or Confucian. Some, such as Singapore, promote a certain brand of nationalism and national identity over and above religion. With regard to democracy, the position also varies greatly. The nature of the 'democracy' that exists in Singapore or Malaysia, for example, is very different from that which existed in Thailand prior to the military coup of September 2006 or that which exists in The Philippines. The Union's primary concern, however, has been to obtain basic commitments to human rights and democracy from all ASEAN states.

One of the grounds of opposition from some of the ASEAN states to such issues as an agenda item in the dialogue with the Union has been on the basis of what is perceived as the imposition of cultural values by the European states: values that some states consider are not relevant to them.[48] The Union, however, has been keen to stress that this is not the imposition of values by one part of the world on another but an affirmation of shared values. The framing of ethical values in this manner does not cut any ice with some of the ASEAN states. Trade and access to markets have been the issues they wish to discuss, and while progress

---

[46] See COM(2003)399/4, p. 10.

[47] See more generally, J. Bauer and D. Bell (eds.), *The East Asian Challenge for Human Rights* (Cambridge: Cambridge University Press, 1999). The ratification of the major UN human rights conventions by these states and the nature of their reservations differ markedly.

[48] Singapore and Malaysia, for example, are well-known exponents of such views.

has been made on these fronts, the Union and its Member States have seen the commitment to human rights by all parties as essential for the dialogue to move forward.[49]

The 2003 Commission Communication, however, very interestingly notes that the clearest shared value between the European Union and ASEAN states is regional integration. As noted above, the Communication also places far greater emphasis on the fight against terror.[50] This does not necessarily mean the abandonment of a commitment to discussion on ethical matters. In the ASEAN-EU Foreign Ministers meeting in January 2003, for example, there was a reaffirmed commitment by all parties to respect the equality of civilizations and to the shared values of human rights, including development and fundamental freedoms.[51] The Nuremburg Declaration, on an EU-ASEAN Enhanced Partnership of 15 March 2007, also refers to human rights, democracy, good governance, justice and the rule of law.[52] Although they are considered to be 'universal values' they are, however, only referred to in the Preamble. The text of the declaration is almost exclusively about cooperation in the political, security, economic, socio-cultural and environmental fields. There is no reference to human rights and democracy, for example, as fields of cooperation.[53] While such texts are not definitive of the Union's approach to such matters, they are illustrative of them. It does seem that while the Union has not abandoned the commitment to such values in its dialogue with the ASEAN states, it has at least subordinated them when other foreign policy objectives have come into sharper focus.

The Union, in pushing ethical values on to the agenda in its dialogue with the ASEAN states, has always essentially adopted a pragmatic view. At the end of 2000, for example, in the Vientiane Declaration adopted by the two blocs, it was stated quite clearly that economic dialogue and

---

[49] This was to some extent achieved as early as 1992. See e.g., Joint Declaration of the Tenth Meeting of the Foreign Ministers of the ASEAN–EC, 29–30 October 1992. All documents from EU-ASEAN meetings are available at the website of the ASEAN Secretariat, www.aseansec.org/

[50] COM(2003)399/4, p. 10. Although the Communication as a whole also refers to, for example, shared values in countering terrorism, the reference to 'regional integration' as a shared value is expressed most strongly.

[51] Joint Co-Chairman's Statement of the Fourteenth EU-ASEAN Ministerial Meeting, 28 January 2003, para. 5.

[52] Joint Co-Chairman's Statement of the Sixteenth EU-ASEAN Ministerial Meeting, 15 March 2007.

[53] Ibid.

cooperation was to be intensified. ASEAN-EU programmes in intellectual property had to be seen as a priority, along with questions of market access.[54] Human rights, democracy and other fundamental freedoms were nowhere to be found as far as cooperation between the blocs was concerned, although both the Union and ASEAN states 'committed' themselves in the Declaration to promote and protect all human rights and the Declaration noted that they had a frank discussion on developments in Myanmar, which was by then a party to such meetings.[55]

The Union has clearly adopted an approach of obtaining basic commitments to human rights and democracy, among others, from third states, whenever it is a party to dialogue with them. This fact is borne out by the other case studies. The commitments obtained add nothing to the legal obligations states are under. All fora where such commitments have been made, no matter how weak they are, present opportunities for the Union to discuss such matters and utilise diplomatic pressure to that end. This is valuable in itself to the extent it allows the Union to emphasise consistently the importance it attaches to, for example, democracy and human rights, and that such matters and any shortcomings in this respect will be a legitimate subject of discussion. Such commitments do not, however, provide any real value beyond this.

4.1.2 Bilateral Dealings with Myanmar

The nature of the regime in Myanmar and its practices have, as noted above, resulted in the Union's refusal in the past to accept that country as a party to inter-regional dialogue. Notwithstanding the general situation in Myanmar since 1961, and some limited punitive measures that the Community adopted in 1991, the relationship between Myanmar and the Union only took a decisive turn for the worse when the Danish Consul in Rangoon, James Leander Nichols, was arrested for the unauthorised use of fax machines and telephones and subsequently died in custody in 1996. Nichols was the honorary consul of Denmark but also represented Finland, Norway and Switzerland. In a Presidency statement issued on 5 July 1996 by the Irish Presidency, the European Union indicated that it was very concerned with the situation in Myanmar and that it expected a full and satisfactory explanation of

---

[54] Vientiane Declaration, Thirteenth ASEAN-EU Ministerial Meeting, 11–12 December 2000, paras. 21–4.
[55] Ibid. paras. 9–10. See further the discussion below.

the death from the authorities.[56] It also called for an investigation into the death by the UN Special Rapporteur.[57] The death of a consular official provided impetus for action and led to a very swift response by Denmark, which pushed vociferously for the imposition of economic sanctions by the Union.[58] As a consequence of Nichols's death the Union decided to adopt a parallel approach towards Myanmar. Diplomatic measures would be utilised, on the one hand, and, on the other, punitive measures would be adopted via the CFSP and Community. These will be analysed in turn.

4.1.2.1 Diplomatic Measures and Myanmar

Following the death of Nichols, the European Union met with Myanmar's Minister of Foreign Affairs on three occasions.[59] The Union insisted that the SPDC must, without delay, respect human rights and release immediately and unconditionally all members of the National League for Democracy and all other political prisoners. It also insisted that the ruling junta enter into meaningful dialogue with the pro-democracy movement and all other national minorities to bring about reconciliation and democratic reform. It further insisted that Myanmar fully explain the death of Nichols.[60] The unrealistic nature of such demands is more than apparent but what the death of the Danish consul provided for the Union was a focal point and reason for it to amalgamate all its objectives and press for them collectively.

Reacting to what it considered an unsatisfactory response to its demands, the Union subsequently asked the UN Special Rapporteur (who had already been denied entry to the country) and the Working Group on Arbitrary Detention and Imprisonment to visit the country, as well as urging the Commission on Human Rights to take action against Myanmar.[61] The Union's deteriorating diplomatic relationship with

---

[56] See (1996) 7/8 Bull. EU 1.4.7.   [57] Ibid.

[58] See [1996] OJ C347/84, 18 November 1996, para. 11 and [1999] OJ C135/69, 14 May 1999. In the latter, Denmark is not expressly named.

[59] At the margins of the APMC in July 1996 and Troika meetings at the margins of the UN General Assembly in July and October 1996. The meetings were described as being 'most unsatisfactory' and 'a disappointment' by the European Union. See [1997] OJ C83/3, 14 March 1997.

[60] See ibid., Council Conclusions, 16 July 1996, (1996) 7/8 Bull. EU 1.2.4 and the Presidency Statement, 5 July 1996, (1996) 7/8 Bull. EU 1.4.7.

[61] Ibid. Myanmar was in fact already an annual topic of debate in the Commission on Human Rights. See further the discussion below.

Myanmar (due to the death of the Danish consul) further came to a head when the other ASEAN states decided to accept Myanmar's application to join them.[62] On 26 June 1997 the Council confirmed its attachment to the EU-ASEAN dialogue, in particular human rights, and expressed the view that the EU-ASEAN dialogue was a forum which the Union should use to raise the issue of human rights in Myanmar.[63] The Council made clear, however, that the current human rights situation in Myanmar precluded starting negotiations on that country's accession to the EC-ASEAN Cooperation Agreement and that membership of ASEAN did not automatically imply involvement in the dialogue between the blocs.[64] Furthermore, the Union had already withdrawn the GSP benefits Myanmar enjoyed and had adopted a Common Position concerning Myanmar; such a measure would have had to be repealed first, which Denmark would have strongly opposed.[65] The Union's approach towards Myanmar caused substantial diplomatic problems in the relationship with the other ASEAN states, as the Union also attempted to chastise them for admitting Myanmar.[66]

ASEAN now had a member state against whom the Union had already taken the punitive measures prescribed in a number of Common Positions. The accession of Myanmar to ASEAN, however, opened the door for a more critical dialogue with Indonesia on the situation in East Timor, something the Portuguese had long been pressing for. This consequently pushed human rights further up the agenda of issues to be discussed. The tactic to be adopted with regard to Myanmar's accession to ASEAN caused problems, though, between EU Member States themselves. Germany advocated Myanmar's participation in the EU-ASEM meeting in Berlin in March 1999, provided human rights were on the agenda. Denmark refused to take part in meetings if Myanmar was a party to the discussion. Eventually a compromise position was agreed between ASEAN states and the European Union and between the EU Member States as well. Myanmar was allowed to be

---

[62] The European Parliament in a resolution strongly condemned ASEAN for admitting Myanmar, see [1997] OJ C200/174, 30 June 1997, para. 6. The Council also commented on this but was more measured in its statement, see (1997) 6 *Bull. EU* 1.4.10.

[63] General Affairs Council, 26 June 1997, (1997) 6 *Bull. EU* 1.4.112.   [64] *Ibid.*

[65] See below the discussion on both the GSP and the Common Position.

[66] See the Statement on the Accession of Cambodia, Laos and Burma/Myanmar to ASEAN, (1997) 6 *Bull. EU* 1.4.10. Also see (1997) 1/2 *Bull. EU* 1.3.115 on the Twelfth EU-ASEAN Ministerial Meeting and [1998] OJ C134/20, 30 April 1998.

present at meetings, but only as a silent observer. Due to the debate over the accession of Myanmar to ASEAN, EU-ASEAN Ministerial Meetings were not held for three years.[67]

The Thirteenth ASEAN-EU Ministerial Meeting, held in Vientiane in December 2000, resolved the position. Laos, Cambodia and Myanmar all participated for the first time at the meeting as full members.[68] With Myanmar attending meetings since 2000 as a full member, the Union has used the opportunity to have discussions on the situation there. Although, as noted above, the Nuremburg Declaration adopted in March 2007 only made passing reference to human rights and democracy, the Joint Co-Chairman's statement of the Nuremburg meeting does make it clear that during the meeting 'ministers had a frank exchange of views on the situation in Myanmar'.[69]

As noted above, however, only Laos and Cambodia have become parties to the EC-ASEAN Cooperation Agreement of 1980. The Union has consistently argued that it is within its prerogative to decide whether to extend the Agreement to new ASEAN states and it will refuse to do so with regard to Myanmar until a democratic government with a commitment to human rights is installed. Until 2003, however, the Community had not sought to negotiate a third generation Agreement with all the ASEAN states, contrary to its practice elsewhere.[70] The historic reason for this had been Portugal's refusal to consent to a Commission mandate to negotiate Agreements with these countries as a group, due to its animosity (over East Timor) with Indonesia.[71] Rather than agreeing to a mandate with the ASEAN states, except Indonesia and Myanmar, which would have been politically very damaging to interests in the region, the Commission attempted to make do with

---

[67] See (2000) 12 *Bull. EU* 1.6.78; [1996] OJ C365/49, 4 April 1996; [1997] OJ C83/3, 14 March 1997; and [1999] OJ C297/153, 15 October 1999. Attempts at arranging, e.g., Troika visits to Rangoon were, however, ongoing. See (2000) 12 *Bull. EU* 1.6.10.

[68] See (2000) 12 *Bull. EU* 1.6.78 and the Vientiane Declaration, para. 1.

[69] Joint Co-Chairman's Statement of the Sixteenth EU-ASEAN Ministerial Meeting, Nuremberg, 15 March 2007, para. 20. The reference to a 'frank discussion' about Myanmar is common place in documents adopted at the end of such meetings.

[70] COM(2003)399/4. 'Third generation' Agreements not only contain 'essential elements' clauses but also deal with cooperation in areas which 'second generation' Agreements did not. As noted above, the Community has negotiated third generation Agreements with some of the ASEAN states, e.g., Cambodia and Laos.

[71] See COM(1996)314, p. 8. Portugal is not named. Although see [1997] OJ C325/16, 27 October 1997, para. 17 where the European Parliament names Portugal in this regard.

the 1980 Agreement.[72] East Timor is now no longer a problem in relations with the ASEAN states and consequently the 2003 Communication on the relationship with them allows for the negotiation of Agreements with the ASEAN states individually.[73] To date, after the 2003 Communication was approved, no new third generation agreements have been negotiated with ASEAN states. As noted above, however, the Council in April 2007 issued a mandate to the Commission to negotiate Free Trade Agreements with the ASEAN states.[74] In the future these Agreements will be the basis for enhanced relations with the ASEAN states. As ASEAN does not have international legal personality, individual Agreements are necessary, allowing the Community to exclude Myanmar. In the past, excluding one state ran the risk of damaging relations with the ASEAN states as a group. This is now less likely due to the increasing impatience of some ASEAN states towards the regime in Myanmar.

The Union has on occasion also arranged *ad hoc* bilateral meetings with representatives of the military junta on the fringes of the UN General Assembly.[75] These meetings have been set up through a network of contacts at embassy level.[76] Such meetings have not been conducive to re-establishing relations. Persuading the other ASEAN states, who have much more influence in Myanmar than the Union, of the benefits of a democratic and free Myanmar may achieve better results. This is in particular the case as the ASEAN states have since 2003 begun publicly to disagree among themselves over how best to deal with Myanmar and the failure of the authorities there to commit to and implement meaningful reform. At the ASEAN summit in June 2003, for example, the other ASEAN states issued a very rare public rebuke to Myanmar over the treatment of Aung San Suu Kyi.[77] Malaysia suggested that Myanmar be expelled unless it reformed, whereas Thailand pressed

---

[72] The General Affairs Council, 24 March 1997, Doc. 6491/97, approved a package of measures proposed in COM(1996)314 which were seen as an alternative to a third generation Agreement.

[73] COM(2003)399/4. East Timor is, further to a decision of the ACP-EC Council of Ministers, 16 May 2003, now a member of the ACP Group of States, (2003) 5 *Bull. EU* 1.6.107.

[74] General Affairs and External Relations Council, 23 April 2007, Doc. 8425/07. Mandates were also issued for India and South Korea.

[75] See [1997] OJ C83/3, 14 March 1997.

[76] I am grateful to Commission desk-officers for this insight.

[77] 'Japan Halts Aid to Burmese over Democracy Leader's Detention', *IHT*, 26 June 2003.

for it to be given more time to allow it to reform.[78] The situation in Myanmar has become a regular topic of discussion in ASEAN meetings.

As an ASEAN state, Myanmar was due to take its turn as Chair in 2006. In July 2005, however, the regime announced that it would postpone its turn in order to focus on national reconciliation and democratisation.[79] The ASEAN summit of December 2005 highlighted clearly how ASEAN states were becoming more impatient with the situation in Myanmar.[80] The Joint Communiqué of the Thirty-ninth ASEAN Ministerial Meeting in July 2006 was, however, ground-breaking in this regard.[81] Although the communiqué is couched in diplomatic language, its importance lies in the fact that ASEAN member states do not tend to comment publicly on each other's 'internal affairs'. Furthermore, ASEAN's expectations vis-à-vis internal reform and democracy in one of its member states were made express in the final text adopted by the Ministerial Meeting. The opportunity is now very ripe for the Union to utilise its leverage and to press the other ASEAN states to further use their political influence in Myanmar. Although the other ASEAN states are very important to Myanmar and it does have, relatively speaking, good relations with them, it is South Korea, China and India who are investing most in Myanmar and who are helping to exploit Myanmar's natural resources. It has been estimated, for example, that the gas project that the Daewoo Corporation of South Korea is involved in off the coast of Myanmar will reap between US$12 and $17 billion for the military regime over the next two decades.[82] To be effective, therefore, the Union must also push for action in other fora such as ASEM and the United Nations. The Union has discussed the issue in ASEM but, as discussed above, such matters are raised but not always forcefully. The Union has been more forthright at the United Nations.

The European Parliament, the Council and Presidency have all regularly adopted démarches, resolutions, declarations and statements, as appropriate, on developments in Myanmar.[83] The Union has also

---

[78] 'Burma Stays Silent on Suu Kyi's Fate as Dissidents are Freed', *Independent*, 24 July 2003.

[79] FCO, *Annual Human Rights Report 2006* (London: HMSO, 2007) p. 38.

[80] Chairman's Statement of the Eleventh ASEAN Summit, Kuala Lumpur, 12 December 2005.

[81] Joint Communiqué of the Thirty-ninth ASEAN Ministerial Meeting, Kuala Lumpur, 25 July 2006, paras. 79–80.

[82] 'The Never-Ending Myanmar Nightmare', *Spiegel Online*, 27 September 2006.

[83] The European Parliament has been extremely active in adopting resolutions on Myanmar, see e.g., [1989] OJ C291/94, 20 November 1989; [1991] OJ C240/180,

pushed for or supported measures against Myanmar in the Commission on Human Rights and General Assembly. The Commission on Human Rights first appointed a Special Rapporteur (Professor Yozo Yokota) on Myanmar in 1992. Since then the human rights situation in Myanmar has regularly been the subject of resolutions of the General Assembly or (until it ceased functioning) the Commission on Human Rights.[84] The EU Member States have either sponsored or at the least supported such measures. For example, at the Sixtieth session of the General Assembly in 2006, the Union drafted and sponsored the resolution which was ultimately adopted.[85] The resolution is couched in strong terms, it is very extensive in its coverage of the violations committed by the authorities and also in demanding action from the military authorities.

EU Member States have, to the extent they have been involved, also supported proposed measures with regard to Myanmar in the Security Council. In January 2007, the United Kingdom and United States sponsored a draft non-punitive resolution on Myanmar. The text received nine votes in favour, the necessary number for a majority, but was vetoed by China and Russia, with South Africa voting against it. Indonesia, an ASEAN state, Qatar and the Republic of Congo abstained.[86] China strongly opposed the draft resolution as it considered (legally incorrectly as discussed in Chapter 2) that the situation in Myanmar was mainly the 'internal affairs of a sovereign state'.[87] China, with a number of other states such as Russia, Congo and South Africa, also did not consider the situation in Myanmar to pose a threat to international peace and security. Indonesia, very importantly as an ASEAN state, stressed that the situation in Myanmar should be tackled by effective measures but also did not think the situation posed a threat to international peace and security.[88] All the EU Member States in the Security Council at the time (France, Italy, Belgium, Slovakia and United Kingdom) voted in favour of the draft resolution. Italy in particular stressed that it had voted in favour of the draft resolution as it reflected

---

16 September 1991; [1995] OJ C166/128, 3 July 1995; [1996] OJ C347/84, 18 November 1996; [1998] OJ C80/235, 16 March 1998; and [2003] OJ C127E/681, 29 May 2003.

[84] See e.g., A/RES/44/144, A/RES/48/150, A/RES/51/117, A/RES/53/162, E/CN.4/RES/1992/58, E/CN.4/RES/94/85 and E/CN.4/RES/2003/12.

[85] Situation of Human Rights in Myanmar, A/RES/60/223, 23 March 2006.

[86] 5619th Meeting of the Security Council, SC/8939, 12 January 2007.   [87] *Ibid.*

[88] Such a determination is, of course, entirely at the political discretion of the Security Council. The situation in Haiti in 1994 where the use of force was authorised to restore a democratically elected government, for example, was deemed to amount to a threat to international peace and security. Security Council Resolution 940 (1994), 31 July 1994.

the concerns expressed by the EU Common Position on Myanmar.[89] It is to such measures that the discussion now turns.

4.1.2.2 Utilisation of Punitive Legal Instruments by the Union against Myanmar

Under European Political Cooperation (EPC), the Community and its Member States had adopted statements on the human rights situation in Myanmar prior to the 1990 elections.[90] The expressed concern about some of the practices of the military regime, however, did not stop the Commission in 1988 discussing the upgrading of relations between the Community and Myanmar.[91] The tone of the démarches and statements issued became more exasperated, however, when it was apparent that there would not be a restoration to democracy in the aftermath of the 1990 elections.[92] In mid-1991 the Community declared itself 'appalled' at the failure to respect the wishes of the population.[93] At this stage the Community and its Member States decided to suspend all non-humanitarian development aid to Myanmar.[94] Economic and trade relations were also reduced to a minimum.[95]

The fact that the Community was reducing aid to a country, due to the failure of a regime to hand over power to a democratically elected body prior to the 1991 June Resolution of the Luxembourg Council, is a clear indication that the resolution was not only establishing guidelines for action but was also building upon existing practice.[96] Gross and systematic violations of fundamental norms since 1962 had until then not prompted any other response from the Community. In the Luxembourg Declaration of 4 January 1991 on Myanmar, however, the Community and its Member States stated that, in the aftermath of the election and the refusal of the military to cede power, the Community and Member States had a 'legitimate concern for … civil and democratic rights' and a call to respect human rights cannot be

---

[89] 5619th Meeting of the Security Council, SC/8939.

[90] See e.g., the joint statements adopted by the Twelve, (1988) 7/8 *Bull. EC* 2.4.7 and (1988) 7/8 *Bull. EC* 2.4.4.

[91] For example, in 1988 a Commission delegation visited Myanmar, at the invitation of the Deputy Prime Minister, with a view to reviewing and upgrading cooperation. See (1988) 7/8 *Bull. EC* 2.2.38.

[92] See e.g., (1990) 6 *Bull. EC* 1.5.2 on the election itself and subsequently (1990) 6 *Bull. EC* 1.5.10, (1991) 1/2 *Bull. EC* 1.4.3 and (1991) 5 *Bull. EC* 1.4.10.

[93] See (1991) 7/8 *Bull. EC* 1.4.10.   [94] (1991) 1/2 *Bull. EC* 1.4.3.

[95] *Ibid.*   [96] See the discussion in Chapter 2.

dismissed as 'interference in the domestic affairs of other states'.[97] As the discussion in Chapter 2 highlights, in particular with regard to the issue of democracy, this is not an uncontroversial statement. Nevertheless, the situation in Myanmar presented one of the first opportunities for the Community and later the Union to apply its new and more robust guidelines to the situation in a third state.

As a direct response to the annulled election, the Heads of Mission of the then twelve Member States issued statements on the detention of Aung San Suu Kyi in November 1991.[98] The Member States also agreed in 1991 to refuse to sell any military equipment to Myanmar and asked all other third countries also to do so.[99] While there was some downgrading of military cooperation, the lucrative trade between Britain and France and Myanmar in armaments, many of which were used in internal repression, was not expressly and more comprehensively prohibited until a Common Position was implemented by Community measures in 2000.[100]

In the light of several strongly worded declarations and a number of Presidency statements and resolutions of the European Parliament on the various consequences of the activities of the regime in Myanmar, the response of the Community is noteworthy. Development assistance projects were wound down, trade and economic relations reduced to a minimum and a decision (even if at that time it made very little real difference) not to sell arms to Myanmar had been taken.

The impetus for the Union to take further punitive measures was, as noted above, the death in 1996 of the Danish consul and also the submission of a complaint from the International Confederation of Free Trade Unions (ICFTU) concerning the use of forced labour in Myanmar. The Union responded in two distinct ways.

The death of the Danish consul in 1996, as noted above, led to Denmark pushing very strongly for the imposition of full economic sanctions against Myanmar. Aung San Suu Kyi, the leader of the

---

[97] (1991) 1/2 *Bull. EC* 1.4.3.   [98] (1991) 11 *Bull. EC* 1.4.14.

[99] (1991) 7/8 *Bull. EC* 1.4.10. This statement was made on 29 July 1991. In a statement on 4 January 1991, (1991) 1/2 *Bull. EC* 1.4.3, it was stated that 'for some time the Member States of the Community have not sold arms to Burma'. The July statement, however, seems to be the formal decision not to sell arms as opposed to the January statement.

[100] Council Regulation 1081/2000, [2000] OJ L122/29, 24 May 2000. Common Position 1996/635/CFSP, [1996] OJ L287/1, 8 November 1996, did not apply to contracts for such goods, which were already in force. See further the discussion below. The 1998 Code of Conduct on Arms Exports, however, may have been used by some Member States to limit arms sales to Myanmar between 1998 and 2000.

pro-democracy movement in Myanmar, whom the Union continually asserts it is supporting and assisting, has at various stages urged the Union to implement such measures.[101] Damrosch has argued that it is legally justifiable for third states to impose and maintain punitive measures against a regime where local leaders, who are being supported by the international community, call for them.[102] As Chapter 2 highlights, there are limits to the legality of such measures. The Union's rhetoric at times, however, certainly leads to the impression that it will implement the measures which have been called for by Suu Kyi and at times refers to her calls, but in a much more limited manner. For example, the Union in 1998 in a declaration stated that it 'echoes the view expressed by Daw Aung San Suu Kyi, that, in the present situation, it is inappropriate for tourists to visit Burma'.[103] The fact, however, as noted above, is that Daw Aung San Suu Kyi has called for full economic sanctions against Myanmar, not just a tourist boycott.

In order to protect the trading interests of their companies, in 1996 both France and the United Kingdom opposed the adoption of punitive measures which would have restricted all commerce with Myanmar. The lack of consensus on the imposition of punitive measures existed because companies such as Total (and ELF Aquitaine prior to the two companies merging) was (and still is) heavily involved in pipe-line projects in Myanmar.[104] EU-based multinational oil companies have in the past provided one-third of all foreign investment in Myanmar.[105] While trade between the European Union and Myanmar may not have been significant in relative terms, investment from EU-based companies has been far from negligible. The Member States whose companies would have been most affected were only prepared to agree to relatively weak punitive measures.

---

[101] The resolutions of the European Parliament regularly refer to this; see e.g., [1997] OJ C200/174, 30 June 1997, para. 3.

[102] L. Damrosch, 'Enforcing International Law Through Non-Forcible Measures' (1997) 269 *RDC* 19, 149.

[103] Declaration by the European Union on Burma, Doc. 12281/98.

[104] See e.g., http://burmacampaign.org.uk/total.html although see Total's position on its investments in Myanmar at http://burma.total.com/ Total has challenged the accusations against it and notes, '[u]nfortunately, the world's oil and gas reserves are not necessarily located in democracies'. See also the questions asked in the European Parliament, e.g., [1996] OJ C365/80, 4 December 1996 and the European Parliament Resolution at [1996] OJ C347/84, 18 November 1996, para. 8.

[105] [1998] OJ C313/181, 12 October 1998, para. g. The figure now is likely to be less due to the involvement of South Korean, Indian and Chinese companies in projects in Myanmar. Accurate trade figures for Myanmar are very difficult to find.

In October 1996, after a good deal of negotiation, a Common Position was adopted which reaffirmed some of the measures, discussed above, which had been adopted after the annulled election of May 1990.[106] This Common Position did not distinguish between the Community and CFSP aspects, although it should be noted that it did not actually require any action on behalf of the Community. The Preamble to the 1996 Common Position provides clear clues as to the rationale behind it. The Union considered itself 'disappointed at the result of the meetings in Jakarta and New York' (the diplomatic negotiations over the death of Nichols, which were discussed above). Only having highlighted this was the absence of progress towards democratisation and the continuing violation of human rights mentioned. What is equally interesting about the 1996 Common Position is the fact that it also calls upon Myanmar to act in certain ways, for example, freeing political prisoners and entering into meaningful dialogue with pro-democracy groups. The punitive measures introduced by the Union aimed to promote progress towards democratisation and securing the immediate and unconditional release of detained political prisoners.

The new measures introduced by the 1996 Common Position were limited to banning entry visas for certain senior members of the military regime and their families as well as the suspension of high-level bilateral governmental visits to Myanmar. The continuing 'further deterioration in the political situation' in Myanmar has led to the original 1996 Common Position being consistently renewed and amended by the Council.[107] In practice, the Common Position has been subsequently amended in a number of significant ways. First, the Council has routinely extended the scope of the visa ban and the persons affected by it. Secondly, in the Common Position adopted in April 2000, the Council agreed to the funds being frozen of those persons affected by the visa ban.[108] Thirdly, the Common Position of April 2000 also prohibited the sale, supply and export of equipment which might be used for internal repression or terrorism.[109] Finally, in 2004 the Council introduced a prohibition on the making of financial loans or credits to state-owned companies in Myanmar.[110]

---

[106] Common Position 96/635/CFSP, [1996] OJ L287/1, 8 November 1996.
[107] See e.g., the Preamble to Common Position 2003/297/CFSP, [2003] OJ L106/36, 29 April 2003. This rationale is routinely cited in the Common Positions.
[108] Article 1 of Common Position 2000/346/CFSP, [2000] OJ L122/1, 24 May 2000.   [109] Ibid.
[110] Common Position 2004/730/CFSP, [2004] OJ L323/17, 26 October 2004.

Despite being consistently amended since 1996, the Common Positions against Myanmar have only very gradually become more comprehensive.[111] The provisions on the suspension of military aid, in the original 1996 Common Position, for example, did not apply to contracts already entered into; thus they continued to be honoured. The Common Positions do not, for example, forbid non-military trade between the Union and Myanmar. This is not to say, however, that certain governments do not pressurise some of their companies to withdraw from Myanmar.[112] The absence of a prohibition on non-military trade between the Union and Myanmar is not unexpected. The Common Positions also do not forbid the investment or the granting of loans to companies in Myanmar, so long as those companies are not state-owned.[113] Annex IV to Regulation 817/2006 lists state-owned companies but it is simple to envisage methods to get around the prohibition.

The freezing of funds concerns individual funds as owned by persons (or their family members) specifically identified in Annex III to the Regulation or those of companies associated with those identified persons. As is the case with the investment ban, for those affected by them, getting around the freezing of personal assets and funds which are held in EU Member States will not be very difficult.[114] Measures such as the freezing of some personal funds and the limited investment ban may make life a little financially trickier for those who are targeted, but whether it is all the Union can do is questionable. There is, however, for the Union a difficult balance to be struck – this is in particular the case with the investment ban.

On the one hand, considering the brutally oppressive nature of the regime in Myanmar and how it permeates every strata of society, it is difficult to see how companies based in Myanmar which trade with the Union cannot be in some way or other linked directly or indirectly to members of the military regime. Thus, any investment in Myanmar will also benefit those individuals. The freezing of assets held in the European Union will only have a limited impact, while European

---

[111] At the time of writing the current measure is Common Position 2007/248/CFSP, [2007] OJ L107/8, 25 April 2007.

[112] The British government, ironically, requested the voluntary withdrawal of British American Tobacco and welcomed it when in November 2003 it did so. In the past, as noted above, the government had been protective of UK companies which had economic interests in Myanmar.

[113] Article 9 of Regulation 817/2006, [2006] OJ L148/1, 2 June 2006.

[114] See *ibid.* Article 6.

investment which seeks to exploit Myanmar's abundant natural resources is permitted. It is in the laying of pipe-lines and exploiting other natural resources that NGOs routinely cite the worst violations of human rights by the military and those companies which invest in Myanmar. The campaigns currently mounted against Total, due to their alleged complicity in slave-like practices, are based on such allegations. In this respect, a complete investment ban would be the most effective measure that can be adopted.[115]

On the other hand, it must be asked what the banning of all European investment in Myanmar would actually achieve? There is no shortage of investors from, for example, India, China or South Korea willing to invest in Myanmar. As noted above, the Daewoo Corporation is involved in projects which will result in billions of dollars in revenue for the military regime. If one considers what happened to the trade between the Union and Myanmar in goods which can be used for internal repression, the point is clear. The regulation implemented to give effect to those parts of the April 2000 Common Position prohibiting the sale and supply of equipment which might be used for internal repression[116] simply resulted in Myanmar signing a trade deal with Russia which now allows it to import the equipment it requires from there.[117] Russia is now by far the largest exporter of weapons and armoury to the developing world and pays no regard to a state's human rights record or how democratic (or not) it is.[118] When weaponry and other instruments have not been legally available from EU-based companies, those based elsewhere have been happy to fill the void. The 2006 Common Position maintains the ban on selling such equipment, yet it makes no practical difference to the situation in Myanmar.

In July 2003 the US Congress adopted the Burmese Freedom and Democracy Act[119] which goes further than the EU Common Positions and bans the import into the United States of all goods produced in Myanmar.[120] Furthermore, this act obliges the United States to oppose

---

[115] If any of the Member States have an Investment Protection and Promotion Agreement with Myanmar this will limit the possibilities for any joint action in this regard under the CFSP. The United Kingdom does not. See the answer by Mr Hain, Hansard HC, 600W, 22 March 2000.

[116] Council Regulation 1081/2000 as amended by Regulation 798/2004.

[117] ICFTU Press Release, 23 July 2001.

[118] See CRS Report for Congress, *Conventional Arms Transfers to Developing Nations, 1998–2005* (Washington, DC: Library of Congress, 2006).

[119] 117 Stat. 864.   [120] *Ibid.* section 3.

the adoption of any loans by international financial institutions to Myanmar.[121] In a number of other respects the Act is very similar to the Union's Common Positions, requiring the freezing of assets and the imposition of a visa ban. As with the EU Common Positions, there is no blanket prohibition on investment by US companies in Myanmar.

For the European Union there is, as noted above, a tricky balance to be struck. On the one hand, the Union could take measures that are as effective as they can be even if the impact is negligible in real terms upon the targeted regime but not without financial impact to the EU Member States. On the other hand, by recognising that any measures taken will have little, if any, real impact, the Union could decide not to take any measures at all as they will not make any real difference. The Union has adopted an approach which is somewhere between these two options; it has taken some measures, which are not without cost, but has not taken all the measures it could have taken. The Union's attempts to bring pressure to bear upon the regime to reform have not so far worked. The change that can be brought about in any third state due to external action short of the use of force is in any case limited. The Union has expressed displeasure but the reality is that if it wishes to send the strongest signal it can, within the limited range of options it has, then a complete investment ban will have to be adopted. Furthermore, as is the case with the United States, the Union will also have to ban all trade with Myanmar. Anything less opens it up to accusations of its actions not matching its rhetoric. However, there are also economic realities: why should companies based in the Union be prohibited from investing in a resource-rich state, so long as this does not directly help to prop up the military regime? If they do not invest there, someone else will. If there is a trade ban, again this will not be without cost to the Member States and again will make little difference to the regime in Myanmar which has no shortage of other trading partners. The correct balance, if indeed there is one, is not an easy one to find.

The Community has defended its current approach towards Myanmar in an *amicus curiae* brief before the US Court of Appeals.[122] The Community opposed a 1996 Massachusetts State Act which regulated

---

[121] *Ibid.* section 4.
[122] *National Foreign Trade Council* v. *Andrew S. Natsios and Philmore Anderson, III*, 118 F.3d.38 (1999). Although the brief is worded in terms of the Union it is technically the Community which was competent to make the submission.

companies doing business with or in Myanmar.[123] Apart from essentially making submissions with regard to the Act interfering with the Union's ability to conduct foreign policy with the United States, the Community also opposed the Act as it is 'deliberately aimed at influencing the foreign policy choices of the European Union'.[124] The Massachusetts Act essentially sought to force all companies doing business with Myanmar to stop doing so. The Community argued that it had 'specifically chosen not to ban such activities in favour of other policy measures towards Burma'.[125] It makes clear, however, as the discussion above has illustrated, that the Union is not indifferent to the human rights situation in Myanmar; it is simply that it has decided to adopt other measures towards Myanmar. One of the other measures referred to is the suspension of the GSP scheme. This is the other major respect in which punitive measures have been adopted against Myanmar and it is to this aspect that the discussion now turns.

The ICFTU complaint, referred to above, related to Myanmar benefiting from the GSP.[126] This eventually led, as discussed in Chapter 3, to a 1997 regulation suspending the GSP in respect of Myanmar. The blatant refusal of the authorities in Myanmar to cooperate with the Commission team which was sent to investigate the allegations played almost as much of a role in the withdrawal of benefits as the forced labour practices themselves. The authorities in Myanmar claimed that there was nothing to investigate and consequently denied the investigatory team entry to the country in November 1996. It was also argued that the forced labour practices were based on Buddhist traditions.[127] A number of MEPs, however, visited Myanmar on tourist visas and in an individual capacity to try and verify the existence of forced labour practices there.[128] The Commission also considered evidence from a wide range of bodies on the practices of the authorities in Myanmar.[129] With a

---

[123] An Act regulating State Contracts with Companies Doing Business with or in Burma (Myanmar), 1996. The Act was declared invalid by the Supreme Court in *Crosby* v. *National Foreign Trade Council*, 530 US 363 (2000).

[124] EU Amicus Brief, p. 5.   [125] *Ibid.*

[126] See [1996] OJ C15/1, 20 January 1996.   [127] See [1997] OJ C133/47, 28 April 1997.

[128] See [1996] OJ C490/185, 13 November 1996.

[129] See [1997] OJ C133/47, 28 April 1997, para. 3. The action taken by and view of the ILO were considered to be very important in the decision to suspend the GSP to Myanmar. Myanmar has continued to be under discussion in the ILO, which has taken further action against it. See further, e.g., the deliberations and discussions during the 294th Session of the Governing Body of the ILO, Geneva 2005, on the Forced Labour Convention, 1930 and the situation in Myanmar, GB.294/6/2. See more generally,

small amount of trade, in relative terms, between the Union and Myanmar, the practical impact of such a measure is not very great. It is admittedly more important now in the context of the revised GSP and GSP+ schemes which Myanmar is expressly excluded from in the new GSP Regulation.[130] Furthermore, such action sets an important precedent, as was evidenced in the case of Belarus.[131]

If one considers the seriousness of Myanmar's legal violations, however, the practical consequences and impact of the measures implemented are still not particularly significant but, as noted above, it must be questioned whether the other available options would in practice achieve anything more effective. It should also be remembered, as discussed in Chapter 2, that the prohibition on forced labour and slavery-like practices are obligations *erga omnes*, which *oblige* the Community and its Member States to act, although the nature of the action that must be taken is unclear. The fact that some lawful measures have been taken to that end in international law terms is sufficient. The suspension of the GSP, even for violations of obligations *erga omnes*, does not, however, automatically mean that all other development aid is cut off. There is no mechanism to that effect.[132]

The Council has repeatedly offered to open discussions with the regime in Myanmar if it essentially takes steps to restore democracy and the human rights situation there improves.[133] In a Council meeting in 1998, for example, it stated that the reconvening of Parliament, the adoption of a new democratic constitution and the holding of free and fair elections would constitute such a move.[134] The imprisoning of opposition activists has specifically been considered to be a move away from democracy.[135] With the exception of occasionally opening a dialogue with the opposition (through initiating a blatantly false 'road-map to democracy' and organising a 'National Convention') and in the past occasionally temporarily releasing Aung San Suu Kyi, the

---

F. Maupin, 'Is the ILO Effective in Upholding Workers' Rights?: Reflections on the Myanmar Experience' in P. Alston (ed.), *Labour Rights as Human Rights* (Oxford: Oxford University Press, 2005) p. 85.

[130] Preamble para. 19 to Council Regulation 980/2005 Applying a Scheme of Generalised Tariff Preferences, [2005] OJ L169/1, 30 June 2005.

[131] See Regulation 1933/2006 Temporarily Withdrawing Access to the Generalised Tariff Preferences from the Republic of Belarus, [2006] OJ L405/35, 30 December 2006.

[132] For confirmation of this view in the past see [1998] OJ C21/75, 22 January 1998.

[133] (1999) 4 *Bull. EU* 1.4.92.   [134] (1998) 10 *Bull. EU* 1.3.11.

[135] See (1998) 9 *Bull. EU* 1.3.16. See also, Common Position 2003/461/CFSP and Common Position 2006/318/CFSP, [2006] OJ L116/77, 29 April 2006.

authorities in Myanmar have shown little inclination to give effect to any of these measures.[136]

The death of James Nichols in 1996 was the primary reason behind the first Common Position, as aggravated by the human rights situation, not the other way around. Since the original Common Position, however, its renewal and strengthening has been due to a perceived deterioration in the human rights situation and the continued absence of democracy in that country. The steps actually taken, however, do not always correlate to the Union's rhetoric. The Union has become increasingly detailed in its demands but does not follow them up in as meaningful a way as may be possible, which is not to deny that the impact of such measures may be limited at best.[137] There is still a continuing feeling, however, that despite the measures being strengthened, initiatives which would affect the general commercial interests of some of the Member States have not been adopted, despite systematic and gross breaches of some of the most fundamental international norms and the continued calls from the democracy movement in Myanmar for such measures to be adopted.

4.1.2.3 Promotion of Values and Principles in Myanmar

Despite the scaling down of development assistance from the Community, it has continued to fund projects in Myanmar which are aimed at helping to alleviate the suffering of the most vulnerable sections of the population. The original 1996 Common Position excluded such measures from its scope and urged the focus of development assistance upon such projects and the provision of humanitarian aid.[138] This approach has been maintained in the subsequent Common Positions. The establishing and running of such projects is in practice very difficult for the Community. Such projects must be undertaken in the context of decentralised cooperation through local civilian authorities and NGOs. Human Rights Watch and Amnesty International have both, for a number of years now, in their annual reports, considered that

---

[136] The Spanish Presidency welcomed Suu Kyi's release in a declaration on 8 May 2002, Doc. 8778/02, although it did not consider this alone to be sufficient for the removal of punitive measures. Suu Kyi's subsequent rearrest led to the adoption of Common Position 2003/297/CFSP. Suu Kyi has always been subsequently rearrested whenever she has been released, or had her period of house arrest extended. Each such incident is accompanied by a condemning statement from the Presidency, see e.g., (2004) 12 *Bull. EU* 1.6.23. Suu Kyi has more or less been under house arrest since 1989.
[137] See e.g., (2003) 1/2 *Bull. EU* 1.6.29.   [138] Article 5(ii) 96/635/CFSP.

non-governmental human rights organisations have not been permitted to function in that country. The number of and activities of other organisations has also been severely curtailed by the authorities. The International Committee of the Red Cross, for example, was forced to close its field office in Myanmar in 2006.[139] In this context it is highly difficult for the Community or any other donor to make anything but the most marginal of contributions.

It is difficult to know how projects which promote democracy, for example, are being implemented in the absence of organisations with the capacity to do so and indeed what difference, if any, they can make at either a local, regional or national level. The Community, however, has still attempted to fund democracy-related projects in Myanmar.[140] Of the other projects the Community has funded, most have been concerned with humanitarian aid. The policies of the authorities in Myanmar have caused an outpouring of refugees into surrounding states, very few of whom are repatriated, as well as large numbers of internally displaced persons.[141] Aid has been provided to finance projects which assist uprooted people, thus improving the quality of life of vulnerable sections of the population in the State of Rakhine and the refugee populations therein.[142] Humanitarian aid budget lines have also been used to assist certain populations. For example, in 2005 the Commission allocated over €16 million to vulnerable populations in Myanmar and refugees on the Myanmar-Thai border and in January 2007 allocated a further €15 million to the same groups.[143]

Beyond this, however, it is difficult, if not impossible, for the Union to make any other contribution to improving the human rights situation in that country by working with NGOs. The Commission has adopted a pragmatic approach, however, towards a number of projects, where it has worked with the authorities in Myanmar. The Commission's approach has been to minimise project aid to the government and to

---

[139] The Presidency issued a declaration condemning this on 5 December 2006 and asked the authorities to reconsider, so as to allow the reopening of the five ICRC field offices in Myanmar. See Doc. 16207/06. The ICRC in June 2007 publicly denounced major and repeated violations of international humanitarian law in Myanmar. See ICRC Press Release 82/07. As discussed in Chapter 6, such statements by the ICRC are exceptionally rare. The European Commission supported the ICRC's stance, see IP/07/1012.

[140] See e.g., (2000) 9 *Bull. EU* 1.2.12.

[141] See P. Crépin, *Evaluation of ECHO Actions in favour of Burmese Refugees in Thailand: Final Report* (Brussels: Pro Logue Consult, 2002).

[142] See e.g., (1998) 12 *Bull. EU* 1.3.121 and (2000) 12 *Bull. EU* 1.6.83.

[143] See IP/05/1694 and IP/07/27.

assist the most vulnerable sections of society. Where it is impossible for NGOs to function, the Commission must work with the regime to achieve a particular objective. Thus, for example, projects funded under the HIV/AIDS budget line have been conducted in conjunction with the Health Ministry so that provision for aid can be made to those most in need.[144] Projects concerned with tackling tuberculosis and malaria have also been funded using the humanitarian aid budget lines.

The regime in Myanmar has shown itself to be insensitive to both positive and negative measures. The tactical approach now adopted by the Union towards Myanmar is almost entirely negative in nature. Dialogue is infrequent and *ad hoc* and only when it can be agreed upon. The Common Positions are prohibitive in nature and reduce all aspects of dialogue and downgrade the relationship between the parties. The death of the Danish consul, not the human rights situation, was the spur for more punitive measures to be adopted after the annulled election but in the circumstances it is difficult to see what difference the Union can make, and indeed what else it should do.

4.2 Pakistan

Pakistan has enjoyed wide-ranging bilateral treaty relations with the Community since 1976, shortly after its former colonial ruler, the United Kingdom, itself acceded to the Community in 1973.[145] Although the Lomé/Cotonou Conventions have been extended to almost all other developing Commonwealth states, the Asian sub-continent has been excluded from this trend. The sheer scale in terms of size and population is no doubt a major factor in this decision. Relations between the Union and Pakistan have blossomed since the end of 2001, despite all but having broken down in 1999. The second generation Agreement, which had been in force since 1986, had expired[146] and a third generation

---

[144] See [1998] OJ C117/160, 16 April 1998.

[145] Commercial Cooperation Agreement between the EEC and the Islamic Republic of Pakistan, [1976] OJ L168/2, 28 June 1976. Diplomatic relations between the Community and Pakistan were first established in 1962. The first Agreement between the Community and Pakistan was in 1969, see Agreement between the European Economic Community and the Islamic Republic of Pakistan on the Supply of Common Wheat as Food Aid, [1969] OJ L175/2, 16 July 1969.

[146] Agreement for Commercial, Economic and Development Cooperation between the EEC and the Islamic Republic of Pakistan, [1986] OJ L108/1, 25 April 1986. Under Article 10, the Agreement was valid for a period of five years, renewable for one-year periods on the agreement of both parties.

Agreement had been negotiated and initialled in April 1998 but it was not signed due, among other reasons, to the coming to power of the military regime of General Pervez Musharraf in October 1999.[147] General Musharraf's coming to power in 1999 led to the Council and Parliament adopting measures, condemning the coup in strong language and calling for the restoration of democracy.[148] The attacks on New York and Washington in September 2001, however, led to the complete rehabilitation of the military dictatorship and Pakistan was welcomed back into a warm embrace by, among others, the European Union and the United States. One of the consequences of this was the signing of the initialled third generation Agreement in November 2001. Before discussing the basis for relations between the Union and Pakistan, it is worth briefly discussing the prevailing political situation in Pakistan.

Civilian rule in Pakistan, since independence in 1947, has routinely been interrupted by the military seizing power. To date, no civilian government has ever completed its full term in office. The second generation Agreement between the Community and Pakistan was concluded with the very brutal, repressive and religiously conservative military regime of General Zia ul-Haq.[149] Pakistani governments of all persuasions have always considered that as Pakistan is a signatory to the Universal Declaration on Human Rights, 1948, this is sufficient evidence of its commitment to the idea of human rights as understood in international law. Pakistan is also party to the 1926 Slavery Convention, the Genocide Convention, the Children's Convention,[150] the Women's Convention and the Convention on the Elimination of

---

[147] See e.g., the comments of former Commissioner Patten at [2001] OJ C350E/137, 11 December 2001.

[148] See European Union Declaration, 16 October 1999, (1999) 10 *Bull. EU* 1.5.17; General Affairs Council, 15 November 1999, (1999) 11 *Bull. EU* 1.5.93; and Parliament Resolution on the State of Emergency Declared in Pakistan, 18 November 1999, (1999) 11 *Bull. EU* 1.5.94.

[149] The Community did raise the issue of human rights with the military regime of Zia ul-Haq as and when the opportunity presented itself. See e.g., (1987) 4 *Bull. EC* 2.2.26 which notes a meeting between Pakistani and Commission officials. The impact of discussion of human rights on such a regime would have been negligible at best.

[150] Pakistan has signed but not ratified the additional Protocols to the CRC: Optional Protocol to the Convention on the Rights of the Child on the Involvement of Children in Armed Conflict, UNGA Res. 54/263, 25 May 2000 and Optional Protocol to the Convention on the Rights of the Child on the Sale of Children, Child Prostitution and Child Pornography, UNGA Res. 54/263, 25 May 2000.

Racial Discrimination.[151] In November 2004, Pakistan signed the International Covenant on Economic, Social and Cultural Rights, 1966, although it has yet to ratify it.[152] Furthermore, it is party to five of the ILO's 'core' conventions, including those which deal with bonded labour and slavery.[153] Pakistan is party to the Four Geneva Conventions of 1949 but not to the Additional Protocols, nor is it a party to the Statute of the International Criminal Court.[154]

In terms of human rights issues, it is well documented that in Pakistan problems exist with regard to: restrictions on the rights to association and expression; anti-terrorist legislation; forced disappearances; abuse of the laws on blasphemy; minority rights; women's rights; religious persecution; the rule of law; child and bonded labour; slavery and slavery-like practices; and the systematic use of torture by security forces.[155] Freedom House ranks the civil liberties situation in Pakistan at 5 out of 7 and political rights at 6, which equates to a country considered to be 'Not Free'.[156] According to Transparency International, Pakistan has consistently been considered one of the most corrupt countries in the world.[157] According to the Fund for Peace and Foreign Policy 'Failed

---

[151] International Convention on the Elimination of All Forms of Racial Discrimination, 1966, 660 UNTS 195. Pakistan has entered a number of 'declarations', as opposed to reservations, to the UN human rights treaties to which it is a party, although see Article 2(d) of the Vienna Convention on the Law of Treaties, 1969, 1155 UNTS 331.

[152] International Covenant on Economic, Social and Cultural Rights, 1966, 993 UNTS 3.

[153] Convention No. 29; Convention No. 87, Freedom of Association and Protection of the Right to Organise Convention, 1948, 68 UNTS 17; Convention No. 98, Right to Organise and Collective Bargaining Convention, 1949, 96 UNTS 257; Convention No. 105, Abolition of Forced Labour Convention, 1957, 320 UNTS 291; and Convention No. 111, Discrimination (Employment and Occupation) Convention, 1958, 363 UNTS 31.

[154] Protocol Additional to the Geneva Conventions of 12 August 1949, and Relating to the Protection of Victims of International Armed Conflicts (Protocol I), 8 June 1977, 1125 UNTS 3; Protocol Additional to the Geneva Conventions of 12 August 1949, and relating to the Protection of Victims of Non-International Armed Conflicts (Protocol II), 8 June 1977, 1125 UNTS 609; Rome Statute of the International Criminal Court, 1998, 2187 UNTS 90.

[155] See, for examples, HRW, *Contemporary Forms of Slavery in Pakistan* (New York: Human Rights Watch, 1995); Amnesty International, *Women in Pakistan: Disadvantaged and Denied their Rights* (London: Amnesty International, 1995); the report of the Special Rapporteur on Torture, E/CN.4/1997/Add.2; and the report of the Special Rapporteur on Intolerance and Discrimination based on Religion or Belief, E/CN.4/1996/95/Add.1.

[156] See www.freedomhouse.org/template.cfm?page=22&year=2006&country=7033

[157] The Transparency International Corruption Perception Index Tables can be found at www.transparency.org/policy_research/surveys_indices/cpi. In 1996 Pakistan was considered after Nigeria to be the most corrupt country in the world. (This led to an in-joke that Pakistan was actually more corrupt than Nigeria but that some Pakistanis

States Index' it was the ninth most unstable state in 2006, which was substantially worse than the situation in 2005 when it was the thirty-fourth most unstable state.[158]

It is estimated that one-fifth of the Pakistani population of over 165 million live in absolute poverty on under US$1 per day and a staggering 73 per cent on under US$2 per day.[159] Furthermore, due to Pakistan's relatively low per capita gross national income (GNI) of US$690, which places it 160th of the 208 economies measured by the World Bank,[160] Pakistan is classified as a low-income country. Pakistan was the recipient of around €423 million in aid from the Union between 1976 and 2001. Since the end of 2001, however, it has received larger amounts of assistance and greater benefits as a reward for its role in the fight against terrorism. Since the start of 2002 this has amounted to over €150 million, in addition to which there has been over €200 million worth of ongoing development programmes from the Union. A further €200 million has been earmarked for the period 2007–2011.[161] Pakistan has also received substantial amounts of humanitarian aid from the Union, which has primarily been aimed at the three million or so Afghani refugees in Pakistan but more recently was targeted at the devastation following the earthquake in northern Pakistan in October 2005. This alone has amounted to over €100 million since 2005.[162]

In terms of trade, the European Union is Pakistan's largest trading partner. Just under one-third of Pakistani exports (in particular, rice, textiles, leather and sporting goods) are destined for the Union. Approximately one-fifth of Pakistan's imports are from EU countries. The overall volume in trade between Pakistan and the European Union has since 2004 annually been worth over €5 billion.[163]

4.2.1 Legal and Political Structure of EU Dialogue with Pakistan

The Union has maintained political dialogue with Pakistan on a number of levels, both regional and bilateral. Dialogue exists with Pakistan

---

had bribed officials from Transparency International to make Nigeria appear more corrupt than Pakistan.)

[158] The Fund for Peace and Foreign Policy 'Failed States Index' can be found at www.fundforpeace.org/programs/fsi/fsindex.php

[159] World Bank, *World Development Indicators 2006*, Table 2.7.

[160] *Ibid.*   [161] See IP/07/115.

[162] See the Commission financing decisions for humanitarian aid operations regularly published in the *Bulletin of the European Union*, e.g., (2006) 1/2 *Bull. EU* 1.29.1.

[163] See the webpage of the EU Delegation in Pakistan for a full breakdown, www.delpak. cec.eu.int/EU-Pak-trade-2004/EU-Pak-Trade-01–03l.xls

through Union meetings with the South Asian Association for Regional Cooperation (SAARC)[164] as well as Troika meetings. The scheduling of SAARC meetings, however, has not been regular. SAARC did not function properly between 1998 and 2004, due to Indian objections over the general situation in southern Asia – a euphemism for the Kashmir issue and alleged Pakistani support for Kashmiri 'terrorists'.[165] Bilateral meetings between representatives of Pakistan and the Union have not always been held regularly, although since 2002 meetings have become more frequent. When representatives of Pakistan and the Union have met, the Union has raised its concerns over, among others, Pakistan's (now formally former) support for the Taliban, the Kashmir issue, nuclear testing and proliferation, the trade in narcotics, international terrorism, the rule of law and various human rights issues such as the death penalty, child labour, discrimination against women and religious minorities and the (ab)use of the blasphemy laws. Other issues have also been raised in these meetings, in particular, the restoration of democracy. Furthermore, the 1986 Agreement between Pakistan and the Community established a Joint Cooperation Committee (JCC) which was supposedly to meet on an annual basis.[166] It did not do so, with the last meeting being in 1996. The third generation Agreement between the parties, which was signed in November 2001 and approved by the European Parliament on 22 April 2004,[167] also establishes a Joint Commission which has not met to date.[168] The Union's discussion with Pakistan on certain values and principles, in these different fora, has tended to concentrate upon a number of key issues. The discussion

---

[164] SAARC's main aims are economic and social development among its member states. It was established in 1985.

[165] Informal summits were held on the fringe of the General Assembly, during this period. The Presidency has welcomed the resumption of regular SAARC Meetings, see (2004) 1/2 *Bull. EU* 1.6.154. The European Union has since 2006 had observer status at SAARC summits.

[166] Article 7(1)(d).

[167] The delay was caused by a large number of MEPs being opposed to the Agreement entering into force. See e.g., 'Pakistan's Human Rights Record Delays EU Accord' (2003) 9(38) *European Voice*, 13 November 2003. When the European Parliament approved the Association Agreement on 22 April 2004 it also adopted a separate resolution expressing concerns about numerous issues, such as human rights, nuclear proliferation and the role of the military in politics, see [2004] OJ C104E/1040, 30 April 2004.

[168] Cooperation Agreement between the European Community and the Islamic Republic of Pakistan on Partnership and Development, [2004] OJ L378/23, 23 December 2004. Article 16 establishes a Joint Commission which is required to meet on at least an annual basis; a meeting was scheduled for early 2007.

below will look in detail at the negotiation of the third generation Agreement with Pakistan and the numerous problems which had to be overcome. It will then move on to the other measures adopted by the Union to promote and protect the values in Pakistan it considers most important.

4.2.2 Democracy, Human Rights, the Union and Pakistan

As discussed in Chapter 3, the Union has elevated democracy to a level at least equivalent to that of fundamental human rights, even though, as Chapter 2 argues, there is still no real legal basis in international law for it to do so. Removing or suspending democratic institutions, the annulling of free elections and *coup d'etats* are more tangible in terms of assessment for the suspension of Agreements, than violations of human rights and fundamental freedoms. In Pakistan, however, the situation has not been so straightforward for the Union.

4.2.2.1 Negotiating the Third Generation Agreement

A third generation Agreement between the Community and Pakistan has, as noted above, now been concluded. This is the same Agreement that was initialled in April 1998 but not signed until November 2001. As also noted above, one of the reasons for this delay was the coming to power of General Musharraf in October 1999. The coup, which was bloodless,[169] brought to power a regime which in many circles is considered to be more committed to economic and social reform and promoting human rights, tackling religious extremism and poverty and rooting out corruption than the government it replaced. It should be borne in mind that in the context of Pakistan, this is relative.[170] Due to the government's military nature and its coming to power in a coup,

---

[169] For Musharraf's version of the coup and its background see P. Musharraf, *In the Line of Fire: a Memoir* (London: Simon and Schuster, 2006) p. 119 *et seq.*

[170] The military government under Musharraf has introduced measures such as the Protection of Women (Criminal Laws Amendment) Act, 2006, which repeals part of Pakistan's antediluvian evidence rules which discriminate very heavily against women. The Pakistan Muslim League-Quaid (PML-Q) (a faction of a long-standing political party under Musharraf's 'guidance') has also introduced a Prevention of Anti-Women Practices Bill, which aims to promote and protect women's rights in Pakistan. It is worth noting that 'secular' parties who have under Nawaz Sharif and Benazir Bhutto held power in civilian governments have never actually been willing to take on the religious parties and repeal, for example, the evidential laws concerning women, which were introduced in the Hudood Ordinance, 1979, by the military government of General Zia ul-Haq. It should also be remembered, as will be discussed below, that Musharraf has also widely abused power to secure continued

however, which the Supreme Court of Pakistan unsurprisingly validated on the basis of the doctrine of necessity,[171] the Community initially refused to sign the Agreement. Having previously refused to acknowledge the validity of the Supreme Court judgment, the Union has, in part, used it to support its normalisation of relations with Pakistan since the end of 2001.[172]

The entire process of the negotiation of the Agreement was tied up with human rights and other ethical issues. The Union, via the Troika and the Commission, were not only concerned with inserting an 'essential elements' clause in the Agreement but had also identified a number of human rights problems in Pakistan, in particular child labour, which needed to be addressed. These human rights concerns were integral to the entire negotiation of the Agreement. In 1996 the then Commissioner for Development, Manuel Marin, visited the then President and Prime Minister of Pakistan (Farooq Leghari and Benazir Bhutto respectively) and discussed the negotiation of the Agreement.[173] Particular emphasis was placed by the Commission on the preparation of a campaign against child labour in Pakistan. The discussion also encompassed drug exportation and support for international terrorism, both of which were related to Pakistan's then links with the Taliban

favours for the armed forces (see A. Siddiqa, *Military Inc: Inside Pakistan's Military Economy* (London: Pluto Press, 2007)) and to maintain his grip on power but in relative terms his regime is neither as despotic nor corrupt as the civilian regimes in power between 1988 and 1999 nor the military rule of, in particular, Zia ul-Haq. Musharraf, for example, manipulated the judiciary to try to ensure that his constitutional amendments could not be overridden and his grip on power challenged by essentially forcing members of the judiciary to either swear allegiance to the military government or be removed from office. This has been through the adoption of the Oath of Office (Judges) Order 2000 which required all judges of the superior courts to take an oath that they would perform their function in accordance with the 1999 Proclamation of Emergency, the measure adopted to constitutionally validate Musharraf's 1999 coup. Musharraf has subsequently amended the Constitution via the Constitution (Seventeenth Amendment) Act, 2003 which affirmed the validity of, *inter alia*, his Presidential orders and the 1999 Proclamation of Emergency.

[171] See *Zafar Ali Shah* v. *Pervez Musharraf* (2000) 52 PLD 869. As Hamid Khan has noted with regard to the Supreme Court giving the military government the latitude it wished to consolidate power, 'the military government could not have asked for more'. H. Khan, *Constitutional and Political History of Pakistan* (Karachi: Oxford University Press, 2006) p. 493. The Supreme Court has not to date failed to validate a government which has come to power via a military coup in Pakistan.

[172] See the discussion below.

[173] Benazir Bhutto had come to power again after general elections in October 1993. The Community and Member States welcomed the elections and an EC election monitoring team had observed the elections and considered them to be generally free and fair. See (1993) 10 *Bull. EC* 1.4.4.

regime in Afghanistan and, with regard to the latter only, the situation in Kashmir.[174]

The actual Agreement, which is non-preferential and has no budget line associated with it, was initialled in April 1998.[175] The discussion at that time primarily centred on strengthening economic and political ties between the parties. Although the Kashmir issue, the economic and social reforms undertaken by Pakistan and Community anti-dumping rules were also discussed, particular attention was once again paid to the question of child labour. At this stage the Commission proposed ECU 71 million to support a programme already launched by the Pakistani government, in conjunction with an earlier Commission project, the ILO and UNICEF, which aimed to improve the education and health of children and eradicate the use of such labour.[176]

The successful negotiation of the Agreement itself had to overcome a substantial number of differences between the parties. Two rounds of negotiations in December 1996 and April 1997 had failed due to a lack of agreement on a number of issues, namely intellectual property rights, maritime transport, the social clause and a declaration on illegal Pakistani immigrants in the EU Member States. Informal talks held in 1998 eventually led to a compromise.[177] Differences of opinion are still apparent with regard to, for example, illegal immigrants.[178] The agreed 'essential elements' clause in the Agreement reaffirms the importance the Community and Pakistan attach to the principles of the Universal Declaration of Human Rights and 'democratic principles'.[179] The democratic process (whatever the distinction between it and democratic principles) and its continued existence are not essential elements. Respect for democratic principles, however, is.

One of the main objectives of the Agreement is to 'support Pakistan's efforts for comprehensive and sustainable development, including economic and social development policies which take account of the poor and disadvantaged sections of its population, particularly women in these sections, as well as sustainable management of natural

---

[174] (1998) 7/8 Bull. EU 1.4.13.   [175] (1998) 1 Bull. EU 3.76.
[176] On the earlier project see [1996] OJ C305/122, 15 October 1996.
[177] See COM(1998)357.
[178] The joint declaration on the readmission of illegal immigrants is not considered to be a part of the Agreement and Pakistan also made a unilateral declaration on this point.
[179] Article 1 of the Cooperation Agreement between the European Community and Pakistan on Partnership and Development.

resources'.[180] Women's sectors have accordingly been receiving extra funding and have been highlighted as a priority area of funding.[181] As the legal basis for the Agreement is Articles 133, 228 and 179 TEC, other issues can also be addressed. One of the most important provisions of the Agreement, as far as the Community is concerned, is the provision concerning the protection of intellectual, industrial and commercial property rights, in conformity with international standards.[182] With regard to the promotion and protection of human rights Article 4, which outlines the basis for development cooperation, is the most important. Priority for funding is to be given to projects which promote and emphasise health education, human resource development specifically for women, population welfare, environment and rural development specifically targeted towards the poorer and disadvantaged sections of the population.

While the provisions of the Agreement are not in any way unique, what is worth noting is that the Agreement would, in all likelihood, have been ratified in 1999 by both parties, if the military coup of October 1999 had not taken place. The Community had obtained the inclusion of an 'essential elements' clause and the Pakistani government was prepared, as the Community insisted, to initiate programmes aimed at alleviating child labour.

In terms of human rights commitments, the Commission was satisfied. This is notwithstanding the fact that Nawaz Sharif, the democratically elected leader of Pakistan at the time, was during his period in office systematically dismantling the country's democratic institutions.[183] Sharif's instigating of a constitutional crisis, due to his interference with the Supreme Court and compelling the Lahore High Court to dismiss the Chief Justice, was widely reported. Alterations to the

---

[180] *Ibid.* Article 2(2).

[181] Until the end of 1996 this was conducted on an *ad hoc* basis under the ALA Regulation and Council Regulation 975/1999, [1999] OJ L120/1, 8 May 1999. Since the start of 2007, Regulation 1905/2006 Establishing a Financing Instrument for Development Cooperation, [2006] OJ L378/41, 27 December 2006 and Council Regulation 1889/2006 Establishing a Financing Instrument for the Promotion of Democracy and Human Rights Worldwide, [2006] OJ L386/1, 29 December 2006, can be used.

[182] See Article 3(4)(b) of the Cooperation Agreement between the European Community and Pakistan on Partnership and Development.

[183] The EU Election Observer Group on the Pakistani election of 1997, which swept Sharif to power, considered that although malpractice existed, on the whole, the election was fair. See [1997] OJ C373/19, 9 December 1997.

Constitution and the make-up of the courts had ensured that there was no de facto method (in the absence of a coup) by which to call or force an election and thus remove Sharif from power.[184] Amnesty International, in a report on Pakistan at the time, noted a 'very sharp downturn in the protection of human rights under the Sharif regime', with NGOs 'routinely being harassed and very high levels of corruption'.[185] The EU Presidency, however, ignoring the bigger picture limited itself at this time to issuing a statement expressing its concern on the issue of 'honour killings' which the Sharif government had refused to declare as murder.[186] Although the issue of 'honour killings' is an important one and the problem endemic in Pakistan, at the time it was certainly not the most important human rights problem in Pakistan. The Community was prepared to negotiate with the Sharif government and apparently turn a blind eye to some of its activities, despite concerns from its delegation in Islamabad, so long as the Pakistani government was prepared to make a basic commitment to human rights and democratic principles.[187]

The initialled Agreement was not signed for three years. There were a number of reasons for the delay. One delay on the part of the Community was due to the kidnapping of a prominent Pakistani journalist, Najam Sethi, who had been very critical of the government. Sethi was kidnapped by a group who are widely suspected to have been acting on the instructions of Sharif. The constitutional crisis, referred to above, which further undermined the rule of law and separation of powers, barely raised an eyebrow in the Union.[188] The kidnapping of a journalist, however, provoked an international response which eventually led to his release.[189] Another delay in signing the Agreement was occasioned by the nuclear tests conducted by both India and Pakistan, which are discussed below, and later in October 1999 by the military coup. The Community's original stance was that it simply would not countenance signature of the Agreement until a legitimate democratic government was installed.

From the perspective of ethical values, the entire episode of negotiating the Agreement was fraught with problems. The Community, as far

---

[184] See e.g., Constitution (Fourteenth Amendment) Act, 1997.
[185] Amnesty International, *World Report 2000: Pakistan*, npg.   [186] (1999) 7/8 *Bull. EU* 1.4.21.
[187] I am grateful to the Commission delegation official in Islamabad who disclosed this.
[188] There are no Presidency statements or declarations on this issue.
[189] The Presidency issued a declaration on this matter, see (1999) 5 *Bull. EU* 1.3.16. Sethi became part of a subsequent Amnesty International campaign.

as it was concerned, when dealing with the Sharif government, was negotiating with a regime legitimately in power. That is certainly true, but the danger signs were more than apparent that Sharif was engaging in and behind some very unsavoury practices. Extra-judicial killings, arbitrary arrests and detentions were widely being used against opposition politicians. His government was massively corrupt, inefficient and despotic. The fact that Sharif had come to power via Community-observed elections seemed to counter that. If ultimately the regime engaged in widespread and systematic breaches on a scale beyond those already occurring, then from the Community's perspective the 'essential elements' clause which had been agreed upon could be invoked. The Pakistani nuclear tests of May 1998, however, ensured that they did not have to rely upon the clause.

Further to Pakistan's six nuclear tests in response to India's five tests in May 1998, the Union unequivocally threatened to take negative action against Pakistan. Signature of the initialled Agreement was completely off the agenda. The Presidency issued a statement in May 1998 following the nuclear tests and again in June of that year.[190] The Council also adopted a Common Position concerning the European Union's contribution to the promotion of non-proliferation and confidence building in the South Asia region.[191] The Presidency statement condemned the tests which it considered ran counter to the wishes of the (then) 149 states which had signed the Comprehensive Test Ban Treaty (CTBT).[192] The Council felt that India had undermined stability in the region and that Pakistan was making it worse.

It was not in the Common Position, however, that the Union threatened to take negative measures but in the Presidency statements it issued. If such commitments had been undertaken in Common Positions this would oblige the Union to take further action in accordance with its terms. Presidency statements thus allowed condemnation and a threat to be issued without any legal obligation to pursue the matter further. The Presidency in its statement of 29 May 1998 assured India and Pakistan that it would take 'all necessary measures' if they did

---

[190] See (1998) 5 *Bull. EU* 1.3.17 and (1998) 6 *Bull. EU* 1.4.19.
[191] Common Position 98/606/CFSP, [1998] OJ L290/1, 29 October 1998. See also, the Conclusions of the Cardiff European Council, 15–16 June 1998 on the tests, (1998) 6 *Bull. EU* I.28.88.
[192] Comprehensive Nuclear Test Ban Treaty, 1996, GA Resolution A/RES/50/245. The treaty is not yet in force as the required forty-four states listed in its Annex 2, including India and Pakistan, have not yet ratified it.

not ratify the CTBT without conditions. The statement condemned the nuclear tests as it was felt they posed a 'grave threat to international peace and security'. The Presidency asked the Commission to consider review of the GSP following India's tests and now asked it to open and extend this consideration to Pakistan as well. After India's tests the Presidency statement had condemned India but did not hint at suspending the Agreement with India. The Member States instead worked for a delay in consideration of loans to India from the World Bank.[193] As a consequence of the Indian tests, the Council had attempted to persuade Pakistan not to carry out tests by asking the Commission to expedite signature of the EC-Pakistan Agreement and to examine the scope for enhanced development and economic assistance. Other concerns over human rights, which had already in part delayed the signing of the Agreement with Pakistan, would be set aside in an attempt to persuade Pakistan not to test such devices.

It is difficult to see how subsequent nuclear tests by Pakistan would have breached the Agreement, which had been initialled, if it had already entered into force. Ratification of the Treaty on the Non-Proliferation of Nuclear Weapons (NPT)[194] and the CTBT was always considered by the Union to be an essential political prerequisite for the ratification of the Agreement with Pakistan.[195] It had repeatedly been raised in Troika meetings and Commission officials were adamant that while it was not a legal requirement for Pakistan to ratify those treaties, politically it was very desirable, if not essential.[196] The timing for the Community was thus ideal, as it could further utilise the Agreement for the purposes of leverage.

There was certainly no attempt on the Community's behalf to suspend the Agreement with India, which was already in force, and in which the relevant provisions are very similar. Following Pakistan's tests, however, the Council withdrew the request to the Commission to expedite the Agreement with Pakistan and asked for an examination of the possible suspension of the GSP, as well as attempting to delay World Bank

---

[193] (1998) 5 *Bull. EU* 1.3.9.

[194] Treaty on the Non-Proliferation of Nuclear Weapons, 1968, 729 UNTS 10485.

[195] Pakistan is party to the Convention on the Physical Protection of Nuclear Material, 1980, 1456 UNTS 101. The Council has entered an objection on behalf of the European Atomic Energy Community to a reservation formulated by Pakistan at the time of its accession to the Convention. See (2001) 10 *Bull. EU* I.4.51.

[196] I am grateful to officials in the Pakistani Foreign Ministry and the EC Delegation to Pakistan for confirming this.

loans.[197] The GSP Regulation at the time clearly did not envisage the withdrawal of benefits in the event of nuclear testing and subsequent versions do not do so either.[198] As a unilateral instrument, however, the Community can lawfully withdraw the benefit of the GSP to a particular third state, if they so wish. The Commission did not reopen the GSP procedure as requested. The reason behind this is unclear. It may be that the Commission did not wish to set a precedent, whereby the Community withdrew the GSP to express displeasure with a third state, for acts not envisaged in the text of the regulation. In any case the effect of such a response upon the Pakistani government would have been marginal at best. With regard to the Member States delaying World Bank loans to Pakistan, the very real fear of Pakistan defaulting on its other loan commitments ensured that any delay was not lengthy.[199]

The reaction of the Union to the nuclear tests is interesting on a number of levels. At no stage did the Union consider Pakistan's legitimate security interests or the other factors which led to the nuclear tests. Pakistan's much larger, powerful and indeed hostile neighbour India had already tested such weapons.[200] Admittedly this was a case of India sabre-rattling with an eye to China, rather than to Pakistan, but it was provocative at the very least and Pakistan felt exceptionally threatened. Nawaz Sharif at the time stated '[t]he pressure was irresistible at home. It was mounting on the government every day, every hour ... we have been holding on and exercising the utmost restraint. We were disappointed that the world community really failed to take strong action again India.'[201] Sharif would have had a 'moral edge' over India by not ordering the nuclear tests and was being offered numerous financial inducements not to do so. The inducements were coming

---

[197] (1998) 6 *Bull. EU* 1.4.19.

[198] See Article 9 of Council Regulation 3281/94, [1994] OJ L348/1, 31 December 1994; Article 26 of Council Regulation 2501/2001, [2001] OJ L346/1, 31 December 2001; and Article 16 of Council Regulation 980/2005 applying a Scheme of Generalised Tariff Preferences, [2005] OJ L169/1, 30 June 2005.

[199] In January 1999, the World Bank loaned Pakistan a further US$350 million to help improve public sector governance. World Bank News Releases, Pakistan, 21 January 1999.

[200] At the time Atal Bihari Vajpayee was in charge of a nationalist Hindu (Bharatiya Janata Party) government in India and essentially took the decision to test India's nuclear devices for his short-term political survival.

[201] Cited by O. Bennett-Jones, *Pakistan: Eye of the Storm* (New Haven: Yale University Press, 2003) p. 192.

from the United States, however, and not the European Union.[202] Sharif had asked President Clinton for the end of US sanctions and also the extension of IMF loans.[203] Clinton for his part offered to treble Pakistan's US$1.6 billion facility with the IMF, to write off US$3 billion in bilateral debt and to put pressure on Japan to write off Pakistan's US$9 billion debt. He could not, however, offer to end the economic sanctions that had already been activated, as that decision lay with Congress, nor could he give the security guarantees that Sharif requested.[204] Sharif had been advised, however, that if Pakistan had the same level of sanctions imposed against it as India, then Pakistan would have no problem withstanding them. Sharif further felt that

---

[202] It is worth noting that many Pakistanis feel that the United States owes Pakistan a huge moral debt as it has suffered substantially as a consequence of being used as a conduit by the United States to defeat the Soviets in Afghanistan. In essence it is felt that Pakistan paid the price for the West to win the Cold War. See Musharraf to this effect, 'West "Will Fail" Without Pakistan', http://news.bbc.co.uk/1/hi/world/south_asia/5394278.stm, 30 September 2006.

[203] The so-called Symington Amendment 1976 (section 101 of the Arms Export Control Act, formerly section 669 of the Foreign Assistance Act, 1961) prohibits most US assistance to any country found trafficking in nuclear enrichment equipment or technology. Jimmy Carter found Pakistan in violation of the Symington Amendment in 1979 because of Pakistan's clandestine construction of a uranium enrichment plant. Due to US support for the Mujahadeen (who were funded and supported primarily by the United States and Saudia Arabia via Pakistan) after the Soviet invasion in 1979, however, it did not have practical effect for a number of years as Presidential waivers were used to override it. The so-called Glenn Amendment 1977 (section 102(b) of the Arms Export Control Act, formerly section 670 of the Foreign Assistance Act, 1961) prohibits US foreign assistance to any non-nuclear-weapon state (as defined by the NPT) that, among other things, detonates a nuclear device. President Clinton invoked the Glenn Amendment against India on 13 May 1998 and against Pakistan on 30 May 1998. The so-called Pressler Amendment, 1985 (section 620[e] of the Foreign Assistance Act, 1961) originally banned most economic and military assistance to Pakistan unless the US President certified, on an annual basis, that Pakistan did not possess nuclear weapons and that the provision of US aid would significantly reduce the risk of Pakistan possessing such a device. In October 1990, President George H. Bush was unable to issue this certification, which triggered economic measures against Pakistan. President George W. Bush overrode all such measures against Pakistan in the aftermath of the attacks of 11 September 2001. It has been estimated that the United States has made aid payments of over US$28 billion to Pakistan between September 2001 and the end of 2006, see 'Pressuring Pakistan', *IHT*, 23 February 2007 and also Centre for Public Integrity, 'Billions in Aid, with No Accountability: Pakistan Receives the Most Post-9/11 U.S. Military Funding, Yet has Failed to Ferret out Al Qaeda, Taliban Leaders', 31 May 2007, available at www.publicintegrity.org/militaryaid/report.aspx?aid=877. The Centre for Public Integrity report gives a figure of US$5 billion in military aid alone after September 2001.

[204] 'Enemies Go Nuclear', *Time Magazine*, 8 June 1998. See also, Bennett-Jones, *Pakistan: Eye of the Storm*, p. 193 *et seq.*

Pakistan could in any case mitigate the effect of any such measures by obtaining finances from elsewhere.[205] The carrot being offered to Pakistan, in particular by the United States, was not an appetising one and the stick with which India had been beaten for its tests was not a particularly painful one. Furthermore, Sharif's decision to test the nuclear devices also avoided a possible rift with the army over the bellicose statements coming from India at the time, as well as securing his own political future. Sharif has stated that he would not have lasted more than two or three days in office if he had not given the go-ahead for the nuclear tests.[206]

The Union, for its part, has recognised and indeed provided scope for exceptions from treaty obligations based on security interests in, for example, the Association Agreements concluded under the Barcelona Process.[207] Yet, no such allowances were made with regard to either India or Pakistan. Additionally, the Union had no regard to Pakistan or India's legal obligations; neither is a party to the CTBT or NPT. Furthermore France, for example, only became party to the CTBT after it had carried out nuclear tests in 1995.[208] As is the case with the European Union's dealings with Iran at present, it does seem somewhat hypocritical for the Union to have insisted that both India and Pakistan not carry out tests and ratify treaties to which some of its own Member States only became party after they had themselves tested similar devices.[209] It is also the case that ratification of those treaties was not a central issue in negotiations on the third generation Agreement with India, but it was with Pakistan. The long-standing suspicion over Pakistani officials (with state complicity) being central to the illegal selling of nuclear proliferation technology to Iran, Libya and North Korea, among others, no doubt played a role in this being one of the reasons behind such an approach being adopted towards Pakistan but not India.[210]

[205] Bennett-Jones, *Pakistan: Eye of the Storm*, p. 193.
[206] 'Enemies Go Nuclear', *Time Magazine*, 8 June 1998.   [207] See the discussion in Chapter 5.
[208] France deposited its instrument of ratification on 6 April 1998. The European Parliament condemned the French tests in the strongest terms, see [1995] OJ C269/61, 16 October 1995.
[209] See the discussion in Chapter 3.
[210] The exposure of the so-called 'A.Q. Khan network' has now proved that Pakistani officials were behind the selling of such secrets and technology. See further IISS, *Nuclear Black Markets: Pakistan, A.Q. Khan and the Rise of Proliferation Networks – a Net Assessment* (London: IISS, 2007). The Commission in 1980 had a very different attitude towards Pakistan's then nuclear programme, see [1980] OJ C156/34, 25 June 1980.

On another level, however, the reaction does demonstrate some consistency. The Presidency was as harsh on India after its nuclear tests as it was on Pakistan, despite the fact that it has far more to lose in trade terms with the former than the latter. In the case of Pakistan, the Union was still in a position to withhold the benefits it was about to grant under the initialled Cooperation Agreement and did so. Ultimately the GSP was not suspended and World Bank loans were not delayed with regard to either country. It should also not be overlooked that the Union was, for obvious reasons, unable to respond after France's nuclear tests. The Union's policy can be considered to be one of the containment of nuclear weapons *if* it is in a position to exert pressure.[211]

4.2.2.2 Signature of the Third Generation Agreement with Pakistan

Events subsequent to those discussed above display the relativity of ethical foreign policies as far as relations between the Union and Pakistan are concerned. Within two weeks of the attacks on New York and Washington in September 2001 the EU Troika was in Pakistan. The General Affairs Council, meeting on 8 and 9 October 2001, completely reformulated policy towards Pakistan. The Council essentially wished to reaffirm its commitment to the 'global coalition against terrorism' and considered global terror to pose a real challenge for it, as well as a threat to 'our security and stability'.[212] No other reason was considered necessary. The political decision was taken, regardless of all other considerations. Dialogue with Pakistan had to be 'continued and developed', in particular by signing the third generation Agreement.[213] In the Special Council Meeting of 12 September 2001, it had already been identified that the attack on the United States was not only an attack on it but also 'against humanity itself and the values and freedoms we all share'.[214] The justification for the change in policy towards Pakistan was solely to ensure that the 'coalition against terror' was effective.

---

[211] Nuclear non-proliferation has also been central to relations with, for example, North Korea and Libya. Nothing has, however, ever been publicly said by the Union about Israel's possession of such weapons. See also, Council Joint Action 2004/495/CFSP on Support for IAEA Activities under its Nuclear Safety Programme and in the Framework of the EU Strategy Against Proliferation of Weapons of Mass Destruction, [2004] OJ L182/46, 19 May 2004 and the discussion in Chapter 3.

[212] General Affairs Council, 8–9 October 2001, Doc. 12330/01, para. 1.   [213] *Ibid.* para. 8.

[214] Declaration of the Special European Council, 12 September 2001, Doc. 11795/01.

In a Commission Communication of September 2001 concerning the GSP, for example, the justification given for including Pakistan among those states which would benefit under the drugs incentive scheme of the 2001 version of the GSP, was to help 'stabilise its economic and social structures and thus consolidate the institutions that uphold the rule of law'.[215] The argument was that by further engaging politically with Pakistan and providing additional development aid, the Community would help to stabilise the region and more specifically Pakistan and pave the way for democratic reforms to be effectively implemented. If this was the case, it is difficult to see why this realisation had not occurred to the Council and Commission prior to September 2001. After all, the conflict in Kargil had already taken place and led to exceptionally high tensions between Pakistan and India. If the Union wanted to restore international peace and stability to the region this would have been an appropriate step to take earlier. The benefits under the GSP drug incentive schemes were simply part of the 'pay-off' for the Pakistani government formally siding with the United States-led coalition against the Pakistani Inter-Services Intelligence's own protégé, the Taliban and Al-Qaeda.[216]

Such incentives to Pakistan did not come without cost to the Union. The United Kingdom and France, in an attempt to placate India over the benefits being awarded to Pakistan, publicly began to support India's claim for a permanent seat in the Security Council of the United Nations.[217] India, as discussed in Chapter 3, successfully challenged the manner in which states could benefit from the drugs incentive scheme under the GSP and, in particular, felt that Pakistan had done nothing in that regard to be eligible for such benefits. In part, as a consequence, the EC had to reformulate its GSP scheme. Pakistan does not benefit under the new incentive scheme and has made representations to the Commission to the effect that this is proving harmful.[218]

---

[215] See COM(2001)131, p. 2.

[216] It is worth pointing out that what became the Taliban and other such movements can be traced in part to clandestine financial support from the United States and Saudi Arabia to the Mujahadeen in their fight against the Soviet Union after the Soviet invasion of Afghanistan. It is further noteworthy that in his decision to side against the Taliban, President Musharraf's Chief of Intelligence was allegedly told by former US Deputy Secretary of State, Richard Armitage that if he did not do so, the United States would bomb Pakistan 'back to the Stone Age'. See Musharraf, *In the Line of Fire*, p. 201.

[217] See C. Hill, 'Renationalising or Regrouping? EU Foreign Policy Since 11 September 2001' (2004) 42 *JCMS* 143.

[218] See Press Release of the Luxembourg Presidency, Talks on GSP+ between Nicolas Schmit and the Pakistani Minister for Trade, 19 January 2005, available at www.eu2005.lu/en/actualites/communiques/2005/01/1903-ns-khan/index.html

The Union's turnaround in relations with Pakistan is not, however, as stark as it may at first seem. The extent of the Community's engagement and funding of projects in Pakistan during the period between the expiry of the second generation Agreement and the signing of the third, also illustrates a difference of approach towards military dictatorships. In Myanmar the Community is, by and large, funding humanitarian work. In Pakistan it was still clearly working with the military government in development projects. In this sense, the Commission is in practice differentiating between military regimes, probably depending on the extent of their repressiveness.

What they are normally not prepared to do now, however, is to sign a bilateral Agreement with a military government. What the Community objected to in the case of Pakistan was not the government in power or its policies *per se*, but the manner in which it came to power. They simply did not wish to be seen to be dealing openly with a military regime. This would open a Pandora's Box, as it would lead to exceptional difficulties in attempting to differentiate why it is was concluding Agreements with one military regime and not another.

The simpler approach was not to sign any Agreements with military regimes and in practice to cooperate with more moderate ones by implementing and funding programmes which are directed towards the most disadvantaged sectors of society. Thus in early 2001, for example, in Pakistan funds were primarily being aimed at social sector development, such as primary education, eradicating child labour, reproductive health and drug rehabilitation. Other projects, which included road and school building, development programmes concerned with the Social Action Programme aiming to improve the quality of elementary education, health, population and sanitation and water quality were also being funded.[219]

Despite the still widespread violation of the values that the Union wishes to promote in Pakistan, as noted above, many positive moves have been made under the military regime both prior to and subsequent to the ratification of the third generation Agreement. Extra-judicial executions have declined sharply since 2000, a National Commission on the Status of Women has been set up to protect women's rights, the Protection of Women Act 2006, which in particular tackles the evidential burden in rape trials has been adopted, and in April 2000 President

---

[219] This is based upon information provided by members of the Commission delegation in Islamabad in December 2001.

Musharraf announced that 'honour killings' would in future be tried as murder.[220] Furthermore, in 2000 the Juvenile Justice System Ordinance (JJSO) was adopted to bring Pakistani penal laws with regard to minors further into line with Pakistan's obligations under the UN Convention on the Rights of the Child.[221] In particular, the JJSO prohibits the execution of minors,[222] arguably an obligation *erga omnes*.[223] Bonded labour, however, remains a grave problem, but as Commission officials admit, this has no short-term or immediate solutions and is more a case of structural and social reform.[224] What is most interesting is that there have been widespread reforms under the military government and, *inter alia*, a stronger commitment to improving (some) human rights, reducing extreme poverty and tackling corruption.[225] In some respects it is arguable that the Union prefers to deal openly with a democratically elected but despotic and corrupt government, as opposed to a non-democratically elected regime which has a commitment to societal and structural reform, which is similar in scope to some of the policies the Union wishes to promote.

The irony, however, is that President Musharraf, has increasingly begun to engage in the systematic dismantling of the separation of powers; he has very substantially interfered with the judiciary, he has amended the Constitution so that it is much more difficult to remove him from power and he has also institutionalised the role of the military in politics. His regime is making the most of its current

---

[220] Something which has long been raised by the Union see e.g., (1999) 7/8 *Bull. EU* 1.4.21. The law was changed by the Criminal Law Amendment Act, 2004. The 2004 Act made various amendments to the Pakistan Penal Code, 1860 and the Code of Criminal Procedure, 1898.

[221] Former Commissioner Patten acknowledged in an answer to a parliamentary question that under Musharraf a number of such steps, such as the enactment of the JJSO, were positive as far as the protection of human rights in Pakistan was concerned. See [2003] OJ C92E/17, 17 April 2003.

[222] Section 12 JJSO 2000.

[223] Article 37 of the Children's Convention; Article 6(5) ICCPR; Article 4(5) of the American Convention on Human Rights, 1969, 114 UNTS 146; and Article 5(3) of the African Charter on Human and Peoples' Rights, 1981, 1520 UNTS 26, 363 all prohibit capital punishment for those under eighteen. Justice Kennedy, giving the lead judgment of the US Supreme Court in *Roper* v. *Simmons*, 543 US 551 (2005), accepted that the United States in 2005 was the last country in the world still to legally allow the execution of children (Pakistan was one of only seven other countries to have executed children since 1990).

[224] Interview with Commission officials, Islamabad, December 2005.

[225] For discussion of many of the recent reforms, see L. Ziring, *Pakistan: At the Cross Roads of History* (Oxford: Oneworld, 2003).

immunity from US and Union criticism.[226] This is more than apparent in two respects.

First, if one considers the elections held as part of the Pakistani 'road-map to democracy': the Pakistani elections held in October 2002 were welcomed by the Presidency and considered to be a 'step in the gradual transition to full democracy' although it did note 'some concerns about reports of manipulation'.[227] The Union's Election Observation Mission (EU EOM) was much more critical. It is worthy of note that a Presidency statement was only issued after the mission's preliminary report and not after the final more comprehensive and critical report was published.[228] The judgment of the Supreme Court validating the coup of October 1999, which is now relied upon by the Union in part to legitimise relations, especially forbade the changing of the fundamental features of the Constitution. Musharraf has done so on numerous occasions to ensure that he maintains overall political control.[229] The EU EOM had serious misgivings about the Legal Framework Order 2002[230] and considered that it had 'grave concerns' about the process and that 'at best Pakistan will be a "guided democracy", far short of international standards'.[231] Serious concerns were also expressed by the Commonwealth Observer Group, which stated that 'we have observed an incomplete democratic process. We look forward to the

---

[226] The Council still issues routine statements on relations with India, for example, but has been sparing when criticising 'internal matters'. The one exception is the Presidency Statement of 20 April 2004 on the conviction and sentencing to twenty-three years' imprisonment of Javed Hashmi (an opposition politician) for treason and mutiny. The statement is worded in notably muted terms.

[227] See the Presidency Statement of 16 October 2002, (2002) 11 *Bull. EU* 1.6.21 and the more critical European Parliament resolution, [2004] OJ C25E/380, 29 January 2004. See further on the elections Z. Ansari and A. Moten, 'From Crisis to Crisis: Musharraf's Personal Rule and the 2002 Elections in Pakistan' (2003) 93 *The Muslim World* 373.

[228] Both reports are available at http://ec.europa.eu/external_relations/human_rights/eu_election_ass_observ/pak/index.htm

[229] Musharraf, for example, declared himself President in June 2001 contrary to the Supreme Court's judgment and has subsequently pushed through the National Security Council Act, 2004, which indefinitely institutionalises the role of the military in civilian politics.

[230] The Order essentially manipulated the electoral process to ensure that overall political control was maintained by the military. The Order in section 5(3) forbids any legal challenge to it.

[231] EU EOM, *Pakistan National and Provincial Assembly Election, 10 October 2002, Final Report,* p. 17.

restoration of democracy in Pakistan.'[232] As a consequence Pakistan was not readmitted back to the Commonwealth after the elections.[233] Yet, the EU Presidency subsequently welcomed the 'transfer of power' to a civilian regime when Zafarullah Khan Jamali was sworn in as Prime Minister.[234]

Secondly, Musharraf not only appointed himself as President but has arranged a blatantly rigged referendum to justify his continued grip on power. After he had appointed himself President of Pakistan in June 2001, an EU Presidency statement was issued within a few days. The statement noted 'the installation of General Musharraf as President of Pakistan and reiterates its call for a transition to democracy'. The Presidency further stated that it was concerned 'that this act *could* jeopardise the progress that *has been made* on this path'.[235] At this point Musharraf was still very much an international pariah as far as the Union and its Member States were concerned.

In April 2002 Musharraf, with his new circle of friends, held a referendum to allow him to continue in power as President beyond the term permitted by the Supreme Court. Referenda have been a favoured ploy whenever the military has seized power throughout Pakistani history. Both General Ayub Khan in 1960 and General Zia ul-Haq in 1984 held referenda to assume the office of the President. Musharraf did so in 2002.[236] It was perceived that a 'yes' vote could give him greater legitimacy. Despite a low turn-out, allegedly 97 per cent of voters backed

---

[232] Commonwealth Observer Group, *Report of the Commonwealth Observer Group: Pakistan National and Provisional Assembly Elections, 10 October 2002* (London: Commonwealth Secretariat, 2002) p. 47.

[233] See Concluding Statement of the Twentieth Meeting of the Commonwealth Ministerial Action Group (CMAG) on the Harare Declaration, 1 November 2002. The US State Department did not send its own observer mission. See also, Human Rights Watch, *Pakistan: Entire Election Process 'Deeply Flawed'*, 9 October 2002. The Commonwealth, with reservations, readmitted Pakistan in June 2004 under very strong pressure from Australia, the United Kingdom and externally the United States. This was a reward for its role in the 'war on terror'. This was only made possible, though, due to the thaw in relations between India and Pakistan.

[234] (2002) 11 *Bull. EU* 1.6.13. The military regime has in the past been referred to by the Union as the 'present interim government'; see *National Indicative Programme, 2003–2005*, p. 7.

[235] (2001) 6 *Bull. EU* 1.6.16. Emphasis added.

[236] The question was framed as follows: 'For the survival of the local government system, establishment of democracy, continuity of reforms, end to sectarianism and extremism, and to fulfil the vision of Quaid-e-Azam, would you like to elect General Pervez Musharraf President for five years?'

Musharraf as President for the next five years.[237] Even Musharraf was embarrassed at the scale of the result and has admitted to some officials having been 'over enthusiastic', a euphemism for going too far in rigging the vote.[238] The referendum has not resulted in any statements from the Council or Presidency, although the European Parliament has not shied away from condemning it.[239] The absence of a formal statement or declaration by the Council or Presidency is very notable, as such a document, whether commending or condemning developments, is issued after almost all plebiscites in third states.

Differences between the Member States as to how to react to a now crucial ally rigging a referendum to stay in power would be a plausible explanation for the silence, although there may well be others. The EU Country Strategy Paper (CSP) which was adopted a short time before the referendum notes Pakistan's geostrategic importance to the Union and how in essence it could not afford to ostracise General Musharraf's regime. The CSP states:

> Given Pakistan's location in a volatile region, with widespread incidence of drugs and arms trafficking as well as illegal migration, it is important for the EU to engage the country for geo-political reasons. Above all, the EU has an interest in fostering peace and stability in South Asia. The constructive behaviour of Pakistan's government during the American intervention in neighbouring Afghanistan made a sustained contribution towards stabilizing the entire region and thus contributed decisively to the fight against international terrorism. The European Commission as a donor should aim to assist in this ongoing process and contribute towards Pakistan's engagement with the international community.[240]

This sequence of events displays the relativity of an ethical foreign policy. The primary purpose of any foreign policy is the defence of the physical and political character of the state.[241] The exportation of values and the achievement of a stable world order will always be subservient to the physical protection of the state. As noted above, the Special Council meeting of 12 September 2001 noted that the alliance against

---

[237] For discussion of the referendum see Ansari and Moten, 'From Crisis to Crisis'.

[238] See Musharraf, *In the Line of Fire*, p. 168.

[239] See the Parliament's resolution on the election in Pakistan, [2004] OJ C25E/380, 29 January 2004.

[240] *Pakistan Country Strategy Paper, 2002–2006*, p. 4. Available at http://ec.europa.eu/external_relations/pakistan/csp/02_06_en.pdf

[241] See E. Denza, *The Intergovernmental Pillars of the European Union* (Oxford: Oxford University Press, 2002) p. 85.

terror had to be as effective as possible. Due to the physical proximity of Pakistan to Afghanistan and the links between the Pakistani government and the Taliban, Pakistani cooperation was imperative if effective action was to be taken against Al-Qaeda. Notwithstanding their concerns, the Member States of the Union had to upgrade their relations with Pakistan and needed enticements to that end. This has consequently placed limitations upon the Union's ability to act against it and is potentially of serious detriment to the situation in Pakistan.

The Union has, in the past, actually had notable success in pursuing its ethical objectives in Pakistan through a combination of targeted condemnation, dialogue and further complementing this with the funding of appropriate projects. Results have not been achieved across the board but with regard to particular situations. The following discussion will look briefly at the problems of blasphemy and child labour, as examples of how the Union has made a noteworthy contribution to the protection of some of the values it wishes to protect in Pakistan.

4.2.3 The Union's Successes in Promoting Ethical Values in Pakistan

4.2.3.1 Pakistani Law on Blasphemy and the Union

The UN Special Rapporteur on Religious Intolerance has considered that the blasphemy laws in Pakistan are applied in a prejudicial manner so as to persecute all minority religious groups, but in particular Christians and Ahmadhis.[242] The European Parliament, Council and Troika have always expressed disquiet about this issue and the Union has responded to this situation, in a concerted way, on two occasions: first in 1995 and then subsequently in 1998. The Union's earlier intervention led to a marked (albeit short-term) improvement in the position of Ahmadhis in Pakistan, although not of the Christian minority. Ahmadhis are in a more vulnerable position, as compared to Christians, as they are considered by some to be heretics, something which has been considered to be punishable by execution in some orthodox Islamic circles.[243] Early in 1995 the Union carried out a series of confidential démarches with the Pakistani authorities on the issue of religious persecution and, in particular, the law on blasphemy. It was assured at the highest level that adequate steps would be taken, if not to repeal the law, then at least to force through amendments and give clear instructions, at the

---

[242] See Report of the Special Rapporteur, E/CN.4/1996/95/Add.1.
[243] For detailed discussion, see M. Eltayeb, *A Human Rights Approach to Combating Religious Persecution* (Oxford: Hart, 2001) p. 55 *et seq.*

administrative level, to prevent any misuse of the law. The issue was also debated during the meeting of the EU-Asia Directors Troika in late October 1995. The validity of the administrative approach to tackle the problem was clear, with many at the time suspected of committing such a crime being acquitted. These steps were duly welcomed by a public declaration of the European Union which undertook to continue mon-itoring the law's application.[244] Although the persecution of Ahmadhis had not been eradicated by the time of the Union's 1998 interventions, the situation had improved.

Various resolutions of the European Parliament led in 1998 to the issue being reopened, this time with particular focus on the Christian minority in Pakistan.[245] The Union Troika again carried out a démarche on the blasphemy laws to the Pakistani Minister of Law and expressed a 'great deal of discomfort' over the presence of the death penalty for the crime.[246] The Commission also sent a delegation on a fact-finding mis-sion to Faisalabad concerning the infamous cases of Ayub Masih and the self-immolation of the Archbishop of Faisalabad, John Joseph.[247] The Council did admit, however, that despite the issuing of several démarches on this issue, which had been raised systematically in the institutional political dialogue with the Pakistani authorities, little had been achieved despite assurances to the contrary by the government.[248]

The later intervention did not substantially improve the situation for the Christian minority and the improvement for the Ahmadhi minority had only been temporary and limited to blasphemy cases being dismissed

---

[244] In political dialogue held in December 1993, the European Union pointed out the problems with regard to the situation of Ahmadhis in Pakistan. Furthermore, with regard to the question of religious intolerance in Pakistan, in a meeting between the Union and Pakistan in Bonn in November 1994, the Union urged Pakistan to repeal the laws on blasphemy. At this meeting the issue of Ahmadhis being declared non–Muslims was also raised. The question of religious identity on identity cards as a basis for persecution was raised by the Presidency in a meeting in November 1992. See the answer to Question No. 11 (H-0023/96) by Anita Pollack to the Council, *Annex to the Official Journal: Debates of the European Parliament*, No. 475, p. 150; [1993] OJ C106/50, 16 April 1993; and [1996] OJ C297/129, 8 October 1996.

[245] See e.g., [1998] OJ C210/211, 6 July 1998 and later [1999] OJ C98/295, 9 April 1999.

[246] See [1999] OJ C96/86, 8 April 1999.

[247] Ayub Masih was falsely accused of blaspheming Islam (due to a dispute over land) and sentenced to death in 1996 by a court in Sahiwal, Punjab. He subsequently became a *cause célèbre* for the global campaign concerning the prejudicial application of Pakistan's blasphemy laws against its Christian minority. He was acquitted in 2002. Archbishop John Joseph shot himself in 1998 to gain national and international attention for the persecution of the Christian minority in Pakistan.

[248] See [1999] OJ C13/136, 18 January 1999 and [1999] OJ C96/146, 8 April 1999.

and did not relate to other discriminatory behaviour being tackled. The Union has continued to raise the treatment of religious minorities whenever the opportunity has arisen. While relations with Pakistan were strained immediately after the military coup, religious intolerance could only be discussed on an *ad hoc* basis and the EU Heads of Mission had the responsibility to raise individual cases directly with the Pakistani authorities.[249] *Ad hoc* political talks between the Troika and Pakistan did take place in November 1999 and November 2000, for example, and the issue was discussed.[250] In the latter meeting, the Pakistani authorities acknowledged that a number of blasphemy cases against Ahmadhis had created anxiety in official circles in Pakistan and the then Pakistani Minister for the Interior promised 'renewed reform efforts'.[251] The Troika reminded the Minister that the Council would keep the situation in Pakistan under review and, if necessary, raise the issue again.[252] It should be recalled that these undertakings were made at a time when relations between the Union and Pakistan were still strained further to the military coup. Post-September 2001, the Troika has continued to raise the matter in meetings between the sides which are now being held more regularly. For example, the EU Troika held a meeting with Pakistani officials in September 2005 where the issue was again discussed.[253]

The failure of the Pakistani authorities to suitably permanently amend the blasphemy laws' application with regard to religious minorities is not due to the shortcomings of the Union's approach. Persecution of all religious minorities in Pakistan is a legacy of the Islamisation of policies which has been pursued, for political reasons, since the 1970s by various governments.[254] It is not so much the manner

---

[249] See [2001] OJ C81E/128, 13 March 2001.
[250] See [2001] OJ C163E/57, 6 June 2001 and [2002] OJ C93E/140, 18 April 2002.
[251] See [2001] OJ C163E/57, 6 June 2001 and [2001] OJ C174E/122, 19 June 2001.
[252] [2001] OJ C174E/122, 19 June 2001. The Council has also issued declarations following attacks on churches in Pakistan in August and September 2002, see (2002) 7/8 *Bull. EU* 1.6.17 and (2002) 9 *Bull. EU* 1.6.21.
[253] FCO, *Annual Human Rights Report, 2006* (London: HMSO, 2006) p. 223.
[254] The trend was started by the supposedly 'secular' Zulfiquar Ai Bhutto, who in 1974 had the Ahmadhis declared non-Muslims so as to placate the religious right and in an attempt to prop up his own unpopular regime. It was under General Zia ul-Haq's regime that the Islamisation policy was accelerated. It should also be noted that Nawaz Sharif sought to prop up his despotic, hugely corrupt and unpopular government by amending the Constitution so as to make Islam the supreme law of the country. See the proposed Constitution (Fifteenth Amendment) Bill, 1998, which was never adopted, in part because Sharif was ousted in a coup by Musharraf, two months after the Bill was presented.

in which the law is framed, however, that is problematic but its ability to be abused in the registering of false accusations against members of religious minorities, often to settle personal vendettas.[255] Endemic corruption in the police force and judicial system results in those accused potentially spending years on remand and, if not acquitted, being executed. Repealing the law in its entirety is not a viable option for any government in power – undertakings to the Union always extend to reviewing its application. The continued existence of the law thus ensures that its abuse is ongoing. What is important is that the Union has been in a position of influence, which is why a commitment to reform has been made by the Pakistani government on more than one occasion. When the European Parliament passed a resolution on the freedom of religion and human rights in Pakistan in June 1998,[256] this was integrated into the discussion between the EC and the Pakistani government, as the initialled third generation Agreement had not then been concluded. Dialogue and discussion have led to an atmosphere which has been conducive to a commitment to reform and the undertaking of measures, even though satisfactory reform has not been forthcoming. What is particularly worthy of note is that the issue of blasphemy has no direct link with any other issue. It is a case of rights which the Union considers to be fundamental being violated. It has thus pursued discussion on that issue with little or no benefit to it and the Member States.

4.2.3.2 Child Labour in Pakistan and the Union

The situation in Pakistan with regard to child labour, especially bonded child labour, is notoriously bad. In 1995, Human Rights Watch put the figure at 20 million bonded child labourers although ILO figures tend to be lower.[257] While the international community has been primarily concerned with those children working in the carpet, textile and football industries, the mistreatment and working conditions of those in

---

[255] The law can be found in Chapter XV of the Pakistan Penal Code, 1860.

[256] [1998] OJ C210/211, 6 July 1998.

[257] See Human Rights Watch, *Contemporary Forms of Slavery*. ILO, 'Child Labour and Responses: Overview Note – Pakistan' does not provide an independent figure for bonded child labour but relies on Pakistani official statistics from 1996 which considered 3.3 million of the 40 million children then in Pakistan to be economically active on a full-time basis. Available at www.ilo.org/public/english/region/asro/newdelhi/ipec/download/pakistan.pdf

mines and brick kilns is equally bad, if not significantly worse.[258] Adult bonded labour is also very widespread yet has received relatively little international attention. When the ICFTU complained to the Commission with regard to Myanmar, vis-à-vis the GSP, it simultaneously complained about Pakistan. The European Parliament in 1996 also passed a resolution on the application of the social clause in the GSP to Pakistan and Myanmar.[259] This led to the opening of an investigation into practices in Pakistan. There was particular concern at the level of forced and bonded child labour, which was considered to breach ILO Conventions Nos. 29 and 105.[260] The Economic and Social Committee (ESC) in its opinion on the Proposal for a Regulation Withdrawing the GSP from Burma[261] asked for the investigation on Pakistan to be reopened, as it was not convinced that adequate measures had been taken.[262] While the European Parliament and ESC pushed for further measures, the Council, for the reasons discussed below, did not proceed with withdrawing the GSP. Such a step would have had important consequences for both the Union and Pakistan.

The Union is the largest importer of Pakistani textiles and arrangements exist to regulate this trade.[263] Furthermore, the Community must tread carefully if it wishes to suspend the GSP vis-à-vis Pakistan. Such practices, which are not state policy as is the case in Myanmar, are also widespread outside of Pakistan. Furthermore, a ban on products produced by such labour would cause other social problems within Pakistan.[264] Withdrawing the GSP would also affect industries other than those which were being targeted. Dialogue and appropriately targeted projects which have in the past produced significant results are therefore the preferred option.

In a Troika meeting in October 1995, for example, the European Union strongly expressed its concerns regarding child labour and the

---

[258] See Human Rights Watch, *Contemporary Forms of Slavery*. Brick kilns, of course, do not result in goods for export unlike the leather or carpet industries.

[259] [1996] OJ C17/201, 22 January 1996.

[260] It would now also violate ILO Convention No. 182, Worst Forms of Child Labour Convention, to which Pakistan is party.

[261] [1997] OJ C133/47, 28 April 1997.   [262] *Ibid.* para. 12.

[263] See e.g., Memorandum of Understanding between the European Community and the Islamic Republic of Pakistan on Transitional Arrangements in the Field of Market Access for Textile and Clothing Products, [2001] OJ L345/81, 29 December 2001.

[264] See [1996] OJ C305/122, 15 October 1996, e.g., where the Commission acknowledged this.

case of Iqbal Masih to the Pakistani authorities.[265] The threat of with-drawing the GSP was put off, however, as the Pakistani authorities undertook measures in response to earlier criticism. The Commission considered that this was, temporarily at least, enough. As with the blasphemy laws, the situation was kept under review.[266] This issue has been specifically targeted by the Commission, the ILO and UNDP for funding, especially in assisting the enforcement of laws which prohibit such activities. The Community has achieved significant results. The problem has been far from eradicated, but governments in Pakistan have undertaken steps and some reform due to cajoling, and consistent and systematic discussion on the issue in institutional dia-logue between Pakistan and the Union.[267]

In the above examples, a sparing use of condemnation, a substantial amount of dialogue and funding, where appropriate, have secured some improvement in the situation. Commission officials consider that in their discussions, Pakistani officials are frank and constructive in their approach. The Pakistanis are also considered to be receptive and indeed obliging when such issues have been raised with them. EU Heads of Mission are now conducting a regular dialogue on human rights with Pakistani government officials. This dialogue particularly focuses on the misuse of the blasphemy laws, violence against women, minority rights, police behaviour, torture, the death penalty and freedom of expression.[268] It is considered that while there is usually a will to under-take reform, the requisite capacity to give effect to it in Pakistan does not always exist.[269] There is currently, however, little need for the Pakistanis to be too receptive to the Union's demands if they do not wish to be so.

---

[265] [1995] OJ C196/67, 31 July 1995. Iqbal Masih was an ex-bonded child labourer who escaped and became an international spokesperson for the global campaign against child labour. He was assassinated, in 1995, aged twelve in Pakistan. He had been awarded the Reebok Human Rights Youth in Action Award, 1994, and was posthumously awarded in 2000 (alongside Anne Frank) the first World Children's Prize. The European Parliament adopted a resolution following his murder, [1995] OJ C151/276, 19 June 1995.

[266] See [1998] OJ C21/148, 22 January 1998.

[267] E.g., in May 2000, the military government announced the National Policy and Action Plan to Combat Child Labour to which the European Union then contributed €990,000.

[268] FCO, *Annual Human Rights Report 2005* (London: HMSO, 2006) p. 113.

[269] I base this upon several interviews with desk-officers in Brussels and members of the EC Delegation in Islamabad.

President Musharraf was obliged to hold elections by the end of 2007 and, after having reneged on his statement to do so in 2004, was also required by then to cede either his post as Chief of the Army or as President.[270] Both the Commonwealth and the United States publicly put pressure on him to ensure an open and fair election and also to cede one of his posts.[271] President Musharraf eventually stepped down as Chief of the Army in November 2007. With a view to ensuring that any further judicial challenges to his authority did not derail any of his plans, in March 2007 he had dismissed the Chief Justice of Pakistan, Iftikhar Mohammad Chaudhry.

Chief Justice Chaudhry, however, refused to stand aside quietly and became a focal point for all opposition to Musharraf's regime and the move back-fired when amidst intense international attention the Supreme Court in July 2007 refused to validate the Chief Justice's dismissal.[272] This is the first occasion in Pakistan's judicial history that the Supreme Court has taken a stand of this nature against the incumbent regime. The entire episode accentuated the repressive tendencies inherent in military rule, even if the regime is relatively-speaking liberal. A number of independent national television stations were attacked by members of the army and taken off air for reporting on opposition rallies in support of the Chief Justice. A number of other clear warnings were given and intimidation of the media was widespread. The Heads of Mission in Islamabad of the Member States and Commission in June 2007 issued a press release in which they stressed the importance of 'freedom of the media as crucial elements for a successful *democratic* process'.[273] As was the case with Sharif's meddling and Musharraf's prior interference with the judiciary, the Council and Presidency did not comment on the issue in any public statements.

---

[270] Under the terms of the 2002 referendum he was elected President for a five-year period.

[271] 'Commonwealth Pushes for Change in Pakistan: End of Year Deadline for Musharraf's Dual Posts', *Dawn*, 26 April 2007 and 'US Says Pakistan Election Must be Fair', *IHT*, 14 June 2007.

[272] Constitution Petition No. 21 of 2007, *Chief Justice of Pakistan – Mr. Justice Iftikhar Muhammad Chaudhry* v. *President of Pakistan through the Secretary and others*, judgment 20 July 2007, nyr.

[273] European Commission Delegation Islamabad, Press Release: Statement by the Heads of Mission in Islamabad of EU Member States and the European Commission on the Current Situation in Pakistan, Islamabad, 7 June 2007, no further references given. Emphasis added. The reference to democracy is with a view to the planned elections in late 2007.

In the light of close scrutiny from the international community Musharraf announced that he would respect the decision of the Supreme Court to reinstate Chief Justice Chaudhry. The Presidency issued a declaration welcoming this announcement.[274] The statement stressed the importance of the rule of law and the independence of the judiciary as key elements of democracy, in particular in view of the forthcoming elections.

The Union and Pakistan in early 2007 had adopted a joint declaration and agreed to intensify their relations.[275] Javier Solana in a meeting with Pakistani Prime Minister Shaukat Aziz in January 2007 stressed the need for Pakistan to maintain its commitment to democratisation.[276] In the light of the above events, it is clear that Pakistan is about to undergo another testing and turbulent period. The Union, however, is also aware just how important President Musharraf and Pakistan's support is in tackling Al-Qaeda. The Union's attitude towards the election process in Pakistan will be crucial. Stability in Pakistan at the price of free and open democratic elections may be the price the Union is willing or has to pay if Musharraf again reneges on his promises. Such an approach, however, would leave the Union with little credibility in promoting democracy in other third states. There will be a difficult balance to strike but the Union has to accept the reality of the situation. Having sided with a military government, the Union now has to live with the consequences of that decision. The Union, while still funding valuable projects in Pakistan through the Community, seems, for the time being at least, to have lost a fair amount of its political leverage in relations with Pakistan or at least seems not to be using that which it still has. This state of affairs will continue to exist while Pakistan (and Musharraf in particular) is perceived to be a vital partner in the pursuance of other geopolitical objectives, such as fighting the 'war on terror'.

4.3 Nigeria

As Nigeria is an ACP state, its relationship with the Union has primarily been through the Lomé/Cotonou Conventions. These Conventions are between the ACP states, on the one hand, and, on the other, the

---

[274] Presidency Declaration, 25 July 2007, Doc. 12165/07.
[275] See EU-Pakistan Joint Declaration, Berlin, 8 February 2007. Musharraf visited Brussels in September 2006 and Prime Minister Shaukat Aziz did so in January 2007.
[276] Press Release, 30 January 2007, S035/07.

Community and Member States. Nigeria, the most populous and one of the most important African nations, has been subjected to the full range of Community and Union punitive measures. These have subsequently been revoked by the Union, as it was felt that enough reforms had taken place for them to be no longer appropriate. The following section will look briefly at the political and economic situation in Nigeria and provide some background to put the following analysis into context. This is followed by a discussion of the Lomé/Cotonou institutions and instruments and the action in that fora as a response to events in Nigeria. The discussion finally examines the punitive and positive action taken under the CFSP and Community pillars.

Since gaining independence in 1960 from the United Kingdom, Nigeria has enjoyed several periods of democracy, although military rule has been more common.[277] In June 1993 Presidential elections, organised by a military government, were held and subsequently annulled. In November 1993, as a consequence of the ensuing turmoil and civil disturbances, the then Nigerian Defence Minister Sani Abacha assumed power. He dissolved all democratic political institutions and replaced elected governors with military officers. In late 1994, the military government established the Ogoni Civil Disturbances Special Tribunal. This was set up to try prominent Ogoni activists, including Ken Saro-Wiwa, for their alleged roles in the killings of four politicians in May 1994. In October 1995, the tribunal sentenced Saro-Wiwa and eight others to death and they were subsequently executed in November 1995. In 1995, the military government also alleged that forty military officers and civilians, mostly journalists and human rights activists, were engaged in a coup plot. A secret tribunal convicted most of the accused and thirteen death sentences were handed down.

In June 1998, Abacha died and was replaced by General Abubaker who undertook a very different course of action from his predecessor. The Provisional Ruling Council commuted the death sentences of a number of political opponents and also released a substantial number of political prisoners. The government also took several steps towards restoring workers' rights, which had deteriorated seriously under previous military regimes. In August 1998, the National Electoral Commission (NEC) was ordered to conduct elections which were held in May 1999 and won by Chief Olusegun Obasanjo, who was sworn in as the democratically-elected President of the Federal Republic of Nigeria. He

---

[277] Nigeria was under military rule between 1966 and 1979 and between 1983 and 1999.

was subsequently re-elected in 2003.[278] In April 2007, state and federal elections were held which, although widely considered to be deficient, returned Umaru Yar'Adua of the ruling People's Democratic Party as President. This was the first time in Nigeria's history that power was successfully democratically transferred from one civilian leader to another.

Nigeria has a population of around 130 million, which is made up of about 200 ethnic groups, 500 indigenous languages, and two major religions, Islam and Christianity. As a consequence of tensions between its various religious and ethnic communities, Nigeria has suffered from very serious intercommunal violence throughout its history. This can be evidenced not only by the Biafran civil war of the late 1960s but also more recent events such as the killing of about 700 people in 2004 as a consequence of intercommunal violence in Plateau State.[279] Human Rights Watch has described intercommunal violence as 'the most serious human rights concern in Nigeria'.[280]

In terms of human rights obligations, Nigeria is a party to the ICCPR;[281] the ICESCR; the Convention Against Torture;[282] the Children's Convention;[283] the Women's Convention; five of the ILO's core conventions;[284] and the African Charter.[285] It is also party to the Four Geneva Conventions of 1949 and both Additional Protocols of 1977. It is also a party to the Statute of the International Criminal Court. The concluding comments of the Human Rights Committee,[286] Committee on

---

[278] The account is derived in part from the Reports of the Special Rapporteurs on Nigeria, A/51538, E/CN.4/1997/62/Add.1 and E/CN.4/1997/62; S. Skogly, 'Complexities in Human Rights Protection: Actors and Rights Involved in the Ogoni Conflict in Nigeria' (1997) 15 NQHR 47; and E. Osaghae, *Crippled Giant, Nigeria Since Independence* (Bloomington, IN.: Indiana University Press, 1998).

[279] Both the Presidency and European Parliament issued a number of statements condemning these killings. See e.g., the Presidency Statements of 13 May 2004, (2004) 5 *Bull. EU* 1.6.14 and of 28 May 2004, (2004) 5 *Bull. EU* 1.6.15 and European Parliament Resolution of 22 April 2004, (2004) 4 *Bull. EU* 1.2.9.

[280] Human Rights Watch, *Human Rights Watch Annual Report, 2005* (New York: Human Rights Watch, 2005) npg.

[281] International Covenant on Civil and Political Rights, 1966, 999 UNTS 171.

[282] Convention Against Torture and Other Cruel, Inhuman or Degrading Treatment or Punishment, 1984, 1465 UNTS 85.

[283] Nigeria has signed but not ratified the two optional protocols to the CRC.

[284] Convention No. 100, Equal Remuneration Convention, 1951, 165 UNTS No. 304 and ILO Convention Nos. 29, 87, 98 and 105.

[285] African Charter on Human and Peoples' Rights, 1981, 1520 UNTS 26, 363.

[286] Doc. CCPR/C/79/Add.64, CCPR/C/79/Add.65 and A/51/40 paras. 267–305.

Economic, Social and Cultural Rights,[287] Committee on Women's Rights[288] and Committee on the Elimination of Racial Discrimination,[289] which relate to the period prior to 1998, paint a very bleak picture. Arbitrary arrest, summary execution and other extra-judicial killings, torture, restrictions on the freedom of expression and association, widespread discrimination on the basis of ethnicity, race and gender, executive control over the judiciary, as well as an ineffective and poorly functioning judiciary were among a host of problems identified as being widespread. The situation was such that a Special Rapporteur was appointed in 1995 by the Commission on Human Rights solely to deal with Nigeria, and the reports of the Special Rapporteurs on extra-judicial, summary or arbitrary executions and independence of judges and lawyers confirm the extent of the problems that existed at the time. The general view of the human rights situation now is that while it is far from perfect, it has improved significantly since the return to democratic government in 1999.[290] The NGO Freedom House currently rates the civil liberties situation in Nigeria at 4 and political rights are also rated at 4, which accordingly classifies it as a 'Partly Free' state.[291] According to Transparency International, Nigeria has consistently been considered one of the most corrupt countries in the world.[292] According to the Fund for Peace and Foreign Policy 'Failed

---

[287] Doc. E/C.12/1/Add.23.   [288] Doc. A/53/38/Rev.1 paras. 138–174.

[289] Doc. A/50/18, paras. 598–636.

[290] See e.g., A/51538, E/CN.4/1997/62/Add.1 and E/CN.4/1997/62. More recent visits by the Special Rapporteurs on Extrajudicial, Summary or Arbitrary Executions (E/CN.4/2006/53/Add.4); Human Rights Defenders (E/CN.4/2006/95/Add.2); and Freedom of Religion or Belief (E/CN.4/2006/5/Add.2) all highlight that the situation while still serious has improved in recent years. More recent Concluding Comments by treaty bodies include those by CERD (CERD/C/NGA/CO/18) and CEDAW (CEDAW/C/2004/I/CRP.3/Add.2).

[291] See www.freedomhouse.org/template.cfm?page=22&year=2006&country=7030.

[292] The Transparency International Corruption Perception Index Tables can be found at www.transparency.org/policy_research/surveys_indices/cpi. As noted above, in 1996 it was considered the most corrupt country in the world although at the time the number of countries Transparency International considered was not as extensive as it is now. The Economic and Financial Crimes Commission of Nigeria has announced that it considers Nigerian leaders have stolen an estimated US$380 billion since 1960. The Commission indicted both (then) President Obasanjo and (then) Vice President Atiku Abubakar for corruption. No action is planned, however, until after May 2007 at the earliest. For further information see www.efccnigeria.org/. Abubakar claimed the allegations were politically motivated as he had fallen out with President Obasanjo. He was subsequently denied the opportunity to run for President.

States Index' it was the twenty-second most unstable state in 2006.[293] In 2005 Nigeria had a per capita GNI of US$560, placing it 170th out of the 208 economies measured by the World Bank.[294] Over 70 per cent of the population lives below the internationally recognised absolute poverty line of US$1 per day and over 90 per cent on under US$2 per day.[295] It is classified as a low-income country.

The annual trade between Nigeria and the EU Member States has been worth at least €10 billion per annum since 2001 and reached €13 billion in 2005. Approximately one-quarter of all Nigerian trade is with the EU Member States, second only to the United States, which accounts for approximately one-third of all Nigerian trade. The Nigerian economy depends heavily on the oil and gas sector. As is to be expected, therefore, Nigeria's largest export in terms of value to the European Union is petroleum, a trade which since 1990 has been worth at least €2 billion per annum. Petroleum and gas-based products have consistently accounted for over 85 per cent of the value of Nigerian exports to the Union. The Union is thus vital to the sustainability and survival of the Nigerian industries involved and its markets are a major foreign currency earner for Nigeria. Nigeria accounts for approximately half of 1 per cent of all EU exports.[296] The diversity of products exported to Nigeria by the Union means that the Nigerian market is unlikely to sustain or be crucial to any particular industries in the Union.

4.3.1 Dialogue between Nigeria and the Union

Although a number of other fora, such as summits between the European and African Unions[297] and EU relations with NEPAD[298] and ECOWAS[299] exist, the most important fora for dialogue and discussion

---

[293] The Fund for Peace and Foreign Policy 'Failed States Index' can be found at http://www.fundforpeace.org/programs/fsi/fsindex.php

[294] World Bank, *World Development Indicators 2006*, Table 2.7.   [295] *Ibid.*

[296] All the above statistics are derived from information available on the webpage of the European Commission to Nigeria at http://trade.ec.europa.eu/doclib/docs/2006/september/tradoc_113427.pdf

[297] Summits have been held, e.g., in 2000, 2003, 2004 and 2006. See further COM(2003)316.

[298] The New African Partnership for Development. See e.g., Presidency Statement at the General Assembly of the United Nations, 25 September 2002, Pres02-246EN.

[299] Economic Community of West African States. The EU and ECOWAS have held a number of Ministerial Meetings to date, e.g., the ninth Ministerial Troika meeting was held in May 2006.

between the EU Member States and Nigeria are the institutions estab-
lished by the successive Lomé Conventions[300] and the Cotonou
Agreement.[301] The institutional structure of these treaties establishes
a Council of Ministers (ACP-EC Council, formally known as the Lomé
Council),[302] a Committee of Ambassadors[303] and a Joint Parliamentary
Assembly (JPA).[304] The ACP-EC Council consists of members of the
Council and Commission of the European Union, on the one hand,
and, on the other, a representative of each of the ACP states. The
ACP-EC Council's main functions are to conduct political dialogue,
adopt policy guidelines and take the necessary decisions for the implementation of the provisions of the Treaty.[305] The Committee of
Ambassadors is composed, on the one hand, of the permanent representative of each Member State to the European Union and a
Commission representative and, on the other, the Head of the Mission
of each ACP state to the Union. The main function of the Committee is
to assist the ACP-EC Council in the fulfilment of its tasks and to carry out
any mandate entrusted to it.[306] The JPA is composed of equal numbers
of EU and ACP representatives. It is composed of members of the
European Parliament, on the one hand, and, on the other, Members
of Parliament or failing this, representatives designated by the
Parliament of each ACP state. The JPA is a consultative body which
aims to promote democratic processes through dialogue and consultation. It can and does adopt resolutions and make recommendations to

---

[300] ACP-EEC Convention of Lomé, [1976] OJ L25/2, 30 January 1976; Second
ACP-EEC Convention, [1980] OJ L347/1, 22 December 1980; Third ACP-EEC Convention,
[1986] OJ L86/3, 31 March 1986 ; Fourth ACP-EEC Convention, [1991] OJ L229/3,
17 August 1991; and the Agreement Amending the Fourth ACP-EEC Convention, [1998]
OJ L156/3, 29 May 1998.

[301] Partnership Agreement between the Members of the African, Caribbean and Pacific
Group of States, of the one Part, and the European Community and its Member States,
of the other Part, [2000] OJ L317/3, 15 December 2000 as revised [2005] OJ L209/27, 11
August 2005. The most important provision regarding dialogue is Article 8 which has
been substantially revised. Guidelines for conducting the dialogue were approved by
the ACP-EC Council of Ministers in May 2003. One of the objectives of the dialogue is to
promote a stable democratic environment, and topics to be included are human rights,
democracy, the rule of law, good governance, peace and security and gender, ethnic or
racial discrimination.

[302] Article 15 Cotonou Agreement and Article 30 Lomé IV (bis).

[303] Article 16 Cotonou Agreement and Article 31 Lomé IV (bis).

[304] Article 17 Cotonou Agreement and Article 32 Lomé IV (bis).

[305] Article 15 Cotonou Agreement. The objectives of the Agreement are set out in Article 1.

[306] Article 16 Cotonou Agreement.

the ACP-EC Council with a view to achieving the objectives of the Agreement.[307]

As discussed in Chapter 3, Article 366a of Lomé IV (bis) established a consultation procedure, although it was not always used.[308] It was not utilised in the case of Nigeria, as the Member States, initially through European Political Cooperation (EPC) and later the CFSP and Community, decided to implement unilateral punitive measures. The discussion below will initially deal with the measures that were taken by the (then) Lomé institutions before examining those adopted under EPC, the CFSP and the Community.

4.3.2 Action against Nigeria under Lomé IV

Lomé IV, which was signed at the end of 1989, was concluded for a period of ten years, with a mid-term review due in 1994. Human rights and democracy were not essential elements of the Agreement (they became so in Lomé IV bis) but the formula in Article 5 Lomé IV left little doubt as to the importance of their role in the cooperation that had been established between the states party to it. Article 5, however, was not formulated so as to impose concrete obligations. Consequently, it was difficult to determine exactly when a state did not comply with the general obligations laid down in it.[309]

The Article 366a procedure was not yet available to respond to the annulling of the elections in Nigeria in 1993. Rather than denounce the Convention with Nigeria upon six months' notice, which was provided for in Lomé IV,[310] the Community and its Member States simply decided upon unilateral measures. The Member States did not engage in any dialogue and discussion with Nigeria concerning suspension, but exercised the unilateral power of assessment they had reserved for themselves.[311]

---

[307] Article 17 Cotonou Agreement.

[308] The European Union suspended all aid to Niger, for example, within 48 hours of a coup in January 1996, see (1996) 1/2 *Bull. EU* 1.4.15. The equivalent provision now is Article 96 Cotonou Agreement. A number of amendments have been made to Article 96 of the Agreement in the 2005 revision of it.

[309] K. Arts, *Integrating Human Rights into Development Cooperation: the Case of the Lomé Conventions* (The Hague: Kluwer, 2000) p. 197.

[310] Article 367 Lomé IV. This was invoked, for example, in the case of Haiti.

[311] The ACP states have on numerous occasions argued for the establishment of a judicial body to determine material breaches of the Convention by either party, see M. Holland, *The European Union and Third World* (Basingstoke: Palgrave, 2002) p. 123.

It is arguable, however, that even if Article 366a had been in place, it would not have been used. Article 366a and the decision implemented to give effect to the procedure was permeated with compromise over questions of competence.[312] Furthermore, it is difficult to consider that the annulling of the elections would have constituted a manifest breach of the essential elements of the Convention at the time. In the case of Nigeria, the Convention had already been negotiated and concluded with a military regime. The military's continued rule of the country did not amount to a fundamental change in circumstance as required by Article 62 of the Vienna Convention on the Law of Treaties, 1969. As Lomé IV had been concluded in 1989, the mid-term review obviously could not exclude states already party to it. Once changes to the Convention came into force, however, it was a different matter for subsequent events, especially as the Union's approach to non-democratic regimes had undergone a transformation in the intervening years.

Other measures were adopted by the Lomé institutions. The problem in discussing dialogue and action in the ACP institutions, however, is that relatively little information tends to enter the public domain other than the resolutions and minutes of the meetings of the JPA.[313] It is thus difficult to know the content of the discussion on Nigeria in the then Lomé Council, although it is likely that confidential measures were adopted.[314] Anecdotal evidence suggests that the debates were heated and intense but few, if any, concrete measures were adopted.[315] The records of the JPA, however, do reveal that there was substantial disagreement between EU representatives and those of the ACP states as to how to react to the situation in Nigeria.

Resolutions concerning Nigeria were adopted at the JPA meetings in October 1994 in Libreville,[316] in March 1996 in Windhoek,[317] in September 1996 in Luxembourg,[318] in March 1997 in Brussels[319] and in April 1998 in Mauritius.[320] The JPA was unable to adopt proposed

---

[312] See the discussion in Chapter 3.
[313] The *Official Journal* and *Bulletin* do not tend to provide any real information.
[314] Arts, *Integrating Human Rights*, p. 254, notes that measures on individual country situations were not common and usually in non-traceable documents or other confidential settings.
[315] I am grateful to a Commission desk-officer for this information.
[316] [1994] OJ C381/48, 31 December 1994.   [317] [1996] OJ C254/46, 2 September 1996.
[318] [1997] OJ C62/25, 27 February 1997.   [319] [1997] OJ C308/37, 9 October 1997.
[320] [1998] OJ C274/49, 2 September 1998.

resolutions concerning the situation in Nigeria at the meetings in Brussels in 1995 and in Togo in 1997. Since 1996, resolutions can be adopted in the JPA by a procedure which is both secret and split (ACP and European Union separately), in response apparently to increasingly critical individual country resolutions.[321] Where the procedure has been used this has resulted in it becoming more difficult to adopt critical country resolutions in the JPA, as it requires a separate majority among both the ACP and the EU members. Arts considers that in the October 1997 JPA in Togo, a resolution critical of Nigeria was not adopted because of this procedure.[322] By contrast, the procedure was not used when a resolution was successfully adopted, for example, at the meeting in October 1994 in Libreville. Notably, however, resolutions critical of Nigeria were adopted at the JPA meetings in March 1996 in Windhoek, in September 1996 in Luxembourg, in March 1997 in Brussels and in April 1998 in Mauritius,[323] where the secret procedure was used on each occasion. In the resolution adopted in the meeting in Mauritius, for example, the ACP states voted in favour of condemning Nigeria by twenty-four votes to twenty-three with three abstentions. The EU members unanimously voted for the measure.[324]

With the exception of the resolution adopted in Libreville in 1994, the other resolutions adopted by the JPA strongly condemned the Nigerian authorities. It is clear that the secret procedure, which was designed to stop condemnatory resolutions, did not always achieve that objective, due to opposition to the activities of the Nigerian regime by other ACP states.[325]

The JPA had been unable to agree a resolution condemning Nigeria at the meeting in Brussels in 1995, as differences between the ACP and EU members had arisen and greater support seemed to be forthcoming for the view that this was tantamount to meddling with a state's internal affairs.[326] It is possible, however, that the failure to adopt such a

---

[321] See S. Horner 'Joint Assembly in Lomé, October 27–30: a Harmonious Prelude' (1998) 167 *The Courier* 11 and Arts, *Integrating Human Rights*, p. 248.

[322] Arts, *Integrating Human Rights*, p. 248, note 137.

[323] [1998] OJ C274, Annex III, 2 September 1998.

[324] [1998] OJ C274/11, 2 September 1998. In the resolutions adopted, for example, at the meetings in Windhoek and Luxembourg, the secret vote was used and the ACP states by a large majority voted in favour of the proposed resolution, but it seems to have been crucial that the resolutions were toned down prior to the vote taking place, see [1996] OJ C254/13, 2 September 1996 and [1997] OJ C62/12, 27 February 1997.

[325] See e.g., Joint Assembly Resolution on Nigeria, [1997] OJ C62/25, 27 February 1997.

[326] See [1996] OJ C96/286, 1 April 1996 and [1996] OJ C254/46, 2 September 1996, para. C.

measure was because the vote was not secret and the 'internal affairs' argument was relied upon so as not to condemn a fellow ACP state. The distinguishing factor, however, with the resolutions actually adopted in 1996 in Windhoek and Luxembourg, which seems to have been decisive for some ACP states, was the execution of the Ogoni leaders in November 1995.[327] The real importance of the 1996 resolutions lies not in the fact that they insisted that the Nigerian regime respect human rights and restore democracy, but in making numerous recommendations to the EU institutions. The resolution adopted at Windhoek in March 1996, for example, noted that international sanctions designed to isolate the Nigerian authorities economically, diplomatically and politically, if applied effectively could bring pressure to establish a democratic constitutional regime and put a halt to its human rights abuses.[328] The Luxembourg resolution adopted in September 1996 called for a total ban on arms exports to Nigeria from the European Union, including exports relating to contracts signed before the embargo came into effect, which was aimed at the lacuna in the Common Positions which had then already been adopted.[329]

The JPA in its resolutions further recognised the alleged complicity of EU-based multinationals in the human rights abuses and environmental degradation in Nigeria. Shell, in particular, was mentioned in JPA resolutions and also those resolutions adopted by the European Parliament at the time.[330] No measure adopted by the EU Member States in any other fora addressed this issue.[331] The Abacha regime may have been

---

[327] See in particular, [1996] OJ C254/46, 2 September 1996, para. 1. This is the resolution adopted in Windhoek in March 1996, the first JPA meeting after the executions. The resolution on Nigeria adopted at the JPA meeting in Libreville in 1994, by contrast, is gentle in its tone, see [1994] OJ C381/48, 31 December 1994.

[328] See [1997] OJ C62/25, 27 February 1997, para. 8.

[329] See [1996] OJ C254/46, 2 September 1996, para. 8 and the discussion below.

[330] See the ACP-EU Joint Assembly Resolution on Nigeria, [1996] OJ C254/46, 2 September 1996, para. F and the European Parliament Resolution on Nigeria, [1995] OJ C323/91, 4 December 1995, para. H. Shell has always denied the allegations but has been highlighted by Greenpeace as being complicit in atrocities and severe environmental degradation in Nigeria. See the discussion paper on Shell's policies at http://archive. greenpeace.org/comms/ken/hell.html. In February 2006, the Federal High Court in Nigeria upheld a fine of US$1.5 billion imposed upon Shell for the environmental degradation caused and the consequential damage suffered by the Ijaw community. *Shell v. Ijaw Aborigines of Bayelsa State*, 24 February 2006, nyr. See further, G. Akpan, 'The Failure of Environmental Governance and Implications for Foreign Investors and Host States: a Study of the Niger Delta Region of Nigeria' (2006) 1 *International Energy Law and Taxation Review* 1.

[331] See e.g., [1997] OJ C62/59, 27 February 1997 and [1997] OJ C308/37, 9 October 1997.

brutal and repressive but EU-based companies were allegedly profiting handsomely from it. The practical results of the resolutions of the JPA on Nigeria, which are legally non-binding, however, were negligible. While in psychological terms they were important in the context of the discussion of human rights and democracy in the JPA, they did not have any real effect. Common Positions, however, which are legally binding and far more important than resolutions of the JPA, had already been adopted by the Council under the CFSP. It is to these the discussion turns.

4.3.3 Action against Nigeria under the CFSP

The annulling of the Nigerian elections of June 1993 led to the Presidency issuing a statement 'deploring' the decision to annul the elections and suspend the NEC.[332] In July 1993, a month after the elections, the Community and its Member States decided to suspend all military cooperation with Nigeria, as well as to impose visa restrictions for the members of the military and security forces and suspend all visits to the EU Member States by members of the Nigerian military. Furthermore, all further cooperation aid would be suspended, although allowances were made for projects which promoted human rights and democracy.[333] The initial action taken by the Community and Member States after the annulled election in Nigeria provoked a stronger response than that which followed the annulled election in Myanmar two years earlier. The annulled elections in Nigeria, in many senses, presented an ideal opportunity for the then newly created Union to assert its identity on the international scene. While Common Positions and Joint Actions could have been adopted after the TEU came into force in 1993, the first such measures with regard to Nigeria were not taken until November 1995. In the meantime, elections had been annulled and the trials of the Ogoni leaders had taken place, as had the sentencing to death of opposition leaders in secret military trials on the basis of an alleged coup.[334] The Commonwealth Ministerial Action Group (CMAG) meeting in Auckland in November 1995 had suspended Nigeria, pending compliance with the 1991 Harare

---

[332] (1993) 6 *Bull. EC* 1.4.11.   [333] (1993) 7/8 *Bull. EC* 1.4.6.

[334] The sentencing to death of thirteen of the alleged coup leaders was condemned in a resolution adopted by the European Parliament, see [1995] OJ C287/196, 30 October 1995, para. E. The Presidency issued statements after Abacha decided to commute the death sentences welcoming this but expressed its disappointment at the severe sentences for the alleged coup plotters. See (1995) 10 *Bull. EU* 1.4.7 and (1995) 10 *Bull. EU* 1.4.8.

Declaration. In a meeting on 23 April 1996 it was pushing for further restrictive measures.[335] Pressure for action thus existed in numerous multilateral fora.

The Union was under considerable pressure to be seen to be acting but the measures adopted reflect the disagreement between the Member States as to the action to be taken. Britain had reportedly already agreed (with its Commonwealth partners) that an oil embargo and general economic sanctions would not be imposed, on the basis that they would hurt the Nigerian population.[336] On the basis of the then Article J.2 TEU the Council adopted two Common Positions, the first on 20 November 1995[337] and subsequently another on 4 December 1995.[338] The Common Positions were a direct response to the execution of the Ogoni activists as opposed to the annulling of the elections. The execution of the Ogoni activists was perceived to be a failure by Nigeria to comply with its international treaty obligations. The Common Positions also strongly hint that one of the primary reasons behind their adoption was the failure of the Nigerian authorities to comply with EU requests for clemency for the Ogoni leaders.

The first Common Position strongly condemned the execution of Ken Saro-Wiwa and his eight co-defendants but followed this with a relatively weak operative part. There is value in (what were then) relatively new legally binding powers being utilised but if such responses are to be anything other than token gestures then the operative part of a Common Position should reflect the sentiments expressed in the declaratory part. In this case, the operative part simply reiterated many of the measures already adopted in 1993 under EPC.[339] It, therefore, gave the impression of taking new steps under the CFSP, when many of the measures in question were already in place, something

---

[335] See Commonwealth Secretariat Press Release, 'Commonwealth Talks with Nigeria', 4 June 1996 and Statement by the Chairman of the CMAG on the Harare Declaration at the Conclusion of the Group's Mission to Nigeria, 26 November 1996.

[336] 'Countries Agree Nigeria Sanctions', *Glasgow Herald*, 24 April 1996. The Vice-Chairman of the CMAG is quoted as saying '[w]e realise an oil embargo is totally impractical. We are trying to target members of the regime and not hurt 100 million Nigerians.'

[337] 95/515/CFSP, Common Position of 20 November 1995 defined by the Council on the Basis of Article J.2 of the Treaty on European Union, on Nigeria, [1995] OJ L298/1, 11 November 1995.

[338] 95/544/CFSP, Common Position of 4 December 1995 defined by the Council on the Basis of Article J.2 of the Treaty on European Union, on Nigeria, [1995] OJ L309/1, 21 December 1995.

[339] See (1993) 7/8 *Bull. EC* 1.4.6.

surprisingly not criticised by the European Parliament in its resolutions.[340] The Common Position did, however, introduce visa restrictions on members of the Provisional Ruling Council and the Federal Executive Council and their families. The decision in 1993 adopted under EPC only extended to visa restrictions for members of the military or the security forces, and their families. The Common Position also encompassed an embargo on arms, munitions and military equipment which also covered spare parts, repairs, maintenance and transfer of military technology. The Common Position made clear, however, that contracts entered into prior to the date of entry into force of the embargo were not affected.[341] Previously only cooperation with the military had been suspended. With no shortage of countries exporting arms, the void this may have left was easy enough to fill. The all important oil embargo was nowhere to be seen. The Common Position of December 1995 added legal force to the existing measures as well stipulating that there was to be an interruption of all contacts in the field of sports through the denial of visas to official delegations and national teams.

In the December Common Position, the Union also committed itself to pursue the adoption of a resolution on Nigeria at the Fiftieth UN General Assembly and the inclusion of Nigeria on the agenda of the Commission on Human Rights. In practical terms there was already significant pressure for this and the Union had adopted a practice under EPC to use the Commission on Human Rights and the General Assembly to condemn third states. The more practical measure to undertake, however (which was supported by the Union in practice), was the adoption of a resolution providing for a UN Special Rapporteur on Nigeria.[342] While this policy was adopted in practice, the Common

---

[340] The European Parliament adopted various resolutions on Nigeria at the time. Among many others, see [1998] OJ C80/233, 16 March 1998 and [1998] OJ C292/154, 21 September 1998.

[341] The arms embargo also did not extend to dual-use goods but these were subject to the dual-use goods regulation then in force. See further, [1996] OJ C280/3, 25 September 1996 on the arms embargo and Nigeria and the discussion and literature cited in Chapter 3 on dual-use goods. The European Parliament in a number of resolutions asked for the arms embargo to be extended to previously negotiated contracts, see e.g., [1996] OJ C362/261, 2 December 1996.

[342] Statement in the Third Committee of the Fiftieth UN General Assembly on the Introduction of Draft Resolution A/C.3/50/50/L.66 on the Human Rights Situation in Nigeria, 11 December 1995. Nigeria initially refused to admit the Special Rapporteurs on the Independence of Judges and Lawyers, and on Extrajudicial, Arbitrary and Summary Executions which the JPA condemned, see [1997] OJ C308/37, 9 October 1997.

Position did not refer to it, yet in many respects it was one of the most important measures the Union could have undertaken in a non-EU context.

Considering the threats and language used by the Council after the Ogoni executions, the measures adopted are a good example of the European Union not following up its words with sufficiently strong action. The Council declarations of 9[343] and 10[344] November (adopted prior and subsequent to the Ogoni executions) provide a clear example. The Council in the latter stated that it 'condemns this cruel and callous act carried out in contempt of the appeal of the European Union (made on 9 November) and those of the whole international community. The Council will consider the immediate steps it will take in its relations with Nigeria and also asks the Commission to make appropriate proposals.' No further proposals were forthcoming from the Commission, however, and the Council only adopted the Common Positions discussed above. The view of the Council was that as a consequence of the Common Positions and the measures implemented by it, 'the members of the shameful military regime in Nigeria will take thought and, if they cannot bring back to life Ken Saro-Wiwa and the eight others executed with him, at least we trust that their sacrifice will not have been in vain'.[345] As the majority of the measures in question had been in place since 1993, repackaging them into Common Positions was not about to make the Abacha regime reconsider its policies and practices. Significantly, what the Union did do, however, was step up the diplomatic crusade. It made representations through the Troika and Presidency to the Nigerian authorities as well as issuing numerous declarations, in particular referring to the detentions and imprisonments of opposition leaders.[346] Also acting on behalf of the Presidency, the French Ambassador to Nigeria made representations to the Nigerian Minister for Foreign Affairs to express the Union's concern at the lack of a precise timetable for a return to a constitutional regime and at the human rights situation.[347]

The limited regime imposed by the Common Positions did not stand the test of time. The European Parliament, for example, regularly condemned the sanctions as not being effective enough and asked for an oil embargo.[348] The Council in the Common Position adopted in December

---

[343] (1995) 11 *Bull. EU* 1.4.6.   [344] (1995) 11 *Bull. EU* 1.4.7.   [345] *Ibid.*
[346] See e.g., (1993) 11 *Bull. EU* 1.4.7; (1993) 6 *Bull. EU* 1.3.13 and (1995) 3 *Bull. EU* 1.4.11.
[347] See [1995] OJ C273/7, 18 October 1995.
[348] See e.g., [1996] OJ C362/261, 2 December 1996 and [1996] OJ C166/200, 10 June 1996.

1995 had stated that 'further measures will be considered, including sanctions, if specific steps are not taken by the Nigerian authorities'.[349] No agreement, however, was reached to take further measures as none were adopted by the Union. The Clinton Presidency in March 1996, for example, was publicly proposing to ban all foreign investment in Nigeria and freeze all assets abroad belonging to the military regime.[350] British Foreign Office officials stated, at this time, that any measures agreed upon by the European Union would not be effective without the United States also imposing an oil embargo, as it was buying 60 per cent of Nigeria's output at the time. The Clinton government was not countenancing such a measure, due to the impact this would have had on the US economy.[351] The then British Foreign Office Minister, Baroness Chalker, however, was opposed to even the relatively limited measures being proposed by the United States. In particular, the Treasury was reluctant to damage London's position as an international financial centre and was thus against the freezing of the Nigerian military's assets.[352]

The coming to power of General Abubaker in 1997, however, ensured that any remaining determination among some EU Member States to impose more punitive measures soon became unlikely. Upon assuming power Abubaker undertook reforms almost immediately. Whatever the reasons, it was clear that Abubaker's regime was much more receptive towards the European Union than his predecessor's in engaging in dialogue and discourse regarding its internal situation. This allowed for much less hostile discussion which proved beneficial to all those involved. The Union felt it was now increasingly able to make headway with the regime and its concerns were being taken on board. This mellowing by the Nigerian authorities further weakened the resolve of some EU Member States, in particular, France and Germany. In contrast to the French and German governments and the previous British Conservative government, Robin Cook, the then Foreign Secretary of the new Labour government, stated at this time that human rights would 'dominate British policy concerning Nigeria' and that strict sanctions should be imposed on Nigeria.[353] France and

---

[349] 95/544/CFSP, para. 3.
[350] 'Allies at Odds Over Nigeria', *Guardian*, 13 March 1996.   [351] *Ibid.*
[352] *Ibid.* It should also be noted that a Dutch, French, Italian and British consortium at this time signed a US$3.8 billion contract with the Nigerian government to build a natural gas plant. It is, of course, unknown if this influenced the approach taken in any way.
[353] Quoted in Human Rights Watch, *World Report 1998: Nigeria* (New York: Human Rights Watch, 1998) npg.

Germany, however, had started to call for most of the existing measures against Nigeria to be lifted.

The Common Position was designed to be renewed every six months to take account of changing circumstances. This is a standard formula allowing the imposition of further measures if the situation so dictates. Its downside is that measures can also be weakened by the intransigence of a Member State in the pursuit of a particular interest, which when it is a short-term one can be especially damaging to the Union's position. In November 1997 the Council, pushed by France and Germany, voted to relax existing visa restrictions. The two states had different reasons. France wished to ensure that the Nigerian football team could play in the 1998 World Cup and also wished to allow exceptions to visa restrictions on 'humanitarian grounds' – a euphemism for private medical care. With regard to the World Cup finals at least, France had prior to the adoption of the 1995 Common Position entered into a binding contract with the Federation of International Football Associations (FIFA) to admit the national teams of all those countries which reached the finals. On this basis there was agreement in the Council that Member States could decide not to apply the visa ban on sporting events in order to fulfil prior undertakings given in that respect.[354]

Germany was motivated by more altruistic reasons. It did not wish for the Nigerian authorities to be further isolated and wanted to encourage dialogue and discussion. As Abubaker had displayed willingness to engage in dialogue, the German approach had much to commend it. The Common Position was thus amended to accommodate France, which was prepared to take a more intransigent line than Germany by vetoing its renewal.[355] To placate the more hawkish line being taken by some other Member States, especially the United Kingdom, however, the General Affairs Council of 28 November 1997 also undertook that if the elections which Abubaker had announced for 1998 failed to permit a return to democracy and the rule of law, then measures in addition to those outlined in the 1995 Common Position would be adopted.[356]

---

[354] See 97/820/CFSP, Council Decision of 28 November 1997 on the Implementation of Common Position 95/544/CFSP on Nigeria, [1997] OJ L338/7, 9 December 1997, para. 2. An exception was also made for the World Basketball Championships which were held in 1998 in Greece.

[355] See Article 1(2) of Council Decision 97/820/CFSP, [1997] OJ L338/1, 9 December 1997 and [1998] OJ C323/129, 21 October 1998.

[356] See (1997) 11 Bull. EU 1.4.96.

There was no need, however, to adopt such measures as the weakening consensus on Nigeria began to disintegrate further, once the promised transition to democracy became a reality. While Abubaker's regime was still engaging in significant breaches of Nigeria's international treaty commitments, they were not on the scale prevalent under Abacha.[357] Once a process towards democracy and the holding of elections became apparent, the Union was true to its word and involved itself in the election process by sending observers. Many of Abubaker's actions, the release of prisoners, for example, were seen in a very positive light by the European Union. As a result the Commission was prepared to intensify the dialogue between it and the Member States, on the one hand, and Nigeria, on the other, including its role in the framework of the Lomé Convention.[358]

The announcement of the holding of elections by Abubaker and the transition of power led to the Union not only issuing Presidency statements endorsing the process but also to the further weakening of the Common Position and the adoption of Joint Actions, so as to establish election monitoring teams. In a Common Position of 30 October 1998, prior to the elections being held, the Council repealed the 1995 Common Position, subject to the proviso that there would be no military cooperation, and an arms embargo would stay in place.[359] Between the coming into force of the new Common Position and the restoration of democracy, however, development cooperation could only continue for actions supporting human rights and democracy, which is exactly as it was before.[360] The significance of this Common Position cannot be overestimated. In practical terms it removed all remaining visa restrictions on the regime and their families, as well as those concerning the recall of European military attachés posted to Nigeria. The other limited sanctions remained. The basic premise is that steps towards democracy, despite continuing concern about human rights problems, were enough for the loose consensus that existed to break down. There did not have to be an improvement in human rights abuses, although there was one, which the Common Position noted, but democracy had to be in place or measures to give effect to it had to be undertaken. Developments which should have led to a civilian government coming

---

[357] Human Rights Watch, *World Report 1999* (New York: Human Rights Watch, 1999) npg, noted a substantial improvement in the situation under Abubaker.

[358] See [1999] OJ C188/1, 29 April 1999.

[359] Common Position 1998/614/CFSP, [1998] OJ L293/77, 31 October 1998.

[360] Articles 1–4 of 1998/614/CFSP.

to power, at some stage in the future, were sufficient for most of the restrictive measures in place, as limited as they were, to be lifted. The Union for its part considered that 'the current democratisation process, should permit the normalisation of ... relations and enable Nigeria to regain a place within the international community in keeping with its aspirations and capabilities'.[361]

The Union did consider, however, that any elections must at least be multiparty elections with universal suffrage based on democratic principles.[362] To this end, as noted above, the Union established an election monitoring team.[363] The Joint Action which was the basis for this, was the Union's concrete measure in response to a number of earlier statements and declarations, which indicated the European Union's willingness to support the legislative and Presidential elections which had been announced.[364] The Commission, acting on behalf of the European Community and its Member States, undertook a number of activities to provide assistance for the preparation of, and observers for, the elections, including support to the functioning of the Nigerian Independent National Election Commission. On 3 March 1999, the Presidency issued a declaration on the elections considering that they were fair and based upon democratic principles and expressed its willingness to cooperate and help with the reforms, as needed, for the strengthening of the rule of law, respect of human rights and good governance.[365] Common Position 1999/347/CFSP[366] accordingly repealed the remaining punitive measures.

4.3.4 Positive Action regarding Ethical Values and Nigeria

Further to the repealing of punitive measures against Nigeria, as discussed above, the Union has reiterated its willingness to cooperate with the authorities to help improve the human rights situation and the quality of democracy in Nigeria. With regard to the former it has acted in numerous ways and these are discussed below. The Union has also very importantly involved itself in both sets of elections in Nigeria in 2003 and 2007 to try and ensure that they are as free and fair as possible. These will be discussed first.

---

[361] [1998] OJ L293/77, 31 October 1998.   [362] See (1999) 3 *Bull. EU* 1.4.12.
[363] Joint Action 98/735/CFSP, [1998] OJ L354/1, 30 December 1998.
[364] See e.g., (1998) 4 *Bull. EU* 1.3.9, (1998) 6 *Bull. EU* 1.4.22 and (1998) 6 *Bull. EU* 1.4.12.
[365] See (1999) 3 *Bull. EU* 1.4.12.   [366] [1999] OJ L133/5, 28 May 1999.

For both the elections in April 2003, in which President Obasanjo was re-elected, and those of April 2007 in which Umaru Yar'Adua of the ruling People's Democratic Party was elected as President, the Union was involved by sending an EU Election Observation Mission (EU EOM).[367] In contrast to the 1999 elections which were seen as being fair and free, in both 2003 and 2007 the EU EOM had serious misgivings about the conduct of the elections. In the 2003 elections, for example, there were widespread allegations of vote rigging and the Final Report of the EU EOM, which was invited to observe the elections, referred to 'serious inconsistencies in the legal framework, significant evidence of malpractice ... and ... the Presidential elections ... being ... marred by serious irregularities and fraud'.[368] The EU Presidency, while expressing some concerns about the conduct of the election, accepted the outcome.[369] In the overall context of relations with Nigeria, the fact that elections had actually been held, despite their shortcomings, and that they were conducted peacefully in most parts of the country, was more important for the Union. As the Presidency statement noted, the elections further consolidated democracy in Nigeria.[370]

The Union's approach to the 2007 elections has been more or less the same. The EU EOM's preliminary statement and final report has made it clear that it felt that both the State and Federal elections have 'fallen far short of basic international and regional standards for democratic elections. They were marred by poor organisation, lack of essential transparency, widespread procedural irregularities, significant evidence of fraud, particularly during the result collation process, voter disenfranchisement at different stages of the process, lack of equal conditions for contestants and numerous incidents of violence.'[371] The EU EOM had deployed over 150 observers to the elections and its findings have been corroborated by the Commonwealth Observer Group, who felt that the 2007 Nigerian elections fell short of the standards set in the 2003

---

[367] This is, of course, in addition to the 1999 elections, as mentioned above.

[368] Final Report of the EU EOM to Nigeria available at www.eueomnigeria.org/media.html

[369] (2003) 5 *Bull. EU* 1.6.16. The European Parliament resolution adopted on 5 June 2003 was couched (unsurprisingly) in less diplomatic language, see [2004] OJ C68E/599, 18 March 2004.

[370] (2003) 5 *Bull. EU* 1.6.16.

[371] EU EOM, Federal Republic of Nigeria, *Statement of Preliminary Findings and Conclusions*, 23 April 2007, para. 1 and EU EOM, *Final Report: Gubernatorial and State Houses of Assembly Elections, 14 April 2007 and Presidential and National Assembly Elections 21 April 2007*, p. 1.

elections.[372] The Presidency statement which was issued after the elections, while condemning the procedural irregularities and fraud, accepts the overall outcome.[373]

In many senses the fact that there has, despite some violence, been a generally peaceful transfer of power from one civilian regime to another for the first time in Nigeria's history is, looking at the bigger picture, more important. As noted in Chapters 2 and 3, the Union has elevated the importance of the democratic process beyond that which can currently be sustained in international law. The reality, however, is that national and local elections, with few exceptions, regardless of the country in which they take place, tend to be marred by some irregularities. The question is one of degree: an election which is so corrupt as not to be at all credible is quite different from one where the scale of irregularities does not negate the overall validity of the outcome. Overly critical statements by the EU Presidency, for example, along with those by other international bodies may inadvertently inflame tensions between competing communities and thus lead to further violence and the breakdown of civil order. In a state such as Nigeria, where intercommunal violence is endemic, such a risk is very real. On a practical level, therefore, it makes sense for the Union to express concern at the irregularities and to try and invest its energies elsewhere to sustain civilian rule. The Union adopted this approach almost immediately after the Nigerian elections of 1999 and continues to do so to the present.

For example, the Presidency in a statement issued after the 1999 elections acknowledged that the incoming government would face serious problems. It thus expressed a willingness to 'continue to promote political and economic reforms ... to cooperate with the elected authorities towards strengthening the rule of law ... respect of human rights and good governance'.[374] As the Community's powers for positive action were fairly limited prior to the TEU coming into force, the extent to which it had previously promoted ethical values in Nigeria is highly questionable.[375] The only activities it had really engaged in since it did obtain the requisite competence in 1993 were punitive. Since the

---

[372] See Chair of the Commonwealth Observer Group, *Interim Statement on Nigeria's Election of April 2007*, 22 April 2007 and *Departure Statement on Nigeria's Election of April 2007*, 27 April 2007.

[373] EU Presidency Statement on the Elections in Nigeria, 27 April 2007, Doc. 8953/07.

[374] (1999) 3 *Bull. EU* 1.4.12.

[375] See Common Position 98/350/CFSP, [1998] OJ L158/1, 2 June 1998.

1999 election, however, the Union has placed greater emphasis on cooperation and engagement in an attempt to help eradicate poverty, assist the development process in Nigeria and, *inter alia*, promote and protect democracy, the rule of law, good governance and human rights. This approach is evident in a number of different policy documents which have been adopted. The Country Strategy Paper which has been agreed between the EC and the Nigerian government makes very clear that projects which seek to reduce poverty and, *inter alia*, promote the aforementioned objectives will receive funding.[376]

In 2001 the Council adopted a Common Position regarding the objectives of the Union's relations with Nigeria.[377] While most of the objectives mentioned overlap with those found in the Community's development cooperation provisions, the emphasis on human rights, civil society, the consolidation of democracy and the democratic process is very noticeable.[378] The 2001 Common Position has now been replaced by Council Conclusions adopted in 2003 which set out Union policy towards Nigeria.[379] In the 2003 Council Conclusions on Nigeria, the Council identifies five key areas where the European Union will support Nigerian efforts.[380] Specifically identified are the development of a democratic culture which respects, promotes and fulfils human rights; institutional capacity building; poverty reduction; economic growth and development; and strengthening Nigeria's capacity to contribute to conflict prevention in West Africa.[381]

---

[376] Nigeria – European Community, *Country Support Strategy and Indicative Programme for the Period 2001–2007*, available at www.delnga.ec.europa.eu/docs/CountryStrategy.pdf

[377] See Common Position 2001/373/CFSP, [2001] OJ L132/1, 15 May 2001.

[378] Articles 1–3 of 2001/373/CFSP.

[379] Relations with Nigeria, Council Conclusions, 17 November 2003, Doc. 14486/03. Common Position 2001/373/CFSP was amended by Common Position 2002/401/CFSP, [2002] OJ L139/1, 29 May 2002 but it was repealed by Common Position 2005/82/CFSP, [2005] OJ L29/49, 2 February 2005 as it was felt the Council Conclusions of 17 November 2003 set out broader EU policy with regard to Nigeria. Common Position 2005/82/CFSP as printed in the *Official Journal* refers to the Council Conclusions on Nigeria of 17 May 2003. The Council Conclusions setting out policy on Nigeria, however, were adopted on 17 November 2003; it is those which are discussed here. Common Position 98/350/CFSP on Human Rights, Democratic Principles, the Rule of Law and Good Governance in Africa, [1998] OJ L158/1, 2 June 1998 has not proved a major source of projects for Nigeria.

[380] Many of these overlap very substantially with those set out in Common Position 2001/373/CFSP.

[381] Relations with Nigeria, General Affairs Council Conclusions, 17 November 2003, Doc. 11486/03, para. 4.

The Union certainly has recognised that projects which will contribute to these ends will require substantial amounts of funding and the CSP for the period 2002–2007 identified €366 million to that end from the Eighth and Ninth EDF funds.[382] For the period between 2006 and 2011, a further €40 million has been earmarked under the Ninth EDF to assist with organising elections in Nigeria, some of which will have already been used in the 2007 election.[383] The majority of non-election-related funding has been absorbed by development projects and, considering the size of the population living in poverty and the shortcomings of the infrastructure that exists, such funding has not gone far. It is for this reason that the funding to be provided seeks not only to assist Nigeria's own reform projects but also will be concentrated in six of Nigeria's thirty-six States.[384] This thus ensures ownership of the projects which exist, which (as discussed in Chapter 3) is considered important for their success. Where the Union's priorities do not coincide with those already identified by the Nigerian authorities, however, the impact any funded projects have will be marginal at best.

Since the democratic elections of 1999 the Community has consistently provided funding for macro-projects which do contribute to the protection and promotion of the values and principles the Commission considers important. In 2000, for example, straight after the election, €1.5 million was provided in funding for a number of projects which contribute to justice being accessible to all, information networks on civil society and the promotion of international human rights.[385] Several budget lines have been tinkered with since to ensure that funds can be channelled to the sophisticated human rights groups which now operate freely in Nigeria. A Special Programme for Democracy and Good Governance in Nigeria Budget Line has also been used to fund a number of EU-based organisations which have helped to develop democracy through, for example, support for the media or the training of judges.[386] Former Commissioner Patten did state in 2001, however, that the quality of most of the submitted projects for Nigeria had been disappointing.[387] As civil society in Nigeria has become increasingly sophisticated, the number of macro-projects now being

---

[382] *Nigeria: EC CSP*, p. 2.   [383] (2006) 7/8 *Bull. EU* 1.33.59.
[384] *Nigeria: EC CSP*, p. 7.   [385] (2000) 12 *Bull. EU* 1.2.11.
[386] This information is derived from the *EIDHR Compendiums* 2000–2004.
[387] See [2001] OJ C113/244E, 18 April 2001.

funded seems to imply that the quality of projects is no longer as problematic as it was.

Finally, since democratic elections were held in Nigeria in 1999 the Union has taken a far less interventionist approach. There has generally speaking been little or no public scrutiny of the general situation prevalent in Nigeria – unlike prior to the military handing power over to a civilian government. The Presidency has in fact had the opportunity to welcome the settling of the dispute between Nigeria and Cameroon over the Bakassi Peninsula and requesting that the decision of the International Court of Justice was fully respected.[388] The Presidency and Parliament have commented, as noted above, on the deaths resulting from the periodic intercommunal violence in Nigeria. There is one set of related events, however, where both the Parliament and Presidency have taken a more critical approach. This is with regard to the introduction of very orthodox religious laws in some of Nigeria's northern states, most importantly Zamfara.

In October 1999, the Governor of Zamfara signed into law two bills aimed at instituting *Shari'a* into state legislation. The Parliament[389] and Presidency[390] have reserved their condemnation, however, to particular incidents as opposed to criticising the imposition of an Islamic penal code more generally. This is part of a more recent overall strategy in relations with Nigeria, where the Union has sought to take positive action to help consolidate, *inter alia*, democracy and promote human rights and to use condemnation as sparingly as possible. Some of these incidents are also interesting as the Presidency, for example, has very specifically referred to Nigeria's international human rights obligations in commenting upon some incidents. For example, in January 2001 an underage girl was flogged in Zamfara State having been sentenced under Zamfara State legislation. The Presidency considered this to be a violation of the Children's Convention, Article 7 ICCPR and Article 5 of the Universal Declaration of Human Rights, 1948, as it violated the prohibition on torture, cruel, inhuman or degrading treatment or punishment.[391] This is one of the relatively few examples of where the

---

[388] *Cameroon v. Nigeria, Equatorial Guinea Intervening – Land and Maritime Boundary between Cameroon and Nigeria* [2002] ICJ Reports 303. See the Declaration by the Presidency, 20 June 2006, Doc. 10691/06.

[389] See, for examples [2001] OJ C276/284, 1 October 2001; [2003] OJ C127E/686, 29 May 2003; and [2003] OJ C272E/486, 13 November 2003.

[390] See e.g., (2001) 1/2 Bull. *EU* 1.6.30 and (2002) 7/8 Bull. *EU* 1.6.24.

[391] (2001) 1/2 Bull. *EU* 1.6.30.

Presidency refers to the specific legal obligations Nigeria (or any state) owes under international human rights treaties in condemning third state behaviour.[392] It is also the case that at the time the Presidency issued the statement, all EU Member States were bound by the provisions of the Children's Convention and the ICCPR and, as discussed in Chapter 2, are on sound legal ground in taking such a step. The Member States thus have a right to do so under international law.

4.4 Conclusions

This chapter set out to investigate the manner in which the Union has, in practice, aimed to promote and protect ethical values in its dealings with certain third states. The case studies allow a number of conclusions to be drawn. In the first instance the Union has, as an actor promoting such values, an identity closely related to but separate to that of its Member States. As a collective, the Union has the capacity to address and to tackle, or at least contribute to, global and regional issues in a manner that the individual Member States cannot match. For example, further to the Common Position on Myanmar in April 2006 being adopted, the (then) twenty-five Member States were joined by the (then) acceding countries (Bulgaria and Romania) as well as nine other states, consisting of either candidate countries, potential candidate countries, countries of the Stabilisation and Association Process, EFTA countries and Moldova. All of these countries undertook to ensure that their domestic legislation was in conformity with the Common Position.[393] The impact of collective action by twenty-seven, or in this case thirty-six, states is significant by any yardstick. The action the Union can take, however, reflects only those elements on which views are shared by all of its Member States. Effective policy is hostage to the individual perspective of each and every Member State. This is why it can be argued that despite having its own identity, the Union does not have its own dynamic, separate from the Member States. It only acts where interests and values shared by all the

---

[392] Reference to provisions of international humanitarian law treaties is more common. See further the discussion of practice in the context of the Israeli-Arab conflict in Chapter 5.

[393] See Declaration by the Presidency on behalf of the European Union concerning Council Common Position 2006/318/CFSP Renewing Restrictive Measures Against Burma/Myanmar, 6 June 2006, Doc. 10105/06.

Member States are affected. The foreign policy of the Union is, of course, a common, not a single, one.

The Union has introduced discussion and dialogue concerning human rights and democracy, among other ethical values, into its dealings with all third states. In setting out to achieve its objectives the Union has used, among other instruments, diplomatic pressure, threats, dialogue, legally binding instruments and financial inducements. The 'requests' made have included abstention from certain activities, for example, testing nuclear devices, as well as specific actions, for example, the holding of democratic elections. The approach adopted is a multifaceted one. The problem with such an approach is one of coordination and consistency with regard to each particular state. The boundaries between Union and Community competence have not, on the whole, been problematic.

In taking action there has, in the case studies at least, been little conscious reference to some of the international legal obligations of the Member States and the third states in question. Torture and slavery as state policies do not by themselves usually provoke a result any different from restrictions on, for example, freedom of expression. The Union has been working to its own agenda and attempting to promote and protect those values which it considers important. The Union has condemned and indeed imposed some punitive measures for breaches of democratic principles, the normative status of which is still questionable. The Union, however, is contributing to the formation of a customary norm in this regard. Much like self-determination, democracy is now for the EU Member States a part of the equation when recognising a state or deciding whether to deal with a government. Annulled elections in the case studies, however, only led to limited punitive measures being imposed. More extensive punitive measures have only been acceptable when the third state(s) in question have further acted in a way considered objectionable by the Union – the death of the Danish consul in Myanmar and the execution of the Ogoni activists in Nigeria. The extent of cooperation that is forthcoming from the third state in question is also clearly an important consideration for the Union in determining what punitive action to take. The execution of Ken Saro-Wiwa, despite a plea for clemency, and the failure of the authorities in Myanmar to cooperate with the Union over either Nichols's death or the GSP investigation were important considerations in taking punitive measures. The willingness of the Pakistani authorities to cooperate and to take Union concerns on board ensured that the GSP was not withdrawn against Pakistan.

No matter how systematic the human rights abuses in the case studies, in the absence of an annulled election or *coup d'etat*, the Union has not downgraded development cooperation.[394]

Even when it has acted, however, the punitive measures have sent out mixed messages. The measures still in force against Myanmar and now repealed against Nigeria simply were not and are not strong enough to compel a regime to act in a particular way. Any proposed action has to consider the legality of such action, including the impact of such measures upon a population and the targeted regime, as well as the interests of the Member States themselves. A total trade embargo and investment ban by twenty-seven states would clearly have some impact on the regime in Myanmar beyond the measures already in place. The Presidency and Member States have in the relevant organs of the United Nations consistently voted against resolutions aimed at classifying economic sanctions as a means of political and economic coercion against developing countries.[395] It clearly wishes to be able to resort to such measures when they are considered appropriate. It is simply a question of whether the political will exists among all of the Member States and if there is a perceived need for such measures to be adopted.

Although the case study on relations with Pakistan can be used to criticise the inconsistency of the Union's practice in response to breaches of democracy and to illustrate the relativity of ethical values, one overall conclusion at the end of these case studies is inescapable. Ethical considerations are now an established part of the equation in the Union's dealings with third states. The weight they are given in

---

[394] See [2003] OJ C280/62E, 21 November 2003, where it was stated in answer to a parliamentary question that 'as of today, no Agreement containing a human rights "essential elements" clause has been suspended' because of violations of such rights. The Union has done so outside of the context of the case studies, for example, in the context of the ACP states where aspects of relations have been downgraded. Outside of the ACP context, aspects of relations under the Agreement with Uzbekistan, for example, have been downgraded further to the killings in Andijan in May 2005: Partnership and Cooperation Agreement Establishing a Partnership between the European Communities and their Member States, of the one Part, and the Republic of Uzbekistan, of the other Part, [1999] OJ L229/3, 31 August 1999. Parts of the Agreement were suspended further to the meeting of the External Relations Council, 3 October 2005, Doc. 12515/1/05REV 1. The Council decided 'to immediately suspend *sine die* all scheduled technical meetings under the PCA. Furthermore, the Council supports the Commission's re-orientation and proposed reduction of its TACIS programme in order to support increased focus on the needs of the population, democracy and human rights, as well as to foster closer links with Uzbek civil society.'

[395] See the discussion in Chapter 2.

determining what action, if any, to take in any given situation will depend on a number of other considerations. It is unlikely that any state or organisation will prioritise concerns about certain values and principles in a third state over its own security and wellbeing. Such matters cannot stand alone from, for example, security considerations, relations with vital allies and trading links. There are at times real shortcomings with the Union's approach, as there are in all policies, but there is clearly a concerted and at times valuable contribution being made to the promotion of the values and principles the Union and its Member States consider most important.

5   Ethical Values and Foreign Policy
     in Practice: the Role of the Union
     in the Middle East Peace Process
     and Relations with the Palestinian
     Authority and Israel

It is arguable that one of the reasons for the Union's somewhat ambivalent responses to the violation of certain values, as was seen in the case studies examined in Chapter 4, is due to the lack of tangible benefits to it in promoting those values at the expense of other interests. It is an inescapable fact that the violation of norms and the failure to respect certain values in far off countries, no matter how abhorrent they may be, do not usually directly threaten a state's fundamental interests. The Union's commitment to the Western Balkans, for example, has been precisely because the detriment to the interests of the Union and its Member States, if further instability breaks out on its borders, is obvious.[1] The former External Relations Commissioner, Chris Patten has noted with regard to the Union's relationship with North Africa, for example, that '[n]othing matters more to Europe than the way we handle our relationship with this sharp edge of the Islamic world. Get it wrong, politically and economically, and our borders will be subjected to unmanageable migratory pressures; the tensions in Arab countries will spill over into our own societies; and our tolerance will be tested to breaking point.'[2]

A major distinguishing feature, therefore, between the previous case studies and those under examination in this chapter, is physical proximity. The Union's direct interest in stability and peace in the Middle East, the Mediterranean region and its 'Neighbourhood' has been made clear on a number of occasions. Examples include the initiation

---

[1] See M. Cremona, 'Creating the New Europe: the Stability Pact for South-Eastern Europe in the Context of EU-SEE Relations' (1999) 2 *CYELS* 463 and COM(2003)104 on the Wider Europe Neighbourhood.
[2] C. Patten, *Not Quite the Diplomat* (London: Penguin Books, 2006) p. 180.

of the Euro-Mediterranean Partnership (the Barcelona Process),[3] the 1996 Florence European Council,[4] the Mediterranean Common Strategy of June 2000[5] and in the formulation in 2004 of the European Neighbourhood Policy (ENP).[6] Furthermore, the historical involvement of some of the Member States has ensured that the Middle East Peace Process (MEPP) is a major issue in the foreign policies of the Union and some of its Member States.

Relations between the Union, on the one hand, and, on the other, Israel and the Palestinian Administered Territories, also differ from those with Myanmar, Nigeria and Pakistan (described in the previous chapter) in a number of other ways. In the first instance, Israel does not have an Agreement with a development cooperation-based focus with the Community, such as exists for the benefit of the Palestinian Authority.[7] The 1995 Agreement with Israel is mixed in nature and is primarily concerned with expanding trade, services and economic cooperation between the parties as well as establishing political

---

[3] The 'Barcelona Declaration' adopted at the Euro-Mediterranean Conference, Barcelona, 27–28 November 1995.

[4] 'Declaration on the Middle East Peace Process' (1996) 6 *Bull. EU* 21/23.

[5] Common Strategy on the Mediterranean Region, 2000/458/CFSP, [2000] OJ L183/5, 22 July 2000. Paragraph 36 of the Common Strategy limits its duration to four years. The Common Strategy was renewed until 23 January 2006 but has not been renewed subsequently. See 2004/763/CFSP, Decision of the European Council of 5 November 2004 amending Common Strategy 2000/458/CFSP on the Mediterranean Region in order to Extend the Period of its Application, [2004] OJ L337/72, 13 November 2004. Articles 6 and 15 of the Common Strategy outlined part of the Union's contribution to the MEPP.

[6] The initial Communication is COM(2003)104. The strategy for the European Neighbourhood Policy was formally articulated in COM(2004)373 and further developed in COM(2006)726. The Presidency Progress Report, *Strengthening the European Neighbourhood Policy* adopted by the General Affairs and External Relations Council, 18 and 19 June 2007, para. 1, states '[t]he European Neighbourhood Policy remains a core priority of the EU's foreign policy. There is a clear geopolitical imperative to foster stability, the rule of law and human rights, better governance and economic modernization in our neighbourhood.'

[7] Euro-Mediterranean Interim Association Agreement on Trade and Cooperation between the European Community, of the one Part, and the Palestine Liberation Organization for the Benefit of the Palestinian Authority of the West Bank and the Gaza Strip, of the other Part, [1997] OJ L187/3, 16 July 1997. The Agreement does not refer to a legal base but Article 1(2), which sets out the objectives of the Agreement, makes clear that Articles 181 and 133 TEC are among the legal bases used. The objectives of the Agreement include establishing the conditions for the progressive liberalisation of trade, fostering the development of balanced economic and social relations between the parties through dialogue and cooperation, and contributing to the social and economic development of the West Bank and Gaza Strip. See further, E. Paasivirta, 'EU Trading with Israel and Palestine: Parallel Legal Frameworks and Triangular Issues' (1999) 4 *EFARev.* 305.

dialogue and encouraging regional cooperation.[8] The dynamic of relations is thus different. Israel is not a developing country and this book
focuses mainly on relations between the Union and such countries. As
noted in Chapter 1, the primary focus of this chapter is the relationship
between the Union and the Palestinian Authority and the role ethical
values play in that relationship. This cannot be examined in isolation,
however, from the prevailing political situation in the region and the
Union's relations with Israel.

The rule of law, good governance, human rights and other ethical values
are not only discussed within the confines of the institutional structure
established by the respective bilateral treaties but are also closely tied up
with the MEPP and the Union's policy towards the Mediterranean region
as a whole. The Euro-Mediterranean Policy, the European Neighbourhood
Policy and the European Neighbourhood and Partnership Instrument
(ENPI)[9] between them complement and support the dialogue and relations
between the Union, on the one hand, and, on the other, either Israel or
the Palestinian Authority. The Union's engagement with Israel and
the Palestinians involves most, if not all, of the competences discussed
in Chapter 3. A myriad of EU policies, instruments and individuals play
a role in relations with Israel and the Palestinian Territories that
is unmatched, as far as the Union's external relations are concerned, in
terms of complexity or symbolic importance on the global level.

The aim of the following sections is to discuss the role that ethical
values and principles have played in the Union's discussion with the

---

[8] Euro-Mediterranean Agreement Establishing an Agreement between the European
Communities and their Member States, of the one Part, and the State of Israel, of the other
Part, Article 1, [2000] OJ L147/3, 21 June 2000. The Agreement entered into force on 1 June
2000. See further generally on the Agreement, M. Hirsch, 'The 1995 Trade Agreement
between the European Communities and Israel: Three Unresolved Issues' (1996) 1 EFARev.
87. This Agreement also does not refer to a legal base which is commonplace in those
Euro-Mediterranean Agreements which are mixed in nature. See e.g., Euro-Mediterranean
Agreement Establishing an Association between the European Communities and their
Member States, of the one Part, and the Kingdom of Morocco, of the other Part, [2000] OJ
L70/2, 18 March 2000 and Euro-Mediterranean Agreement Establishing an Agreement
between the European Communities and their Member States and the Republic of Tunisia,
OJ L97/2, 30 March 1998. The Member States are party to the Agreements for those matters
which fall within their competence.

[9] Regulation 1638/2006 Laying Down General Provisions Establishing a European
Neighbourhood and Partnership Instrument, [2006] OJ L310/1, 9 November 2006 (ENPI).
The ENPI, as discussed in chapter 3, replaced a number of earlier regulations. It, in
particular, replaced Council Regulation 2698/2000, [2000] OJ L331/1, 12 December 2000
(MEDA II) which in turn had replaced Council Regulation 1488/96, [1996] OJ L189/1,
30 July 1996 (MEDA I).

region as a whole and to then focus upon relations with the Palestinian Authority and Israel. The discussion will initially examine the role of the Union in the Middle East Peace Process. It will then examine the role of values such as human rights and democracy in the context of the European Neighbourhood Policy and the Barcelona Process. The discussion will then examine in detail the bilateral relations with Israel and the Palestinian Territories, paying specific attention to how the Union has tried to deal with issues such as human rights in the context of bilateral relations and the overall context of the peace process. In the discussion on relations with Israel, particular attention will be paid to the 'essential elements' clause of the Agreement as this has been crucial. In the discussion on relations with the Palestinian Authority particular attention will be paid to the positive measures adopted by the Union as these have been most important in that relationship.

5.1 Ethical Values and the Middle East Peace Process, the Barcelona Process and the European Neighbourhood Policy

The Union, which perceives itself as a promoter of a just and lasting peace in the Middle East, has essentially sought to make the MEPP and the Barcelona Process 'separate but complementary'.[10] The European Neighbourhood Policy, which is a later initiative, by seeking to contribute to the 'fight against terrorism and the proliferation of weapons of mass destruction, as well as abidance by international law and the efforts to achieve conflict resolution' is also part of the Union's approach towards Israel and the Palestinian Territories.[11] The Action Plans for Israel and the Palestinian Territories which have been adopted under the European Neighbourhood Policy make this aspect of the Union's policy very clear.[12] The Barcelona Process and the other institutional aspects to this dimension of EU policy have, however, been affected by the tensions and problems of the peace process.[13] They are inextricably tied up, despite attempts to keep them separate. It is, in particular,

---

[10] See the Preamble to the Barcelona Declaration.   [11] COM(2004)373, p. 3.

[12] See EU/Palestinian Authority Action Plan and EU/Israel Action Plan (both available at http://ec.europa.eu/world/enp/documents_en.htm) and the European Neighbourhood Policy Country Report: Palestinian Authority of the West Bank and Gaza Strip, SEC(2004)565 and European Neighbourhood Policy Country Report: Israel, SEC(2004)568.

[13] See e.g., the Presidency Conclusions of the Fifth Euro-Mediterranean Conference of Foreign Ministers, Valencia, 22–23 April 2002, Doc. 8254/02.

perceived that stimulating economic growth and development and enhancing dialogue and cooperation may lead to a lasting peace.[14] It is equally apparent that a lasting peace will lead to economic and social development in the region. Israel is, however, usually able to withstand pressure of every sort from the European Union as it can almost always court and rely upon economic, political and moral support from the United States to counterbalance it.[15] It is for this reason that the Union attempts to maintain the separate identities of the different policies and approaches it has adopted. The problem is one of maintaining a consistent approach. The timescale of the objectives and priorities which are being pursued are different and the emphasis they place on certain facets of the dialogue also differs.[16] The discussion will now address the role of the Union in the Middle East Peace Process before moving onto the role of, *inter alia*, human rights and democracy in the Union's policy towards the Mediterranean region and its other neighbours.

5.1.1 The Union and the MEPP

While a general discussion of the MEPP is beyond the scope of the chapter, it is necessary to make a few initial observations, so as to provide some context for the discussion below. A number of the Member States, in particular the United Kingdom, France and increasingly Germany, are major players in the MEPP. Domestic politics, as can be expected, play a major role in the stance taken. France, with its traditional ties with the Arab world has, except for a brief period in the 1950s, generally adopted

---

[14] For criticism of this see V. Nienhaus, 'Promoting Development and Stability through a Euro-Mediterranean Free Trade Zone' (1999) 4 *EFARev.* 501.

[15] See P. Marr, 'The United States, Europe and the Middle East: Cooperation, Cooptation or Confrontation?' in B. Robertson (ed.), *The Middle East and Europe: The Power Deficit* (London: Routledge, 1998) p. 74 and D. Lesch, (ed.), *The Middle East and the United States: a Historical and Political Reassessment*, 2nd edn (Oxford: Westview Press, 1999). See also, J. Mearsheimer and S. Walt, 'The Israel Lobby and US Foreign Policy' (2006) XIII *Middle East Policy* 29, who argue that the central feature of US Middle Eastern foreign policy has not been what is in the best interests of the United States but its relationship with Israel. A paper for the Congressional Research Service has estimated that since 1985, Israel has received over US$3 billion annually in aid from the United States; this is in military and development aid. See C. Mark, *CRS Issue Brief for Congress: Israel – US Foreign Assistance* (2005) available at www.fas.org/sgp/crs/mideast/IB85066.pdf

[16] See further, G. Edwards and E. Philippart, 'The Euro-Mediterranean Partnership: Fragmentation and Reconstruction' (1997) 2 *EFARev.* 465; F. Pierros, J. Meunier and S. Abrams, *Bridges and Barriers: the European Union's Mediterranean Policy* (Ashgate: Aldershot, 1999) and R. Nathanson and S. Stetter (eds.), *The Israeli European Policy Network* (Tel Aviv: Friedrich Ebert Stiftung, 2005).

a critical approach towards Israel. French support for Israel in the 1950s was allegedly seen by General De Gaulle as a way to extract a degree of revenge against Egypt, which supported the Algerians in their independence struggle against the French.[17] France is widely considered to have supplied nuclear technology to Israel and has in the past also sold a substantial amount of arms to Israel. France now, however, is consistently one of Israel's most vociferous European critics. President Chirac, for example, was at the vanguard of criticising the lack of a coherent European response to the Israeli invasion of southern Lebanon in the summer of 2006.[18] Germany, on the other hand, has historically felt a moral responsibility to support Israel and has taken a very placating approach towards it.[19] Britain, due to its empire and historical connection to the region, has in some way or other been long involved in the affairs of the Middle East. Britain has generally speaking not been very critical of Israeli practices and policies.

The articulation of a coherent policy by the Community and later Union has not been straightforward. There are clear differences of approach between some of the Member States, as well as the desire of a number of them also to maintain an individual presence. The importance of the issue has meant, however, that the Member States have attempted to formulate a common policy since the early 1970s.[20] The most important document on the MEPP under European Political Cooperation (EPC) is the declaration adopted by the Venice European

---

[17] See A. La Guardia, *War Without End: Israelis, Palestinians and the Struggle for a Promised Land* (New York: St Martin's Press, 2001) p. 354 *et seq.*

[18] President Chirac, for example, in July 2006 sent a letter to the Finnish President, Matti Vanhanen, during the Finnish Presidency, complaining about the failure of the Member States to provide Javier Solana, the EU's High Representative for the Common Foreign and Security Policy, with a suitable mandate to ensure an effective European response to the Israeli invasion of southern Lebanon.

[19] Germany stopped providing unqualified support to Israel in the 1970s and has in more recent years sometimes publicly condemned Israel. See e.g., 'German Harsh Words for Israel', *IHT*, 10 April 2002. In general terms, however, outside of the EU context it does take a very non-critical approach towards Israel.

[20] One of the first important statements made by the then Nine was on the Yom Kippur War in 1973, see 'Declaration by the Nine on the Situation in the Middle East' (1973) 10 *Bull. EC* 2502. For a historical perspective of the Community and later Union's approach see B. Soetendorp, *Foreign Policy in the European Union* (London: Longman, 1999) p. 99 *et seq.*; B. Soetendorp, 'The EU's Involvement in the Israeli-Palestinian Peace Process: the Building of a Visible International Identity' (2002) 7 *EFARev.* 283; and E. Aoun, 'European Foreign Policy and the Arab-Israeli Dispute: Much Ado About Nothing?' (2003) 8 *EFARev.* 289.

Council of June 1980.[21] In this declaration, which largely forms the basis of the Union's approach, the Heads of States and Governments considered that the traditional and common ties between them and the other parties obliged them to play a special role and work towards peace.[22] The position of the Member States with regard to Israeli practices and the occupation of certain territories highlighted, however, that the Community (and later Union), despite internal differences, was generally adopting a more critical approach to Israel's policies and practices than the United States.[23] The 1980 Venice Declaration, for example, at a relatively early stage supported Palestinian self-rule, considered Israeli settlements in the Occupied Territories to be illegal, and has been the basis for the Union repeatedly demanding that Israel comply with, *inter alia*, Security Council Resolutions 242[24] and 338[25] which Israel has consistently failed to respect.[26] The Nine in the Venice Declaration and at all times subsequently have strongly condemned the use of force by all sides and consistently stressed the right to exist of a secure Israel.[27]

Due in part to the fact that it has not provided uncritical support for Israel and has stressed compliance with Security Council Resolutions which Israel considers detrimental to its interests, the Community/Union and its representatives have, by and large, been treated with a degree of suspicion, if not outright hostility, by some Likud, Labour and more recently Kadima politicians. The 1980 Venice Declaration led to an official Israeli response which stated, '[o]nly a memory of the sea will

---

[21] (1980) 6 *Bull. EC* 1.1.6. For a detailed explanation of the Venice Declaration, see the address by Mr Thorn, 24 July 1980, at the UN General Assembly Special Session on the Palestinian Problem, (1980) 6 *Bull. EC* 2.2.69.

[22] Venice Declaration, para. 2. The Union has added to the Venice Declaration through a number of later declarations. Notable among these is the declaration on the Middle East Peace Process adopted by the Berlin European Council, 24–25 March 1999, (1999) 3 *Bull. EU* I.42, in which it was stated, '[t]he European Union is convinced that the creation of a democratic, viable and peaceful sovereign Palestinian State on the basis of existing agreements and through negotiations would be the best guarantee of Israel's security and Israel's acceptance as an equal partner in the region'.

[23] This is not to say that certain US administrations have not been critical of Israeli polices. President Carter, for example, is widely regarded as being the modern US President who took the toughest line with Israel.

[24] Security Council Resolution 242 (1967), 22 November 1967.

[25] Security Council Resolution 338 (1973), 22 October 1973.

[26] See e.g., the declaration adopted by the Berlin European Council, 24–25 March 1999, (1999) 3 *Bull. EU* I.42.

[27] Venice Declaration, paras. 3, 4 and 5, the address by Mr Thorn at the UN General Assembly Special Session on the Palestinian Problem, and the discussion below.

survive the Venice Declaration. The Declaration calls on us, and other nations, to cooperate in the peace process with the Arab S.S. named "The Organisation for the Liberation of Palestine".'[28] Some Israeli politicians have been openly contemptuous of the Union and the role it plays in the MEPP. It has, for example, at times been suggested that the Union should limit itself to funding Palestinian reform.[29] A widely held perception in Israel and the United States, as expressed by Henry Kissinger, is that there is nothing to be gained by engaging 'Europe' as it is 'keen to preserve its links with the Arabs and unlikely to ask of them the sacrifices needed'.[30] Ariel Sharon, for example, when Prime Minister, unequivocally stated that Israel would only be prepared to allow the Union to play a greater role in the MEPP if it took a 'more even-handed approach'.[31] Ehud Olmert in August 2006 responded to European criticism following the deaths of civilians in Qana, Lebanon, as a consequence of Israeli military incursions, by stating that further to their intervention in Kosovo the Europeans had no right to preach to Israel. He further implied that anti-Semitism played a role in European criticism but stated that such criticism was mainly due to ignorance and short-sightedness.[32]

The promotion and establishment of peace and stability, not only in Europe but globally as well, is mentioned as an objective in the Preambles to both the EC and EU Treaties as well as in the proposed Constitutional Treaty.[33] Such activities in third states are a part of the foreign policy of the Union. The ultimate objective of the role the Union seeks to play in the MEPP is the normalisation of relations between Israel and its Arab neighbours. Helping to broker a solution

---

[28] Cabinet statement, 15 June 1980 in response to the Resolution of the Heads of Government and Ministers of Foreign Affairs of the European Council (Venice Declaration), 13 June 1980, available at www.mfa.gov.il

[29] 'Israel Says EU Should Stay out of Middle East Peace Process', *KnowEurope*, 18 July 2002.

[30] H. Kissinger, *Toward a Diplomacy for the Twenty-First Century* (London: Simon and Schuster, 2001) p. 184.

[31] 'Sharon Pours Scorn on European Peace Efforts', *Guardian*, 29 January 2003.

[32] 'Sie haben Israel sowieso gehasst', *Welt am Sonntag*, 6 August 2006. I am grateful to my friend and colleague Beke Zwingmann for translating this interview for me. On the killings of civilians in Qana, Javier Solana stated 'nothing can justify that' and described the killings as 'unjustifiable' and 'deplorable'. See statement of 30 July 2006, S222/06.

[33] Article I-3(4) of the Constitutional Treaty. At the informal European Council held in Lisbon on 18–19 October 2007, the Treaty amending the Treaty on European Union and the Treaty Establishing the European Community, which is to replace the Constitutional Treaty, was agreed. See further the Table of Equivalences between the Constitutional Treaty and the Reform Treaty.

to the 'Palestinian issue' and helping to sustain it will lead to a greater degree of stability in that region and should have an appreciable effect on the protection and promotion of those values to which the Union is committed. The discussion now turns to the Union as an actor in the MEPP.

The Union contributes to the MEPP in various differing ways. The first is as a member of the Quartet, an *ad hoc* arrangement alongside the United States, United Nations and Russia, which first met in April 2002. The Quartet was established with two main aims: to help to broker a solution to the situation in the Middle East and in the intermediate to allow the partners to take collective action in response to events on the ground. It is no secret, however, that the United States is the primary member of the Quartet and often acts on its own outside of it. Ariel Sharon, while he was Prime Minister, stated that as far as Israel is concerned the 'Quartet is nothing ... only the US matters'.[34] Sharon's courting only of President George W. Bush in April 2004 to approve Israel's planned unilateral withdrawal from Gaza, is evidence of this. Alvaro De Soto, the former UN Secretary-General's Envoy to the Quartet, has stated that, '[w]hatever the Quartet was at the inception ...: today, as a practical matter, the Quartet is pretty much a group of friends of the US – and the US doesn't feel the need to consult closely with the Quartet except when it suits it'.[35]

The ultimate aim of the Quartet is to implement the 'Roadmap' to peace which will lead to a two-state solution, as well as resolution of the Israeli-Syrian and Israeli-Lebanese conflicts.[36] The Roadmap takes an incremental approach to achieving the ultimate objective of a Palestinian and Israeli state living side by side. Under the terms of the Roadmap, Phase I, which was to be completed by May 2003, involves the ending of violence between the parties, normalising Palestinian life and building Palestinian institutions. Phase II is a transition phase prior to Phase III which is the brokering of a permanent status agreement

[34] 'Sharon Rejects "Irrelevant" Mediators', *The Times*, 20 January 2003. Franco Frattini, during the Italian Presidency, was candid enough to state that the Union was only a minor partner in the Quartet: 'Les priorités européennes de Franco Frattini', *Le Figaro*, 17 July 2003.

[35] A. De Soto, *End of Mission Report* (May 2007) para. 63. The confidential report was leaked and is available at http://image.guardian.co.uk/sys-files/Guardian/documents/2007/06/12/DeSotoReport.pdf

[36] The Secretary-General, *A Performance-Based Roadmap to a Permanent Two-State Solution to the Israeli-Palestinian Conflict*, 7 May 2003, UN Doc. S/2003/529 ('Roadmap').

and the end of the Palestinian-Israeli conflict. Under the terms of the Roadmap, Phase III should have been achieved by the end of 2005.

The Roadmap essentially requires that the government in Israel genuinely believes in the creation of a Palestinian state which is not only economically and politically viable but also independent of Israeli rule. It further requires Israeli leaders to convince the Israeli population that a Palestinian state is the only method by which a secure Israel with normalised relations with all its neighbours can exist; otherwise a conflict of varying degrees of intensity will continue. The price to be paid for normalised relations with its neighbours by Israel will be the dismantling of (some) settlements with land swaps to compensate for those that are retained, and joint sovereignty over Jerusalem. On the Palestinian side, the Roadmap requires the Palestinian leaders to have the will and ability to win the argument that a Palestinian state can only be achieved by peaceful means and that any settlement reached thus will be the best that can be achieved. It further requires the Palestinians (and the Arab states in which many Palestinians now reside) to accept that most, if not all, Palestinian refugees will not have the right to return to Israel and that they will have to finally accept the consequences of the creation of Israel and the loss of their homes and land.

One of the fourteen reservations Israel put forward in accepting the Roadmap was that it did not accept the legitimacy of the Quartet.[37] Thus, when Sharon received the Roadmap in April 2003 he only allowed the US Ambassador, Dan Kurtzer, to come and see him, not representatives of all Quartet members. Similarly, at the meeting in June 2003 at Aqaba of Bush, Sharon and the then Prime Minister of the Palestinian Authority, Mahmoud Abbas (also known as Abu Mazen) to implement the Roadmap, the European Union's participation was vetoed by Israel as Sharon refused to meet Javier Solana, the EU High Representative for Common Foreign and Security Policy, for having the temerity to have earlier met Yasser Arafat, then Chairman of the Palestinian Liberation Organisation (PLO) and President of the

---

[37] See 'Israel's Response to the Roadmap', 25 May 2003, in particular Reservation 4, available on the webpage of the Israeli Knesset at www.knesset.gov.il/process/docs/ roadmap_response_eng.htm. See further, communiqués issued by the Israeli government: 'Government Meeting about the Prime Minister's Statement on the Roadmap', 25 May 2003 and 'Statement on UN Security Council Roadmap Resolution', 20 November 2003 both available at www.mfa.gov.il/mfa/government/ communiques/2003/

Palestinian Authority.[38] Subsequently, Israel has in practice dealt with and accepted the role played by the Quartet but its formal reservations to its legitimacy and the Roadmap still stand.

The Quartet's effective functioning is dependent upon agreement between all its members, which involves the search for a solution acceptable to and with the support of all. This is clearly a difficult condition to meet. The differing approach of the United States and Union to Arafat, especially after the efforts of Israel and the United States to render him irrelevant, was an example of differences between the parties. While Arafat was alive the Union considered him to be the legitimate interlocutor for the Palestinians.[39] The United States and Israel, however, considered him tainted by terror. President Bush, in a major policy speech in June 2002, asked the Palestinians to elect new leaders in democratic elections but, without any sense of irony, made clear that when exercising their democratic choice they should not choose Arafat.[40] In September 2003 Israel decided, in principle, to 'remove' him.[41] A proposed Security Council Resolution condemning the Israeli threat was vetoed by the United States, with the United Kingdom abstaining. France and Germany, along with nine others, voted in favour of the resolution.[42] Three days later the General Assembly adopted a resolution condemning Israel by 133 votes to 4. All (then) fifteen EU Member States voted in favour of the resolution after amendments, inserting stronger language condemning both Israel and the Palestinian Authority, were accepted.[43] In October 2003, Sharon stated that Israel would not assassinate Arafat,

---

[38] Similarly, on 1 September 2003, Sharon cancelled a meeting with Solana, due to the European Union's refusal to sideline Arafat. See 'Sharon Cancels Solana Meeting', *EU Observer*, 2 September 2003.

[39] See e.g., the Conclusions of the Fifth Euro-Mediterranean Conference of Foreign Ministers, Valencia, 22–23 April 2002, Doc. 8254/02, Presidency Conclusions para. 13.

[40] 'President Bush Calls for New Palestinian Leadership', 24 June 2002, available at www.whitehouse.gov/news/releases/2002/06/20020624-3.html. President Bush did not actually name Arafat but left no doubt as to whom he was referring.

[41] See Israeli government communiqué, 11 September 2003. The External Relations Council meeting on 29 September 2003 in its conclusions urged 'the Israeli Government to refrain from executing its decision in principle to remove the elected President of the Palestinian Authority, which would be counter productive to the efforts at reaching a peaceful solution to the conflict'. Doc. 12294/03, Council Conclusions – Middle East, para. 4.

[42] 'US Vetoes Security Council Resolution Demanding Israel not Deport Arafat', UN News Centre, 16 September 2003. The debate and position of the Member States can be found in Security Council, 4828th Meeting, S/PV.4828, 16 September 2003.

[43] Press Release GA/10152, 19 September 2003.

although in April 2004 he reneged on his pledge not to harm him.[44] Until Arafat's death in November 2004, a compromise existed where Arafat was still recognised as a legitimate representative by the European Union (but not the United States) but, under tremendous pressure from the United States and Union, Arafat had ceded some of his power to a Prime Minister (initially Mahmoud Abbas and subsequently Ahmed Qurei') with whom Israel and the United States nominally dealt.[45] Even here, however, the Union's unified approach to Arafat could not be sustained. Prior to assuming the Presidency in the latter half of 2003, Italian representatives made clear that they would not deal with Arafat. In retaliation, Mahmoud Abbas, who was then the Prime Minister of the Palestinian Authority, refused to meet with the then Italian Prime Minister, Silvio Berlusconi.[46] Throughout the Italian Presidency, Franco Frattini, the then Italian Foreign Minister, insisted upon meeting only Abbas and subsequently Qurei' while other EU actors continued to meet Arafat.

This difference of views among the different EU actors is not surprising. The Union has three representatives in the Quartet: the External Relations Commissioner, the High Representative for the Common Foreign and Security Policy and a representative from the Member State which holds the Presidency at the time. Chris Patten has wryly referred to the Quartet as 'all six of us'.[47] The representative of the Presidency reflects the perspective of that particular Member State in the Quartet and thus the approach is usually subtly, sometimes markedly, different from one Presidency to the next. Alvaro De Soto has referred to 'sniggering in the corridors' when the Union's role in the Quartet was being discussed for, as he states, 'it has three representatives which hampers its ability to present their position forcefully' but concedes that this 'does result in greater representativity'.[48] Although there have been differences of view between the representatives of the Union, let alone the Quartet, the manner in

---

[44] See 'Israel "Will not Kill" Arafat', http://news.bbc.co.uk/1/hi/world/middle_east/3217581.stm, 27 October 2003 and 'Sharon: "We May Kill Arafat"', *Guardian*, 24 April 2004.

[45] The position of the Prime Minister of the Palestinian Authority was created by amending the Palestinian Basic Law. See the Explanatory Memorandum for the Amended Basic Law, *Official Gazette*, 19 March 2003.

[46] See 'Abbas Refuses to Meet Italian PM: Protest over Arafat Boycott', *Dawn*, 10 June 2003 and 'Abbas Snubs Berlusconi for not Meeting Arafat', *Jerusalem Post*, 10 June 2003.

[47] Patten, *Not Quite the Diplomat*, p. 196.   [48] De Soto, *End of Mission Report*, para. 84.

which the United States dominates the Quartet is more than apparent considering the way in which the Union has usually tried to align itself with the perspective of the United States, so as not to be marginalised in the peace process. Chris Patten has noted, albeit slightly harshly, when discussing the Union's approach to the Quartet and the views of the United States that:

[w]hat was certain was that a Pavlovian rejection of any course of action that might distance us from the Americans was the main determinant of our political behaviour ... We had, at least in theory, the same objectives as the Americans. But declaring those aims too strongly, along with proposals for trying to achieve them, risked opening up some clear water between us and Washington. While we were prepared to do this from time to time, for example over the Israeli fence, on the whole we preferred to delude ourselves that Washington was as committed to an end to settlements, and to an agreement based on the 1967 borders, as we were ourselves.[49]

What it is important to bear in mind at this point is that the Union, as part of the Quartet, is not attempting to impose a solution regardless of the context and views of the parties involved. The ultimate goal of the Quartet, as noted above, is to find a two-state solution to the Palestinian-Israeli dispute. No matter how unviable or unlikely a Palestinian state may at times appear to be, all parties are publicly at least still committed to the Roadmap, although how this is to be achieved and the details a number of years after it was due to be fully implemented are still unclear.

Despite the public commitment of the Union to the Roadmap, France, Belgium and Ireland have championed an alternative peace plan, known either as the 'Geneva Accords' or 'Geneva Initiative'.[50] These states, much to the annoyance of Israel, attempted to persuade the other EU Member States to adopt this alternative plan as their formal policy and the Union has funded projects under the Rapid Reaction Mechanism to that effect.[51] They have not yet succeeded. In November 2006, France,

---

[49] Patten, *Not Quite the Diplomat*, p. 197.
[50] The Presidency has welcomed the initiative. See Presidency Statement on the Initiatives by the Israeli and Palestinian Civil Societies, 2 December 2003, Doc. 15583/03.
[51] See 'France, Belgium Draw Israeli Ire over Geneva Accord', *Euractiv.com*, 6 November 2003. Colin Powell was also attacked by Israel for his support for the Accord. See 'Israel Criticised Powell for "Mistake" over Peace Plan', *Independent*, 3 December 2003. Under the Rapid Reaction Mechanism (Council Regulation 381/2001, Creating a Rapid Reaction Mechanism, [2001] OJ L57/5, 27 February 2001) on 23 March 2004 the Union provided €950,000 in support of measures to help with the Geneva Initiative. The

Spain and Italy launched another EU Middle East Peace Initiative. These states felt that the United Kingdom's membership of the Union and its uncritical support for Israel was damaging to the Union's ability to act as an 'honest broker' in the peace process. Although the then British Foreign Secretary, Margaret Beckett subsequently argued that the United Kingdom was seen as an 'honest broker' by Arab politicians in the Middle East Peace Process, a view which in the aftermath of British support for the US-led invasions of Afghanistan and Iraq is at best naïve, it is clear that a number of other European Heads of State have at times felt it wise to leave Britain out of any 'European' peace initiative.[52] Italy (under Romano Prodi as opposed to Silvio Berlusconi), Spain and France, in particular, wished to exclude the United Kingdom as it is reported that Margaret Beckett substantially watered down a Presidency statement condemning Israeli actions in the Occupied Palestinian Territories, to the chagrin of a number of other Member States.[53]

As nothing has really come of any initiative, including the Roadmap, and despite problems and differences of view among the Union's representatives and Member States, the Union still routinely reaffirms its commitment to the Quartet and the Security Council still considers the Roadmap to be the current best mechanism by which a solution can be brokered.[54]

The Union is also directly involved in the MEPP outside of the Quartet. The Presidency, Troika,[55] President of the Commission, Commissioner

Geneva Initiative was launched on 1 December 2003 and the funding was used to finance a public information campaign about it in the Palestinian Territories and Israel.

[52] Hansard HC col. 1437, 24 January 2007.

[53] See 'Blair Snubbed by Europe's Middle East Initiative', *Independent*, 17 November 2006. The snub was in the aftermath of events in Beit Hanoun, which are discussed in detail below.

[54] See e.g., Security Council Resolution 1397(2002), 12 March 2002 and Security Council Resolution 1515(2003), 19 November 2003. In March 2002, King Abdullah of Saudi Arabia put forward an Arab League proposal for peace. This envisages Israel withdrawing to the 1967 boundaries, the dismantling of all settlements in the Occupied Territories, a solution for Palestinian refugees and with regard to Jerusalem, and the creation of a viable Palestinian state in return for all Arab League states recognising Israel and normalising relations with it. This proposal, which is not incompatible with the Roadmap, is at the time of writing seen by some commentators as the most viable initiative.

[55] Troika visits have at times been controversial, e.g., when Robin Cook during the British Presidency in March 1998 visited Palestinian officials in East Jerusalem and was subsequently snubbed by then Israeli Prime Minister, Benjamin Netanyahu. As a consequence, a number of Troika visits were cancelled.

for External Relations, Commissioner for Development and Humanitarian Aid, High Representative of the Common Foreign and Security
Policy (CFSP) and the Special Representative for the Middle East Peace
Process have, as noted above, all made different and at times differing
contributions to it. The Special Representative, who is accountable to
the Council,[56] acts independently of the Troika and High Representative
in an attempt to help broker deals, in accordance with the terms of
his mandate.

The post of Special Representative for the MEPP was initially created by the General Affairs Council of 28 October 1996, with Miguel
Moratinos being appointed.[57] On 14 July 2003, he was replaced by Marc
Otte.[58] The Joint Actions which establish the mandate use Articles 14
and 18(5) TEU as their legal bases. Article 14 provides for Joint Actions,
requiring commitments of money, men or both, to be taken by the
Union, whereas Article 18(5) TEU provides the Council with a specific
power to appoint 'whenever it deems necessary' a Special Representative
with a 'mandate in relation to particular policy issues'. The use of
both legal bases is a consequence of the structure and provisions of
the Treaty on European Union.

Javier Solana (who was a part of the Mitchell Commission, which in
part asked for an end to Palestinian terrorism)[59] has generally been
treated and seen as being more impartial by the Israelis, whereas
Moratinos (the first Special Representative) was generally seen as
being favourable to the Palestinians, although not anti-Israeli *per se*.[60]
For a substantial period of time the Israelis vetoed all contact with the

[56] Article 18(5) TEU. Although see Article 4(1) of Joint Action 2003/837/CFSP, [2003] OJ
L326/46, 13 December 2003, which states that the Special Representative is accountable
to the High Representative. The same is true of Article 4(1) of Joint Action 2007/110/
CFSP, [2007] OJ L46/71, 16 February 2007, which is the current legal base for the Special
Representative's mandate.

[57] General Affairs Council, 28 October 1996, Doc. 11052/96, Council Conclusions – Middle
East Peace Process.

[58] Joint Action 2003/537/CFSP, [2003] OJ L184/45, 23 July 2003.

[59] *Report of the Sharm el-Sheikh Fact Finding Mission* (30 April 2000).

[60] When Moratinos was Special Representative, his webpage essentially confirmed this.
Moratinos annoyed a number of influential and important players in the MEPP by
leaking or at least allowing to be leaked his record, which all accept as being accurate,
of the negotiations between the Israelis and Palestinians at Taba in January 2001. The
record of the Taba negotiations known as the 'Moratinos Document' has entered
Middle East folklore. Some see the negotiations at Taba between Yasser Arafat and Ehud
Barak (with the very substantial involvement of President Clinton) as the nearest the
Middle East has come in recent years to a peace settlement. The 'conventional wisdom'
is that Arafat was offered 97 per cent of the West Bank and Gaza and just about

current Special Representative, Marc Otte, due to his insistence on meeting Arafat while he was still alive and the democratically legitimate representative of the Palestinians.[61] The attitude of the Israelis towards the Special Representative has more recently eased, especially after Arafat's death. For example, in 2005 he was instrumental in helping to establish the EU Border Assistance Mission (EU BAM) at Rafah so as to allow movement across the border between Gaza and Egypt and he is also involved with the EU police training and reform mission in the Palestinian Territories.[62] Despite Otte's increased contribution, Solana, the High Representative, is and has historically been preferred by both the Israelis and Palestinians to Otte whose post was specifically created to increase the Union's contribution to the MEPP.[63]

The mandate of the Special Representative is primarily to work with the various parties involved in the peace process and to try and provide good offices and contribute to and ensure the smooth implementation of the agreements reached. He also works as a conduit between the parties to the peace process and the Council to provide information

everything else he asked for and still turned it down. Dennis Ross, the long standing US Middle East advisor, squarely laid the blame for the failure for the talks to succeed on Arafat, as did Barak and Clinton; in fact, Ross seems to squarely lay the blame for much of the malaise in the Middle East on Arafat. See D. Ross, *The Missing Peace: the Inside Story of the Fight for Middle East Peace* (New York: Farrar, Straus and Giroux, 2005) *passim*. See also, B. Rubin and J. Rubin, *Arafat: a Political Biography* (London: Continuum, 2003) who are not particularly flattering about Arafat either. The view that the failure to agree a negotiated solution at Taba was entirely Arafat's fault has increasingly been challenged by President Jimmy Carter and respected Middle East commentators such as Deborah Sontag, Robert Mallay and Hussain Agha. Malley and Agha have argued that Taba and Camp David were opportunities missed 'less by design than by mistake, more through miscalculation than through mischief'. See R. Malley and H. Agha, 'Three Men in a Boat' (2003) 50 *NYRB*, 14 August 2003. Sontag has argued that the Taba discussions were held up due to the pending Israeli elections (in which Barak was voted out of power) and not because of the attitude of Arafat. See D. Sontag, 'Quest for Mideast Peace: How and Why it Failed: Many Now Agree that All Parties, not Just Arafat were to Blame', *New York Times*, 26 July 2001. See also, J. Carter, *Palestine: Peace not Apartheid* (New York: Simon Schuster, 2006) p. 152 *et seq.* who also makes it very clear that Arafat was made a scapegoat for the shortcomings of all the protagonists.

[61] See EU Declaration at the Fourth Meeting of the EU-Israel Association Council, 17–18 November 2003, Doc. 14796/03, para. 2.

[62] Otte's mandate was amended to accommodate the police reform mission, see Article 3 of Joint Action 2006/119/CFSP, [2006] OJ L49/8, 21 February 2006 as subsequently amended by Joint Action 2007/110/CFSP. See further the discussion below on both the EU BAM and the police reform mission.

[63] The envoy was originally appointed by Joint Action 1996/676/CFSP, [1996] OJ L315/1, 4 December 1996. Joint Action 2000/794/CFSP, [2000] OJ L318/5, 16 December 2000 renamed the envoy as a representative.

on the initiatives and interventions the Council may wish to make.[64] With regard to human rights and democracy in particular, the Special Representative has two important functions. First, he is required to engage constructively with signatories to agreements, within the framework of the peace process, in order to promote compliance with the basic norms of democracy, including respect for human rights and the rule of law.[65] Since February 2007, the Special Representative is also required to contribute to the implementation of EU human rights policy in the region.[66] As the Special Representative is to contribute to the implementation of 'agreements reached between the parties' his engagement until February 2007 seemed to link to the human rights and fundamental freedom clauses which have been inserted in the various agreements brokered between the parties. It was not a mandate until then independently to promote human rights or the rule of law in the region, as a part of the process. As 'human rights clauses' are increasingly a standard feature in internationally sponsored peace agreements, the Special Representative potentially has a major task on his hands, with regard to this aspect of his mandate.[67] This has not, however, in practice been a major part of his work. The Special Representative has been far more concerned with ensuring that the peace process, as a whole, stays on track. From the limited information available, it seems that the human rights and rule of law aspect of his mandate has not received a great deal of attention, although it is too early as yet to tell if the amendment made to the Special Representative's mandate in February 2007 will make a difference in this regard.[68]

The second aspect of the Special Representative's mandate, in this context, is his responsibility to report to the Council on possible initiatives it may wish to take in the peace process. In this context, the Special Representative can advise on which development projects should be

---

[64] Article 3 of Joint Action 2007/110/CFSP.
[65] *Ibid.* Article 3(g).   [66] *Ibid.* Article 3(h).
[67] See C. Bell, *Peace Agreements and Human Rights* (Oxford: Oxford University Press, 2000) Ch. 4 and G. Watson, *The Oslo Accords: International Law and the Israeli-Palestinian Peace Agreements* (Oxford: Oxford University Press, 2000) Chs. 9 and 13. The Roadmap does not envisage such clauses and has been condemned by a number of NGOs for this. For example, see ICG, *A Time to Lead: the International Community and the Israeli-Palestinian Conflict* (New York: ICG, 2002).
[68] This is based upon discussion with members of the Special Representative's staff and the answers given by the Special Representative at the end of a lecture at Cambridge University in February 2005.

pursued or indeed suspended, due to their impact or interference with the peace process. Again, whether any initiatives concerning human rights, democracy or the rule of law, for example, have been taken specifically as a result of the Special Representative's work is uncertain.[69] What this does further prove, however, is the close relationship between the different aspects of the dialogue. The Special Representative can potentially have a major influence on the development of projects and the objectives and priorities they pursue, which the Commission is then likely to redesign or amend accordingly. To date, very few, if any, such projects seem to have been specifically designed due to recommendations by the Special Representative.

5.1.2 The Union, Ethical Values, the Barcelona Process and the European Neighbourhood Policy

The Barcelona Process, which was a Spanish-led initiative seeking a European policy towards the Mediterranean region, and the European Neighbourhood Policy (ENP), to the extent they overlap, represent complementary strategies towards peace and stability in the wider Mediterranean region.[70] The discussion will initially deal with the Barcelona Process and then with the European Neighbourhood Policy.

The Barcelona Process aims to create economic prosperity, by establishing a free trade area.[71] As noted above, peace and stability in the region may stem from peace negotiations or economic interdependence. Indeed, in many respects they will succeed or fail together.[72]

The Mediterranean region is not homogeneous, from either a political, economic, social or cultural perspective. Due to the different relationships and political conditions within the wider Mediterranean

---

[69] A number of Commission desk-officers did not recall any specific such projects and no references could be found either.

[70] See more generally, F. Hakura, 'The Euro-Mediterranean Policy: the Implication of the Barcelona Declaration' (1997) 34 *CMLRev.* 337; S. Stavridis and J. Hutchence, 'Mediterranean Challenges to the EU's Foreign Policy' (2000) 5 *EFARev.* 35; and M. Emerson, S. Aydin, G. Noutcheva, N. Tocci, M. Vahl and R. Youngs, *The Reluctant Debutante: the European Union as Promoter of Democracy in its Neighbourhood*, CEPS Working Doc. No. 223 (2005).

[71] *Euro-Med Regional Strategy Paper 2002–2006* and *Regional Indicative Programme 2002–2004* both attempt to reinvigorate this. Chris Patten has argued that the Union has been far more concerned with creating the 'free trade area' as opposed to promoting free trade, which is what he feels will lead to the identified objectives being fulfilled. Patten, *Not Quite the Diplomat*, p. 92 *et seq.*

[72] The Presidency Conclusions at the Fifth Euro-Mediterranean Conference, e.g., illustrate this clearly.

region, the Union had, until the Barcelona Declaration, adopted a very piecemeal approach to these countries.[73] Remnants of this approach still exist. The individual Association Agreements, for example, differ in their legal bases and nature. As noted above, the Agreement with Israel is mixed and does not have a development-based focus. The Member States are not parties, however, to the Agreement with the Palestinian Liberation Organisation for the benefit of the Palestinian Authority, which does have a development-based focus.[74]

The main goals of the European Union's Mediterranean policy are set out in the Barcelona Declaration, which develops an earlier Commission Communication,[75] as supplemented by the Common Strategy adopted at the Feira European Council, the Conclusions of the Conferences of Foreign Ministers[76] and, where they overlap, with the ENP. The most important objective of the Mediterranean policy, for our purposes, is to create an area of peace and stability based on fundamental principles, including respect for human rights and democracy.[77] The Barcelona Declaration identifies a number of principles with regard to both internal and external security, which are aimed at promoting and upholding human rights and other values. With regard to the internal dimension, each partner is committed to the principles in the United Nations Charter and the Universal Declaration; the development of the rule of law; good governance; and democracy in the form of holding free and regular elections. Furthermore, the parties have committed themselves to the fundamental freedoms of expression, association for peaceful purposes, thought, conscience, religion, pluralism and tolerance between different groups in society, as well as non-discrimination with regard to race, nationality, language, religion and sex. With regard to external security, the most relevant commitments in the Barcelona Declaration are a commitment by each party to respect the sovereign equality of other partners in accordance with international law; a commitment to non-interference in the internal affairs of other partners;

---

[73] For a historical perspective see Pierros, Meunier and Abrams, *Bridges and Barriers*.

[74] Euro-Mediterranean Interim Association Agreement on Trade and Cooperation between the European Community and the Palestine Liberation Organisation.

[75] COM(1994)427. See also, COM(1995)72.

[76] These are available at http://europa.eu.int/comm/external_relations/euromed/

[77] The Barcelona Declaration establishes three areas of cooperation: political and security, with a view to establishing a common area of peace and security; an economic and financial partnership, with a view to creating an area of shared prosperity; and a partnership in social, cultural and human affairs.

respect for the territorial integrity of the other partners; and the peaceful settlement of disputes.[78]

Although the first pillar of the Barcelona Process (political and security cooperation) contains broad-ranging commitments to human rights and democracy, the question of cooperation on such issues is reserved to a relatively narrowly focused range of activities in the third pillar. The third pillar (social, cultural and human affairs) among its other objectives, aims to 'support ... democratic institutions ... the rule of law and civil society'. A dialogue on ethical values does exist within the Euro-Mediterranean Ministerial Conferences established by the Barcelona Process, although it has not been very extensive or indeed pushed vigorously by either side. In fact, the Ministerial Conferences only seem to have reiterated support for those principles espoused in the original Ministerial meeting at Barcelona,[79] although there has since 2001 been an increasing focus on combating terrorism.[80]

In a number of Mediterranean countries, human rights and democracy are particularly sensitive and in an area which comes within the final areas of cooperation, discussion was thin on the ground. Edwards and Phillipart noted in 1997 that only the European Parliament sought to give human rights a high profile image in the context of the Barcelona strategy.[81] The Commission in its 2000 Communication, *Reinvigorating the Barcelona Process*,[82] recognised that the lack of focus on human rights issues had been one of the major shortcomings of the process since it came into being. It was felt that there had not been a sufficiently frank or serious dialogue on human rights or the prevention of terrorism and migration. It also noted that human rights policy in the region had lacked consistency and that more needed to be done.[83] The Fifth Euro-Med Conference at Valencia expressly recognised the failure to pursue and have frank and constructive discussions on these issues.[84]

---

[78] These commitments are contained in the Political and Security Pillar of the Declaration. See also, e.g., the Presidency Conclusions, Cannes European Council, 26–27 June 1995, (1995) 6 *Bull. EU* 1.1.

[79] See e.g., the Conclusions of the Foreign Ministers Conferences held in Malta, 15–16 April 1997; Palermo, 4–5 May 1998; Stuttgart, 15–16 April 1999; and Marseilles, 15–16 November 2000.

[80] See e.g., the Conclusions of the Foreign Ministers Conferences held in Naples, 2–3 December 2003; Luxembourg, 30–31 May 2005; and Tampere, 27–28 November 2006.

[81] Edwards and Phillippart, 'Euro-Mediterranean Partnership', 465.

[82] COM(2000)497.   [83] *Ibid.* p. 4.

[84] Conclusions of the Fifth Euro-Mediterranean Conference of Ministers of Foreign Affairs, Valencia, 22–23 April 2002, para. 3.

A number of initiatives have been adopted to address these short-comings. The Commission in 2003 adopted a Communication which identified strategic guidelines to reinvigorate the promotion and protection of human rights and democracy in relations with all the Mediterranean partners subsequent to the Euro-Med Conference in Valencia in 2002.[85] The 2003 Communication proposed ten recommendations to improve the human rights and democracy-related dialogue between the European Union and its Mediterranean partners. Some of these recommendations, such as increasing institutional knowledge on the key issues in each partner country, were essentially meaningless and unlikely to make any difference at all.[86] The lack of information as to the situation in a partner country is not really a problem, it is how or if the issues are to be addressed and in which forum, considering other objectives and priorities. The Communication highlighted that religious extremism and internal security concerns, especially in the light of the 'war on terror', were seen as issues which compounded the human rights shortcomings. This clearly illustrates the sensitivity of these issues and the difficult balance that the Union has had to adopt in this regard.[87] On the one hand, the Union needs its partners in the process to clamp down on religious extremism, due to its links to international terrorism but, on the other, does not wish to give them a blank cheque which can be used as an excuse to suppress opposition to the incumbent regime, as has been the case in Egypt.

The 2003 Communication did note with regard to the Arab-Israeli conflict that Israel was seen as possessing distinct characteristics in the region. The Communication highlighted that Israel functions as a well-established democracy, has an effective separation of powers and that sophisticated civil society organisations operate freely. The Commission did note, however, that the Jewish nature of the state caused problems as far as the rights of the non-Jewish minority were concerned. It further stressed that the violation of human rights in the context of the occupation of the Palestinian Territories needed to be urgently addressed so as to ensure compliance by all parties with international human rights standards and humanitarian law. The Commission also noted that this will require a special effort by the European Union and the setting up of an appropriate strategy.[88] In the context of the Barcelona Process, however, there have not been any specific strategies to tackle these identified shortcomings.

---

[85] COM(2003)294.   [86] Ibid. p. 12.   [87] Ibid. p. 4.   [88] Ibid. p. 5.

A further Communication adopted in April 2005, prior to the tenth anniversary of the Barcelona Declaration, identified a number of short and medium-term challenges 'faced by our Partners' which included human rights and democracy, sustainable economic growth and reform, and education.[89] The 2005 Communication was considered by the Commission to be building upon the 2003 Communication and argued that greater emphasis has been placed on cooperation in these areas since 2003. The list of initiatives in the 2005 Communication includes conferences on human rights and the proposal to organise further ones on democracy and human rights.[90] These do not appear to be proposals which will have any tangible impact and it seems to be more a case of the Commission trying to argue that at least something is being done to address perceived shortcomings, as opposed to something actually having been done to address them.

The conclusions of the Seventh Euro-Med Conference in Luxembourg in 2005, on the tenth anniversary of the Barcelona Declaration, expressly recognised that while there were positive achievements in the Barcelona Process much still remained to be done, although values such as human rights and democracy are not expressly mentioned in this regard. The conclusions did not really address the lack of progress on human rights issues, but in the section on good governance and democracy it is recognised that the Arab-Israeli conflict has affected the progress of the partnership.[91] Another Communication, this time adopted in 2006, entitled 'The Euro-Mediterranean Partnership: Time to Deliver', also noted how the ongoing conflict, especially after the conflict had spread to Lebanon again, adversely affected the partnership and why as a consequence the partnership was even more important as an inclusive structure of regional cooperation.[92] References to human rights, democracy and good governance are thin on the ground, although the Communication does laud the adoption and implementation of the Euro-Med Code of Conduct on Countering Terrorism, which is seen as playing a significant role in sharing experiences and providing an appropriate platform for enhanced cooperation in this respect.[93]

---

[89] COM(2005)139, p. 4.   [90] *Ibid.* p. 5.
[91] Conclusions of the Seventh Euro-Mediterranean Conference of Ministers of Foreign Affairs, Luxembourg, 30–31 May 2005, para. 20.
[92] COM(2006)620, p. 1.   [93] *Ibid.* p. 5.

The Barcelona Process has not and does not provide a particularly effective forum in which principles such as human rights, democracy and good governance can be effectively pursued. The 2003 Communication discussed above identified a number of recommendations but these have made little, if any, difference. With the Union's increasing emphasis on the fight against terror, especially that related to religious extremism, the emphasis on human rights and democracy is less of a priority in the Barcelona Process. What is also clear is that the European Neighbourhood Policy, and in particular the European Neighbourhood Policy Instrument (ENPI) which can be used to fund initiatives which help to promote values such as democracy, human rights and good governance, is a more suitable avenue for the Union to pursue these objectives and this is implicitly or expressly recognised in the three Communications discussed above. The discussion thus now moves on to the European Neighbourhood Policy.

The Community, as noted above, had adopted the MEDA Regulations (MEDA I which was repealed by MEDA II) which set out the details of the Community's internal competence to fund human rights and democracy programmes in the Euro-Med region.[94] These regulations were in addition to the European Initiative for Democracy and Human Rights, which was discussed in Chapter 3, and the funding available under that initiative. As was also noted above, the MEDA II Regulation has now been repealed and replaced by the ENPI.

The ENPI provides a consolidated legal instrument which can be used to fund initiatives which pursue the Union's objectives in that geographic area which is seen as encompassing the Union's 'neighbourhood'.[95] The ENPI, which entered into force in January 2007, was specifically adopted so as to give effect to the European Neighbourhood Policy, which was developed in 2004.[96] The ENP, which was initiated as a response to what was then the Union's pending enlargement, has since

---

[94] Council Regulation 2698/2000 (MEDA II), which had replaced Council Regulation 1488/96 (MEDA I).

[95] See COM(2003)393 and COM(2004)628, which is the later proposal for what became Regulation 1638/2006, which is the ENPI. Sixteen partners are included in the ENP, they are: Algeria, Armenia, Azerbaijan, Belarus, Egypt, Georgia, Israel, Jordan, Lebanon, Libya, Moldova, Morocco, Palestinian Authority, Syria, Tunisia and Ukraine. The Union has a strategic partnership with Russia even though it geographically shares a border with a number of EU Member States.

[96] The ENP was proposed in COM(2003)104 and developed in a Strategy Paper which was published as COM(2004)373.

its inception placed a substantial amount of stress on values such as democracy, human rights and the rule of law. The European Council of 17–18 June 2004, which welcomed the Commission's proposal for a European Neighbourhood Policy, reiterated the importance the Union attached to strengthening cooperation with its neighbours and expressly stressed that the Union felt it important that this was 'on the basis of partnership and joint ownership and building on shared values of democracy and respect for human rights'.[97]

The General Affairs Council of 25 April 2005 also reaffirmed the value that the Union assigns to its neighbours and stressed that links with the Union will be maintained 'on the basis of common values of democracy, the rule of law, good governance, respect for human rights, including freedom of the media, and common interests, as defined in the framework of the ENP'.[98]

Under the ENP, the Commission has adopted a Country Report for each state and Action Plans have been negotiated with each partner. Each Country Report has fairly detailed sections on, *inter alia*, the general political situation, human rights, fundamental freedoms, the rule of law and democracy. The Action Plans set out a relatively comprehensive set of priorities, which cover areas within the scope of the Partnership and Cooperation and Association Agreements which the Community (and in some cases also the Member States) have with these states.[99] The External Relations Council of 16 June 2003 and the General Affairs Council of 14 June 2004 were quite clear that each Action Plan was to be agreed jointly with the neighbouring country concerned. Each Action Plan was also to be 'differentiated' taking into account the specific circumstances and conditions prevalent in each neighbour and the relations it enjoyed with the Union.[100]

This differentiated approach has not meant that the Action Plans adopted have watered down the treatment of human rights or the rule of law as far as certain partners are concerned. In each Action Plan the Union has identified that it will pay particular attention to strengthening democratic institutions and respect for human rights

---

[97] European Council, 17–18 June 2004, Doc. 10679/2/04.
[98] General Affairs Council, 25 April 2005, Doc. 8035/05, p. 11.
[99] At the time of writing, Action Plans have been agreed for twelve of the sixteen states. Action Plans have not yet been adopted for Algeria, Belarus, Libya and Syria.
[100] External Relations Council, 16 June 2003, Doc. 10369/03, p. V *et seq.* and General Affairs Council, 14 June 2004, Doc. 10189/04, p. 11 *et seq.* See also, COM(2004)373.

and fundamental freedoms. The protection of such values and principles is in no sense *the* or even *an* overriding priority for the ENP. The
major objective of the ENP is to create a 'circle of friends' around the
Union and thus prevent 'the emergence of new dividing lines'.[101] This
approach is perceived as enhancing security and stability, in accordance with the 2003 European Security Strategy, and also trying to
increase prosperity for all. It is clear, however, that a greater emphasis
is being placed on values such as human rights, democracy and the
rule of law under the ENP than is the case with the Barcelona Process,
although it should again be stressed that the ENP and Barcelona
Process are complementary fora. As far as the Mediterranean neighbours are concerned, the ENP is to be implemented through the
Barcelona Process, the ENPI and the Association Agreements with each
partner country.[102] As has been discussed above, this dimension has not
been strongly pursued through the Barcelona Process and it is thus the
Association Agreements and projects funded under the ENPI, as supplemented by the EIDHR, which will be the primary vehicles for giving
these objectives effect.

In many senses the emphasis on human rights, democracy and
the rule of law which the ENP documentation considers to be the
shared values upon which the partnership is built, can be seen to be
supplementary to the 'essential elements' clauses which, as discussed
in Chapter 3, are a standard feature of the Community's third generation Agreements. The ENP adds value to these clauses in that the
Action Plans and Country Reports under the ENP have identified priorities for the political discussion which takes place in the Association
Councils established by the various Agreements. It is the relevant provisions of the Association Agreements in conjunction with the EIDHR
and ENPI which provide the Community with the competence to fund
programmes in the Mediterranean region which pursue objectives such
as the promotion of human rights, democracy and the rule of law.[103]
The way in which such programmes have been funded in Israel and the
Palestinian Territories will be assessed below.

---

[101] See COM(2004)795, p. 2.
[102] This is implicit in most ENP documentation, but for an express statement to this
effect see the European Neighbourhood Policy, Strategy Paper published as COM(2004)
373, p. 6.
[103] For an assessment of the utility of the MEDA Regulations more generally, see Court
of Auditors, *Special Report No. 5/2006, Concerning the MEDA Programme*, [2006] OJ C200/1,
24 August 2006.

5.2 Ethical Values and Bilateral Relations with Israel and the Palestinian Authority

5.2.1 Ethical Values, Israel and Bilateral Relations

The current basis for the Union's bilateral dialogue on ethical values with Israel is a part of the general political dialogue that has been established under Article 3 of the 1995 Association Agreement. For example, in the first meeting of the Israel–EU Association Council, human rights were raised in the dialogue alongside other political and economic issues. The President of the EU Council especially recalled that human rights were an 'essential element' of the Agreement and used the opportunity to welcome a then recent judgment of the Israeli Supreme Court which outlawed the widespread use of 'moderate physical pressure' by the Israeli security forces.[104] The four priorities of the Agreement highlighted, however, were concerned with trade issues. What is particularly noteworthy is that the Agreement does not make cooperation in human rights or other ethical values a specific field of activity. In the *Portugal* case, one of the reasons why the ECJ held that Article 177 TEC was a valid legal basis for the Agreement with India was precisely because human rights was not a field of cooperation.[105] In this instance, where there is a mixed Agreement, the Member States clearly have such a competence and there is no legal reason why it has not been specifically addressed.

Extensive and detailed discussion on ethical values with Israel is imperative to placate some of the Union's Member States.[106] Israel is party to the International Covenant on Civil and Political Rights;[107] the International Covenant on Economic, Social and Cultural Rights;[108] the Convention Against Torture;[109] the Race Convention;[110] the Women's

---

[104] See (2000) 6 *Bull. EU* 1.6.57. The decision being referred to was *Public Committee Against Torture in Israel* v. *State of Israel*, HCJ 5100/94, Supreme Court of Israel, Sitting as the High Court, 26 May 1999, 53(4) P.D. 817.

[105] Case C-268/94 *Portuguese Republic* v. *Council of the European Union* [1996] ECR I-6177.

[106] Austria, Belgium, Finland, France, Ireland, Sweden and Spain tend to adopt a more critical approach towards Israel than a number of the other Member States.

[107] International Covenant on Civil and Political Rights, 1966, 999 UNTS 171.

[108] International Covenant on Economic, Social and Cultural Rights, 1966, 993 UNTS 3.

[109] Convention Against Torture and Other Cruel, Inhuman or Degrading Treatment or Punishment, 1984, 1465 UNTS 85.

[110] International Convention on the Elimination of All Forms of Racial Discrimination, 1966, 660 UNTS 195.

Convention;[111] the Children's Convention and the 2000 Protocol on Children in Armed Conflict;[112] the 1926 Slavery Convention;[113] the Genocide Convention;[114] and forty-five ILO Conventions, including five of the eight core conventions.[115] It is also party to the Four Geneva Conventions of 1949.[116] It is not party to the 1977 Additional Protocols to the 1949 Conventions,[117] nor the Rome Statute of the International Criminal Court, a body which the Union has long championed.[118] The non-governmental organisation (NGO) Freedom House ranks the civil liberties situation in Israel at 2 and political rights at 1, deeming it a 'Free State'.[119] In the Israeli Occupied Territories, Freedom House ranks the civil liberties situation at 5 and political rights at 6, which classifies them as 'Not Free'. Transparency International in 2006 ranked Israel as the thirty-fourth least corrupt country, which made it less corrupt than eleven EU Members States.[120]

---

[111] Convention on the Elimination of All Forms of Discrimination Against Women, 1979, 1249 UNTS 13.

[112] Convention on the Rights of the Child, 1989, 1577 UNTS 3; Optional Protocol to the Convention on the Rights of the Child on the Involvement of Children in Armed Conflicts, UNGA Res. 54/263, 25 May 2000.

[113] Slavery Convention, 1926, 60 LNTS 253.

[114] Convention on the Prevention and Punishment of the Crime of Genocide, 1948, 78 UNTS 277.

[115] Convention No. 29, Forced Labour Convention, 1930, 39 UNTS 55; Convention No. 87, Freedom of Association and Protection of the Right to Organise Convention, 1948, 68 UNTS 17; Convention No. 98, Right to Organise and Collective Bargaining Convention, 1949, 96 UNTS 257; Convention No. 105, Abolition of Forced Labour Convention, 1957, 320 UNTS 291; and Convention No. 111, Discrimination (Employment and Occupation) Convention, 1958, 363 UNTS 31.

[116] Geneva Convention for the Amelioration of the Condition of the Wounded and Sick in Armed Forces in the Field, 1949 (Geneva Convention I) 75 UNTS 31; Geneva Convention for the Amelioration of the Condition of the Wounded, Sick and Shipwrecked Members of the Armed Forces at Sea, 1949 (Geneva Convention II) 75 UNTS 85; Geneva Convention Relative to the Treatment of Prisoners of War, 1949 (Geneva Convention III) 75 UNTS 135; and Geneva Convention Relative to the Protection of Civilian Persons in Time of War, 1949 (Geneva Convention IV) 75 UNTS 287.

[117] Protocol Additional to the Geneva Conventions of 12 August 1949, and Relating to the Protection of Victims of International Armed Conflicts (Protocol I), 8 June 1977, 1125 UNTS 3 and Protocol Additional to the Geneva Conventions of 12 August 1949, and Relating to the Protection of Victims of Non-International Armed Conflicts (Protocol II), 8 June 1977, 1125 UNTS 609.

[118] Rome Statute of the International Criminal Court, 1998, 2187 UNTS 90.

[119] See www.freedomhouse.org/template.cfm?page=363&year=2006&country=6985

[120] The Transparency International Corruption Perception Index Table can be found at www.transparency.org/policy_research/surveys_indices/cpi/2006

Israel is one of the few functioning democracies in the region, in which most issues, bar nuclear capabilities, are openly discussed and it has a thriving and sophisticated civil society.[121] Israel, however, also engages in systematic and gross violations of numerous international norms. The Jewish nature of the state, in particular, causes significant problems for non-Jewish minorities.[122] Israel does not have any basic laws providing for equality. The Committee on the Elimination of Racial Discrimination (CERD), the Human Rights Committee (HRC) and the Committee on the Elimination of Discrimination Against Women (CEDAW) have found that Israeli laws systematically discriminate against the Arab minorities, who make up 20 per cent of the population.[123] Israel's Nationality and Entry into Israel Law (Temporary Order) of 31 July 2003 is seen as being particularly problematic in this regard. The law suspends the possibility, subject to limited and very subjective exceptions, of family reunification, especially in cases of marriages between an Israeli citizen and a person residing in the Occupied Territories.[124] There have been attempts to classify some of Israel's discriminatory practices and policies towards its Arab populations as apartheid, genocide and ethnic cleansing and the issue of 'Zionism as Racism' has in the past been a regular feature on the agenda of the General Assembly, as well as causing a major schism

---

[121] Mordechai Vanunu has become (in)famous for publicly discussing Israel's nuclear policy and being imprisoned for eighteen years as a consequence. In December 2006, the Israeli Prime Minister, Ehud Olmert inadvertently admitted that Israel had nuclear weapons, see 'Calls for Olmert to Resign after Nuclear Gaffe', *Guardian*, 13 December 2006. Israel has traditionally adopted a 'no comment' approach to the issue of its nuclear capabilities. Israel has signed but not ratified the Comprehensive Nuclear Test Ban Treaty, 1996, GA Res. A/RES/50/245. The treaty is not yet in force. Israel is not party to the Treaty on the Non-Proliferation of Nuclear Weapons, 1968, 729 UNTS 10485.

[122] As noted above, see COM(2003)294 where the Union recognises this.

[123] See Concluding Comments of the CERD: Doc.A/50/18; Concluding Observations of the HRC: Israel CCPR/C/79/Add.93 and CCPR/CO/78/ISR; and Concluding Comments of the CEDAW: CEDAW: Israel, 22 July 2005, A/60/38, paras. 221–68. The EU Member States Consuls General in Jerusalem and Heads of Mission in Tel Aviv also have in the past regularly compiled an *EU Human Rights Watch Report: Occupied Territories* describing human rights abuses in the Occupied Palestinian Territories. No new reports have been published since 2001.

[124] CEDAW (A/60/38, para. 254), CERD (CERD/C/65/Dec.2) and the HRC (Israel, 21 August 2003, CCPR/CO/78/ISR, para. 21) have all expressed serious concerns about the law which is applied in a highly discriminatory manner. To some extent, Israel accepts this but justifies it on security grounds. See the Addendum to Israel's Report to the CERD, CERD/C/471/Add.21, 1 September 2005, para. 279 *et seq*.

at the World Conference on Racism held in Durban in September 2001.[125] Israeli Arabs are also disproportionately subjected to torture, inhuman and degrading treatment.[126] Israel has been described by the Committee Against Torture (CAT) as the only democracy where legally sanctioned inhuman treatment still exists.[127] The CAT has noted Israel's security concerns, but has stated that they cannot be used to justify torture. The legality of its continued use of derogations from its commitments under UN human rights treaties is also widely questioned.[128]

Israel's practices in the Occupied Territories are also a major issue. Israel has consistently refused to accept that its international legal obligations extend to the Occupied Territories, whereas the various human rights treaties bodies and also the International Court of Justice in its *Wall Opinion* have made it perfectly clear that this is not the case.[129] In the aftermath of the unilateral Israeli withdrawal or 'disengagement' from Gaza in September 2005, the Israeli position has consistently been to argue that as it no longer occupies Gaza, Israel is no longer legally obliged in any respect as far as that territory and its population is concerned.[130] Professor Crawford has noted, however, that the partial withdrawal in the case of Gaza has no legal significance and the status of the Occupied Palestinian Territories remains unchanged pending a comprehensive settlement.[131] The Israeli argument is legally disingenuous as under the Hague Conventions the test for occupation is effective

---

[125] See more generally, M. Bishara, *Palestine/Israel: Peace or Apartheid – Occupations, Terrorism and the Future* (London: Zed Books, 2001) and Carter, *Palestine: Peace not Apartheid*.

[126] Concluding Comments of the CERD: Israel CERD 304/Add.45; Concluding Comments of the CAT: Israel, 9 May 1997, A/52/44 paras. 253–60; and Concluding Comments of the HRC: Israel, 21 August 2003, CCPR/CO/78/ISR.

[127] See Concluding Comments of the CAT: Israel, 23 November 2001, CAT/C/XXVII/Conc.5.

[128] See Concluding Comments of the CAT, Israel, 23 November 2001, CAT/C/XXVII/Conc.5 and Concluding Observations of the HRC: CCPR/CO/78/ISR. The HRC's General Comment 29, 31 August 2001, CCPR/C/21/Rev.1/Add.11, makes clear the limitations on lawful derogations from the ICCPR. The HRC has expressly drawn Israel's attention to the incompatibility in its approach to derogations and obligations under the Covenant.

[129] Advisory Opinion, *Legal Consequences of the Construction of a Wall in the Occupied Palestinian Territory* [2004] ICJ Reports 136, para. 109 *et seq.* See also, e.g., Concluding Observations of the HRC: Israel, CCPR/C/79/Add.93, para. 10; CCPR/C/77/L/ISR, 27 November 2002; and Concluding Comments of the HRC: Israel, 21 August 2003, CCPR/CO/78/ISR, para. 11.

[130] See the detailed documents available from webpage of the Israeli Ministry of Foreign Affairs at www.israel-mfa.gov.il

[131] J. Crawford, *The Creation of States in International Law*, 2nd edn (Oxford: Oxford University Press, 2006) p. 448, note 286.

control.[132] Israel retains full effective control over the border between Gaza and Israel and also between Gaza and Egypt, as well as over the airspace over Gaza and access to the sea. The situation in the Occupied Territories has been recognised as being of such gravity that the now defunct Commission on Human Rights appointed a Special Rapporteur on Occupied Palestine, with whom Israel has consistently refused to cooperate.[133]

There are thus numerous relevant issues and concerns with regard to ethical values in relations with Israel and many of these are discussed further below. In practice, one of the most important issues has been the application of the 'essential elements' clause in the 1995 Agreement. The clause, however, and the applicability and continuance of the Agreement, are inextricably tied up with the MEPP and the survival of the Palestinian Authority. The discussion will thus turn to the relationship between the Union and the Palestinian Authority before examining the relevance of the essential elements clause and its application. Before doing so, however, it is necessary to briefly discuss economic relations between the Union and Israel to provide some context for the discussion below.

Economic relations between the Community and Israel have grown steadily closer. The Essen European Council of 1994 had, in the context

---

[132] Article 42 of Regulations Respecting the Laws and Customs of War on Land Annexed to the Fourth Hague Convention of 18 October 1907, (1910) UKTS 9. For the customary international law status of this provision see Advisory Opinion, *Legal Consequences of the Construction of a Wall*, n. 129 above para. 78.

[133] The current Special Rapporteur is Prof. John Dugard. He has published a number of reports on the situation and has taken a very rigorous approach towards Israel. The Special Rapporteur has a limited mandate which does not permit him to examine Palestinian violations. As a consequence, Israel has refused to cooperate with him. Professor Dugard has been as even-handed as possible and at every opportunity highlighted the inherent bias in his mandate and in his reports he makes clear that the Palestinians also engage in gross violations of the rights of Israelis. See e.g., *Update to the Mission Report on Israel's Violations of Human Rights in the Palestinian Territories Occupied Since 1967*, E/CN.4/2001/30, 21 March 2001 (hereinafter '*Special Rapporteur's 2001 Report*'); Report of the Special Rapporteur of the Commission on Human Rights, *On the Situation in the Palestinian Territories Occupied by Israel Since 1967*, E/CN.4/2002/32, 6 March 2002 (hereinafter '*Special Rapporteur's 2002 Report*'); Report of the Special Rapporteur of the Commission on Human Rights, *On the Situation in the Palestinian Territories Occupied by Israel Since 1967*, E/CN.4/2004/6, 8 September 2003 (hereinafter '*Special Rapporteur's 2003 Report*'); Report of the Special Rapporteur, *On the Situation of Human Rights in the Palestinian Territories Occupied Since 1967*, A/HRC/2/5, 5 September 2006; and Report of the Special Rapporteur, *On the Situation of Human Rights in the Palestinian Territories Occupied Since 1967*, A/HRC/4/17, 29 January 2007 (hereinafter '*Special Rapporteur's 2007 Report*').

of relations with the Mediterranean region, identified that Israel 'on account of its high level of economic development, should enjoy special status in its relations with the European Union on the basis of reciprocity and common interests'.[134] The various Agreements negotiated between the parties have ensured that the Union has become Israel's largest trading partner.[135] The Union is the largest importer of Israeli goods, although the United States exports more goods to it than the Union.[136] In 2005, 38 per cent of all Israeli imports, worth in excess of €14 billion, were from the Union. Twenty-eight per cent of all Israeli exports, worth just over €9 billion, were to the Union. As far as the Union is concerned, trade with Israel is worth less than 1 per cent of its total imports or exports. Since 2001, the volume of trade between Israel and the European Union, despite the latter's expansion, has in real terms been decreasing.

The various financial protocols which have been signed with Israel by the Community and the Member States are, by and large, less favourable than those granted to other states in the region. Israel is economically more prosperous than those other states, it has a per capita gross national income of over US$18,500.[137] For this reason aid is largely limited to European Investment Bank (EIB) loans and other loans for cooperation projects. Israel, while not entitled to development funding as such, is eligible for regional or decentralised cooperation projects. The MEDA Regulations and now the ENPI, which provides the legal basis for funding such projects, goes beyond the framework of traditional development assistance and is intended also to apply to countries that are not classifiable as developing, as can be witnessed by the reliance upon Articles 179 and 181a TEC as legal bases.

The attitude of the Union to providing assistance to Israel can be contrasted with that of the United States. Notwithstanding the fact that Israel is a high-income country, according to the World Bank, in 2000 it received US$800 million in official development assistance.[138]

---

[134] Essen European Council, 9–10 December 1994, (1994) 12 *Bull. EU* I.14.
[135] In addition to the 1995 Euro-Mediterranean Agreement there was an EC-Israel Interim Agreement on Trade and Trade Related Matters, which entered into force on 1 January 1996, [1996] OJ L71/1, 21 March 1996. This sought to update the 1975 Agreement until the 1995 Agreement with Israel entered into force.
[136] See DG Trade, *Israel: EU Bilateral Trade*, available at http://trade.ec.europa.eu/doclib/docs/2006/september/tradoc_113402.pdf
[137] World Bank, *World Development Indicators 2006*, Table 2.7.   [138] *Ibid.*

The United States is by far the largest bilateral donor to Israel. Since 1985, the United States has annually provided US$3 billion in grants to Israel, a substantial percentage of which is in military aid. Since 1976, Israel has been the largest annual recipient of US foreign assistance, and is the largest cumulative recipient of such aid since the Second World War.[139]

5.2.2 Ethical Values, the Palestinian Authority and Bilateral Relations

The Agreement between the Community and the Palestinian Liberation Organisation for the benefit of the Palestinian Authority currently represents the only development cooperation Agreement the Community has with a non-state entity.[140] Unlike the Agreement with Israel, mainly for political and legal reasons, it is not mixed in nature. The Agreement aims to establish a free trade area between the Community and the West Bank and Gaza by the end of 2001, something that has not been achieved and, considering the political situation at the time of writing, it is unlikely to be achieved at any time in the near future. Article 1 of the Agreement states that its objectives shall include providing an appropriate framework for a comprehensive dialogue. Article 2 is the 'essential elements' clause and Article 70 is a suspension clause. In substantive terms these are identical to those in the Agreement with Israel. Furthermore, Article 68 articulates the 'security interests' exception, which is more or less identical to that in the other Euro-Mediterranean Agreements.

Relations between the Palestinian Authority, a non-state entity, and the Union must take account of various special factors. In those territories where the Palestinian Authority has control its powers and

---

[139] Statistics on US aid are derived from C. Mark, *CRS Issue Brief for Congress: Israel – US Foreign Assistance* (2005). With a population of just under seven million, it is often argued that per capita Israel is the largest recipient of aid in the world. While technically correct, this is misleading as over US$2 billion of the annual US$3 billion in US aid to Israel is in military assistance.

[140] Under Article 310 TEC, the Community 'may conclude with one or more States or international organisations agreements establishing an association involving reciprocal rights and obligations'. The Palestinian Liberation Organisation is neither a state nor an 'international organisation' as that term is normally understood in international law. Paasivirta, 'EU Trading with Israel and Palestine', 309, note 19 has argued, however, that the term 'international organisation' in this context can extend to the PLO and the Palestinian Authority, although she then concedes, 'though this would admittedly give an extended meaning to the term "international organization"'.

competences are less than those of a state.[141] Further to the outbreak of what is commonly known as the Al-Aqsa Intifada in September 2000, those arrangements that were in place after the Oslo Peace Accords have not survived following Israeli military incursions and at times occupation of territory that should be under the control of the Palestinian Authority.[142] A distinction should be drawn between the Gaza Strip and the Palestinian Territories of the West Bank. Further to the 'disengagement' from Gaza in September 2005, Israel controls all access to and from Gaza but Israel is not involved in any way in Gaza's internal administration.[143] Israel is involved in the administration of the West Bank due to the building of a large number of settlements and 'illegal outposts', but some aspects of administration are under the control of the Palestinian Authority.[144]

---

[141] See Israel–Palestinian Liberation Organisation: Declaration of Principles on Interim Self-Government Arrangements, 13 September 1993, (1993) 32 *ILM* 1525 (Oslo I) and Israeli-Palestinian Interim Agreement on the West Bank and the Gaza Strip, 24 September 1995, (1997) 36 *ILM* 557 (Oslo II). See further, P. Malunczuk, 'Some Basic Aspects of the Agreements between Israel and the Palestinian Liberation Organisation from the Perspective of International Law' (1996) 7 *EJIL* 485 and Watson, *The Oslo Accords, passim*. R. Falk, 'Some International Law Implications of the Oslo/Cairo Framework for the PLO/Israeli Peace Process' in S. Brown (ed.), *Human Rights, Self Determination and Political Change in the Occupied Political Territories* (The Hague: Martinus Nijhoff Publishers, 1997) pp. 1, 4, notes that a disparity in power, wealth, influence, information and negotiating skill between Israel and the PLO has pervaded all phases of negotiation and this multilayered disparity has also pervaded implementation. There is a strong tendency in international law to respect whatever framework parties to a conflict agree upon to resolve their differences and any disparities in power are legally irrelevant.

[142] For a legal discussion on the first *intifada* and an example of the passions the Middle East conflict can evoke even in academic literature, see R. Falk and B. Weston, 'The Relevance of International Law to Palestinian Rights in the West Bank and Gaza: in Legal Defense of the Intifada' (1991) 32 *Harvard ILJ* 129. In reply, see M. Curtis, 'International Law and the Territories' (1991) 32 *Harvard ILJ* 457 and consequently R. Falk and B. Weston, 'The Israeli-Occupied Territories, International Law and the Boundaries of Scholarly Discourse: a Reply to Michael Curtis' (1992) 33 *Harvard ILJ* 191.

[143] Special Rapporteur John Dugard has stated with regard to Gaza that 'in effect, following Israel's withdrawal, Gaza became a sealed off, imprisoned and occupied territory': *Special Rapporteur's 2007 Report*, p. 7. For discussion of the Gaza disengagement from an Israeli legal perspective, see S. Navot, 'The Israeli Withdrawal from Gaza: a Constitutional Perspective' (2006) 12 *EPL* 17.

[144] The term 'illegal outposts', which is regularly used, is a misnomer as under the Fourth Geneva Convention all Israeli settlements in land occupied by Israel after the 1967 war are illegal. The term 'illegal' outposts', however, is used to distinguish between settlements which are built with the cooperation of the Government of Israel as opposed to those which do not have official sanction. The World Bank in 2007 estimated that there are 100 'illegal' outposts but notes that they cannot be built

The Palestinian Authority is a very dysfunctional entity. During the last years of his life, while Arafat still symbolised the Palestinian cause, he was politically a discredited figure in the West, large parts of the Arab world and also among many Palestinians. Sharon, his old adversary from the Lebanon conflict of 1982, in deciding to surround Arafat's compound (the *Muqata'a*) in Ramallah in 2001 essentially gave Arafat a new lease of political life and legitimacy in the eyes of many, despite the corruption and incompetence of Arafat's Fatah party.[145] After Arafat's death in November 2004, the long-standing simmering tensions between different Palestinian factions and the widespread public disenchantment with Fatah came further to the fore. Arafat's death ensured that Presidential elections had to be held. In such circumstances, according to Palestinian law, Presidential elections must be held within sixty days and in January 2005, Mahmoud Abbas, a member of Fatah, was declared victorious in what were considered to be fair and free elections.[146]

Abbas is a hugely important figure in the Palestinian cause. Alongside Arafat he is accredited with helping to found Fatah and after Arafat's death he became not only Chairman of the PLO but also the head of Fatah. Abbas is considered by the Union, Russia and the United Nations as someone they are able to deal with. The same is very importantly also true of both the United States and Israel, as he is considered and referred to by them as a 'moderate'.[147]

The elections to the Palestinian Legislative Council (PLC) in January 2006, however, which were secure, free and fair according to EU and other international observers, led to a victory for the more militant Hamas.[148] This outcome has been described as a 'seismic shift' in

without a substantial degree of official complicity: World Bank, *Movement and Access Restrictions in the West Bank: Uncertainty and Inefficiency in the Palestinian Economy*, (9 May 2007) p. 6, available at http://siteresources.worldbank.org/INTWESTBANKGAZA/Resources/WestBankrestrictions9Mayfinal.pdf

[145] See further the discussion below.

[146] Article 37(2) of Amended Basic Law, 2003. See European Union Election Observation Mission, West Bank and Gaza 2005, *Final Report on the Presidential Elections, 9 January 2005* and the discussion below.

[147] The use of the term 'moderates' and 'extremists' when referring to Muslims in the context of the 'war on terror' is highly selective and the label is applied for political expedience, much like the use of the terms 'totalitarian' and 'authoritarian' during the Cold War. For an outstanding discussion, see M. Mamdani, *Good Muslim, Bad Muslim: America, the Cold War and the Roots of Terror* (New York: Random House, 2005).

[148] See the discussion below.

Palestinian politics.[149] Hamas won 74 out of 132 parliamentary seats with 45 per cent of the vote. Fatah won 45 seats. Hamas was successful for a number of reasons, primarily Fatah's inefficiency, corruption and the building up of debts; Fatah's failure to make progress in the peace process and to improve living conditions for Palestinians; a limited growth in Islamic fundamentalism; and the strong commitment of Hamas to social welfare.

As will be discussed further below, the subsequent formation of a democratically elected Hamas-led government resulted in an interruption to contacts between the European Union, Israel and the United States, on the one hand, and, on the other, the Hamas-led government. The Union and United States also stopped all direct financial aid to the Palestinian Authority. This interruption was due to the refusal of Hamas to meet the demands of the Quartet and in particular to expressly renounce violence and recognise Israel. Further to the adoption of a Common Position in December 2001, Hamas-Izz al-Din al-Qassem (identified in the Common Position as the terrorist wing of Hamas) and Palestinian factions, such as Islamic Jihad, were classified alongside, *inter alia*, the Basque separatists ETA and certain Irish nationalist groups as terrorists and were subject to punitive measures.[150] Subsequently this has been changed and both the political wing of Hamas and Hamas-Izz al-Din al-Qassem have been considered to be terrorist organisations and subject to the punitive measures set out in the 2001 Common Position. Unlike, for example, members of Al-Qaeda, persons associated with Hamas have not to date been classified as 'terrorists' by the Security Council of the United Nations.[151] The Union, Israel and the United States refused to have any contact with Hamas which led the government, but not with President Abbas.[152]

---

[149] R. Malley 'A New Middle East' (2006) 54 *NYRB*, 21 September 2006. Malley has argued that the 2006 election result is the most radical shift in Palestinian politics since Arafat and his Fatah movement took over the PLO following the 1967 war.

[150] Council Common Position, 2001/931/CFSP, On the Application of Specific Measures to Combat Terrorism, [2001] OJ L344/93, 28 December 2001, as amended most recently by Council Common Position, 2007/448/CFSP, Updating Common Position 2001/931/CFSP on the Application of Specific Measures to Combat Terrorism, [2007] OJ L169/69, 29 June 2007.

[151] See Security Council Resolution 1267(1999), 15 October 1999, as subsequently amended most recently by Security Council Resolution 1735(2006), 22 December 2006.

[152] Israel does not distinguish between the 'political' and 'terrorist' wings of Hamas. In the aftermath of the January 2006 election, an Israeli Cabinet communiqué stated that as Hamas had been elected the 'entire Palestinian Authority' must be considered a

When Arafat was alive, he was pressed by the Union and the United States to create the post of Prime Minister and to have a Cabinet so that he would have to cede some of his powers.[153] Under those arrangements, following the 2006 elections and the formation of a Hamas-led government, the Prime Minister (Ismail Haniya of Hamas) was Chairman of the Palestinian Security Council and the Interior Minister (Sa'id Siyam, also a member of Hamas) was in charge of the security forces. Hamas thus controlled the Parliament and government but Fatah retained the Presidency as well as control over the PLO. The security forces and civil service were still dominated by Fatah supporters even though they should have been under the control of the Interior Minister, a member of Hamas. The diplomatic isolation of Hamas also meant that international diplomacy was conducted by Abbas, a Fatah member. Thus in reality, despite the Hamas victory in the 2006 elections, a fractious, corrosive, dual-power structure existed.[154] The power struggle between Hamas and Fatah took on another dimension when in June 2007 Hamas effectively secured full control of the Gaza Strip after a violent confrontation with forces loyal to Fatah. Abbas, as President, established an emergency administration without Hamas members based in the West Bank. The West Bank is at the time of writing under the control of forces loyal to Fatah.

Prior to the current disintegration of the Palestinian Authority, a Select Committee of the House of Commons in 2003 had described it as having no de facto or *de jure* control over any territory.[155] Furthermore, there is no geographical continuity between the West Bank and Gaza. Palestinians are, therefore, dependent upon the Israeli authorities for permission to travel between the two territories or indeed between towns and villages within the West Bank, as well as to go to Israel to work, as many Palestinians have traditionally done.[156] Israel is also responsible

'terrorist organisation'. Cabinet communiqué, 19 February 2006, available at www.israel-mfa.gov.il/mfa/mfaarchive/2000_2009/2006
[153] See the Amended Basic Law, 2003, for the respective powers of the President (Title Three), Legislative Council (Title Four), and the Executive Authority which includes the Prime Minister (Title Five).
[154] See H. Agha and R. Malley 'The Road from Mecca' (2007) 54 *NYRB*, 10 May 2007 and Malley, 'A New Middle East'.
[155] House of Commons Select Committee on International Development, *Development Assistance and the Occupied Palestinian Territories*, Second Report of the Session 2003–2004 (London: HMSO, 2004) p. 10.
[156] Further to the Gaza 'disengagement', Israel does not restrict movement within Gaza in the manner it did previously. As will be discussed below, restrictions on Palestinian movement are severely curtailed in the West Bank.

under the terms of the 1994 Protocol on Economic Relations Between the Government of Israel and the Palestinian Liberation Organisation (the Paris Protocol)[157] for collecting and handing over to the Palestinian Authority all the customs duties it is owed as goods travel between the Palestinian Territories and Israel. Under the terms of the Protocol, Israel has no claim to these tax revenues. The Palestinian Authority is heavily reliant upon Israel and the payment of these taxes for its financial survival. In the past, over 90 per cent of all imports came from Israel and over 80 per cent of all exports went to it.[158] These revenues, which amount to between US$50 and US$60 million per month, provide almost half of the Palestinian Authority's monthly budget. As and when there is increased tension between the parties, Israel unlawfully withholds such payments, although it in the past released some of the funds at a later stage. Following the election success of Hamas in January 2006, Israel ceased transferring such payments to the Palestinian Authority.[159] In June 2007 when Abbas dismissed the Hamas-led administration and appointed an emergency government, Israel announced it would, subject to conditions, transfer the revenue to Abbas's government.[160]

Furthermore, Israel employs the policy of 'closure' when tensions rise between it and the Palestinian Authority. This policy blocks the flow of goods, services and employment between Israel and the Palestinian Territories and in conjunction with the withholding of taxes brings the Palestinian Authority to the verge of collapse and greatly exacerbates the humanitarian crisis in the Palestinian Territories.[161] Israel's security needs are compelling and the policy of 'closure' is in part a response to those needs, but the manner in which the policy is

---

[157] Annex V Oslo II.

[158] US Department of State, *Human Rights Reports: the Occupied Territories 1998* (Washington DC: US Department of State, 1999) npg. For detailed discussion on the economic crisis in the Palestinian Territories, see IMF-World Bank, *West Bank and Gaza: Economic Developments in 2006 – A First Assessment* (March 2007).

[159] Although Israel reportedly often uses such funds to pay approximately US$5.5 million per month to Israeli utility companies for the monies owed by the Palestinian Authority for the supply of, for example, water. See 'Israel to Buy Supplies for Gaza Hospitals', *New York Times*, 19 May 2006.

[160] Cabinet communiqué, 24 June 2007, available at www.israel-mfa.gov.il/MFA/Government/Communiques/2007/Cabinet%20Commuique%2024-Jun-2007

[161] The policy of closure is long-standing; for early discussion on the policy see, Palestinian Centre for Human Rights, *The Israeli Policy of Closure* (Gaza: Mansour Press, ndg) and HRW, *Israel's Closure of the West Bank and Gaza* (New York: Human Rights Watch, 1996). For recent assessment, see World Bank, *Movement and Access Restrictions in the West Bank*.

implemented points directly at a number of other objectives. In 2007, a World Bank Technical Team noted that while 'Israeli security concerns are undeniable and must be addressed, it is often difficult to reconcile the use of movement and access restrictions for security purposes from their use to expand and protect settlement activity and the relatively unhindered movement of settler and other Israelis in and out of the West Bank'.[162] The World Bank paper further noted, 'in the West Bank, closure is implemented through an agglomeration of policies, practices and physical impediments which have fragmented the territory into ever smaller and disconnected cantons'.[163] Over 50 per cent of the land of the West Bank is estimated to be subject to 'closure'.[164]

The policy of closure is often, although certainly not always, used following attacks on the Israeli Defence Force (IDF) in the Occupied Territories or attacks on Israeli citizens either from within the West Bank or Gaza or by means such as suicide-bombings in Israeli cities. The policy of closure, as a form of collective punishment, is clearly prohibited by Article 49 of the Fourth Geneva Convention, 1949. It is also a violation of the terms of the Oslo Accords and the terms of the Roadmap.[165] Notwithstanding Israel's security concerns, it is difficult to argue that such measures are proportionate responses even to what are clearly illegal and prohibited acts.

Occupation of the Palestinian Territories by Israel has also ensured that there is little or no infrastructure in place and thus the economy is small and poorly developed and highly reliant upon agriculture, services and some light manufacturing. Levels of malnutrition in the Palestinian Territories in 2003 reached a level commensurate with sub-Saharan Africa.[166] By 2007, the World Bank estimated that approximately 70 per cent of households in the Palestinian Territories were living on less than US$2 per day.[167] Many of these considerations make the promotion of ethical values particularly difficult. The Union has in

---

[162] World Bank, *Movement and Access Restrictions in the West Bank*, p. 2.
[163] *Ibid*. p. 12.   [164] *Ibid*.
[165] See Article IX(2)(a) of Annex I Oslo II and Phase I of the Roadmap.
[166] World Bank, *Two Years of Intifada, Closures and the Palestinian Economic Crisis: an Assessment* (Washington DC: World Bank, 2003).
[167] House of Commons Select Committee on International Development, *Development Assistance and the Occupied Palestinian Territories*, Fourth Report of the Session 2006–2007 (London: HMSO, 2007) vol. II, Evidence, Question 24. Olmert has as recently as 2006 argued that the scale of the humanitarian situation in the Palestinian Territories is 'total propaganda' but this is clearly not the case. See 'Israel to Buy Supplies for Gaza Hospitals', *New York Times*, 19 May 2006.

place, however, a sophisticated and complex set of programmes which aim to both support the infrastructure and the civil society which exists, as well as promoting ethical values. These are discussed further below.

Unlike Israel, the Palestinian Authority cannot be a party to multilateral human rights treaties which are only open to states. It is bound, however, to respect those rights that have entered the corpus of custom and obligations *erga omnes*. Despite the relatively limited scope of these provisions, it is clear that the Palestinian Authority engages in, or is complicit in, systematic and gross violations of acts that are contrary to these norms. As in Israel, torture of suspected terrorists by members of the security forces is widespread.[168] Prolonged detention and lack of due process are also legally very problematic. Arbitrary arrest, unfair trials and impunity for those violating rights, as well as extra-judicial and political killings and kidnappings, are commonplace.[169] Furthermore, the Palestinian Authority, depending on the point of view, is either complicit in or unwilling or unable to stop attacks on Israeli civilians and the IDF. These attacks include the launching of attacks on the Israeli population using Qassem missiles and suicide missions. Such practices are very clear violations of international humanitarian law. It is also the case that in the internal fighting between Palestinian factions, grave violations of international humanitarian law regularly occur.[170]

Human Rights Watch has in the past described the human rights situation in the Palestinian Territories as 'deplorable'.[171] A 1998 study commissioned by the European Commission to investigate the utility of the MEDA Regulations found that in the areas under the control of the Palestinian Authority, there was no separation of powers; the rule of law was fundamentally deficient; censorship was widespread; intimidation of journalists and opposition parties was widespread; and rights to association were relatively limited.[172] The reports of various human rights organisations highlight that the situation is no better now.

---

[168] Select Committee, *Development Assistance and the Occupied Palestinian Territories 2004*, p. 65.
[169] See the Amnesty International and Human Rights Watch Reports for the Palestinian Territories for the period between 1997 and 2006 for examples of such acts.
[170] See e.g., the Presidency statements of 16 May 2007, 13 June 2007 and 15 June 2007 on, *inter alia*, such incidents.
[171] Human Rights Watch, *Palestinian Self-Rule Areas: Human Rights under the Palestinian Authority* (New York: Human Rights Watch, 1997) p. 1.
[172] N. Karkutli and D. Bützler, *Evaluation of the MEDA Democracy Programme 1996–1998* (1998) *passim*.

Husseini has argued that although political developments have hindered the ability of the Palestinian Authority to govern effectively, its overall record has been one of substantial improvement.[173] Israeli action and curfews have allegedly undermined it and exposed its weakness.[174] It is certainly the case that Palestinian judicial, security and administrative infrastructure has been destroyed by Israel in its military incursions, especially in Gaza. These weaknesses have subsequently been used against it, leading to an international consensus that reform must be undertaken, while some of the blame certainly does not lie at the Palestinian Authority's door.[175] It is undeniable that some of the abuses, discussed above, have been a direct result of the intense pressure the Palestinian Authority has been put under by Israel, the United States and the European Union to curb and control factions which conduct and engage in attacks against Israel. The 'essential elements' clause of the Agreement has, as is the case with Israel, played a role in relations between the parties and it is to these we now turn.

5.2.3 Relevance of the Essential Elements Clauses in the Agreements with Israel and the Palestinian Authority

5.2.3.1 Essential Elements Clause and Relations with Israel

The 'essential elements' clause in the Agreement with Israel has been relevant in the context of Israeli practices in both the Occupied Territories and those areas nominally under the control of the Palestinian Authority. It has not been particularly significant, in practice, with regard to the situation within Israel's internationally recognised boundaries, even though systematic discrimination on the basis of race exists. This is despite the fact that a Joint Declaration on Article 2 (the 'essential elements' clause) was attached to the Agreement which noted that the parties 'reaffirm the importance they attach to the respect of human rights as set out in the UN Charter including the struggle against xenophobia, anti-Semitism and *racism*'.[176] As noted above, the Human Rights Committee, the Committee on the Elimination of Racial Discrimination and the Committee Against Torture have all highlighted how Israeli

---

[173] H. Husseini, 'Challenges and Reforms in the Palestinian Authority' (2003) 26 *Fordham ILJ* 500, 532.

[174] *Ibid.*

[175] See e.g., Conclusions of the Seville European Council, 21–22 June 2002, (2002) 6 *Bull. EU* I.32, where it is noted, '[t]he reform of the Palestinian Authority is essential'.

[176] Joint Declaration relating to Article 2, [2000] OJ L147/163, 21 June 2000. Emphasis added.

Arabs are systematically discriminated against. Such widespread and systematic racial discrimination, which is sanctioned by the state, is arguably a violation of an obligation *erga omnes* and, as discussed in Chapter 2, such obligations require the Member States of the Union to take some action in response.

The adoption of the Joint Declaration on Article 2 when the Agreement with Israel was signed underscored the human rights aspects of it and the fact that persistent abuse of such rights would be a breach of the Agreement. Article 79 of the Agreement contains a more or less standard version of the 'non-execution' clause. The Preamble to the Agreement refers to economic freedom and the principles of the United Nations Charter, particularly human rights and democracy (which is not mentioned in the Charter) as forming the 'very basis of the Association'. Article 2 of the Agreement (the 'essential elements' clause) simply notes that '[r]elations between the parties, as well as the provisions of the Agreement itself, shall be based upon respect for human rights and democratic principles which guides their internal and international policy'.

Where human rights concerns have been raised by the Community and Member States, Israel has consistently invoked its security interests. The European Council, whenever it discusses such issues, recognises the legitimacy of Israel's security concerns, meaning that Israel will have to submit convincing arguments primarily with regard to the question of proportionality as opposed to necessity.[177] As that issue is a more subjective one, it makes it more difficult for the Member States to come to any agreement on Israeli preemptive or retaliatory attacks. As part of the Barcelona Process, the Union and Member States have effectively allowed the parties on the other side to take any measures that they consider essential to their own security 'in the event of internal disturbances affecting the maintenance of law and order, in time of war or serious international tension constituting threat of war'.[178] This has

---

[177] The Union in every almost statement on the MEPP recognises Israel's legitimate security interests. For example, European Council, *EU Annual Report on Human Rights 2005* (Luxembourg: OOPEC, 2005) p. 99 notes 'like all countries, Israel has the right to self-defence and a duty to protect its citizens against the real threat from terrorist groups. While condemning all acts of terrorism and violence, the EU recognises Israel's legitimate right to protect its citizens from terrorist attacks. However, the Government of Israel must exercise this right within the boundaries of international law.'

[178] Wording in, e.g., Article 76 of Israel-EC Association Agreement and Article 68 of Association Agreement with the PLO for the Benefit of the Palestinian Authority.

ensured that Israel is able to rely upon this provision of the Agreement, in an attempt to justify its policies and practices. The issue of proportionality, however, is clearly legitimate. Unless the Union is permitted to send fact-finding missions or have observers in place, it is more difficult for them to judge what is or is not proportionate. Israel considers that it is for it to determine the measures needed to counter the threats and danger it is under and has consistently refused to allow any fact-finding missions from either the United Nations or the Union when such requests have been made.[179] The disproportionate and illegal nature of some Israeli activities is, however, more than apparent and the Union regularly makes statements to this effect.[180] This brings into focus the applicability of the 'essential elements' clause. The discussion below will look at three case studies to highlight the role played by the essential elements clause in relations between Israel and the Union. The first case studies will look at the Union's response to the Israeli military incursions in Jenin in 2002 and Beit Hanoun in 2006.[181] The third case study will look at the Union's response to the building of the Israeli 'Security-Barrier', 'Fence' or 'Wall' in the area in and around the West Bank.[182] The discussion will then look specifically at the relevance of the essential elements clause to these case studies.

---

[179] This is a long-standing practice. The Security Council in 1979, e.g., strongly condemned Israel for its refusal to cooperate with a Commission which had been established into Israel's settlement activities, see Security Council Resolution 452 (1979), 20 July 1979. See further the discussion below on the continued practice.

[180] For example, the Finnish Presidency issued a statement in November 2006 which stated, '[t]he Presidency deplores the growing number of civilian casualties the Israeli military operation has caused. The right of all states to defend themselves does not justify disproportionate use of violence or actions which are contrary to international humanitarian law.' EU Presidency Statement on Increased Violence in Gaza, 4 November 2006, Press Release 444/2006.

[181] The are a number of other examples one can choose from, e.g., the incursions, occupations and destruction in Nablus, Bethlehem, Rafah and Ramallah, respectively, since 2002.

[182] Israel describes the structure as a 'fence' or 'security barrier', whereas the International Court of Justice adopted the terminology of the General Assembly which in its request to the Court used the term 'Wall'. None of the different terms is any more accurate than the others when considering the actual structure in question. As the ICJ noted, 'the "Wall" in question is a complex construction, so that that term cannot be understood in a limited physical sense. However, the other terms used, either by Israel ("fence") or by the Secretary-General ("barrier"), are no more accurate if understood in the physical sense.' Advisory Opinion, *Legal Consequences of the Construction of a Wall*, n. 129 above, para. 67. The term 'Wall' will be used in this discussion as it has achieved the most widespread use.

5.2.3.1(a) Israeli Military Incursions into Palestinian Territory and the Essential Elements Clause

Between March and May 2002, the Israeli Defence Forces carried out major incursions into Palestinian Territories. On 3 April 2002, the IDF launched a major offensive on the refugee camp in Jenin. It is widely accepted that the overwhelming majority of persons in the camp were civilians. Israel argued that a number of persons responsible for attacks on Israeli civilians were taking refuge in the camp. It is undeniable that Palestinian militants were present as there was vicious and sustained fighting between Palestinian militants and the IDF. The IDF, however, did not distinguish between civilians and combatants and acted in an indiscriminate manner. Over 4,000 people, one-quarter of the camp's population, were made homeless and entire districts were bulldozed as the IDF destroyed houses, supposedly to allow tanks and other heavy armour to penetrate deep into the camp. Serious damage was also done to utilities such as water and electrical infrastructure. It was estimated that over fifty civilians were killed as a result of the IDF operation.

Widespread international calls for observers and fact-finding missions to verify what had actually happened in Jenin, by among others the Security Council, were ignored by the Israelis who subsequently refused access to a team sent by the Secretary-General of the United Nations to establish events.[183] In its relations with Myanmar, as discussed in Chapter 4, the Union has been very critical of the authorities for their refusal to allow access to the Special Rapporteur and the Special Envoy, and used this as part of its rationale for restrictive measures. In the case of Israel such condemnation, not only with regard to events in Jenin but also of the continuing refusal to cooperate with the Special Rapporteur for Occupied Palestine, has not so far resulted in such action. As discussed in Chapter 3, the Vienna Convention on the Law of Treaties, 1969 imposes restrictions on the circumstances in which the 'essential elements' clause can be legitimately used.[184] Events in Jenin, however, give a very clear indication of the lack of political agreement with regard to its use among the Member States, even where the legal requirements are satisfied.

---

[183] Security Council Resolution 1405(2002), 19 April 2002. See further *Report of the Secretary General prepared pursuant to General Assembly Resolution ES-10/10.A/ES-10/186* (the '*Jenin Report*').

[184] Vienna Convention on the Law of Treaties, 1969, 1155 UNTS 331.

The Secretary-General's Report on events in Jenin considered both the Israeli and Palestinian authorities to be culpable.[185] Both are considered to have engaged in violations of provisions of the relevant Geneva Conventions of 1949. The Report indicates, however, that the breaches by Israel were substantially graver, with some of the acts prima facie amounting to 'war crimes' as defined under the Rome Statute of the International Criminal Court.[186] In July 2002, thirty aid agencies, in the aftermath of the Israeli occupation of Jenin, issued a formal and unprecedented joint statement condemning the Israeli action that impeded and hindered their work and further worsened a dire humanitarian crisis.[187]

The Spanish Presidency, at this time not only summoned the Israeli ambassador to register its protest at Israeli activities but was also very critical of the Israeli action in public meetings of the Security Council, specifically with regard to events to Jenin. The Presidency considered that the action Israel had taken could in no way be justified.[188] In the Security Council it was particularly condemnatory of the humiliation of Arafat and destruction of Palestinian infrastructure.[189] A delegation of MEPs also considered that the situation in Jenin amounted to war crimes.[190] In the United Nations, a number of EU statements recognised the right of Israel to combat terror but its condemnation and its

---

[185] It should be stressed that the team compiling the report were not allowed access to Jenin by Israel and had to reach their conclusions as best they could without visiting the relevant sites or being able to interview many of those with first-hand experience of events.

[186] Although the Statute of the Court is not binding on Israel, the definition of war crimes is widely seen as representative of custom. Israel is a party to the Fourth Geneva Convention, 1949, which prohibits many of those same acts.

[187] 'International Aid Agencies Condemn Israel', http://news.bbc.co.uk/1/hi/world/middle_east/2093120.stm, 4 July 2002. See also, 'Israeli Army Warned by UN for Shooting at Aid Workers', *Independent*, 28 November 2003.

[188] On 8 February 2002, Spain summoned the Israeli ambassador to explain and justify the attacks in Ramallah.

[189] See statement by H.E. Mr Inocencio Arias, Permanent Representative of Spain to the United Nations, on behalf of the European Union at the Meeting of the Security Council on the Situation in the Middle East, including the Palestinian Question, New York, 18 April 2002, PRES02-065EN, and then subsequently, statement by H.E. Ambassador Ellen Margrethe Løj, Permanent Representative of Denmark to the United Nations, on behalf of the European Union on the Resumed Tenth Emergency Special Session of the General Assembly: Jenin, New York, 5 August 2002.

[190] 'EP Delegation Denounces War Crimes against Palestinians', European Parliament Press Release, 25 April 2002.

assessment in political, if not legal, terms of Israeli practices was more than enough to justify suspension of the Association Agreement. A statement on 18 April 2002 noted that:

The virtual destruction of the Palestinian Authority and its infrastructure, the continued isolation of Chairman Arafat, the humiliation, confinement and disregard of the Palestinian civilian population and their most fundamental rights, and the violations of international humanitarian law are unacceptable. These actions must end immediately; they are contrary to international law and unjustified. Israel must immediately stop extra-judicial killings, lift the closures and restrictions in the Territories and reverse its settlement policy.[191]

A statement made on 3 May 2002 in the Security Council further noted:

The EU is extremely concerned at the destruction of the basic structures of the Palestinian Authority. These actions are unacceptable and counterproductive. They diminish the capability of the Palestinian Authority to enforce the rule of law and may lead to a dangerous security vacuum and, in the longer term, to an even greater risk for the security of Israel. At the same time the unprecedented damage caused by the recent Israeli military operations to Palestinian civil infrastructure and private property, and the disruption of basic social services with no security role whatsoever, cannot be justified on the basis of Israel's legitimate fight against terrorism. These actions in violation of international law must end immediately . . . [w]e call on Israel to put an immediate end to the economic strangulation of the Palestinian Territories, the tight closures, restrictions and checkpoints in the Territories, the isolation and confinement of populations and the severe limitations to the movement of people and goods.[192]

There was substantial pressure on the Union to take action against Israel.[193] This was particularly important because at the same time the Union had begun to introduce restrictive measures against Zimbabwe for the abuse of human rights and it would appear to be very selective and inconsistent if action was taken against Zimbabwe but not Israel, particularly in the light of the statements that were being made about Israel's conduct.[194]

---

[191] Statement by Mr Inocencio Arias, 18 April 2002.
[192] EU statement at the Security Council on the Middle East, 3 May 2002, PRES02-074EN.
[193] See e.g., 'LAW Tells European Union: No More Words but Decisive Action', 7 February 2002.
[194] See Common Position 2002/145/CFSP, [2002] OJ L50/1, 21 February 2002. At the time of writing, the measure is Common Position 2007/120/CFSP, [2007] OJ L51/25, 20 February 2007.

In response to events in Jenin, the imposition of punitive measures was discussed by the Union, especially the suspension of arms sales which was being called for by resolutions of the European Parliament,[195] at the Quartet meeting held in April 2002.[196] No such measures were taken. Romano Prodi, the then President of the Commission, had warned, however, that unless Israel withdrew from the Palestinian Administered Territories the Agreement would be suspended.[197] It is likely, though, that the refusal of the Israelis to allow Josep Piqué (of the Spanish Presidency) and Romano Prodi to meet Yasser Arafat, a few days earlier in Ramallah, played a role in his threat, as a day prior to the proposed meeting with Arafat Prodi had reportedly stated that the Agreement with Israel could *not* be suspended as it provided 'a forum for dialogue and was not there for the purposes of blackmail'.[198] After the events in Jenin, the Member States could not agree to call an emergency meeting of the EU-Israel Association Council.[199] Both the Fifth Euro-Med Conference in Valencia in April 2002 and the Seville European Council of June 2002 were used to express concern at the situation but nothing beyond that was done.[200]

The second case study which could legally justify the suspension of the Association Agreement with Israel occurred in 2006, with Israeli operations in Gaza, in particular the unwarranted killing of civilians in Beit Hanoun. In response, in part, to the kidnapping of Corporal Gilad Shalit and primarily the continued firing of home-made Qassem rockets into Israel, the IDF launched 'Operation Summer Rains' and 'Operation

---

[195] [2003] OJ C127E/589, 29 May 2003, para. 7.
[196] 'Middle East Turmoil; Europeans Press Demands on Israel', *New York Times*, 11 April 2002.
[197] 'Withdraw Now or Face EU Sanctions', *Guardian*, 9 April 2002.
[198] 'Palestinians Seek EU Arms Ban on Israel', *Know Europe*, 4 April 2002.
[199] Due to the lack of unanimity among the fifteen. The third meeting of the EU-Israel Association Council was held on 21 October 2002. The Union acknowledged that Israel's security concerns were legitimate, but reiterated that they must be addressed with full respect for human rights and the rule of law. It further urged Israel to put an end to activities inconsistent with international humanitarian law, to abstain from all acts of collective punishment, to cease settlement activities, to abstain from deportations of members of Palestinian families, to give full access to international personnel necessary for humanitarian projects in the Palestinian territories, and to cease the systematic destruction of Palestinian infrastructures, including those financed by the European Union. See (2002) 10 *Bull. EU* 1.6.83.
[200] In the Conclusions of the Seville European Council, 21–22 June 2002, (2002) 6 *Bull. EU* I.32, the Union uses stronger language with regard to Israel than in the Fifth Euro-Mediterranean Conference of Foreign Ministers, Valencia, 22-23 April 2002, Doc. 8254/02, Presidency Conclusions, paras. 6–13.

Autumn Clouds'.[201] The Israeli Prime Minister Ehud Olmert instructed the IDF and the Israeli security establishment 'to do everything' in order to bring Shalit back and stated 'when I say everything, I mean everything, whatever is possible, whatever is necessary'.[202]

As part of 'Operation Summer Rains' and 'Operation Autumn Clouds' the IDF made military incursions using heavy artillery shelling, air to surface missile attacks and bulldozers to destroy or damage, homes, schools, hospitals, mosques, public buildings and bridges. On 27 June 2006, during the height of summer, the IDF destroyed the only electricity plant which supplied over 40 per cent of the electricity to Gaza and for several months over half of the population of Gaza was without electricity.[203] Water pipelines were also routinely destroyed and a substantial amount of agricultural land was levelled. The illegal nature of such acts was recognised by the External Relations Commissioner, Benita Ferrero-Waldner when in a speech to the European Parliament the following week she stated 'the Israeli incursion into the Gaza Strip and the destruction of civilian infrastructure there punishes Palestinians collectively and puts civilian lives at risk. It raises questions about the respect of international law.'[204]

Israel justified its military operations on three grounds: finding Shalit, eradicating those militant groups who operated from Gaza, and above all stopping Qassem rocket fire into southern Israel. It should be noted that over 1,700 home-made rockets had reportedly been fired into Israel by this point.[205] The majority of these rockets had been

[201] Some of these operations coincided in time with the Israeli incursions into Lebanon in summer 2006. On 25 June 2006, members of Palestinian organisations including Hamas attacked an Israeli military base, killed two soldiers and seized a third, Corporal Gilad Shalit. On 12 July 2006, twelve Hezbollah members crossed into Israel, captured two soldiers, and killed eight others. This led to Israeli incursions into both Gaza and Lebanon. The Israeli incursion into Lebanon and the Union's response to that conflict is beyond the scope of this discussion.

[202] Cabinet communiqué, 2 July 2006, available at www.mfa.gov.il/MFA/Government/Communiques/2006/Cabinet+Communique+2-Jul-2006.htm

[203] For the impact of this act see the report by the Israeli human rights organisation B'Tselem, *Act of Vengeance: Israel's Bombing of the Gaza Power Plant and its Effects* (September 2006), available at www.btselem.org/english/Publications/Summaries/200609_Act_of_Vengeance.asp. Sweden and Egypt funded the repairs to the electricity plant while the Union paid for electricity supplies to key institutions such as hospitals. See further the discussion below.

[204] B. Ferrero-Waldner, 'The Situation in the Palestinian Territories', 5 July 2006, Speech/06/434.

[205] While Palestinian militants have fired around 1,700 rockets, according to Human Rights Watch, since September 2005, Israel had fired about 15,000 rounds into

launched from Beit Hanoun and it was this town which was subjected to the most brutal attack.

In November 2006, the IDF led a six-day incursion into Beit Hanoun. Eighty-two Palestinians were killed with over half of them being civilians, including 21 children. Over 200 adults and over 60 children were injured, some very seriously, as a result of the incursion and hundreds of males between the ages of sixteen and forty were arbitrarily arrested. All 40,000 people in the town were confined to their homes for the duration of the incursion due to the imposition of a curfew. In the town, the IDF destroyed 279 homes, an 850-year old mosque, schools and a substantial amount of the civilian infrastructure. The starkest event, however, was on 8 November 2006, when the IDF shelled a house, killing 19 and wounding 55 others.[206] The house was in the middle of a densely populated residential area. All those killed were members of one family and civilians. Prime Minister Olmert expressed sorrow over the killings but blamed the shelling on a 'technical failure'.[207] Such a 'technical' error was likely to happen sooner or later, however, as in April 2006 the IDF had reportedly narrowed the 'safety zone', allowing shelling within 100 metres of civilian areas, which makes such events more probable.[208] The Israel Foreign Minister, Tzipi Livni was contrite when she stated that 'unfortunately, in the course of battle, regrettable incidents such as that which occurred this morning do happen'.[209]

In contrast to the responses from Olmert and Livni, the ICRC, which very rarely condemns belligerents in a conflict, and UNICEF used stronger language when both were reported to have been 'appalled' at the killings in Beit Hanoun.[210] The EU's External Relations Commissioner, Benita Ferrero-Waldner, who had earlier expressed doubts about the legality of Israeli incursions into Gaza, said, 'the killing this morning

Gaza. See Human Rights Watch, *Israel: IDF Probe No Substitute for Real Investigation*, 10 November 2006, available at http://hrw.org/english/docs/2006/11/10/ isrlpa14550.htm

[206] For UNRWA's assessment of events, see UNRWA, *Beit Hanoun: Flash Appeal*, available at www.reliefweb.int/library/documents/2006/unrwa-pse-19nov.pdf

[207] See 'Grief Turns to Rage as Beit Hanoun Buries its Dead', *Guardian*, 10 November 2006. It is worth noting that such events are not rare. The Israeli assault on Qana in Lebanon, e.g., as noted above, led to a similar incident in July 2006, which also led to widespread outrage.

[208] See 'How Israel Put Gaza Civilians in Firing Line', *Observer*, 12 November 2006.

[209] 'Statement by FM Livni on Beit Hanoun', 8 November 2006, available at www.israel-mfa.gov.il

[210] 'Aid Agencies Condemn Gaza Carnage', http://news.bbc.co.uk/1/hi/world/middle_east/ 6131042.stm, 11 November 2006.

of so many civilians in Gaza, including many children, is a profoundly shocking event. Israel has a right to defend itself, but not at the price of the lives of the innocent.'[211] Javier Solana, the High Representative for the CFSP, 'deplored' the Israeli military operation in Beit Hanoun whereas Alvaro de Soto, then the Secretary-General's Envoy to the Quartet, stated 'I'm appalled and shocked. It's really condemnable. This has just gone too far.'[212] Louise Arbour, the United Nations High Commissioner for Human Rights, when visiting Beit Hanoun after the IDF incursion, stated that she felt that Palestinians living in the Gaza strip had been subjected to 'massive' human rights violations.[213]

The Security Council debated the Israeli incursion into Gaza and events in Beit Hanoun. A proposed draft which condemned the attack and asked for an investigation to be launched on 11 November 2006 was vetoed by the United States.[214] The United Kingdom, Denmark and Slovakia abstained whereas France, Italy and Belgium all voted in favour of what was an even-handed proposal. The General Assembly, however, adopted a resolution which was very similar in content. The resolution condemned all parties, 'deeply deploring' the actions of Israel and the 'firing of rockets from Gaza into Israel'.[215] During the debate prior to the General Assembly resolution being adopted, the Finnish representative on behalf of the European Union made it clear that the Union 'condemned the recent incidents in Beit Hanoun, as well as all other acts of violence against civilians on both sides'.[216] The resolution which was eventually adopted condemned Israel for its military incursion and the loss of civilian life and the destruction of infrastructure and included a call on the Palestinian Authority 'to take immediate and sustained action to bring an end to violence, including the firing of rockets on Israeli territory'.[217] The resolution also called upon the Secretary-General to establish a fact-finding mission.

---

[211] Ibid.
[212] See Javier Solana, 'EU High Representative for the CFSP, Deplores the Israeli Military Operation at Beit Hanoun', S/306/06 and 'Aid Agencies Condemn Gaza Carnage', 11 November 2006.
[213] 'UN Condemns Massive Human Rights Abuses in Gaza Strip', Guardian, 21 November 2006.
[214] Security Council, 5565th Meeting, Draft Resolution S/2006/878, para. 3.
[215] A/RES/ES-10/16, 4 April 2007. The Resolution was adopted on 17 November 2006 but was reissued for technical reasons.
[216] See General Assembly Press Release, 17 November 2006, GA/10534.
[217] Ibid. para. 5.

The Human Rights Council (which Israel has subsequently denounced as suffering from severe politicisation and political diversion)[218] also discussed the incident in Beit Hanoun and adopted a resolution to that end.[219] The statement by the Finnish representative on behalf of the European Union during the debate condemned Israel's operations in Gaza and the incident in Beit Hanoun in strong language. It noted that 'the EU strongly deplores the Israeli military action in Gaza resulting in growing numbers of civilian casualties, including women and children, and deplores the unacceptable military operation in Beit Hanoun … We deeply regret the … destruction of houses and other civilian infrastructure.'[220] Displaying commendable even-handedness, a rare quality in the context of the Arab-Israeli conflict, the statement also strongly deplored the firing of rockets into Israel and called on the Palestinian leadership to bring such acts to an end and to release Corporal Gilad Shalit. The Union also called upon Israel to release the Palestinian ministers and legislators, who Israel had decided to arbitrarily detain in Israel.[221]

The resolutions adopted by the General Assembly and the Human Rights Council reflected the seriousness of the Israeli incursions into Gaza and events in Beit Hanoun. On a practical level, the resolution adopted by the Human Rights Council also proposed an independent investigation into events in Beit Hanoun, which when it was established was led by Archbishop Desmond Tutu. In June 2007, the fact-finding body led by Archbishop Tutu published its report.[222] The mission had twice applied for and not been granted permission by Israel to travel to Beit Hanoun. As the mandate of the mission required it, *inter alia*, to assess the needs of the victims of the incident, the refusal of travel to Beit Hanoun resulted in the mission not being able to fulfil its mandate. The report reiterated in the strongest terms that 'a duly mandated

---

[218] See 'Israel Protests Human Rights Council Decision', *MFA Newsletter*, 21 June 2007.
[219] See *Human Rights Violations Emanating from Israeli Military Incursions in the Occupied Palestinian Territory, including the Recent One in Northern Gaza and the Assault on Beit Hanoun*, A/HRC/S-3/1. Archbishop Desmond Tutu was appointed on 29 November 2006 to lead the mission and Prof. Christine Chinkin of the London School of Economics was appointed as a member of the mission.
[220] 'EU Statement at the UN Human Rights Council on the Situation in Gaza', Third Special Session, 15 November 2006, available at www.eu2006.fi/news_and_documents/ speeches/vko46/en_GB/1163600049946
[221] *Ibid.*
[222] *Report of the High-Level Fact-Finding Mission to Beit Hanoun Established under Resolution*, S-3/1, A/HRC/5/20.

mission … has been and is being prevented from addressing a critical human rights situation due to the non-cooperation of a concerned Government'.[223] As the report notes, Israel refused to cooperate with the mission as it perceives the Human Rights Council to be biased against it.[224] On the basis of the information available to them, however, the mission did suggest that grave human rights violations had been committed by the Israeli military incursion. This was a consequence not only of the deaths and injuries of civilians but also of the widespread destruction of civilian infrastructure.[225]

It is very clear that extremely serious and grave abuses of international human rights law and international humanitarian law were committed during the IDF's incursions into Gaza in 2006, in particular in Beit Hanoun. It is difficult to expect Israel or indeed any state to exercise complete restraint when it is constantly subject to attacks from missiles and bombings emanating from outside its territory. Notwithstanding the International Court of Justice's wholly unsatisfactory discussion of Israel's right to self-defence against attacks from non-state groups in the *Wall Opinion*, Israel clearly has a right to self-defence; the issue is whether the responses are proportionate or not.[226]

Approximately 1,700 Qassem rockets have been fired into Israel in recent years, members of the IDF have been kidnapped and suicide-bombings targeting civilians have taken place since the start of the Al-Aqsa Intifada. Such acts clearly amount to serious violations of international humanitarian law. The crucial distinction between the acts of the Palestinians and the Israelis, however, is that the Palestinians do not illegally occupy Israeli territory and, notwithstanding the abhorrent nature of some of the Palestinian violations, they are simply not on the same scale as those committed by Israel. It is difficult to assess the scale of response which would be proportionate and legitimate for Israel to engage in when responding to the attacks it is subjected to.

---

[223] *Ibid.* para. 12.   [224] *Ibid.*   [225] *Ibid.* para. 14.
[226] Advisory Opinion, *Legal Consequences of the Construction of a Wall*, n. 129 above, para. 138 *et seq.* For critique of the Opinion see the Agora published in the *American Journal of International Law* and the Symposium in the *European Journal of International Law*, both in 2005. On the issue of self-defence, see C. Tams, 'Light Treatment of a Complex Problem: the Law of Self-Defence in the Wall Case' (2005) 17 *EJIL* 793; R. Wedgewood, 'The ICJ Advisory Opinion on the Israeli Security Fence and the Limits of Self-Defense' (2005) 99 *AJIL* 52; and S. Murphy, 'Self-Defense and the Israeli Wall Advisory Opinion: an Ipse Dixit from the ICJ?' (2005) 99 *AJIL* 62. More generally on the issue of self-defence in the context of the 'war against terror', see the excellent discussion in C. Gray, *International Law and the Use of Force*, 2nd edn (Oxford: Oxford University Press, 2004) p. 159 *et seq.*

What is clear, however, is that the random and deliberate destruction of civilian infrastructure, such as primary healthcare facilities, schools, bridges, power plants and places of worship, as well as the indiscriminate killings of civilians by the IDF, undeniably amounts to what the UN Special Rapporteur, Professor John Dugard considers to be 'serious war crimes'.[227]

'Operation Summer Rains' and 'Operation Autumn Clouds' and more specifically the events in Beit Hanoun in November 2006 at the least violate Article 33 (the prohibition on collective punishments and the spreading of terror) and Article 147 (wilfully killing or causing great suffering and extensive destruction and appropriation of property, not justified by military necessity and carried out unlawfully and wantonly) of the Fourth Geneva Convention, 1949, to which Israel is party. Although Israel is not party to the 1977 Protocols, many of the prohibitions contained therein do represent rules of custom[228] and the events under discussion amount to clear violations of the prohibitions in Article 48 (the obligation to distinguish between the civilian population and combatants and between civilian objects and military objectives),[229] Article 51 (the obligation to protect the civilian population)[230] and Article 52 (the general obligation to protect civilian objects)[231] of the First Additional Protocol of 1977. The Palestinian Authority can also be seen to be in violation of the relevant obligations under the Geneva Conventions and 1977 Additional Protocols which represent customary rules.[232]

Furthermore, despite its assertions to the contrary, Israel's jurisdiction extends to the Occupied Palestinian Territories and events such as those in Beit Hanoun are such that Israel is in breach of many of its international human rights obligations. At the very least, events in Beit Hanoun involve gross and systematic violations of Article 6 (right to life), Article 7 (prohibition on ill-treatment), Article 9 (prohibition on arbitrary arrest and detention) and Article 12 (liberty of movement) of

---

[227] *Special Rapporteur's 2007 Report*, p. 2.
[228] See the discussion in Jean-Marie Henckaerts and L. Doswald-Beck, *Customary International Humanitarian Law*, vol. I, *Rules* (Cambridge: Cambridge University Press, 2005).
[229] *Ibid.* p. 3 *et seq.*   [230] *Ibid.*   [231] *Ibid.* p. 25 *et seq.*
[232] For discussion on armed non-state groups and international humanitarian law, see S. Sivakumaran, 'Binding Armed Opposition Groups' (2006) 55 *ICLQ* 369. Sivakumaran's argument that legislative jurisdiction can be the basis for such obligations does not apply to Palestinian groups.

the International Covenant on Civil and Political Rights, 1966. Article 11 (right to food) and Article 12 (right to health) of the International Covenant on Economic, Social and Cultural Rights, 1966 were certainly also violated. The Israeli army is widely regarded to be a disciplined and sophisticated army and it is not acting of its own volition when engaging in gross and systematic violations of such obligations. The Israeli state is clearly responsible for the violations the IDF commits.

The Union's response to the Israeli incursions in Gaza in 2006 and events in Beit Hanoun, as was the case with Jenin, has been weak. It has criticised some of the more excessive violations of international norms and used condemnatory language but has not responded in a manner commensurate to the seriousness of the violations of international rules. This is also true with regard to the third case study, which concerns the building of the Wall in the area in and around the West Bank. The Wall, however, presents the greatest challenge to the Union's policy objectives as it is de facto creating events on the ground which makes the securing of a sustainable peace much more difficult.

5.2.3.1(b) The Wall and the Essential Elements Clause
As is well known, Israel has since June 2002 been constructing a Wall for, it argues, security reasons. It is contended by Israel that the construction of the Wall will and does stop suicide-bombing and other attacks on Israeli citizens by Palestinian terrorists.[233] In October 2003, the Israeli Cabinet approved a route which will form one continuous line stretching approximately 720 kilometres along the West Bank.[234] At the time of writing, the Wall has not been completed although approximately 60 per cent of it is in place.[235]

The physical structure of the Wall differs along its length.[236] Where it has been built it is composed of sections which consist of a combination of the following: a concrete wall several metres high; a fence with electronic sensors; a ditch up to four metres deep; a two-lane asphalt

---

[233] See, *inter alia*, the official Israeli arguments in favour of the Wall at www.israel-mfa. gov.il/mfa/mfaarchive/2000_2009/2003/11/saving%20lives-%20israel-s%20anti-terrorist %20fence%20-%20answ

[234] Advisory Opinion, *Legal Consequences of the Construction of a Wall*, n. 129 above, para. 80 *et seq.*

[235] See the information available at www.israel-mfa.gov.il/mfa/mfaarchive/2000_2009/ 2003/11/saving%20lives-%20israel-s%20anti-terrorist%20fence%20-%20answ

[236] The following description of the Wall is derived from Advisory Opinion, *Legal Consequences of the Construction of a Wall*, n. 129 above, para. 80 *et seq.* The factual description of the structure and its route are not contentious.

patrol road; a trace road (a strip of sand smoothed to detect footprints) running parallel to the fence; or a stack of six coils of barbed wire marking the perimeter of the complex.[237] Israel is without any doubt legally entitled to build any structure it so wishes on its territory. The problem with the Wall, however, is that it deviates in places substantially from the Green Line (the 1949 armistice line which prior to 1967 was the boundary between Israel and Jordan) and encroaches into and envelops Occupied Palestinian Territory. The Special Rapporteur in his 2007 report has argued that 80 per cent of the Wall is built within the Palestinian Territory itself and in order to incorporate the Ariel settlement block, it extends over twenty kilometres into the West Bank.[238] It is estimated that when the Wall is complete, over 60,000 West Bank Palestinians living in forty-two villages and towns will reside in a 'closed zone' – the area of land between the Green Line and the Wall. It is also highly pertinent to note that the 'closed zone' also includes many of the West Bank's most valuable water resources. Approximately one-third of all the West Bank's Palestinians need a permit to exit the 'closed zone', so as to tend their lands, visit relatives or to get to their places of employment. In this regard it is worth quoting the Special Rapporteur in detail. He notes:

The Wall has serious humanitarian consequences for Palestinians living within the closed zone. They are cut off from places of employment, schools, universities and specialized medical care, and community life is seriously fragmented. Moreover they do not have 24-hour access to emergency health services. Palestinians who live on the eastern side of the Wall but whose land lies in the closed zone face serious economic hardship as a result of the fact that they are not able to reach their land to harvest crops or to graze their animals without permits. Permits are not easily granted. A host of obstacles are placed in the way of obtaining a permit. Bureaucratic procedures for obtaining permits are humiliating and obstructive. The United Nations Office for the Coordination of Humanitarian Affairs (OCHA) has estimated that 60 per cent of the farming families with land to the west of the Wall could no longer access their land. To aggravate matters the opening and closing of the gates leading to the closed zone are regulated in a highly arbitrary manner ... Hardships experienced by Palestinians living within the closed zone and in the precincts of the Wall have already resulted in the displacement of some 15,000 persons, but it is feared that more will leave this area as life is made intolerable for them by the IDF and settlers.[239]

---

[237] Ibid. para. 82.   [238] Special Rapporteur's 2007 Report, p. 12.
[239] Ibid. (references omitted).

The permit system operating in conjunction with the Wall has been considered by the Special Rapporteur to be analogous to that used by the South African apartheid regimes.[240] The World Bank in 2007 noted that where the Wall exists, it in practice deprives Palestinians of all rights to access their land.[241] The World Bank also noted that the route of the Wall almost totally ignores the daily needs of the Palestinian population and is 'focused almost exclusively on the desire to maintain the fabric of life of the Israeli settlers'.[242]

Israel has, as a consequence of constructing the Wall, also exacerbated the continuing humanitarian emergency in the West Bank. Even this, however, is not the most serious issue.[243] The Wall, where it deviates from the Green Line, very clearly amounts to 'de facto annexation' of Palestinian territory and a denial of Palestinian rights to self-determination, fundamental breaches of international law and its principles.[244] The Special Rapporteur considers that Israel's arguments (vis-à-vis justifications for the Wall) 'are simply not supported by the facts' and that the construction of the Wall violates the right to self-determination, an obligation *erga omnes*, and also amounts to the forcible acquisition of territory.[245]

The Special Rapporteur also considers Israel's actions to be disproportionate, even after according it a 'wide margin of appreciation' in responding to terror.[246] The Wall is also fundamentally incompatible with the Roadmap itself. It protects illegal settlements, some of which Israel is obliged to dismantle under the plan, and makes the two-state solution impossible to implement as it prejudges the boundaries between Israel and any future Palestinian state.[247] Israel has consistently refused to recognise that it is illegally annexing territory; nor does it recognise the 1967 borders. The Israeli Foreign Minister, Tzipi Livni in January 2007, for example, argued that since there was no Palestinian state in 1967 and no connection between Gaza and the West Bank, new

---

[240] Special Rapporteur John Dugard, statement to Fifty-ninth Session of the General Assembly, Third Committee, Item 105(c), New York, 28 October 2004. Dugard noted in his statement that the permit system of the Wall is similar to the 'pass laws' of the apartheid regime of South Africa, only far more arbitrary and inconsistent.
[241] World Bank, *Movement and Access Restrictions in the West Bank*, p. 10. The World Bank is as scathing as the Special Rapporteur on the consequences of the Wall.
[242] *Ibid.*
[243] *Special Rapporteur's 2003 Report*, para. 21, considers that the humanitarian crisis is caused almost entirely by Israel.
[244] *Ibid.* paras. 6–16.   [245] *Ibid.*   [246] *Ibid.* para. 5.   [247] Phase I of the Roadmap.

borders will have to be worked out.[248] While it is undeniably true that new borders and some land exchanges will have to be negotiated to ensure that a viable Palestinian state and secure Israel can exist side by side, by building a permanent structure Israel is unilaterally deciding those borders. This is in clear contravention of various agreements with the Palestinians to which Israel is party and the expectations of the international community, including the Union.[249]

As is well known, in July 2004 the International Court of Justice (ICJ) delivered an Advisory Opinion on the consequences of the construction of the Wall. Israel contested the Court's jurisdiction to give an Advisory Opinion and refused to cooperate further with the Court. The ICJ, therefore, was obliged to base its understanding on other accounts of the facts, including the Special Rapporteur's 2003 Report. The Court, by a majority of fourteen to one, considered the Wall, where it enters the Occupied Palestinian Territory, including in and around East Jerusalem, to be contrary to international law.[250]

As noted above, the ICJ's discussion of Israel's right to self-defence was wholly unsatisfactory. One of the Israeli contentions had been that the Wall was essential to protect Israel from attacks stemming from within the Palestinian Territories. The Court dismissed the contention that Article 51 UNC was applicable, however, because the attacks on Israel were not imputable to a foreign state.[251] This approach, which is consistent with the Court's decision in the *Nicaragua* case, has also been maintained in subsequent cases.[252] For states such as Israel this approach is wholly unsatisfactory as, unlike in the case of Hezbollah, for example, whose acts may be imputable to Lebanon or Syria, the acts

---

[248] 'FM Livni Participates in Discussion of Israel-Palestinian Conflict in Davos', 25 January 2007, available at www.mfa.gov.il

[249] See e.g., European Council, 24–25 March 2004, Doc. 9048/04, Presidency Conclusions, para. 54, where it is stated, '[t]he European Council renewed its commitment to a negotiated agreement resulting in two viable, sovereign and independent states, Israel and Palestine, based on the borders of 1967, living side by side in peace and security, in the framework of a comprehensive peace in the Middle East, as laid out in the RoadMap drawn up by the Quartet. The European Union will not recognise any change to the pre-1967 borders other than those arrived at by agreement between the parties.'

[250] Judge Buergenthal, dissenting.

[251] Advisory Opinion, *Legal Consequences of the Construction of a Wall*, n. 129 above, para. 139.

[252] *Nicaragua v. United States of America – Case Concerning Military and Paramilitary Activities in and Against Nicaragua* [1986] ICJ Reports 14, para. 115 establishes an 'effective control' test for such acts to be attributable to a state. See also, *Democratic Republic of Congo v. Uganda – Armed Activities on the Territory of the Congo* [2005] ICJ Reports 116, para. 147.

of groups based in the Palestinian Territories are much more difficult to impute to a state.[253] Even if the Palestinian Territories are treated for this matter as being akin to a state and thus Israel has the right to self-defence under Article 51 UNC, the route of parts of the Wall still cannot be justified on that basis.

The ICJ noted, as has the World Bank, that the right to self-defence and security concerns do not justify the route along which the Wall was being built.[254] It is worth stressing again that the Court did not dispute Israel's right to build the structure so long as it is built in what is undisputedly Israeli territory. Considering the route followed, the Court concluded that the Wall severely impedes the Palestinian's right to self-determination;[255] violates a number of international human rights and humanitarian law obligations incumbent upon Israel;[256] was tantamount to de facto annexation;[257] and took a route which was not essential for security purposes.[258] In sum, the Court concluded that 'Israel cannot rely on a right to self-defence or on a state of necessity in order to preclude the wrongfulness of the construction of the Wall'.[259]

Sharon immediately denounced the ICJ's Opinion.[260] The Dutch Presidency, clearly wishing not to commit itself for the time being, stated that the Court's Opinion 'will need to be studied carefully' and further noted that 'it will now be up to the political bodies of the United Nations to decide how to act upon the Court's Advisory Opinion'.[261] Studying the Union's pronouncements and approach towards the situation in the Middle East, it is very clear that with the exception of the treatment of Israel's right to self-defence, the ICJ's *Wall Opinion* closely reflects the position that the Union has continuously adopted.

---

[253] For an excellent discussion, see G. Capaldo, 'Providing a Right to Self-Defense against Large-Scale Attacks by Irregular Forces: the Israeli-Hezbollah Conflict' (2007) 48 *Harvard ILJ* 101.

[254] See World Bank, *Movement and Access Restrictions in the West Bank*, p. 9.

[255] Advisory Opinion, *Legal Consequences of the Construction of a Wall*, n. 129 above, para. 122.

[256] *Ibid.* paras. 123–37.   [257] *Ibid.* para. 121.

[258] *Ibid.* paras. 114–37.   [259] *Ibid.* para. 142.

[260] See 'Sharon Pledges to Defy Court on Barrier', *New York Times*, 12 July 2004 and 'Sacred Right to Fight Terror Overrides Court, Says Sharon', *Guardian*, 12 July 2004.

[261] General Affairs and External Relations Council, 12–13 July 2004, Doc. 1105/05. Javier Solana was also cautious in his response. See 'Comments by Javier Solana on Today's ICJ Opinion', 9 July 2004, SO189/04.

The Opinion of the ICJ was delivered nine days after a decision of the Israeli Supreme Court which considered that specific parts of the Wall caused unjustifiable harm and suffering to certain Palestinians.[262] As opposed to the Opinion of the ICJ, the basis for the decision of the Israeli Supreme Court was the violation of Palestinian rights to property and freedom of movement.[263] In September 2005, in another challenge to the route of the Wall, the Israeli Supreme Court was rather dismissive of the ICJ's Opinion because it considered that the ICJ had not adequately taken account of Israel's security concerns.[264]

More recently, however, the bases for these decisions of the Israeli Supreme Court have been questioned. The Israeli government has admitted that the Wall serves a political purpose and not an exclusively security one.[265] The government has also admitted that the Wall has in part been built to include West Bank settlements so as to bring them within Israel's direct protection.[266] As of 2007, there are over one-quarter of a million settlers in the West Bank.[267] Over three-quarters of the West Bank settler population is enclosed within the Wall, this makes it exceptionally difficult to refute that the Wall is not concerned with annexing land. The Israeli High Court has, as a consequence of the government's admissions, rebuked it for providing misleading information in the *Mara'abe* hearing and other challenges to the legality of the Wall and its route.[268] Whether the Israeli Supreme Court will take a different approach in subsequent challenges to the route of the Wall, at the time of writing, remains to be seen.

The route of the Wall through Jerusalem is particularly contentious. Jerusalem, of course, holds great symbolic value for Christians, Jews and Muslims alike. Jerusalem has been declared by Israel as its complete

---

[262] *Beit Sourik Village Council* v. *Government of Israel and the Commander of the IDF Forces in the West Bank*, HCJ 2056/04, Supreme Court of Israel Sitting as the High Court of Justice, 30 June 2004, (2004) 43 *ILM* 1099.

[263] *Ibid*. para. 60.

[264] *Mara'abe* v. *Prime Minister of Israel*, HCJ 7957/04, Supreme Court of Israel Sitting as the High Court of Justice, 15 September 2005, (2006) 45 *ILM* 202.

[265] See World Bank, *Movement and Access Restrictions in the West Bank*, p. 9.

[266] *Ibid.*

[267] *Ibid*. p. 6. This figure does not include those Israelis living in East Jerusalem nor those living in 'illegal outposts'.

[268] See *Head of the Azzun Municipal Council, Abed Alatif Hassin and others* v. *State of Israel and the Military Commander of the West Bank*, HCJ 2733/05, cited in *Special Rapporteur's 2007 Report*, para. 24.

and united capital.[269] East Jerusalem, however, is illegally occupied by Israel. In the Venice Declaration the special importance of Jerusalem for all the concerned parties was recognised by the then nine Member States. They further noted that 'they will not accept any unilateral initiative designed to change the status of Jerusalem' before stressing the need for Israel to put to an end its territorial occupation of land captured since 1967.[270] Accordingly, Israel's annexation of East Jerusalem is not recognised. As a consequence, in line with the practice of almost all other states, the EU Member States' embassies and the Commission delegation are based in Tel Aviv.[271]

Approximately seventy-five kilometres of the Wall passes through Jerusalem and it has been argued that the route has been chosen with a view to 'social engineering' and 'designed to achieve the Judaization of Jerusalem by reducing the number of Palestinians in the city'.[272] The Special Rapportuer has argued that the route chosen 'cannot conceivably be justified on security grounds' and has 'serious implications for the human rights' of the one-quarter million or so Palestinians living in Jerusalem.[273] The World Bank's assessment is very similar.[274]

The Union is not oblivious to the consequences for Palestinians of Israeli polices in East Jerusalem. The Commission since 2002 has been active in providing support to the Arab population of East Jerusalem due to the impact of Israeli policies.[275] In 2005, the EU Heads of Mission in Jerusalem and Ramallah compiled a report on the Israeli annexation of East Jerusalem which was very critical of Israeli practices. Under the Presidency of the United Kingdom, the then British Foreign Secretary,

---

[269] Jerusalem, Capital of Israel Law, 1980, 30 July 1980, available at www.mfa.gov.il/
In response to this law, the Security Council adopted Resolution 478(1980), 20 August 1980. It was stated that the Security Council, '[c]ensures in the strongest terms the enactment by Israel of the "basic law" on Jerusalem'. In Security Council Resolution 252(1968), 21 May 1968, the Council had first made it clear 'that all legislative and administrative measures and actions taken by Israel, including expropriation of land and properties thereon, which tend to change the legal status of Jerusalem are invalid and cannot change that status'.

[270] Venice Declaration, paras. 8–9.

[271] Due to the EU Member States' refusal to recognise the Israeli occupation of East Jerusalem, diplomats from, among others, EU Member States and the EU Commission refused, to the consternation of Israeli officials, to attend functions to celebrate the fortieth anniversary of the 'unification' of Jerusalem. See 'EU Boycotts "Provocative" Israeli Anniversary Party', *Independent*, 14 May 2007.

[272] *Special Rapporteur's 2007 Report*, para. 26.   [273] *Ibid.* para. 27.

[274] World Bank, *Movement and Access Restrictions in the West Bank*, p. 11.

[275] See COM(2005)458, p. 7.

Jack Straw decided to suppress the report.[276] The report, however, was subsequently leaked.[277] The report is very clear that Israel is turning the 'annexation of East Jerusalem into a concrete fact' and that 'Israel's activities in Jerusalem are in violation of both its Roadmap obligations and international law'.[278] The Heads of Mission suggested a number of proposals, both operational and political, to try and mitigate the impact of Israeli policy and practice. One of these was that the European Union and Quartet make clear statements that Jerusalem remains an issue for negotiation between the two sides and that Israel should desist from all measures designed to preempt such negotiations.

The Wall is not only manifestly illegal where it departs from the Green Line, it is also a structure which makes the Union's objective of a viable two-state solution increasingly improbable. The Union, however, has at no point responded to the building of the Wall in general or in East Jerusalem in particular in a manner commensurate to the seriousness of the violation of those norms it stresses its commitment to at every opportunity.

A proposed resolution in the Security Council in 2003, condemning the Wall and Israel's continued settlement activities, was vetoed by the United States.[279] The United Kingdom and Germany both abstained, whereas France voted in favour of the resolution. In the General Assembly, however, the (then) fifteen Member States co-sponsored the resolution condemning the Wall which was finally adopted.[280] The (then) Member States abstained from General Assembly Resolution ES-10/14 which requested the ICJ for an Advisory Opinion on the legality of the Wall. This is not because the Member States doubted that the Wall, where it deviates from the 1949 armistice line, is unlawful.[281] Indeed, it was clear that the Wall was a development the Member States objected to on both legal and political grounds. In the Seville European Council of June 2002, for example, the Union had declared in the context of the Middle East that, '[w]alls will not bring peace'.[282] The

---

[276] See 'EU won't Publish East Jerusalem Report', *Jerusalem Post*, 12 December 2005.
[277] Jerusalem and Ramallah Heads of Mission, *Report on East Jerusalem* (2005). The report is available at www.ejjp.org/bijlagen/EU%20report%20on%20Jerusalem.pdf
[278] *Ibid.*
[279] Press Release SC/7896, 14 October 2003.
[280] Resolution ES-10/13, 21 October 2003.
[281] See the statement by the Italian representative, Marcello Spatafora on behalf of the EU Presidency at the Tenth Emergency Session of the General Assembly, 8 December 2003, Press Release GA/10216.
[282] Seville European Council, 21–22 June 2002, (2002) 6 *Bull. EU* I.32.

EU Member States abstained from the General Assembly Resolution requesting an Advisory Opinion on the legality of the Wall because they felt that such an Opinion was not conducive to relaunching political dialogue.[283] Prior to delivering its Advisory Opinion, it was conceivable that if the International Court of Justice condemned the Wall in strong language, then the Union would be under severe pressure to act in a manner commensurate to the seriousness of those violations of international law that the Court considered were occurring. The Court condemned the Wall accordingly, but the Union has not responded as it should have.

The Union has discussed the issue of the Wall with Israel in bilateral negotiations. It has, as noted above, also occasionally condemned the Wall at the United Nations. In bilateral meetings, the issue was not initially raised consistently although as its illegality has become increasingly apparent it has become a regular feature of all discussions between the parties. In the third meeting of the EU-Israel Association Council held in October 2002, for example, there was no mention of the Wall in the European Union's declaration, despite a long list of other concerns, such as extra-judicial killings and collective punishments, being raised by the Union.[284] In the fourth meeting of the Association Council in November 2003, the Union did raise the issue of the Wall, using much of the language it had already adopted in the Presidency Conclusions of the October 2003 European Council.[285] In the declaration of the fourth meeting, the Union recognised that the Wall results in a de facto change of the legal status of many Palestinian villages and requests that Israel dismantle the Wall, something Sharon had repeatedly refused to do, a policy continued by his successor, Ehud Olmert.[286]

In the fifth meeting of the EU-Israel Association Council, which met on 13 December 2004 under the Dutch Presidency, the Union discussed a number of Israeli policies and practices to which it was opposed. The fifth meeting of the EU-Israel Association Council took place five

---

[283] *Ibid.* Nine of the then fifteen Member States, as well as the Irish Presidency, submitted written observations to the ICJ on the request for an Advisory Opinion.

[284] Declaration of the European Union at the Third Meeting of the EU-Israel Association Council, 21 October 2002.

[285] European Council, 16–17 October 2003, Doc. 15188/03, Presidency Conclusions, p. 13 *et seq.* and Declaration of the European Union at the Fourth Meeting of the EU-Israel Association Council, 19 November 2003, para. 4.

[286] The Quartet has also long recognised that the Wall prejudges the final borders between the parties. See e.g., Quartet statement, 26 September 2003.

months after the ICJ's *Wall Opinion* was delivered and with regard to the Wall the Union asked Israel to halt its construction inside Occupied Palestinian Territory, including in and around East Jerusalem, and to ensure that the Wall's route is on or behind the Green Line.[287] The European Union also called upon Israel to ease the policy of 'closure', freeze all settlement expansion, cease its practice of extra-judicial killings and house demolitions, as well as act with restraint in the face of Palestinian violence. The Union further raised its concerns about collective punishments, and called on Israel to ensure that any abuses by members of the Israeli Defence Forces, settlers and others are properly investigated and that the perpetrators are prosecuted. The Union, while stressing Israel's right to protect its citizens from terrorist attacks, reiterated that this right must be exercised 'within the boundaries of international law'.[288]

In the sixth meeting in June 2006, the Union again raised the issue and did so in stronger language. The Union reiterated that it felt that the Wall threatened to make any solution based on the coexistence of two states physically impossible. The issue had also been discussed in the Association Committee on 17 May 2006.[289] Under the framework of the EU-Israel European Neighbourhood Policy Action Plan, both sides had agreed to achieve closer political cooperation and to engage in dialogue on the basis of what were identified as their common values: respect for human rights and fundamental freedoms, democracy, good governance and international humanitarian law. The EU-Israel Action Plan contains a specific section on human rights and fundamental freedoms and an EU-Israel Human Rights Working Group was established at the Subcommittee on Political Dialogue and Cooperation meeting of 21 November 2005. The EU-Israel Human Rights Working Group held its first meeting on 7 June 2006. The working group provided another opportunity for the Union to discuss, among other issues, the effect of the Wall and the restrictions Israel was placing on movement within the Palestinian Territories and the impact these were having on the lives and livelihood of the Palestinians.[290]

The issue of the Wall is now being raised in bilateral discussion consistently by the Union. The Union is also routinely referring to the

---

[287] See statement of the European Union at the Fifth Meeting of the EU-Israel Association Council, 10 December 2004.
[288] *Ibid.*
[289] European Council, *Annual Report on Human Rights, 2006* (Luxembourg: OOPEC, 2006) p. 70.
[290] *Ibid.*

Wall in the declarations adopted after Council Meetings and this is regularly in strong terms. In the Presidency Conclusions adopted after the Council meeting in December 2003, for example, while referring to the Wall and its consequences for the free movement of the Palestinians of the West Bank, it was stated 'the EU is alarmed by the creation of a closed zone between this "fence" and the Green Line'.[291] As far as the Union is concerned, the Wall should not be used by Israel to annex Palestinian land and should take a different route from that which is currently being taken. The Israeli government has, however, only in the light of the Israeli Supreme Court's decisions (not the Opinion of the ICJ) agreed to reconsider certain parts of the route taken by the Wall.[292] The Israeli Supreme Court does not require the Wall to be dismantled, only partially rerouted.[293] The de facto annexation of land or the denial of Palestinian self-determination referred to by the ICJ has not been of central concern to the Israeli Supreme Court. The fundamental problem with the Wall, however, as far as the Union is concerned, is that it is unilaterally establishing a permanent border, which illegally annexes land and denies the Palestinian's right to self-determination. It makes the creation of a viable Palestinian state, which is also in Israel's interests, far more difficult to achieve and this is contrary to everything the Union has sought to achieve in its interventions in the Middle East Peace Process.

5.2.3.1(c) Israeli Violations of International Norms and the Essential Elements Clause

The detailed discussion on the Wall and events in Jenin and Beit Hanoun provide clear examples of Israeli violations of international law that are legally more than enough to justify suspension of the Association Agreement or at the very least the introduction of some sort of punitive measures. It is difficult to consider that any state other than Israel, for political and historical reasons, would be granted such latitude in this regard by the Union and its Member States. The adoption of punitive measures against, for example, Uzbekistan and Zimbabwe provide

---

[291] European Council, 12–13 December 2003, Doc. 5381/04, Presidency Conclusions, para. 59.

[292] See the maps available at the website of the Israeli human rights NGO B'Tselem on the route taken by the Wall and the adjustments made in the light of Israeli Supreme Court decisions at www.btselem.org/English/Maps/Index.asp

[293] See e.g., *Beit Sourik Village Council* v. *Government of Israel*, n. 262 above, and *Mara'abe* v. *Prime Minister of Israel*, n. 264 above.

interesting comparisons. With regard to Uzbekistan, further to the killings of hundreds of people in Andijan, the Union has not only adopted a Common Position[294] but a decision has also been taken to suspend all scheduled technical meetings under the Partnership and Cooperation Agreement between the Community and Member States, on the one hand, and Uzbekistan, on the other. The Commission accordingly has reoriented and reduced its programmes to focus on the needs of the population and promote democracy and human rights.[295] With regard to Zimbabwe, the Union adopted a Common Position in 2002 for human rights violations and the erosion of democracy.[296] This Common Position as subsequently amended, *inter alia*, imposes visa restrictions on members of President Mugabe's regime, imposes restrictions on their assets, as well as banning the sale of arms and other related goods to Zimbabwe.[297] Under the Cotonou Convention, Article 96 consultations commenced with Zimbabwe in 2001.[298] From 2002 onwards, direct financial support under the various European Development Funds to Zimbabwe has been suspended and funding reoriented to support human rights, democracy and the rule of law.[299]

The Israeli army, of course, has not massacred hundreds of innocent demonstrators, as seems to have happened in Andijan, nor has the government of Israel essentially eroded the rule of law or democracy to retain power. However, there is little doubt that Israel routinely and

---

[294] Common Position 2005/792/CFSP, Concerning Restrictive Measures against Uzbekistan, [2005] OJ L299/72, 16 November 2005, as most recently amended by Common Position 2007/338/CFSP, Renewing Certain Restrictive Measures against Uzbekistan, [2007] OJ L128/50, 16 May 2007.

[295] Partnership and Cooperation Agreement Establishing a Partnership between the European Communities and their Member States and the Republic of Uzbekistan, [1999] OJ L229/3, 31 August 1999. Parts of the Agreement were suspended further to the meeting of the External Relations Council, 3 October 2005, Doc. 12515/1/05REV 1.

[296] Common Position 2002/145/CFSP, Concerning Restrictive Measures against Zimbabwe, as subsequently amended by, *inter alia*, Common Position 2007/120/CFSP, Renewing Restrictive Measures against Zimbabwe, [2007] OJ L51/25, 20 February 2007.

[297] Some of these measures are implemented in the Community legal order by Commission Regulation 777/2007, Concerning Certain Restrictive Measures in respect of Zimbabwe, [2007] OJ L173/3, 3 July 2007.

[298] See COM(2001)623.

[299] Council Decision 2002/148/EC, Concluding Consultations with Zimbabwe under Article 96 of the ACP-EC Partnership Agreement, [2002] OJ L50/64, 21 February 2002, as subsequently amended by, *inter alia*, Council Decision extending the Period of Application of the Measures in Decision 2002/148/EC Concluding Consultations with Zimbabwe under Article 96 of the ACP-EC Partnership Agreement, [2007] OJ L53/23, 22 February 2007.

systematically violates some of the fundamental norms of international law and yet enjoys immunity from the sorts of measures that some other third states are subjected to. In the cases of Jenin and Beit Hanoun, prima facie grave breaches of the principles of international humanitarian law and human rights law were committed by Israel. Collective punishments, the stifling of humanitarian aid, the destruction of infrastructure[300] and civilian property and extra-judicial killings were all rife and part of a systematic policy.[301] While there is little doubt that the Palestinian Authority was also guilty of seriously violating international humanitarian law and human rights at these times, those independent experts who have examined events consider that culpability primarily lies with the Israelis.[302] With regard to the Wall, the violations of international law are at least as stark. The ICJ in its Advisory Opinion considered that all states, while respecting international law, must try to bring the impediment to the Palestinian's right to self-determination to an end.[303] It further stated that all states parties to the Fourth Geneva Convention (which includes all of the Union's Member States) are under a similar obligation with regard to violations of that Convention.[304] The Union, as discussed in Chapter 3, has introduced Guidelines on Promoting Compliance with International Humanitarian Law, which attempt to ensure that states and non-state actors act in accordance with these norms.[305] In the case of Jenin, the Union used language which suggested that suspension of the Agreement was a very real possibility. This has not yet been the case as far as events in Beit Hanoun or the building of the Wall have

---

[300] World Bank, *Twenty Seven Months – Intifada, Closures and the Palestinian Economic Crisis: an Assessment* (Washington DC: World Bank, 2003) p. 19 considers that Israel had destroyed US$930 million worth of Palestinian infrastructure during its incursion into Jenin.

[301] In response to events in Jenin, the EU Presidency asked for an inventory of the damage, see the speech by Commissioner Patten, 68 *EuropaWorld*, 8 February 2002. No request has been made in the aftermath of the incursions into Beit Hanoun, see Development Committee, *Development Assistance and the Occupied Palestinian Territories 2007*, Evidence, Question 308.

[302] See *Special Rapporteur's 2003 Report*, para. 55 with regard to Jenin and *Report of the High-Level Fact-Finding Mission to Beit Hanoun*, para. 12 with regard to Beit Hanoun. The latter report is in particular scathing of the culture of impunity that exists among both Israelis and Palestinians for grave human rights violations.

[303] Although see the criticisms of this discussed in Chapter 2.

[304] Advisory Opinion, *Legal Consequences of the Construction of a Wall*, n. 129 above, para. 159.

[305] European Union Guidelines on Promoting Compliance with International Humanitarian Law, [2005] OJ C327/4, 23 December 2005.

been concerned. A clear difference of approach is clearly being taken by the Union towards Israel as opposed to its approach and policy towards third states.

Suspending the Agreement with Israel is difficult for the Community and its Member States because of its mixed nature, although this did not cause any problems in the case of Uzbekistan, where the Agreement is also mixed. Article 79 of the Agreement with Israel contains a more or less standard version of the non-execution clause that is now inserted in all Agreements with third states to which the Community becomes party. Under the non-execution clause, if one party considers that the other has failed to fulfil its obligations under the Agreement, it may take appropriate measures to that effect. Before doing so, however, it must supply the Association Council with sufficient information to allow a thorough investigation of the situation. The only exception to this is in cases of special urgency. The Association Council, as established by Article 69 of the Agreement with Israel, is composed of representatives of the Members of the Council of the European Union and Commission, on the one hand, and, on the other, Israel. Thus, Israel is able to put forward its arguments concerning the alleged breach of the essential elements of the Agreement. These are invariably based upon state security. For the Agreement to be suspended, the consent of all the Union's Member States as well as the Commission is required. Despite the fact that the Union has taken a more critical line on Israel than the United States, this is highly unlikely to happen. While provision is made for such an eventuality, the reality of the situation is different. There are a number of reasons for this.

First, Commission officials consider Israeli delegations, not only in the Association Council but also in Troika meetings, Euro-Med Conferences, ENP meetings and any other forum, to have a very business-like and professional approach to the issue of human rights and other ethical values. Israeli delegations are generally considered to be very well briefed, highly professional and at least prepared to discuss concerns raised by the Member States or Commission in their meetings.[306] Commitments to keep the 'situation under review' and 'necessity' have so far always been enough to placate some of the Member States. Furthermore, on a number of occasions Israel has also, to some extent or other, responded to criticism. Israeli diplomats, due to differences between the perspectives of the Member States, by strategically making

---

[306] I base this upon several interviews with Commission officials.

some concessions are able to ensure that any consensus to take action by the Member States which may have existed breaks down.[307]

Secondly, even in the event that agreement can be reached between the Member States that the Agreement should be suspended, the Union is well aware that if this were done Israel would be likely to refuse to agree to its further participation in any negotiations concerning the MEPP or at least try and relegate it to an ancillary role. The tension between the Community and Israel was apparent, for example, at the signing of the peace agreements in Madrid in 1991. Israel had initially refused to let the Community take part in the negotiations. Only once the Community had agreed, and negotiations had taken place to update the 1975 Agreement with Israel, did it consider the Community's participation to be acceptable.[308] The difference in the balance of power can be seen in the fact that Israel was largely dictating the agenda. The Community's role was still limited to a minor one, working on regional economic development.[309] Having obtained a more important role in the MEPP, and in an attempt to maintain and promote itself as an

[307] An example from the early 1990s illustrates this. Israel initially consistently failed to comply with a series of Security Council Resolutions, such as Resolution 799 (1992), 18 December 1992, on the deportation of 415 Palestinians, who were members of Hamas. The deportations were subsequently discussed in the EC/Israel Cooperation Council on 1 February 1993, under the 1975 Agreement, where the Community raised its concerns. It was argued by the EC Council that the continuance of discussion and non-suspension of that Agreement (which did not have an 'essential elements' clause) provided the Community and its Member States with 'another opportunity to exert pressure on the Israelis to take immediate action with regard to the deportees'. As a consequence of not only European but also global condemnation, the then Israeli Foreign Secretary, Shimon Peres informed the EC Foreign Ministers that 100 deportees had been allowed to return and the duration of the exile period had been halved for the others. The Community and its Member States considered this to be an important step forward in complying with Security Council Resolution 799, although it fell considerably short of what was actually stipulated, and thus felt their approach was vindicated. In the Cooperation Council, the Community had stated that it did not wish to be put in a position where it would have to adopt a position on the 415 deported Palestinians while negotiating the 1995 Agreement. The Israelis, by making some concessions, ensured that they did not have to. (See the answers to Question No. 48 by Mr Dessylas (H-0386/93) to European Political Cooperation: the 415 Deported Palestinians and EEC-Israel Relations, *Annex to the Official Journal: Debates of the European Parliament*, No. 430, p. 176 and Question No. 39 by Mr Dessylas (H-0088/93) to European Political Cooperation: the 415 Deported and Exiled Palestinians, International Law and UN Security Council Resolutions, *Annex to the Official Journal: Debates of the European Parliament*, No. 429, p. 142.)

[308] See A. Tovia, 'The EU's Mediterranean Policies under Pressure' in R. Gillespie (ed.), *Mediterranean Politics* (London: Frank Cass, 1996) vol. II, p. 14.

[309] See COM(1993)305.

international actor, the Union has condemned Israel as and when considered necessary but as a consequence it is unlikely the Association Agreement will be suspended. In this respect the general idea, in practice, seems to be that the peace process and the Union's role in it must take priority and the possibility of maintaining some influence over Israel comes first. Unlike many other third states, Israel can also rely on the United States to counter the effect of any punitive Union action, and indeed count on the United States to diplomatically lobby the Union on Israel's behalf not to take such action in the first place. This is closely linked to the subservient role the Union plays to the United States in the Quartet. The Union does not wish to lose influence in the Quartet; the suspension of the Association Agreement with Israel by the Union would lead to it being further sidelined by the United States and shunned by the Israelis.

Thirdly, due to the dependence of the Palestinian Territories upon Israel for their economic survival, the Member States consider that suspension of the Agreement with Israel is likely to have an adverse economic effect on the Palestinians. While the economic and physical wellbeing of Israel has been a cornerstone of US foreign policy in the Middle East since 1948, it can be argued that since it has taken a stand on the MEPP in 1980, the Community and later Union has been attempting to give effect to the UN Security Council Resolutions that deal with the region. Protecting Palestinian rights has been central to the approach adopted by the Union. This has included attempting to lessen the impact of certain Israeli practices upon those most affected by them. A punitive approach has not been adopted towards Israel, even where it has destroyed infrastructure in the Palestinian Authority which the Community and EU Member States have paid for. Every tension and turn in relations between Israel and the Palestinian Authority has a direct impact on the viability and survival of the area nominally under the latter's control. Israel has, as mentioned above and as will be further discussed in detail below, on numerous occasions withheld tax transfers to the Palestinian Authority, which has always brought the Palestinian Authority to the verge of collapse.[310] Negotiation and dialogue have thus been maintained at all costs. A number of Member States generally consider the continuance of the Association Agreement

---

[310] The Union has consistently asked Israel to transfer such funds to the Palestinian Authority, which Israel has refused to do until such time as it has deemed appropriate. See further the discussion below.

with Israel to be vital if the peace process is to be kept on track. On numerous occasions when the suspension of the Agreement has been raised, the Council has stated that it did not consider the breaking-off of relations to be conducive to the resolution of the situation. 'Discussion not threats' is seen as the 'method' to employ with regard to Israel.[311] Ex-Commissioner, Manuel Marin-González stated, for example, that ratification of the Agreement ensured that the Community is 'in a better position to exercise a positive influence regarding all human rights related issues in the framework of the political dialogue'.[312] Benjamin Netanyahu, when Prime Minister of Israel, adopted a similar approach. He warned the Union against imposing sanctions, as they supposedly would have no effect and would lead to deteriorating relations between the Union and Israel as a result.[313] The Council's 2006 *Annual Human Rights Report* makes clear that although the essential elements clause allows sanctions to be adopted 'in response to serious violations of human rights or of the democratic process ... the principal role of the clause is to provide the EU with a basis for positive engagement on human rights and democracy issues with third countries'.[314] On the basis of the clause in the Agreement with Israel, the Commission has under the European Neighbourhood Policy established, as noted above, a Working Group on Human Rights which held its first meeting in June 2006. In relations with Israel at least, the clause is seen as almost exclusively providing a basis for negotiation and discussion and not punitive action, as has been the case with some other third states.

Finally, it is politically increasingly difficult for the Union's Member States to suspend the Agreement. The refusal to suspend it, following events that have already occurred, may mean that in future the violations will have to be even more serious before all the Member States agree to suspend it. In legal terms the position has probably not changed, although Israel may be able to argue that estoppel is now a relevant consideration. The Member States have never stated, however, that Israel's

---

[311] See the answers to Question No. 19 by Mr Wibe (H-0787/96) to the Council: Measures against the State of Israel, *Annex to the Official Journal: Debates of the European Parliament*, No. 489, p. 180; Question No. 5 by Mr Wibe (H-0868/97) to the Council: EU Relations with Israel and Palestine, *Annex to the Official Journal: Debates of the European Parliament*, No. 511, p. 181; and Question No. 8 by Mr Wibe (H-0414/98) to the Council: Economic Sanctions against Israel, *Annex to the Official Journal: Debates of the European Parliament*, No. 519, p. 199.

[312] See [1998] OJ C117/86, 16 April 1998.

[313] 'Israel Urges Blair to Veto Arab Lobby', *Daily Telegraph*, 21 July 1998.

[314] European Council, *Annual Report on Human Rights, 2006*, p. 20.

assassinations of Palestinian leaders, widespread arbitrary detentions or the systematic racial discrimination against Arab Israelis do not amount to a 'material breach' of the Association Agreement, as that term is understood in Article 60 of the Vienna Convention on the Law of Treaties.[315] With regard to the Israeli practice of building settlements in land occupied after 1967, however, the legal position is different. As has been noted above, and will be discussed in detail below, the Heads of Government under EPC and subsequently the Union have since 1979 consistently objected to the building of settlements and have made clear that they consider it a breach of the Fourth Geneva Convention. Having entered into treaty relations with Israel, the Community and Member States are restricted by Article 45 of the Vienna Convention from claiming a 'material breach' of the Association Agreement by Israel as far as some of Israel's settlement activity is concerned.[316] The Community and Member States, if they were to claim a 'material breach' on the basis of Israeli settlements policy, can theoretically do so only with regard to settlement activity which has occurred once the Agreement came into force in June 2000. Otherwise, treaty relations would have been entered into with one side already in 'material breach' of the treaty. The Community and Member States have in effect acquiesced to those settlements which already existed in June 2000 as far as the Agreement with Israel is concerned.

The Union in its declarations subsequent to the Agreement coming into force has drawn a clear distinction between those settlements built after March 2001, which it considers Israel must dismantle, and those built prior to then.[317] It was in March 2001 that an Israeli coalition government with Ariel Sharon as Prime Minister declared that, 'the Government will not establish new settlements' although it did make

---

[315] Israel's targeted assassination policy has been discussed by the Israeli Supreme Court in *Public Committee Against Torture in Israel* v. *Government of Israel*, HCJ 769/02, Supreme Court of Israel Sitting as the High Court of Justice, 11 December 2005, (2007) 46 *ILM* 375. The Court was clear that it is not always possible to determine in advance whether a targeted killing will be illegal or not. See more generally, D. Kretzmer, 'Targeted Killing of Suspected Terrorists: Extra-Judicial Executions or Legitimate Means of Defence?' (2005) 16 *EJIL* 171, who argues that the current international legal position and that of the Government of Israel are both difficult to justify.

[316] Article 45 VCLT, for these purposes, prevents a state from claiming a material breach under Article 60 if by reason of its conduct it can be considered to have acquiesced to the maintenance in force of the treaty in the light of the conduct of the other party.

[317] See e.g., European Council, 12–13 December 2003, Doc. 5381/04, Presidency Conclusions, para. 59.

clear that existing settlements would be further developed.[318] Legally, therefore, while the 'essential elements' clause could have been invoked for all settlement activity after June 2000, due to what amounts to its further acquiescence the clause can in all probability now only be invoked by the Community and Member States with regard to settlement activity since March 2001.

There is, however, one further complication. The 'essential elements' clause in the Agreement with Israel does not refer to respect for international law in general but specifically refers to 'respect for human rights and democratic principles'. Israeli settlement activity is a violation of Article 49 of the Fourth Geneva Convention. Although technically this is a part of international humanitarian law, there is no doubt that settlement activity and the consequences of protecting settlers also involve serious violations of the human rights obligations Israel legally owes to those affected Palestinians. Settlement policy, for example, when seen cumulatively, in no small part contributes alongside other policies to the denial of Palestinian self-determination. Other human rights obligations upon Israel stemming from both treaty obligations and customary international law are also relevant. As international humanitarian law treaties, such as the Geneva Conventions of 1949 and the Additional Protocols of 1977, aim also to protect human dignity and to lessen human suffering, the term 'human rights' in Article 2 of the Agreement with Israel should be read to encompass the relevant provisions of these treaties also. The 'essential elements' clause in the Agreement with Israel can, therefore, be legally invoked by the Community and Member States for Israeli settlement activity, but it is more than likely that this is only with regard to that activity which has occurred after March 2001. With regard to other matters, the clause can be legally invoked for all other serious violations of human rights, such as the denial of Palestinian self-determination or violation of Palestinian property rights through the building of the Wall, but only if all the Member States consider such activity to amount to a 'material breach' of the Agreement.

It is clear, however, that historically the Community usually only downgrades development cooperation and assistance and the Union takes punitive measures through the adoption of Common Positions if there has either at some stage been an effective suspension of the

---

[318] Basic Guidelines of the Government of Israel, 7 March 2001, para. 2.9, available at www.mfa.gov.il

democratic process (as is the case in Zimbabwe), or there has not been one at all (as in the case of Uzbekistan) and widespread human rights violations occur. In practice, human rights violations have not been the primary reason for such reactions but if the reference to 'human rights' in Community 'essential elements' clauses is to have any significance then systematic violations of such obligations must also be seen as material breaches of the Agreement in the absence of democracy being suspended. The political reality, however, is that as this has not occurred to date despite the scale of the violations committed by Israel, only graver and more fundamental breaches of the relevant norms in the future will lead to such a course of action being seriously considered in relations with Israel.

In fact, until Israel complied with the demands of the Union in November 2003, it was always much more likely that the Association Agreement with Israel would be suspended over a dispute as to whether products from Israeli settlements in the Occupied Territories are entitled under the Association Agreement to preferential access to the Community market.[319] Former External Relations Commissioner, Chris Patten at a plenary session of the European Parliament in 2001, for example, made it very clear that the Israel-EU Agreement accord was likely to be suspended due to the dispute.[320] At the fourth meeting of the Association Council, held a week before the Israeli announcement, the Union continued to express regret that the dispute had not been resolved.[321]

Numerous allegations of trade impropriety by Israel exist in this respect. As disputes over agriculture were the most difficult in the negotiation of the 1995 Agreement, the Commission took the issue very seriously and, for example, called the twelfth meeting of the Community-Israel Cooperation Committee specifically to discuss the issue.[322] The Union's position over rules of origin is closely tied up to its overall approach to the MEPP. The Union cannot publicly declare that the settlements are illegal under international law and then accept goods produced in

---

[319] Rules of origin are set out in Articles 2–5 of Protocol 4 to the Agreement. On 25 November 2003, Ehud Olmert, who was then Trade and Industry Minister, announced that Israel would geographically label goods produced in settlements in the Occupied Territories.

[320] C. Patten, 'Statement on Situation in the Middle East', 16 May 2001, Speech 01/222.

[321] Declaration of the European Union, Fourth Meeting of the EU-Israel Association Council, 17–18 November 2003, Doc. 14796/03, para. 15.

[322] See [1998] OJ C304/106, 2 October 1998.

them, which help to finance the settlements, as being entitled to preferential access as a part of Israeli territory.[323] Exports to the Union from the settlements in 2003 were worth approximately €140 million per year.[324] Israeli exports to the Union, as noted above, are worth over €9 billion.

Before the House of Commons Select Committee, a Commission representative in 2003 had argued that suspending the Agreement with Israel may do more harm to the European Union than Israel due to the trade balance being 'very very heavily' in the Union's favour.[325] Despite this, suspension of the Agreement due to the dispute over goods produced in the settlements was a real possibility. It made sense for Israel to agree to pay customs duties on €140 million worth of exports rather than risk losing benefits on all of them. The damage to the economic interests of the Union would have been shared by the Member States. Israel alone would have suffered on the other side. As noted above, trade and economic relations with Israel are necessary for the Union if it wishes to maintain political relations with it and a role in the MEPP. Although the amounts involved are relatively minor and the issue not so fundamental (since Israel does not consider the payment of customs duties prejudicial to its sovereignty over the settlements) the resolution of this dispute does highlight that by taking a tough approach, the Union can compel Israel to compromise.

The difference in approach to events, on the one hand, in Jenin, Beit Hanoun or the building of the Wall and, on the other, Israeli exports from the settlements is not due to the priority given to trade over ethical values by the Union. If the 'essential elements' clause is relied upon, the Union may find that suspension of the Agreement has little effect upon Israel's behaviour; the Agreement and clause would in turn no longer serve any real purpose and the Union will have lost much of the influence it has. In the context of trade, countermeasures are not unusual. The suspension of an Agreement for human rights violations is far less common. Suspension of the Agreement over exports from the

---

[323] See M. Hirsch, 'Rules of Origin as Trade or Foreign Policy Instruments? The European Union Policy on Products Manufactured in the Settlements in the West Bank and Gaza Strip' (2003) 26 *Fordham ILJ* 572 and C. Hauswaldt, 'Problems under the EC-Israel Association Agreement: the Export of Goods Produced in the West Bank and Gaza Strip under the EC-Israel Association Agreement' (2003) 14 *EJIL* 591.

[324] Editorial, *Haaretz*, 26 November 2003.

[325] Development Committee, *Development Assistance and the Occupied Palestinian Territories 2004*, p. 65.

settlements, by contrast, would not cause as much collateral damage to EU-Israeli relations as the use of the 'essential elements' clause for human rights violations.

The failure to suspend the Agreement with Israel does not mean that the Union is not condemnatory of Israeli practices. There has, as noted above, traditionally been relatively little public criticism of Israel's discriminatory legislation or its legislation allowing administrative detention within Israel. Prior to 2000 there were relatively few public démarches on such issues. More recently, there has been a noticeable shift from this approach and the Union has become more vociferous in its public condemnation. The Swedish Presidency, for example, was publicly critical of Israel and its human rights record towards its Arab populations at the Fifty-seventh Session of the Commission on Human Rights.[326] The Union is also becoming increasingly stringent in trying to hold Israel to account for such policies and practices in bilateral discussions. The EU-Israel Human Rights Working Group, which held its first meeting on 7 June 2006, discussed the situation of minorities in Israel and the Union, for example, raised the issue of the Nationality and Entry into Israel Law which is highly discriminatory on the basis of race against Arab Israelis. A number of other human rights issues were also raised in the meeting and the 2006 *Annual Report on Human Rights* notes 'the meeting concluded on an understanding that both sides saw value in continuing this dialogue' – clearly a euphemism for the fact that both parties seemed to have very different opinions on the matters discussed.[327]

With regard to Israel's behaviour in the Occupied Territories, the situation is, as noted above, quite different and the Union has always been relatively vocal on such matters. For example, Israel has, as is well known, drawn up 'hit lists' of Palestinians to be assassinated. After one of the first such incidents, the European Union almost immediately issued a strong statement on extra-judicial killings by Israel of Palestinians and a démarche reflecting this concern was made to the Israeli Foreign Ministry. The Union described Israel's activities as unacceptable and contrary to the rule of law and international law.[328] Each subsequent assassination by Israel has been followed by condemnation by the Union. The assassination in 2004 of Sheikh Ahmed Yassin,

---

[326] Available at www.eu2001.se/eu2001/news/news_read.asp?iInformationID=13758
[327] European Council, *Annual Report on Human Rights, 2006*, p. 71.
[328] (2000) 1/2 *Bull. EU* 1.6.27.

the paraplegic spiritual leader of Hamas, for example, was strongly condemned by the Council.[329]

The Israeli practice of establishing and expanding settlements in the Occupied Territories has, as noted above, long been a policy that the Member States and later Union has strongly opposed.[330] In 1979, the Foreign Ministers of the then nine Member States issued a statement on the situation in the Middle East in which they stated that they 'deplore any action or declaration which might stand in the way of the quest for peace. They consider, in particular, that certain attitudes and declarations of the Israeli Government are such as to create obstacles in the search for a comprehensive settlement of this kind, notably ... [t]he policy of the establishment of settlements pursued by the Israeli Government in the occupied territories, which is illegal in international law.'[331] The statement of the Foreign Ministers repeatedly referred to Israel's legal responsibilities under the Fourth Geneva Convention of 1949, which Israel continues to violate. In the Venice Declaration of 1980 the Nine had stated that, '[t]hey are deeply convinced that the Israeli settlements constitute a serious obstacle to the peace process in the Middle East ... these settlements, as well as the modification in population and property in the occupied Arab territories, are illegal under international law'.[332] In 1980, the Security Council for the first time adopted a very strongly worded condemnation of Israel's settlement policy.[333]

---

[329] (2004) 3 *Bull. EU* 1.6.83.
[330] The EU Member States Consuls General in Jerusalem and Heads of Mission in Tel Aviv in addition to their *EU Human Rights Watch Reports* also compile *Settlements' Watch Reports*.
[331] Statement by the Council of Foreign Ministers of the European Economic Community, 18 June 1979, (1979) 6 *Bull. EC* 2.2.59. Israel issued a reaction to the statement the day after, in which it stated '[t]he Government of Israel totally rejects the Middle East statement of the Foreign Ministers of the European Community of June 18th and views it as injurious to the entire process of negotiations in the area and to the search for a comprehensive settlement'. The Israeli response is available at www.israel-mfa.gov.il/ The condemning of settlements became an established practice under European Political Cooperation. For an example of another strongly worded statement on Israeli settlement activity under EPC, see Joint Statement by the Twelve on Israeli Activities in the Occupied Territories (1988) 4 *Bull. EC* 2.4.3.
[332] Venice Declaration, para. 9.
[333] Security Resolution 465(1980), 1 March 1980. The Resolution which also refers to Israel's obligations under the Fourth Geneva Convention, 1949, 'deplored' the decision 'of the Government of Israel to officially support Israeli settlement in the Palestinian and other Arab territories occupied since 1967'. The Council had earlier adopted Security Council Resolution 446(1979), 22 March 1979 and Security Council Resolution

The Union has continued to issue démarches or strongly worded statements in response to settlement activity and the settler violence which accompanies it. Démarches have been issued on settler harassment and violence in, for example, 2002 and 2005.[334] The Union has been stringent in its criticism of Israeli settlement policy, as not only is it illegal under the Geneva Convention, it is also contrary to the Roadmap and makes the finding of a final solution much more difficult by 'creating facts on the ground'. The Council meeting in June 2004, for example, stated very clearly that a two-state solution was becoming increasingly difficult due to Israeli settlement activity.[335]

In the aftermath of the Israeli 'disengagement' from Gaza, Israel has moved some settlers from Gaza to the West Bank and as a consequence has had to build new or expand existing settlements to accommodate them. This practice has met with strong criticism from the Union. The Union, in 'accepting' the disengagement plan, had made it clear that the transferring of settlements to the West Bank was not acceptable to it.[336] In September 2006, for example, the Finnish Presidency issued a statement condemning the Israeli government's announcement that it was building new housing units in existing settlements in the West Bank. The Presidency statement demanded that Israel freeze all settlement activity, including the natural growth of settlements, as is stipulated in the Roadmap, because such practices threaten the two-state solution and 'like all settlement activity it is contrary to international law, in particular Article 49 of the Fourth Geneva Convention'.[337]

452(1979), 20 July 1979, but these had condemned Israel's failure to comply with a number of earlier resolutions and its failure to comply with the Commission to investigate settlements policy and had not specifically condemned settlement policy.

[334] A démarche on settler violence was issued on 14 March 2002 and was published on the Spanish Presidency's webpage. The UK Presidency on 19 December 2005 and 23 December 2005 issued a Troika démarche and Presidency démarche respectively on Israeli settlement policy. These were referred to in a speech on 1 February 2006 by Austrian Secretary of State Winkler to the European Parliament, available at www.ue2006.at/en/News/Speeches_Interviews/index.html

[335] European Council, 17–18 June 2004, Doc. 10679/2/04, Presidency Conclusions, p. 25.

[336] European Council, 24–25 March 2004, Doc. 9048/04, Presidency Conclusions, para. 55.

[337] Se the EU Presidency statement on Renewed Israeli Settlement Activity, 3 September 2006, Press Release 347/2006. See also, Presidency statement of 27 December 2006, Press Release 544/2006, where the Presidency expressed 'deep concern' at the news that the Israeli government authorised construction of the Maskiot settlement in the West Bank. Javier Solana has expressed 'shock' at the scale of Israeli settlement activity in the West Bank in recent years; see 'Solana Shocked at Growth of Israeli Settlements in West Bank', *Haaretz*, 22 January 2007.

The Union has recognised that the Wall and settlement activity in conjunction with collective punishments, the destruction of infrastructure and the policy of closure threaten 'to make any solution based on the co-existence of two states physically impossible'.[338] Notwithstanding the Union's condemnation of such policies and practices, however, its overall approach towards Israel has been to emphasise dialogue and discussion and to resort to condemnation as sparingly as possible. Israeli politicians tend to be far more concerned with their domestic constituency and the view of the United States than with other international pressure. They thus carry out the acts they so wish, such as the building of settlements, destruction of property and assassinations, with little regard to the views of others, including the Union.

5.2.3.2 Essential Elements Clause and Relations with the Palestinian Administered Territories

In terms of possible suspension, the Union has far more leverage in the case of the Palestinian Authority than it does with Israel. Paasivirta has noted, for example, that upon the ratification of the Agreement the President of the EU Council stressed 'Mr Arafat will do everything possible to promote human rights'.[339] The situation in the Palestinian Territories with regard to the rule of law and human rights has at times been appalling. One of the ironies of the approach adopted by the Union and Member States towards Israel, however, has been that they are equally unlikely to suspend this Agreement, even though it is far easier to do so institutionally, procedurally and politically. This is the case notwithstanding the Palestinian Authority's own practices and the activities of certain groups that are based in the territory which is nominally under its control, who engage in destructive activities in Israel itself or in the settlements in the Occupied Territories. It is also the case notwithstanding the coming into power of a Hamas-led government in 2006. At no point has the European Union seriously considered suspending the Interim Association Agreement, even though it ceased to provide direct assistance to the Hamas-led government of the Palestinian Authority, as will be discussed below.

Israeli practices in the Palestinian Territories have had a direct and detrimental effect on many projects and objectives identified by the

---

[338] European Council, *Annual Report on Human Rights, 2006*, p. 70.
[339] Europe No. 6922, 29 February 1997, p. 4 cited by Paasivirta, 'EU Trading with Israel and Palestine', 311, note 25.

Community for development funding.[340] The Community and EU Member States have poured millions of euros into the Palestinian Territories, in an effort to help develop an embryonic Palestinian state, only often to find these efforts thwarted by the Israelis. In the Palestinian Territories, the Community's development projects face considerable logistical problems. The lack of geographical continuity between Gaza and the West Bank compounds these problems. In Gaza, for example, forty years of occupation have led to problems such as inadequate health-care and basic sanitation facilities in some areas. Setbacks in the peace process and the policy of 'closure' which usually accompanies them directly affect the projects attempting to address such problems. If the Community and Member States suspend the Association Agreement with Israel, then they have less leverage in persuading the Israeli authorities in permitting or at least not hindering their work in the Palestinian Territories. Conversely, suspending the Agreement with the Palestinian Authority and all aid is likely to contribute to the total collapse of the Palestinian Authority, exacerbate the humanitarian crisis and in turn the failure of the MEPP. It is thus equally unlikely. This is despite the fact that the lack of a countervailing power, such as the United States, who can nullify the effects of suspension, has made the Palestinian Authority more pliable to the demands of the Union. Whereas it was argued above that the 'essential elements' clause is now of limited value in relations with Israel, the situation is different with regard to relations with the Palestinian Authority. In de facto terms, however, there is little value in the Association Agreement as far as trade between them is concerned. Israel's policies of closure, the levelling of agricultural land or its confiscation, the scorched earth policy in Gaza and the restrictions on water have ensured that little, if any, produce leaves the Palestinian Territories for export anywhere, let alone the EU Member States.

Notwithstanding the lack of trade between the Union and the Palestinian Territories, the Union enjoys tremendous political influence with those Palestinians led by Mahmoud Abbas, although the Union's influence over other groups, such as Hamas, if it exists at all, is far more limited. The Union's influence in relations with Abbas and in turn Fatah is directly related both to the scale of financial assistance it provides and the extent to which the Union attempts to mitigate, both practically and politically, the impact of Israeli policies which affect the Palestinian

---

[340] See Court of Auditors, *Special Report No. 19/2000, On the Management by the Commission of the Programme of Assistance to Palestinian Society*, p. 16 *et seq.*

Territories. The Union's ability to exert pressure upon and obtain results in its relations with the Palestinians is, however, limited by events on the ground, which have been dictated by the actions of Israel. Prior to 2005, the Union concentrated on administrative reform and building infrastructure throughout both the West Bank and Gaza. After the Israeli 'disengagement' from Gaza in 2005, the economic and social viability of that strip of land became a central focus for Union action. In 2006, once the Hamas-led government came to power, the Union's focus shifted to trying to limit the humanitarian emergency which was afflicting the Palestinians as the Union refused to have formal contact with Hamas and its representatives.

There are many examples of the Union exercising and using its influence so as to achieve the outcomes it seeks in its relations with the Palestinians. In June 2001, for example, when the situation between the Palestinians and Israelis was extremely dire, with reprisal killings endemic between the parties, rather than put huge amounts of pressure on the Israelis (although diplomacy was also at work there), it was Arafat who was targeted by the Union. The Union eventually managed to obtain Arafat's agreement to a truce. The methodology of 'threats' which has been seen as inappropriate for Israel was ideal for the Palestinians. It was reported that Arafat only agreed to a truce with Israel after a heated debate with Joschka Fischer and the threat to cut off all Union aid if he did not agree.[341] The extent of the Palestinian Authority's basic reliance upon Union aid could be seen from the fact that the European Union at this time bailed it out of a financial crisis, due to the implications of the Israeli policy of closure, and had to pay the salaries of those providing basic services. In return for this aid, the Palestinian Authority had to agree, which it did, to a strictly controlled austerity budget.[342]

The Community has also used simplified versions of 'essential elements' clauses in some of the specific legislation it is implementing to deal with various issues in the Palestinian Territories. As noted above, one of the major and persistent problems in relations between Israel and the Palestinian Authority has been that of acts of terrorism by Palestinian groups such as Hamas, the Al-Aqsa Martyrs Brigade and

---

[341] 'German Threat Forces Arafat to Declare Truce', *The Times*, 4 June 2001.
[342] 'Europe Throws £37m Lifeline to Palestinians', *Guardian*, 1 June 2001. See further the discussion in N. Brown, *The Palestinian Reform Agenda*, Peaceworks Paper 48 (Washington DC: United States Institute of Peace, 2002).

Islamic Jihad against Israelis.[343] The pressure on the Palestinian Authority to clamp down upon such activists has been one of the major factors contributing to unfair trials, arbitrary detention and torture in the Palestinian Administered Territories.[344] The Union has assisted in the implementation and funding of projects specifically designed to help the Palestinian Authority in countering the activities of such groups as well as its own excesses. The Joint Action, which acts as the legal base for funding such activity, specifically states that the European Union will suspend the programme if the Palestinian Authority either refuses to cooperate *fully* with the Union; fails to allow the Union to monitor and carry out evaluations of the project; or fails to take appropriate measures to ensure respect for human rights in the implementation of the programme.[345]

The Joint Action itself is based upon Articles 14 and 18(2) TEU and was adopted to help further the Union's role in the MEPP and especially to make an important contribution to the 'objectives pursued by the European Union in supporting the Palestinian Authority in its efforts to counter terrorist activity'.[346] The basic approach is that the Union will only contribute money (the Joint Action has a budget of €10 million) if it is satisfied that the programme implemented is effective according to a committee established by the Union and, furthermore, that it respects human rights. Evaluation committees where Community funds are allocated may be part of the parcel but what is unclear is who will assess the compatibility of human rights standards with the programme, and

---

[343] As noted above, these groups are classified as being engaged in terrorist activity by the Union and thus subject to punitive measures.

[344] The Palestinian Authority when it was run by Fatah argued that it had little control over these groups, especially Hamas. The Israelis regularly contended, however, that all such groups were directly accountable to Arafat (when he was alive) even though it is clear that Hamas and Fatah have long been involved in a struggle for power. Fatah certainly did and does have some control over groups such as the Al-Aqsa Martyrs Brigade. See further the discussion below.

[345] Article 7 of Joint Action 2000/298/CSFP on a European Union Assistance Programme to Support the Palestinian Authority in its Efforts to Counter Terrorist Activities Emanating from the Territories under its Control, [2000] OJ L97/4, 19 April 2000. Article 1 establishes that the programme should be extended for three years (from 2003) but has not at the time of writing been repealed or directly replaced by another such programme. The 2000 Joint Action replaced a 1997 Joint Action which had similar objectives, see Joint Action 97/289/CFSP on the Establishment of a European Union Assistance Programme to Support the Palestinian Authority in its Efforts to Counter Terrorist Activities Emanating from the Territories under its Control, [1997] OJ L120/2, 12 May 1997.

[346] Article 3 of Joint Action 2000/298/CSFP.

further, by what standards? Human rights conditionality in such circumstances is not unreasonable but clearly guidelines and the human
rights standards involved need to be established. None are articulated or
provided in the Joint Actions.

In essence, programmes have to be entirely planned and designed in
consultation with the Community and subject to its scrutiny, otherwise
they are not to be funded. The problem for the Palestinians, however,
has been that where they have designed counter-terrorism projects, the
allocation of funds from the Community has sometimes been from
different budget heads depending on the exact project in question,
each having its own procedures and financing decisions. This has at
times caused inordinate delay in some projects which have had to be
cancelled as they were no longer of relevance, and led to additional
complications in the working of the programmes.[347] Furthermore,
the destruction of Palestinian infrastructure by the Israelis has often
destroyed the very apparatus which is essential for such projects to be
effective.[348] This in turn alleviates some pressure on the Palestinians
as they can justifiably highlight that such institutions need to be re-
established rather than simply reformed. The vast majority of the
Union's involvement with the Palestinians, however, has not been
centred on the 'essential elements' clause but has been through programmes which aim to improve the situation in the Palestinian
Territories. It is to such projects in both Israel and the Palestinian
Territories that the discussion now turns.

5.2.4 Promotion of Ethical Values

5.2.4.1 Positive Measures and Israel

Civil society in Israel, unlike in its Arab neighbours, is well developed.
The majority of funding made available under the EIDHR, the MEDA
Regulations, the MEDA Democracy Programme (MDP) and European
Neighbourhood Policy has, therefore, been to those NGOs addressing issues which the Community has identified as its priorities. A
substantial percentage of the projects funded by Community budget
lines attempt to address discrimination against Arab-Israelis. As noted
above, although the Union does not very often publicly condemn Israel
for anti-Arab discrimination, it is well aware of the problem and tries to

---

[347] See Court of Auditors, *Special Report No. 19/2000*, para. 76.
[348] This is recognised by the Union. See the statement, noted above, made in the Security
Council further to the Israeli incursion into Jenin, 3 May 2002.

tackle it through promoting understanding between the various communities in Israel.[349] As the Member States have a legal interest in such discrimination, the approach adopted is an interesting one.

The Union is aware that in the overall context of the MEPP, routine public condemnation of discriminatory treatment in Israel will achieve little. Promoting understanding between the communities may contribute something. For this reason, among others, priority has been given to projects which are directed towards confidence building and dealing generally with Palestinian-Israeli issues on all levels and attempting to improve relations between the different groups, as well as the different Jewish communities in Israel.[350] In December 2005, for example, a 'Transformation in Israel' project was started. The project aims to combat racism and transform intercommunal relations between the Jewish majority, the Arab minority and ethnic groups, including the Russians and Ethiopians. The project also aims to reform Jewish communities in Israel, by improving intercommunal understanding, respect for the rights of all minorities, and the eventual prevention of inter-group conflict and violence. The project aims to achieve this by, *inter alia*, monitoring hate crimes, providing legal advice to groups and individuals, launching media campaigns and monitoring the implementation of international agreements to which Israel is a party. The project has been awarded approximately €300,000 through the EIDHR.[351]

The Union is also aware that there is little in the overall context of the MEPP it can currently do to stop some of the human rights abuses committed against the Palestinians by the Israelis. For that reason, the Community funds a number of projects which provide legal aid to Palestinian/Arab victims of Israeli human rights abuses.[352] The funding of such projects by the Community again illustrates the reality of the situation; such matters can at best only be partially addressed by providing funding to appropriately designed projects.

It is also noteworthy that no project has to date been funded which targets the Israeli security forces, the main perpetrators of some of the violations of international law that the Union and Member States are opposed to. As the Union does not help pay for the security services in Israel, as it has in the case of the Palestinian Authority, it has no leverage

---

[349] Under Article XXII Oslo II, both parties agreed to seek to foster mutual understanding and tolerance between themselves.

[350] Two-thirds of all Community funding has at times been directed at such projects.

[351] European Council, *Annual Report on Human Rights, 2006*, p. 55.

[352] See Karkutli and Bützler, *Evaluation*, p. 144.

in this regard. In general, the amounts spent in Israel under the various programmes are comparatively small when compared to the funds committed by the EU Member States and from the EC budget to the Palestinian Territories. This funding has not only been in terms of infrastructure projects or those which promote ethical values, such as human rights, democracy and the rule of law, but also humanitarian aid.

5.2.4.2 Positive Measures and the Palestinian Authority

The Union has placed far greater emphasis on positive measures in its relationship with the Palestinian Authority than it has in relations with Israel. The reasons for this are obvious. The Palestinian Territories have, as a consequence of conflict and occupation, little infrastructure and thus institution building and their reform have been priorities. The Union has also been heavily involved in other regards. The discussion will initially look at the earlier interventions of the Union, in particular after the Oslo Accords. It will also look at the reform efforts that the Union has engaged in with regard to Palestinian institutions. The discussion will then examine the Union's response to the Israeli 'disengagement' from Gaza and the EU border mission at Rafah as an example of the Union's intervention. It will finally discuss the Union's response to the Hamas victory in the 2006 Palestinian Legislative Council Elections and the establishment of the Temporary International Mechanism as a response.

5.2.4.2(a) Positive Measures and Reforming the Palestinian Authority

The Oslo Accords of 1993 (Oslo I) are considered by the international community to have introduced a new phase in the relationship between the Palestinian and Israeli communities and prompted promises of huge amounts of assistance. The Community has historically provided assistance to Palestinian society through funding to the United Nations Relief and Works Agency (UNRWA). Through UNRWA the Community between 1971 and 1989 provided ECU388 million worth of aid to Palestinian society.[353] In the late 1980s and early 1990s, in response to the increasingly desperate situation in the Occupied Territories and the prospects for peace which were then on the horizon,[354] the Member

---

[353] Strasbourg European Council, 8–9 December 1989, Declaration on the Middle East, (1989) 12 *Bull. EC* 1.1.21.

[354] The Twelve repeatedly made clear that they would contribute to the search for peace. See e.g., Conclusions of the Madrid European Council, 26–27 June 1989, Declaration on the Middle East, (1989) 6 *Bull. EC* 1.1.23, where it is stated '[t]he Community and its

States decided to 'increase substantially their aid to inhabitants of these Territories'.[355] In the Strasbourg European Council of 1989 it was agreed that by 1992 aid would double to Palestinian society.[356] It was not until the October 1993 donors' conference in Washington where the Community pledged US$2.5 billion between 1994 and 1998 to the Palestinian Territories that its funding took on another dimension.[357] As a direct consequence of this, the Community adopted Regulation 1734/94.[358] A Commission document in 1997 estimated that Palestinians received €258 per head of a population as opposed to €23 for the ACP states and €11 for the other Mediterranean countries.[359] By 2006, the European Union had contributed over €6 billion in aid to the Palestinian Authority since 1994, making it by far the largest donor to Palestinian society.[360] The Community and Member States have continued to be the largest donors of aid even allowing for the suspension of direct aid to the Hamas-led government in 2006. The number of budget heads which have been used to fund the Community commitment, however, are difficult to pin down. In the past, Council Regulation 1734/94, the EC-UNRWA Conventions and the MEDA Regulations formed the legal bases for some expenditure. Three separate budget heads were used to fund the Palestinian commitment, B7–4200 which was concerned with the Israel-PLO Peace Agreement, UNRWA was funded through B7–4210 and B7–4100 which was also used to fund all other projects to Mediterranean non-member countries.[361] When assessing the legal bases for expenditure in 2000, the Court of Auditors identified a further twelve different budget headings for projects for the Palestinian Authority.[362] Some of these were concerned with the EIDHR as this was (and the

Member States have demonstrated their readiness to participate actively in the search for a negotiated solution to the conflict, and to cooperate fully in the economic and social development of the people of the region.'

[355] Strasbourg European Council, 8–9 December 1989.   [356] *Ibid.*

[357] Court of Auditors, *Special Report No. 19/2000*, para. 6.

[358] Council Regulation 1734/94, on Financial and Technical Cooperation with the Occupied Territories, [1994] OJ L182/4, 16 July 1994, as subsequently amended most recently by Council Regulation 669/2004, Amending Council Regulation 1734/94 on Financial and Technical Cooperation with the West Bank and the Gaza Strip, [2004] OJ L105/1, 14 April 2004.

[359] COM(1997)715.

[360] See COM(2005)458, p. 2 for confirmation of the amounts the European Union has annually granted in aid to the Palestinian Territories. Approximately half of the funding comes from the EC budget and the rest from bilateral EU Member State funding.

[361] Court of Auditors, *Special Report No. 19/2000*, para. 8 *et seq.*   [362] *Ibid.*

current version of the Regulation still is) a more specific budget line in terms of the objectives of some projects. The Community has also sent a significant amount of humanitarian aid to populations in the Palestinian Territories.

In a 1995 Communication, the Commission had already adopted an approach attempting to set out the future relationship between the Community and the West Bank and Gaza Strip and the economic assistance to be provided.[363] The European Parliament for its part adopted a report which called for 'support for an independent and democratic Palestine which is respectful of human rights and a free press'.[364] The Union's first major project and concrete measure outside of direct dialogue and negotiation concerning the MEPP, therefore, was the sending of monitors to elections to the Palestinian Legislative Council in 1996.

Article 5 of Joint Action 94/267/CFSP in support of the MEPP, based upon Article 13 TEU, provided for a European contribution to the preparation of the observing of elections, if requested, in the Occupied Territories.[365] The precise arrangements were subject to Council Decision 95/205/CFSP of June 1995,[366] which provided for ECU10 million to be charged to the general budget of the EC, and Council Decision 95/403/CFSP of September 1995,[367] which established a European Union Electoral Unit (EUEU) which was involved with the detailed aspects of the administrative and financial procedures for observing the elections. Council Decision 95/403/CFSP set out the objectives of the EUEU as well as its composition. The elections themselves took place on 20 January 1996.

Due to financial irregularities in complying with Community procedures, the observation was not as effective as had been hoped. There had additionally been a degree of uncertainty over the timing of the elections which had hindered the observations. There were also problems with logistic support, which had gone out to competitive tender. The preferred support was not put in place, therefore, due to cost restrictions. Some of expense of the observations was borne by Member States and some by budget line B8–103. The wrong budget heads were also used to fund some programmes, such as a seminar on the work of the

---

[363] COM(1995)505.
[364] See European Parliament Report, A4–0129/96, 24 May 1996.
[365] [1994] OJ L119/1, 7 May 1994. It was then Article J.3 TEU.
[366] [1995] OJ L130/1, 14 June 1995.   [367] [1995] OJ L238/4, 6 October 1995.

EUEU, due to the restrictions imposed by the Council and Parliament on the use of CFSP funds.[368]

The election itself was won by Yasser Arafat and candidates from his Fatah party, who won 60 per cent of the seats. The Presidency expressed its 'deep satisfaction' with the election and on the commitment to human rights in the areas under the control of the Palestinian Authority.[369] What is most surprising about the Union's involvement in the election is the assessment that an election in which the rules had been manipulated to provide for an Arafat victory was deemed satisfactory. The EUEU observed an election whose actual conduct was, according to most accounts, free of major malpractice. The mandate of the EUEU did not extend to assessing the design of the election. Yet Arafat had himself appointed a Commission which designed the election in such a manner that winning 30 per cent of the vote gained his party over 60 per cent of the seats. Conversely, those who won 60 per cent of the vote only gained twenty-three seats out of eighty-eight. A significant number of important parties, such as Hamas, mostly opposed to the Oslo Accords, boycotted the election as it gave them little or no chance of winning a seat. Despite this the Union, no doubt with an eye on the MEPP having a greater chance of success if Arafat had a semblance of democratic legitimacy and a strong mandate, wholeheartedly approved of the election.

Arafat and his Fatah movement, despite all his and their shortcomings, were (and in the case of Fatah still are) seen by the Union as being vastly preferable to groups such as Hamas and Islamic Jihad. At the Laeken European Council, for example, it was expressly demanded that Arafat dismantle Hamas and Islamic Jihad's terror networks as a part of the two-state solution.[370] Hamas's victory in the 2006 Palestinian Legislative Elections is, however, testament to the continuing support in the Palestinian Territories that it enjoys. Hamas has long been and continues to be able to challenge Fatah for both physical and political control of the Palestinian Territories. In 1996, however, as Arafat was perceived by the international community as the democratically legitimate leader of the Palestinians, he was in a position to negotiate with

---

[368] See Court of Auditors, *Special Report No. 4/1996, Concerning the Observation of the Palestinian Elections*, [1997] OJ C57/1, 24 February 1997.

[369] (1996) 1/2 *Bull. EU* 1.4.17.

[370] Declaration on the Situation in the Middle East, (2001) 12 *Bull. EU* 4.54.

and expect international donors to deliver on the promises they had made of assistance as inducements to ease the peace process along.

The Union, for its part, adopted a multiheaded approach to its activities in the Palestinian Territories. However, a lack of relevance and appropriateness, especially in the early years of Community funding, has been one of the recurring features of some of the projects identified and funded by the Community. In the first instance, projects under the MEDA Regulations, even though they went beyond the framework of traditional development assistance, could not extend to public authority tasks. In the Palestinian Administered Territories, institution building was and continues to be a key priority to ensure that basic tasks are being performed. The decision-making procedure for those projects which were identified by the Commission for funding, however, tended to be heavily layered and complex, so that decision-making was slow, cumbersome and at times unclear.[371] Furthermore, the Commission for much of the time had been in the almost unique position of having too many funds on its hands to be able to deal with. In conjunction with a cumbersome decision-making procedure this resulted in the Commission not being able to set up a proper and effective scheme to ensure that projects were identified and prepared and approved as a continuous process.[372]

Many project decisions were made under intense pressure to ensure that the funds allocated were actually being spent. This resulted in little consideration being given to the size of the project portfolio which could be effectively managed and the ability of the Palestinian Authority to absorb and use the help that was being given.[373] A specific example of Community projects being badly designed and of limited utility is the Palestinian Housing Council. This was a project specifically designed to provide low cost housing and indeed spun by the Commission as a contribution to housing rights. The units, however, became far too expensive due allegedly in part to the extensive use of Italian marble in the design (as a consequence of poor design as opposed to tied procurement) which contributed to the increases in price, taking them out of the reach of the low-income families they were meant to be helping.[374]

---

[371] It has also often been duplicitous and not very effective. See COM(1999)494, p. 2.
[372] Ibid. p. 47. See also, COM(1998)524.
[373] See Court of Auditors, *Special Report No. 19/2000*, para. 69 *et seq.*
[374] Ibid.

Other projects have been more successful, in that they have been designed and properly implemented, although it is difficult to determine the effect of many of them. Projects which raise awareness of human rights issues, promote harmonious relations with Israel and fund NGOs who provide legal assistance to those seeking to use the courts in an effort to gain compensation, must all contribute, however marginally, to ensuring that various ethical values are being promoted and respected.[375] Unlike in the case of Israel, the Community has funded human rights courses for Palestinian security forces to ensure they are knowledgeable about the permissible limits on the use of force.[376] In the case of Israel they are unlikely to be given permission to do so and, even if they are, the rules of engagement will not change. In the case of the Palestinian Authority, the Union is aware that such projects may make a difference due to the leverage it usually enjoys in the overall political relationship. The Community also continues to regularly commit funds to assist in the rehabilitation of torture victims, of both the Palestinian Authority and Israel.[377]

The Union has, as noted above, in its programmes in the Palestinian Territories consistently prioritised building up the capacity of and reforming Palestinian institutions. Chris Patten, for example, when he was External Relations Commissioner, made very clear in 2002 that the Union needed to act to create the conditions such that, as and when a peace settlement was reached, the Palestinian institutions were already in place to ensure that they could comply with their obligations. To that end, Patten stated the Union needed to help: create a constitutional government by shaping the institutions foreseen in the Basic Law and make them efficient and accountable; establish an independent judiciary and a harmonised national legal and regulatory framework more suitable to a free society and market; abolish state security courts; establish a pluralist society; and encourage financial openness and accountability.[378] The March 2005 London Meeting on Supporting the Palestinian Authority, at which the Quartet and World Bank among others were present, also identified a number of similar priorities. The European Commission, Norway, the World Bank and United States all

---

[375] The information on the projects is from Karkutli and Bützler, *Evaluation*.

[376] See e.g., (2000) 12 *Bull. EU* 1.2.11.

[377] See e.g., (2000) 10 *Bull. EU* 1.2.7 and European Council, *Annual Report on Human Rights, 2006*, p. 87.

[378] Statement by Chris Patten to the Foreign Affairs Committee of the European Parliament, Brussels, 19 June 2002, Speech/02/293.

undertook to follow up the commitments made by the Palestinian Authority and those made by the international community.[379] The 2005 Commission Communication on the Gaza 'disengagement' also makes clear that reform of the Palestinian Authority is imperative if the two-state solution is to be realised.[380] The 2005 Communication building upon the ENP Action Plan made very clear that establishing a functioning judiciary, the effective enforcement of legislation and strengthening the rule of law, strengthening institutions, and reinforcing administrative capacity were all priorities.[381]

The constant and long-standing emphasis on reforming the institutions of the Palestinian Authority indicates that although calls for such reform have been influential at the theoretical level, they have not always resulted in practical change. The Union, however, as noted above, has more influence and capacity in assisting reform of the Palestinian institutions than any other actor including the United States. The Union has never been shy to call for a greater emphasis on democracy and human rights, nor has it shied away from the implications of such calls. As discussed above, the Union did not ostracise Arafat and ask for him to be replaced in the manner that the United States did.

Brown has argued that one of the most remarkable differences between US and European reform agendas, however, has not been in their content but in the reaction they have provoked.[382] He gives the example of the calls for reform in 2002, such as those by Chris Patten noted above. Brown argues that US calls for reform were greeted cynically by all Palestinians, even by many reformers, who doubted not only the sincerity of the United States but were also worried that overly close association with the United States would damage their cause and sully their nationalist reputations. The European Union, he argues, by contrast, was able to issue far more direct calls for reform without provoking any criticism. He gives the example in May 2002 when the Community formally conditioned its continued assistance, which kept the Palestinian Authority afloat, on a detailed reform programme, including measures such as approval of the long-delayed law on the judiciary.[383]

---

[379] Documentation from the meeting is available at www.fco.gov.uk/servlet/Front?
pagename=OpenMarket/Xcelerate/ShowPage&c=Page&cid=1107298460718
[380] COM(2005)458.   [381] Ibid. p. 4.
[382] Brown, *The Palestinian Reform Agenda*, p. 44.   [383] Ibid.

Even well-designed projects which can potentially make an important contribution to reform and increase the efficiency of public administration in the Palestinian Territories are hostage to overall political developments in the Middle East. For example, in November 2005, a Council Joint Action was adopted which launched a European Security and Defence Policy (ESDP) initiative, the EU Police Mission for the Palestinian Territories (EUPOL COPPS).[384] As with the earlier ESDP police missions, the legal basis for the Joint Action is Articles 14 and 25 TEU.[385] EUPOL COPPS is designed to build upon the ongoing work of the EU Coordinating Office for Palestinian Police Support (known by the acronym EU COPPS) which had been established in April 2005 following an Exchange of Letters between the Palestinian Prime Minister (Ahmed Qurei' of Fatah at the time) and Marc Otte, the EU's Special Representative to the Middle East Peace Process.[386] There are approximately 19,000 members of the civilian police force in the Palestinian Territories.[387] As noted above, these forces have been responsible for routine acts of torture and other forms of ill-treatment, arbitrary arrests and, in part, the failure to stem lawlessness in the Palestinian Territories.

EUPOL COPPS, which has a mandate until the end of 2009, has approximately thirty police and civilian experts who provide support to the Palestinian Civil Police in identifying immediate operational priorities and also assist with designing the Palestinian Civil Police Development Programme (PCPDP). This is with a view to contributing to the long-term transformation and reform of the Palestinian Civil

---

[384] Joint Action 2005/797/CFSP, on the European Union Police Mission for the Palestinian Territories, [2005] OJ L300/65, 17 November 2005. The acronym EUPOL COPPS is shorthand for the European Union Coordinating Office for Palestinian Police Support, see Article 1 of Joint Action 2005/797/CFSP.

[385] The earlier EU police missions under the ESDP were in: Bosnia and Herzegovina (EUPM, Council Joint Action, 2002/201/CFSP, [2002] OJ L70/1, 13 March 2002, as subsequently amended); the former Yugoslav Republic of Macedonia (EUPOL PROXIMA, Council Joint Action 2003/681/CFSP, [2003] OJ L249/66, 1 October 2003, as subsequently amended); and in the Democratic Republic of Congo (EUPOL Kinshasa, Council Joint Action 2004/847/CFSP, [2004] OJ L367/30, 14 December 2004). For discussion of these missions see M. Merlingen and R. Ostrauskaite, 'ESDP Police Missions: Meaning, Context and Operational Challenges' (2005) 10 *EFARev*. 215. The Union has subsequently also established a police mission in Afghanistan, see Council Joint Action 2007/369/CFSP, [2007] OJ L139/33, 31 May 2007. The legal basis for this Joint Action is also Articles 14 and 25 TEU.

[386] Ahmed Qurei' is also known as Abu Ala.

[387] EU COPPS and Palestinian Civil Police Development Programme, Fact-sheet, available at www.consilium.europa.eu/uedocs/cmsUpload/EUCOPPShandoutFeb2006.pdf

Police.[388] The Union perceives the mission to be part of its contribution to the ongoing peace efforts in the region and expects that it will assist the Palestinians to comply with their Roadmap obligations, in particular, with regard to security and institution building.[389] One of the objectives of the investment was to wrest the security forces and their power away from the President so that democratic parliamentary control could be exercised over the civil police.[390]

Such projects are clearly needed and a well-designed reform programme for the Palestinian Civil Police could make a substantial difference in this regard. A group of British MPs, who met with representatives from EU COPPS, were told that US$50 million had to date been invested in buildings, equipment and vehicles to assist with policing in the Palestinian Territories. There are, however, two problems. First, the Palestinian Interior Ministry was under the control of Hamas after it won the Legislative Council election in January 2006. Until June 2007, when the Hamas-led government was dismissed by President Abbas, EU COPPS and EUPOL COPPS could not deal with the Palestinian police as they were under the authority of a Minister, Sa'id Siyam, who is a member of Hamas and the Union has no formal contact with that organisation.[391] The earlier strategy of trying to ensure that democratic parliamentary control could be exercised over the civil police and wrested away from the President seems to have been abandoned once Hamas was in power. Secondly, IDF incursions during the course of 2006 had 'completely destroyed' buildings and what equipment there was.[392] It should be borne in mind that Israel expects every act of Palestinian terror to be stopped before it considers the Palestinian Authority to be complying with its obligations under Phase I of the Roadmap. This is notwithstanding the fact that even when Israel has sent its troops into the Palestinian Territories, it cannot stop attacks on Israeli citizens and that Israel has on more than one occasion destroyed the very infrastructure that the Palestinians need to stop attacks on Israelis themselves.

If the mandate of EUPOL COPPS is extended and further financial commitments are made, then the project may still make an important contribution to police reform, but substantial investment will again be needed to pay for equipment and infrastructure before it can even start

---

[388] Article 3 of Joint Action 2005/797/CFSP.
[389] See the Preamble to Joint Action 2005/797/CFSP.
[390] Development Committee, *Development Assistance and the Occupied Palestinian Territories 2007*, Evidence, Question 307.
[391] *Ibid.*   [392] *Ibid.*

to try and help reform the Palestinian Civil Police. It is unlikely, however, that the initiative as it currently stands will assist the Palestinian Authority enough to allow it to comply with its Roadmap obligations, as interpreted by Israel, with regard to security and institution building.

There are other examples of well thought-out EU initiatives, the effect and impact of which has also been negated. An example of where the Union has designed and funded an important and potentially very valuable initiative, which the Israelis have initially agreed to and then subsequently undermined the effectiveness of is, the EU Border Mission at Rafah (EU BAM). This was designed in light of the Union's response to the 'disengagement' of Gaza and is discussed in that context.

5.2.4.2(b) Positive Measures and the Gaza 'Disengagement'

In withdrawing from Gaza, Israel acted in a unilateral manner and although it was presented as a move towards peace by Sharon and his government, it is clear that this was not the primary motive.[393] A senior advisor to Sharon, Dov Weisglass, stated unequivocally that, 'the significance of the plan is the freezing of the peace process'.[394] This view of the 'disengagement' is very different from that of the Union. The European Council meeting in March 2004, for example, made very clear that, 'such a withdrawal could represent a significant step towards the implementation of the Road Map'.[395] This is certainly true, as Phase III of the Roadmap (Permanent Status Agreement and End of the Israeli-Palestinian Conflict) envisages Israel dismantling some settlements. The Roadmap has, however, never yet moved beyond Phase I (Ending Terror and Violence, Normalising Palestinian Life and Building Palestinian Institutions). The Council nevertheless felt that 'disengagement' was a step towards peace and a two-state solution, provided it took place in the context of the Roadmap; so long as it did not involve a transfer of settlement activity to the West Bank; that there was an organised and negotiated handover of responsibility to the Palestinian Authority; and that Israel facilitated the rehabilitation and reconstruction of Gaza.[396]

---

[393] The Union has described the disengagement as 'unilateral' on a number of occasions. See e.g., the Preamble to Council Joint Action 2005/889/CFSP on Establishing a European Union Border Assistance Mission for the Rafah Crossing Point (EU BAM Rafah), [2005] OJ L327/28, 14 December 2005.
[394] 'Top PM Aide: Gaza Plan Aims to Freeze the Peace Process', *Haaretz*, 6 October 2004.
[395] European Council, 24–25 March 2004, Doc. 9048/04, Presidency Conclusions, para. 55.
[396] *Ibid.*

Sharon was in no way (re)acting in response to the 'conditions' being set by the Union. The 'disengagement' was a unilateral action designed to serve Israeli economic, security and political interests and not about implementing the Roadmap. Notwithstanding the fact that this was clear, it did present an opportunity for some progress, no matter how limited, in Palestinian-Israeli affairs.[397] Javier Solana was heavily involved in shuttle diplomacy with the Israelis in trying to ensure that the process as a whole would allow something tangible to be achieved once Israel had withdrawn from Gaza. The EU Special Envoy to the Middle East Peace Process, Marc Otte, was working with the detail of what the Union could actually do on the ground. The fact that the Israelis were dictating the agenda was clear when Solana stated in a meeting in Israel that, 'the EU wants to be part of the solution, not part of the problem, and will work to make this a reality'.[398] Trying to ensure that something positive could be achieved was not an easy undertaking for the Union.

The Union continually stressed the need to ensure the social and economic viability of Gaza following the 'disengagement'. A Commission Communication adopted to that end and the ENP Action Plan for the Palestinian Authority made this priority clear.[399] The Quartet appointed James Wolfensohn, the former World Bank President, to serve as its Special Envoy for the Gaza Disengagement. The Commission seconded staff to his team and also made available €60 million for projects which needed immediate financial support.[400]

The 2005 Communication on 'disengagement' also stressed that Gaza and the West Bank need to be economically viable if a Palestinian state is to exist and recommended measures to be taken to that end.[401] One of the most pressing needs in this regard was and still is for goods and persons to be able to enter and leave the Gaza Strip. Not only does this facilitate economic development but it also allows humanitarian assistance to be delivered to populations in need. Due to Israel's complete control over exit and entry to Gaza, Israel's withdrawal from that territory meant that the international crossing point between Egypt and Gaza at Rafah was (apart from in exceptional circumstances) closed.

---

[397] Although the Union did seem to overplay this. See e.g., COM(2005)458, p. 2.
[398] See 'FM Shalom Meets with EU High Representative Solana', 28 August 2005, available at www.mfa.gov.il
[399] COM(2005)458.   [400] *Ibid.*   [401] *Ibid.* p. 8.

To that end an Agreement on Movement and Access and Agreed Principles for Rafah Crossing were agreed upon with the US Secretary of State Condoleezza Rice, Javier Solana and James Wolfensohn facilitating the negotiations between the Israelis and Palestinians.[402] In the Agreed Principles for Rafah Crossing, a 'third party', which is identified as being the European Union, has the authority to ensure that the Palestinian Authority complies with 'all applicable rules and regulations' concerning the Agreement. Under the Agreed Principles, the Union is also to 'assist the PA to build capacity-training, equipment and technical assistance on border management and customs'.[403] The Israelis wanted to ensure that the Palestinians complied with their obligations and, in particular, that the Rafah crossing was not used to traffic weapons. The presence of a third party assuaged some of their concerns and also ensured that aid deliveries could reach the Palestinians. Marc Otte was heavily involved in determining the Union's role as that 'third party'.

In the framework of an ESDP mission, the Council adopted a Joint Action and the Union established the EU Border Assistance Mission (EU BAM) at Rafah.[404] The mission started operating and the border was opened on 25 November 2005 as the Agreement on Movement and Access identifies. The Joint Action utilises, as is to be expected, Articles 14 and 25 TEU as legal bases. As with the EU police missions in the Palestinian Territories, EU BAM is also seen as fulfilling one of the objectives of the Union's Common Foreign and Security Policy, articulated in Article 11 TEU, by helping to preserve peace and strengthen international security. EU BAM's role, as agreed with the Palestinians and Israelis, is to monitor, verify and evaluate the Palestinians' compliance with the Agreements between the parties.[405] Approximately €7.6 million was allocated to the mission between November 2005

---

[402] Agreement on Movement and Access, 15 November 2005 and Agreed Principles for Rafah Crossing, 15 November 2005. It is important to note that these agreements explicitly state that the Paris Protocol, under which customs duties are to be paid by the Israelis to the Palestinian Authority, continues to apply.

[403] *Ibid.* The Union was formally invited by letter by the Palestinians and Israelis, respectively, to establish the mission, once the various agreements had been concluded.

[404] Council Joint Action 2005/889/CFSP, Establishing a European Union Border Assistance Mission for the Rafah Crossing Point (EU BAM Rafah), [2005] OJ L327/28, 14 December 2005. The mandate of the mission has been extended and amended most recently by Joint Action 2007/359/CFSP, [2007] OJ L133/51, 25 May 2007.

[405] Article 2 of Joint Action 2005/889/CFSP.

(when it was set up) and May 2007 (when the mandate was initially due to end) and 80 or so police officers and 100 monitors seconded from the Member States have worked with it.[406]

To begin with, the mission worked relatively well and over one-quarter of a million individuals were processed in the six months the border operated more or less as it should have. Operations Summer Rains and Autumn Clouds in 2006, however, meant that Israel unilaterally closed the border crossing at Rafah. This was despite the fact that no evidence of any impropriety at Rafah during this period has become apparent and the functioning of the border was not in any way directly connected to the kidnapping of Corporal Gilad Shalit or the firing of Qassem rockets into Israel from the Gaza Strip.

In the ten months between 25 June 2006 and the end of April 2007, for example, the border crossing was open for sixty-four days. Even some of this limited time was due in part to Javier Solana trying to broker the opening of the border crossing so as to allow Muslim pilgrims to leave Gaza to perform *Hajj* and for humanitarian reasons.[407] The Union also tried to negotiate another mandate for a mission similar to that at Rafah for the border crossing point between Gaza and Israel at Karni. Once hostilities had again escalated between the Palestinians and Israelis, this was never a serious proposition.[408]

The closing of the border at Rafah for most of the time it should have been operational is another clear example of Israel collectively punishing an entire population for the abhorrent misdeeds of a few and doing so in contravention of the Fourth Geneva Convention. The Union was unable to convince the Israelis to allow the normal operation of the border crossing and, as a Hamas-led government was in power, the chances of the border being reopened while it remained in power were non-existent. The dismissal of the Hamas-led government in June 2007 has not changed this as Hamas is still, at the time of writing, in control of Gaza. Israel did, however, in May 2007 ask the Union to

---

[406] The mandate has been extended until May 2008 by Article 1 of Joint Action 2007/359/CFSP. The financial envelope for the period May 2007–May 2008 is €7 million.

[407] Solana on a visit to Ramallah in August 2006, for example, tried to broker the opening of the Rafah border crossing. See Summary of Remarks to the Press by Javier Solana, EU High Representative for the CFSP, 13 August 2006, Doc. S228/06. Alvaro De Soto has stated that EU BAM has only been open for 14 per cent of the time stipulated in the November 2005 Agreements. See De Soto, *End of Mission Report*, p. 9.

[408] See Summary of the Address by Javier Solana to the European Parliament Foreign Affairs Committee, Brussels, Doc. S278/06, 4 October 2006.

extend the mandate of the mission for twelve months.[409] This is clearly with a view to the mission being able to operate if Israel deems appropriate at some point during its extended mandate.

As is obvious from the preceding discussion, the Union's fundamental problem in helping in the reform of Palestinian institutions or promoting and protecting ethical values in the Palestinian Territories is that events on the ground move so quickly. This is especially the case after the outbreak of the Al-Aqsa Intifada in September 2000: Arafat died, Israel 'disengaged' from Gaza, Sharon left the political scene, an Israeli general election took place, Hamas won elections in the Palestinian Territories, and a major Israeli incursion in Gaza and south Lebanon in the summer of 2006 all occurred in the space of eighteen months. Each of these events on their own, let alone when considered together, is of tremendous importance. It is difficult to overestimate the seismic impact some of them have had on the ground. As a consequence, the Union's efforts have largely been engaged in damage limitation exercises by trying to prevent the humanitarian and political situation deteriorating further, as opposed to improving it *per se*. The Union has also responded to events, such as the Israeli dismantling of settlements in Gaza, by trying to make the most of any opportunities that arise with a view to the peace process progressing. The Union has continually stressed the virtues of democracy, human rights and the rule of law in its relations with the Palestinian Authority. As discussed above, the Union did not ostracise Arafat despite tremendous pressure from the United States and Israel to do so, because he was the democratically elected Palestinian leader. In the context of the ongoing 'war on terror', however, a Hamas election victory in the Palestinian Legislative Council Elections in January 2006 presented new dilemmas for the Union. It is to this election and its consequences that the discussion now turns.

5.2.4.2(c) 2006 Palestinian Elections and the Temporary International Mechanism

The election laws which had led to an Arafat victory in the 1996 elections had, as discussed above, been designed with a view to ensuring a Fatah victory. The Palestinian Legislative Council Elections of 2006 were held under a new Election Law whereby half of the Palestinian Legislative Council (PLC) seats were apportioned from a proportional representation contest and the other half through majoritarian races.

---

[409] Preamble, para. 3 to Joint Action 2007/359/CFSP.

The Election Law had actually been amended in the light of the recommendations contained in a report issued by the EU Election Observation Mission (EU EOM) in the aftermath of the 2005 Presidential Elections.[410] The 2006 elections were the first to be held for the PLC since 1996. Furthermore, whereas numerous groups had boycotted the 1996 PLC elections, representatives from the full spectrum of Palestinian perspectives planned to participate in the 2006 elections. Hamas, which had boycotted both the 1996 PLC elections and the 2005 Presidential elections, was to participate for the first time. All in all, if the 2006 PLC elections were conducted fairly, they would be the first genuinely democratic elections to the Legislative Council. This would lead to that body acquiring much needed democratic legitimacy and credibility, both amongst Palestinians and in relations with Israel and the international community as a whole.

Some members of the international community had since mid-2005 been discussing the possible consequences if Hamas, who were expected to do well, were able to form a government on the basis of the outcome of the election. In the Quartet meeting in September 2005 there was a great deal of debate as to whether the Quartet should say anything publicly about the consequences or the implications of a Hamas victory. The view that prevailed was that it would be inappropriate to attempt to influence the democratic choices of the Palestinians. A member of the British delegation at the meeting (which was held during the UK Presidency) has stated that nothing was said, 'precisely because we thought it could easily be counter-productive and inappropriate for the international community to be attempting, as it were, to influence the outcome of these elections'.[411] The Quartet Statement issued on 20 September 2005, therefore, only made a short reference to the then forthcoming PLC elections, stating '[t]he Quartet calls for an end to all violence and terror ... the PA leadership has condemned violence and has sought to encourage Palestinian groups who have engaged in terrorism to abandon this course and engage in the democratic process ... The Quartet also welcomes the announcement of Palestinian Legislative Council elections and upcoming municipal elections.'

---

[410] European Union Election Observation Mission, West Bank and Gaza 2005, *Final Report on the Presidential Elections, 9 January 2005*.

[411] Development Committee, *Development Assistance and the Occupied Palestinian Territories 2007*, Evidence, Question 2.

In December 2005, however, when it was clearer that a Hamas victory was a very real possibility, the Quartet changed its approach. The earlier view that it was inappropriate for the international community to attempt to influence the outcome of the elections was abandoned and a clear warning shot was sent to the Palestinian electorate and Hamas. The Quartet Statement of 28 December 2005, a month prior to the elections, stated 'those who want to be part of the political process should not engage in armed group or militia activities, for there is a fundamental contradiction between such activities and the building of a democratic state. In this regard, the Quartet calls on all participants to renounce violence, recognise Israel's right to exist, and disarm.' More problematically, the Quartet also put pressure on the Palestinian Authority prior to the election being held to:

take additional steps to ensure the democratic process remains untainted by violence, by prohibiting political parties from pursuing their aims through violent means, and by moving expeditiously to codify this as Palestinian law ... In particular, the Quartet expressed its view that a future Palestinian Authority Cabinet should include *no* member who has not committed to the principles of Israel's right to exist in peace and security and an unequivocal end to violence and terrorism.[412]

This part of the statement implied that the Quartet wanted President Abbas to take steps to prohibit Hamas from participating in the forthcoming elections and also made clear that the Quartet members would not accept a Hamas-led government, a Unity government or even a Fatah-led government if it contained *a single* member of Hamas.[413] By December 2005, the Quartet had no compunction in making clear what they thought the composition of any government after the Palestinian elections should be. In early January 2006, Solana made it publicly known that if there was a Hamas election victory, one of the consequences that may follow would be the Union cutting funding to the Palestinians.[414] The Union was thus making its position clearer prior

---

[412] Quartet statement, 28 December 2005. Emphasis added.

[413] The Union has on other occasions also issued statements prior to democratic elections being held in an effort to influence the outcome. One of the starkest examples was a week prior to the Serbian elections of September 2000, where the Union stated that if Milosevic was defeated the Union would, *inter alia*, lift sanctions against Serbia, provide economic aid and support the reintegration of Serbia into the international community. See Message to the Serbian People, 19 September 2000, Doc. 11422/00.

[414] See 'EU Election Monitors Face Risks in Palestine', *euobserver.com*, 3 January 2006.

ETHICAL DIMENSIONS OF THE FOREIGN POLICY

to the election: if there was a Hamas election victory there would be negative consequences for the Palestinians.

As far as the 2006 PLC elections themselves were concerned, the Union sent 240 election observers, one of its largest ever monitoring missions, and spent over €18 million on supporting the electoral process. The Union's level of engagement reflected the importance of these elections in the context of the Middle East Peace Process. The Roadmap states that elections for democratic Palestinian institutions are fundamental to the peace process and the Quartet, in one of its statements prior to the elections, had noted that it 'welcomes the upcoming Palestinian Legislative Council elections as a positive step toward consolidation of Palestinian democracy and the goal of a two-state solution to the Israeli-Palestinian conflict'.[415] The EU EOM, which was headed by Véronique De Keyser MEP, was deployed between 13 December 2005 and 13 February 2006 to observe the preparation for the elections and the process. The assessment of the EU EOM was that the new Election Law, despite some shortcomings, provided an effective basis for the conduct of democratic elections.[416] With regard to the conduct of the elections and the results, the EU EOM noted:

elections to the Palestinian Legislative Council (PLC) reflected an open and fairly-contested electoral process that was efficiently administered ... Overall, the elections saw impressive voter participation, demonstrating ... an overwhelming commitment by the Palestinian people to determine their political future via democratic means ... Overall, the legal framework for elections provided an effective basis for the conduct of democratic elections ... The CEC (Central Elections Commission) oversaw the election in a proper and impartial manner ... The CEC commanded a high degree of public confidence in its professionalism and independence. It maintained integrity in the face of intimidation ... Candidates from across the whole political spectrum participated in the elections through an inclusive and open candidate registration process ... These elections were held under an occupation by Israeli military forces that, by its nature, reduced the scope for genuinely free elections. Severe restrictions by Israeli forces on the freedom of movement by candidates and voters were widespread across the West Bank.[417]

The US-based National Democratic Institute, in conjunction with the Carter Center, which had also sent a team of observers, was similarly

---

[415] Phase I of the Roadmap; Quartet statement, 28 December 2005.
[416] European Union Election Observation Mission, West Bank and Gaza 2006, *Final Report on the Palestinian Legislative Council Elections, 25 January 2006*, p. 8.
[417] *Ibid.* p. 1 *et seq.*

positive in its assessment of the election process.[418] An EU Presidency statement issued the day after the elections perceived them positively in terms of democratic expression.[419] The Presidency statement considered the PLC elections to be open and fairly contested and an important step in strengthening Palestinian democracy and in implementing the Roadmap. The statement also expressed the view that there was no place in the political process for groups or individuals who advocate violence.[420]

The External Relations Council which met at the end of January 2006 essentially reiterated the Presidency statement but added that the 'Council underlined that violence and terror are incompatible with democratic processes and urged Hamas and all other factions to renounce violence, to recognise Israel's right to exist, and to disarm'.[421] The Council further stated that it 'expects the newly elected PLC to support the formation of a government committed to a peaceful and negotiated solution of the conflict with Israel based on existing agreements and the Roadmap as well as to the rule of law, reform and sound fiscal management'.[422] There was no express mention in the Council Conclusions of the Union stopping or reconsidering its financial assistance to the Palestinian Authority. That was made abundantly clear in the Quartet statement issued on 30 January 2006. The Quartet expressly stated that all donors would review future assistance to the new government against its commitment to the 'principles of non violence, recognition of Israel, and acceptance of previous agreements and obligations, including the Roadmap'.[423] The Quartet statement, which was

---

[418] See Carter Center, Preliminary Statement of the NDI/Carter Center International Observer Delegation to the Palestinian Legislative Council Elections, 26 January 2006, available at www.cartercenter.org/news/documents/doc2283.html. For President Carter's account of the election and some of the problems faced, see Carter, *Palestine: Peace not Apartheid*, p. 177 *et seq.*

[419] Presidency statement on the Palestinian Legislative Council Elections, 26 January 2006, Doc. 5738/06.

[420] *Ibid.*   [421] External Relations Council, 30–31 January 2006, Doc. 5565/06, p. 16.

[422] *Ibid.*

[423] Quartet statement, 30 January 2006. De Soto has stated that the Quartet did not set the conditions. They were, he argues, set by the Union and United States and that the Quartet 'provides a shield for what the US and EU do'. De Soto, *End of Mission Report*, para. 79. De Soto's position is somewhat contradicted, however, by both the wording of the statement ('[i]t is the view of the Quartet that all members of a future Palestinian government must be committed to') and the statement by Kofi Annan in the press conference after the Quartet meeting in which he used the exact language of the Quartet statement. There is no doubt, however, with regard to the Union's position which was made clear in the Council Conclusions of 30–31 January 2006.

worded in stronger terms than the European Council conclusions, also stipulated more or less identical conditions on the newly elected PLC with regard to commitments to a peaceful and negotiated solution to the conflict and relations with Israel.

The Quartet statements of December 2005 and January 2006 made its approach abundantly clear. Any new Palestinian government could not contain any members who had not denounced violence, who refused to recognise Israel and who would not agree to respect the previous Agreements with Israel. The Quartet's stipulations on the composition of the government essentially meant that Hamas had to renounce part of its political platform, if it was to be able to form a government that the Quartet considered acceptable. If this did not happen and any of its members wished to join the new government, they would have to expressly renounce violence and basically also leave Hamas. The Quartet members would consider a government which contained *any* Hamas members to be unacceptable.[424] If such a government was formed, the Quartet was leaving little doubt that direct assistance to the Palestinian Authority would stop.

At the time of the elections, total direct aid to the Palestinian Authority's budget from international donors, primarily the EC budget and the EU Member States, amounted to approximately US$20 million per month.[425] In the immediate aftermath of the election Israel, as noted above, stopped transferring all customs duties to the Palestinians; this amounted to between US$50 and US$60 million per month. The Palestinian Authority's expenditure needs at the time were estimated to be approximately US$165 million per month.[426] As the Palestinian Authority was already in the midst of a severe budgetary crisis, the options for those trying to form a new government were stark.[427]

---

[424] See e.g., Quartet statement, 28 December 2005, discussed above.

[425] Department for International Development, *Memorandum Submitted by the Department for International Development to the House of Commons International Development Select Committee*; Development Committee, *Development Assistance and the Occupied Palestinian Territories 2007*, pp. 73, 79.

[426] *Ibid.*

[427] At the end of February 2006, a letter from James Wolfensohn, the Quartet's Special Envoy to the Quartet Principals, was leaked to the Reuters News Agency. In the letter Wolfensohn argued that the dire financial crisis of the Palestinian Authority meant that it was unable to pay salaries to civil servants and security forces alike and that this would have grave consequences. He further argued that as a consequence of the Israeli decision to withhold tax transfers, the Palestinian Authority faced collapse within two weeks. Immediately after the election, while negotiations on the composition of a

Attempts, however, were still made to form a Unity government involving Hamas, Fatah and independent politicians during February and March 2006. De Soto has stated that the United States intimated to Abbas that they did not wish to see any blurring of the lines between Hamas and other Palestinians and this was part of the reason why Abbas and Fatah were not prepared to be part of a Unity government.[428] If a Unity government had been formed in early 2006, and if the Quartet had been prepared to deal with it, this would have not only respected the outcome of the election but it would also have meant that the peace process, no matter how feeble, would not have been completely frozen.[429] By stipulating to President Abbas that Fatah should not form a Unity government involving members from Hamas, the United States, and by extension the Union in the Quartet, were basically forcing Hamas to govern alone but the Quartet members knew full well that due to the budgetary crisis Hamas would not be able to do so. The approach essentially adopted was that as Hamas had won, it must denounce violence; if it did not, it had to govern so that it could be isolated and forced to fail.

Somewhat unsurprisingly, therefore, a Hamas-led government with Ismail Haniya as Prime Minister and no Fatah members was formed on 29 March 2006, just over two months after the election. A Quartet statement issued the day after again stated that the government was expected to comply with the three conditions that had been stipulated.[430] The Quartet statement of 30 March 2006 also reiterated that all donor assistance would be measured against the Hamas-led government's commitment to the three conditions that had been stipulated.

new government were ongoing, an interim technocratic government was established in the Palestinian Territories. Wolfensohn thus approached a number of Arab governments to try and make up the budgetary shortfall. See 'Palestinians on Financial Brink Warns Envoy', *Washington Post*, 28 February 2006. Wolfensohn's letter is available at www.washingtonpost.com/wp-dyn/content/article/2006/02/28/AR2006022800278.html

[428] De Soto, *End of Mission Report*, para. 55.

[429] A Unity government was eventually formed after the Mecca Agreement in March 2007, with independent politicians as well as Hamas and Fatah members. The Presidency adopted a declaration once the Unity government had been formed, and welcomed its creation, but continued to insist that the new government accepted all the principles established by the Quartet: Declaration by the Presidency of the EU on the Formation of a Palestinian Government of National Unity, 17 March 2007. The Quartet issued a statement four days later to the same effect, see Quartet statement, 21 March 2007 and further the discussion below.

[430] Quartet statement, 30 March 2006.

Having won an election in part on the basis of its long-standing opposition to the existence of Israel and the armed struggle against it, Hamas was clearly not going to immediately comply with the conditions set out by the Quartet. Hamas was, however, observing a ceasefire (the *hudna*) and had done so since August 2004 and, by and large, it had not been violated. Although Hamas had not renounced violence, in practice a ceasefire was being observed. Hamas refused to expressly accept Israel's right to exist but did make a number of ambiguous and at times conflicting statements with reference to this issue.[431] With regard to accepting all previous agreements, including the Roadmap, the Hamas leadership at times argued that it did accept some of these, implicitly recognising Israel, but also pointed out, with some justification, that Israel failed to respect those agreements as well.[432] Israel, for example, has not at any point agreed to return to the 1967 borders, nor has it in practice stopped settlement activity or rerouted the Wall, which the Quartet has asked Israel to do.[433]

Javier Solana, appearing before the European Parliament a week after the Hamas-led government took office, articulated the Union's position.[434] He stated that the new Palestinian government's programme was 'unacceptable to the international community'. The reason for this was because the Hamas government was not prepared to respect the

---

[431] At times Hamas has implicitly recognised Israel, see, 'Climbdown as Hamas Agrees to Israeli State', *Guardian*, 22 June 2006 and 'Hamas Touts 10 Year Ceasefire Plan Instead of Recognising Israel', *Guardian*, 1 November 2006. At other times, Hamas has stated that it will never recognise Israel, see 'Hamas Deals Swift Blow to Peace Deal Hopes', *Guardian*, 10 February 2007.

[432] See Carter, *Palestine: Peace not Apartheid*, p. 184 *et seq.* The Wye River Memorandum of 23 October 1998, (1998) 37 *ILM* 1251 (which was intended to clarify some of the ambiguities in earlier agreements) is a clear example of Israel agreeing to and then reneging on its obligations. This was heavily criticised by the Union, see Presidency statement, 4 December 1998, Doc. 13679/98 and Presidency Declaration on the Decision by the Israeli Government to Halt Implementation of the Wye Memorandum, 23 December 1998, Doc. 14388/98. The Union has also heavily criticised settlement activity, in particular in Jerusalem, as being contrary to Israel's obligations under Oslo I, see e.g., Presidency statement, 15 May 1995, (1995) 5 *Bull. EU* 1.4.10.

[433] See e.g., Quartet statements of 9 May 2005 and 20 September 2005. In October 2006, it was reported that Hamas was prepared to accept all previous Palestinian agreements with Israel although no express statement was later made to this effect. See 'Hamas Ready to Accept Prior Agreements with Israel', *Haaretz*, 11 October 2006. As noted above, the Israeli government has rerouted parts of the Wall but only further to judgments of the Israeli Supreme Court.

[434] J. Solana, 'Middle East Peace Process: Appearance before the European Parliament', 5 April 2006, S101/06.

principles stipulated by the Union (and Quartet, as they were the same). Solana pointed out that the three principles stipulated were the minimum requirements if the ideal of a two-state solution was to be achievable. He further noted, 'there can be no negotiation if the parties do not recognise one another. There can be no peaceful settlement if the parties resort to arms in order to resolve the conflict.'[435] Solana further relied upon the principle in Article 26 of the Vienna Convention on the Law of Treaties, 1969, arguing that no solution based on the principles of international law could be reached if the parties disregarded the principle that previous agreements binding upon them are to be honoured.[436]

Solana's most important comment was that the Union did 'not want on principle to see the Hamas government fail'. He stated, '[w]hat we want is for that government, besides respecting the Quartet's three principles, also to apply those of the rule of law, a state based on it and democratic transfer of power, and to maintain the pluralistic nature of Palestinian society. If it does so, Hamas can be regarded as a fully-fledged political entity.'[437]

Whether Hamas, as Solana contends, fails to respect the rule of law, would not allow the democratic transfer of power and would eradicate the pluralism of Palestinian society is very debatable. In the first instance, it is dubious whether the Hamas-led government was any less committed to the rule of law than the Fatah one, whose commitment to it was poor to say the least. It is unclear on what basis Solana was making such a judgment. Furthermore, there was no evidence that Hamas would not transfer power if it lost the next election. In fact, members of the security forces who were loyal to Fatah were not agreeing to work with the Hamas-led government and this resulted in inter-factional fighting.

With regard to Hamas undermining the pluralistic nature of Palestinian society, while it is certainly true that Fatah has historically been more secular and thus more tolerant of pluralism than Hamas, Fatah has recently increasingly used Islam for political purposes. Fatah has not, for example, been adverse to using religious labels. The now common description of the 'Second Intifada' as the 'Al-Aqsa Intifada' to describe the Palestinian uprising in the aftermath of Sharon's deliberately provocative and strategically timed visit to the Al-Aqsa mosque compound is clearly a resort to Islam as a rallying call

---

[435] *Ibid.*   [436] *Ibid.*   [437] *Ibid.*

against Israel.[438] There is no clear evidence that Hamas would undermine the pluralistic nature of Palestinian society. The alleged absence of a commitment to the rule of law by Hamas or their undermining of pluralism simply does not stand up to scrutiny. In essence, it is debatable with regard to the issues mentioned by Solana, if Hamas was or is any worse than Fatah. Solana actually failed to mention that in terms of good governance and the eradication of corruption, Hamas has a far better record than Fatah. The Community has committed millions of euros in an attempt to reform the Palestinian institutions and in part to eradicate corruption. Fatah was universally seen as corrupt and inept and part of the reason it lost the PLC elections was because Hamas was considered by the electorate to be far less corrupt than Fatah.

Simply put, the most important issue for the Union was that Hamas was not renouncing violence or recognising Israel. Although Hamas did not expressly comply with the conditions stipulated by the Union, the differences between Hamas and Fatah are not as radically different as the Union's attitude (and that of the United States and in particular Israel) towards them suggests. As abhorrent as the practice of suicide-bombings is, Hamas is not alone among Palestinian factions in resorting to them. Various other groups closely connected to Fatah, such as Islamic Jihad, also use them.

An important, if not the *key*, difference between Hamas and Fatah is in their official positions. Hamas, as was the case with the Palestinian Liberation Organisation in the past, is still officially committed to the destruction of Israel but has at times observed ceasefires. With regard to recognising Israel, as noted above, Hamas has made ambiguous and sometimes conflicting statements but the position is no longer as unequivocal as it once was; there are competing and at times conflicting voices within Hamas. The PLO (which Fatah dominates), on the other hand, now officially recognises Israel but groups affiliated or in complicity with Fatah are involved in attacks on Israelis.[439] It is crucial,

---

[438] The French Presidency issued a statement on 2 October 2000 calling on the leaders of both parties to ensure that 'new provocative action is avoided', (2000) 10 *Bull. EU* 1.6.18. The European Parliament was much more forthright in a resolution adopted on 5 October 2000 on the Situation in the Middle East, [2001] OJ C178/283, 22 June 2001. It noted, 'the bloodshed which has claimed so many victims was sparked off by the provocative action of Mr. Ariel Sharon who decided, at a time of extreme tension in this area, to visit the Muslim religious compound housing the Dome of the Rock'.

[439] It should be noted, however, that the approach of the Union towards the PLO was not as stringent as it has been towards Hamas. In 1988, the Palestinian National Council

however, to note that while Israel was required to recognise the PLO, Israel has never been required to expressly recognise, prior to any negotiations with the Palestinians, that the Palestinians have a right to a state or that they accept all previous agreements with the Palestinians.[440] Israel, as noted above, routinely violates its legal obligations under these agreements, as do the Palestinians.

For the Union, the theory as opposed to the practice seems to be the most important issue as far as Hamas are concerned. Fatah is theoretically committed through peaceful means to find a negotiated solution to the 'Palestinian issue', despite some of its practices. In the same respect, the Union considers Israel a partner in peace yet it has only accepted the Roadmap with reservations and in practice continues systematically to act in contravention of it. With regard to Hamas, Solana has been clear that it can become a partner for Europe in the peace process. He has noted 'Hamas cannot change its past, but ... if it decides that there is no place in that future for terror, violence or negation of the reality of the State of Israel, the EU will be able to respond appropriately, as it has always done'.[441]

The Union, as noted above, has adopted a Common Position and designated Hamas as a terrorist organisation and has imposed punitive measures against its members. No such measures have been taken against Fatah. The Union was not credibly able to deal with a Hamas-led government as things then stood. Hamas either had to make significant changes to its political ideology and stop supporting and organising acts of violence against Israel or, in the alternative, the Union had to decide that it no longer considered Hamas to be a terrorist organisation. As neither of these alternatives was about to be realised in the short term, a Hamas-led government, which was democratically

---

condemned terrorism but only implicitly recognised the right of Israel to exist. This was welcomed in a declaration by the Twelve, see (1988) 11 *Bull. EC* 2.4.4. The Union dealt with the PLO for a number of years prior to the Palestinian National Council on 24 April 1996 specifically amending the Palestinian Charter (reproduced (1997) 36 *ILM* 771) so that it no longer denied the right of Israel to exist. The Presidency welcomed amendment to the Charter in a statement, see (1996) 4 *Bull. EU* 1.4.13.

[440] Under the terms of the Oslo Accords, this is not the case. Although Israel has accepted the Roadmap which aims to work towards a two-state solution, this is still formally with reservations and Israel's recognition of Palestinian statehood is only implicit. See Reservation 5, Israel's Response to the Roadmap. Israeli politicians do regularly now refer to a Palestinian state but the point is that they have not been expressly required to do so prior to and as a part of any negotiations with the Palestinians.

[441] Solana, 'Middle East Peace Process'.

legitimate, was considered unacceptable by the Union because it refused to comply with the established conditions.

Although the terms 'recognition' and 'legitimacy' were widely used, it is doubtful that the Union refused to 'recognise' the Hamas-led Palestinian government or its 'domestic legitimacy' in the legal sense.[442] Where states still recognise new governments, and it is increasingly rare, it is usually part of the legal process of recognising entities as new states.[443] In this case, the various Presidency Statements, Council Conclusions and pronunciations by, for example, Solana make clear that the Union considered the Hamas-led government to be, in legal terms, the legitimate government of the Palestinian Territories.[444] The questioning of the Hamas-led government's legitimacy in legal terms was not on the domestic plane. The Union may, however, have questioned the legitimacy of the Hamas-led government on the international level in the sense that part of Hamas's political platform, in particular the commitment to eradicate the State of Israel, is fundamentally incompatible with the tenets of international law. There is, however, no evidence to suggest that the Union was drawing such nuanced distinctions and it is likely that terms such as 'recognition' and 'legitimacy' were used in the political sense without any reference to their legal significance. It is within the discretion of the government of any state whether it wishes to deal with another, and in this instance the Union and its Member States did not wish to have direct contact with the Hamas-led government. The Union clearly is choosing, when other priorities and interests do not come to the fore, only to deal with democratically elected governments who subscribe to a liberal agenda, commensurate (theoretically at least) to that of its own Member States. Not only must the process by which a government comes to power be acceptable to the Union, so must the platform on which they have been elected. The approach towards Hamas is neither surprising nor new. The Union after all maintained relations with Algeria when the 1991 elections were halted by the military after the first round of

---

[442] For example, in the Presidency Declaration on the Unity government, it was stated, '[t]he Presidency of the EU recalls the readiness of the EU to work with and to resume its assistance to a *legitimate* Palestinian government adopting a platform reflecting the Quartet principles'. Emphasis added.

[443] For outstanding discussion, see further, C. Warbrick, 'States and Recognition in International Law' in M. Evans (ed.), *International Law*, 2nd edn (Oxford: Oxford University Press, 2006) pp. 218, 253 *et seq.* and B. Roth, *Governmental Illegitimacy in International Law* (Oxford: Oxford University Press, 1999) p. 121 *et seq.*

[444] See Title Four (The Legislative Authority) and Title Five (The Executive Authority), Amended Basic Law, 2003.

voting, when it was clear that the Front Islamique du Salut would in all probability be victorious.[445]

As was to be expected in the light of the Quartet Statements, the European Council meeting on 10 April 2006 thus formally took the decision to stop all direct assistance to the Palestinian Authority.[446] It can be argued that by taking this approach, the Union punished the Palestinian population for exercising their democratic rights and having the temerity to elect those standing on a political platform of which the Union did not approve. Subsequent to the suspension of direct EU funding to the Palestinian Authority, Javier Solana in the Arab daily *Al-Hayat* argued that the Union respects 'the Palestinian's democratic choices; we do not intend to punish them or to blackmail the Government they have chosen'. He continued, however, 'if the party in power no longer shares the peace agenda underpinning our partnership or visions of a pluralist Palestinian society attached to the rule of law and respect for human rights, we are obliged to reflect on the conditions under which the European Community and the Governments of the Union may continue to use European taxpayers' money in the context of assistance to the Palestinians and their institutions'.[447]

Although the Quartet statement of 30 March 2006 made clear that all donors would review the commitment of the Hamas-led government to the three conditions set out in the statement of 30 January 2006, and the Union had acted accordingly, it is clear that not all Quartet members subscribed to the view that direct aid should be cut. De Soto has stated that he, as the Secretary-General's Special Envoy to the Quartet, argued at the meetings prior to that statement being adopted for a 'common but differentiated approach' which allowed the United Nations to

---

[445] For discussion of the elections and subsequent events, see J. Ruedy, *Modern Algeria: the Origins and Development of Nations*, 2nd edn (Bloomington: Indiana University Press, 2005) p. 257 *et seq*. The Community and Member States now have a Euro-Med Association Agreement with Algeria which came into force after the 2004 elections were fairly won by Abdelaziz Bouteflika: Euro-Mediterranean Agreement Establishing an Association between the European Community and its Member States, of the one Part, and the People's Democratic Republic of Algeria, of the other Part, [2005] OJ L265/12, 10 October 2005. In the 1999 elections, all the other Presidential candidates withdrew due to Bouteflika having the support of the military. The Presidency statement on the 1999 election, however, makes no mention of the fact that the election was heavily influenced by the army. See (1999) 4 *EU Bull.* 1.4.3.

[446] See External Relations Council, 10–11 April 2006, Doc. 7939/06, Conclusions on the Middle East Peace Process.

[447] J. Solana, 'Europe's Unwavering Support to the Palestinian People', *Al Hayat*, 24 April 2006.

engage with Hamas so as to allow it to evolve politically.[448] The Quartet Statement issued makes clear that this approach was not acceptable to some Quartet members.[449] In contrast, it was widely reported that at the time that the Union and United States stopped all aid payments, Russia made direct payments to the Hamas-led government.[450] The Russian Foreign Minister, Sergey Lavrov in the press conference after the May 2006 Quartet meeting made clear that Russia felt that isolating Hamas 'will not help us to achieve the goal we wish to reach' and that it was 'essential to continue to work with the Hamas government'.[451] Russia subsequently maintained diplomatic relations with the Hamas-led government.

The balance which the Union had to strike once Hamas won the 2006 PLC elections and formed a government was an extremely difficult one. As discussed above, the preferred option, which was unrealistic, was for Hamas to be pressurised to accept the conditions stipulated by the Union and, *inter alia*, renounce violence and recognise Israel. As that strategy did not succeed the Union, if it was to act credibly in the light of the Quartet statements, was left with little choice but to stop all direct assistance to the Palestinian Authority. The Union, however, had to consider the implications of the attempt to isolate Hamas with its established policies and practices and any other consequences that may follow.

First, the Union in line with its long-term policy in the Palestinian Territories, ideally needed to try and maintain the Palestinian Authority's institutional fabric.[452] The Union has over the years, as discussed above, consistently invested heavily in terms of money and effort in Palestinian institutions in the hope that when a peace agreement is reached, the basics of a Palestinian state already exist. If the rule of law was to be observed and lawlessness and attacks on Israel stemmed to any extent, then the institutions and security services which already existed had to be supported or at least not further undermined, even if they were now

---

[448] De Soto, *End of Mission Report*, para. 44.
[449] De Soto states that the United States initially implied that funding to the United Nations was at stake if it did not get its way but subsequently receded from this threat. De Soto, *End of Mission Report*, para. 49.
[450] 'Palestinians to Get Russian Aid', 15 April 2006, http://news.bbc.co.uk/2/hi/middle_east/4911310.stm
[451] Transcript of Press Conference, 9 May 2006, www.unorg/news/press/docs/2006/sgsm10453.doc.htm
[452] See External Relations Council, 10–11 April 2006, Doc. 7939/06, Conclusions on the Middle East Peace Process.

under the control of Hamas. If the Union did not support or work with these institutions, then it was essentially completely reversing one of the established pillars of its approach towards the Palestinian–Israeli conflict. Solana and the Council on a number of occasions expressed support for President Mahmoud Abbas and by implication the institutions under his (and Fatah's) effective control.[453] The Union did not wish to undermine any Palestinian institutions but Ismail Haniya, a member of Hamas, was legitimately Prime Minister. The effect of the Union's refusal to have contact with Hamas and supporting its rival Fatah was essentially to undermine institutions and offices it had been influential in creating and heavily financially sustaining because they were now under the control of Hamas.

Secondly, the Union needed to continue its humanitarian aid supplies to the Palestinians not only due to the scale of the emergency but also if the Union was to try and avoid being perceived as punishing the Palestinians for democratically electing Hamas. The need and desire to continue humanitarian aid supplies was made clear in numerous Council Conclusions and in the Quartet statement of 30 March 2006.[454] Solana noted in this regard that the 'EU will ... continue its aid for the Palestinian people, firstly, because this is a moral imperative which the EU cannot shirk and, secondly, because the humanitarian crisis and instability in the Occupied Territories do no good to anyone, starting with Israel itself'.[455] The Union's decision to suspend direct aid to the Hamas-led government would undeniably compound the effects on the Palestinian population of the Israeli decision to withhold customs transfers and the existing financial and humanitarian crisis.[456] The budgetary shortfall already meant that, for example, the salaries of members of the security forces were not being paid and social services, education

---

[453] See for examples, Solana, 'Middle East Peace Process' and External Relations Council, 16–17 October 2006, Doc. 13340/06, where it was stated, '[t]he Council expressed its support to President Abbas and called on the Palestinians to join his efforts towards national unity and the formation of a government with a platform reflecting the Quartet principles and allowing for early engagement'.

[454] See e.g., European Council, 15–16 June 2006, Doc. 10633/1/06, Annex V, Declaration on the Middle East Peace Process.

[455] Solana, 'Middle East Peace Process'.

[456] The Union on numerous occasions requested the Israelis to transfer the money to the Palestinian Authority. See e.g., European Council, 15–16 June 2006, Declaration on the Middle East Peace Process. No statement adopted by the Quartet has requested Israel to do this.

and healthcare provision, to the extent they still existed, had deteriorated further.[457]

Thirdly, the Union needed to consider if the suspension of direct aid to the Hamas-led government could lead to other negative consequences in the overall context of the Middle East. Once a Hamas-led government was formed in early 2006, James Wolfensohn as the Quartet's envoy could not seek funds, as he had done prior to the 2006 election, for the Palestinian Authority.[458] The Palestinian budgetary crisis meant that to stop the Palestinian Authority from collapsing the Hamas-led government had to turn to other donors. Some donors such as Iran (which has at times funded Hamas and added the further complication of a Shia/Sunni dimension to inter-Palestinian fighting, even though both Hamas and Fatah membership is almost exclusively drawn from Sunni Muslims) and Syria, are involved in proxy wars against Israel. The giving of any aid by these states could strengthen the position of hardliners in Hamas and make any peaceful negotiation between the Palestinian factions and in particular with Israel even less likely.[459]

Fourthly, a number of the Member States felt that Hamas was undergoing (and continues to undergo) an evolutionary process into a political body. The difference in views became apparent when some Member States argued to this effect in European Council meetings both prior to and subsequent to the Mecca Agreement of February 2007, in which Fatah and Hamas members along with independent members finally

---

[457] De Soto, *End of Mission Report*, para. 51.
[458] Wolfensohn stepped down soon after in April 2006 as he was unclear about the scope of his mandate. The post was vacant until June 2007 when the former British Prime Minister, Tony Blair was appointed as the Special Envoy.
[459] Javier Solana has warned against this. See e.g., Solana, 'Middle East Peace Process' where he states, '[w]e must not forget that the Palestinian-Israeli conflict is part of the serious crisis which the Middle East region is undergoing. In working on the peace process, we have to bear in mind the role of States which may exert a positive but also a negative influence and the repercussions of the situation in Iraq.' At the time the European Union and United States stopped direct aid payments to the Palestinian Authority (April 2006), an agreement also existed among some Arab states not to send direct aid to the Hamas-led government. This agreement collapsed in November 2006 once, as discussed above, a resolution proposed by Qatar in the Security Council condemning Israel for events in Beit Hanoun was vetoed by the United States. The vetoing of the Security Council resolution led to a statement by the Foreign Ministers of the Arab League in which they declared that they would now send aid directly to the Hamas-led government. See 'Arabs "to Break Hamas Aid Freeze"', http://news.bbc.co.uk/2/hi/middle_east/6142094.stm 12 November 2006. Any aid sent had to avoid the imposition of punitive measures against Hamas in the United States and European Union.

did create a Unity government. The then Finnish Foreign Minister, Erkki Tuomioja, during the Finnish Presidency of the second half of 2006, for example, was reportedly very keen on dealing with the Hamas-led government. It was argued during an informal Foreign Ministers meeting that the peace process could only be moved along by engaging with the Hamas-led government as well as Fatah and the Israelis. It was reported, however, that the United Kingdom and Germany in particular were very concerned about the consequences such a move would have on relations with Israel and thus there was no change in approach towards Hamas.[460] Further to the Mecca Agreement and the Unity government being formed in early 2007, the divisions between the Member States over whether to deal with Hamas and the Unity government became far more pronounced. President Abbas tried to convince both Chancellor Merkel (Germany held the Presidency at the time) and the US Secretary of State Dr Rice, to give the new Unity government a chance. The United States did not change its point of view but other states did. Norway, for example, normalised relations with the Palestinian Authority in March 2007. As far as the EU Member States were concerned, France, Ireland, Spain and Sweden reportedly pressed the other Member States to change the Union's approach and deal with the new government which contained Hamas members. The Netherlands, Germany and the United Kingdom were much more inflexible in their approach and refused to do so.

The differing views of the Members States towards Hamas and the implications of attempting to isolate Hamas as opposed to continuing with the Union's established policies and practices in the Palestinian Territories posed a dilemma for the Council. In April 2006, when a Hamas-led government was initially formed, the proposed solution to the conflict between, on the one hand, the Union's agreed approach in the Quartet to suspend direct aid and, on the other, its established practices and the different views of its Member States regarding Hamas, was to press the other Quartet members to establish what became the Temporary International Mechanism (TIM) to fund programmes and projects in the Palestinian Territories. The Quartet statement of 9 May 2006 noted in this regard:

---

[460] See 'EU Foreign Ministers Unite to Call for Revival of Middle East Peace Process', 1 September 2006, www.eu2006.fi/news_and_documents/other_documents/vko35/en_GB/1157129388944/; 'EU Urged to Make Contact with Hamas', *Financial Times*, 31 August 2006; and 'EU Plans to Hold Talks with *Hamas* Cause Divisions', *EU Observer. com*, 1 September 2006.

The Quartet expressed serious concern about deteriorating conditions in the West Bank and Gaza, and about the delivery of humanitarian assistance, economic life, social cohesion and Palestinian institutions. We call on the international community to respond urgently to assistance requests by international organizations, especially UN agencies, and urge both parties to take concrete steps to implement their obligations under the Agreement on Movement and Access.

We also expressed our willingness to endorse a temporary international mechanism, *limited in duration and scope and fully accountable, that ensures direct delivery of any assistance to the Palestinian people*. The Quartet welcomed the EU's offer to develop and propose such a mechanism, and invites donors and international organizations to consider participating. The Quartet urges Israel, in parallel, to take steps to improve the humanitarian situation of the Palestinian people.[461]

The proposed mechanism was an EU initiative as opposed to being something which the Union agreed to develop as a part of the Quartet. At the meeting of the Quartet on 9 May 2006, the External Relations Commissioner, Benita Ferrero-Waldner proposed to set up a mechanism because it had become clear that the Commission's emergency package to the Palestinian Authority of €120 million at the end of February 2006 was insufficient, having run out more quickly than anticipated.[462] The United States was reported to be strongly opposed to the then proposed mechanism being established and even subsequently only wanted to agree to it having a very narrow scope, primarily limited to humanitarian aid.[463] Other Quartet members wanted it to be far wider. The disagreements were about what the coverage should be in terms of assisting those who were employed by the Palestinian Authority, and what kind of services it should target.[464]

---

[461] Emphasis added.

[462] At the end of February 2006, the European Commission tried to help fill the budgetary shortfall in the Palestinian Authority's budget and put together an emergency package totalling €120 million. Of this money, €40 million would be used to pay fuel bills, €64 million would help refugees through UNRWA, and €17.5 million was in the form of budget support. Prior to the Hamas-led government being formed at the end of March 2006, as noted above, a technocratic interim government was in place. It was this administration which received the budgetary support. See IP/06/235, 27 February 2006.

[463] See De Soto, *End of Mission Report*, para. 80 and 'America Bows to EU Pressure to Allow Aid for Palestinians', *Independent*, 10 May 2006.

[464] Development Committee, *Development Assistance and the Occupied Palestinian Territories 2007*, Evidence, Question 172 *et seq*. The TIM which was eventually agreed upon has been described as being 'somewhere in the middle', although the US Secretary of State Dr Rice has implied that it is at the narrower end of the spectrum, in line with

The proposed mechanism also first had to be approved by the European Council. It was to be administered by a Management Unit based in Jerusalem with staff from the Commission and EU Member States seconded to it. Budgetary allocations for existing funding initiatives were effectively to be reallocated. The Council did not need to adopt a new legal instrument, simply to approve the proposal. The European Council of 15 and 16 June 2006 adopted a Declaration on the Middle East Peace Process which, with regard to the proposed mechanism, stated:

The European Council stresses the need for a coordinated international response to the deterioration of the humanitarian, economic and financial situation in the West Bank and Gaza Strip.

The European Council endorses the proposed temporary international mechanism to channel assistance *directly to the Palestinian people*, which has been drawn up by the Commission following consultations within the EU as well as with Quartet members, major donors, international financial institutions and partners in the region. The European Council appreciates the Commission's work so far and requests it to continue urgently establishing the mechanism, in conjunction with Quartet members, other key international partners *and the PA President's Office*.

The European Council agrees that, in order to achieve an immediate impact, the mechanism will focus on essential supplies and running costs for social services and health, supply of utilities including fuel, and social allowances. Other donors, including Arab States, are invited to provide funding and to consider early and substantial contributions. The Community stands ready to contribute a substantial amount to the international mechanism.[465]

A number of the Member States made it clear that their approval in the European Council of what became the TIM was conditional upon the other Quartet partners agreeing to it.[466] This was duly forthcoming and the Quartet, meeting the day after the European Council approved the TIM, again articulated that it was to be 'limited in scope and duration'

---

the US position. She stated in this regard that, 'we looked at several proposals. We have said that after three months this will be evaluated. The goal here is ... to provide assistance to the Palestinian people so that they do not suffer deprivation and do not suffer humanitarian crisis. That's the goal here. That's why it's of limited duration and of limited scope.' Comments made after the Quartet meeting, 9 May 2006, available at www.un.org/News/Press/docs//2006/sgsm10453.doc.htm

[465] European Council, 15–16 June 2006, Doc. 10633/1/06 REV1, Annex V, Declaration on the Middle East Peace Process. Emphasis added.

[466] Development Committee, *Development Assistance and the Occupied Palestinian Territories 2007*, Evidence, Question 172 *et seq*. This is likely to have been part of the trade-off in the Council of 10 April 2006 over the decision to suspend direct aid to the Hamas-led government.

and must operate with 'full transparency and accountability'.[467] The statement further made clear that the TIM would be reviewed by the Quartet after three months and would only continue to function if all Quartet members agreed to this.[468]

The mechanism agreed upon was to facilitate 'needs-based assistance directly to the Palestinian people, including essential equipment, supplies, and support for health services, support for the uninterrupted supply of fuel and utilities, and basic needs allowances to poor Palestinians'.[469] Between 9 May 2006, when the Quartet statement which initially referred to what became the TIM was adopted, and 17 June 2006, when the Quartet approved its establishment, the Union had negotiated the essentials with the other Quartet members. As a consequence, the TIM was up and running almost immediately after approval, with the TIM Management Unit opening an office on 26 June 2006 in Jerusalem.[470] There had, however, been a very strong view within the Quartet that part of the mechanism should be delivered through the World Bank and not the European Commission. It rapidly became apparent, however, that the World Bank did not have the capacity on the ground to implement the TIM within the envisaged timescale.[471]

The TIM, which is still operational at the time of writing, has three 'windows'. Window I is funded primarily by the EC and EU Member States and pays for essential supplies and covers running costs for health, education and social services for the Palestinians. It is now implemented through the World Bank's Emergency Services Support Programme. To May 2007, over €49 million had been contributed to Window I, with the largest contributions coming from the EC budget, Spain and the United Kingdom. Due to the World Bank not being able

---

[467] Quartet statement, 17 June 2006.
[468] In the Quartet statements of 20 September 2006 and 2 February 2007, the TIM was extended and in the latter also developed.
[469] Quartet statement, 17 June 2006. The Quartet meeting of 2 February 2007 subsequently agreed to further develop the TIM 'to support the political process, to identify suitable projects for international support in the areas of governance, institution building and economic development, and urged other members of the international community to consider practical support to the parties': Quartet statement, 2 February 2007. The mandate of the TIM was extended until September 2007.
[470] Development Committee, *Development Assistance and the Occupied Palestinian Territories 2007*, Evidence, Question 172 *et seq.*
[471] *Ibid.* and Quartet statement, 20 September 2006.

to get their operations up and running quickly, Window I has been seen as the least effective part of the mechanism, although it seems to have operated more effectively since November 2006.[472]

Windows II and III are the responsibility of the European Commission and both are considered to have functioned well.[473] Window II seeks to ensure access to electricity, healthcare and sanitation. Until May 2007, Window II had a budget of €75 million which has been funded entirely from the EC budget.[474] Over €37 million from a total budget of €75 million has been spent providing electricity for Gaza.[475] Two days after the TIM office was opened in Jerusalem, Israel bombed the only electricity plant in Gaza. On 4 July 2006, President Abbas requested the TIM to begin emergency fuel deliveries to hospitals, which were started a week later, and on 20 July 2006 fuel deliveries to water installations commenced.[476]

Window III has been allocated just under €190 million. This has been funded from the EC budget alongside contributions from the EU Member States and other donors. Window III seeks to provide support to vulnerable Palestinians, through the payment of social allowances to the poorest part of the population and to key workers delivering essential public services. Window III has, according to the Commission, provided relief to nearly a million of the poorest and most vulnerable Palestinians through direct cash assistance.[477] One of the other major priorities of the TIM has been to meet the needs of the health service in the Palestinian Territories, in particular to ensure that emergency services continued to exist. This is why payments have also been made under Window III to those who work in the public services and to healthcare providers, as their salaries have not been paid due to the Palestinian budgetary crisis. This is to try and ensure that they have an

---

[472] Development Committee, *Development Assistance and the Occupied Palestinian Territories 2007*, Evidence, Question 41.

[473] *Ibid.* Question 172 *et seq.* It should be noted this was the opinion of Alan Seatter, who, at the time of giving evidence, was Head of the Near East Unit, Directorate-General for External Relations in the European Commission.

[474] See Temporary International Mechanism Management Unit, *Overall Implementation Progress*, available at www.delwbg.cec.eu.int/en/tim/tim_implementation.pdf

[475] *Ibid.*

[476] Development Committee, *Development Assistance and the Occupied Palestinian Territories 2007*, Evidence, Question 174.

[477] Approximately 150,000 heads of household have received payment under Window III. The TIM Management Unit estimates that as each household has six members, this equates to helping approximately one million of the poorest and most vulnerable in Palestinian society.

incentive to continue working, which in turn assists with the functioning of the health service.

Although the Union suspended direct assistance to the Hamas-led
government, the amount of aid from the EC budget to the Palestinians
has at least stayed the same, if not increased. In 2006, for example,
assistance to the Palestinians from the Community budget amounted to
just under €340 million. For 2007, the commitment amounts to just
over €336 million.[478] Apart from the fact that over half of the 2007
budget is destined for Windows II and III of the TIM, there is actually
very little difference between the allocations for 2006 and 2007.
Ostensibly, the amount allocated for humanitarian aid in 2007 halved,
even though the humanitarian emergency has continued to intensify
since 2002, but the fact is that this has been shifted to Window III which,
in part, pays social allowances, and is in all but name humanitarian
assistance.[479]

The reality of the TIM is that there was no actual suspension of aid to
the Palestinian Territories by the Union. The gesture as far as relations
with Hamas were concerned had been made – budgetary assistance and
direct financial aid were stopped. Different priorities and beneficiaries were identified, and a new mechanism was established to that
end; however, the assistance in financial terms to Palestinian society
continued.

The EU Member States and the Community as donors have a discretion with regard to the aid they provide and indeed whether they
provide it or not. As discussed in Chapter 2, a unilateral decision to
stop aid to a government is usually not illegal under international law.
With one exception, the decision to redirect aid does not seem to come
within those limited circumstances in which such a decision may be
unlawful. The Community has not, in spite of the scale of assistance
provided, at any stage undertaken unilateral obligations to fund
Palestinian institutions or assist infrastructure projects which entail
legally binding obligations that the Community may be estopped from
rescinding. Nor is it the case that the Community has suspended or
downgraded treaty relations with the Palestinian Authority. As noted in
Chapter 2, however, suspension of bilateral aid can potentially lead to

---

[478] These figures are derived from the DFID, *Memorandum Submitted to the Select Committee*,
and the data available at the webpage of the Commission delegation to the West
Bank and Gaza, www.delwbg.cec.eu.int/en/eu_and_palestine/overview.htm

[479] On the humanitarian crisis, see IMF-World Bank, *West Bank and Gaza: Economic
Developments in 2006*.

the legal responsibility of the former donor, for violations of economic, social and cultural rights in the target state.[480]

The suspension of direct aid exacerbated poverty in the Palestinian Territories and the suffering of civilians. Even in the light of the TIM being established, in particular Window III which has targeted the neediest in the Territories, the redirection of aid led to further humanitarian damage among the Palestinian populations.[481] Although the situation would have been substantially worse without this assistance, the problem lies in the fact that the decision to stop direct assistance undermined Palestinian institutions. These institutions, which were bypassed by the TIM, were the very same institutions which were established, reformed and sustained with the assistance of the Community. These were the very same institutions which were designed to assist with running the Territories, addressing the needs of citizens and alleviating their suffering. While some, if not most, of the blame for the humanitarian crises lies with Israel for blocking access and travel to and from the Palestinian Territories and refusing to transfer customs duties to the Palestinian Authority, the Union is not without fault. The redirection of aid through the TIM, however, cannot be seen to amount to a violation by the Union of the economic and social rights of the Palestinians.

The Union's attempts to influence the outcome of the election and the composition of the new government and subsequently to isolate and undermine the Hamas-led government that was formed also raise legal issues. As discussed in Chapter 2, states must not intervene in the internal affairs of another. Although the Palestinian Territories are not a state, it is credible to argue that the same restriction applies as far as its 'domestic jurisdiction' is concerned as exists in international law generally.

The Union, as part of the Quartet, tried to influence the outcome of the 2006 PLC election and the composition of the government to be formed after the outcome was known. The Quartet statement of 28 December 2005, Solana's comment on 3 January 2006 about aid

---

[480] See General Comment 8 of the Committee of Economic, Social and Cultural Rights (CESCR), E/C.12/1997/8, para. 11 *et seq.*

[481] Oxfam, for example, has been very critical of the TIM and has stated that it has not prevented the decline in the emergency situation in the Palestinian Territories and argued that the TIM has been restricted by flawed policy constraints set by the Member States. See Oxfam Briefing Note, *Poverty in Palestine: the Human Cost of the Financial Boycott,* 13 April 2007.

possibly being cut, and the Quartet statement of 30 January 2006, were designed to highlight to the Palestinians that the Quartet members would not deal with a government which contained Hamas members and that the United States and European Union would consider their assistance programmes if such a government were formed. The Union's views on Hamas are, of course, publicly well known and long-standing; Hamas were first legally classified as a terrorist organisation by the Union in 2001 and its practices have been condemned by the Union on many occasions.[482] Statements to the effect that the Union, as part of the Quartet, would not deal with a Hamas-led government or may not provide funding to it, came as no real surprise and cannot be seen as satisfying the threshold needed for such acts to amount to intervention.

The refusal to deal with a government which contained a single Hamas member is legally less straightforward, especially after the election results were known and a government was formed. As discussed above, the strategy was to compel Hamas to denounce violence and, if it did not, to force it to govern alone. Once in government, the aim was to further isolate Hamas but to support President Abbas (and by extension the opposition Fatah party) and precipitate Hamas's failure. If the strategy is considered as a whole then it can be considered to satisfy the necessary threshold to amount to intervention. The most problematic part of the policy is the supporting of Fatah.

The Union sought as a donor to bypass the democratically elected government and some Palestinian institutions to directly assist beneficiaries. The TIM, however, needed a Palestinian partner, and as the conclusions of the European Council of 15 and 16 June 2006 made clear, that was to be President Abbas. The President's Office identified those who were to benefit from the TIM. The TIM Unit then validated and audited the funds to be transferred. The TIM worked closely with the President's Office. For example, as noted above, much of the budget from Window II was spent on emergency fuel deliveries further to a specific request from President Abbas. With regard to those individuals and institutions which benefited, in the context of vicious inter-Palestinian factional fighting and a power struggle, it is inconceivable that beneficiaries would be identified who were not at least

---

[482] Common Position, 2001/931/CFSP, as noted above, this initially only extended to the terrorist wing of Hamas. The United States first classified Hamas in its entirety as a terrorist organisation in 1995, pursuant to Executive Order 12947, Prohibiting Transactions with Terrorists who Threaten to Disrupt the Middle East Peace Process, 23 January 1995.

sympathetic to Fatah no matter how thorough the auditing of their needs.[483] In choosing between a democratically legitimate government and a democratically elected President, the Union, by siding with Abbas, also allowed him to display to the Palestinians that he can promise and deliver on assistance from the international community, which Hamas cannot. As well intentioned as the TIM may be with regard to alleviating Palestinian suffering, it has also intentionally supported an opposition politician, albeit one with a democratically legitimate mandate, against a democratically elected government.

Council Conclusions, statements by Solana and the Quartet among others consistently referred to supporting President Abbas and the institutions under his effective control.[484] The TIM sought to alleviate suffering but also supported Abbas and Fatah while trying to isolate Hamas. It does not matter how undesirable the Union and some of its Member States may find Hamas; such action clearly 'intervenes' in the legal sense in the internal affairs of the Palestinian Territories. As discussed in Chapter 2, the International Court of Justice made clear in the *Nicaragua* case that the principle of non-intervention, 'forbids all States or groups of States to intervene directly or indirectly in the internal or external affairs of other States'.[485] The 'choice of political, economic, social and cultural system and the formulation of foreign policy' are all matters within the domestic jurisdiction of a state.[486]

The unequivocal welcoming by the Union and Quartet of President Abbas's actions in dismissing the Unity government (which was formed in March 2007 after the Mecca Agreement, with independent members as well as Hamas and Fatah politicians) in the context of vicious fighting between forces loyal to either Hamas or Fatah further highlights the fact that the Union wishes to support him in his opposition to Hamas. The Quartet statement of 16 June 2007 'expressed understanding and support for President Abbas' decisions to dissolve the Cabinet and

---

[483] De Soto has stated that the US envoy to the Quartet expressed delight vis-à-vis the Palestinian inter-factional fighting as the US envoy felt it meant that 'other Palestinians are resisting Hamas'. De Soto, *End of Mission Report*, para. 56.

[484] For example, in Presidency statement on the Situation in the Palestinian Territories, 15 June 2007, it was stated, '[t]he EU Presidency once again reiterates its complete support for President Abbas, who is our partner and whom we regard as a partner for the Israeli government'. See also European Council Declaration, 15–16 June 2006, text accompanying n. 465 above.

[485] *Nicaragua* v. *United States*, n. 252 above, para. 205.

[486] *Ibid.*

declare an emergency'. Equally importantly, the Quartet 'recognised the necessity and legitimacy of these decisions, taken under Palestinian law'.[487] The External Relations Council of 18 June expressed 'its full support for President Abbas and his decision taken within his mandate to declare a state of emergency and to install an emergency government for the Palestinian Territories under Prime Minister Fayyad, underlining the importance of the Palestinian Basic Law'.[488] The Council also decided as a consequence of the dismissal of the Unity government to 'resume normal relations with the Palestinian Authority immediately'. This includes direct financial support to the government and support for the resumption of EUPOL COPPS, and the EUBAM at Rafah.[489]

The Quartet and European Council fully accepted the legality of Abbas's decision. However, the legal issues are not clear-cut. Under Title Seven of the Palestinian Basic Law, which contains the 'Provisions of the State of Emergency', President Abbas has the power to declare a state of emergency for a period not to exceed thirty days when there is a threat to national security caused by war, invasion or armed insurrection.[490] This period can be extended for another thirty days but only if it is approved by two-thirds of the Legislative Council, which after the 2006 PLC election is dominated by Hamas.[491] As obvious as it may seem, the Palestinian Territories are in a political and constitutional crisis. If this had happened elsewhere, the almost certain response of the Union would have been for the Presidency or Council to adopt a document in which it expressed the sentiment that the Union expects the crisis to be resolved peacefully using the judicial process with all parties respecting the rule of law and the decisions of judicial bodies. It is difficult to think of another recent occasion on which a democratically legitimate government has been dismissed by an opposition politician in the context of a violent power struggle between the protagonists and immediately been welcomed as legitimate by the Union. In many senses, this again highlights the uniqueness of the situation between the Palestinians and Israelis. The Union acts in a manner and tolerates legal violations by all sides which it is difficult to consider it would accept in any other

---

[487] Quartet statement, 16 June 2007.
[488] External Relations Council, 18 June 2007, Doc. 10657/07, Conclusions on the Middle East Peace Process, para. 3.
[489] *Ibid.* para. 6.   [490] Article 110(1) of Amended Basic Law, 2003.
[491] *Ibid.* Article 110(2).

circumstances. This raises the most fundamental of questions. What is the meaning of an 'ethical foreign policy' for the Union in the context of the Middle East? This is discussed in the conclusions below.

5.3 Conclusions

Relations with Israel and the Palestinian Territories and resolution of the Arab-Israeli conflict are one of the most important, yet simultaneously probably the most difficult, foreign policy issues for the Union. The Union's relationships with the Palestinians and Israelis, bilaterally, regionally and in the context of the Middle East Peace Process, are hugely complex. The relationships exist on many levels involving a number of policies, a large number of actors and various different objectives. As is to be expected in the context of relations with Israel and the Palestinians, which can involve very emotive issues, the perspectives of the various Union actors often differ.

The Union's attempt to promote and protect certain values and principles in the political context of relations with the Israelis and Palestinians raises a number of questions about what such foreign policies seek to achieve. For the Union, foreign policy formulation which has both an ethical dimension to it, while simultaneously working towards a solution to the region's conflicts, is compatible in the long term. A balance between these objectives, which will sometimes compete with one another, must also be struck as needed in the short term. The Union's ultimate policy objective in the region is to help find a solution to and sustain any settlement in the dispute between Israel and some of its Arab neighbours. In the light of this objective, keeping the peace process on track is undisputedly the Union's top priority. There is much to be said in support of the Union's overall approach. It takes a long-term perspective and attempts to tackle the root cause of the region's problems, which have taken on an even greater importance in the context of recent developments in global affairs. Having an ethical dimension to its foreign policies in relations with all third states, however, means that the manner in which the Union responds to events in one part of the world will be compared to its practice elsewhere.[492]

---

[492] As discussed in Chapter 3, although the Community does not have an 'essential elements clause' in its treaty relations with all third states, the Union does seek to promote values such as human rights and democracy in its relations with all third states. The question is one of emphasis.

To be credible, the Union's attempt at promoting and protecting certain values and principles must be as consistent as possible in relations with all third states. Allowing one state to systematically violate the basic norms of international law without taking punitive action against it, while taking such action against other states for similar or lesser transgressions, can be hugely damaging to such an approach. Even allowing for the Union's overall objectives and priorities in relations with Israel and the Palestinian Territories, there are problems with the current balance being struck by the Union between its long-term objectives in the region, its ethical foreign policies and events on the ground.

The first problem is the utility of the 'essential elements' clause in the respective Agreements with Israel and the Palestinians as an instrument to maintain dialogue on such issues and to have an impact on practice and policy. The clause only has value if there is a point at which it will be activated. If there is a failure to use the clause in relations with a party which is committing systematic and gross violations of international norms, the clause will be rendered increasingly redundant as an instrument for meaningful dialogue as the other party will know that it is unlikely to be relied upon. In the context of relations with Israel and the Palestinians and the Union's overall objectives, the ignoring of systematic violations of fundamental norms is only understandable in policy terms as long as a viable peace between them is still possible. As and when either the Israelis or Palestinians make the achievement of this objective very difficult, if not impossible, then a change of policy is imperative. If there is not a change in approach, then the clause is rendered increasingly meaningless and the clause (and Union to boot) loses credibility in this regard in relations with all third states.

The Union's approach towards the Israelis and Palestinians and the relevance of the 'essential elements' clauses in treaty relations with them have differed. With regard to Israel, much of the dialogue regardless of the forum has existed due to the 'essential elements' clause in bilateral treaty relations. Israel has on numerous occasions grossly violated the basic tenets of international law. At the very least, Israel's building of the Wall, where it deviates from the Green Line and its establishment of de facto permanent boundaries, and the continued expansion and building of settlements has surely reached the point at which the Community and Member States must seriously consider taking punitive action by using the 'essential elements' clause. This is the case even if it means, as it will, that relations between Israel and the Union will deteriorate as a consequence. The humanitarian consequences of the Wall for some Palestinians are well documented but there are, as the ICJ has stated, other fundamental issues also at stake: violation of the right to self-determination and the forcible acquisition of territory.

The Union's entire policy towards Israel and the Palestinians has been predicated on finding a just and lasting peace in the Middle East, through the creation of a viable Palestinian state and a secure Israel. It is difficult not to feel that Israel has, in part, used the Roadmap as a delaying tactic by always considering that the conditions for progress from one phase to the next have not been met by the Palestinians, while in the meantime acting in a manner that contributes toward imposing a unilateral solution. As things stand, unless the manner in which the West Bank has been split up by the Wall and the settlements is tackled, then although the Palestinians will be free to call the entity created at the end of any final peace agreement a 'state' it will be unlike any other in history and Israel will not be secure. The Council has on numerous occasions made statements to the effect that it recognises that the two-state solution is becoming impossible due to Israel's actions, yet it does not take any action against Israel which is commensurate with the activities Israel engages in. As things stand, the Union refuses to take punitive action against Israel as it hopes to maintain influence with it, while in the interim the Union's ultimate objective is increasingly being rendered unachievable by the Israelis.

With regard to the Palestinians, the essential elements clause has not been nearly as crucial to relations as it has with the Israelis. Prior to the Hamas election victory, the Union was in a stronger position of influence than any other external actor with regard to the establishment and reform of institutions. In the light of events on the ground, the EU Member States and EC budget very significantly ensured that the Palestinian Authority was at least able to stagger from one crisis to the next. Without this support, the Palestinian Authority in the light of Israel's military incursions and withholding of tax transfers, would have collapsed long ago. The basic vulnerability of the Palestinian Authority ensured that prior to 2006 it was pliable to the demands of the Union. If the Palestinian Authority refused to try and accommodate the Union, there was a danger that the Palestinians would ostracise their major financial backer and international supporter. The Union, for the five or so years between 1995 and the outbreak of the Al-Aqsa Intifada in 2000, was in the almost unique position in the Palestinian

Territories of dealing with a small territory and, relatively speaking, an excess of funds. A very substantial contribution could have been made towards the economic development of the Palestinian Territories as well as the creation of a pluralistic area with human rights respected and the rule of law and democracy established and protected. Up until the point of the Hamas-led government being formed, however, the Agreement and relations with the Palestinian Authority were being hindered by Israel, a country which is itself benefiting from its own Agreement with the Community and its Member States. Israel's policies and practices have ensured that in terms of trade, the Agreement between the Community and the Palestinian Authority is effectively meaningless. The Union's leverage in the political relationship has existed as a consequence of financial assistance – the Palestinian Authority derives little, if any, benefit from the Association Agreement.

The Union, between September 2000 and the Hamas-led government being formed in March 2006, essentially helped stop the Palestinian Authority collapsing and primarily sought to try and prevent the political, financial and humanitarian situation in the Palestinian Territories from deteriorating even further. The Union's actions in its relations with the Palestinians were largely reactive and not proactive, and tried to make the best of the situation, as the discussion on the Union's response to the Gaza 'disengagement' highlights. The Union quite rightly placed tremendous pressure on the Palestinian Authority to clamp down on attacks on Israelis and to reform its institutions, but the Union's reaction to the election victory of Hamas in January 2006 has damaged its credibility with some as an actor in the Middle East Peace Process and as the promoter of an ethical and principled foreign policy.

The Union's reaction to the Hamas-led victory is closely related to the second and third problems in the current balance being struck by the Union between long-term objectives in the region, events on the ground and the pursuance of an ethical foreign policy. These are both closely connected to the Union's current structure.

The second problem with the Union's current approach is that it does not have the confidence to implement the steps required to give effect to those objectives it can agree. The contribution of the Union to the promotion and protection of ethical values in relations with the Palestinian Authority and Israel highlights very clearly that collective action is a double-edged sword. On the one hand, the Union has made a far more valuable contribution to the Middle East Peace Process than the Member States would have been able to individually. It is because of the Union consistently pushing the two-state solution, for example, that it is now the preferred international approach. The collective voice of the Member States is a powerful one. On the other hand, the need for unanimity has been a hindrance. The Member States sometimes cannot agree how to act due to their own historic and domestic considerations. The need for unanimity among the Member States for them to take action has meant that Israel has ultimately been able to rely upon the United States not to withdraw support (indeed, under the second Bush Presidency for the United States to acquiesce to whatever unilateral steps Israel takes) and the Union, due to differences between the Member States, not to act to curtail it. It is for this reason, among others, that on a political level the Union plays a minor role compared to the United States.

If the Member States could agree and took action against Israel then, despite the bravado of a number of Israeli politicians, it would have very serious consequences for Israel. This will still be the case if the United States tries to mitigate the impact of such measures. Israeli politicians have to tread a difficult balance between their economic reliance upon the Union with regard to trade and the Palestinian Authority's reliance upon the Union for financial assistance, with the political disdain of 'European' interventions that is still prevalent in Israeli society.

The EU Member States, however, at times pull in different directions and the compromises that have to be reached to accommodate these differing views undermine the effectiveness of EU actions. The Union's reaction to the Hamas victory in the 2006 Palestinian Legislative Council elections is a classic example of this. Javier Solana made clear that the peace process would have no chance of success while Hamas was in power. It is equally arguable, however, that the decision to ostracise Hamas was short-sighted. Disenchantment with Fatah's corruption and ineptitude and a lack of progress in the peace process, as well as the commitment of Hamas to social welfare programmes, were major factors in Hamas doing well in the 2006 PLC elections. Whether the policies, practices and views of Hamas vis-à-vis Israel and the commitment to an armed struggle were primary factors or not in their election success, it is clear that opposition to the current situation resonated with enough voters for them to find Hamas an acceptable alternative to Fatah.

The Member States clearly differed in their views as to how they should respond to the Hamas election victory. One option was to continue to refuse to deal with Hamas. The other was to engage with it at some level or other, as a consequence of the elections, so as to try and recognise the new political reality and to encourage Hamas to further evolve in the same way as they had done with the PLO previously. The Union chose the former. It must be seriously doubted, however, whether the Union would have boycotted all contact with, for example, a Unity government containing Hamas, Fatah and independent politicians if it had not been the approach of the United States in the Quartet to set conditions which were unrealistic. The Union, to its continuing credit, backed Arafat and considered him the democratically elected leader of the Palestinians, despite pressure to marginalise him from the United States and Israel. The initial decision to back Arafat, however, had ignored the quite legitimate concerns expressed by other Palestinians. It was with a view to the overall success of the peace process that Arafat was backed by all. The failure of that process has in part been because views held by groups such as Hamas continue to enjoy support among many Palestinians, as the 2006 PLC elections proved. The agreement of all the Member States to stop direct financial aid to the Palestinian Authority was clearly conditioned upon some of the Member States insisting that what became the TIM was established, so as to try not to further undermine Palestinian institutions and worsen the humanitarian situation.

The TIM was the worst of all worlds. Despite the money which was spent under the Community budget to fund the TIM and even though the humanitarian situation would have been even more dire without it, the TIM still contributed to undermining some of those very same Palestinian institutions which the Union had long championed and assisted. The TIM did not manage to neutralise the impression that the Union was punishing the Palestinians for exercising their democratic choices, as they had long been told to do as a part of the peace process. In addition, the Union, in seeking to support Fatah, was intervening in the internal affairs of the Palestinians.

The Union did not need to align itself with the United States in the Quartet as far as the three conditions were concerned; it could have adopted its own approach and worked pragmatically with some of the members of a democratically legitimate Palestinian government. Without US strong-arm tactics, it is possible that a Unity government could have been established in early 2006 which the Union could have worked with. The Union did not need to work with all members of such a government but it could have at least worked with some of them. This would not have undermined the Palestinian Authority in the same way and it could have also helped avoid the power struggle which ensued and has left Gaza an even more isolated and desperate territory than it previously was. The Union and United States may say similar things on the settlements or the route of the Wall, but their perspectives *are* really quite different. Due to US opposition, the Quartet has not once asked Israel to transfer the tax duties it was unlawfully withholding from the Palestinian Authority. The Union routinely made reference to this matter and the harm it was causing. The creation of the TIM does highlight, however, that even the United States, in the face of concerted opposition from the other Quartet members, especially the Union (which economically at least is the only one that actually matters), does compromise.

Essentially the Union, having gained a role in the MEPP, has been keen to ensure that it maintains it. The Union does not wish to be sidelined, even as a member of the Quartet, in the peace process, which is why it aligns itself with the United States. Even allowing for the differences between the Member States, there is an EU perspective which is distinct from that of the United States and other actors, such as the Arab League or Russia. As things stood after Oslo, the Union allowed itself to be marginalised and was expected to pay the bill for the agreement reached by others, in many senses a payer not a player. Many Israeli politicians and members of the public are generally still suspicious of the motives of 'Europe'. It should be stressed, however, that despite a perception to the contrary which exists in some quarters, the Union is *not* pro-Palestinian and anti-Israeli. Notwithstanding the shortcomings of its practice, the Union's approach is an even-handed one based upon compliance by all sides with the relevant Security Council resolutions and international legal obligations. The Union is seen with suspicion in Israel, in part, because it questions the moral and legal basis of many Israeli practices. Israel, however, cannot now effectively veto the participation of the Union in the peace process. The Palestinian Territories are simply not viable, politically and economically without the Union's backing. There will be no peace and solution to the situation in the Middle East without the widespread consent of most Palestinians. For this reason, the Union will be guaranteed a place at the negotiating table in the search for peace.

The third problem with the Union's current approach, which is again closely related to its structure, is that the Union still has too many different voices in its relations with Israel and the Palestinian Authority.

The approach adopted by the Presidency, some of the Member States, the High Representative, the Special Representative and the External Relations Commissioner have at times in the past differed. These differing voices are especially damaging when they are part of the Union's contribution to the Quartet, hence the reference to 'sniggering in the corridors'. In the context of relations with Israel and the Palestinians, some of the Member States are perfectly aware that they cannot emphasise the virtues of 'European values' without being routinely reminded, and rightly so, of the legacy of European anti-Semitism and colonialism. Whereas such retorts may have limited effect in the Union's relations with many other third states, in the Union's relations with Israel they still carry a very particular resonance. A number of the Member States wish to ensure that their separate voices are always heard, whereas for others the Presidency is the platform to be used. Although the plethora of views further serves to highlight the complexity and emotive nature of the issues involved, for the effectiveness of the Union's contribution to be enhanced, there need to be fewer, clearer voices.

Foreign policy formulation when dealing with Israeli-Arab relations will never be straightforward. Things move incredibly quickly on the ground. The Union certainly cannot be blamed for the malaise that exists. No external actor, be it the Union, the United States, the United Nations or the Arab League, can impose a solution. The fundamental issues are for the Palestinians and Israelis to work out. The question is whether the political will exists among the protagonists to find a long-term solution to their conflict and to make the sacrifices that will be needed on both sides to ensure it is implemented. External actors can only help to create the conditions in which such a solution can be found and to help ensure it is implemented and respected.

With regard to the Union's attempt to promote ethical values in relations with all third states, it is inconceivable that as much latitude as has been granted to the Palestinians and Israelis would be afforded in the absence of the overall objective of finding a solution to the Middle East conflict. If the Arab-Israeli dispute is resolved and relations normalise between the protagonists, then the Union's approach towards both the Israelis and Palestinians must become consistent with that towards all other third states. Despite the conflicting national perspectives of some of the Member States and its shortcomings, however, the Union's contribution to the pursuance of ethical values in the context of the Palestinian-Israeli dispute on balance has been a positive one, but it has certainly not been as positive as it could have. The Union's contribution has had its shortcomings for the reasons outlined above. One test, however, to evaluate the Union's role is not to consider its failings but to try to envisage the situation if the Union played no role in the region at all. On this basis, the value of the Union's contribution is more than apparent.

6   Ethical Values and Foreign Policy in Practice: Humanitarian Aid and the European Union

This final substantive chapter of the book examines the role played by the humanitarian aid policy of the European Union in promoting ethical values in its foreign policy. As noted in Chapter 1, humanitarian aid is an ideal litmus test to assess the implementation of a foreign policy which seeks to promote and protect certain values and principles. Poul Nielson, the former Commissioner for Development Cooperation and Humanitarian Aid has stated:

Humanitarian assistance is viewed as a true 'success story' of Community external relations, not only by the European institutions but more importantly by the international community. Community humanitarian assistance has indeed become the expression of the values of humanity on which the EU is founded.[1]

The EU is the largest humanitarian aid donor in the world.[2] The theory of humanitarian assistance subscribed to by not only the Union but also organisations such as the International Committee of the Red Cross (ICRC) is one based solely upon need.[3] It should not be influenced by any other interests or geopolitical considerations.[4] As the Preamble to the 1996 Regulation on Humanitarian Aid notes:

---

[1] WG VII-Working Document 48, *Note from Mr Poul Nielson, Member of the European Commission on Humanitarian Assistance.*

[2] In 2006, for example, the European Union collectively (through both the EC budget and the bilateral contributions of the Member States) contributed over €2 billion worth of humanitarian aid. This amounted to over 40 per cent of all officially reported international humanitarian assistance. See COM(2007)317, p. 4.

[3] For a detailed account of the history, policies and principles of the ICRC, see D. Forsythe, *The Humanitarians: the International Committee of the Red Cross* (Cambridge: Cambridge University Press, 2005).

[4] See the Statute and Rules of Procedure of the International Red Cross and Red Crescent Movement and General Assembly Resolution 46/182, Strengthening of the

humanitarian aid the sole aim of which is to prevent or relieve human suffering, is accorded to victims without discrimination ... and must not be guided by, or subject to, political consideration ... decisions must be taken impartially and solely according to the victim's needs and interests.[5]

In a 2007 Communication which aims to set out the principles underpinning EU policy in this field, the Commission notes that the European Union 'has a firm commitment to the fundamental humanitarian principles' of, *inter alia*, neutrality and impartiality.[6] The commitment to these two principles can, however, present problems for the Union, in particular due to the place of humanitarian aid within the overall context of the Union's foreign policy. The first part of the discussion, therefore, looks briefly at the basic principles of humanitarian aid, namely neutrality and impartiality, to provide a framework for discussion. The chapter then goes on to examine the role of humanitarian aid as an instrument of the Union and its relationship with different EU policies. The chapter finally looks at practice and the use of humanitarian aid by the Union to pursue more general foreign policy and political objectives.

Coordination of Humanitarian Emergency Assistance of the United Nations, A/RES/46,182, 19 December 1991. See also, for examples, DG ECHO, *ECHO Aid Strategy 2005*, p. 1; DG ECHO, *2006 Operational Strategy*, p. 1; and DG ECHO, *Operational Strategy 2007*, SEC (2006)1626, p. 1.

[5] Council Regulation 1257/96, [1996] OJ L163/1, 2 July 1996. The emphasis on these principles is also clear in Article III-321(2) of the proposed Constitutional Treaty which states that humanitarian aid operations 'shall be conducted in compliance with the principles of international law and with the principles of impartiality, neutrality and non-discrimination'. At the informal European Council held in Lisbon on 18–19 October 2007, the Treaty Amending the Treaty on European Union and the Treaty Establishing the European Community, which is to replace the Constitutional Treaty, was agreed. See further the Table of Equivalences between the Constitutional Treaty and the Reform Treaty.

[6] COM(2007)317, p. 3. The two other fundamental principles mentioned in the Communication are 'humanity' and 'independence'. Humanity is defined as meaning that 'humankind shall be treated humanely in all circumstances by saving lives and alleviating suffering, while respecting the individual'. Independence is defined as '[h]umanitarian agencies must formulate and implement their own policies independently of (other) government policies or actions'. See COM(2007)317, p. 14. Humanity and independence as defined in the Communication do not lead to any separate legal issues as far as the Union's practices are concerned and will not be specifically discussed in detail. The 2007 Communication (COM(2007)317) is entitled 'Towards a European Consensus on Humanitarian Aid' and is seen by the Commission as leading to the humanitarian aid equivalent of the European Consensus on Development, which was discussed in Chapter 3.

6.1 Concepts of Neutrality and Impartiality and their Relationship with Humanitarian Aid

The 2007 Communication on humanitarian aid policy defines neutrality as 'not taking sides in hostilities or engaging at any time in controversies of a political, racial, religious or ideological nature'.[7] Neutrality is essentially a principle of abstention. In the context of a natural disaster, neutrality means that assistance must be given solely on the basis of need. In the context of an ongoing conflict, it means that humanitarian actors must not act in a way which will assist or hinder the belligerents in their military objectives.[8] Yet relieving the warring factions of any obligations they may have towards civilian populations, for example, by feeding them or providing shelter, does assist belligerents by releasing resources and indeed may perpetuate conflict in some instances or lead to a dependency upon such aid.[9] In such cases, non-involvement in the hostilities is the key indicator of neutrality.[10] Maintaining neutrality is exceptionally difficult, however, especially where in civil war situations, for example, the objective of one of the parties is the eradication of another ethnic or religious group.[11]

Different organisations take differing approaches to what neutrality encompasses for them in practice. The ICRC, for example, refused to denounce publicly or report the scale of atrocities committed by Nigerian troops in the Biafra conflict in the late 1960s as this would

---

[7] COM(2007)317, p. 14.

[8] See D. Curtis, *Politics and Humanitarian Aid: Debates, Dilemmas and Dissension*, Humanitarian Policy Group Report 10 (London: ODI, 2001).

[9] See M. Anderson, *Do No Harm: How Aid Can Support Peace – or War* (Boulder, CO: Lynne Rienner Publishers, 1999) and P. Hervey and J. Lind, *Dependency and Humanitarian Relief: a Critical Analysis*, Humanitarian Policy Group Report 19 (London: ODI, 2005). See also, Article 23(c) of Geneva Convention Relative to the Protection of Civilian Persons in Time of War, 1949 (Geneva Convention IV) 75 UNTS 287 which recognises that although states party to it must allow the free passage of consignments of medical and hospital stores, they do not have to do so if the military efforts or economy of the recipient state will gain a definite advantage as a consequence.

[10] Curtis, *Politics and Humanitarian Aid*. See more generally, C. Pirotte, B. Husson and F. Grunewald, *Responding to Emergencies and Fostering Development: the Dilemmas of Humanitarian Aid* (London: Zed Books, 1999); G. von Dok, C. Varg and R. Schroeder, *Humanitarian Challenges: the Political Dilemmas of Emergency Aid* (Lucerne/Luxembourg: Caritas, 2005) and for a more scathing view, D. Rieff, *A Bed for the Night: Humanitarianism in Crisis* (London: Vintage, 2002) p. 31 *et seq.*

[11] DAC, *DAC Guidelines on Conflict, Peace and Development Cooperation* (Paris: OECD, 1997) p. 30.

have, as it saw it, compromised its neutrality. It was the ICRC's silence on this matter which led to the founding of Médecin Sans Frontières (MSF) in 1971 by some disenchanted French doctors who had volunteered for the ICRC in Nigeria. The ICRC to date has very rarely publicly denounced any regime for its practices, as this may compromise its neutrality and thus access to those in need.[12] MSF, however, does denounce regimes which engage in atrocities but considers that this is not compromising its neutrality in providing aid to those in need; it is simply breaking with the ICRC's tradition of silence.[13] Publicly denouncing a regime is not, however, without cost. Oxfam, for example, was 'asked' to leave Sudan and wrap up its valuable projects in response to its director making a public statement that the Security Council was not doing enough to address the atrocities being committed in Darfur.[14] It is clear that to be practicable, neutrality must have some limits.[15] For the ICRC, for example, the Taliban's treatment of women in Afghanistan was not their business. Interference with an ICRC male doctor treating a female patient in an ICRC hospital would, however, have been the ICRC's business.[16]

With regard to impartiality, the 2007 Communication notes that the '[p]rovision of humanitarian assistance must be impartial and not based on nationality, race, religion, or political point of view. It must be based on need alone.'[17] Impartiality does not mean that the same amount of assistance is distributed to all. It requires an assessment of needs and that aid is distributed accordingly on an objective basis, without any regard to other considerations.[18] Non-discrimination,

---

[12] As discussed in Chapter 4, the ICRC was expelled from Myanmar in 2006 and in June 2007 publicly condemned the regime in Myanmar for gross and repeated violations of international humanitarian law. See ICRC Press Release 82/07.

[13] K. Anderson, 'Humanitarian Inviolability in Crisis: the Meaning of Impartiality and Neutrality for UN and NGO Agencies following the 2003–2004 Afghanistan and Iraq Conflicts' (2004) 17 *HHRJ* 41, 68.

[14] Cited by A. Bonwick, 'Advocates or Aid Worker? Approaches to Human Rights in Humanitarian Crises' in T. O'Neil (ed.), *Human Rights and Poverty Reduction: Realities, Controversies and Strategies – an ODI Meeting Series* (London: ODI, 2006) pp. 108, 109.

[15] *Ibid.* See also, Anderson, 'Humanitarian Inviolability in Crisis'.

[16] L. Minear, 'The Theory and Practice of Neutrality: Some Thoughts on the Tensions' (1999) 833 *IRRC* 63.

[17] COM(2007)317, p. 14.

[18] The manner in which needs are assessed by agencies differs, which can lead to various outcomes. See J. Darcy and C. Hofman, *According to Need? Needs Assessment and Decision-Making in the Humanitarian Sector*, Humanitarian Policy Group Report 15 (London: ODI, 2003).

proportionality and the absence of all subjective distinctions are essential. Abiding by the principle is again exceptionally difficult, especially for organisations such as the European Union. The Directorate-General for Humanitarian Aid (DG ECHO), for example, will often fund non-governmental organisations (NGOs), international organisations or specialised agencies of the United Nations that are providing aid in a conflict, whilst at the same time the Union will be involved in UN or other efforts at negotiating an end to the hostilities.[19] International pressure to end hostilities can lead to a temptation to provide less assistance to one side or the other, regardless of need, depending on the strength of the legal and moral culpability of the belligerents.[20] This ensures that impartiality is difficult to achieve. This is especially the case where one of the parties has a strong legal claim to being the victim of an act of aggression.

Neutrality and impartiality do not mean indifference to the plight of groups; they are operational principles. Humanitarian action, even if impartial and neutral, is a political act and will have a political effect. It should not, however, have a political intention in the sense of trying to influence events beyond relieving suffering.[21] After the fall of the Taliban in Afghanistan and the ousting of the Baathist regime in Iraq, a number of humanitarian organisations have engaged in what in effect amounts to nation building. Although some of these organisations claim their activities are neutral, such activities are not apolitical.[22]

---

[19] A recent example which in fact led to a positive, as opposed to a detrimental, outcome was in the aftermath of the Indian Ocean tsunami in December 2004. DG ECHO was funding humanitarian operations for affected populations in Indonesia but the Rapid Reaction Mechanism (Council Regulation 381/2001, Creating a Rapid Reaction Mechanism, [2001] OJ L57/5, 27 February 2001) was being used to finance mediation efforts between the Indonesian government and the Free Aceh Movement, which strengthened the reconstruction efforts. Cited by Court of Auditors, *Special Report No. 3/2006, Concerning the European Commission Humanitarian Aid Response to the Tsunami together with the Commission's Replies*, [2006] OJ C170/1, 21 July 2006, para. 26.

[20] See H. Baitenmann, 'NGOs and the Afghan War: the Politicisation of Humanitarian Aid' (1990) 12 *Third World Quarterly* 62 and COM(2001)231.

[21] See J. Macrae and N. Leander, *Shifting Sands: the Search for Coherence between Political and Humanitarian Responses to Complex Emergencies*, Humanitarian Policy Group Report 8 (London: ODI, 2000) and N. Middleton and P. O'Keefe, *Disaster and Development: the Politics of Humanitarian Aid* (London: Pluto Press, 1998).

[22] Anderson, 'Humanitarian Inviolability in Crisis', 42 cites the August 2003 attack on the UN headquarters and October 2003 attack on the ICRC headquarters, both in Baghdad, as examples of bodies which claimed to be acting neutrally but were perceived as being partisan and thus were attacked as expressions of opposition to the changing

6.2 Humanitarian Aid as a Foreign Policy Instrument of the Union

Humanitarian aid is one of the Union's most important external policies and DG ECHO is widely respected as a humanitarian aid donor.[23] Although DG ECHO has field experts working in different parts of the world to oversee the implementation of funding, it is not an 'aid agency' in the sense of having its own aid workers. DG ECHO instead funds either the governments of states where there is a humanitarian need or more usually other organisations which provide aid and assistance on the ground. These organisations are either NGOs, for example, Save the Children and Oxfam; intergovernmental agencies, for example, the ICRC; or UN specialised agencies, for example, the World Food Programme or the United Nations High Commissioner for Refugees. All organisations funded by DG ECHO must have a Framework Partnership Agreement (FPA) with it.[24] The relationship between DG ECHO and the NGO sector on the whole works effectively but at times the relationship with some NGOs has been conflictual.[25]

In 2006 humanitarian aid from the EC budget assisted 100 million people in seventy-five different countries.[26] The majority of DG ECHO's funding decisions are made on the basis of a scientific 'needs-based

political order. While there is some justification in seeing the United Nations as partisan (in particular, considering that the entire Iraqi sanctions regime was under the auspices of the United Nations) it is more difficult objectively to see ICRC operations in Iraq at the time as anything other than neutral.

[23] VOICE, *The Strengthening of EU Crisis Capabilities: What Impact on Humanitarian Aid?*, Voice Briefing Paper (October 2006) p. 3. VOICE is a consortium of ninety European NGOs who work with DG ECHO and represent approximately half of all the NGOs who have an FPA with DG ECHO.

[24] The exception to this is the relationship between UN specialised agencies and DG ECHO, which is defined in the Financial and Administrative Framework Agreement. The terms and conditions as to whom DG ECHO can provide funding to are set out in Articles 6–12 of Regulation 1257/96. There are approximately 200 FPAs currently in force.

[25] See the evidence of Johannes Luchner, who at the time was Head of Unit at DG ECHO, House of Commons International Development Select Committee, *Humanitarian Responses to Natural Disasters*, Seventh Report of the Session 2005–2006 (London: HMSO, 2006) vol. II, Evidence, Question, 176.

[26] COM(2007)317, p. 4. The average annual EC budget for humanitarian aid (as opposed to EU aid which includes both the EC budget and the bilateral humanitarian aid contributions made by the Member States) has been approximately €600 million. See DG ECHO, *Annual Report 2003*, COM(2004)583, p. 4 and DG ECHO, *Annual Report 2005*, COM(2006)441, p. 5. The financial envelope for humanitarian and food aid for 2007 is approximately €732 million.

analysis' and for those emergencies classified as 'forgotten emergencies' on a methodology which identifies emergencies where humanitarian needs are far outstripping funding and where other donors are not contributing to the needs situation.[27] DG ECHO's work cannot but be very valuable in helping to preserve life.

The geostrategic interests of donor states, however, rarely coincide with those of the victims of a humanitarian disaster. DG ECHO's mandate may require it not to be swayed by any political considerations, but that does not stop it being used as a general foreign policy instrument of the Union, if the need arises. Efforts to make humanitarian aid more efficient and to have less recourse to it have led to attempts to coordinate and indeed make the Union's different external relations policies complementary and coherent.[28] Complementarity requires action at differing levels to improve the effectiveness of that action. Coherence must imply that humanitarian aid is part of a set of responses to a particular situation. This requires the working out of overall strategies between different EU bodies and Directorates-General of the Commission and giving effect to their various responsibilities.[29] The link between development and humanitarian aid in the context of the Community, as discussed in Chapter 3, is the most obvious.[30]

The Community's development cooperation policy is far from impartial or neutral and makes no pretences to that effect. Humanitarian aid, however, is often portrayed as being separate and distinct from the politics of not only foreign policy but also development cooperation. As MacFarlane notes, humanitarian actors, in their most condescending form, consider themselves superior to both politics and foreign policy.[31]

---

[27] The technical manner in which DG ECHO carries out its 'needs-based' and 'forgotten emergency' assessments is described in DG ECHO, *Technical Note: Assessment of Humanitarian Needs and Identification of 'Forgotten Crises'*, 4 August 2006. The 'needs-based' assessment covers approximately 70 per cent of DG ECHO's annual budget.

[28] See COM(2007)317, p. 3 and the discussion below.

[29] There is a need, depending on the context, for coordination between the activities of DG ECHO, on the one hand, and, on the other either, DG RELEX, DG EuropeAid (AIDCO) or DG Environment.

[30] See ICEA/DPPC, *Development and Humanitarian Assistance of the European Union: an Evaluation of the Instruments and Programme Managed by the European Commission*, Final Synthesis Report (1999); COM(2001)231; and House of Commons International Development Select Committee, *Humanitarian Responses to Natural Disasters*, Seventh Report of the Session 2005–2006 (London: HMSO, 2006) vol. I.

[31] N. MacFarlane, *Politics and Humanitarian Action*, Thomas J. Watson Jr Institute Occasional Paper 41 (2000).

In the context of the Union, the relationship between humanitarian aid and development cooperation is not the only issue. There is also a strong relationship between crisis management and humanitarian aid. The Rapid Reaction Mechanism (RRM)[32] was a much broader instrument than the provision of emergency assistance and was, with regard to some activities, a potentially competing instrument. In the light of the new external relations legal architecture, the Stability Instrument, which has replaced the RRM, presents similar dilemmas.[33] The discussion will, therefore, initially examine the relationship between development and humanitarian aid before examining the relationship between humanitarian aid and other EU polices and instruments.

6.2.1 Relationship between Humanitarian Aid and Development Cooperation

The general relationship between development and humanitarian aid is, as discussed in Chapter 3, a natural one. An emergency intervention in the aftermath of a disaster often addresses the acute manifestation of chronic needs which had previously been addressed by development actors. Efforts by humanitarian actors to address acute needs often impact on prospects for the reduction of chronic needs, the long-term aim of development actors.[34] As development actors have increasingly identified poverty eradication as their key objective, it is clear that complex emergencies (whether primarily man-made or natural) impact upon the development process. Development funds allocated to mitigating or preventing disasters, therefore, will strengthen poverty reduction strategies, whereas failing to act may undermine or destroy them. A continuum thus exists between development and humanitarian aid, one that increasingly politicises all assistance to third states.

Structural approaches to development can help to reduce vulnerability in a natural disaster and DG ECHO, as mandated by the Regulation on Humanitarian Aid, spends a proportion of its budget on disaster preparation.[35] In the case of complex emergencies, development assistance

---

[32] Regulation 381/2001.
[33] Regulation 1717/2006, Establishing an Instrument for Stability ('Stability Instrument').
[34] See International Development Committee, *Humanitarian Responses to Natural Disasters*, vol. I, para. 17.
[35] Article 2(f) of Council Regulation 1257/97. This is known by the acronym DIPECHO (Disaster Preparedness ECHO). In the more general humanitarian aid industry such measures are known as disaster risk reduction (DRR). In the United Kingdom, the Department for International Development (DFID) now allocates 10 per cent of its

may help to contribute against the slide into conflict and the crises that would ensue. The relationship between development and humanitarian aid is, however, at times a delicate one and care must be taken to ensure that projects which are making a valuable contribution on the ground are not abandoned during the transition from one type of aid to the other. The end of an emergency and the return to development simply may mean disengagement by those providing assistance.[36]

The major problem in the relationship between humanitarian and development aid is that of politicising the former by linking it with the more overtly political objectives of development cooperation and foreign policy in general. In the United Kingdom, for example, the Department for International Development (DFID) which also acts in humanitarian emergencies was specifically created to distinguish it from the more politically driven Foreign and Commonwealth Office (FCO) and to avoid its work being compromised by the FCO.

In the EU context, the Commissioner for External Relations and the High Representative for the Common Foreign and Security Policy, of course, have distinct portfolios from those concerning development and humanitarian aid, although this is not to say that they are completely distinct areas of policy, as the discussion in Chapter 3 highlights. As far as humanitarian aid is concerned, Emma Bonino was the Commissioner for Humanitarian Aid only in the Santer Commission. Her successor, Poul Nielson, was the Commissioner for both Development Cooperation and Humanitarian Aid. This is also the case with the office holder at the time of writing, Louis Michel. A clear distinction is maintained in practice between DG ECHO and EuropeAid,[37] which is responsible for the implementation of non-humanitarian aid. EuropeAid is part of the portfolio of the External Relations Commissioner whereas DG ECHO is the responsibility of the Commissioner for Development Cooperation and Humanitarian Aid. Notwithstanding the separation of DG ECHO from EuropeAid, the 'two-hatted' portfolio of both development cooperation and humanitarian aid still increases the danger of EC humanitarian aid being influenced by the more general foreign policy objectives that have

---

budget for such measures. Johannes Luchner has noted how DG ECHO has traditionally focused on small-scale community-based DRR projects, but was now trying to mainstream disaster preparedness into all its programmes. See International Development Committee, *Humanitarian Responses to Natural Disasters*, vol. I para. 172.

[36] See I. Smillie, *Relief and Development: the Struggle for Synergy*, HWP Occasional Paper 33 (1998).

[37] Also known as AIDCO.

become increasingly prominent in Community development policy. An advantage of this approach, however, is that with one set of political guidance (as opposed to two, which would be the case if the portfolio was split up) it can be much easier for delegations in third countries, to whom much of the aid-making decisions have been delegated, to ensure that projects are as properly designed, implemented and effective as can be in the circumstances. This does require, however, effective coordination between the activities of DG ECHO and EuropeAid.

European humanitarian assistance is intrinsically linked with the EC's development cooperation policies due to the 'grey zone': the period of time after an emergency but before longer-term development programmes, if any, commence in the affected region. DG ECHO's strategy papers, for example from 2001 and 2003, talk of streamlining the grey zone, which necessitates a coherent and effective linkage between the handover phases of assistance as well as coordination with other actors.[38] Policy papers emanating from DG ECHO have also long emphasised the linking of relief, rehabilitation and development (LRRD).[39] As DG ECHO functions through funding partners, this can be difficult to achieve at the practical level for some organisations. The different types of work tend to be specialised, and historically most NGOs have primarily focused on either humanitarian or development aid.[40] Some intergovernmental agencies (as opposed to NGOs), however, have broadened their work, thus increasingly politicising the allocation of aid. The World Bank and the Development Assistance Committee (DAC) of the OECD, for example, now increasingly deal

---

[38] See DG ECHO, *ECHO Aid Strategy 2001* and DG ECHO, *ECHO Aid Strategy 2003*. This streamlining of the grey zone was welcomed in the so-called Carlotti Report, A5-0433/2002, which was endorsed in a resolution of the European Parliament, see [2004] OJ C38E/35, 12 February 2004.

[39] See DG ECHO, *Operational Strategy 2007*, SEC(2006)1626, p. 5, COM(2007)317, p. 10 and COM(2005)153. For the definitions and assessments of LRRD in the Community context, see COM(1996)153, SEC(2000)514 and COM(2001)153. The European Consensus on Development (Joint Statement by the Council and the Representatives of the Governments of the Member States Meeting within the Council, the European Parliament and the Commission, The European Consensus on Development, 22 November 2005, [2006] OJ C46/1, 24 February 2006) para. 21 also strongly commits the European Union to linking emergency aid, rehabilitation and development aid.

[40] J. Macrae (ed.), *The New Humanitarianisms: a Review of Trends in Global Humanitarian Action*, Humanitarian Policy Group Report 11 (London: ODI, 2002). Some NGOs, such as Oxfam, Save the Children, CARE and World Vision, are exceptions and have always been at a competitive advantage in receiving allocations of aid.

with conflict situations, while the United Nations High Commissioner for Refugees (UNHCR) and the Inter-Agency Standing Committee on Humanitarian Affairs have also moved into development.[41]

The grey zone has historically come within DG ECHO's competence due to the absence of flexible and rapid instruments in other parts of the Commission and because of the awareness of the relationship between development and humanitarian aid. It has, on the whole, been easier and quicker to obtain funding from DG ECHO than under all other Community programmes and it has often been used for that reason, even in the absence of an emergency.[42] Since its 2001 Strategy Paper, DG ECHO has identified a concentration on its core mandate, that is, to save and preserve lives in emergencies, as a priority. This does give a clearer indication to agencies and NGOs as to the scale of the European Union's intervention and its form, in turn allowing them to plan with greater accuracy. The problem this leads to, however, is one of having to coordinate activities and programmes with other parts of the Commission and ensuring that a vacuum does not exist between relief and development. The aim should be to avoid a hiatus in the Union's external action during the different phases of relief, rehabilitation and development.

A distinction should be drawn, however, between the effectiveness of linking relief, rehabilitation and development assistance in the aftermath of natural disasters as opposed to during man-made crises.[43] In a

---

[41] Macrae, *The New Humanitarianisms*.

[42] See Court of Auditors, *Special Report No. 2/97, Concerning Humanitarian Aid from the European Union between 1992 and 1995*, [1997] OJ C143/1, 12 May 1997 and ICEA/DPPC, *Development Assistance*. SEC(2001)873 established a procedure which streamlined humanitarian decision-making, allowing DG ECHO to take decisions for primary emergency aid of up to €3 million for a period of three months. The Commissioner responsible for humanitarian aid has the power to take emergency decisions for sums up to €30 million for operations for a period of six months. The Rapid Reaction Mechanism (Regulation 381/2001) was established to allow the Commission to respond quickly to emergencies and to provide aid which is not solely humanitarian.

[43] The distinction between natural and man-made disasters is, of course, an artificial one. Most emergencies or disasters combine natural hazards with human vulnerability. Natural hazards can be either weather-related (for example, storms, drought or flooding) or geophysical (for example, earthquakes, volcanoes or landslides). Vulnerability can be defined as 'the extent to which a person or group is likely to be affected by adverse circumstances'. The vulnerability of a population to disasters depends on many variables, for example, poor governance, civil war, economic policies and the prevalence of epidemic diseases. A natural hazard will only lead to a disaster if it affects a population which is vulnerable to it. Furthermore, the extent of the impact of the disaster will be determined by the ability of the population to anticipate, cope

natural disaster, for example the Indian Ocean tsunami of December 2004 or the earthquake in northern Pakistan in October 2005, there is in many senses a linear progression. The regime(s) in power are usually not hostile to such aid and the key issues are ensuring that the assistance received is not detrimental to long-term development assistance, while ensuring that urgently needed aid is being supplied.[44] Clearly this requires coordination and consistency in operations and a close working relationship with those actually assisting on the ground. Emergencies which are primarily caused by conflicts, however, are much more difficult. There is usually no linear change and the intensity of the fighting will differ from one part of the affected region to another. Furthermore, the various factions will also have their own agendas as to the types of aid provided and to whom. The situation can, therefore, change continuously. Any infrastructure which is replaced (or has been built for the first time) is still in danger of being destroyed.[45] In such circumstances it often becomes very difficult to distinguish between humanitarian (short-term relief aid supplied to those in desperate need), rehabilitation (assistance which aims to stabilise the situation and prepare for development) and development aid.

Defined in the strict sense, humanitarian aid is provided where, for whatever reasons, development cooperation policies have failed in their objectives and slippage into 'disaster' has occurred. Humanitarian aid, where it is being provided as part of a continuum of responses, is also concerned with sustainability and long-term needs, which may not equate with the immediate needs on the ground.[46] Subordinating humanitarian aid to longer-term objectives can in these circumstances cost more lives. Humanitarian aid thus is no longer about simply relieving suffering. It is also about ensuring sustainability and is part and parcel of the instruments used to achieve long-term development

with and recover from it. On this basis there are no purely natural disasters; human and natural elements are always inextricably linked. This discussion draws heavily from International Development Committee, *Humanitarian Responses to Natural Disasters*, vol. I, para. 11.

[44] See United Nations Office for the Coordination of Humanitarian Affairs, *Humanitarian Report 1997: the Link between Relief and Development* (New York: United Nations, 1997). See further Court of Auditors, *Special Report No. 3/2006*.

[45] Rieff, *A Bed for the Night*, p. 22 gives the example of the Italian UN official who had organised the building of a hospital in Afghanistan on the same spot three times and on each occasion it was destroyed by the forces of the Uzbek warlord, Abdul Rashid Dostam. The aid worker felt he could not do it a fourth time.

[46] This idea is recognised in Articles 1–3 of Regulation 1257/96.

objectives. Seeing humanitarian aid as part of a package of measures and responses can divert attention from just how limited the impact of such aid can be in alleviating suffering. As Sadako Ogata, the former United Nations High Commissioner for Refugees, has been quoted as saying, 'there are no humanitarian solutions to humanitarian problems'.[47]

The rationale behind linking the different types of aid was that humanitarian aid created dependency and did little to assist in tackling the root causes of emergencies. This approach to humanitarian aid, where it is used as a component of an overall strategy to reform and create desirable circumstances in third countries, is part of what has been called 'a new humanitarianism'.[48] The end of the Cold War and the absence of competing sources of funding and ideologies has led to a broader spectrum of views as to what humanitarian aid should be aiming to achieve.[49] DG ECHO has been part of this shift and in practice has been funding projects which aim to achieve more than simply relieving basic suffering in an emergency situation. The blurring of the different types of aid, while understandable in the context of the long-term effectiveness of assistance, is a step backwards as far as the non-political nature of humanitarian aid, which DG ECHO has always professed, is concerned and furthermore may detract from essential life-sustaining assistance.

DG ECHO has increasingly tried to plan and has an annual strategy in place; global plans accordingly now exist, which set out priorities, objectives and budgets for each given region.[50] The problem, however, is that in the context of sub-Saharan Africa, for example, given the enormity of the needs situation, projects have barely had enough funding to focus on basic life-sustaining aid let alone tackle other objectives. Despite the impressive size of its budget, DG ECHO cannot realistically pursue other objectives as well. In Kosovo, for example, at the turn of the Millennium assistance varied from core humanitarian aid to

---

[47] Cited by Rieff, A Bed for the Night, p. 22.
[48] See MacFarlane, Politics and Humanitarian Action and Macrae, The New Humanitarianisms.
[49] See N. Leander and J. Macrae (eds.), Terms of Engagement: Conditions and Conditionality in Humanitarian Action, Humanitarian Policy Group Report 6 (London: ODI, 2002) and Macrae and Leander, Shifting Sands.
[50] Each annual strategy paper identifies the priority countries for each region as well as cross-cutting priorities. In the most recent strategy papers, children who are suffering as a consequence of humanitarian crises and water sanitation have also been identified as priorities for funding.

rehabilitation and resettlement aid and also aimed to help with the effects of the transition to a market economy.[51] Even allowing for the links being made between the different types of assistance, given the enormity of the situation elsewhere, it is difficult to see how in the light of its mandate this was a priority for funding from DG ECHO.

For emergency and longer-term aid to be complementary to one another, it is not only DG ECHO but also the other Directorates-General of the Commission which must consider the link between them. In practice this has at times been difficult for the other Directorates-General because of the scope of the regulations concerned with a certain region. For example, the Regulation for Uprooted Persons in Asia and Latin America contained provisions on better linkage between development, rehabilitation and relief aid.[52] Other regulations, however, such as the TACIS Regulation, did not allow for rehabilitation and thus other budget lines had to be used for such activities, making it more difficult to link up the different types of aid.[53]

Even where the various Directorates-General of the Commission do have the competence to ensure that there is no hiatus in the provision of assistance, they do not always coordinate their activities as well as they should. For example, after the Indian Ocean tsunami of December 2004, in addition to DG ECHO acting and the Humanitarian Aid Regulation being relied upon, a number of other instruments and Commission Directorates-General were also involved in the emergency effort. Initially, the Community Civil Protection Mechanism (CCPM) based in DG Environment was used to send experts to the affected regions to help assess the situation and coordinate the arrival and distribution

---

[51] See Court of Auditors, *Special Report No. 2/2001, Concerning the Management of Emergency Humanitarian Aid for the Victims of the Kosovo Crisis*, [2001] OJ C16/1, 12 June 2001 and the discussion further below.

[52] See Articles 2 and 3 of Council Regulation 443/97, on Operations to Aid Uprooted People in Asian and Latin American Developing Countries, [1997] OJ L68/1, 8 March 1997, which has been repealed and replaced by Regulation 1905/2006, Establishing a Financing Instrument for Development Cooperation, [2006] OJ L378/41, 27 December 2006. The Preamble to Regulation 1905/2006 emphasises the link between the different types of aid.

[53] Council Regulation 99/2000, Concerning the Provision of Assistance to the Partner States in Eastern Europe and Central Asia, [2000] OJ L12/1, 18 January 2000, repealed and replaced by Regulation 1085/2006, Establishing an Instrument for Pre-Accession Assistance, [2006] OJ L210/82, 31 July 2006. Regulation 1085/2006, does not refer to the link between the different types of aid.

of the civil protection assistance offered by the Member States.[54] Furthermore, the Rapid Reaction Mechanism, which was based in the Directorate-General for External Relations (DG RELEX), was also used to allow the Commission to respond in a rapid and flexible manner to the unfolding crises so as to try and create conditions under which longer-term development objectives could be pursued.[55] Longer-term rehabilitation, reconstruction and recovery aid were also sent under the responsibility of DG RELEX and EuropeAid.

Notwithstanding the scale of the disaster and the fact that it happened during the holiday period, DG ECHO was still able to make funding decisions and allocated €23 million of aid within five days of the tsunami striking.[56] There was an overwhelming response to the disaster and the scale of the funding donated, including that from DG ECHO, was such that it exceeded the ability of some partners (who quickly arrived in the affected areas) to fully utilise the aid. This, of course, is not something the Commission can be blamed for. Where there was a substantial shortcoming in the Commission's response, however, was in the coordination between the different Directorates-General of the Commission.

It is somewhat ironic that DG ECHO granted €1 million to support the United Nations Office for the Coordination of Humanitarian Affairs, so as to assist with the coordination, implementing and monitoring of the aid coming in, yet the Court of Auditors found that in the Commission's own response to the tsunami there was inadequate coordination between the different Directorates-General. In particular, DG Environment (who were involved due to the use of the Community Civil Protection Mechanism) and DG ECHO in both Sri Lanka and Indonesia did not adequately exchange information or coordinate their work.[57] Nevertheless, there has been an improvement in the Commission's performance. In 2000, the Court of Auditors, when examining the relationship between the work of (what are now) DG ECHO and DG Development in ACP states, found that their programming had been *ad hoc* and unsystematic. The Court of Auditors considered that at that

---

[54] Court of Auditors, *Special Report No. 3/2006*, para. 6. The Community Civil Protection Mechanism was established by Council Decision 2001/792/EC, Euratom of 23 October 2001, [2001] OJ L57/5, 27 February 2001. This decision has now been supplemented by Council Decision 2007/162/EC, Euratom of 5 March 2007, [2007] OJ L71/9, 10 March 2007 which establishes a financial instrument.

[55] Court of Auditors, *Special Report No. 3/2006*, para. 7.

[56] *Ibid.* para. 12.   [57] *Ibid.* para. 24.

time DG ECHO and DG Development often acted as different donors rather than complementary units in the same organisation.[58] In the aftermath of the Indian Ocean tsunami, the Commission adopted a further communication on how EU disaster and crisis responses in third countries could be reinforced.[59] The underlying emphasis of the Communication is again how all EU action should be coordinated, coherent and complementary. Whether this will lead to a further improvement in the coordination and coherence of Commission responses to major emergencies remains to be seen.

6.2.2 Relationship between Humanitarian Aid and Other EU Foreign Policy Instruments

The relationship between humanitarian aid and development cooperation, as noted above, is not the only issue in the overall structure of the Union's external relations architecture. Johannes Luchner, at the time of writing the Head of DG ECHO, has argued that there has been a 'fundamental sea-change' in European humanitarian aid since the tsunami of 2004, in that civil protection and military authorities have started to become interested in humanitarian aid and civil protection in third states.[60] The tsunami was the major natural disaster which accelerated the already increasing use of both civilian and military instruments to tackle crises in third states.

The use of both means by the Union and or its Member States in a disaster situation is, however, not a new one. The Helsinki European Council of December 1999, for example, had called on the Commission to take specific measures to set up a 'non-military crisis management mechanism ... to coordinate and make more effective the various civilian means and resources, in parallel with the military ones, at the disposal of the Union and the Member States'.[61] This implies that

---

[58] Court of Auditors, *Special Report No. 4/2000, On Rehabilitation Actions for ACP Countries as an Instrument to Prepare for Normal Development Aid*, [2000] OJ C113/1, 19 April 2000.

[59] COM(2005)153. There has also been a major report commissioned by Jan Egeland, the United Nations Under-Secretary General for Humanitarian Affairs, *Humanitarian Response Review* (New York and Geneva: United Nations, 2005) which makes recommendations addressed to all involved in the humanitarian aid industry as to how to achieve better coordination and results in humanitarian operations.

[60] International Development Committee, *Humanitarian Responses to Natural Disasters*, vol. II, Evidence, Question 157.

[61] The Helsinki European Council, 10 and 11 December 1999, (1999) 12 *Bull. EU* I.1, Annex IV. The Helsinki European Council was further developing the work of the Cologne European Council, 3 and 4 June 1999, (1999) 6 *Bull. EU* I.1.

humanitarian aid is perceived to be part and parcel of non-military and military responses to a crisis. The Commission confirmed this view in its Communication on the issue, when it stated, '[r]ecent conflicts ... have shown that the EU possesses a wide range of humanitarian, economic, financial and civilian resources'.[62] The European Security Strategy gives the same impression.[63] The proposed Constitutional Treaty in Article I-41 notes when referring to the Common Security and Defence Policy that it shall provide the Union with an operational capacity drawing on civil and military assets. Article III-309, when referring to Article I-41, specifically mentions humanitarian aid as one of the civilian means to be used.

The idea that humanitarian aid is simply one of the tools at the disposal of the Union to further achieve its foreign policy objectives is thus not new. An important legal development which in part contributed to the blurring of humanitarian and other EU capacities was the adoption in 2001 of a Regulation Establishing the Rapid Reaction Mechanism (RRM). As noted above, the Regulation Establishing the RRM has at the start of 2007 been repealed by the Regulation Establishing a Stability Instrument. As it is too early as yet to tell to what extent the Stability Instrument in practice will impact upon EU humanitarian aid policy, practice under the RRM will be examined before discussing the Stability Instrument.

The aim of the RRM was not to create new instruments *per se* but to use those that already existed.[64] It was a complementary mechanism which aimed to improve the capacity for rapid and flexible EU action. The overall objective was for the RRM and the Commission's crisis management unit to facilitate early intervention and overall coherence in disasters.[65]

The RRM was conceived to allow the European Union to respond quickly to emergencies without having to engage in cumbersome lengthy bureaucracy. As the RRM Regulation noted, one of its aims is to 're-establish in situations of crisis or emerging crisis, the conditions of stability essential to the proper implementation and success of these aid, assistance and cooperation policies and programmes'.[66] On 13 June 2001, however, a primary emergency operation procedure

[62] COM(2000)119.
[63] J. Solana, *A Secure Europe in a Better World: European Security Strategy*, p. 13, approved by the European Council, 12–13 December 2003, Doc. 5381/04.
[64] See the Annex to Regulation 381/2001.
[65] *Ibid.*   [66] Article 3 of Regulation 381/2001.

also came into force for DG ECHO.[67] The Commission decided that DG ECHO should have an instant response capacity to add to its existing capability. In theory, the two procedures should have been complementary.

The distinction drawn between humanitarian aid and the RRM by the Commission (which unlike the Council tried to maintain one) was that DG ECHO's objective is to alleviate the suffering of the individual from man-made and natural disasters, while the RRM was intended to provide resources for urgent operations of crisis management and conflict prevention linked into the overall context of the CFSP and the European Security and Defence Policy (ESDP).[68] This division of responsibilities can raise problems, however, for humanitarian aid actors. It can cause confusion between humanitarian and non-humanitarian actors in the delivery of relief. This may result in some humanitarian actors withdrawing as the overlap compromises, or at least threatens, their neutrality and impartiality. There are numerous instances in the past of NGOs refusing to accept funding or working with DG ECHO as it has been perceived to be too politically loaded and often also a part of a 'political' crisis-management operation.[69]

The legal base of Article 308 TEC for the RRM did distinguish it, to some extent, from humanitarian and development aid but the competing, if not overlapping, objectives of the RRM and humanitarian aid were more than apparent. The RRM Regulation was explicit that activities covered by the Humanitarian Aid Regulation should not be funded under it.[70] DG ECHO has, however, in practice, focused on complex emergencies as opposed to 'pure' natural disasters (which due to their unpredictability make long-term planning difficult) and thus the overlap between different activities funded under the RRM, development cooperation policy and humanitarian aid have at times been clear. To take one example, de-mining operations have been funded by DG ECHO, under development cooperation policies and under the RRM.[71]

---

[67] See SEC(2001)873 and the discussion above.

[68] See COM(2000)119 and *EU Crisis Response Capability: Institutions and Processes for Conflict Prevention and Management*, IGC Issues Report No. 2 (2001) p. 9.

[69] See S. Jaspers, *Solidarity and Soup Kitchens: a Review of Principles and Practice for Food Distribution in Conflict*, Humanitarian Policy Group Report 7 (London: ODI, 2000) and further VOICE, *Strengthening of EU Crisis Capabilities*.

[70] See the Preamble to and Article 2 of Regulation 381/2001.

[71] See COM(2000)119. See further, European Commission Conflict Prevention and Crisis Management Unit, *Rapid Reaction Mechanism End of Programme Report* (December 2003) s. 4.4.

Examining the five instances in which the RRM was used in 2001 (twice in Macedonia, once in Afghanistan and the Congo, and in one programme which covered Indonesia, Nepal and the Pacific), it appears that with the exception of the last programme, DG ECHO could have acted instead with regard to part of each of these programmes. For the period between 2002 and the end of 2006, however, the position is different. In the first year of the RRM's operation there was a clear overlap with some of the work being carried out by DG ECHO. But for the period between 2002 and the end of 2006 there was a noticeable shift away from such work. The RRM was instead being used, for example, to sustain democracy in Bolivia, to support the Benghazi Aids Action Plan in Libya and the rule of law in Georgia.[72]

The RRM, in this sense, was a welcome development for DG ECHO if it genuinely wished to ensure its neutrality and concentrate on the core of its mandate. The RRM could be seen as a substitute for part of the work DG ECHO was involved in where the European Union wished to overtly influence a particular course of events in a security-related crisis but maintain the neutrality and impartiality of humanitarian aid. The other side of the coin, however, was that any RRM-based intervention clearly further politicised the Union's intervention in every situation it was involved in and by association the work of organisations funded by and working with DG ECHO. As the RRM budget was relatively small, at €25 million per year, however, and any operations funded by it limited in time to six months duration, it was unable to significantly overlap in practice with humanitarian aid.[73] Such limitations do not now exist under the terms of the Stability Instrument, which is also much wider in its ambit than the RRM.[74]

The Stability Instrument has a financial envelope of over €2 billion for the six year period from 2007–2013.[75] Unlike the RRM, therefore, projects funded under the Stability Instrument will not be severely limited by budgetary constraints. Considering the very broad scope of activities that the Stability Instrument covers, the overlap with some of

[72] Information concerning all RRM projects is available at http://ec.europa.eu/external_relations/cfsp/cpcm/rrm/
[73] The budget was initially limited to €25 million per annum. For 2005 it was €30 million. Under Article 8 of Regulation 381/2001, any RRM action had to be limited to a maximum duration of six months.
[74] For background on the instrument see COM(2004)630.
[75] Article 24 of Regulation 1717/2006.

DG ECHO's work is very clear.[76] It is thus imperative that if humanitarian aid policy is to remain as neutral and impartial as possible, a clear distinction between the work of DG RELEX (under the Stability Instrument) and DG ECHO (under the Humanitarian Aid Regulation) needs to be maintained. It is apparent that despite the palpable danger that the RRM would supersede humanitarian aid policy, in practice this did not really materialise. The Preamble to the Stability Instrument, however, emphasises that the European Security Strategy, the fight against terrorism and the objectives of the CFSP are all relevant to the projects to be funded under it. The far greater scope of the Stability Instrument, the competence it confers to intervene, and the continuing emphasis on the coherence of the Union's response to a crisis, all ensure that there is a greater risk that EU humanitarian aid policy will be affected by it. Further to the adoption of the Stability Instrument there are two possible dangers for the Union's humanitarian aid policy. Humanitarian aid may increasingly be marginalised to those emergencies in which the Union has little geopolitical interest and thus be seen as a policy of limited importance. In the alternative, where humanitarian assistance is granted in those emergencies where the Union has a political interest, it will be integrated into the political, military or security agendas of the Union and its Member States, further compromising the neutrality and impartiality of the policy.

The military and security agendas of states are an inherent part of their political priorities and where military operations have become involved in the delivery of humanitarian aid this has caused real problems with trying to respect the principles of neutrality and impartiality. This has become apparent, in particular, in the aftermath of the Indian Ocean tsunami and the 2005 earthquake in northern Pakistan. In many senses, however, both of these disasters are atypical; most of DG ECHO's work does not involve emergencies on such a large scale. But it is precisely in emergencies of such scale that the logistical support and capacities of the military are most valuable. In the context of the Pakistani earthquake, a number of European NGOs expressed extreme discomfort at the Pakistani military invading the 'humanitarian space' which humanitarian agencies need to maintain their neutrality and impartiality. ActionAid, the British Red Cross, Care International and the International Crisis Group have all been very critical of the role played

---

[76] See Article 3 of Regulation 1717/2006.

by the military during the Pakistani earthquake.[77] Despite these reservations, it was also widely recognised that without the role that was played by the military, the relief effort would have been even more severely hampered in the delivery of the necessary aid by the weather conditions, the inhospitable nature of the landscape, the remoteness of some of the affected areas and the sheer scale of the destruction.[78]

Johannes Luchner has argued that despite the reticence about the military increasingly becoming involved in the distribution of European humanitarian aid, there are two options. He has stated, 'either the military hugs us or we give them a hug. I prefer the second one'. Two sets of guidelines have been adopted under the auspices of the UN Office for the Coordinator of Humanitarian Affairs on the role of the military in a humanitarian crisis. Both make it very clear that the military should only be used in humanitarian emergencies as a very last resort.[79]

Notwithstanding reservations about the role to be played by the military in emergencies, the Union has taken steps to ensure that there is a greater degree of civil–military coordination in EU crisis management. The Civilian Headline Goal 2008, for example, as part of the ESDP, calls for the ensuring of 'close cooperation and coordination with the military efforts throughout all phases of the operations. When necessary, civilian crisis management missions must be able to draw on military enabling capabilities.'[80] In the aftermath of the Indian Ocean tsunami, the Commission adopted an important Communication which sought to reinforce EU disaster and crisis response in third states. This again emphasised the relationship between EU civilian and military

---

[77] See International Development Committee, *Humanitarian Responses to Natural Disasters*, vol. I, para. 138. See also, the more general position on the very limited role which should be played by the military adopted by VOICE, VOICE Statement on the Humanitarian Aid Policy of the European Union, 5 March 2007.

[78] See IRIN, *When Disaster Strikes: the Response to the South Asian Earthquake* (June 2006) p. 11 *et seq.* which is very detailed on the role of the military in Pakistan and how its work was essential.

[79] See Guidelines on the Use of Military and Civil Defence Assets to Support United Nations Humanitarian Activities in Complex Emergencies, March 2003 (representatives from DG ECHO, the EC and twelve Member States helped draft the guidelines) and Guidelines on the Use of Military and Civil Defence Assets to Support United Nations Humanitarian Activities in Disaster Relief, as revised, October 2006.

[80] Civilian Headline Goal 2008, 7 December 2004, Doc. 15863/04. For detailed discussion, see A. Nowak (ed.), *Civilian Crisis Managements: the EU Way*, Chaillot Paper No. 90 (Paris: ISS, 2006).

capabilities.[81] Where EU military operations have been deployed, the legal mandate has made clear that there must be a coherent EU response and that all Community action will be consistent with the military operation.[82] Where military operations are sent to an area where an ongoing emergency exists, the danger that humanitarian aid policy will simply be absorbed into the overall EU response to a crisis is very clear. In such circumstances, any needs-based assessment of the situation may simply be relegated in comparison to the Union's political priorities which may, depending upon the circumstances, cost lives.

Speaking in 2006 in the context of military involvement in humanitarian emergencies, Johannes Luchner stated, 'I have not had one incident, I have not seen one programming year where we were under any kind of political pressure, for instance, to change our needs assessment or to disregard our needs assessment at a global level. We have had no change in the principle that we do the needs assessment and seventy per cent of our funds are pre-programmed to make sure we have the coverage.'[83] As the Union's capabilities to respond to crises in third states develop, there is a real danger that the pressure to move away from a solely needs-based assessment for an emergency becomes greater. The massive over-distribution of humanitarian aid in Kosovo or the change in approach towards Afghanistan (both are discussed below) make it clear that while DG ECHO's core budget may largely remain intact, extra funding is found as and when needed to pay for humanitarian operations which reflect general foreign policy objectives.

The other point that Luchner's assertion overlooks is that although there may not to date have been any pressure to change the 'needs-based assessment', as the Union becomes further drawn into and involved in any crisis, the organisations it provides funds to deliver humanitarian aid to will increasingly feel that their neutrality and impartiality is compromised by being associated with DG ECHO. Some organisations may as a consequence refuse to work with DG ECHO and

---

[81] COM(2005)153, p. 4.

[82] See, for examples, Articles 5 and 14 of Joint Action 2005/557/CFSP, on the European Union Civilian-Military Supporting Action to the African Union Mission in the Darfur Region of Sudan, [2005] OJ L188/46, 20 July 2005 and Articles 8 and 11 of Joint Action 2006/319/CFSP, on the European Union Military Operation in Support of the United Nations Organisation Mission in the Democratic Republic of the Congo during the Election Process, [2006] OJ L116/98, 29 April 2006.

[83] International Development Committee, *Humanitarian Responses to Natural Disasters*, vol. II, Evidence, Question 176.

seek to distance themselves from it. As noted above, this has certainly happened in the past. Furthermore, VOICE (a coalition of ninety EU-based NGOs, all of whom have an FPA with DG ECHO) has made it clear in a statement that, in the EU context, any further blurring of the boundaries between civilian and military responses to crises will lead in the 'long term to the erosion of humanitarian principles, reduced access to affected populations and potential implications for the security of professional humanitarian workers'.[84]

Even where military capabilities are not deployed as part of the Union's response to a crisis, civilian crisis instruments can substantially impact upon the role of the Union's humanitarian aid policy. As noted above, there is a Community Civil Protection Mechanism (CCPM).[85] The CCPM, which is based in the Directorate-General for the Environment, supports and facilitates the mobilisation of vital civil protection assistance for the immediate needs of disaster-stricken countries. It can be used to provide assistance to both EU Member States and third countries. It has since 2001 been used to provide assistance in, for example, France following the flooding in 2003, Portugal to deal with forest fires in 2004 and Iran following the Bam earthquake in 2003. Further to the Indian Ocean tsunami, the General Affairs and External Relations Council in January 2005 sought in part to examine how the mechanism should be improved.[86] A Council Decision establishing a financial instrument has now been adopted using Articles 308 TEC and 203 Euratom as legal bases, to try and ensure that the CCPM can continue to function and is more effective than it was.[87]

Although the decision states that it cannot be used to finance activities covered by the Humanitarian Aid Regulation, the clearly overlapping objectives of the CCPM and Humanitarian Aid Regulation simply cannot be ignored.[88] The Commission proposal on improving the CCPM notes that '[c]ivil protection is about immediate relief in the first hours and days of a disaster'.[89] It is thus identical in its objectives

---

[84] VOICE, Statement on Humanitarian Aid Policy.
[85] See further COM(2005)137, COM(2005)153 and COM(2006)29 as well as M. Barnier, *For a European Civil Protection Force: Europe Aid* (May 2006) ('Barnier Report') as to how the system should be reformed. The report has not been favourably received by all EU institutions.
[86] Extraordinary Meeting of the General Affairs and External Relations Council, 7 January 2005, Doc. 5142/05.
[87] Council Decision 2007/162/EC, Euratom, [2007] OJ L71/9, 10 March 2007.
[88] Preamble to Council Decision 2007/162/EC, Euratom.
[89] COM(2005)137, p. 3.

to humanitarian aid in that its purpose is to save lives and alleviate the effects of a disaster in its immediate aftermath. It will differ, of course, in that humanitarian aid is also used in complex emergencies, whereas the CCPM is for use in the aftermath of a disaster which exists primarily due to natural causes, such as earthquakes and flooding. The Communication does note, however, that there are four differences between humanitarian aid and the CCPM: civil protection assistance can address the environmental consequences of disasters as well as their humanitarian impact; civil protection assistance is provided through teams, experts and equipment provided by the governments participating in the mechanism, rather than through the humanitarian organisations used by DG ECHO; civil protection assistance may be delivered both inside and outside the European Union whereas human-itarian assistance can only be supplied to third states; and the CCPM can be used also as a tool for facilitating and supporting CFSP crisis-management operations.[90]

Although a joint Council–Commission Declaration was adopted (on 29 September 2003) which sets out the specific rules for the use of the CCPM in CFSP crisis management operations, and no exact equivalent exists for humanitarian aid, it is clear that humanitarian aid is part and parcel of the Union's instruments in response to crises in any part of the world. The other three distinctions drawn by the Commission between the role of the CCPM and humanitarian aid are largely meaningless. The institutions and bodies which are involved may differ but the objectives of the CCPM and humanitarian aid as far as natural disasters in third states are concerned are largely identical and where the CCPM is used, the different Directorates-General of the Commission will at times compete with one another.

This competition was very clear in the response to the Indian Ocean tsunami. The CCPM has a Civil Protection Monitoring and Information Centre (MIC) based and operated by DG Environment which has been established to coordinate the participation of the thirty European states who pool their civil protection resources, resources which can then be made available to any disaster-stricken state which asks for assistance. In the context of the tsunami, despite the existence of mechanisms to coordinate operations between the MIC and DG ECHO, the Court of Auditors noted that the MIC 'had not confined itself to civil protection activities, but had overlapped with the humanitarian field which is

---

[90] *Ibid.*

beyond their role and given the impression that it was coordinating *all* EU assistance'.[91]

Considering the number of instruments and their respective objectives, there has long been a fundamental problem in obtaining a coherent response to a crisis from the Union.[92] What is required is the linking of crisis management (whether military or civilian) to development cooperation objectives while simultaneously maintaining a distinction from humanitarian aid. But at the same time, the link between humanitarian and rehabilitation and reconstruction aid must be ensured and the delivery of all aid must be coordinated with aid agencies. This is never going to be straightforward. It is very clear that the CCPM with its identical objectives and broader scope is yet another instrument competing with the Humanitarian Aid Regulation. The CCPM potentially can further marginalise the role of the genuine 'needs-based' assessments of Community humanitarian aid to those emergencies which are of marginal importance to the geopolitical interests of the Union and its Member States.

6.3 Humanitarian Assistance and the Promotion of Political Objectives and the Protection of Human Rights

6.3.1 Using Humanitarian Aid to Assist with Political Objectives

Humanitarian aid, a very blunt instrument, is now the primary form of geopolitical intervention in a complex crisis which is of no, or little, strategic importance to the European Union.[93] The Council can use DG ECHO's activities as evidence of foreign policy intervention to persuade its political constituencies, if they express concern, that they are active in a situation. At times that engagement may actually be quite minimal; in fact it can be argued that the funding of humanitarian aid operations is the contracting out to civil society of foreign policy.

There is currently no internationally agreed method for determining need in an emergency situation.[94] However, comparing apparent or estimated need to the commitments made and paid by donors, while crude, is a fair indicator of the importance to a donor of an emergency.

---

[91] Court of Auditors, *Special Report No. 3/2006*, para. 25. Emphasis added.
[92] See A. Missiroli, 'European Security Policy: the Challenge of Coherence' (2001) 6 *EFARev.* 177, 194.
[93] Macrae and Leander, *Shifting Sands*.
[94] One of the first in-depth studies on this issue is Darcy and Hofman, *According to Need?*

DG ECHO's Annual Reports illustrate a heavy bias in the assistance provided which is skewed to the Union pursuing more general foreign policy objectives as and when the need arises.[95] The Kosovo crisis can be invoked to illustrate how DG ECHO and its activities can reflect the more general foreign policy objectives of the Union and its Member States.[96] The approach towards Afghanistan and Iraq can also be used to that end. They will each briefly be discussed in turn.

Kosovo, in percentage terms, has received more aid from the European Union than any other emergency.[97] For example, 42 per cent of DG ECHO's total budget in 1999 of €813 million went to Europe, and of this 55 per cent went to Kosovo.[98] In Kosovo, as far as nutrition levels were concerned, the major problem was not malnutrition but obesity. The number of malnourished children was steady at less than 2 per cent. Forty per cent of women and children were clinically obese or their body mass index classified them as substantially overweight.[99] Yet the scale of the humanitarian response from DG ECHO was unprecedented in volume and cash terms. Until the Indian Ocean tsunami in 2005, Kosovo was the only occasion, as far as is known, when the World Food Programme (WFP) and United Nations more generally received more aid than the estimated need.[100] DG ECHO actually sent out unsolicited funds for the purchase of fresh fruit and vegetables, Mars bars, Turkish delight and cakes.[101] In a fast-changing situation, DG ECHO was unable to deal with the situation at hand. It intended to deliver two kilograms of food per person in

---

[95] The statistics as to the payments made are not entirely accurate, as they reflect the use of DG ECHO budget lines for rehabilitation as well as emergency aid. The proportion of DG ECHO's budget which is used for rehabilitation aid is not, however, significant.

[96] See more generally, Court of Auditors, *Special Report No. 2/2001*. It should be noted that DG ECHO was part of a very complex group providing aid, including other Commission Directorates-General such as Development and External Relations, the EU Member States and national agencies from other states, as well as NGOs and the UN family. Another good example is assistance to Turkey following the Gulf Conflict of 1991/2 and the subsequent exodus of Kurds to south-east Turkey and Iran. According to MacFarlane, *Politics and Humanitarian Action*, all Turkish claims for assistance, as opposed to 10 per cent of those by Iran, were met.

[97] See COM(2000)784.

[98] See COM(2000)784 which is the 1999 ECHO Annual Report.

[99] This information is derived from Jaspers, *Solidarity and Soup Kitchens*.

[100] See COM(2000)784. In the aftermath of the Asian tsunami, certain regions, for example parts of Sri Lanka, received more aid than the agencies on the ground could use, whereas other regions received far less than the needs assessments considered was required. See Court of Auditors, *Special Report No. 3/2006*, para. 23.

[101] Jaspers, *Solidarity and Soup Kitchens*. See also, COM(1999)468.

refugee camps in Kosovo, yet twelve kilograms per person was being delivered to spend funds. The allocation in other camps, during the same crises, was less than one-fifth of a kilogram per person.[102]

Food rations were, for probably the first time in an emergency, based on supply and not need. Much of this was in an attempt to display to the population that alliance with the West was beneficial to the average person and to help stir up opposition to the incumbent regime. Such actions are possibly in violation of the obligations owed by all the Member States as parties to the International Covenant on Economic, Social and Cultural Rights, 1966.[103] In General Comment 12 on Article 11 of the Covenant (on the Right to Food) the CESCR stated that it is clear that 'food should never be used as an instrument of political and economic pressure'.[104] Yet this is exactly what it was used for in Kosovo by the European Union.[105] Rieff has argued that the approach to Kosovo was about containing a crisis through charity.[106] The Union's action seems to have been primarily driven by pragmatism and self-interest and not the humanitarian imperative. In DG ECHO's Annual Review of 2000, for example, it was noted:

> it is not just a matter of moral duty, it is a matter of self interest. If the EU wants to avoid having thousands of refugees ... knocking on its door as asylum seekers, it is in its interests to help them out on the spot. The cost per head of emergency ... aid is always much lower than, and cannot remotely be compared with, the legal and social costs of an asylum seeker.[107]

This is hardly any different from the way in which development assistance, as discussed in Chapter 3, has been used. In Afghanistan, humanitarian aid has also been used for political purposes.[108] In the aftermath of the Soviet Union being defeated in Afghanistan and the consequent civil war and droughts, Afghanistan witnessed a massive humanitarian crisis. Prior to the US-led invasion in 2001, the amount of

---

[102] COM(1999)468.
[103] International Covenant on Economic, Social and Cultural Rights, 1966, 993 UNTS 3.
[104] General Comment 12 on Article 11 of the ICESCR, E/C.12/1995/5 CESCR, para. 37.
[105] See further below.
[106] Rieff, A Bed for the Night, p. 131. Rieff has argued that the scale of aid given to the victims of the conflict in the former Yugoslavia was also due to a level of affinity with those suffering which simply does not exist when the victims are not European.
[107] DG ECHO, Humanitarian Crises Out of the Spotlight (2000) p. 8.
[108] See more generally, C. Johnson 'Afghanistan and the "War on Terror"' in J. Macrae and A Harmer (eds.), Humanitarian Action and the 'Global War on Terror': a Review of Trends and Issues, Humanitarian Policy Group Report 14 (London: ODI, 2003) p. 49.

international humanitarian aid being sent to Afghanistan was far below estimated needs.[109] Once US bombing started in 2001, however, the amount of aid sent by donors such as DG ECHO went up very substantially. In 1998, when there was a major earthquake in Afghanistan in February of that year, EU humanitarian aid amounted to €46 million. In 2000, it amounted to €19 million. By the end of 2001, however, €354 million had been pledged with the European Council of 17 October 2001 alone committing €320 million in emergency aid.[110] While the humanitarian crisis undeniably worsened once hostilities broke out, it had not worsened eighteen-fold. It is futile even to attempt to argue that the level of emergency aid being granted by the Union was unrelated to support for the United States in its attempt to overthrow the Taliban regime after 2001. Humanitarian aid was no doubt also used to highlight to those opposed to the military intervention in the Member States and elsewhere that the needs of Afghani civilians were being addressed during the conflict. Furthermore, the delivery of such aid could illustrate to the Afghani population that it would be beneficial to turn against the Taliban and support the West, as their needs would be met if Afghanistan was again a full member of the international community and no longer a pariah state.

The example of Afghanistan above can be contrasted with decisions concerning the funding of humanitarian aid operations in Iraq prior to the US-led invasion in March 2003. This can be used to highlight that a decision not to fund humanitarian operations can also be overtly politically driven. In this instance, a substantial number of powerful EU Member States were not sympathetic to the policies of the United States. Prior to the invasion of Iraq in March 2003, in the aftermath of the most comprehensive sanctions regime in UN history, there was a very substantial humanitarian crisis affecting the general population. Torrente has argued, however, that in late 2002 the majority of EU Member States refused to agree to the granting of millions of extra

---

[109] The consolidated fund for 2000, for example, received 45 per cent of estimated needs. See House of Commons International Development Committee, *The Humanitarian Crisis in Afghanistan and the Surrounding Region* (London: HMSO, 2001) vol. I, para. 7.

[110] Council Conclusions, 17 October 2001, (2001) 10 *Bull. EU* 1.6.83. These figures are derived from the humanitarian aid decisions published in the *EU Bulletin* for the respective years. These disbursements are assumed to be separate from the pledges made by the Member States and those under the terms of the Bonn Agreement (Agreement on Provisional Arrangements in Afghanistan, pending the Reestablishment of Permanent Government Institutions, Bonn, 5 December 2001) as they relate only to emergency aid.

euros in humanitarian aid to Iraq.[111] If the decision had been made on a 'needs basis', in particular bearing in mind that 'disaster preparation' was an urgent priority as there was likely to be an even more acute crisis if there was an armed conflict, it is clear that a decision to substantially increase the funding available to DG ECHO for that purpose should have been made. Yet, Torrente has argued that some Member States refused to do so as they felt that the granting of such aid would have amounted to accepting the inevitability of a US-led attack on Iraq.[112] As some EU Member States were vehemently opposed to such a course of events, rather than act in a manner which assisted a genuinely needy population, it was decided it was preferable not to act.[113] The fact that Iraq has now been identified as a country having very high needs by DG ECHO and a priority for humanitarian aid allocations simply highlights how politically driven and short-sighted the Council decision was not to make more funding available prior to the US-led invasion. Whereas the humanitarian situation could have been mitigated, even marginally, by disaster preparation projects, the decision by some Member States to make a political point by refusing to grant aid ensured that not only have lives almost certainly unnecessarily been lost but also that all subsequent aid efforts had to start from a lower base level.

6.3.2 Using Humanitarian Aid to Promote and Protect Human Rights

Most international agencies and NGOs have for some time now been considering the human rights implications of their humanitarian aid operations. Adopting a human rights-based approach seems to have become an imperative for many organisations and Save the Children, Oxfam, ActionAid, CARE, UNHCR, WFP and UNICEF, among others, now describe their humanitarian operation in human rights terms.[114]

---

[111] N. Torrente, 'Humanitarian Action under Attack: Reflections on the Iraq War' (2004) 17 *HHRJ* 1, 7.

[112] *Ibid.*

[113] For 2001 and 2002, EU humanitarian aid to Iraq totalled €26 million. In 2003 alone such aid amounted to €102 million. The figures are derived from the humanitarian aid decisions published in the *EU Bulletin* for the respective years. On any needs-based analysis, the situation was not approximately eight times worse in 2003 than it was in either of the two preceding years.

[114] See M. Frohardt, D. Paul and L. Minear, *Protecting Human Rights: the Challenge to Humanitarian Organisations*, HWP Occasional Paper 35 (1999); K. Kenny, *When Needs are Rights: an Overview of UN Efforts to Integrate Human Rights into Humanitarian Action*, HWP Occasional Paper 38 (2000); and L. Cotterell, 'Approaches to Human Rights in Humanitarian Crises' in T. O'Neil (ed.), *Human Rights and Poverty Reduction: Realities, Controversies and Strategies – an ODI Meeting Series* (London: ODI, 2006) p. 111.

O'Brien has argued, however, that aid agencies have utilised human rights language to give legitimacy to the work they are already doing and to try to keep up with changes in thinking.[115] A major exception to this trend is the ICRC, which does not use human rights language to describe its work, for fear of compromising its neutrality.

In this general recognition of the need for an examination of the relationship between humanitarian activities and human rights, DG ECHO was very much at the rearguard. Although Commissioners for Humanitarian Aid have been very keen on espousing the contribution of DG ECHO's work to protecting human rights, it was not until a 1999 internal discussion paper was circulated by DG ECHO to the NGO sector that the link was extensively explored.[116] The response of the NGO sector was on the whole not unfavourable. Considering the lack of conceptual analysis and formulation of concrete policy in the human rights discussion paper, this is not surprising.[117]

The DG ECHO human rights discussion paper considers that humanitarian aid has lost its innocence and although impartiality and neutrality should be ensured, the paper does not address the biases of DG ECHO's activities. The basic premise of the paper is that DG ECHO is 'a human rights actor as it funds the delivery of rights such as food and shelter'.[118] A major issue not directly addressed by the paper is how to integrate human rights considerations into humanitarian aid activities. DG ECHO's 2001 and 2003 aid strategy papers to some extent address this.[119] The aid strategy papers from the period after 2003 do not directly refer to or discuss this issue. What these later strategy papers do firmly stress, however, is that a 'needs-based' approach, as opposed to a 'rights-based' one, will be taken at all times to humanitarian aid.[120] Although 'needs-based' and 'rights-based' approaches to humanitarian

---

[115] P. O'Brien, 'Rights Based Responses to Aid Politicization in Afghanistan' in P. Gready and J. Ensor (eds.), *Reinventing Development: Translating Right-Based Approaches from Theory into Practice* (London: Zed Books, 2005) p. 201.

[116] The discussion paper is an internal DG ECHO document (hereinafter 'DG ECHO Discussion Paper'). I am grateful to an official in DG ECHO for providing me with a copy of it.

[117] See e.g., the discussion in the paper issued by Voice, *The Future of European Humanitarian Aid* (1999).

[118] DG ECHO Discussion Paper.

[119] DG ECHO, *ECHO Aid Strategy 2001* and DG ECHO, *ECHO Aid Strategy 2003.*

[120] DG ECHO, *ECHO Aid Strategy 2005*, p. 1; DG ECHO, *Operational Strategy 2006*, p. 1; and DG ECHO, *Operational Strategy 2007*, SEC(2006)1626, p. 3. Although this is not to say that a needs-based approach is not also emphasised in, for example, the strategy paper for 2003.

aid are often seen as being in opposition, they are not necessarily incompatible, although they may sometimes lead to different outcomes.[121]

To take an example from practice, the ICRC, UNICEF and Save the Children were all active in those parts of Afghanistan under the control of the Taliban during the late 1990s. UNICEF and Save the Children, as noted above, define their work in terms of human rights, with both using the 1989 Children's Convention as their normative document.[122] Both UNICEF and Save the Children consider that they have regard to all the implications of both acting and not acting where there is a humanitarian need.[123] In the Taliban-controlled areas of Afghanistan, both UNICEF and Save the Children stopped their programmes in the late 1990s due to their objections to the Taliban's discriminatory policies and practices against women and children.

The fact that the Taliban were not concerned in the slightest with the perceptions of such actors (or indeed Western governments) and were not susceptible to conditionality was ignored. To be capable of guiding conduct, a rights-based assessment of humanitarian assistance must provide a way of balancing competing rights and interests. The suspending of projects by UNICEF and Save the Children may have further highlighted the wholly exceptional nature of the Taliban's practices to the international community, but it is difficult to determine how the balance between various rights was struck. The opposition of UNICEF and Save the Children to the Taliban's insistence that there were no educational facilities for women and girls subsequently, for example, led to no schools in certain districts for boys either, where the schools were run by those agencies. Furthermore, food which was previously entering the country as a result of those agencies' work no longer did so, which must have led to an inflationary effect as demand continued to further outstrip supply. The ICRC, however, which adopts a 'needs-based' approach, did not pull out of Afghanistan.[124]

DG ECHO, as noted above, is now very firmly committed to a 'needs-based' approach when it comes to aid distribution and has developed a very scientific methodology to that end. It must not, however, ignore the consequences of the distribution of that aid. The European Commission and ten Member States are signatories

[121] See Darcy and Hofman, *According to Need* and further the discussion below.
[122] Convention on the Rights of the Child, 1989, 1577 UNTS 3.
[123] See Kenny, *When Needs are Rights.*
[124] See A. Rashid, *Taliban: the Story of the Afghan Warlords* (Basingstoke: Pan Books, 2000) p. 113.

to the 2003 Stockholm Principles on Humanitarian Donorship ('Stockholm Principles').[125] General Principle 4 of the Stockholm Principles requires donors to 'respect and promote the implementation of international humanitarian law, refugee law and human rights'. Article III-321 of the proposed Constitutional Treaty also refers to such obligations when it states that the 'Union's operations in the field of humanitarian aid shall be conducted within the framework of the principles and objectives of the external action of the Union'. Article III-292, which in part establishes such objectives, notes that the 'Union's action on the international scene shall be guided by the principles which have inspired its own creation, development and enlargement, and which it seeks to advance in the wider world: democracy, the rule of law, the universality and indivisibility of human rights and fundamental freedoms, respect for human dignity ... and respect for the principles of the United Nations Charter and international law'. Article III-321(2) also stresses that humanitarian aid operations shall 'be conducted in compliance with the principles of international law'. As discussed in Chapter 3, guidelines on promoting compliance with international humanitarian law were adopted by the Council in 2005.[126] Finally, the 2007 Communication on the principles underpinning EU humanitarian aid notes in the light of the 2005 guidelines on how respect for international law is essential for such assistance to be given and that 'a proactive approach to preserving the conditions necessary for humanitarian action' should be adopted.[127]

By reading these documents in conjunction with DG ECHO's strategy papers, especially from 2001, and the 1999 human rights discussion paper, it is clear that human rights-related considerations must be taken into account by DG ECHO when making decisions about humanitarian aid.[128] The approach espoused attempts to ensure that the distribution of aid does not lead to any detrimental side effects. This requires that all non-urgent proposals address two fundamental issues: first, does a project proposal consider the human rights situation in the

---

[125] Principles and Good Practice of Humanitarian Donorship, Stockholm, 17 June 2003.
[126] European Union Guidelines on Promoting Compliance with International Humanitarian Law, [2005] OJ C327/4, 23 December 2005.
[127] COM(2007)317, p. 3
[128] This is the case notwithstanding the fact that neither the abandoned Constitutional Treaty nor the EU Reform Treaty which replaced it is in force at the time of writing.

field? Secondly, does it consider if and how it will impact on the protection of human rights?[129]

The basic premise for DG ECHO, therefore, is that any aid provided has to be 'human rights conscious' but what the consequences of any such assessment are is unclear. A human rights assessment with regard to humanitarian action requires that the impact on human rights of acting, or not, as the case may be, are considered. This seems to assume, however, that in a complex situation there is a 'correct' answer in balancing the inevitably competing rights of different individuals, which may dictate how DG ECHO should respond. This can equate to the idea that assistance should not be provided if it will worsen the human rights situation overall. Similarly, it must be asked if this means that aid should not be granted if the collateral effects will on an overall assessment be negative. Despite methodologies having been adopted for the identification of greatest global needs and indeed the needs of a population, no methodology has been worked out to quantify if providing aid is the most effective way to relieve suffering, bearing in mind the collateral consequences of that act.

Humanitarian action, if seen through a human rights prism can be seen as an attempt to both protect and also provide relief from harm. In its documentation, DG ECHO does not tend to elaborate on aspects of the former. In practice, it seems to be primarily concerned with relief from harm and not protecting, even though the latter can be seen to be part of its mandate.[130] Assisting in isolation from the commitment to protect is short-sighted; there is often talk of the 'well-fed dead syndrome'; those who are being fed should not simply be kept alive so that they can be killed by a repressive regime or belligerents. For DG ECHO, however, it is a question of weighing up the options and taking the approach which is considered to be the most effective in terms of protecting rights even in the light of a needs-based assessment.[131]

---

[129] DG ECHO, *ECHO Aid Strategy 2001.*
[130] DG ECHO Discussion Paper. See further Article 1 of Regulation 1257/96. COM(2007)317 which, as noted above, sets out the main principles underlying EU humanitarian aid, refers to the 'responsibility to protect' but does so with reference to the obligations upon states to protect populations within their jurisdiction and of the international community acting under the auspices of the UN Charter. It does not refer to the general 'responsibility to protect' in the sense of states owing an obligation to protect populations in third states from harm.
[131] See DG ECHO, *ECHO Aid Strategy 2001.*

In practice, such an approach amounts to conditionality even though conditionality should have no role to play in a humanitarian aid policy which is neutral and impartial.[132] Speaking in 2000, Mikael Barfod, the then Head of Policy Analysis at DG ECHO, argued that DG ECHO uses three different types of humanitarian aid conditionality: impact conditionality, legal conditionality and political conditionality.[133] As the discussion above notes, some of these types of conditionality have been expressly or implicitly referred to in the 1999 human rights discussion paper or the subsequent strategy papers. Others are apparent in practice. Each will be discussed in turn.

Impact conditionality essentially adopts a utilitarian approach to the distribution of aid. As the 2001 Strategy Paper notes, aid should not be distributed if it results in negative consequences.[134] Unwelcome side-effects, however, such as population movements or the possible manipulation of conflict in an effort to gain more aid, are commonplace in contemporary complex emergencies. It is sometimes very difficult, if not impossible, to balance the benefits to a population in desperate need of aid against the collateral effects of such action. Taken to an extreme, impact conditionality can result in the conclusion that if the distribution of humanitarian aid is likely to do some harm, then no aid is likely to do less. A solely 'needs-based' approach would clearly reject such an approach. For impact conditionality to be workable, a 'tipping-point' needs to be identified. If that point is reached then any assistance being provided must be withdrawn. In a practical context, this is a difficult choice to make. In the conflicts in Angola, Sudan, Ethiopia and Bosnia, for example, it has been clear that the humanitarian aid supplied to desperately needy populations has helped perpetuate conflict and contributed to the abuse of rights.

The conflict in Ethiopia is a classic example of some of the dilemmas involved.[135] Humanitarian assistance from the international community, including DG ECHO, was perceived to be assisting the war effort.

---

[132] See also, M. Duffield, *Aid Policy and Post Modern Conflict: a Critical Review*, International Department, School of Public Policy, University of Birmingham, Discussion Paper 19.

[133] M. Barfod, 'Humanitarian Aid and Conditionality: ECHO's Experience and Prospects under the CFSP' in Leander and Macrae, *Terms of Engagement*.

[134] DG ECHO, *ECHO Aid Strategy 2001*.

[135] See J. Borton, *The Changing Role of NGOs in the Provision of Relief and Rehabilitation Assistance: Case Study 3 – Northern Ethiopia and Eritrea*, ODI Working Paper 76 (London: ODI, 1994); J. Tanguy and F. Terry, 'Humanitarian Responsibility and Committed Action: Response to Principles, Politics, and Humanitarian Action' (1999) 13 *Ethics and International Affairs*, www.cceia.org/; and Barfod, 'Humanitarian Aid and Conditionality'.

The international community paid for improvements to ports and transport links to ease the movement of such assistance. Those same facilities were also being used by the warring factions to move their arms. Aid was also leading to population movements and a dependency upon aid.[136] The essential question in such circumstances is, should a population in distress be allowed to starve due to the fact that in the short to medium term the provision of assistance will lead to other negative consequences? Essentially, is starvation a morally and ethically acceptable alternative?

The danger of such conditionality becomes most acute where humanitarian aid is seen by European policy-makers, especially in the Council, as being a viable substitute for political action.[137] In such circumstances, where foreign policy (in)action is effectively delegated to DG ECHO, this particular 'human rights approach', if it is used, can become positively detrimental to the population in need. Such an approach is also in conflict with the Humanitarian Aid Regulation, which in its Preamble states:

people in distress, victims of natural disasters, wars and outbreaks of fighting, or other comparable exceptional circumstances have a right to international humanitarian assistance where their own authorities prove unable to provide effective relief . . . humanitarian aid decisions must be taken . . . *solely according to the victims' needs and interests.* [138]

Notwithstanding the apparent conflict between impact conditionality and the 1996 Humanitarian Aid Regulation, such an approach is unlikely to be a violation of the legal obligations of the Member States under the International Covenant on Economic, Social and Cultural Rights.[139] Despite the fact that he was speaking in 2000, Barfod's contention, that there have been relatively few, if any, examples of DG ECHO adopting this approach in practice, still holds true.[140]

DG ECHO's aid strategy papers from 2001 and 2003, the Stockholm Principles, the Council's International Humanitarian Law Guidelines, the Commission's 2007 Communication on the principles underpinning humanitarian aid and the proposed Constitutional Treaty also

---

[136] Barfod, 'Humanitarian Aid and Conditionality'.
[137] Although in the Madrid Declaration it is stated quite clearly that it will not be. Declaration of the Humanitarian Summit, Madrid, 15 December 1995, para. 1.
[138] Preamble, paras. 3 and 10 to Regulation 1257/96. Emphasis added.
[139] See the discussion in Chapter 2.   [140] Barfod, 'Humanitarian Aid and Conditionality'.

refer, as noted above, to using humanitarian aid in an emergency to create respect for both the individual recipient's human rights and international humanitarian law. This is what Barfod refers to as 'legal conditionality'.[141] According to this approach, violations of international humanitarian law or international human rights law will lead to any humanitarian assistance to those in need being withdrawn (if it is already being distributed) or not being granted until such norms are respected. This type of conditionality is only relevant in a man-made emergency, although the situation can be compounded by natural factors, such as drought. In contrast to the relationship between impact conditionality and the Humanitarian Aid Regulation, legal conditionality is in accordance with the terms of the Regulation. The Preamble states:

civilian operations to protect the victims of fighting or of comparable exceptional circumstances are governed by international humanitarian law and should accordingly be considered part of humanitarian action.[142]

Furthermore, the EU Member States, as parties to the Four Geneva Conventions of 1949, are obliged, in accordance with Common Article 1, to 'undertake to respect and to ensure respect for the ... Convention in all circumstances'.[143] In practice, legal conditionality is used in two distinct ways. Under the first approach, where the conditions to work in a principled way do not exist (for example, humanitarian workers are being attacked), no aid will be supplied until a secure environment is allowed to exist.[144] The second approach is that assistance will be provided only if the state or militia in question comply with a number of conditions, such as stopping certain human rights abuses.

---

[141] *Ibid.*   [142] Preamble to Regulation 1257/96.

[143] Geneva Convention for the Amelioration of the Condition of the Wounded and Sick in Armed Forces in the Field, 1949 (Geneva Convention I) 75 UNTS 31; Geneva Convention for the Amelioration of the Condition of the Wounded, Sick and Shipwrecked Members of the Armed Forces at Sea, 1949 (Geneva Convention II) 75 UNTS 85; Geneva Convention Relative to the Treatment of Prisoners of War, 1949 (Geneva Convention III) 75 UNTS 135; and Geneva Convention Relative to the Protection of Civilian Persons in Time of War, 1949. See further on this point, Advisory Opinion, *Legal Consequences of the Construction of a Wall in the Occupied Palestinian Territory* [2005] ICJ Reports 136, paras. 96 and 158.

[144] For example, this occurred in Iraq in autumn 2003 when the ICRC, Oxfam and Save the Children, among others, pulled out after the attacks on the UN and ICRC headquarters in Baghdad. The ICRC returned relatively quickly once guarantees for their safety were forthcoming.

It is difficult, however, to ascertain the exact relevance of violations of international human rights and humanitarian law for this type of conditionality. O'Brien has argued that as the rules of humanitarianism are now being written in places like Iraq and Afghanistan, humanitarian actors are misconceived if they feel that through aid they can stop serious human rights violations or change attitudes.[145] This has also been true in earlier conflicts where, for example, there has been hostility between ethnic groups. In such cases eradication of, for example, an ethnic group or a religious minority may be an inherent purpose of the conflict. Yet the withholding of aid in, for example, the former Yugoslavia would have been untenable for the Union. In practice, however, there are examples of the imposition of this type of conditionality but only where the violations have not been central to the situation and the emergency of relatively little political importance to the Union and its Member States.

DG ECHO, for example, has in the past withdrawn assistance to southern Sudan due to attacks on projects funded by it. As the then Commissioner responsible for humanitarian aid, Poul Nielson noted, the reason for the withdrawal was due to a 'serious breach of international humanitarian law'.[146] Yet in the Palestinian Territories, serious attacks by both Palestinian groups and the Israeli Defence Force (IDF) upon the ICRC and other humanitarian workers funded by DG ECHO, during the occupation of Jenin in 2002 for example, did not lead to such a withdrawal.[147] It is difficult to argue that subjective factors do not creep into these determinations and that this type of conditionality is only used where DG ECHO feels it is politically acceptable for it to retract funding until acceptable conditions for providing humanitarian assistance exist.

One of the limitations of legal conditionality is that where the destruction and eradication of other ethnic groups is an objective of the conflict, guarantees with regard to the security of humanitarian workers (who are assisting both sides) and human rights are unlikely to be forthcoming or, if they are, to be respected. Securing or attempting to secure such commitments can, however, further highlight the conduct of the warring parties to the international community. DG ECHO, as noted above, has in the past suspended funding operations in Taliban

---

[145] O'Brien, 'Rights Based Responses to Aid Politicization in Afghanistan', p. 201.
[146] Quoted by Barfod, 'Humanitarian Aid and Conditionality'.
[147] See more generally the discussion in Chapter 5.

controlled areas of Afghanistan. The 1998 ECHO Annual Report notes that aid to Afghanistan was suspended due to 'continued violations of fundamental humanitarian principles' in the sense of targeting and threatening aid workers.[148] This, however, was not the primary reason. Violations, in the sense of targeting aid workers, were at the time relatively rare, although they did exist.[149] The Taliban had no problems with aid agencies, so long as they respected their interpretation of Islam. It was due to the gradually increasing opposition to the policies of the Taliban, in particular from women's groups in the United States and in Europe, that DG ECHO suspended all operations.[150] DG ECHO used legal conditionality in humanitarian aid as part of an overall approach where aid of every kind was eventually used by the Union as an instrument to isolate the Taliban.

The Taliban's treatment of women is closely related to a more fundamental issue in the relationship between legal conditionality in humanitarian aid and human rights. For the Union, discrimination against women was the most important violation of human rights. As objectionable as it may seem, the Union would have been on sounder legal ground for suspending aid for the flagrant and systematic violations of international humanitarian law being committed by all sides in Afghanistan and the Taliban's policies and practices towards certain ethnic and religious groups, such as the Hazaras, which arguably also amounted to genocide.[151] As was discussed in Chapter 2, systematic

---

[148] DG ECHO, *Annual Report on Humanitarian Aid 1998*, p. 18.

[149] It is important to note that both the United States and United Kingdom are widely considered to have used emergency aid as a cover for security operations. This consequently resulted in some attacks on aid convoys by the Taliban. See further, M. Atmar, 'The Politicisation of Humanitarian Aid and its Consequences for Afghans', *Humanitarian Exchange,* September 2001 and MacFarlane, *Politics and Humanitarian Action.*

[150] See the discussion in Rashid, *Taliban,* p. 113 .

[151] The Hazaras are primarily adherents of Shia Islam. The Taliban, as is also the case with other Wahabbi/Deobandi sects, are strongly opposed to Shia Islam and some consider it as being tantamount to heresy. It is well documented that during the course of the civil war, many thousands of Hazaras were massacred by the Taliban. One such incident was in Mazar-e-Sharif in August 1998. The EU Presidency on 23 September 1998 adopted a strongly worded statement condemning the killings, see (1998) 9 *EU Bull.* 1.3.3. Human Rights Watch and a number of other NGOs also issued press releases at the time strongly condemning the widespread killings. Although Human Rights Watch did not use the term genocide, other organisations were using the term (see the written statement submitted by the Society for Threatened Peoples to the Commission on Human Rights, 25 March 1998, E/CN.4/1998/NGO/86). Considering the statements issued by Taliban leaders and the manner and sheer numbers of Hazaras who the

violations of international humanitarian law and acts of genocide are breaches of obligations *erga omnes* and the Member States of the Union are required to take steps to bring such violations to an end.

The then EU Commissioner for Humanitarian Aid, Emma Bonino argued that the approach taken in Afghanistan over women's rights was a principled one.[152] To argue that such a course of action would improve the observance of human rights and international law in Afghanistan was at best naïve. The politics of the Taliban are such that their entire ideological foundation relies upon resorting to selected aspects of society as it existed in seventh-century Arabia, regardless of the societal context. The suppression of women is part of the puritanical trend in Wahabbi/Deobandi traditions. The demonisation and dehumanisation of women, who are considered to provide a distraction from committing 'God's work', and the complete merging of theology and politics, is fundamental to the Taliban's ideology. Conditionality, sanctions or any other external action would under no circumstances lead to a change in that attitude. A perspective based solely upon needs would have allowed the continuation of aid supplies to those Afghanis in desperate need, no matter how repugnant the Taliban's practices were, not only towards women but also religious and ethnic minorities.

The final type of conditionality identified by Barfod is political conditionality.[153] In this case, assistance is used solely to achieve specific foreign policy objectives. The aim, for example, may be to put pressure on a government or faction to end hostilities, to start peace negotiations

---

Taliban massacred (according to Human Rights Watch in Mazar-e-Sharif in August 1998, men had their throats slit while women and young boys had both hands cut off) a case can be made that the Taliban's policy amounted to genocide under the terms of the Convention on the Prevention and Punishment of the Crime of Genocide, 1948, 78 UNTS 277. This should, however, be seen in the light of the ICJ's decision in *Bosnia and Herzegovina* v. *Serbia and Montenegro – Application of the Convention on the Prevention and Punishment of the Crime of Genocide*, judgment 26 February 2007, nyr, paras. 276–77, where the Court lay particular emphasis on the *dolus specialis* (specific intent) of the perpetrators to destroy in whole or part a group. See further, Human Rights Watch, 'UN Urged to Prevent More Killings as Taliban Offensive Continues', Press Release, 14 September 1998; Human Rights Watch, *Afghanistan: the Massacre in Mazar-i-Sharif* (1998) vol. 10 (7); and Rashid, *Taliban*, p. 72 *et seq.*

[152] In a speech entitled, 'Principled Aid in an Unprincipled World' available at http://europa.eu.int/en/comm/spp/rapid.htmlDonald. See also, P. Brandt, 'Relief as Development, but Development as Relief?', www.jha.ac/articles/a024.htm

[153] Barfod, 'Humanitarian Aid and Conditionality'.

or to weaken a regime.[154] Such conditionality sits uneasily with the Humanitarian Aid Regulation, which in its Preamble makes clear that:

humanitarian aid ... is accorded to victims without discrimination on the grounds of race, ethnic group, religion, sex, age, nationality or political affiliation *and must not be guided by, or subject to, political considerations.*[155]

A real danger of humanitarian aid being sucked into a political vacuum exists, however, when no other EU intervention exists. There are clear examples of this. In Cambodia in the 1990s, the European Union was financing a number of NGOs who had a very determined mandate to support opposition parties. The ICRC and Médecins Sans Frontières sought to maximise their distance from all factions. USAID and DG ECHO, however, worked mostly in the north of the country and outside of the public health system and their actions were an inherent part of a political policy and strategy to boost the opposition parties in the run-up to the elections. The intervention was not to boost the general sustainability of the health sector, as was ostensibly the case, but rather to boost the legitimacy and capacity of the opposition.[156]

DG ECHO has on other occasions resisted being overtly used as a foreign policy instrument. In Serbia, for example, before the fall of the nationalist government, DG ECHO provided aid through the ICRC. The Member States, however, wanted to support the opposition and specifically strengthen it. The DG ECHO programme was thus halted and an Energy for Democracy (EfD) programme was started instead, funded by the Directorate-General for External Relations.[157] Allowing the Directorate-General for External Relations to hijack DG ECHO programmes does allow the Commission to argue that humanitarian aid is not biased or tainted, but whether the average Serb was able to distinguish between the different administrative divisions of the Commission remains unclear.[158] The fundamental difference between the situation

---

[154] *Ibid.* For a critical analysis of such efforts in general, see M. Scholms, 'On the (Im)possible Inclusion of Humanitarian Assistance into Peace Building Efforts', *Journal of Humanitarian Assistance,* www.jha.ac.articles/a072.htm

[155] Preamble to Regulation 1257/96. Emphasis added.

[156] See further J. Macrae, *Aiding Recovery? The Crisis of Aid in Chronic Political Emergencies* (London: Zed Books, 2001) p. 85.

[157] On the EfD programme, see Commission MEMO/99/65, 3 December 1999. See also, House of Commons Select Committee on International Development, *The Effectiveness of EC Development Aid,* Ninth Report of the Session 1999–2000 (London: HMSO, 2000).

[158] Macrae, *Aiding Recovery,* p. 42, notes it is significant that the DFID resisted FCO pressure to provide funds to the EfD programme.

in Cambodia and Serbia was that in the latter other EU bodies were active and thus could take over a pre-existing project. In Cambodia, where there was no other foreign policy action, DG ECHO was used for political purposes as it was the only EU actor active at the time that could contribute to more general foreign policy objectives by supporting the opposition.

The use of these types of conditionality in humanitarian aid by DG ECHO and the Union more generally sits somewhat uneasily with the underlying principles of humanitarian assistance. The use of impact and political conditionality in humanitarian aid does not correlate with the 1996 Humanitarian Aid Regulation. The human rights implications of (in)action may be a consideration in whether or not, or indeed how and to whom, to provide aid but they are far from the most important factor when weighing up options. Studies suggest that conditionality is of limited use and influence in such circumstances and is ineffective in forcing factions to respect rights and cajole them towards a political outcome.[159] Furthermore, in many instances the power and legitimacy a group seeks internationally may have little to do with their relationship with their subject population.

6.4 Conclusions

In a panel discussion in 1998, Emma Bonino, the then Commissioner for Humanitarian Aid, observed:

I have my doubts, looking at the array of conflicts in which humanitarian relief is called for today ... that being neutral is still at all possible or indeed ethically just ... should [humanitarian agencies] be unable to distinguish right from wrong, the aggressor from the victim, the killers from the dead bodies? What absurd wisdom could call for this organised ethical confusion?[160]

It is clear that in many situations the neutrality and impartiality of the Union's humanitarian aid policy has been compromised. As Johannes Luchner, at the time of writing the Head of DG ECHO, has stated when talking about the work of DG ECHO, 'we do not work in isolation from the Commission and we do not work in isolation from what is a

---

[159] See P. Uvin, *The Influence of Aid in Situations of Violent Conflict* (Paris: OECD, 1999) and Scholms, 'On the (Im)possible Inclusion'.

[160] Cited by Minear, 'The Theory and Practice', note 12. Bonino was a member of a panel discussion entitled 'Is Neutrality Still Possible?'.

€10 billion development and foreign relations budget'.[161] The erosion of the principles of impartiality and neutrality in humanitarian aid by political actors is something that almost all aid organisations are concerned about. If the politicalisation of the Union's humanitarian aid policy continues, then at some point certain aid organisations will simply refuse to continue to work at all with DG ECHO.

There are a number of options open to the Union as far as the role of DG ECHO is concerned. DG ECHO can solely concentrate on providing aid on a 'needs-based' approach and to those 'forgotten emergencies' for which it has devised methodologies and be kept isolated from the more general foreign policy objectives of the Union and its Member States. An alternative is for DG ECHO to be fully integrated into the Union's arsenal of crisis-management tools. From the perspective of many of the aid agencies funded by DG ECHO, such a development would be undesirable. A final option is that DG ECHO should expressly adopt an approach which is usually referred to as 'third-way humanitarianism'.[162]

This would be the most honest approach to the policies implemented by DG ECHO in practice. The Commission in its 2007 Communication on humanitarian aid has, as discussed above, re-emphasised the importance of, *inter alia*, neutrality and impartiality.[163] In third-way humanitarianism, neutrality is not expressly abandoned.[164] Where neutrality is expressly abandoned, humanitarianism is subordinate to foreign policy objectives, as is the case with USAID. Third-way humanitarianism is also distinguishable from where neutrality is the pre-eminent principle,[165] as in the case of the ICRC. Third-way humanitarianism allows humanitarian assistance to have other objectives, such as peace building and tackling root causes, but is not biased *per se* between the parties to a conflict.[166] Although this approach is unclear about the politics of humanitarian aid and merges increasingly into development assistance, it does provide significant flexibility, tries to ensure there is a

---

[161] International Development Committee, *Humanitarian Responses to Natural Disasters*, vol. II Evidence, Question 157.

[162] See e.g., N. Leander, *The Politics of Principle: the Principles of Humanitarian Action in Practice*, Humanitarian Policy Group Report 2 (London: ODI, 2000); Scholms, 'On the (Im) possible Inclusion'; and D. Hilhorst, 'Being Good at Doing Good?', International Working Conference on Enhancing the Quality of Humanitarian Assistance, 12 October 2001.

[163] COM(2007)317, p. 3.   [164] Leander, *The Politics of Principle*.

[165] *Ibid.*   [166] *Ibid.*

clear continuum between programmes during the different phases of recovery from crisis, and accords with current practice.

Although many aid organisations, such as the ICRC, continue to strictly adhere to the principles of neutrality, impartiality and independence, in the context of current emergencies such as those in Sudan, Iraq and Afghanistan they cannot escape the political implications of their actions. Such an adherence to these principles is in reality not possible for DG ECHO. DG ECHO's role and function in the overall context of EU foreign policy means that the biases in the approach the Union has adopted towards third states in general have seeped into DG ECHO. The temptation to use humanitarian aid as an instrument amongst a myriad of other measures and policies has at times proved overwhelming for the Union. Third-way humanitarianism allows, and importantly recognises, that while addressing acute needs is the primary purpose of humanitarian action, it should do more than simply alleviate suffering. The emphasis on capacity building and the continuum between development and humanitarian aid can thus be strengthened.[167] The emphasis on linking relief, rehabilitation and development in the Commission is really no different from this. There is the danger that by expressly taking such an approach 'forgotten emergencies' (which DG ECHO has identified as a priority) and those which are of little significance to the Union will be moved further out of focus. For such emergencies, a certain percentage of DG ECHO's budget could be ring-fenced so that its very valuable work in those disasters is not affected.

There has in the context of humanitarian aid been little, if any, reference to the legal obligations of the Member States, but this is not surprising. The contribution of DG ECHO to the protection of ethical values in third states has not been consistent. This does not mean, however, that such considerations are not a part of the equation. They clearly are, but the weight given to them sometimes differs when the Union's more general foreign policy objectives come to the fore. But this cannot in any way deny that the work of DG ECHO has made a very significant contribution to the alleviation of suffering in third states. This is where a 'needs-based' approach to aid has been of the greatest value.

[167] Ibid.

7   Conclusions

The European Union has set itself the objective of promoting certain values and principles in its relations with all third states. This book has primarily been concerned with the Union's relations with developing countries. Its aims were to examine the legal basis for the ethical dimension to the Union's foreign policies and their implementation through a series of case studies. Four main conclusions can be drawn. First, seeking to promote and protect values and principles adapts the Union's foreign policies but it has not fundamentally changed them. Secondly, the structure and nature of the Union act as obstacles to it being an effective actor in this regard. Thirdly, EU policies in this area are neither consistent nor coherent but need to be. Finally, despite these shortcomings, the Union does achieve some of the objectives it pursues and in some respects makes an important contribution but it could make a better one. Each of these issues is discussed below.

The measures the Union can take to promote and protect certain values and principles in a third state are determined by the nature of its relationship with that state. As the Union, like other international actors, has no uniform approach either to developing or to developed states or between them, the basis for its relations with each state differs fundamentally. The nature and basis of relations with, for example, Myanmar and the other ASEAN countries, the countries of the Sub-Continent, the Palestinian Authority and the ACP states, all differ. There may be a bilateral or multilateral, a mixed or pure treaty in force to regulate relations, or there may be no treaty relationship at all. Furthermore the various unilateral instruments the Union has adopted have different objectives and priorities, although the new financial external relations regulations should enable a greater degree of coherence than was possible in the past. The instruments, mechanisms and

447

institutions which can be used to conduct relations with Nigeria, for example, will differ from those that can be used with Pakistan, as will the parties to the dialogue.

Classic instruments of diplomacy, such as dialogue and condemnation, as well as positive and punitive measures, are part of the arsenal in relations with all states. The various 'human rights' guidelines which have been adopted set out policy with regard to, for example, the death penalty or human rights dialogues but there is no coherent set of overall guidelines as to which instruments and mechanisms should be used by the Union nor how it should act or react to the situation in a third state. This is, of course, understandable as it provides the flexibility which is essential for states and actors such as the Union to react, all things considered, as they see appropriate. As a consequence, however, the Union's approach to these issues in its international relations is being formulated on an *ad hoc* basis.

The Union initially attempted to forge the ethical dimension to foreign policy by implanting it into the existing frameworks for relations with third states. The transformation in both Community competence and approach over a period of time has at times been significant, for example, in food aid policy. Existing policies, however, on the whole, were not fundamentally reviewed but mutated or adapted. As new unilateral instruments, such as the Development Cooperation Instrument or the GSP Regulation, have been adopted, this dimension has been given greater prominence. By making poverty reduction the overriding principle of Community development cooperation, for example, it is clear that the Community's aid policies and projects are now more effective on the ground than they have often been in the past. The ethical dimension has also been given greater prominence as relations with third states or regions have been reviewed and new treaties negotiated. The approach has not been consistent in relations with all third states but the political reality is that this is to be expected.

There are, as discussed in Chapter 2, numerous statements which place ethical considerations at the heart of the Union's relations with third states. From the case studies it is clear that in practice this is not the case. As many Realists contend, it would be naïve to think it is. But whereas some Realists reject any role for such considerations in policy formulation, in the case of the Union, the pursuit of ethical values is *an* objective alongside others. The constitutive treaties imply this, even if the ECJ took a somewhat different approach to the relationship between development cooperation and human rights in the *Portugal* case. A 1994 Communication on relations with Asia, for example, stated quite clearly that human rights will be *a* 'major objective' of policy with Asia. Ethical considerations are now undeniably an established part of the equation in the Union's dealings with all third states.

The case studies illustrate the role and weight given by the Union to differing considerations and factors in determining its policy toward third states. In its relations with Myanmar, the Community displayed an initial unwillingness to take punitive measures. When the elections were annulled in 1990, the formulation of Community policy was in its infancy. The maintenance of dialogue and possibly influence as well as trade interests, even though relatively unimportant, initially only led to the downgrading of development assistance and the withdrawal of military attachés. The death of the Danish consul and the consequent Danish outrage compelled the Union to take some action. There are no security considerations or major quantities of vital natural resources at stake and the fact that there is an isolationist and repressive regime in power, which is engaging in gross and systemic violations of human rights, should make the formulation of policy relatively straightfor-ward. Historically it is clear that, in the absence of Security Council resolutions, the Union takes punitive measures through the adoption of Common Positions and the Community downgrades development cooperation and assistance only if there has at some stage been an effective suspension of the democratic process, or there has not been one at all, and widespread human rights violations are occurring. Human rights violations are not the primary reason for such a reaction, although they are usually the aggravating factor which can lead to further punitive measures being adopted or their continuation. The studies on both Nigeria and Myanmar in Chapter 4 and on relations with Israel in Chapter 5 illustrate this. In many senses, if the Union takes punitive action in response to gross and systematic violations of certain human rights, as opposed to violations of democratic principles, it is on much sounder legal ground. Due to the approach it has adopted to the relationship between human rights, development and democ-racy, however, it tends to see them as inseparable.

In line with the approach now adopted by the Security Council, the Union is reluctant to unilaterally impose sweeping punitive measures which will have a negative impact on the population of a state at large. The commercial interests and political perspectives of the Member States are also relevant in determining what measures, if any, to adopt. If punitive measures are adopted the Commission refocuses programmes to try and ensure that any such measures against a state have a limited impact upon the population at large and, if possible, to encourage civil society and human rights. The approach is primarily to target those in power with so called 'smart sanctions'. Condemning a third state for whatever reason does not, as discussed in Chapter 2, amount to interference in legal terms. Assuming the political will and capacity exists, taking action which will effectively curtail a regime in a third state, however, may not be legally permissible. Striking the correct balance, bearing in mind all the different factors referred to above, is difficult. As a consequence, many of the measures implemented by the Union have a limited impact upon the regime(s) in question. This leads to routine accusations of, for example, the Union giving priority to trade interests above all other considerations, claims which are not always justifiable.

The Union also sometimes fails to strike the correct balance in the promotion of values. Countless studies and reports criticise the relevance and effectiveness of aspects of the development projects funded by the Community in third states. To a large extent, the Commission is reliant on appropriate projects being proposed by recipient states and the NGOs and agencies working there. Some of its projects, however, do make a substantial and valuable contribution, especially when they work with a government which is implementing a reform agenda. The projects which aim to tackle child labour in Pakistan, as discussed in Chapter 4, are one example. Yet, even these sorts of projects can suffer from problems, the continuity of funding being one. In a number of instances, much of the good work achieved in the short term is later undone by the Community's lack of planning and foresight. This, however, is an ailment which in part exists due to one of the inherent contradictions in granting conditional aid. On the one hand, donors aspire to have the long-term, predictable aid partnerships which are necessary to effect the deep structural changes which are needed to achieve their objectives but, on the other hand, donors have a deep-seated need for mechanisms allowing them to rescind their assistance, for whatever reason, if they unilaterally decide to do so.

The structure and nature of the Union also makes it difficult for it to effectively implement its policies in this regard. Although the interests and views of the Member States largely coincide, there are invariably issues where they have different opinions, priorities and interests. The recent expansions of the Union exacerbate these differences, which are sometimes a major factor in inhibiting the ability of the Union to take a principled and effective stance. States rarely publicly acknowledge their order of priorities as far as international affairs are concerned. These priorities and the emphasis to be given to them are a product of history, as well as the state's political, economic and security considerations. The Scandinavian Member States, for example, are considered (especially when holding the Presidency of the Council) to be more vociferous and determined in the pursuance of ethical values than some of the other Member States. At times, this can adversely affect other aspects of the relationship with a third state. Some other Member States, for example France and the United Kingdom, are seen as being politically tainted by some third states and this can harm any action by the Council vis-à-vis certain issues, especially when these states hold the Presidency. In the context of the Middle East, for example, the United Kingdom has little credibility in some parts of the Arab (and more generally Muslim) world, especially on the 'Arab street'. This is due not only to its historical involvement in the region but also its eager participation in the US-led invasions of Afghanistan and Iraq. France, however, is seen as being a more trustworthy partner by parts of the Arab world, despite its equally chequered past in the region, but not by Israel.

The Union has at its disposal an impressively broad array of powers by which to give effect to foreign policies which pursue certain values and principles. The competence derived from the development cooperation provisions of the EC Treaty, for example, ensures that if the Community wishes to inform journalists in third states about the virtues of freedom of expression (if they need to be told), if elections are to be monitored or water purified, then a legal base exists. Competence can also be derived from, among others, Articles 310, 308 and 133 TEC or under the CFSP. There are, however, sometimes problems of consistency in the exercise of different policies. Development cooperation, on the one hand, and trade policy and general foreign policy objectives, on the other, do not always coincide and despite the provisions contained in proposals for treaty reform, this is unlikely to change any time soon.

The fundamental problems that currently stand in the way of a more articulate, coherent and effective set of policies is the structure of the Union and its approach to relations with third states. The organisation of the Commission, the structure and mechanics of the Union and the use of differing competences, to name a few, make such issues very difficult to work out in a consistent and credible manner. The Union usually has too many voices for its position in foreign policy matters to be clear and authoritative. The High Representative for the CFSP, the Council, the Commissioner for External Relations, the Commissioner for Development Cooperation and Humanitarian Aid, the Presidency, the various Member States, the relevant Directorates-General of the Commission through Communications, the European Parliament through the adoption of resolutions and, in the context of their mandates, the Special Representatives, can all legitimately comment on the same issue. It is thus not surprising that they do not always sing from the same hymn sheet. The creation of an EU Minister for Foreign Affairs in the proposed Constitutional Treaty was seen as a partial solution to this problem. This will not deprive the others, in particular the Member States, of their prerogative to comment on issues of concern to them.

Any policy aimed at promoting and protecting certain values and principles in all third countries, to be credible and principled, must be coherent and consistent, with little regard to the strategic or economic importance of a third state or the historical considerations that continue to exist in relations with some third states. Inconsistency in application, in particular, between developed and developing states and the use of conditionality in relations with the latter, exposes the Union to the accusation of cultural imperialism. As far as Community Agreements with third states are concerned, reference is usually made to the outcomes of those international conferences, treaties and declarations which all parties to the Agreement have accepted. Thus, reference to the Universal Declaration of Human Rights is commonplace, even though the scope and content of some of the rights it contains is uncertain. The Union, however, also attempts directly to transplant and promote the principles and values it considers relevant to third states, sometimes without enough regard to their appropriateness or the difficulty those states will face in giving effect to them. Good governance and democracy are examples, in particular as the legal content of these principles is unclear in international law and the Union rarely articulates what it means by them – although it is increasingly willing to accept that these principles are variable and that there is no omnipresent model.

In the Union's actions and responses in both promoting and protecting ethical values in third states, with the notable exception of the implementation of UN sanctions, there is rarely any reference to the legal obligations of the various actors. EU practice is, however, undeniably influencing the content of international law. Responses to the annulment of elections, for example, are part of a trend where

non-democratic regimes are increasingly perceived as being illegiti-
mate. Community Agreements require 'democratic principles' to be
respected. Yet deficiencies in that regard in third states are routinely
overlooked by the Union, if it is politically expedient. The Union advocates the illegitimacy of non-democratic governments yet by being
inconsistent in its attitude towards all such regimes, the Union
regresses and to some extent undermines the normative development
it seeks.

The Union has failed to scrutinise the behaviour of, for example,
many oil rich Middle-Eastern states. It can be argued that the principle
in part being developed by the Union only relates to where the
expressed will of a population in multiparty elections is ignored – it is
not concerned with the (il)legitimacy of regimes, where there has not
been a plebiscite in the first place. Even if this distinction is a valid one,
the intervention of the military after the first round of the democratic
elections in Algeria in 1991 serves to undermine that argument in the
light of the Union's response to, for example, Myanmar after the 1990
election. The Union's response to the situation in Algeria is, however,
about its own perceived security interests (as is the case now in relations
with Pakistan), and it is consistent with its response to the Hamas
election victory in the Palestinian Legislative Council Elections of
2006. In the Palestinian Territories, the Union not only strongly encouraged but also helped fund what were free and fair elections but did not
approve of the outcome. The Union clearly wishes to encourage democracy but will only deal with and assist territories if the democratically
legitimate governments that are elected subscribe to the same values
as the Union and its Member States. The Union's vision of democracy
is one based upon elected governments subscribing to a select part of
the political spectrum; third states should be liberal democracies, not
simply democratically legitimate.

The Union's apparent turnaround in relations with Pakistan, as discussed in Chapter 4, is to some extent distinguishable. 'Exceptional
circumstances' are seen to exist and although the Union is open to
accusations of double standards, the promotion and protection of
ethical values in a third state will never trump the vital security interests of the promoting polity. Relations with Pakistan simply serve to
highlight the relative importance of ethical values in the hierarchy of
the Union's interests and priorities in its international relations.

Not only does the role played by ethical values in the Union's relationships with third states differ but there have also been variable

degrees of success, depending on the state(s) in question. The instruments and mechanisms that are used in relations with different third states vary greatly in their usefulness in pursuing such a policy. In its relations with developed countries the balance of power is also different and, if confronted with resistance, the Union has more to lose if it pushes these issues too hard. In the case of developing countries, the Union has more leverage which, as all donors do, it uses to pursue its objectives.

Notwithstanding these shortcomings, the Union has contributed to global and regional issues in a manner that the individual Member States simply cannot. The impact of collective action by an organisation which now has twenty-seven Member States will always be significant. For example, as Chapter 5 highlights, it is because the Union has pushed the Roadmap and the two-state solution to the conflict in the Middle East that it is now the preferred international approach. In the Middle East Peace Process, however, the Union has failed to take advantage of its own importance due to the Member States's differing opinions and perspectives. The Union and its Member States have not fully used their power and the instruments available to them to put pressure on Israel to rein in its practices in the Palestinian Territories. The failure to respond to fundamental, systematic and gross violations of international human rights law and international humanitarian law raises questions about the credibility of the Union's promotion and protection of such norms in its relations with all third states.

Yet, some of the Union's contributions, for example with regard to food security, are exceptionally valuable. With regard to humanitarian aid, the contribution of the Union is somewhat uneven. Its practice is conceptually ambiguous and there is little or no reference to legal obligations. The Union has struggled to find an appropriate role for humanitarian aid in its foreign policy instruments. It is not always clear, in practice, if it sees it as a part of the political process or apart from it. Due to the nature of the activity, it cannot but help make a positive contribution to the survival of those in need but, as discussed in Chapter 6, the provision of such aid is intrinsically bound up with many other ethical problems and political considerations to which the Union (and indeed many of the organisations it funds) does not always have a clear approach. Funds are not always spent where the absolute need is greatest and it is at times clear that insufficient coordination exists between programmes providing the different types of Community aid.

It is important not to overlook the fact that any foreign policy will always be limited in what it can achieve. Regardless of how well-designed or coherent a policy is, it is usually difficult, while respecting international legal obligations, to influence the situation in a third state so that the desired outcome is attained. Soft power has its limitations, as does military power. Many such matters are simply outside of the control of a state or, in our case, the Union. For example, as noted in Chapter 4, the refusal of the Union and its Member States to sell arms and instruments of oppression to Myanmar has simply resulted in the military regime sourcing those goods from elsewhere. In practice, the impact of these measures in Myanmar has been negligible but it has not been without cost to manufacturers of those goods in the EU Member States. Furthermore, the Union has pumped billions of euros into the Palestinian Territories in an effort to build a viable entity. The ongoing conflict has resulted in the Union, however, having to make damage limitation, the basic viability of the entity and the survival of its population its primary objectives, as opposed to supporting civil society, building an infrastructure and developing the Palestinian economy.

Even allowing for matters outside of its control, the Union, bearing in mind its wealth and political power, currently makes a less positive contribution in this regard than it should. This is not to deny the value of the contribution it does make. Simply put, it can make a more significant one. The promotion of ethical values in third states is not a purely altruistic endeavour. The Union promotes these values and norms because it believes in their inherent value and it also considers that it will in turn derive benefits from them. Foreign policies which emphasise certain values can make an important contribution to protecting the interests of the promoting entity and strengthening the pillars of the international legal order. The Union and its Member States will be more successful in 'exporting' their own political philosophy if their actions are perceived to be principled, consistent and beneficial. This needs to be supplemented by creating or supporting conditions and institutions which provide the target states with the capacity to 'import' the values in question and to implement them. It is, therefore, in the Union's interests to consider reform of its policies and practice.

A number of different aspects of the policy can be improved without the need for major reform. In terms of positive action, there must be a clearer identification of where development needs are the greatest and what contribution can be made by funding a project. Although this approach has been adopted in policy terms, it has not been properly implemented. There are many instances in which projects are funded and where a more substantial contribution could have been made elsewhere.

Where the greatest contribution can be made is with regard to poverty reduction. Poverty reduction is considered to be *the* major human rights challenge of this century. The most concrete contribution that the Union can make is by targeting those populations most in need, regardless of the strategic and political importance of the states they are in. Humanitarian, food and development aid and cooperation (depending on the circumstances) should be targeted at these populations to alleviate their suffering. Subject to scrutiny, all projects should work towards that end. Furthermore, the EBA initiative can be further amended to take account of any produce that is exported by such populations, regardless of its sensitivity. If there is no such produce, then projects can work towards establishing either an agricultural base or an industrial one so that goods which will earn much needed foreign currency can be exported to the Union. The Union should complement this initiative by targeting any adverse effects such a policy has on other populations in developing countries, in particular those who export competing produce, by providing them with additional support and benefits. This approach has the advantage of not only assisting those in most need but is clearly where funds can be most effectively spent. It requires a long-term commitment which is not sacrificed to short-term objectives and priorities.

Poverty reduction *is* considered to be the overwhelming priority of Community development cooperation but some projects have been poorly designed and poverty reduction policies have been all too easily compromised when other political considerations have come to the fore. The 'war against terror' and security are increasingly taking priority. While emphasis on the 'war against terror' is understandable, the Union should not relegate the importance of poverty reduction. Effective poverty reduction strategies can help break the cycle of dependency, create wealth and contribute to better governance and development. In any case, poverty reduction should contribute to a safer world and a securer global environment. There is a clear commitment to the Millennium Development Goals and these are being used as a yardstick, but the danger is that all development projects are being spun as being poverty orientated when this is sometimes difficult to justify. A genuinely expansive 'capabilities' approach to poverty is to be welcomed but it is, simply put, difficult to see how some Community-funded projects effectively reduce poverty for the targeted population.

Aspects of the 'essential elements' clause should also be reconsidered. The failure to use it against, for example, Israel means that the Union loses further credibility when the clause is invoked for similar or lesser violations by other states. Accusations of double standards are particularly harmful to the Union's credibility in this regard, which is essential. This does not mean that 'essential elements' clauses are of little or no use, but each principle in the clause could be defined more clearly so that all parties understand what they actually mean and when it is likely to be relied upon in case of violations of the principles referred to.

If any Agreement in whole or in part is suspended then it should also automatically follow that benefits under the GSP, GSP+ and EBA initiatives, as appropriate, for the state in question, are reviewed. In third generation Agreements there is currently no link with suspension of these benefits. As many third generation Agreements do not have a separate budget line attached to them, review of and possible suspension of the GSP and EBA schemes are a more effective tool, along with dialogue, to achieve a change in the situation which is objected to than is currently the case. The GSP Regulation can be amended to this effect. Any such action should be complemented with programmes and funding at the grass-roots level to ensure that the impact of these measures on the general population is mitigated and, as far as is possible, only affects those in power. This should ensure, in case of any doubt, that by withdrawing unilateral benefits no international legal obligations are violated.

To conclude, numerous shortcomings in the Union's approach in practice have been highlighted in this book. The overall picture of the promotion of ethical values and principles in third states is, however, a positive one. Without reform and reassessment of what it is attempting to achieve and how it should do so, the Union's contribution will continue to be less meaningful than it can be. The question for the Union is to what extent is it really committed to those values and what price is it prepared to pay in pursuing them? The Laeken Declaration of 2001 has been significant in both asking questions and providing answers about the perception that European leaders have as to the Union's values and its role and responsibilities in a globalised world. As the Declaration notes, Europe is the 'continent of humane values, the

Magna Carta, the Bill of Rights . . . the continent of liberty, solidarity and above all diversity . . . A power seeking to set globalisation within a moral framework.' Analysis of practice does display a commitment to these values but not an overriding one. The fact that the Union does not always get things right, however, does not mean that it should not continue with its efforts. It is just that the shortcomings need to be further addressed. On occasion it is difficult not to see the futility of the course of action adopted but, on the whole, this is outweighed by the positive aspects of the policy and there has been a concerted effort to reform aspects of the Union's programmes. Further reform is required on a number of different levels to make the Union's contribution more valuable in the promotion and protection of those values the Union considers are at its own core.

Select Bibliography

Abi-Saab, G., 'The Concept of Sanction in International Law' in Gowlland-Debbas, *United Nations Sanctions and International Law*, p. 29

Addo, M., 'Some Issues in European Community Development Policy and Human Rights' (1988) *LIEI* 55

Agha, H. and Malley, R., 'The Road from Mecca' (2007) 54 *NYRB*, 10 May 2007

Ahmed, T. and Butler, I., 'The European Union and Human Rights: an International Law Perspective' (2006) 17 *EJIL* 771

Akpan, G., 'The Failure of Environmental Governance and Implications for Foreign Investors and Host States: a Study of the Niger Delta Region of Nigeria' (2006) 1 *International Energy Law and Taxation Review* 1

Alston, P., 'Linking Trade and Human Rights' (1980) 23 *GYBIL* 126
  'International Trade as an Instrument of Positive Human Rights Policy' (1982) 4 *HRQ* 155
  (ed.), *The United Nations and Human Rights: a Critical Appraisal* (Oxford: Oxford University Press, 1992)
  (ed.), *People's Rights* (Oxford: Oxford University Press, 2001)
  'Ships Passing in the Night: the Current State of the Human Rights and Development Debate Seen Through the Lens of the Millennium Development Goals' (2005) 27 *HRQ* 755
  (ed.), *Labour Rights as Human Rights* (Oxford: Oxford University Press, 2005)

Alston, P., Bustelo, M. and Heenan, J. (eds.), *The EU and Human Rights* (Oxford: Oxford University Press, 1999)

Alston, P. and Robinson, M. (eds.), *Human Rights and Development: Towards Mutual Recognition* (Oxford: Oxford University Press, 2005)
  'The Challenges of Ensuring the Mutuality of Human Rights and Development Endeavours' in Alston and Robinson, *Human Rights and Development: Towards Mutual Recognition*, p. 1

Alston, P. and Tomasevski, K. (eds.), *The Right to Food* (Utrecht: Martinus Nijhoff, 1984)

Alston, P. and Weiler, J., 'An Ever Closer Union in Need of a Human Rights Policy: the EU and Human Rights' in Alston *et al.*, *The EU and Human Rights*, p. 3

Alvarez, J., 'Do Liberal States Behave Better? A Critique of Slaughter's Liberal Theory' (2001) 12 *EJIL* 183

International Organizations as Law-Makers (Oxford: Oxford University Press, 2005)

Anderson, E., Grimm, S. and Montes, C., *Poverty Focus in EU Support to Middle Income Countries* (London: ODI, 2004)

Anderson, E. and Waddington, H., *Aid and the MDG Poverty Target: How Much is Required and How Should it be Allocated?*, ODI Working Paper 275 (2006)

Anderson, K., 'Humanitarian Inviolability in Crisis: the Meaning of Impartiality and Neutrality for UN and NGO Agencies following the 2003–2004 Afghanistan and Iraq Conflicts' (2004) 17 *HHRJ* 41

Anderson, M., *Do No Harm: How Aid Can Support Peace – or War* (Boulder, CO: Lynne Rienner Publishers, 1999)

Ansari, Z. and Moten, A., 'From Crisis to Crisis: Musharraf's Personal Rule and the 2002 Elections in Pakistan' (2003) 93 *The Muslim World* 373

Aoun, E., 'European Foreign Policy and the Arab-Israeli Dispute: Much Ado About Nothing?' (2003) 8 *EFARev.* 289

Arnull, A., 'Opinion 2/94 and its Implications for the Future Constitution of the Union' in *The Human Rights Opinion of the European Court of Justice and its Constitutional Implications*, CELS Occasional Paper No. 1 (Cambridge: Centre for European Legal Studies, 1996) p. 7

'Left to its Own Devices? *Opinion 2/94* and the Protection of Fundamental Rights in the European Union' in Dashwood and Hillion, *The General Law of EC External Relations*, p. 61

Arts, K., *Integrating Human Rights into Development Co-operation: the Case of the Lomé Convention* (The Hague: Kluwer, 2000)

'ACP-EU Relations in a New Era: the Cotonou Agreement' (2003) 40 *CMLRev.* 95

Asseburg, M., 'The EU and the Middle East Conflict: Tackling the Main Obstacle to Euro-Mediterranean Partnership' (2003) 8 *Mediterranean Politics* 175

Atmar, M., 'The Politicisation of Humanitarian Aid and its Consequences for Afghans' (2001) *Humanitarian Exchange* npg

Attina, F., 'The Euro-Mediterranean Partnership Assessed: the Realist and Liberal Views' (2003) 8 *EFARev.* 181

Aust, A., *Modern Treaty Law and Practice* (Cambridge: Cambridge University Press, 2000)

Babrinde, O. and Faber, G., *The European Union and the Developing Countries: the Cotonou Agreement* (Leiden: Martinus Nijhoff, 2005)

Baehr, P., *The Role of Human Rights in Foreign Policy*, 2nd edn (London: Macmillan, 1996)

Baitenmann, H., 'NGOs and the Afghan War: the Politicisation of Humanitarian Aid' (1990) 12 *Third World Quarterly* 62

Baratta, R., 'Overlaps between European Community Competence and European Union Foreign Policy Activity' in Cannizzaro, *The European Union as an Actor in International Relations*, p. 51

Barfod, M., 'Humanitarian Aid and Conditionality: ECHO's Experience and Prospects under the CFSP' in Leander and Macrae, *Terms of Engagement*

Bartels, L., 'Article XX of GATT and the Problem of Extraterritorial Jurisdiction' (2002) 36 *JWT* 353

'The WTO Enabling Clause and Positive Conditionality in the European Community's GSP Program' (2003) 6 *JIEL* 507

Human Rights Conditionality in the EU's International Agreements (Oxford: Oxford University Press, 2005)

'Conditionality in GSP Programmes' in Cottier *et al.*, *Human Rights and International Trade*, p. 463

Bartels, L. and Ortino, F. (eds.), *Regional Trade Agreements and the WTO Legal System* (Oxford: Oxford University Press, 2006)

Bauer J. and Bell, D. (eds.), *The East Asian Challenge for Human Rights* (Cambridge: Cambridge University Press, 1999)

Baxi, U., *The Future of Human Rights*, 2nd edn (New Delhi: Oxford University Press, 2006)

Beigbeder, Y., *The Role and Status of International Humanitarian Volunteers and Organisations: the Role and Duty to Humanitarian Assistance* (The Hague: Martinus Nijhoff, 1991)

Bennett-Jones, O., *Pakistan: Eye of the Storm*, 2nd edn (New Haven: Yale University Press, 2003)

Benvenisti, E., 'The Israel-Palestinian Declaration of Principles: a Framework for Future Settlement' (1994) 5 *EJIL* 542

Bethlehem, D., 'Regional Interface between Security Council Decisions and Member States Implementation: the Example of the European Union' in Gowlland-Debbas, *United Nations Sanctions and International Law*, p. 291

Bhagwati, J., *In Defence of Globalization* (Oxford: Oxford University Press, 2005)

Bhandari, J. and Sykes, A. (eds.), *Economic Dimensions in International Law: Comparative and Empirical Perspectives* (Cambridge: Cambridge University Press, 1998)

Bishara, M., *Palestine / Israel: Peace or Apartheid – Occupations, Terrorism and the Future* (London: Zed Books, 2001)

Bjørnskov, C. and Lind, K., 'Where Do Developing Countries Go After Doha? An Analysis of WTO Positions and Potential Alliances' (2002) 36 *JWT* 543

Black, J., 'What Kind of Democracy Does the "Democratic Entitlement" Entail?' in Fox and Roth, *Democratic Governance and International Law*, p. 517

Bonwick, A., 'Advocates or Aid Worker? Approaches to Human Rights in Humanitarian Crises' in O'Neil, *Human Rights and Poverty Reduction*, p. 108

Borner, S., Bunetti, A. and Weder, B., *Political Credibility and Economic Development* (London: St Martin's Press, 1995)

Brandtner, B. and Rosas, A., 'Human Rights and the External Relations of the European Community: an Analysis of Doctrine and Practice' (1998) 9 *EJIL* 468

'Trade Preferences and Human Rights' in Alston *et al.*, *The EU and Human Rights*, p. 699

Broadbent, E., 'Human Rights and Democratic Development: Foreign Policy Concerns in the Western World' in Mahoney and Mahoney, *Human Rights in the Twenty-First Century: a Global Challenge*, p. 715

Bronckers, M., 'The Relationship of the EC Courts with Other International Tribunals: Non-Committal, Respectful or Submissive?' (2007) 44 *CMLRev.* 601

Brown, C., 'Universal Human Rights: a Critique' in Dunne and Wheeler, *Human Rights in Global Politics*, p. 103

　'Ethics, Interests and Foreign Policy' in Smith and Light, *Ethics and Foreign Policy*, p. 15

　Understanding International Relations, 2nd edn (Basingstoke: Palgrave, 2001)

　Sovereignty, Rights and Justice: International Political Theory Today (Oxford: Polity Press, 2002)

Brown, S. (ed.), *Human Rights, Self Determination and Political Change in the Occupied Political Territories* (The Hague: Martinus Nijhoff Publishers, 1997)

Brownlie, I., 'The Responsibility of States for the Acts of International Organisations' in Ragazzi, *International Responsibility*, p. 355

Bulterman, M., *Human Rights in the Treaty Relations of the European Community: Real Virtues or Virtual Reality?* (Antwerp: Intersentia, 2001)

Burchill, S., Devetak, R., Linklater, A., Paterson, M., Reus-Smit, C. and True, J., *Theories of International Relations*, 3rd rev. edn (Basingstoke: Palgrave Macmillan, 2005)

Burnside, C. and Dollar, D., 'Aid, Policies and Growth' (2000) 90 *American Economic Review* 847

Byers, M., *Custom, Power and the Power of Rules* (Cambridge: Cambridge University Press, 1999)

　(ed.), *The Role of Law in International Politics: Essays in International Relations and International Law* (Oxford: Oxford University Press, 2000)

Byers, M. and Chesterman, S., 'You the People: Pro Democratic Intervention in International Law' in Fox and Roth, *Democratic Governance and International Law*, p. 259

Byers, M. and Nolte, G. (eds.), *United States Hegemony and the Foundations of International Law* (Cambridge: Cambridge University Press, 2004)

Cannizzaro, E., 'The Role of Proportionality in the Law of International Countermeasures' (2001) 12 *EJIL* 889

　(ed.), *The European Union as an Actor in International Relations* (The Hague: Kluwer, 2002)

Capaldo, G., 'Providing a Right to Self-Defense against Large-Scale Attacks by Irregular Forces: the Israeli-Hezbollah Conflict' (2007) 48 *Harvard ILJ* 101

Capps, P., Evans, M. and Konstadinidis, S. (eds.), *Asserting Jurisdiction: International and European Legal Perspectives* (Oxford: Hart, 2003)

Carothers, T., *Critical Mission: Essays on Democracy Promotion* (Washington DC: Carnegie Endowment for International Peace, 2004)

Carter, J., *Keeping Faith: Memoirs of a President* (New York: Bantam Books, 1982)

　Palestine: Peace Not Apartheid (New York: Simon Schuster, 2006)

Cassese, A., 'The Role of Legal Advisers in Ensuring that Foreign Policy Conforms to International Legal Standards' (1992) 13 *Michigan YBILS* 139

Self-Determination of Peoples: a Legal Reappraisal (Cambridge: Cambridge University Press, 1995)

International Law, 2nd edn (Oxford: Oxford University Press, 2004)

Cassese, A., Clapham, A. and Weiler, J. (eds.), *The European Union: the Human Rights Challenge, vol. II, Human Rights and the European Community: Methods of Protection* (Baden-Baden: Nomos, 1991)

The European Union: the Human Rights Challenge, vol. III, Human Rights and the European Community: Substantive Law (Baden-Baden: Nomos, 1991)

Cathie, J., 'European Food Aid Policy, 1968–1988' in Ruttan, *Why Food Aid?*, p. 174

Cavanaugh, K., 'Selective Justice: the Case of Israel and the Occupied Territories' (2003) 26 *Fordham ILJ* 934

Chinkin, C., 'Human Rights and the Politics of Representation: is there a Role for International Law?' in Byers, *The Role of Law in International Politics: Essays in International Relations and International Law*, p. 131

Chomsky, N., *The Umbrella of U.S. Power: the Universal Declaration of Human Rights and the Contradiction of U.S. Policy* (New York: Seven Stories Press, 1999)

Hegemony or Survival: America's Quest for Global Dominance (London: Penguin, 2004)

Chowdhury, S., Denters, E. and de Waart, P. (eds.), *The Right to Development in International Law* (Dordrecht: Martinus Nijhoff, 1992)

Chua, A., 'The Paradox of Free Market Democracy: Rethinking Development Policy' (2000) 41 *Harvard ILJ* 288

Chun, L., 'Human Rights and Democracy: the Case for Decoupling' (2001) 5 *International Journal of Human Rights* 19

Clapham, A., 'Where is the EU's Human Rights Common Foreign Policy and How is it Manifested in Multilateral Fora?' in Alston *et al.*, *The EU and Human Rights*, p. 627

Human Rights Obligation of Non-State Actors (Oxford: Oxford University Press, 2006)

Clark, J., 'Human Rights and Democratic Development' in Mahoney and Mahoney, *Human Rights in the Twenty First Century*, p. 683

Cleveland, S., 'Human Rights Sanctions and International Trade: a Theory of Compatibility' (2002) 5 *JIEL* 133

Cochran, M., 'A Pragmatist Perspective on Ethical Foreign Policy' in Smith and Light, *Ethics and Foreign Policy*, p. 55

Collier, P. and Dollar, D., 'Can the World Cut Poverty in Half? How Policy Reform and Effective Aid Can Meet International Development Goals' (2001) 29 *World Development* 1787

'Aid Allocation and Poverty Reduction' (2002) 46 *European Economic Review* 1475

Compa, L. and Diamond, S. (eds.), *Human Rights, Labour Rights and International Trade*, 2nd edn (Philadelphia: University of Pennsylvania Press, 1996)

Conway, G., 'Breaches of EC Law and the Responsibility of Member States' (2002) 13 *EJIL* 679

Cosnard, M., 'Sovereign Equality: "the *Wimbledon* Sails On"' in Byers and Nolte, *United States Hegemony and the Foundations of International Law*, p. 117

Cotterell, L., 'Approaches to Human Rights in Humanitarian Crises' in O'Neil, *Human Rights and Poverty Reduction*, p. 111

Cottier, T., 'Trade and Human Rights: a Relationship to Discover' (2002) *JIEL* 111

Cottier, T., Pauwelyn, J. and Bürgi, E. (eds.), *Human Rights and International Trade* (Oxford: Oxford University Press, 2005)

Court, J., Hyden, G. and Mease, K., *Making Sense of Governance: Empirical Evidence from Sixteen Transitional Societies* (London: Lynne Reinner, 2004)

Cox, A. and Chapman, J., *The European Community External Cooperation Programmes: Policies, Management and Distribution* (London: ODI, 1999)

Craig, P., 'Formal and Substantive Conceptions of the Rule of Law: an Analytical Framework' (1997) *Public Law* 467

Craig, P. and de Búrca, G. (eds.), *The Evolution of EU Law* (Oxford: Oxford University Press, 1999)

Craven, M., *The International Covenant on Economic, Social and Cultural Rights: a Perspective on its Development* (Oxford: Oxford University Press, 1998)

'Legal Differentiation and the Concept of the Human Rights Treaty in International Law' (2000) 11 *EJIL* 489

'Humanitarianism and the Quest for Smarter Sanctions' (2002) 13 *EJIL* 43

'"For the 'Common Good": Rights and Interests in the Law of State Responsibility' in Fitzmaurice and Sarooshi, *Issues of State Responsibility before International Judicial Institutions*, p. 105

Crawford, J., 'Democracy and International Law' (1993) 44 *BYBIL* 113

'Democracy and the Body of International Law' in Fox and Roth, *Democratic Governance and International Law*, p. 91

'The Relationship between Sanctions and Countermeasures' in Gowlland-Debbas, *United Nations Sanctions and International Law*, p. 57

The International Law Commission's Articles on State Responsibility: Introduction, Text and Commentaries (Cambridge: Cambridge University Press, 2002)

The Creation of States in International Law, 2nd edn (Oxford: Oxford University Press, 2006)

Cremer, G., 'On the Problem of Misuse in Emergency Aid', www.jha.ac/articles/a042.htm

Cremona, M.,'Human Rights and Democracy Clauses in the EC's Trade Agreements' in Emiliou and O'Keeffe, *The European Union and World Trade Law*, p. 62

'External Relations and External Competence: the Emergence of an Integrated Policy' in Craig and de Búrca, *The Evolution of EU Law*, p. 137

'The EU and the External Dimension of Human Rights Policy' in Konstadinidis, *A People's Europe*, p. 155

'Creating the New Europe: the Stability Pact for South-Eastern Europe in the Context of EU-SEE Relations' (1999) 2 *CYELS* 463

'The Draft Constitutional Treaty: External Relations and External Action' (2003) 40 *CMLRev.* 1347

(ed.), *The Enlargement of the European Union* (Oxford: Oxford University Press, 2003)

'The Union as a Global Actor: Roles Models and Identity' (2004) 41
    CMLRev. 553
Curtin, D., 'The Constitutional Structure of the Union: a Europe of Bits and
    Pieces' (1993) 30 *CMLRev.* 17
Curtin, D. and Dekker, I., 'The EU as a "Layered" International Organisation:
    Institutional Unity in Disguise' in Craig and de Bùrca, *The Evolution of EU
    Law*, p. 83
Curtis, A., *Politics and Humanitarian Aid: Debates, Dilemmas and Dissension*,
    Humanitarian Policy Group Report 10 (London: ODI, 2001)
Curtis, M., 'International Law and the Territories' (1991) 32 *Harvard ILJ* 457
D'Amato, A., 'The Invasion of Panama was a Lawful Response to Tyranny' (1990)
    84 *AJIL* 37
Damrosch, L., 'Politics Across Borders: Non-intervention and Non-forcible
    Influence over Domestic Affairs' (1989) 83 *AJIL* 1
    'Enforcing International Law through Non-Forcible Measures' (1997) 269
    RDC 19
Damrosch, L., Henkin, L., Pugh, R., Schachter, O. and Smit, H., *International Law:
    Cases and Materials*, 4th edn (St Paul, MN: West Publishing, 2001)
Daniels, R. and Trebilcock, M., 'The Political Economy of Rule of Law Reform in
    Developing Countries' (2004) 26 *Michigan JIL* 99
Darcy, J. and Hofman, C., *According to Need? Needs Assessment and Decision-Making
    in the Humanitarian Sector*, Humanitarian Policy Group Report 15 (London:
    ODI, 2003)
Dashwood, A., 'Implied External Competence of the EC' in Koskenniemi,
    International Law Aspects of the European Union, p. 113
Dashwood, A. and Hillion, C. (eds.), *The General Law of EC External Relations*
    (London: Sweet & Maxwell, 1999)
de Feyter, K., *World Development Law: Sharing Responsibility for Development*
    (Antwerp: Intersentia, 2001)
de Soto, A., *End of Mission Report* (May 2007)
de Soto, H., *The Other Path* (New York: Harper and Rowe, 1989)
    The Mystery of Capital: Why Capital Triumphs in the West and Fails Everywhere Else
    (London: Black Swan Books, 2001)
de Waart, P., 'Quality of Life at the Mercy of WTO Panels: GATT's Article XX:
    an Empty Shell?' in De Waart and Weiss, *International Economic Law with a
    Human Face*, p. 109
de Waart, P. and Weiss, F. (eds.), *International Economic Law with a Human Face*
    (Dordrecht: Nijhoff, 1988)
de Witte, B., 'Rules of Change in International Law: How Special is the EC?'
    (1994) 25 *NYBIL* 299
    'The Pillar Structure and the Nature of the European Union: Greek Temple or
    French Gothic Cathedral?' in Heukels, Blokker and Brus, *The European Union
    after Amsterdam*, p. 51
    'The Past and Future Role of the European Court of Justice in the Protection
    of Human Rights' in Alston *et al.*, *The EU and Human Rights*, p. 859

Dehousse, F., 'After Amsterdam: a Report on the Common Foreign and Security Policy of the European Union' (1998) 9 *EJIL* 525

Deng, F. and Lyons, T (eds.), *African Reckoning: a Quest for Good Governance* (Washington DC: Brookings Institute, 1998)

Denza, E., *The Intergovernmental Pillars of the European Union* (Oxford: Oxford University Press, 2002)

'Non-Proliferation of Nuclear Weapons: the European Union and Iran' (2005) 10 *EFARev.* 289

'The Relationship between International and National Law' in Evans, *International Law*, p. 423

Department for International Development, *Realising Human Rights for Poor People* (HMSO: London, 2000)

Development Assistance Committee, *Shaping the 21st Century, Scoping Study, Donor Poverty Reduction and Practices* (Paris: OECD, 1996)

DAC Guidelines on Conflict, Peace and Development Cooperation (Paris: OECD, 1997)

Guidelines on Poverty Reduction (Paris: OECD, 2001)

Donnelly, J., 'Human Rights, Democracy and Development' (1999) 21 *HRQ* 608

Realism and International Relations (Cambridge: Cambridge University Press, 2000)

'An Overview' in Forsythe, *Human Rights and Comparative Foreign Policy*, p. 310

Doyle, M., *Ways of War and Peace* (New York: W.W. Norton & Company, 1997)

Dunne, T. and Wheeler, N. (eds.), *Human Rights in Global Politics* (Cambridge: Cambridge University Press, 1996)

'Blair's Britain: a Force for Good in the World?' in Smith and Light, *Ethics and Foreign Policy*, p. 147

Duquette, E., 'Human Rights in the European Union: Internal Versus External Objectives' (2001) 34 *Cornell ILJ* 363

Dutch Ministry of Foreign Affairs, 'Human Rights and Foreign Policy' (1980) 11 *Netherlands Yearbook of International Law* 193

Dutton, A., 'The Moral Legitimacy of "Conditionality" in Humanitarian Relief' *Journal of Humanitarian Affairs*, www.jha.ac/articles/a070.htm

Easterly, W., 'Can Foreign Aid Buy Growth?' (2003) 17 *Journal of Economic Perspectives* 23

Eaton, M., 'Common Foreign and Security Policy' in O'Keeffe and Twomey, *Legal Issues of the Maastricht Treaty*, p. 215

Edwards, G. and Philippart, E., 'The Euro-Mediterranean Partnership: Fragmentation and Reconstruction' (1997) 2 *EFARev.* 465

Edwards, G. and Regelsberger, E. (eds.), *Europe's Global Links: the European Community and Inter-Regional Cooperation* (London: Pinter, 1990)

Eeckhout, P., *External Relations of the European Union: Legal and Constitutional Foundations* (Oxford: Oxford University Press, 2004)

Eide, A., 'Economic, Social and Cultural Rights as Human Rights' in Eide, Krause and Rosas, *Economic, Social and Cultural Rights: a Textbook*, p. 9

'The Right to an Adequate Standard of Living including the Right to Food' in Eide, Krause and Rosas, *Economic, Social and Cultural Rights: a Textbook*, p. 133

Eide, A., Krause, C. and Rosas, A. (eds.), *Economic, Social and Cultural Rights: a Textbook* (Dordrecht: Nijhoff, 2001)

Elagab, O., *The Legality of Non-Forcible Countermeasures in International Law* (Oxford: Oxford University Press, 1989)

Eltayeb, M., *A Human Rights Approach to Combating Religious Persecution: Cases from Pakistan, Saudi Arabia and Sudan* (Oxford: Hart, 2001)

Emerson, M., Aydin, S., Noutcheva, G., Tocci, N., Vahl, M. and Youngs, R., *The Reluctant Debutante: the European Union as Promoter of Democracy in its Neighbourhood*, CEPS Working Document No. 223 (2005)

Emiliou, N. and O'Keeffe, D. (eds.), *The European Union and World Trade Law: After the GATT Uruguay Round* (Chichester: Wiley, 1996)

Legal Aspects of Integration in the European Union (The Hague: Kluwer, 1997)

Ermacora, F., 'Human Rights and Domestic Jurisdiction (Art.2(7) of the Charter)' (1968) 124 *RDC* 375

European Council, *EU Annual Report on Human Rights, 1998/1999* (Luxembourg: OOPEC, 1999)

EU Annual Report on Human Rights, 2000 (Luxembourg: OOPEC, 2000)

EU Annual Report on Human Rights, 2001 (Luxembourg: OOPEC, 2001)

EU Annual Report on Human Rights, 2002 (Luxembourg: OOPEC, 2002)

EU Annual Report on Human Rights, 2003 (Luxembourg: OOPEC, 2003)

EU Annual Report on Human Rights, 2004 (Luxembourg: OOPEC, 2004)

EU Annual Report on Human Rights, 2005 (Luxembourg: OOPEC, 2005)

EU Annual Report on Human Rights, 2006 (Luxembourg: OOPEC, 2006)

Evans, M. (ed.), *Aspects of Statehood and Institutionalism in Contemporary Europe* (Aldershot: Dartmouth, 1997)

International Law, 2nd edn (Oxford: Oxford University Press, 2006)

Falk, R., 'Some International Law Implications of the Oslo/Cairo Framework for the PLO/Israeli Peace Process' in Brown, *Human Rights, Self Determination and Political Change*, p. 1

'Sovereignty and Human Dignity: the Search for Reconciliation' in Deng and Lyons, *African Reckoning: a Quest for Good Governance*, p. 14

Human Rights Horizons: the Pursuit of Justice in a Globalising World (London: Routledge, 2000)

Falk, R. and Weston, B., 'The Relevance of International Law to Palestinian Rights in the West Bank and Gaza: in Legal Defence of the Intifada' (1991) 32 *Harvard ILJ* 129

'The Israeli-Occupied Territories, International Law and the Boundaries of Scholarly Discourse: a Reply to Michael Curtis' (1992) 33 *Harvard ILJ* 191

Farer, T., 'Promoting Democracy: International Law and Norms' in Newman and Rich, *The UN Role in Promoting Democracy: Between Ideals and Reality*, p. 32

Faundez, J. (ed.), *Good Government and Law: Legal and Institutional Reform in Developing Countries* (London: Macmillan, 1997)

Fierke, K., 'Constructing an Ethical Foreign Policy: Analysis and Practice from Below' in Smith and Light, *Ethics and Foreign Policy*, p. 129

Fierro, E., *The EU's Approach to Human Rights Conditionality in Practice* (The Hague: Kluwer, 2002)

Fink, C., *Living Silence: Burma under Military Rule* (London: Zed Books, 2001)

Fitzmaurice, M. and Sarooshi, D. (eds.), *Issues of State Responsibility before International Judicial Institutions* (Oxford: Hart Publishing, 2004)

Foreign and Commonwealth Office, *British Policy towards the United Nations*, Foreign Policy Doc. No. 26 (London: HMSO, 1978)

Human Rights in Foreign Policy, Foreign Policy Doc. No. 215 (London: HMSO, 1991)

Human Rights in Foreign Policy, Foreign Policy Doc. No. 268 (London: HMSO, 1996)

Human Rights Annual Report 2003 (London: HMSO, 2003)

Human Rights Annual Report 2005 (London: HMSO, 2006)

Active Diplomacy for a Changing World: the UK's International Priorities (London: HMSO, 2006)

Human Rights Annual Report 2006 (London: HMSO, 2006)

Forsythe, D., *Human Rights and World Politics*, 2nd rev. edn (Lincoln, NB: University of Nebraska Press, 1989)

'The United Nations, Human Rights, and Development' (1997) 19 *HRQ* 334

(ed.), *Human Rights and Comparative Foreign Policy* (Tokyo: United Nations University Press, 2000)

Human Rights in International Relations (Cambridge: Cambridge University Press, 2000)

The Humanitarians: the International Committee of the Red Cross (Cambridge: Cambridge University Press, 2005)

Fox, G. and Roth, B. (eds.), *Democratic Governance and International Law* (Cambridge: Cambridge University Press, 2000)

Franck, T., 'The Emerging Right to Democratic Governance' (1992) 86 *AJIL* 46

Fairness in International Law and Institutions (Oxford: Oxford University Press, 1995)

Frohardt, M., Paul, D. and Minear, L., *Protecting Human Rights: the Challenge to Humanitarian Organisations*, HWP Occasional Paper 35 (1999)

Frost, M., *Ethics in International Relations: a Constitutive Theory* (Cambridge: Cambridge University Press, 1996)

Frowein, J., 'Reactions by Not Directly Affected States to Breaches of Public International Law' (1994) 248 (IV) *RDC* 349

Gaga, G., 'Obligations *Erga Omnes*, International Crimes and *Jus Cogens*: a Tentative Analysis of Three Related Concepts' in Weiler *et al.*, *International Crimes of States*, p. 151

'Opinion 2/94' (1996) 33 *CMLRev.* 973

'Do States have a Duty to Ensure Compliance with Obligations *Erga Omnes* by Other States?' in Ragazzi, *International Responsibility*, p. 31

Garcia, F., 'The Global Market and Human Rights: Trading Away the Human Rights Principle' (1999) 25 *Brooklyn JIL* 51

Gardner, P. (ed.), *Human Rights as General Norms and a State's Right to Opt Out* (London: BIICL, 1997)

Gaskarth, J., 'Discourses and Ethics: the Social Construction of British Foreign Policy' (2006) *Foreign Policy Analysis* 325

Ginther, K., Denters, E. and de Waart, P. (eds.), *Sustainable Development and Good Governance* (The Hague: Kluwer, 1995)

Goldstein, J., *International Relations*, 3rd edn (Harlow: Longman, 1999)

Goodrich, L., Hambro, E. and Simins, P., *The Charter of the United Nations: Commentary and Documents*, 3rd edn (New York: Columbia University Press, 1969)

Gosalbo Bono, R., 'Some Reflections on the CFSP Legal Order' (2006) 43 *CMLRev.* 337

Gould, J. (ed.), *The New Conditionality: the Politics of Poverty Reduction Strategies* (London: Zed Books, 2005)

Gowlland-Debbas, V. (ed.), *United Nations Sanctions and International Law* (The Hague: Kluwer, 2001)

Gradstein, M and Milanovic, B., *Does Liberté = Egalité: a Survey of the Empirical Links between Democracy and Inequality with Some Evidence on the Transition Economies*, PRWP 2875 (Washington DC: World Bank, 2002)

Gras, J., *The European Union and Human Rights Monitoring* (Helsinki: University of Helsinki, 2000)

Gray, C., *International Law and the Use of Force*, 2nd edn (Oxford: Oxford University Press, 2004)

Gready, P. and Ensor, J. (eds.), *Reinventing Development: Translating Right-Based Approaches from Theory into Practice* (London: Zed Books, 2005)

Grilli, E., *The European Community and the Developing Countries* (Cambridge: Cambridge University Press, 1993)

Grindle, M., 'Good Enough Governance: Poverty Reduction and Reform in Developing Countries' (2004) 17 *Governance* 525

Hakura, F., 'The Euro-Mediterranean Policy: the Implications of the Barcelona Declaration' (1997) 34 *CMLRev.* 337

Hansen, H. and Tarp, F., 'Aid and Growth Regressions' (2001) 64 *Journal of Development Economics* 547

Harlow, C., 'Global Administrative Law: the Quest for Principles and Values' (2006) 17 *EJIL* 187

Harrison, J., 'Incentives for Development: the EC's Generalized System of Preferences, India's WTO Challenge and Reform' (2005) 42 *CMLRev.* 1663

Hartley, T., 'International Law and the Law of the European Union: a Reassessment' (2001) 72 *BYBIL* 1

Harvey, P., 'Militant Democracy and the European Convention on Human Rights' (2004) *ELRev.* 407

Haslam, J., *No Virtue Like Necessity: Realist Thought in International Relations since Machiavelli* (New Haven: Yale University Press, 2002)

Hatchard, J. and Perry-Kessaris, A. (eds.), *Law and Development: Facing Complexity in the 21st Century* (London: Cavendish, 2003)

Hauswaldt, C., 'Problems under the EC-Israel Association Agreement: the Export of Goods Produced in the West Bank and Gaza Strip under the EC-Israel Association Agreement' (2003) 14 *EJIL* 591

Held, D., *Models of Democracy*, 3rd edn (London: Polity Press, 2006)
Henckaerts, J. M. and Doswald-Beck, L., *Customary International Humanitarian Law, vol. I, Rules* (Cambridge: Cambridge University Press, 2005)
Henkin, L., *How Nations Behave: Law and Foreign Policy*, 2nd edn (New York: F.A. Praeger, 1979)
  'International Law: Politics, Values and Functions' (1989) 216 *RDC* 9
  The Age of Rights (New York: Columbia University Press, 1990)
  'Human Rights and State "Sovereignty"' (1996) 25 *Ga. J Int'l and Comp. L* 31
  'Inter-State Responsibility for Compliance with Human Rights Obligations' in Vohrah *et al.*, *Man's Inhumanity*, p. 383
Hervey, P. and Lind, J., *Dependency and Humanitarian Relief: a Critical Analysis*, Humanitarian Policy Group Report 19 (London: ODI, 2005)
Heukels, T., Blokker, N. and Brus, M. (eds.), *The European Union after Amsterdam* (The Hague: Kluwer, 1998)
Higgins, R., *The Development of International Law through the Political Organs of the United Nations* (London: RIIA and Oxford University Press, 1963)
  'Human Rights and Foreign Policy' (1987) *Rivista di Studi Politici Internazionali* 563
  'The Legal Consequences for Member States of the Non-Fulfilment by International Organisations of their Obligations toward Third Parties' (1995) 66 *AIDI* 249
  'Introduction' in Gardner, *Human Rights as General Norms*, p. vx
Hill, C., 'The Capability–Expectations Gap, or Conceptualising Europe's International Role' (1993) 31 *JCMS* 305
  'The EU's Capacity for Conflict Prevention' (2001) 6 *EFARev.* 315
  'Renationalising or Regrouping? EU Foreign Policy since 11 September 2001' (2004) 42 *JCMS* 143
Hill, D. and Beddard, R. (eds.), *Human Rights and Foreign Policy: Principles and Practice* (Basingstoke: Macmillan, 1989)
Hillion, C. (ed.), *EU Enlargement: a Legal Approach* (Oxford: Hart Publishing, 2004)
Hilpold, P., 'EU Development Cooperation at a Crossroads: the Cotonou Agreement of 23 June 2000 and the Principle of Good Governance' (2002) 7 *EFRARev.* 53
Hirsch, M., *The Responsibility of International Organisations toward Third Parties: Some Basic Principles* (Dordrecht: Martinus Nijhoff, 1995)
  'The 1995 Trade Agreement between the European Communities and Israel: Three Unresolved Issues' (1996) 1 *EFARev.* 87
  'Rules of Origin as Trade or Foreign Policy Instruments? The European Union Policy on Products Manufactured in the Settlements in the West Bank and Gaza Strip' (2003) 26 *Fordham ILJ* 572
Holland, M., *The European Union and the Third World* (Basingstoke: Palgrave, 2002)
Hollis, M. and Smith, S., *Explaining and Understanding International Relations* (Oxford: Clarendon, 1990)
House of Commons Select Committee on International Development, *The Effectiveness of EC Development Aid*, Ninth Report of the Session 1999–2000 (London: HMSO, 2000)

Development Assistance and the Occupied Palestinian Territories, Second Report of the Session 2003–2004 (London: HMSO, 2004)

The Commission for Africa and Policy Coherence for Development: First Do No Harm, First Report of Session 2004–2005 (London: HMSO, 2004)

Fair Trade? The European Union's Trade Agreements with African, Caribbean and Pacific Countries, Sixth Report of the Session 2004–2005 (London: HMSO, 2005)

The WTO Hong Kong Ministerial and the Doha Development Agenda, Third Report of the Session 2005–2006 (London: HMSO, 2006)

Humanitarian Responses to Natural Disasters, Seventh Report of the Session 2005–2006 (London: HMSO, 2006) vols. I and II

Development Assistance and the Occupied Palestinian Territories, Fourth Report of the Session 2006–2007 (London: HMSO, 2007) vols. I and II

EU Development and Trade Polices: an Update, Fifth Report of Session 2006–2007 (London: HMSO, 2007)

House of Lords European Union Committee, *Preventing Proliferation of Weapons of Mass Destruction: the EU Contribution*, Thirteenth Report of the Session 2004–2005 (London: HMSO, 2005)

Too Much or Too Little? Changes to the EU Sugar Regime, Eighteenth Report of the Session 2005–2006 (London: HMSO, 2005) vol. I

Howse, R. and Trebilcock, M., 'The Free Trade–Fair Trade Debate: Trade, Labour and the Environment' in Bhandari and Sykes, *Economic Dimensions in International Law*, p. 186

Human Rights Watch, *Contemporary Forms of Slavery in Pakistan* (New York: Human Rights Watch, 1995)

Husseini, H., 'Challenges and Reforms in the Palestinian Authority' (2003) 26 *Fordham ILJ* 500

Ignatieff, M., *Human Rights as Politics and Idolatry* (Princeton: Princeton University Press, 2003)

Imseis, A., ' "Moderate Torture on Trial": Critical Reflections on the Israeli Supreme Court Judgement Concerning the Legality of the General Security Service Interrogation Methods' (2001) 5 *International Journal of Human Rights* 71

'On the Fourth Geneva Convention and the Occupied Palestinian Territory' (2003) 44 *Harvard ILJ* 65

International Commission of Jurists, *Human Rights in United States and United Kingdom Foreign Policy: a Colloquium* (London: International Commission of Jurists, 1978)

International Commission on Intervention and State Sovereignty, *The Responsibility to Protect* (Ottawa, ON: International Development Research Centre, 2001)

International Institute for Strategic Studies, *Nuclear Black Markets: Pakistan, A.Q. Khan and the Rise of Proliferation Networks: a Net Assessment* (London: IISS, 2007)

Isaac, G., 'Le "pilier" communautaire de l'Union Europe, un "Pilier" pas comme les autres' (2001) 37 *CDE* 45

Jackson, R. and Sørenson, G., *Introduction to International Relations: Theories and Approaches*, 2nd edn (Oxford: Oxford University Press, 2003)

Jaspers, S., *Solidarity and Soup Kitchens: a Review of Principles and Practice for Food Distribution in Conflict*, Humanitarian Policy Group Report 7 (London: ODI, 2000)

Jennings, R. and Watts, A. (eds.), *Oppenheim's International Law*, 9th edn (Harlow: Longman, 1992)

Johnson, C., 'Afghanistan and the "War on Terror"' in Macrae and Harmer, *Humanitarian Action and the 'Global War on Terror'*, p. 49

Jørgensen, K., 'Theoretical Perspectives on the Role of Values, Images and Principles in Foreign Policy' in Lucarelli and Manners, *Values and Principles*, p. 42

Jørgensen, N., *The Responsibility of States for International Crimes* (Oxford: Oxford University Press, 2000)

Kagan, R., *Of Paradise and Power: America and Europe in the New World Order* (New York: Vintage Books, 2004)

Kamminga, M., *Inter-State Accountability for Violations of Human Rights* (Philadelphia: University of Pennsylvania Press, 1992)

Karagiannis, N., *Avoiding Responsibility: the Politics and Discourse of European Development Policy* (London: Pluto Press, 2004)

Kellerman, A. (ed.), *Israel Among Nations* (The Hague: Kluwer, 1998)

Kennedy. D., 'Laws and Development' in Hatchard and Perry-Kessaris, *Law and Development*, p. 17

  The Dark Sides of Virtue: Reassessing International Humanitarianism (Princeton: Princeton University Press, 2004)

Kenny, K., *When Needs are Rights: an Overview of UN Efforts to Integrate Human Rights into Humanitarian Action*, HWP Occasional Paper 38 (2000)

Keohane, R., *International Institutions and State Power: Essays in International Relations Theory* (Boulder: Westview Press, 1989)

Ketvel, M., 'The Jurisdiction of the European Court of Justice in respect of the Common Foreign and Security Policy' (2006) 55 *ICLQ* 77

Khan, H., *Constitutional and Political History of Pakistan* (Oxford: Oxford University Press, 2001)

Killick, T., Gunatilaka, R. and Marr, A., *Aid and the Political Economy of Policy Change* (London: Routledge, 1998)

King, T., 'The European Community and Human Rights in Eastern Europe' (1996) *LIEI* 93

  'Human Rights in the Development Policy of the EC: Towards a European World Order?' (1997) 27 *NYBIL* 51

  'Human Rights in European Foreign Policy: Success or Failure for Post-Modern Diplomacy?' (1999) 10 *EJIL* 313

  'Ensuring Human Rights Review of Intergovernmental Acts in Europe' (2000) 25 *ELRev.* 79

Kissinger, H., *Diplomacy* (New York: Touchstone, 1994)

Toward a Diplomacy for the Twenty-First Century: Does America Need a Foreign Policy? (London: Simon and Schuster, 2001)

Klabbers, J., 'Presumptive Personality: the European Union in International Law' in Koskenniemi, *International Law Aspects of the European Union*, p. 231

'Comment on Case C-162/96, *A. Racke GmbH & Co.v. Hauptzollant Mainz*' (1999) 36 *CMLRev.* 179

'Accepting the Unacceptable: a New Nordic Approach to Reservations to Multilateral Treaties' (2000) 69 *Nordic JIL* 179

'Restraints on the Treaty-Making Powers of Member States deriving from EU Law: Towards a Framework for Analysis' in Cannizzaro, *The European Union as an Actor in International Relations*, p. 151

Klein, P., 'Responsibility for Serious Breaches of Obligations Deriving from Peremptory Norms of International Law and United Nations Law' (2002) 13 *EJIL* 1241

Knack, S., 'Does Foreign Aid Promote Democracy?' (2004) 48 *International Studies Quarterly* 251

Koh, H., 'A United States Human Rights Policy for the 21st Century' (2002) 46 *Saint Louis University Law Journal* 293

Konstadinidis, S. (ed.), *A People's Europe: Turning a Concept into Content* (Aldershot: Dartmouth, 1999)

Koskenniemi, M. (ed.), *International Law Aspects of the European Union* (The Hague: Martinus Nijhoff, 1997)

Koutrakos, P., *Trade, Foreign Policy and Defence in EU Constitutional Law* (Oxford: Hart, 2001)

EU International Relations Law (Oxford: Hart, 2006)

Kretzmer, D., 'Targeted Killing of Suspected Terrorists: Extra-Judicial Executions or Legitimate Means of Defence?' (2005) 16 *EJIL* 171

Kronenberger, V. (ed.), *The European Union and the International Legal Order: Discord or Harmony?* (The Hague: Kluwer, 2001)

Kumado, K., 'An Analysis of the Policy of Linking Development Aid to the Implementation of Human Rights Standards' (1993) 50 *The Review: the ICJ* 23

Kuyper, P., 'Sanctions against Rhodesia and the European Economic Community and the Implementation of General International Legal Rules' (1975) 12 *CMLRev.* 231

'Community Sanctions against Argentina: Lawfulness under Community and International Law' in O'Keeffe and Schermers, *Essays in European Law and Integration*, p. 141

La Guardia, A., *War Without End: Israelis, Palestinians and the Struggle for a Promised Land* (New York: St Martin's Press, 2001)

Langenkamp, D, 'The Victory of Expediency: Afghan Refugees and Pakistan in the 1990s' (2003) *Fletcher Forum of World Affairs* 229

Laurent, P., 'Humanitarian Assistance is a Right' in Pirotte, Husson and Grunewald, *Responding to Emergencies and Fostering Development*, p. 122

Lauterpacht, H., 'The International Protection of Human Rights' (1947) 62 *RDC* 1

Leander, N., *The Politics of Principle: the Principles of Humanitarian Action in Practice*, Humanitarian Policy Group Report 2 (London: ODI, 2000)

Leander, N. and Macrae, J. (eds.), *Terms of Engagement: Conditions and Conditionality in Humanitarian Action*, Humanitarian Policy Group Report 6 (London: ODI, 2002)

Leary, V., 'The WTO and the Social Clause: Post-Singapore' (1997) 7 *EJIL* 118

Leino, P., 'European Universalism? The EU and Human Rights Conditionality' (2005) 24 *YEL* 329

Lenaerts, K. and De Smijter, E., 'The European Community's Treaty Making Competence' (1996) 16 *YEL* 1

'The European Union as an Actor under International Law' (1999/2000) 19 *YEL* 95

Lensink, R. and White, H., 'Are there Negative Returns to Aid?' (2001) 37 *Journal of Development Studies* 42

Lesch, D. (ed.), *The Middle East and the United States: a Historical and Political Reassessment*, 2nd edn (Oxford: Westview, 1999)

Little, R. and Wickham-Jones, M. (eds.), *New Labour's Foreign Policy: a New Moral Crusade?* (Manchester: Manchester University Press, 2000)

Loucaides, L., 'Determining the Extra-territorial Effect of the European Convention: Facts, Jurisprudence and the *Banković* Case' (2006) *EHRLR* 391

Lowe, V., 'Can the European Community Bind Member States on Questions of Customary International Law ?' in Koskenniemi, *International Law Aspects of the European Union*, p. 149

Lowe, V. and Warbrick, C. (eds.), *The United Nations and the Principles of International Law: Essays in Memory of Michael Akehurst* (London: Routledge, 1994)

Lucarelli, S., 'Values, Principles, Identity and European Union Foreign Policy' in Lucarelli and Manners, *Values and Principles in European Union Foreign Policy*, p. 1

Lucarelli, S. and Manners, I. (eds.), *Values and Principles in European Union Foreign Policy* (London: Routledge, 2006)

Macalister-Smith, P., 'The EEC and International Humanitarian Assistance' (1981) *LIEI* 89

MacFarlane, N., *Politics and Humanitarian Action*, Thomas J. Watson Jr Institute Occasional Paper 41 (2000)

Macleod, I., Hendry, I. and Hyett, S., *The External Relations of the European Communities: a Manual of Law and Practice* (Oxford: Oxford University Press, 1996)

Macrae, J., *Aiding Recovery? The Crisis of Aid in Chronic Political Emergencies* (London: Zed Books, 2001)

(ed.), *The New Humanitarianisms: a Review of Trends in Global Humanitarian Action*, Humanitarian Policy Group Report 11 (London: ODI, 2002)

Macrae, J. and Harmer, A. (eds.), *Humanitarian Action and the 'Global War on Terror': a Review of Trends and Issues*, Humanitarian Policy Group Report 14 (London: ODI, 2003)

Macrae, J. and Leander, N., *Shifting Sands: the Search for Coherence between Political and Humanitarian Responses to Complex Emergencies*, Humanitarian Policy Group Report 8 (London: ODI, 2000)

Madsen, H., 'Development Assistance and Human Rights Concerns' (1994) 61/62 *Nordic Journal of International Law* 129

Mahmud, T., 'Freedom of Religion and Religious Minorities in Pakistan: a Study of Judicial Practice' (1995) 19 *Fordham ILJ* 1

Mahncke, D., 'Relations between Europe and South East Asia: the Security Dimension' (1997) 2 *EFARev.* 291

Mahoney, K. and Mahoney, P. (eds.), *Human Rights in the Twenty First Century* (Dordrecht: Martinus Nijhoff, 1993)

Malley, R., 'A New Middle East' (2006) 54 *NYRB*, 21 September 2006

Malley, R. and Agha, H., 'Three Men in a Boat' (2003) 50 *NYRB*, 14 August 2003

Maluka, Z., *The Myth of Constitutionalism* (Karachi: Oxford University Press, 1996)

Malunczuk, P., 'Some Basic Aspects of the Agreements between Israel and the Palestinian Liberation Organisation from the Perspective of International Law' (1996) 7 *EJIL* 485

Mamdani, M., *Good Muslim, Bad Muslim: America, the Cold War and the Roots of Terror* (New York: Random House, 2005)

Manin, P., 'The European Communities and the Vienna Convention on the Law of Treaties between States and International Organisations or between International Organisations' (1987) 24 *CMLRev.* 457

Manners, I., 'Normative Power Europe: a Contradiction in Terms?' (2002) 40 *JCMS* 235

Marantis, D., 'Human Rights, Democracy, and Development: the European Community Model' (1994) 7 *HHRJ* 1

Marks, S., 'The Human Right to Development: Between Rhetoric and Reality' (2004) 17 *HHRJ* 137

'International Law, Democracy and the End of History' in Fox and Roth, *Democratic Governance and International Law*, p. 532

Marr, P., 'The United States, Europe and the Middle East: Cooperation, Cooptation or Confrontation?' in Robertson, *The Middle East and Europe*, p. 74

Maupin, F., 'Is the ILO Effective in Upholding Workers' Rights?: Reflections on the Myanmar Experience' in Alston, *Labour Rights as Human Rights*, p. 85

McGoldrick, D., *The Human Rights Committee* (Oxford: Oxford University Press, 1994)

'Human Rights and Non-Intervention' in Lowe and Warbrick, *The United Nations and the Principles of International Law*, p. 85

'The European Union after Amsterdam: an Organisation with General Human Rights Competence?' in O'Keeffe and Twomey, *Legal Issues of the Amsterdam Treaty*, p. 249

International Relations Law of the European Union (London: Longman, 1997)

'Approaches to the Assertion of International Jurisdiction: the Human Rights Committee' in Capps *et al.*, *Asserting Jurisdiction: International and European Legal Perspectives*, p. 199

McHugo, J., 'Resolution 242: a Legal Appraisal of the Right-Wing Israeli Interpretation of the Withdrawal Phrase with reference to the Conflict between Israel and the Palestinians' (2002) 51 *ICLQ* 851

McMahon, J., *The Development Co-operation Policy of the EC* (The Hague: Kluwer, 1998)

'ASEAN and the Asia-Europe Meeting: Strengthening the European Union's Relationship with South East Asia?' (1998) 3 *EFARev.* 233

'International Agricultural Trade Reform and Developing Countries: the Case of the European Community' (1998) 47 *ICLQ* 632

'Negotiating in a Time of Turbulent Transition: the Future of Lomé' (1999) 36 *CMLRev.* 599

Law of the Common Agricultural Policy (Harlow: Longman, 2000)

Mearsheimer, J. and Walt, S., 'The Israel Lobby and US Foreign Policy' (2006) XIII *Middle East Policy* 29

Meessen, K., 'The Application of Rules of Public International Law within Community Law' (1976) 13 *CMLRev.* 485

Menon, P., 'The Law of Treaties between States and International Organisations or between International Organisations with Special Reference to the Vienna Convention of 1986' (1987) 65 *RDI* 255

Merlingen, M. and Ostrauskaite, R., 'ESDP Police Missions: Meaning, Context and Operational Challenges' (2005) 10 *EFARev.* 215

Mestdagh, P., 'The Right to Development' (1981) 28 *NILR* 30

Michalopoulos, C., *Developing Countries in the WTO* (London: Palgrave, 2001)

Middleton, N. and O'Keefe, P., *Disaster and Development: the Politics of Humanitarian Aid* (London: Pluto Press, 1998)

Minear, L., 'The Theory and Practice of Neutrality: Some Thoughts on the Tensions' (1999) 833 *IRRC* 63

Missiroli, A., 'European Security Policy: the Challenge of Coherence' (2001) 6 *EFARev.* 177

Mols, J., 'Cooperation with ASEAN: a Success Story' in Edwards and Regelsberger, *Europe's Global Links*, p. 66

Morgenthau, H., *Politics Among Nations* (London: McGraw Hill, 1992)

Morphet, S., 'British Foreign Policy and Human Rights: from Low to High Politics' in Forsythe, *Human Rights and Comparative Foreign Policy*, p. 87

Mumtaz, K. and Shaheed, F., *Women of Pakistan: Two Steps Forward, One Step Back?* (London: Zed Books, 1987)

Murphy, S., 'Democratic Legitimacy and the Recognition of States and Governments' (1999) 48 *ICLQ* 545

'Self-Defense and the Israeli Wall Advisory Opinion: an Ipse Dixit from the ICJ?' (2005) 99 *AJIL* 62

Musharraf, P., *In the Line of Fire: A Memoir* (London: Simon and Schuster, 2006)

Mutua, M., 'The Banjul Charter and the African Cultural Fingerprint: an Evaluation of the Language of Duties' (1995) 35 *Virginia JIL* 339

'The Ideology of Human Rights' (1996) 36 *Virginia JIL* 589

'Politics and Human Rights: an Essential Symbiosis' in Byers, *The Role of Law in International Politics*, p. 149

Human Rights: a Political and Cultural Critique (Philadelphia: University of Pennsylvania Press, 2002)

Napoli, D., 'The European Union's Foreign Policy and Human Rights' in
    Neuwahl and Rosas, *The European Union and Human Rights*, p. 297
Nathanson, R. and Stetter, S. (eds.), *The Israeli European Policy Network* (Tel Aviv:
    Friedrich Ebert Stiftung, 2005)
Nayar, M., 'Human Rights and Economic Development: the Legal Foundations'
    (1980) 2 *Universal Human Rights* 55
Neframi, E., 'International Responsibility of the European Community and of
    the Member States under Mixed Agreements' in Cannizzaro, *The European
    Union as an Actor in International Relations*, p. 193
Nelson, J., *'Good Governance: Democracy and Conditional Economic Aid'* in P. Mosley,
    Development Finance and Policy Reform (London: Palgrave Macmillan, 1992)
    p. 309
Nelson, J. and Eglinton, S., *Encouraging Democracy: What Role for Conditioned Aid*
    (Washington DC: Overseas Development Council, 1992)
Neuwahl, N., 'The Treaty on European Union: a Step Forward in the Protection
    of Human Rights?' in Neuwahl and Rosas, *The European Union and Human
    Rights*, p. 1
  'A Partner with a Troubled Personality: EU Treaty Making in Matters of CFSP
    and JHA after Amsterdam' (1998) 3 *EFARev.* 177
  'Legal Personality of the European Union: International and Institutional
    Aspects' in Kronenberger, *The European Union and the International Legal
    Order*, p. 3
Neuwahl, N. and Rosas, A. (eds.), *The European Union and Human Rights* (The Hague:
    Martinus Nijhoff, 1995)
Newman, E. and Rich, R. (eds.), *The UN Role in Promoting Democracy: Between Ideals
    and Reality* (Tokyo: United Nations University Press, 2004)
Nienhaus, V., 'Promoting Development and Stability through a
    Euro-Mediterranean Free Trade Zone' (1999) 4 *EFARev.* 501
Nogueras, D. and Martinez, L., 'Human Rights Conditionality in the External
    Trade of the European Union: Legal and Legitimacy Problems' (2001) 7
    Columbia JIEL 307
Novak, M., 'Human Rights "Conditionality" in Relation to Entry to, and Full
    Participation in, the EU' in Alston *et al.*, *The EU and Human Rights*, p. 687
  U.N. Covenant on Civil and Political Rights: CCPR Commentary, 2nd edn (Kehl: Engel,
    2005)
Nye, J., *The Paradox of American Power: Why the World's Only Superpower Can't Go it
    Alone* (Oxford: Oxford University Press, 2002)
  Soft Power: the Means to Success in World Politics (New York: Public Affairs, 2004)
O'Brien, P., 'Rights Based Responses to Aid Politicization in Afghanistan' in
    Gready and Ensor, *Reinventing Development: Translating Right-Based Approaches
    from Theory into Practice*, p. 201
O'Keeffe, D., 'Community Competencies' in Dashwood and Hillion, *The General
    Law of EC External Relations*, p. 179
O'Keeffe, D. and Schermers, H. (eds.), *Essays in European Law and Integration*
    (The Hague: Kluwer, 1982)

O'Keeffe, D. and Twomey, P. (eds.), *Legal Issues of the Maastricht Treaty* (London: Chancery Law, 1994)

Legal Issues of the Amsterdam Treaty (Oxford: Hart, 1999)

O'Manique, J., 'Human Rights and Development' (1992) 14 *HRQ* 78

'Development, Human Rights and Law' (1992) 14 *HRQ* 383

O'Neil, T. (ed.), *Human Rights and Poverty Reduction: Realities, Controversies and Strategies, an ODI Meeting Series* (London: ODI, 2006)

Office of the United Nations High Commissioner for Human Rights, *Human Rights and Poverty Reduction: a Conceptual Framework* (New York and Geneva: United Nations, 2004)

Orakhelashvili, A., *Peremptory Norms in International Law* (Oxford: Oxford University Press, 2006)

'The Idea of European International Law' (2006) 17 *EJIL* 315

Organisation for Economic Cooperation and Development, *Final Report of the Ad Hoc Working Group on Participatory Development and Good Governance* (Paris: OECD, 1997)

International Trade and Core Labour Standards (Paris: OECD, 2000)

OECD Workshop on the Paris Declaration: Implications and Implementation (Paris: OECD, 2006)

Osaghae, E., *Crippled Giant, Nigeria since Independence* (Lexington: Indiana University Press, 1998)

Owen, P., 'Culture Shock: Obstacles to Bringing Conflict Prevention under the Wing of UN Development and Vice Versa' (2003) 35 *NYUJILP* 671

Paasivirta, E., 'The European Union: from an Aggregate of States to a Legal Person?' (1997) 2 *Hofstra Law and Policy Symposium* 37

'European Union Trading with Israel and Palestine: Parallel Legal Frameworks and Triangular Issues' (1999) 4 *EFARev.* 305

Paasivirta, E. and Rosas, A., 'Sanctions, Countermeasures and Related Actions in the External Relations of the EU: a Search for Legal Frameworks' in Cannizzaro, *The European Union as an Actor in International Relations*, p. 207

Pagani, F., 'A New Gear in the CFSP Machinery: Integration of the Petersburg Tasks in the Treaty on European Union' (1998) 9 *EJIL* 737

Palchetti, P., 'Reactions by the European Union to Breaches of Erga Omnes Obligations' in Cannizzaro, *The European Union as an Actor in International Relations*, p. 219

Patel, D., *Testament of a Liberal* (Karachi: Oxford University Press, 2000)

Patten, C., *Not Quite the Diplomat* (London: Penguin Books, 2006)

Paul, J., 'The Human Right to Development: Its Meaning and Importance' (1992) *Third World Legal Studies* 17

'The United Nations and the Creation of an International Law of Development' (1995) 36 *Harvard ILJ* 307

Pavoni, R., 'UN Sanctions in EU and National Law: the Centro-Com Case' (1999) 48 *ICLQ* 582

Peers, S., 'Comment on Case C-268/94, *Portugal v Council*' (1998) 35 *CMLRev.* 539

'EC Frameworks of International Relations: Co-operation, Partnership, Association' in Dashwood and Hillion, *The General Law of EC External Relations*, p. 160

EU Justice and Home Affairs Law, 2nd edn (Oxford: Oxford University Press, 2006)

Peers, S. and Ward, A. (eds.), *The EU Charter of Fundamental Rights: Politics, Law and Policy* (Oxford: Hart, 2004)

Perez, R., 'Are the Economic Partnership Agreements a First-Best Optimum for the African Caribbean Pacific Countries' (2006) 40 *JWT* 999

Pescatore, P., 'Les relations extérieures des Communautés Européennes' (1961) 103 *RDC* 1

Philippart, E., 'The Euro-Mediterranean Partnership: a Critical Evaluation of an Ambitious Scheme' (2003) 8 *EFARev.* 201

Pierros, F., Meunier, J. and Abrams, S., *Bridges and Barriers: the European Union's Mediterranean Policy, 1961–1998* (Aldershot: Ashgate, 1999)

Piris, J., *The Constitution for Europe: a Legal Analysis* (Cambridge: Cambridge University Press, 2006)

Pirotte, C., Husson, B. and Grunewald, F. (eds.), *Responding to Emergencies and Fostering Development* (London: Zed Books, 1999)

Playfair, E. (ed.), *International Law and the Administration of Occupied Territories* (Oxford: Oxford University Press, 1992)

Pogge, T., *World Poverty and Human Rights: Cosmopolitan Responsibilities and Reforms* (London: Polity Press, 2005)

Preuss, L., 'Article 2, Paragraph 7 of the Charter of the United Nations and Matters of Domestic Jurisdiction' (1949) 74 *RDC* 553

Ragazzi, M., *The Concept of Obligations Erga Omnes* (Oxford: Oxford University Press, 1997)

(ed.), *International Responsibility Today: Essays in Memory of Oscar Schachter* (Leiden: Martinus Nijhoff, 2005)

Rajagopal, B., *International Law from Below: Development, Social Movements and Third World Resistance* (Cambridge: Cambridge University Press, 2003)

Rajan, R. and Subramanian, A., *What Undermines Aid's Impact on Growth*, NBER Working Paper 11657 (2005)

Rashid, A., *Taliban: the Story of the Afghan Warlords* (Basingstoke: Pan Books, 2000)

Raz, J., *The Authority of Law* (Oxford: Oxford University Press, 1979)

Reidel, E. and Will, M., 'Human Rights Clauses in External Agreements of the EC' in Alston *et al.*, *The EU and Human Rights*, p. 723

Reisman, M., 'Sovereignty and Human Rights in Contemporary International Law' (1990) 84 *AJIL* 866

Reiterer, M., 'ASEM: the Third Summit in Seoul 2000: a Roadmap to Consolidate the Partnership between Asia and Europe' (2001) 6 *EFARev.* 1

'The Asia Europe Meeting (ASEM): the Importance of the Fourth ASEM Summit in the light of 11 September' (2002) 7 *EFARev.* 133

Reus-Smit, C., *The Politics of International Law* (Cambridge: Cambridge University Press, 2004)

Richardson, J., 'The European Union in the World: a Community of Values' (2002) 26 *Fordham ILJ* 12

Rideau, J., 'Le rôle de l'Union européenne en matière de protection des droits de l'homme' (1997) 265 *RDC* 9

Riedel, E. and Will, M., 'Human Rights Clauses in External Agreements of the EC' in Alston *et al.*, *The EU and Human Rights*, p. 723

Rieff, D., *A Bed for the Night: Humanitarianism in Crisis* (London: Vintage, 2002)

Risse, T. and Ropp, C., 'International Human Rights Norms and Domestic Change: Conclusions' in Risse *et al.*, *The Power of Human Rights: International Norms and Domestic Change*, p. 234

Risse, T., Ropp, C. and Sikkink, K. (eds.), *The Power of Human Rights: International Norms and Domestic Change* (Cambridge: Cambridge University Press, 1999)

Roberts, A., 'Prolonged Military Occupation: the Israeli-Occupied Territories since 1967' (1990) 84 *AJIL* 44

Robertson, B. (ed.), *The Middle East and Europe: the Power Deficit* (London: Routledge, 1998)

Rosas, A., 'Mixed Union – Mixed Agreements' in Koskenniemi, *International Law Aspects of the European Union*, p. 125

'Comment on Case C-149/96, *Portugal v. Council*' (2000) *CMLRev.* 797

Rosenne, S., *Breach of Treaty* (Cambridge: Grotius, 1985)

Ross, D., *The Missing Peace: the Inside Story of the Fight for Middle East Peace* (New York: Farrar, Straus and Giroux, 2004)

Roth, B., *Governmental Illegitimacy in International Law* (Oxford: Oxford University Press, 1999)

Roy, S., 'Religious Nationalism and the Palestinian-Israeli Conflict: Examining Hamas and the Possibility of Reform' (2004) 5 *Chicago Journal of International Law* 251

Rubin, B. and Rubin, J., *Yasir Arafat: a Political Biography* (London: Continuum, 2003)

Ruedy, J., *Modern Algeria: the Origins and Development of Nations*, 2nd edn (Bloomington: Indiana University Press, 2005)

Ruttan, V. (ed.), *Why Food Aid?* (Baltimore: John Hopkins University Press, 1993)

Sachs, J., *The End of Poverty: How We Can Make it Happen in Our Lifetime* (London: Penguin Books, 2005)

Sano, H., Alfredsson, G. and Clapp, R. (eds.), *Human Rights and Good Governance: Building Bridges* (The Hague: Martinus Nijhoff, 2002)

Sarooshi, D., *International Organizations and their Exercise of Sovereign Powers* (Oxford: Oxford University Press 2005)

Schachter, O., 'International Law Implications of US Human Rights Policies' (1978/9) 24 *NYL Sch. LR* 63

Schenbaum, T., *International Relations: the Path not Taken – Using International Law to Promote World Peace and Security* (Cambridge: Cambridge University Press, 2006)

Scholms, M., 'On the (Im)possible Inclusion of Humanitarian Assistance into Peace Building Efforts', *Journal of Humanitarian Assistance*, www.jha.ac. articles/a072.htm

Schütze, R., 'Organized Change towards an 'Ever Closer Union': Article 308 EC and the Limits to the Community's Legislative Competence' (2003) 22 *YEL* 79

Scobbie, I., 'The Invocation of Responsibility for the Breach of "Obligations under Peremptory Norms of General International Law"' (2002) 13 *EJIL* 1201

Secretary of State for Defence and Secretary of State for Foreign and Commonwealth Affairs, *The Future of the United Kingdom's Nuclear Deterrent*, CM 6994 (London: HMSO, 2006)

Segger, M. and Khalfan, A., *Sustainable Development Law: Principles, Practices and Prospects* (Oxford: Oxford University Press, 2004)

Sen, A., *Inequality Re-examined* (Cambridge: Harvard University Press, 1992)
Development as Freedom (Oxford: Oxford University Press, 1999)

Sengupta, A., 'On the Theory and Practice of the Right to Development' (2002) 24 *HRQ* 837

Shelton, D., 'The Duty to Assist Famine Victims' (1984–85) 70 *Iowa LR* 1279
(ed.), *Commitment and Compliance: the Role of Non-Binding Norms in the International Legal System* (Oxford: Oxford University Press, 2003)

Sherwood, R., Shephard, G. and Marcos de Sousa, C., 'Judicial Systems and Economic Performance' (1994) 34 *Quarterly Review of Economics and Finance* 101

Shihata, I., 'Democracy and Development' (1997) 46 *ICLQ* 635

Siddiqa, A., *Military Inc: Inside Pakistan's Military Economy* (London: Pluto Press, 2007)

Simma, B., 'From Bilateralism to Community Interest in International Law' (1994) 250 (VI) *RDC* 221
(ed.), *The Charter of the United Nations: a Commentary* (Oxford: Oxford University Press, 1994)

Simma, B. and Alston, P., 'The Sources of Human Rights Law: Custom, Jus Cogens and General Principles' (1992) 27 *AYBIL* 82

Simma, B., Aschenbrener, J. and Schulte, C., 'Human Rights Considerations in the Development Cooperation Activities of the EC' in Alston *et al.*, *The EU and Human Rights*, p. 571

Sinclair, I., *The Vienna Convention on the Law of Treaties*, 2nd edn (Manchester: Manchester University Press, 1984)

Sivakumaran, S., 'Binding Armed Opposition Groups' (2006) 55 *ICLQ* 369

Skogly, M., 'Complexities in Human Rights Protection: Actors and Rights Involved in the Ogoni Conflict in Nigeria' (1997) 15 *NQHR* 47

Slaughter, A., 'International Law and International Relations Theory' (1993) 87 *AJIL* 205
'International Law in a World of Liberal States' (1995) 6 *EJIL* 503

Smillie, I., *Relief and Development: the Struggle for Synergy*, HWP Occasional Paper 33

Smith, K., 'The Use of Political Conditionality in the EU's Relations with Third Countries: How Effective?' (1998) 3 *EFARev.* 253
'The EU, Human Rights and Relations with Third Countries: "Foreign Policy" with an Ethical Dimension?' in Smith and Light, *Ethics and Foreign Policy*, p. 185
European Union Foreign Policy in a Changing World (Oxford: Polity Press, 2003)

Smith, K. and Light, M. (eds.), *Ethics and Foreign Policy* (Cambridge: Cambridge University Press, 2001)

Smith, M., *Realist Thought from Weber to Kissinger* (Baton Rouge LA: Louisiana State University Press, 1998)

Snyder, F., 'The European Community's New Food Aid Legislation: Towards a New Development Policy?' in Snyder and Slinn, *International Law of Development: Comparative Perspectives*, p. 271

'European Community Law and Third World Food Entitlements' (1989) 32 *GYBIL* 87

Snyder, F. and Slinn, P. (eds.), *International Law of Development: Comparative Perspectives* (London: Butterworths, 1987)

Soetendorp, B., *Foreign Policy in the European Union* (London: Longman, 1999)

'The EU's Involvement in the Israeli–Palestinian Peace Process: the Building of a Visible International Identity' (2002) 7 *EFARev.* 283

Sogge, D., *Give and Take: What's the Matter with Foreign Aid?* (London: Zed Books, 2002)

Stavridis, S. and Hutchence, J., 'Mediterranean Challenges to the EU's Foreign Policy' (2000) 5 *EFARev.* 35

Stetter, S., 'Democratization Without Democracy? The Assistance of the European Union for the Democratization Process in Palestine' (2003) 8 *Mediterranean Politics* 152

Stevens, A. and Kennan, J., *The Impact of the EU's Everything But Arms Proposal: a Report to Oxfam* (London: Oxfam, 2001)

Stewart, F., 'Basic Needs Strategies, Human Rights and the Right to Development' (1989) 11 *HRQ* 347

Stiglitz, J. and Charlton, A., *Fair Trade for All: How Trade Can Promote Development* (Oxford: Oxford University Press, 2005)

Talmon, S., 'Responsibility of International Organizations: Does the European Union Require Special Treatment?' in Ragazzi, *International Responsibility*, p. 405

Tams, C., 'Light Treatment of a Complex Problem: the Law of Self-Defence in the Wall Case' (2005) 17 *EJIL* 793

Tomaševski, K., *Development Aid and Human Rights Revisited* (London: Pinter, 1993)

Between Sanctions and Elections: Aid Donors and their Human Rights Performance (London: Pinter, 1997)

Responding to Human Rights Violations 1946–1999 (The Hague: Kluwer, 2000)

Tomuschat, C., 'The International Responsibility of the European Union' in Cannizzaro, *The European Union as an Actor in International Relations*, p. 177

Human Rights: Between Idealism and Realism (Oxford: Oxford University Press, 2003)

Torrente, N., 'Humanitarian Action under Attack: Reflections on the Iraq War' (2004) 17 *HHRJ* 1

Tridimas, T. and Nebbia, P. (eds.), *European Union Law for the Twenty First Century: Rethinking the New Legal Order* (Oxford: Hart, 2005)

Trimble, P., 'Human Rights and Foreign Policy' (2002) 46 *Saint Louis University Law Journal* 465

Trindade, A., 'The Domestic Jurisdiction of States in the Practice of the United Nations and Regional Organisations' (1976) 25 *ICLQ* 715

United Nations Development Programme, *Human Development Report 2000, Human Rights and Development* (Oxford: Oxford University Press, 2000)

United Nations Office for the Coordination of Humanitarian Affairs, *Humanitarian Report 1997: the Link Between Relief and Development* (New York: United Nations, 1997)

Uvin, P., *The Influence of Aid in Situations of Violent Conflict* (Paris: OECD, 1999)

Vandenhole, W., 'Third State Obligations under the ICESCR: a Case Study of EU Sugar Policy' (2007) *Nordic Journal of International Law* 73

Vincent, R., *Human Rights and International Relations* (Cambridge: Cambridge University Press, 1986)

Vohrah, L., Pocar, F., Featherstone, Y., Fourmy, O., Graham, C., Hocking, J. and Robson, N. (eds.), *Man's Inhumanity to Man: Essays on International Law in Honour of Antonio Cassese* (The Hague: Kluwer Law International, 2003)

von Bogdandy, A., 'The Legal Case for Unity: the EU as a Single Organisation with a Single Legal System' (1999) 36 *CMLRev.* 887

von Bogdandy, A. and Netteshein, M., 'Ex Pluribus Unum: Fusion of the European Communities into the European Union' (1996) 2 *ELJ* 267

von Dok, G., Varg, C. and Schroeder, R., *Humanitarian Challenges: the Political Dilemmas of Emergency Aid* (Lucerne/Luxembourg: Caritas, 2005)

Waer, P., 'Social Clauses in International Trade' (1996) 30 *JWT* 25

Waldock, H., 'General Course of Public International Law: State Sovereignty and the Reserved Domain of Domestic Jurisdiction' (1962) 106 *RDC* 173

Wallach, J., 'Human Rights as an Ethics of Power' in Wilson, *Human Rights in the 'War on Terror'*, p. 108

Warbrick, C., 'Recognition of States-Part 2' (1993) 43 *ICLQ* 433
    'States and Recognition in International Law' in Evans, *International Law*, p. 218

Warne, W., 'The Quality of Foreign Aid: Country Selectivity or Donors Incentives?', WBPRWP 3325 (Washington DC: World Bank, 2004)

Watson, G., *The Oslo Accords: International Law and the Israeli-Palestinian Peace Agreements* (Oxford: Oxford University Press, 2000)

Wedgewood, R., 'The ICJ Advisory Opinion on the Israeli Security Fence and the Limits of Self-Defense' (2005) 99 *AJIL* 52

Weiler, J., 'The Community System: the Dual Character of Supranationalism' (1981) 1 *YEL* 267
    'The Transformation of Europe' (1991) 100 *Yale Law Journal* 2403

Weiler, J. and Fries, S., 'A Human Rights Policy for the European Community and Union: the Question of Competences' in Alston *et al.*, *The EU and Human Rights*, p. 147

Weiler, J., Spinedi, M. and Cassese A. (eds.), *International Crimes of States: a Critical Analysis of the ILC's Draft Article 19 on State Responsibility* (Berlin: Walter de Gruyter, 1989)

Weiss, F., 'Internationally Recognised Labour Standards and Trade' in Weiss, de Waart and Denters, *International Law and Development*, p. 79

Weiss, F., de Waart, P. and Denters, E. (eds.), *International Law and Development* (Dordrecht: Nijhoff, 1988)

Wellens, K., *Remedies Against International Organisations* (Cambridge: Cambridge University Press, 2002)

Wessel, R., 'The International Legal Status of the European Union' (1997) 2 *EFARev.* 109

    The European Union's Foreign and Security Policy: a Legal Institutional Perspective (The Hague: Kluwer, 1999)

    'The Inside Looking Out: Consistency and Delimitation in EU External Relations' (2000) 37 *CMLRev.* 1135

Wet, E., 'Labour Standards in the Globalised Economy: the Inclusion of a Social Clause in the General Agreement on Tariffs and Trade/World Trade Organisation' (1995) 17 *HRQ* 443

Wheeler, N., *Saving Strangers: Humanitarian Intervention in International Society* (Oxford: Oxford University Press, 2000)

White, B., *Understanding European Foreign Policy* (Basingstoke: Palgrave, 2001)

White, N. and Abass, A., 'Countermeasures and Sanctions' in Evans, *International Law*, p. 509

Williams, A., *EU Human Rights Policies: a Study in Irony* (Oxford: Oxford University Press, 2004)

Wilson R. (ed.), *Human Rights in the 'War on Terror'* (Cambridge: Cambridge University Press, 2006)

Wolfensohn, J., 'Some Reflections on Human Rights and Development' in Alston and Robinson, *Human Rights and Development*, p. 19

World Bank, *Building Poverty Reduction Strategies in Developing Countries* (Washington: World Bank, 1999)

Youngs, R., *The European Union and the Promotion of Democracy* (Oxford: Oxford University Press, 2002)

Zemanek, K., 'Human Rights Protection vs. Non Intervention: a Perennial Conflict?' in Vohrah *et al.*, *Man's Inhumanity to Man*, p. 383

Ziring, L., *Pakistan: at the Cross Roads of History* (Oxford: Oneworld, 2003)

Index

In this Index :-
(1) entries in **bold** denote main entries
(2) the following abbreviations are used:

EU	European Union
EU BAM	EU Border Assistance Mission (Rafah)
EU EOM	EU Electoral Observation Mission
EUEU	European Union Electoral Unit
EUPOL-COPPS	EU Police Mission for the Palestinian Territories
EU 3	France, Germany and United Kingdom
FCO	Foreign and Commonwealth Office
GATT	General Agreement on Tariffs and Trade
GSP	Generalised System of Preferences
HRC	Human Rights Committee
IAEA	International Atomic Energy Agency
ICC	International Criminal Court
ICCPR	International Covenant on Civil and Political Rights
ICESCR	International Covenant on Economic, Social and Cultural Rights
ICFTU	International Confederation of Free Trade Unions
ICJ	International Court of Justice
ICRC	International Committee of the Red Cross
IDF	Israeli Defence Force
IDI	Institut De Droit International
ILC	International Law Commission
ILCASR	International Law Commission's Articles on State Responsibility
ILO	International Labour Organisation
IMF	International Monetary Fund
IPA	Instrument for Pre-Accession Assistance
JHA	Justice and Home Affairs
JPA	Joint Parliamentary Assembly
LDCs	Least Developed Countries
LICs	Low Income Countries
LMICs	Lower Middle Income Countries
LRRD	linking relief, rehabilitation and development
MDGs	Millennium Development Goals
MDP	MEDA Democracy Programme
MEDA	Regulation to implement Euro-Mediterranean Partnership
MEPP	Middle East Peace Process
MIC	Civil Protection Monitoring and Information Centre
MSF	Médecins Sans Frontières
NAS	New Asia Strategy
NGO	Non-Governmental Organisation
NLD	National League for Democracy
NPT	Treaty on the Non-Proliferation of Nuclear Weapons
OAS	Organisation of American States
OCHA	Office for the Coordination of Humanitarian Affairs
OECD	Organisation for Economic Cooperation and Development
PCIJ	Permanent Court of International Justice
PLC	Palestinian Legislative Council
PLO	Palestine Liberation Organisation
RRM	Rapid Reaction Mechanism
SAARC	South Asian Association for Regional Cooperation
SALW	Small Arms and Light Weapons
SPDC	State Peace and Development Council
TEC	Treaty (Establishing the) European Community
TEU	Treaty on European Union
TIM	Temporary International Mechanism
UDHR	Universal Declaration of Human Rights
UMICs	Upper Middle Income Countries
UNC	Charter of the United Nations

UNDP	United Nations Development Programme
UNHCR	United Nations High Commissioner for Refugees
UNICEF	United Nations Children's Fund
UNRWA	United Nations Relief and Works Agency
VCLT	Vienna Convention on the Law of Treaties
VCLTSIO	Vienna Convention on the Law of Treaties between States and International Organisations
WHO	World Health Organisation
WTO	World Trade Organisation